Communications in Computer and Information Science 2935

Series Editors

Rationale

The CCIS series is devoted to the publication of proceedings of computer science conferences. Its aim is to efficiently disseminate original research results in informatics in printed and electronic form. While the focus is on publication of peer-reviewed full papers presenting mature work, inclusion of reviewed short papers reporting on work in progress is welcome, too. Besides globally relevant meetings with internationally representative program committees guaranteeing a strict peer-reviewing and paper selection process, conferences run by societies or of high regional or national relevance are also considered for publication.

Topics

The topical scope of CCIS spans the entire spectrum of informatics ranging from foundational topics in the theory of computing to information and communications science and technology and a broad variety of interdisciplinary application fields.

Information for Volume Editors and Authors

Publication in CCIS is free of charge. No royalties are paid, however, we offer registered conference participants temporary free access to the online version of the conference proceedings on SpringerLink (http://link.springer.com) by means of an http referrer from the conference website and/or a number of complimentary printed copies, as specified in the official acceptance email of the event.

CCIS proceedings can be published in time for distribution at conferences or as post-proceedings, and delivered in the form of printed books and/or electronically as USBs and/or e-content licenses for accessing proceedings at SpringerLink. Furthermore, CCIS proceedings are included in the CCIS electronic book series hosted in the SpringerLink digital library at http://link.springer.com/bookseries/7899. Conferences publishing in CCIS are allowed to use our online conference service (Meteor) for managing the whole proceedings lifecycle (from submission and reviewing to preparing for publication) free of charge.

Publication process

The language of publication is exclusively English. Authors publishing in CCIS have to sign the Springer CCIS copyright transfer form, however, they are free to use their material published in CCIS for substantially changed, more elaborate subsequent publications elsewhere. For the preparation of the camera-ready papers/files, authors have to strictly adhere to the Springer CCIS Authors' Instructions and are strongly encouraged to use the CCIS LaTeX style files or templates.

Abstracting/Indexing

CCIS is abstracted/indexed in DBLP, Google Scholar, EI-Compendex, Mathematical Reviews, SCImago, Scopus. CCIS volumes are also submitted for the inclusion in ISI Proceedings.

How to start

To start the evaluation of your proposal for inclusion in the CCIS series, please send an e-mail to ccis@springer.com

Abeer Alsadoon · Farid Ghareh Mohammadi ·
Farzan Shenavarmasouleh · Soheyla Amirian ·
Hamid R. Arabnia · Leonidas Deligiannidis
Editors

Emerging Trends in Computational Biology, Biomedical Engineering, and Health Informatics

26th International Conference, BIOCOMP 2025, 11th International Conference, BIOENG 2025, and 11th International Conference, HIMS 2025, Held as Part of the World Congress in Computer Science, Computer Engineering, and Applied Computing, CSCE 2025
Las Vegas, NV, USA, July 21–24, 2025
Revised Selected Papers

Editors
Abeer Alsadoon
Charles Sturt University
Bathurst, NSW, Australia

Farid Ghareh Mohammadi
Verify Radiology Images Consultants
Athens, GA, USA

Farzan Shenavarmasouleh
MediaLab, Inc.
Lawrenceville, GA, USA

Soheyla Amirian
Pace University
New York, NY, USA

Hamid R. Arabnia
University of Georgia
Athens, GA, USA

Leonidas Deligiannidis
Wentworth Institute of Technology
Boston, MA, USA

ISSN 1865-0929 ISSN 1865-0937 (electronic)
Communications in Computer and Information Science
ISBN 978-3-032-22198-8 ISBN 978-3-032-22199-5 (eBook)
https://doi.org/10.1007/978-3-032-22199-5

This Springer imprint is published by the registered company Springer Nature Switzerland AG
The registered company address is: Gewerbestrasse 11, 6330 Cham, Switzerland

Preface

It is our great pleasure to introduce this collection of selected papers presented at the 26th International Conference on Bioinformatics & Computational Biology (BIOCOMP 2025), the 11th International Conference on Biomedical Engineering & Sciences (BIOENG 2025), and the 11th International Conference on Health Informatics & Medical Systems (HIMS 2025).

These conferences were held as part of the federated 2025 World Congress in Computer Science, Computer Engineering, and Applied Computing (CSCE 2025), which took place from July 21 to July 24, 2025, in Las Vegas, Nevada, USA.

The CSCE 2025 Congress brought together papers from a diverse array of communities, including researchers from universities, corporations, and government agencies. Accepted papers are published by Springer Nature, and the proceedings showcase solutions to key challenges in various critical areas of Computer Science, Computer Engineering, and Applied Computing.

Computer Science (CS) is the study of computational systems, data processing, information management, and automation. Many applications in CS focus on solving problems that would be impossible or extremely difficult to address without the use of computers. It serves as a bridge between computational science and other scientific fields. The interdisciplinary nature of CS involves leveraging computers to understand and solve complex challenges, making it the science of using computers to advance scientific discovery. Computer Engineering (CE), on the other hand, integrates aspects of computer science, electronic engineering, and electrical engineering. It encompasses the design and production of computer hardware, such as chips, servers, supercomputers, embedded systems, and communication systems, among others.

Considering the above broad outline, the CSCE 2025 Congress was composed of the following focused conferences:

Applied Cognitive Computing (ACC); Bioinformatics & Computational Biology (BIOCOMP); Biomedical Engineering (BIOENG); Scientific Computing (CSC); eLearning, e-Business, Enterprise Information Systems, & e-Government (EEE); Embedded Systems, Cyber-physical Systems, & Applications (ESCS); Foundations of Computer Science (FCS); Frontiers in Education (FECS); Grid, Cloud, & Cluster Computing (GCC); Health Informatics (HIMS); Artificial Intelligence (ICAI); Data Science (ICDATA); Emergent Quantum Technologies (ICEQT); Internet Computing & IoT (ICOMP); Wireless Networks (ICWN); Information & Knowledge Engineering (IKE); Image Processing, Computer Vision, & Pattern Recognition (IPCV); Modeling, Simulation & Visualization Methods (MSV); Parallel & Distributed Processing Techniques & Applications (PDPTA); Security & Management (SAM); and Software Engineering Research & Practice (SERP). The scope of each track can be found at: https://www.american-cse.org/csce2025/conferences

The primary objective of the CSCE Congress and its associated conferences is to foster opportunities for cross-fertilization between the fields of Computer Science (CS)

and Computer Engineering (CE). The CSCE Congress is deeply committed to promoting diversity and eliminating discrimination, both in its role as a conference organizer and as a service provider. Our goal is to create an inclusive culture that respects and values differences, promotes dignity, equality, and diversity, and encourages individuals to reach their full potential. We are also dedicated, wherever possible, to organizing a conference that represents the global community. We sincerely hope that we have succeeded in achieving these important objectives.

The Steering Committee and the Program Committees would like to extend their gratitude to all the authors who submitted papers for consideration. This year's conferences received submissions from 58 countries, with approximately 50% of them coming from outside the USA. Each submitted paper underwent a rigorous peer-review process, with at least two experts (an average of 2.4 referees per paper) evaluating the submissions based on originality, significance, clarity, impact, and soundness. In cases where reviewers' recommendations were contradictory, a program committee member was tasked with making the final decision, often consulting additional referees for further guidance. The Congress followed the guidelines of COPE (Committee on Publication Ethics):

- Typical submissions underwent a single-blind peer review process, in which the authors remained unaware of the identities of the reviewers, while the reviewers were informed of the authors' identities.
- Papers authored by one or more members of the program committee, including co-chairs, were subjected to a double-blind peer review process, ensuring that neither the authors nor the reviewers were aware of each other's identities or affiliations.

The BIOCOMP 2025 Conference received a total of 112 submissions, of which 22 papers were accepted, resulting in a paper acceptance rate of 20%. For this volume we selected only 9 of the papers accepted at BIOCOMP. The BIOENG 2025 Conference received 62 submissions, of which 15 papers were accepted, resulting in a paper acceptance rate of 24%. For this volume we selected only 3 of the papers accepted at BIOENG. The HIMS 2025 Conference received a total of 197 submissions, of which 41 papers were accepted, resulting in a paper acceptance rate of 21%. For this volume we selected only 23 of the papers accepted at HIMS. In addition, the book contains 3 poster papers.

This volume includes 38 of the accepted papers from BIOCOMP 2025, BIOENG 2025, and HIMS 2025.

We are deeply grateful to the many colleagues who contributed their time and effort to organizing the Congress. In particular, we extend our thanks to the members of the Program Committees, the Steering Committee, the referees, and the Chairs and organizers of individual sessions and conferences. We would also like to express our appreciation to the primary sponsor of the conference, the American Council on Science & Education. The list of members of the Program Committee for each track can be found at: https://www.american-cse.org/csce2025/committees

We extend our heartfelt gratitude to all the speakers and authors for their valuable contributions. We would also like to thank the following individuals and organizations for their support: the staff at the Luxor Hotel and the staff of Springer Nature for their assistance in various aspects of the event.

We are pleased to present a curated selection of papers from the BIOCOMP 2025, BIOENG 2025, and HIMS 2025 conferences. These proceedings represent a collection of outstanding research contributions that reflect the diversity and depth of work in core areas of Computational Biology, Biomedical Engineering, and Health Informatics.

August 2025

Abeer Alsadoon
Farid Ghareh Mohammadi
Farzan Shenavarmasouleh
Soheyla Amirian
Hamid R. Arabnia
Leonidas Deligiannidis

Organization

Steering Committee – Co-chairs (CSCE 2025)

Hamid R. Arabnia	University of Georgia, USA
Leonidas Deligiannidis	Wentworth Institute of Technology, USA
Fernando G. Tinetti	Universidad Nacional de La Plata, Argentina
Quoc-Nam Tran	Southeastern Louisiana University, USA

Co-editors of BIOCOMP 2025, BIOENG 2025, and HIMS 2025 Proceedings – Publication Co-chairs

Abeer Alsadoon	Charles Sturt University, Australia
Farid Ghareh Mohammadi	Verify Radiology Images Consultants, LLC, USA
Farzan Shenavarmasouleh	Medialab Inc., USA
Soheyla Amirian	Pace University, USA
Hamid R. Arabnia	University of Georgia, USA
Leonidas Deligiannidis	Wentworth Institute of Technology, USA

Members of Steering Committee (CSCE 2025)

Babak Akhgar	Sheffield Hallam University, UK
Abbas M. Al-Bakry	University of IT & Communications, Iraq
Nizar Al-Holou	University of Detroit Mercy, USA
Hamid R. Arabnia	University of Georgia, USA
Rajab Challoo	Texas A&M University-Kingsville, USA
Chien-Fu Cheng	Tamkang University, Taiwan
Hyunseung Choo	Sungkyunkwan University, South Korea
Kevin Daimi	University of Detroit Mercy, USA
Leonidas Deligiannidis	Wentworth Institute of Technology, USA
Eman M. El-Sheikh	University of West Florida, USA
Mary Mehrnoosh Eshaghian-Wilner	University of California, Los Angeles, USA
David L. Foster	Kettering University, USA
Henry Hexmoor	Southern Illinois University at Carbondale, USA
Ching-Hsien (Robert) Hsu	Chung Hua University, Taiwan
James J. (Jong Hyuk) Park	SeoulTech, South Korea

Research Tracks – Co-chairs (CSCE 2025)

Program Committees of BIOCOMP 2025, BIOENG 2025, and HIMS 2025

Refer to the lists at:
https://www.american-cse.org/csce2025/committees

Contents

11th International Conference on Biomedical Engineering and Sciences (BIOENG'25)

11th International Conference on Health Informatics and Medical Systems (HIMS'25) Section: Health Informatics, Data Science, and Tools

26th International Conference on Bioinformatics and Computational Biology (BIOCOMP'25)

Self-supervised Multimodal Pre-training for Lung Adenocarcinoma Overall Survival Prediction

Francisco Carrillo-Perez[1,2], Marija Pizurica[2,3], Ignacio Rojas[1], Kathleen Marchal[3], Luis Javier Herrera[1(✉)], and Olivier Gevaert[2]

[1] Department of Computer Architecture and Technology, University of Granada, C.I.T.I.C., Periodista Rafael Gómez Montero, 2, 18014 Granada, Spain
{franciscocp,jherrera}@ugr.es

[2] Stanford Center for Biomedical Informatics Research (BMIR), Department of Medicine, Stanford University, 1265 Welch Rd, Stanford, CA 94305, USA
marija.pizurica@ugent.be

[3] Internet Technology and Data Science Lab (IDLab), Ghent University, Technologiepark-Zwijnaarde 126, 9052 Gent, Belgium

Abstract. The collection of multiple modalities of cancer data has increased over the years, allowing research in complex problems such as cancer prognosis. However, given the high-dimensionality of biological data, efficiently training machine learning models when scarce samples are available is still challenging. In this work we propose a novel multi-modal self-supervised learning framework based on neural networks for survival analysis and we evaluate it in a few-shot learning setting for lung adenocarcinoma prognosis. We show that the multimodal self-supervised pre-training is more effective than regular pre-training or training from scratch for two modalities (RNA-Seq and Whole Slide Imaging) when few samples are available. With the multimodal self-supervised learning framework, the relation between the modalities is learned in a pretext task and the leveraged information is successfully used for the relevant downstream task for both modalities, showing the potential of the proposed methodology.

Keywords: Self-supervised learning · Multimodal classification · Survival Analysis · Deep Learning

1 Introduction

Cancer is one of the deadliest diseases around the world. Accurately predicting the survival outcome of the disease is a challenging problem that has been studied in the last decades. To do so, authors have studied the relationships between different variables and the survival outcome, in some cases using parametric or semi-parametric models [22]. One of the most used models in recent years is the

F. Carrillo-Perez and M. Pizurica—These authors contributed equally to this work.

A. Alsadoon et al. (Eds.): CSCE 2025, CCIS 2935, pp. 3–12, 2026.
https://doi.org/10.1007/978-3-032-22199-5_1

Cox proportional hazards model [9]. The Cox proportional hazards model is a statistical method to analyze the effect of several risk factors on survival, or in a more general way, on the time it takes for a specific event to happen. The model makes an assumption about how the predictions affect the hazard function, but not about the baseline hazard function. Given that in most real world scenarios the form of the true hazard function is unknown or too complex to model, it has been the most popular survival analysis method in recent years [16].

Historically, low-dimensional phenotype characteristics (e.g. age, sex or other clinical variables) from patients were used for survival analysis, in combination with more tumor related variables such as stage or grade [19]. Recently, the rise of next-generation sequencing technologies such as RNA-Seq, and the advances in digital imaging of histopathology glass slides to Whole Slide Images (WSIs) have shown their usefulness for survival analysis, particularly when used as input in Deep Neural Networks (DNNs) in combination with regularized Cox models [5,15,18]. However, these techniques require huge amounts of data to be properly trained. An interesting approach to deal with scarce data is to leverage information from other relevant cancer types with more available samples, and transfer knowledge to a rare cancer type with less data. For instance, convolutional neural networks pre-trained on the ImageNet dataset have been successfully used for survival prediction on WSIs [27]. The same holds for meta-learning approaches using RNA-Seq data [25].

In the medical field, often considerably more unlabeled data is available than labeled data. In this context, self-supervised learning (SSL) seems a promising framework for leveraging the information provided from unlabeled data, and using it on downstream tasks. The premise of SSL is to generate weak labels from unlabeled data, and learn important features from pretext tasks. In the case of images, the tasks can be to predict the rotation of an image, or predict which augmentation has been applied [3,7]. On multimodal data, SSL has been used to create similar feature vectors for the audio and frames of the same video [1]. Given the multi-omic and multi-scale nature of cancer data, leveraging information from different modalities is beneficial for downstream tasks, and it has been shown in literature that multimodal models outperform the results of single-modality classifiers on multiple tasks [4,5,17].

In this work, we present a novel multimodal SSL framework that leverages the multi-scale nature of cancer data and use it in few-shot learning setting for lung adenocarcinoma (LUAD) overall survival prediction. In this section an introduction and the motivation to the problem have been outlined. In Sect. 2 the data, preprocessing steps, models and SSL framework are described. The results are presented and discussed in Sect. 3 and finally in Sect. 4 conclusions are drawn and future work is discussed.

2 Materials and Methods

2.1 Data Acquisition and Implementation

In this work we have considered one molecular/genomic modality and one imaging modality: RNA-Seq and WSIs. The data was collected from the The Cancer

Genome Atlas (TCGA) program [26], that is easily accessible from the GDC portal [12]. The preprocessings steps for each of the modalities will be reported in the following subsections. The Case IDs and the code used for this work are available in a Github repository[1]. Nine cancer types were used for the pretext task and one for the downstream task. The information of the cancer types is presented in Table 1.

Table 1. TCGA-Projects used for the pretext and the downstream tasks.

TCGA-Project	Cancer type	# Samples	Task
TCGA-CESC	Cervical Squamous Cell Carcinoma	277	Pretext
TCGA-CHOL	Cholangiocarcinoma	36	Pretext
TCGA-ESCA	Esophageal Carcinoma	156	Pretext
TCGA-GBM	Glioblastoma Multiforme	208	Pretext
TCGA-KIRP	Kidney Renal Papillary Cell Carcinoma	290	Pretext
TCGA-LUAD	Lung Adenocarcinoma	509	Downstream
TCGA-OV	Ovarian Serous Cystadenocarcinoma	82	Pretext
TCGA-PAAD	Pancreatic Adenocarcinoma	201	Pretext
TCGA-PRAD	Prostate Adenocarcinoma	444	Pretext
TCGA-UVM	Uveal Melanoma	80	Pretext

2.2 Self-supervised Learning Multimodal Pre-training

In an SSL setting, we want to learn good features from weakly labeled data in order to improve our performance in a few-shot learning problem. Similarly to Arandjelovic et al. [1], where the authors used an SSL framework to learn similar representations between two modalities, we approached the pretext task as a same-cancer type classification. One encoder is used for each modality, being Resnet-18 [14] for the WSI data and a two-layer neural network for the RNA-seq data. For all the pretext cancer types (see Table 1) we permuted 50% of the samples so, for a given sample, the WSI and the RNA-Seq data do not correspond to the same cancer type. Then, using the SSL framework depicted in Fig. 1, we try to predict whether the tile and the gene expression used as input correspond to the same cancer type, based on the distance between the obtained feature vectors (in our case the Euclidean distance). The aim of this approach is to learn similar feature vectors from multimodal data as a representation of the cancer type, which would allow us to use less data on the downstream task. For the SSL framework, a linear layer with 2 neurons was used previous to the output layer. The AdamW optimizer was used with a learning rate of $3e^{-7}$ for the WSI encoder, and $3e^{-3}$ for the rest, using a weight decay value of 0.1, and the

[1] https://github.com/pacocp/SSL-Survival.

Cross Entropy Loss was used as loss function. The model was trained during 20 epochs using an early-stopping approach with a batch size equal to 16.

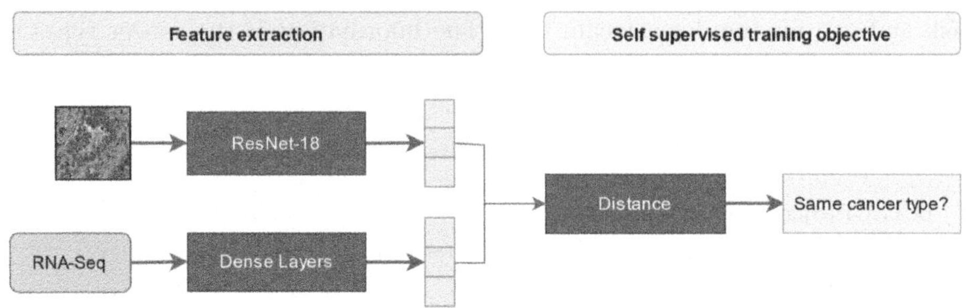

Fig. 1. SSL framework used in this work. The two modalities (RNA-Seq and WSI) are encoded using two different networks. The distance is computed between the feature vectors using the euclidean distance, and the value is forward trough a linear layer. The pretext tasks consists on predicting whether the two modalities are from the same cancer type or not.

2.3 RNA-Seq Preprocessing and Model

For the gene expression data, we followed the preprocessing steps described by Zheng et al. [28]. The raw sequencing reads were aligned to the human transcriptome and quantified using the Kallisto-Sleuth algorithm proposed by Bray et al. [2]. NaN values were removed and we selected those genes that the different cancer types have in common. These preprocessing steps left us with a total of $17,655$ genes that were used as input to the model. The gene expression was normalized with the z-score transformation from the training set values.

As the model we decided to use an architecture formed by two linear layers of 600 and 512 neurons each (the encoder that is trained in the SSL framework), and a final liner layer of 200 neurons. As activation function LeakyReLU was used, the AdamW optimizer with a learning rate of $3e^{-3}$ was employed for the training and the Cox Loss was used as loss function. If SSL pre-trained were not used, the weights were initialized using the Xavier initialization [11]. The networks were training for 20 epochs using an early-stopping approach.

2.4 WSI Preprocessing and Model

Scanned WSIs, stained with hematoxylin and eosin, were acquired in SVS format and downsampled to 20$\times$ magnification ($0.5\mu m$ px^{-1}). Typical WSIs easily supersede $10k \times 10k$ pixels, and can therefore not be directly used as input in deep learning models. Instead, a regular grid was placed over the WSI resulting in smaller, non-overlapping tiles of 256×256 pixels, consistent with related work in state-of-the-art WSI processing [8,20,21]. The Otsu threshold method was used to obtain a mask of the tissue [23]. Tiles containing more than 60% background and with low-contrast were discarded.

The WSI deep learning pipeline uses a bag of $N = 100$ tiles per sample for training and is based on the state-of-the-art [20,21]. Each tile is forwarded through a pre-trained ResNet-18 network, resulting in a lower dimensional representation of the tile. Most weights from the pre-trained ResNet weights were frozen, except for the last convolutional layer. Two modes were used for the ResNet-18, either pre-trained on the ImageNet dataset [10] or acquired by our self-supervised training procedure (described in Sect. 2.2). Once the representations are obtained from all the tiles, they are averaged and forwarded through the Cox regression layer. The procedure is schematically illustrated in Fig. 2b.

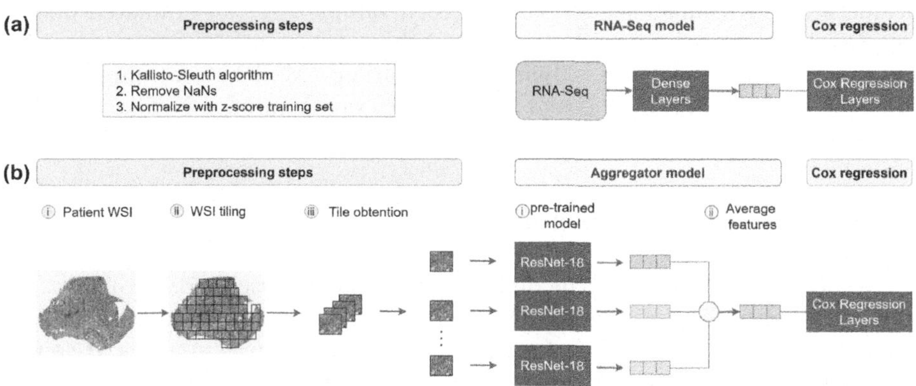

Fig. 2. (a) RNA-Seq training and prediction pipeline. After preprocessing, the data is fed through dense layers for feature extraction. Then, the features are forwarded through the Cox regression layers. (b) WSI training and prediction pipeline. First, the tiles from the slide are obtained. Then, N tiles are selected as a representation of the slide. Each tile is forwarded through a pre-trained ResNet network to obtain a feature vector. The feature vectors are averaged and forwarded through the Cox regression layers.

2.5 Experimental Setup and Implementation Details

For training our models, we relied on the neural network extension of the Cox model [6], which has shown to achieve best performance for high dimensional data [25]. Features from the feature extraction network (as described above) are fed to a Cox loss module which performs the survival prediction (by doing a Cox regression with the features as linear predictors of the hazard [9]). To optimize the parameters β of the Cox module, we minimize the negative of the partial log likelihood:

$$\mathcal{L}(\beta) = - \sum_{y_i = uncensored} (\boldsymbol{z}_i\beta - \log(\sum_{y_j \geq y_i} e^{\boldsymbol{z}_j\beta})) \quad (1)$$

being y_i the survival length for patient i, $\boldsymbol{z}_i$ the patient's features and β the coefficients (weights) between the features and the output. To assess the added value of our SSL method, we evaluate it with two alternative training schemes that are based on the same neural network architecture. For the RNA-Seq model, we compare the performance for survival prediction achieved by training a network directly, i.e. from scratch, with the performance achieved by fine-tuning the network pre-trained with our self supervised learning method. For the WSI model, we compare the performance for survival prediction achieved by fine-tuning a model pre-trained on the ImageNet dataset with the performance after fine-tuning a model pre-trained with our SSL technique. Specifically, to illustrate the effectiveness of the method in case of scarce data, we consider three cases of learning with small sample sizes: a sample size 5, 10 and 20. We also include a larger sample size of 150. For each sample size, we evaluated on the complete held-out test set and we repeated the experiments 10 times, using different random seeds ($99 \times i$, i being the iteration). Models were implemented using the Pytorch library [24] and experiments were run on a Nvidia ™ GTX ® 2080 GPU.

3 Results and Discussion

The results are presented for the different experiments described in Subsect. 2.5 on the test sets. We evaluate the performances with the concordance index (C-index or CI) [13], a standard performance measure in survival analysis. It counts the number of pairs whose predicted survival times are correctly ordered, and divides it by the total number of pairs that can be ordered. Pairs cannot be ordered if the earlier event in a pair is censored or if both events in the pair are censored. The maximum value of the C-index, 1, indicates perfect prediction, while a value of 0.5 indicates random prediction. In Figs. 3 and 4, the boxplot of test set CI over the 10 different runs can be observed.

For the RNA-Seq model (see Fig. 3), using SSL learned weights (ssl) as starting point improves the results over the direct model (direct) in case of using 5 and 20 training samples. Especially for the case of 5 samples the improvement is considerable, showing the potential of SSL when few samples are available. For 10 and 150 samples the obtained CIs are similar, especially for 150 samples, where the direct and SSL methods obtain almost the same median CI.

In the WSI case (see Fig. 4), the model using SSL learned weights (ssl) again outperformed ImageNet (im) in those cases where few samples were available (5 and 10 samples used as training set). For the case of 20 and 150, the results are similar, showing no gain of performance of our proposed SSL method over using ImageNet weights. Specifically, in the case of 150 samples as training set the results are almost identical, with the standard deviation of the runs also consistent for the two approaches.

In terms of the downstream task of survival analysis, RNA-Seq generally outperforms WSI, although the standard deviations obtained across the runs

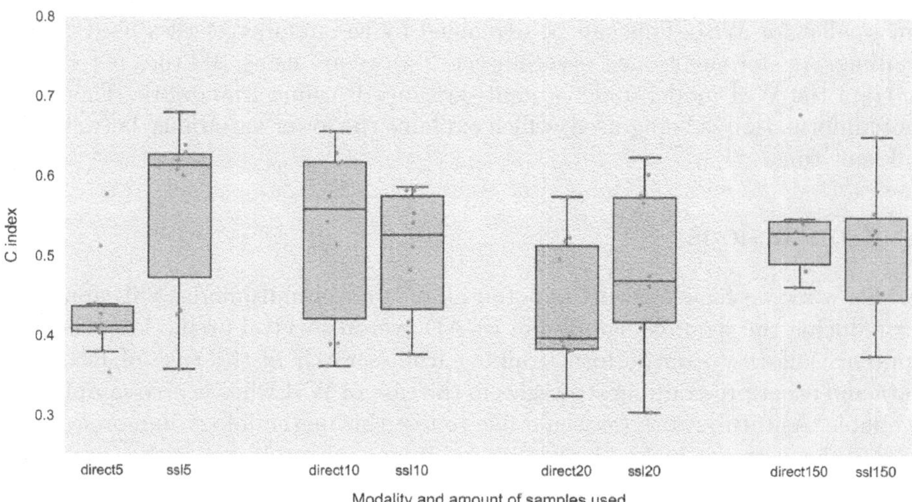

Fig. 3. Comparison of pre-train models for 5, 10, 20 and 150 samples with the RNA-Seq model, each repeated 10 times. In each group of two, the left boxplot represents results without pre-training (direct), while the right one is pre-trained with our self-supervised method (ssl).

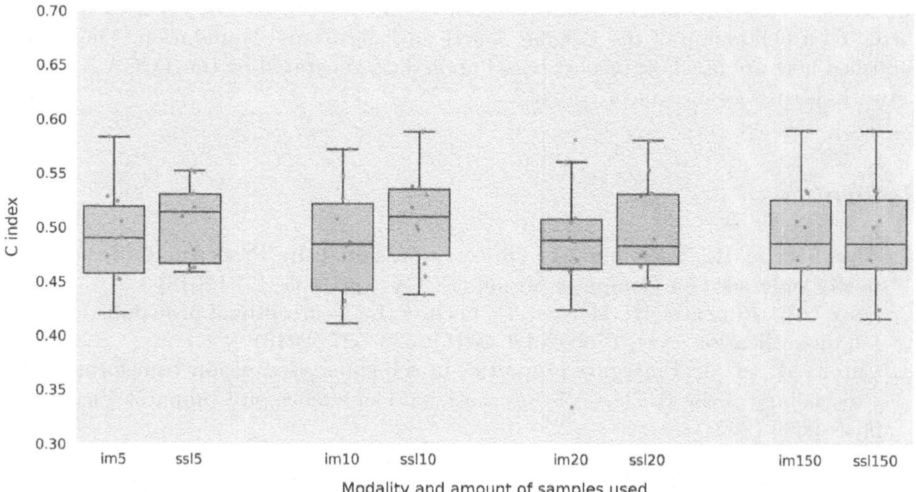

Fig. 4. Comparison of pre-train models for 5, 10, 20 and 150 samples with the WSI model, each repeated 10 times. In each group of two, the left boxplot represents results with a ResNet pre-trained with ImageNet (im), while the right one is pre-trained with our self-supervised method (ssl).

are smaller for WSI. This can be explained by the number of tiles used during training. As aforementioned (see Subsect. 2.4) we are using 100 tiles per sample to train the WSI model under a multi-instance learning framework. Therefore, more information is being used, which explains the lower variability between the different runs.

4 Conclusions

In this work we have shown the potential of a novel multimodal SSL approach for reducing the required samples in LUAD overall survival prediction. The SSL approach allows to outperform training from scratch in the case of RNA-Seq data and other pre-training strategies in the case of WSI when scarce samples are available. As future work we would like to test this methodology in more cancer-related downstream tasks, to show its usefulness on problems with scarce data in contrast to training from scratch or using other pre-training methodologies.

Acknowledgments. This publication is part of the R&D&I project RTI2018-101674-B-I00 and by the Government of Andalusia under the grant CV20-64934 and P20-00163. It is also supported by grants of the Fonds Wetenschappelijk Onderzoek-Vlaanderen (FWO) [G046318, G.0371.06, and 3G045620], and the UGent Bijzonder Onderzoeksfonds. F. Carrillo-Perez was supported by a Predoctoral Fulbright Scholarship funded by the Fulbright Spanish Commission. In addition, M. Pizurica was supported by a Fellowship of the Belgian American Educational Foundation. The results published here are in whole or part based upon data generated by the TCGA Research Network: https://www.cancer.gov/tcga.

References

1. Arandjelovic, R., Zisserman, A.: Objects that sound. In: Proceedings of the European Conference on Computer Vision (ECCV), pp. 435–451 (2018)
2. Bray, N.L., Pimentel, H., Melsted, P., Pachter, L.: Near-optimal probabilistic RNA-seq quantification. Nat. Biotechnol. **34**(5), 525–527 (2016)
3. Caron, M., et al.: Emerging properties in self-supervised vision transformers. In: Proceedings of the IEEE/CVF International Conference on Computer Vision, pp. 9650–9660 (2021)
4. Carrillo-Perez, F., et al.: Non-small-cell lung cancer classification via RNA-seq and histology imaging probability fusion. BMC Bioinfo. **22**(1), 1–19 (2021)
5. Cheerla, A., Gevaert, O.: Deep learning with multimodal representation for pan-cancer prognosis prediction. Bioinformatics **35**(14), i446–i454 (2019)
6. Ching, T., Zhu, X., Garmire, L.X.: Cox-nnet: an artificial neural network method for prognosis prediction of high-throughput omics data. PLoS Comput. Biol. **14**(4), e1006076 (2018)
7. Ciga, O., Xu, T., Martel, A.L.: Self supervised contrastive learning for digital histopathology. Mach. Learn. Appl. **7**, 100198 (2022)
8. Coudray, N., et al.: Classification and mutation prediction from non-small cell lung cancer histopathology images using deep learning. Nat. Med. **24**(10), 1559–1567 (2018)

9. Cox, D.R.: Regression models and life-tables. J. Roy. Stat. Soc.: Ser. B (Methodol.) **34**(2), 187–202 (1972)
10. Deng, J., Dong, W., Socher, R., Li, L.J., Li, K., Fei-Fei, L.: ImageNet: a large-scale hierarchical image database. In: 2009 IEEE Conference on Computer Vision and Pattern Recognition, pp. 248–255. IEEE (2009)
11. Glorot, X., Bengio, Y.: Understanding the difficulty of training deep feedforward neural networks. In: Proceedings of the Thirteenth International Conference on Artificial Intelligence and Statistics, pp. 249–256. JMLR Workshop and Conference Proceedings (2010)
12. Grossman, R.L., et al.: Toward a shared vision for cancer genomic data. N. Engl. J. Med. **375**(12), 1109–1112 (2016)
13. Harrell, Frank E., J., Califf, R.M., Pryor, D.B., Lee, K.L., Rosati, R.A.: Evaluating the Yield of medical tests. JAMA **247**(18), 2543–2546 (1982). https://doi.org/10.1001/jama.1982.03320430047030
14. He, K., Zhang, X., Ren, S., Sun, J.: Deep residual learning for image recognition. In: Proceedings of the IEEE Conference on Computer Vision and Pattern Recognition, pp. 770–778 (2016)
15. Huang, Z., et al.: Deep learning-based cancer survival prognosis from RNA-seq data: approaches and evaluations. BMC Med. Genomics **13**(5), 1–12 (2020)
16. Kleinbaum, D.G., Klein, M.: The cox proportional hazards model and its characteristics. In: Survival Analysis, pp. 97–159. Springer (2012)
17. Lee, T.Y., Huang, K.Y., Chuang, C.H., Lee, C.Y., Chang, T.H.: Incorporating deep learning and multi-omics autoencoding for analysis of lung adenocarcinoma prognostication. Comput. Biol. Chem. **87**, 107277 (2020)
18. Li, R., Yao, J., Zhu, X., Li, Y., Huang, J.: Graph CNN for survival analysis on whole slide pathological images. In: International Conference on Medical Image Computing and Computer-Assisted Intervention, pp. 174–182. Springer (2018)
19. Louis, D.N., et al.: The 2016 world health organization classification of tumors of the central nervous system: a summary. Acta Neuropathol. **131**(6), 803–820 (2016)
20. Lu, M.Y., et al.: Ai-based pathology predicts origins for cancers of unknown primary. Nature **594**(7861), 106–110 (2021)
21. Lu, M.Y., Williamson, D.F., Chen, T.Y., Chen, R.J., Barbieri, M., Mahmood, F.: Data-efficient and weakly supervised computational pathology on whole-slide images. Nature biomed. Eng. **5**(6), 555–570 (2021)
22. Muche, R.: Applied survival analysis: regression modeling of time to event data. dw Hosmer, jr., s Lemeshow. New York: John Wiley, 1999, pp. 386, ISBN: 0-471-15410-5 (2001)
23. Otsu, N.: A threshold selection method from gray-level histograms. IEEE Trans. Syst. Man Cybern. **9**(1), 62–66 (1979)
24. Paszke, A., et al.: PYTorch: an imperative style, high-performance deep learning library. In: Wallach, H., Larochelle, H., Beygelzimer, A., d'Alché-Buc, F., Fox, E., Garnett, R. (eds.) Advances in Neural Information Processing Systems 32, pp. 8024–8035. Curran Associates, Inc. (2019). http://papers.neurips.cc/paper/9015-pytorch-an-imperative-style-high-performance-deep-learning-library.pdf
25. Qiu, Y.L., Zheng, H., Devos, A., Selby, H., Gevaert, O.: A meta-learning approach for genomic survival analysis. Nat. Commun. **11**(1), 1–11 (2020)
26. Weinstein, J.N., et al.: The cancer genome atlas pan-cancer analysis project. Nat. Genet. **45**(10), 1113 (2013)

27. Yao, J., Zhu, X., Jonnagaddala, J., Hawkins, N., Huang, J.: Whole slide images based cancer survival prediction using attention guided deep multiple instance learning networks. Med. Image Anal. **65**, 101789 (2020)
28. Zheng, H., Brennan, K., Hernaez, M., Gevaert, O.: Benchmark of long non-coding RNA quantification for RNA sequencing of cancer samples. GigaScience **8**(12), giz145 (2019)

Robust Unsupervised Classification of *Drosophila* Cell Dynamics Using Dynamic Time Warping and Consensus Clustering of Engineered Features

Tim Rogalsky(✉), Lia Campbell-Enns, Matthaeus Dyck, and Nicolas Malagon

Canadian Mennonite University, Winnipeg, MB, Canada
trogalsky@cmu.ca

Abstract. Understanding the spatio-temporal dynamics of cell development is a key step toward early detection of abnormal growth patterns, including cancer. In this study, we classify size oscillation patterns of epithelial cells in the developing foreleg of *Drosophila melanogaster* using unsupervised machine learning. We began by clustering raw delta-area time series using Dynamic Time Warping (DTW) with hierarchical and Gaussian mixture model (GMM) clustering, which revealed three distinct dynamic patterns of size change. Building on this, we engineered interpretable time series features and applied dimensionality reduction techniques – Principal Component Analysis (PCA) and Non-negative Matrix Factorization (NMF) – each followed by hierarchical and k-means clustering. Finally, we evaluated clustering agreement and applied omnibus statistical tests (ANOVA or Kruskal-Wallis) with effect size ranking to identify the most discriminative features of cell behavior. The results highlight recurring developmental motifs and reveal a reproducible structure underlying the cell dynamics. These methods and findings establish a computational baseline for future comparisons to pathological data and demonstrate the utility of consensus clustering in developmental biology.

Keywords: Cell dynamics · *Drosophila* development · Dynamic time warping · Consensus clustering · Time series clustering · Unsupervised learning

1 Introduction

The sex comb, a male-specific structure on the *Drosophila* foreleg, is essential for courtship behaviors [1]. During development, tissues change in area through complex epithelial reorganization, to facilitate the rotation of the sex comb into its functional position. This process involves expanding and contracting cells in the surrounding foreleg tissue, resulting in non-periodic oscillations in cell area. These oscillations are hypothesized to be an evolved mechanism for identifying and eliminating unfit cells, and serve as a potential baseline for detecting abnormal developmental patterns [2, 3]. However, analyzing such oscillations poses a challenge due to irregular time series length, noise, and variability.

A. Alsadoon et al. (Eds.): CSCE 2025, CCIS 2935, pp. 13–27, 2026.
https://doi.org/10.1007/978-3-032-22199-5_2

To classify these patterns, we applied unsupervised machine learning techniques [4] to a dataset consisting of measurements from 131 epithelial cells captured in three time-lapse movies, each documenting the development of a different *Drosophila melanogaster* specimen [3]. Cells were imaged using live-cell microscopy (Fig. 1) and measured every 20 min in the segment immediately proximal to the sex comb. The data for each specimen contain measurements for 35 to 53 cells, with time series ranging from 39 to 48 time steps. We focused our analysis on the delta-area time series (the change in area between time points), as they capture dynamic cell behavior more directly than absolute area.

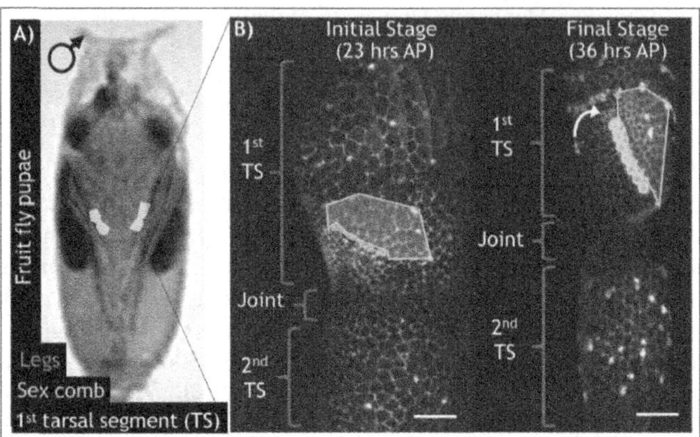

Fig. 1. Visualization of sex comb development in *Drosophila melanogaster* forelegs. A) Ventral view of a male pupa showing the developing forelegs (blue) and the location of the sex comb (yellow) on the first tarsal segment (white). B) Confocal images of the foreleg at two developmental stages: 23 h and 36 h after puparium formation (AP). The first (1st TS) and second (2nd TS) tarsal segments are labeled, with the sex comb in yellow and the surrounding region of interest (ROI), proximal to the comb, outlined in pink. Cells in the ROI exhibit a net reduction in tissue area via irregular oscillations over time. Scale bars: 20 μm. Taken from [3].

We began by applying the DTW metric [5] to the raw delta-area time series. Clustering with Ward's hierarchical agglomerative method and GMM revealed three consistent, distinct clusters of cell behavior. Building on this, we engineered a wide range of interpretable time series features and used two dimensionality reduction techniques – PCA and NMF – to identify structure in the feature space. Each of these was followed by Ward's hierarchical and k-means clustering, producing a total of six clusterings. We then performed a consensus analysis across the six clustering pipelines and, for each engineered feature, applied an omnibus test (one-way ANOVA or Kruskal-Wallis as appropriate) followed by $\eta 2$ effect size ranking to pinpoint the variables that most reliably distinguish cell-behavior patterns; this revealed recurrent developmental motifs that were consistent across methods.

2 Related Work

Unsupervised machine learning has become an increasingly powerful tool in developmental biology, particularly for uncovering latent structure in high-dimensional or time-resolved data. In *Drosophila melanogaster*, early clustering of gene expression time series [6, 7] revealed developmental modules and temporally shifted co-expression patterns. More recent image-based and single-cell approaches have leveraged clustering to identify morphological phenotypes [8] and reconstruct cell-type maps from 3D imaging [9]. Likewise, Moore et al. [10] imaged *C. elegans* embryos in 4-D and extracted hundreds of lineage, positional, and shape features per cell to create a high-resolution wild-type reference atlas. Using hierarchical clustering with Ward's linkage on binary "deviation" vectors derived from mutant embryos, they grouped genes with similar developmental defects entirely through unsupervised classification.

Time-series methods that combine time-warping alignment with later clustering are particularly effective when cellular signals are noisy, irregular, or out of phase. Pioneering this approach, Aach and Church [11] applied dynamic-time-warping algorithms to align gene-expression time courses with differing developmental rates, laying the groundwork for today's widespread use of DTW in bioinformatics time-series analysis.

Feature-based clustering often begins with dimensionality-reduction techniques such as PCA and NMF, which convert high-dimensional biological signals into a few latent components. Demonstrating this power, Brunet et al. [12] used NMF to derive interpretable "metagenes" from cancer-expression microarrays and showed that unsupervised clustering of the metagene profiles recovers clinically relevant tumour subtypes. Unsupervised matrix-factorization and clustering approaches have uncovered key cancer patterns. For example, NMF revealed mutational signatures that expose underlying DNA-damage processes [13], while multi-omic iCluster/NMF analyses identified pan-cancer molecular subtypes with distinct prognoses [14].

Our work builds on this tradition by combining DTW-based alignment with interpretable, feature-driven clustering to distinguish recurring oscillatory motifs in healthy *Drosophila* epithelial cells, laying the groundwork for future anomaly detection in developmental pathologies.

3 Time Series Clustering with DTW

3.1 Data Acquisition and Preprocessing

We analyzed 131 cells from three time-lapse microscopy movies (Movie 1: 43 cells, Movie 2: 35 cells, Movie 3: 53 cells), with measurements recorded every 20 min. Each cell's delta-area (change in area between time steps) was extracted. Time series ranged from 39 to 48 time steps. Missing values were encountered for some cells, indicating instances where accurate data could not be captured, but these were located exclusively at the heads and tails of the series (Fig. 2). Cells were excluded if they had more than 25% NaN values relative to the length of the longest time series. The 108 remaining time series were padded with NaNs at the head and tail to match the longest sequence. No imputation was applied; during DTW computation, alignment was restricted to overlapping regions with valid data, enabling robust comparison despite missing values.

The delta distributions were nearly normal with a slight left skew, and were centered around zero (Fig. 3), which aligns with the oscillatory patterns typically observed in cell development. Many outliers were present, some of them extreme. To enable meaningful comparisons across cells with varying absolute growth rates, the dataset was min-max normalized to the range [0, 1]. Scaling parameters were fit on the complete dataset and then applied identically across all downstream analyses to ensure consistency. This transformation preserves the shape and temporal dynamics of each time series while removing magnitude-based differences, allowing unsupervised classification to focus on relative structural features. All clustering, feature extraction, and statistical analyses were performed on these normalized delta values. Due to left skewness in the original distribution, the median of normalized deltas is approximately 0.6.

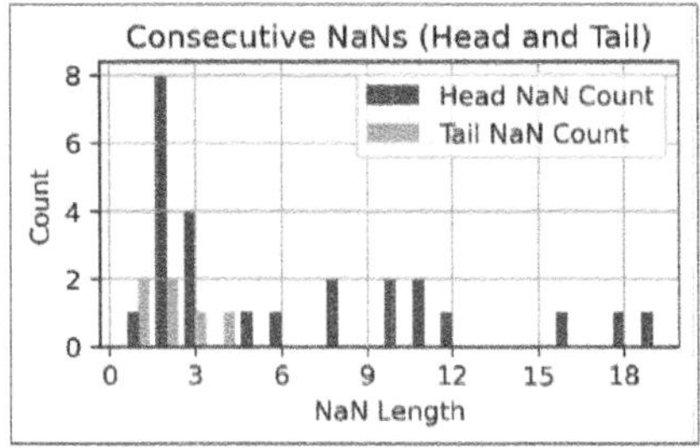

Fig. 2. Distribution of consecutive missing values (NaNs) at the start (Head) and end (Tail) of time series for cell measurements.

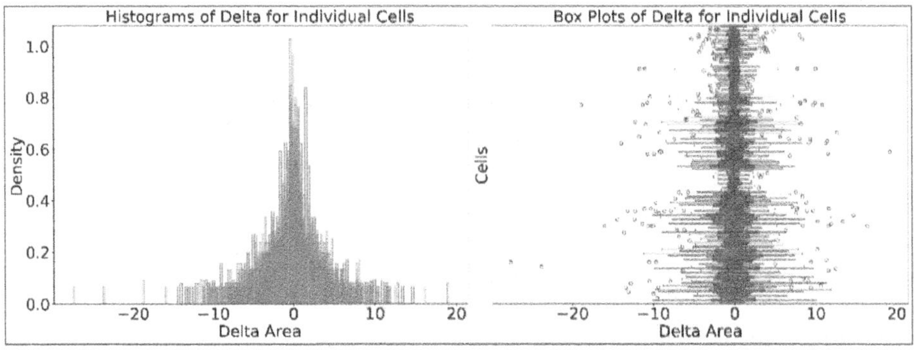

Fig. 3. Distributions of Delta Area for Individual Cells. Left: Histograms showing approximately normal distributions with outliers. Right: Box plots highlighting the spread and variation across individual cells.

3.2 DTW-Based Clustering

Delta-area time series were compared using the dynamic time warping (DTW) metric, which aligns sequences nonlinearly to minimize distances between corresponding points, even when the series differ in length or exhibit temporal shifts. This made DTW particularly effective for our dataset, where some time series were shorter or distorted. Clustering based on DTW distances was performed using hierarchical clustering (Ward's method) and GMM, both of which revealed distinct groupings. Although Ward's linkage is formally defined for Euclidean distances, we applied it with DTW pairwise dissimilarities, following the pragmatic approach adopted in prior time series clustering studies [15]. For GMM, each row of the DTW distance matrix was treated as a feature vector representing a cell's dissimilarity profile, an adaptation that departs from standard GMM usage but yielded complementary cluster structure. In contrast, k-means consistently returned a single cluster for k up to 10, and DBSCAN produced only one cluster across a wide range of eps and min_samples values, with varying levels of noise. These results suggest that the DTW distance space is not well suited to centroid- or density-based clustering.

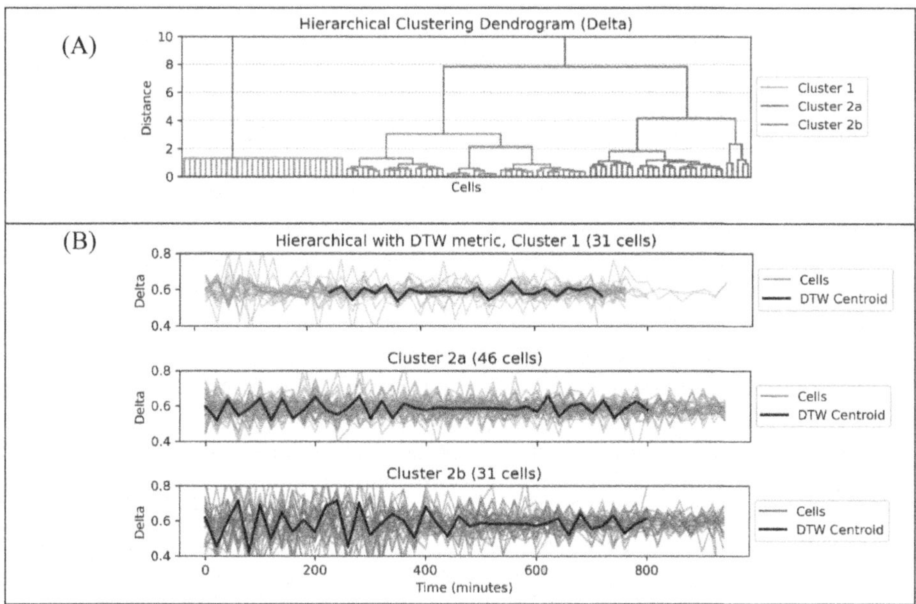

Fig. 4. Hierarchical Clustering for non-imputed Delta time series, using the DTW metric. A) Dendrogram with clusters identified at cut distances of 10 and 6. B) Cluster assignments and DTW barycenters. Time series with more than 25% missing values were excluded, and no truncation was applied.

There were two highly distinct clusters, with one cluster subdividing into two smaller groups, as shown for the hierarchical model in Fig. 4. The clustering results were robust: they remained virtually unchanged across both hierarchical and GMM models, regardless of whether longer series were truncated, and across a range of NaN filtering levels. Significantly, Cluster 1 was composed primarily of cells from Movie 1, suggesting either a spatial/temporal pattern specific to that specimen or a difference in imaging start time. Cluster centroids, calculated with DTW barycenter averaging (DBA), are shown in Fig. 4B. Note that these centroids are shorter than some time series because DBA can only be performed where data exist across all series within a cluster.

Visually, the three DTW-based clusters revealed distinct temporal dynamics in delta-area behavior across Drosophila cells. Cluster 1 exhibited small, stable oscillations with low variance, composed almost entirely of cells from a single movie, suggesting possible biological or technical variation in that sample. Cluster 2a maintained consistent activity throughout the developmental period, while Cluster 2b showed pronounced early-stage fluctuations that gradually tapered off, potentially reflecting tissue remodeling during early rotation of the sex comb. While these observations provide a qualitative view of temporal patterns in cell behavior, further analysis was needed to describe these differences in a more quantitative, systematic, and interpretable way.

3.3 Feature Engineering and Statistical Ranking

To characterize the differences in behavior of individual *Drosophila* cells during development, we extracted a diverse set of engineered features from their normalized delta-area time series and used these to compare clusters statistically. These features spanned seven categories: (a) statistical summaries, which captured the overall distribution of delta values (e.g., mean, skewness, kurtosis); (b) frequency-domain features, which quantified oscillatory strength and regularity using spectral analysis; (c) peak and trough timing, which described the pacing and symmetry of oscillatory events; (d) magnitude features, which examined the strength and progression of oscillation amplitudes; (e) complexity and autocorrelation, which assessed the temporal structure through entropy, short- and long-lag autocorrelations, and the Hurst exponent (interpreted cautiously given the short series); (f) early vs. late behavior, which compared statistical and autocorrelation properties across developmental phases; and (g) oscillation shape features, which captured sharpness, asymmetry, and overall energy. Features showing strong redundancy ($|r| > 0.9$) were pruned in favor of the more interpretable or biologically grounded member of each pair, yielding a final set of 45 complementary descriptors that underpinned all cluster comparisons and the subsequent feature-based clustering analyses.

To interpret differences between the DTW-based clusters, we focused on a preliminary consensus group – a subset of cells whose cluster assignments were consistent across both the hierarchical and GMM models. Cluster 1 was identical in both models, containing the same 31 cells. Cluster 2a showed near-perfect agreement, as 46 of GMM's 47 cells overlapped with the 46 cells in the hierarchical cluster. Similarly, Cluster 2b included 29 overlapping cells, which were exactly the 29 assigned to that cluster by GMM.

For each engineered feature, we performed an omnibus test to identify overall differences among the three clusters: a one-way ANOVA when assumptions of normality and homoskedasticity were met, or a Kruskal-Wallis test otherwise. Features were then ranked by effect size ($\eta 2$), defined as the proportion of total variance attributable to between-group differences. For features with a significant omnibus result, we conducted pairwise comparisons using t-tests (parametric) or Dunn's tests with Holm correction (non-parametric). All reported pairwise differences remained significant after adjustment.

The most discriminative features revealed strong and consistent separation between clusters. The top eight features (Table 1) showed highly significant differences across groups ($p < 0.0001$ for all), with pairwise comparisons remaining significant at $\alpha =$

0.05 after Holm correction. These features followed a clear and consistent gradient: mean values increased progressively from Cluster 1 to 2a to 2b, reflecting a rise in oscillatory intensity and variability from group to group.

Table 1. Top eight features distinguishing DTW clusters, based on Kruskal-Wallis tests. All features had p-values < 0.0001 and are ranked by effect size ($\eta^{2)}$.

Category	Feature	H	η^2
Oscillation Shape	Sharpness index	58.4	0.594
Statistical Summary	Standard deviation	59.6	0.576
Early vs. Late	Early std dev	54.5	0.572
Magnitude Change	Mean rise amplitude	58.4	0.564
Magnitude Change	Mean amplitude	57.5	0.559
Statistical Summary	Range	56.9	0.556
Magnitude Change	Mean fall amplitude	57.6	0.550
Magnitude Change	Std dev of amplitude	54.7	0.549

Figure 5 illustrates this trend using the top two ranked features, sharpness index and standard deviation, which exemplify the broader pattern. Additional features, including spectral power and high-frequency band power, also increased progressively across the cluster trajectory. In contrast, temporal structure features such as autocorrelation and the Hurst exponent decreased significantly from Cluster 1 to 2a to 2b, indicating reduced predictability and greater irregularity in cell dynamics.

Features capturing early-stage oscillations – such as initial rise amplitude, initial fall amplitude, and initial oscillation strength ($\eta 2 = 0.529, 0.479, 0.366$ respectively) – did not differ significantly between Clusters 1 and 2a but showed strong increases from $2^{\text{a to 2b}}$ ($p < 0.001$). This highlights the distinctive early dynamics of Cluster 2b. Similarly spectral flatness ($\eta\ 2 = 0.162$) showed a significant decrease only from Cluster 2a to 2b ($p < 0.01$), suggesting a transition toward more noise-like oscillations.

Taken together, these findings suggest that the DTW-based clustering captured meaningful variation in cell behavior. Cluster 1 represents cells with small, stable oscillations, while Cluster 2a shows moderate increases in variability. Cluster 2b is distinguished by earlier, sharper, and more erratic size fluctuations, coupled with a measurable loss of temporal structure and predictability. Collectively, the three clusters reflect a progression from stability to increasing dynamic intensity and irregularity, pointing to distinct developmental regimes within the epithelial tissue.

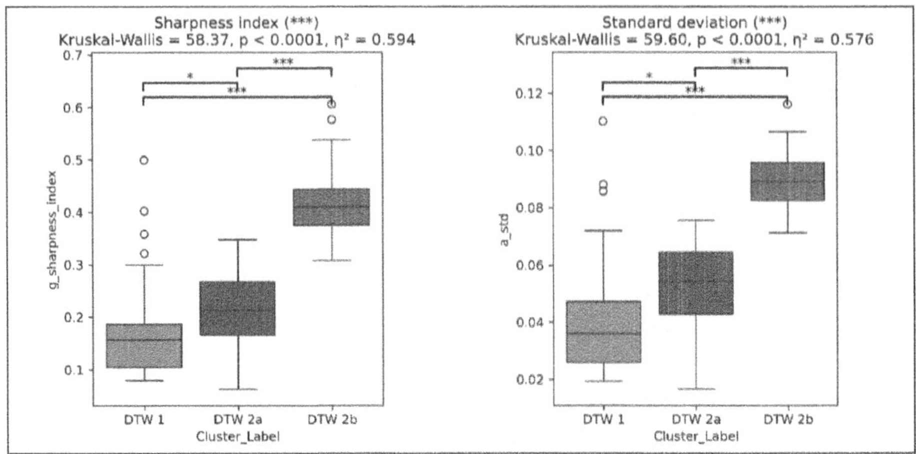

Fig. 5. Top two features distinguishing DTW-based preliminary consensus clusters. Left: Sharpness index. Right: Standard deviation of delta magnitude. Boxplots show cluster-wise distributions with significance levels from Kruskal-Wallis omnibus tests and post hoc pairwise comparisons (Holm-adjusted). $^*p < 0.05$, $^{**}p < 0.01$, $^{***}p < 0.001$.

4 Dimensionality Reduction and Alternative Clusterings

4.1 PCA on Engineered Features

To explore the latent structure in the engineered features, we first applied PCA to reduce dimensionality while retaining most of the dataset's variance. The cumulative explained variance plot showed that the first 12 principal components together accounted for roughly 90% of the total variance. These 12 components were retained for clustering and visualization to strike a balance between dimensionality and interpretability.

Clustering performed on the PCA-reduced space revealed patterns broadly consistent with DTW-based results. Both hierarchical clustering and K-means produced a two-cluster structure with a prominent subcluster. This structure was supported by both dendrogram cut points and elbow curve analysis, each suggesting that three clusters offered an optimal representation of the data. The strong correspondence between the clusters produced by hierarchical clustering and K-means further indicated that the major modes of variation captured by PCA align with biologically meaningful structure. Quantitative comparisons of clustering agreement are presented in a later section.

4.2 NMF on Engineered Features

To further explore the structure of the engineered features, we applied NMF, a dimensionality reduction method that produces interpretable, additive components. A scree plot of the proportion of variance explained (based on Frobenius reconstruction error) for 1 to 30 components revealed an elbow at five components, after which additional components contributed less than 2% to the total variance. The five-component solution explains 80.9% of the total variance, while maintaining interpretable clusters.

Each component emphasized distinct aspects of cell dynamics. Component 1 reflected oscillation strength, long-range autocorrelation, low-frequency fluctuation intensity, and late-phase variability. Component 2 highlighted short-term autocorrelation, early-phase dynamics, and asymmetry in initial oscillatory behavior. Component 3 emphasized late-phase behavior and signal complexity, including reduced predictability and lower regularity. Component 4 captured variability and timing between peaks in the oscillatory signal. Component 5 was shaped by early oscillation strength, low-frequency spectral energy, and early autocorrelation.

Clustering performed in the NMF-reduced space showed strong agreement between hierarchical clustering and K-means. Again, dendrogram cut point and elbow curve analysis supported two main groups with a prominent subcluster. These results closely align with those obtained through DTW and PCA, reinforcing the robustness of the engineered features in capturing biologically meaningful variation. Comparative analyses across all clustering approaches are presented in the next section.

5 Multi-method Consensus Analysis of Clustering Results

5.1 Consensus Patterns and Cross-Method Agreement

To assess the consistency and robustness of unsupervised classification, we compared six clustering pipelines: hierarchical clustering and GMM or K-means, each applied to three feature spaces (DTW, PCA, and NMF). Each pipeline produced a two-cluster solution with a prominent subcluster, as described in Sects. 3 and 4 For consistency, we treated these as three-cluster solutions in all cases, enabling direct comparison of cell-level assignments across methods. Similarity was evaluated using both the Adjusted Rand Index (ARI) and Normalized Mutual Information (NMI). These are complementary metrics: NMI quantifies the mutual information shared between clustering solutions, while ARI assesses pairwise agreement in cluster assignments, correcting for chance.

ARI comparisons revealed strong alignment between methods using the same feature space. DTW-based clusterings (HC and GMM) showed the highest agreement (ARI = 0.976), followed by PCA-based (ARI = 0.924) and NMF-based (ARI = 0.910) pipelines. Cross-feature comparisons between PCA and NMF were also high (ARI = 0.814–0.870), indicating that both captured similar structural variation. Agreement between DTW and feature-based clusterings was moderate (ARI = 0.648–0.678), suggesting that DTW captures different but not contradictory information about cell dynamics. These relationships are visualized in Fig. 6.

Normalized Mutual Information scores supported these trends. DTW methods exhibited strong mutual information (NMI = 0.922), while PCA and NMF pipelines showed moderate-to-strong mutual information (NMI = 0.773–0.787). In contrast, NMI scores between DTW and PCA/NMF clusterings were substantially lower (NMI = 0.275–0.340), indicating lower information overlap and suggesting that these methods may capture distinct aspects of the underlying cell dynamics.

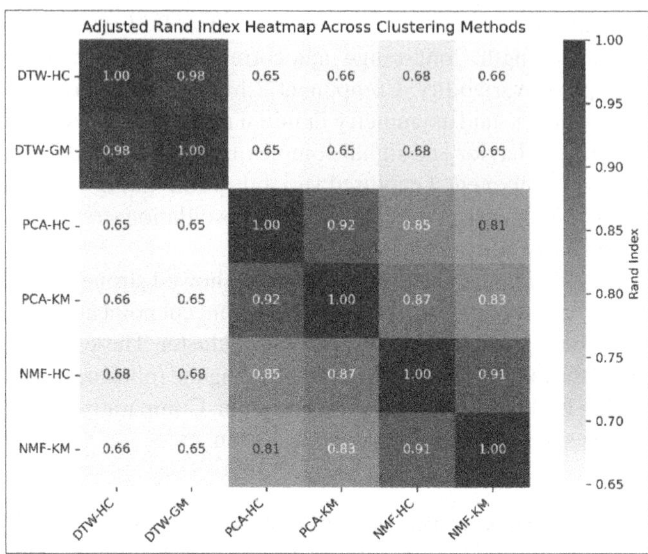

Fig. 6. ARI heatmap showing pairwise similarity between clustering methods. Each method combines a feature extraction technique (DTW, PCA, or NMF) with a clustering algorithm: hierarchical (HC), k-means (KM), or Gaussian mixture model (GM). All pipelines produced three interpretable clusters, enabling direct comparison of cell-level assignments.

To locate the strongest cross-method agreements, we concatenated each cell's six cluster assignments into a single intersection signature (e.g., "2-2-1-1-3-3"). Counting identical signatures across all 108 cells revealed five highly recurrent patterns that together covered 82 cells (76% of the dataset); every other signature occurred three times or fewer, indicating borderline or noisy classifications. To align these consensus groups with the DTW hierarchy, we relabeled the five dominant signatures as 1 (N = 24), 2a.1 (N = 13), 2a.2 (N = 25), 2b.1 (N = 10), and 2b.2 (N = 10), where the 2a and 2b labels preserve the original DTW sub-structure. These consensus groups provide a high-confidence basis for all downstream statistical comparisons and biological interpretation.

5.2 Statistical Ranking of Discriminative Features

To compare the five consensus clusters, each of the retained engineered features was re-tested with the same omnibus procedure described earlier (ANOVA when assumptions held, Kruskal-Wallis otherwise) and ranked by its univariate effect size ($\eta 2$). Table 2 lists the most discriminative features ($p < 0.0001$, $\eta 2 \geq 0.75$), and Fig. 7 shows representative box-plots. Although the feature count was reduced by correlation filtering, the analysis still examines 45 variables against 108 cells; accordingly, ranking is kept strictly univariate to minimize over-fitting. Finally, while three clusters are well populated, two contain only ten cells each; the corresponding results remain internally consistent but should be interpreted with the usual caution applied to small-N subgroups.

Table 2. Top 12 features distinguishing the five consensus-based cluster signatures, based on ANOVA or Kruskal-Wallis tests. All had p-values < 0.0001 and are ranked by effect size (η^2).

Category	Feature	F or H	η^2
Oscillation	Total spectral power	66.0	0.843
Statistical Summary	Standard deviation	65.2	0.832
Magnitude Change	Mean rise amplitude	64.0	0.803
Magnitude Change	Mean amplitude	64.0	0.802
Magnitude Change	Mean fall amplitude	64.1	0.797
Oscillation Shape	Sharpness index	62.4	0.792
Magnitude Change	Initial fall amplitude	51.6	0.791
Magnitude Change	Initial oscillation strength	41.8	0.787
Statistical Summary	Range	61.9	0.783
Early vs. Late Behavior	Early standard deviation	69.5	0.783
Magnitude Change	Initial rise amplitude	55.3	0.772
Magnitude Change	Std dev of amplitude	60.8	0.767

A consistent three-tiered pattern emerged across the top six ranked features in Table 2 – including total spectral power, standard deviation, amplitude features, and sharpness index – with total spectral power (Fig. 7a) serving as a clear representative of this group. Clusters 1 and 2a.1 formed a shared lower tier, with no significant difference between them. Values increased significantly in 2a.2, forming a distinct middle tier, and increased again in clusters 2b.1 and 2b.2, which were statistically indistinguishable from each other and together formed the highest tier. This structure suggests a shared low-amplitude, low-oscillation phenotype in clusters 1 and 2a.1, with a stepwise increase in oscillatory dynamics in 2a.2 and both 2b subgroups.

A second, more graded pattern was observed in early-phase features such as initial fall amplitude, early standard deviation, and initial rise amplitude, with initial fall amplitude (Fig. 7b) illustrating this trend. Again, clusters 1 and 2a.1 were statistically indistinguishable and formed the lower end of the distribution. However, each subsequent group – 2a.1, 2b.1, 2b.2 – showed a statistically significant increase over the previous one, suggesting a smooth continuum of rising early-phase amplitude and variability, rather than discrete transitions.

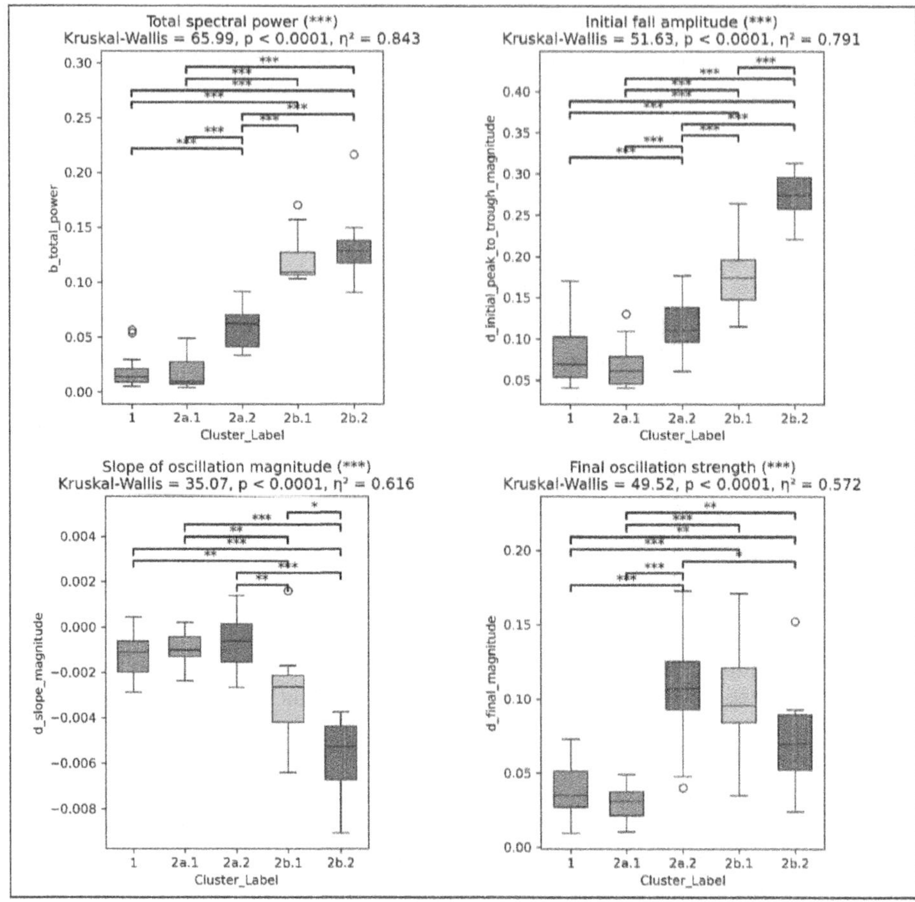

Fig. 7. Four engineered features distinguishing the five final consensus clusters. Top left: Total spectral power. Top right: Initial fall amplitude. Bottom left: Slope of oscillation magnitude. Bottom right: Final oscillation strength. Boxplots show cluster-wise distributions with significance levels from Kruskal-Wallis omnibus tests and post hoc pairwise comparisons (Holm-adjusted). $^{*}p < 0.05$, $^{**}p < 0.01$, $^{***}p < 0.001$.

A third pattern emerged in features related to temporal change, most clearly represented by the slope of oscillation magnitude (Fig. 7c). Here, a reversed three-tiered structure appeared: clusters 1, 2a.1, and 2a.2 formed an upper tier with relatively stable slopes, while clusters 2b.1 and 2b.2 showed significantly more negative values and grouped together in a lower tier. This suggests that only the 2b clusters exhibit a pronounced decline in oscillation strength over time, marking a temporal shift toward reduced activity.

A final set of features is exemplified by final oscillation strength (Fig. 7d). These features showed a two-tiered pattern: clusters 1 and 2a.1 consistently had significantly lower values than the remaining groups. Similar patterns were observed for final rise/fall amplitude and high-frequency band power, indicating that baseline groups remained relatively inactive even at later stages. Conversely, features like late autocorrelation and spectral flatness were higher in clusters 1 and 2a.1, suggesting more regular and predictable behavior, in contrast to the increased irregularity and complexity seen in the 2b clusters.

Despite broad similarity across many features, a few measures did reveal statistically significant but modest differences between clusters 1 and 2a.1. For example, late standard deviation and final rise amplitude were both slightly lower in 2a.1. While these results suggest that 2a.1 cells may end with somewhat more subdued activity, the magnitude of these differences is limited and may reflect subtle developmental timing differences rather than a distinct regulatory program.

5.3 Spatio-Temporal Signatures and Biological Interpretation

The five consensus-based clusters revealed not only consistent statistical differences, but also interpretable spatio-temporal patterns in cell behavior. Clusters 1 and 2a.1 consistently formed a shared lower tier across many of the top-ranked features, showing no significant differences in oscillation strength, amplitude, or early variability. This repeated tiering suggests that these cells may represent a common, stable developmental phase or spatial zone, potentially a baseline state before divergence occurs. Notably, Cluster 1 was composed primarily of cells from one specimen (Movie 1), while 2a.1 included cells from the other two, suggesting that similar behaviors can emerge across different individuals or spatial regions, independent of imaging timing.

In contrast, Clusters 2a.2, 2b.1, and 2b.2 exhibited increasingly dynamic and variable behavior. Cells in 2a.2 showed a marked departure from the baseline, with significantly higher amplitudes and early-phase variability, forming a distinct middle tier. Cells in 2b.1 and 2b.2 extended this trend, with additional increases in oscillation strength and irregularity. These groups also showed more negative slopes in oscillation magnitude, indicating a tapering of oscillatory behavior over time. Reduced values in features such as spectral flatness and Hurst exponent in the 2b clusters further reflect increasingly unpredictable dynamics.

From a biological perspective, these patterns are consistent with the hypothesis that epithelial oscillations near the *Drosophila* sex comb reflect an evolved mechanism to identify and eliminate unfit or non-contributing cells. The reproducibility of the clustering results across DTW-, PCA-, and NMF-based clustering supports the biological robustness of the observed motifs. In particular, the repeated grouping of Clusters 1 and 2a.1 suggests a conserved developmental "baseline," while the progressively more active and irregular behaviors in the 2b clusters may signal cells undergoing late-stage mechanical stress, reorganization, or pruning.

6 Conclusions and Future Work

This study demonstrates a robust and interpretable framework for classifying developmental cell dynamics in *Drosophila melanogaster* using both time-aligned and feature-based unsupervised learning. By combining DTW, engineered time series features, and consensus clustering across six pipelines, we uncovered reproducible patterns in the oscillatory behavior of epithelial cells near the developing sex comb.

The resulting clusters revealed a consistent tiered structure. One group of cells, largely from a single specimen, showed a low-variability, low-amplitude baseline shared with a subset of cells from the other specimens. Other clusters exhibited progressively stronger and less predictable oscillations, suggesting distinct transitions in cell behavior potentially linked to spatial context or regulatory mechanisms. These findings support the idea that non-periodic oscillations may contribute to morphogenesis, possibly by eliminating unfit cells. Our framework thus provides a computational baseline for future comparisons to mutant or pathological datasets.

Future work will extend the analysis to additional specimens to test generalizability, incorporate distal foreleg regions, and integrate spatial metadata such location and neighborhood effects. Longer term, we aim to compare developmental trajectories to mutant lines and investigate whether early deviations in oscillatory behavior can serve as predictive markers of abnormal morphogenesis.

While our framework demonstrates reproducible clustering of Drosophila cell dynamics, several limitations should be noted. First, the dataset was modest in size and drawn from only three specimens, which may limit generalizability. Second, two consensus clusters contained only ten cells each, so their statistical profiles should be interpreted with caution. Finally, although our feature set was broad and carefully pruned for redundancy, unmeasured spatial or temporal factors may also influence clustering outcomes. These constraints highlight the need for larger datasets, expanded spatial coverage, and methodological refinement in future work.

Acknowledgments. This study was funded by a CMU Faculty Research Grant. The authors also used OpenAI's ChatGPT to assist with drafting text, refining wording, and supporting Python coding during data analysis. All scientific content, interpretations, and conclusions remain the sole responsibility of the authors.

Disclosure of Interests. The authors have no competing interests to declare that are relevant to the content of this article.

References

1. Malagon, J., et al.: Evolution of Drosophila sex comb length illustrates the inextricable interplay between selection and variation. PNAS **111**(39), E4103–E4109 (2014). https://doi.org/10.1073/pnas.1322342111
2. Malagon, J., Ho, E., Ahuja, A., Singh, R., Larsen, E.: Rotation of sex comb in Drosophila melanogaster requires precise and coordinated spatio-temporal dynamics from forces generated by epithelial cells. PLoS Comput. Biol. **14**(10), E1006455 (2018). https://doi.org/10.1371/journal.pcbi.1006455
3. Hosseini Moghadam, M., et al.: How Do Small Adjustments in Apical Surface Area Impact Tissue-Wide Homeostasis? microPublication biology (2025). https://doi.org/10.17912/micropub.biology.001727
4. Géron, A.: Hands-On Machine Learning with Scikit-Learn, Keras, and TensorFlow. 3rd ed. Sebastopol, CA: O'Reilly Media (2022)
5. Berndt, D. J., Clifford, J.: Using dynamic time warping to find patterns in time series. In: AAA1–94 Workshop on Knowledge Discovery in Databases, vol. 10(16), pp. 359–370 (1994). https://cdn.aaai.org/Workshops/1994/WS-94-03/WS94-03-031.pdf. (Accessed 31 October 2025)

6. Arbeitman, M.N., et al.: Gene expression during the life cycle of Drosophila melanogaster. Science **297**(5590), 2270–2275 (2002). https://doi.org/10.1126/science.1072152
7. Liu, X., Müller, H.G.: Modes and clustering for time-warped gene expression profile data. Bioinformatics **19**(15), 1937–1944 (2003). https://doi.org/10.1093/bioinformatics/btg257
8. Bakal, C., Aach, J., Church, G., Perrimon, N.: Quantitative morphological signatures define local signaling networks regulating cell morphology. Science **316**(5832), 1753–1756 (2007). https://doi.org/10.1126/science.1140324
9. Zinchenko, V., Hugger, J., Uhlmann, V., Arendt, D., Kreshuk, A.: MorphoFeatures for unsupervised exploration of cell types, tissues, and organs in volume electron microscopy. eLife **12**, e80918 (2023). https://doi.org/10.7554/eLife.80918
10. Moore, J.L., Du, Z., Bao, Z.: Systematic quantification of developmental phenotypes at single-cell resolution during embryogenesis. Development **140**, 3266–3274 (2013). https://doi.org/10.1242/dev.096040
11. Aach, J., Church, G.M.: Aligning gene expression time series with time warping algorithms. Bioinformatics **17**, 495–508 (2001). https://doi.org/10.1093/bioinformatics/17.6.495
12. Brunet, J.-P., Tamayo, P., Golub, T.R., Mesirov, J.P.: Metagenes and molecular pattern discovery using matrix factorization. Proc. Natl. Acad. Sci. **101**, 4164–4169 (2004). https://doi.org/10.1073/pnas.0308531101
13. Alexandrov, L.B., et al.: Signatures of mutational processes in human cancer. Nature **500**, 415–421 (2013). https://doi.org/10.1038/nature12477
14. Hoadley, K.A., et al.: Cell-of-origin patterns dominate the molecular classification of 10,000 tumors from 33 types of cancer. Cell **173**, 291-304.e6 (2018). https://doi.org/10.1016/j.cell.2018.03.022
15. Javed, A., Lee, B.S., Rizzo, D.M.: A benchmark study on time series clustering. Mach. Learn. Appli. **1**, 100001 (2020). https://doi.org/10.1016/j.mlwa.2020.100001

Risk Factors for the Development of Early Onset Cancers

Andrew Stevens[1(✉)], Jing Chen[1], Michael Behring[2], and Katia Maxwell[1]

[1] Department of Computer Science, Athens State University, Athens, AL, USA
Asteven4@my.athens.edu, {Jing.chen,Katia.maxwell}@athens.edu
[2] Department of Behavioral Science, Athens State University, Athens, AL, USA
Michael.Behring@athens.edu

Abstract. Cancers previously considered "cancers of old age" are making a statistically significant shift toward younger diagnoses. Termed Early Onset Cancers (EOC's), EOC's are particularly concerning because current medical research has been unable to identify a reason for this shift. Identifying risk factors for the development of EOC is an area of critical need. Given the unclear clinical application of extant literature, this study applies data clustering, heat maps, and data analysis to EOC data using clinical and genomic data from the publicly available PAN-CAN project. The study focus is to provide novel insights to elucidate risk factors that contribute to the development of EOC's, which will help inform preventative measures to potentially reduce the risk of EOC's.

Keywords: cancer · early onset · data analysis · risk reduction

1 Introduction

Cancer remains a disease of enormous personal, emotional, financial, and societal impact.Despite many decades of research, cancer remains a disease with many unknowns and variables. The quest to better understand, not just the nature of the disease, but also factors that lead to its development, is of paramount importance. An emerging field in cancer research is the growing rise of Early Onset Cancers (EOC's). These are cancers that generally afflict people later in life, usually those 50 years of age or older. However, the past two decades of cancer epidemiological research have shown a clear decrease in the age of diagnosis for a growing number of cancers once considered "cancers of old age" [2]. A thorough review of medical literature and protocols shows that regarding the preventative approaches recommended for EOC's, the evidence is inconclusive and remains a stark mystery [3]. Yet, epidemiological data continues to show a consistent increase in the number of cancer cases below 50 years of age [4].

This paper uses data analysis and data mining techniques with publicly available cancer data to elucidate clinical and genomic factors that could be correlated with a potential increase in risk for the development of EOC's. The goal of this paper is to contribute to a growing body of research providing new insights into EOC's and provide information that meaningfully informs methods and strategies for mitigating risk factors

A. Alsadoon et al. (Eds.): CSCE 2025, CCIS 2935, pp. 28–39, 2026.
https://doi.org/10.1007/978-3-032-22199-5_3

for EOC's. The problem this paper seeks to address is a dearth of knowledge regarding the causative factors and the risks associated with the development of EOC's. This paper is designed to be informational, providing new insights into the PANCAN data that yields useful information to help better inform the understanding of risk factors for EOC's as well as provide a foundation for follow-up and future research.

2 Methodology

For this paper, the publicly available PANCAN database, which provided both clinical and genomic data, was selected as the data source to analyze. Upon obtaining the data, the process of data cleaning was immediately begun. The datasets were obtained in two separate sets: the clinical dataset and the genomic dataset. The datasets were comprised of 10,957 patients across 18 different clinical variables and 20,531 genes. The first method was to determine which of the clinical variables included in the PANCAN clinical dataset would be most insightful for the study. Of the original 747 variables, 18 were selected for the study.

PyCharm, a Python IDE developed by JetBrains, was used to write, edit, modify, debug, and run the scripts.

As Fig. 1 indicates below, the cleaning process had to be performed in several key stages, first excluding metrics outside the scope of the study, and then transposing the genomic data to be compatible with the formatting of the clinical data for a merger.

Once these checks verified that the data had been properly transposed and preserved, the two files were merged into a single file. The final merged dataset appended the genomic columns onto the clinical data. To keep the original data integrity and accuracy, and prevent the program from crashing during analysis, "[Not Available]" was removed from the dataset. After this, additional cleaning needed to be done to represent concepts such as "Male" and "Female" as numerical values. This was done with two other categories, vital status and race. ICD code values and tumor location sites were not modified, however, due to the complexity of the values and the understanding that a numerical transformation would be functionally unnavigable or incomprehensible. Figure 2 shows the second main stage of the data cleaning process.

Once this was performed, data clustering analysis was performed on the training dataset. For this, a KMeans clustering analysis was performed using 2D approaches. As the study's focus is on EOC's, the column, "age_at_initial_pathologic_diagnosis" was compared to "gender", "race", and "vital_status". These clusters were graphed using Python's matplotlib and sklearn libraries.

Following this, the Seaborn and matplotlib packages were used to create heatmaps from the training dataset. These were saved as images.

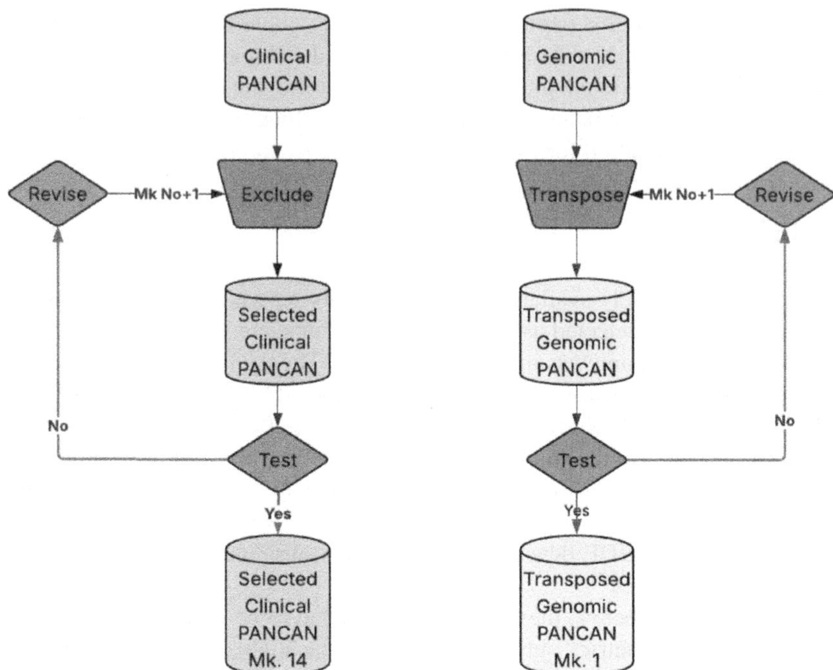

Fig. 1. Flow Chart of the Initial Data Cleaning & Preparation Process

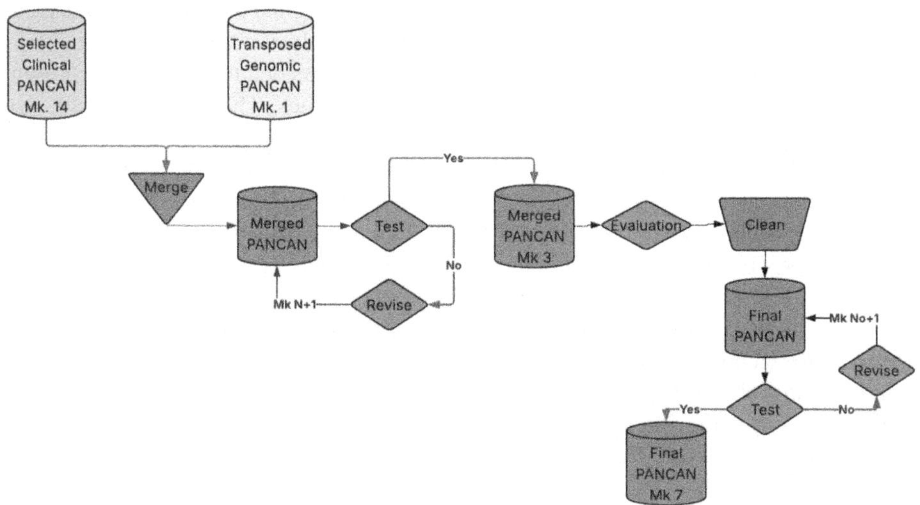

Fig. 2. Merging of the Datasets and Secondary Cleaning

3 Results

As the primary focus of the study is the age of pathological diagnosis in the patients who participated in the PANCAN study, getting an initial understanding of the age spread in the data might yield some important insights. Figure 4 illustrates a general statistical overview of the training dataset used for the paper's analyses (Fig. 3).

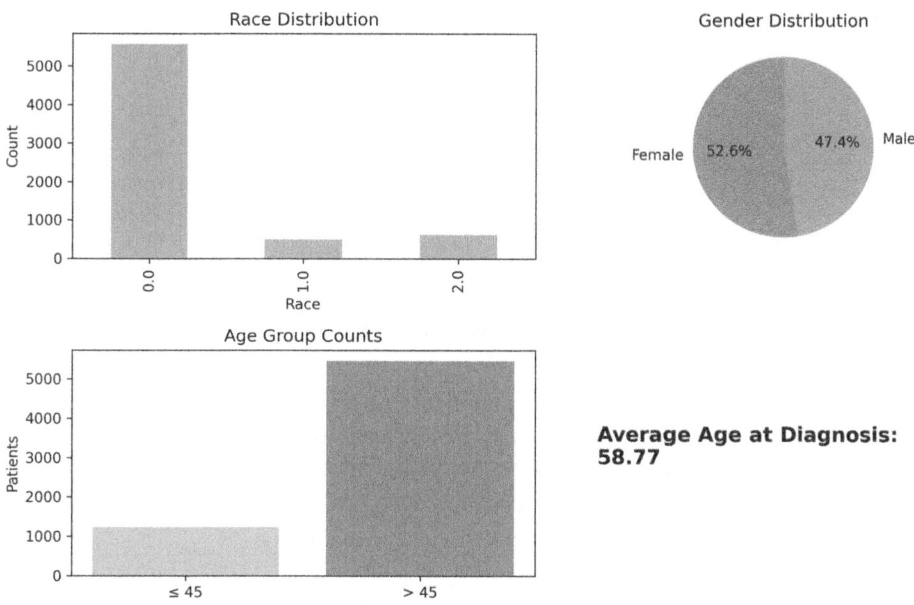

Fig. 3. General statistical analysis of the Paper Dataset

Figure 5 illustrates the age range in the PANCAN population. The general trend of the graph is quite consistent with a standard bell curve, with the peak of the graph falling around 62 years of age. This is consistent with current data, that is, the likelihood of a cancer diagnosis has been consistently shown to increase with age. Because this study focuses on EOC type cancers, the next data analysis was to narrow the age range to patients under 45 and plot the results.

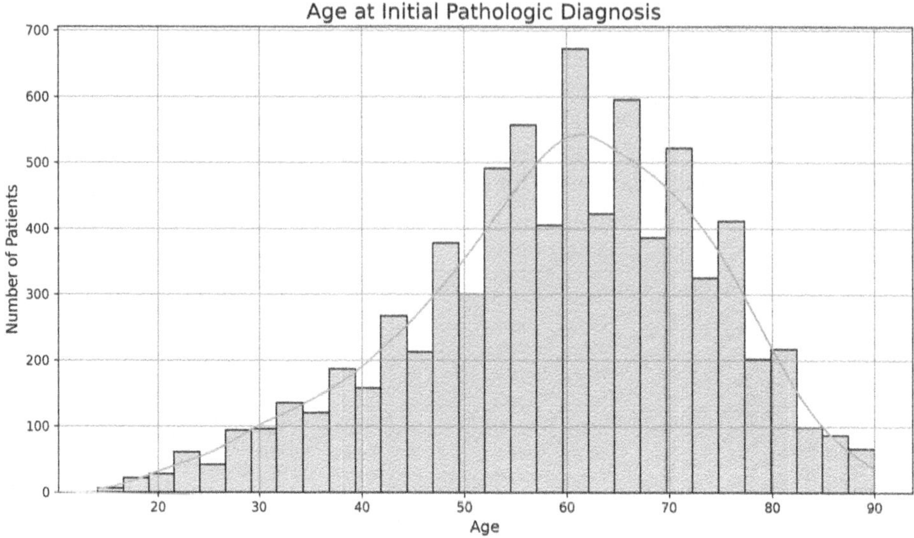

Fig. 4. Age range of patients in the PANCAN study

In reviewing Fig. 6, there were no significant surprises here. Just as was shown in Fig. 5, there is a nearly linear increase in the patient age at diagnosis with each increment. That is, until age 43, where the diagnosis markedly increases.

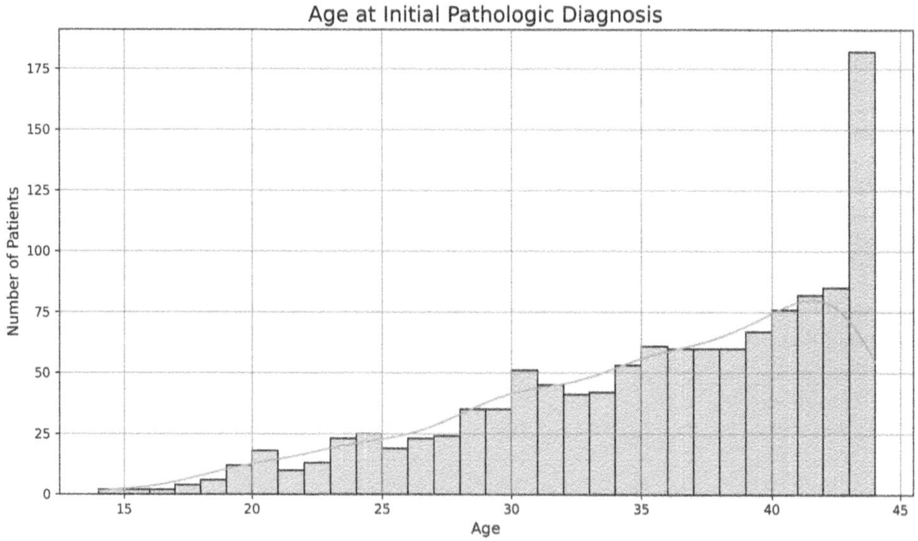

Fig. 5. A selected age range under 45 in the PANCAN dataset

To better understand this phenomenon, an additional demographic analysis was done. In this analysis, as shown in Fig. 7, was to increase the age range to 55 and set the minimum age to 20, in so doing, it helps expand the possible age range to see if Fig. 6's dramatic increase continues, and it also helps exclude pediatric cancers, which have a very different set of factors.

In Fig. 7, the dramatic increase in diagnoses seen in Fig. 6 was not reflected when the age range was expanded by 10 years. Instead, a consistent increase in diagnoses was seen overall. This can be better understood with a numerical comparison of the data within Fig. 7. Within the dataset, there were 225 patients between 20 and 30 years of age, 540 patients between 30 and 40 years of age, and 1,016 patients between 40 and 50 years of age. This would translate to a 41 percent increase in cancer diagnoses between patients in their 20's versus patients in their 30's, and a 54 percent increase in cancer diagnoses between patients in their 30's and 40's. The core statistical data shows that while a statistically significant number of cancers occur in patients younger than 45 years of age, the age demographic with the highest number of diagnoses is consistent with the current general understanding that a patient's age is one of the greatest risk factors for cancer. This is consistent biologically with the accrual of somatic mutations and cellular damage over the life of an individual. Moving into data clustering yielded some additional insights.

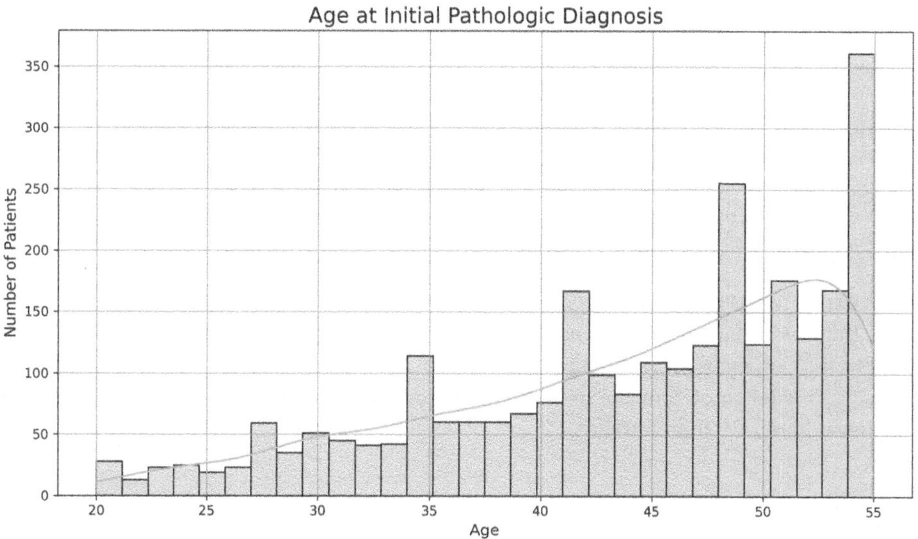

Fig. 6. A modified age ranges from 20 to 55 within the selected PANCAN dataset

Data Clustering

Figure 8 illustrates a clustering of age at diagnosis with vital status. Using numerical categorization, where 0 is equivalent to deceased and 1 is equivalent to living, the analysis breaks diagnosis down into two main groups, and the breakpoint is near the age range shown in the statistical analysis in Figs. 5, 6–7. One trend that is shown here, too is that there is a greater number of living patients post diagnosis under 30 than deceased patients. Based on the data here, it could potentially be inferred that a younger diagnosis is positively correlated with a greater likelihood of survival. This correlation certainly warrants further investigation and study.

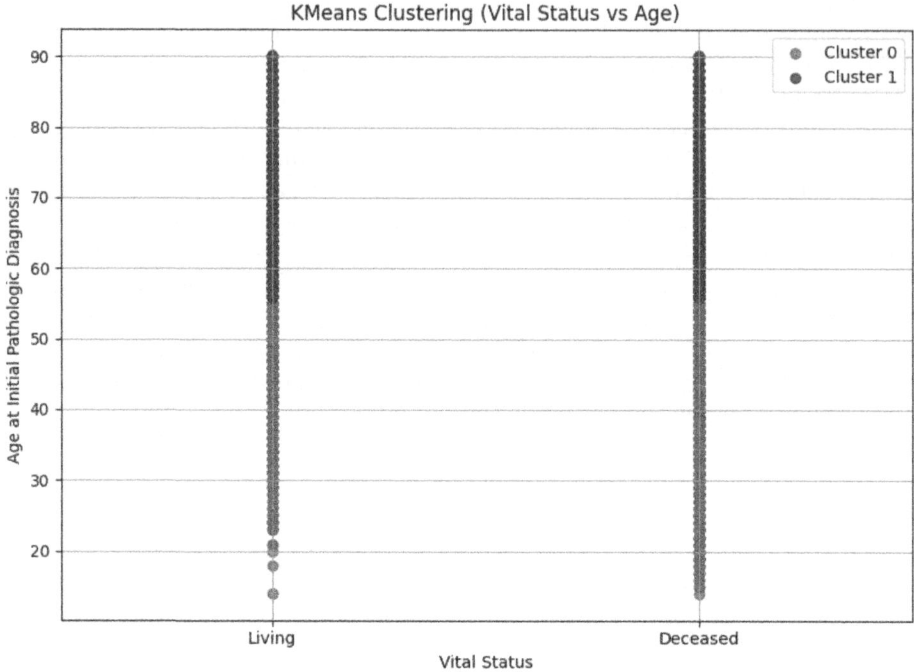

Fig. 7. KMeans cluster analysis of age of diagnosis vs vital status (survival)

In exploring gender versus age of diagnosis, a similar trend emerges. Figure 9 illustrates that a similar breakpoint is placed around 55 years of age that divides the two clusters. For analysis, females are categorized as 0, and males as 1. Here, given the quite close balance of females to males, it appears there might be slightly more males diagnosed under 20 than females.

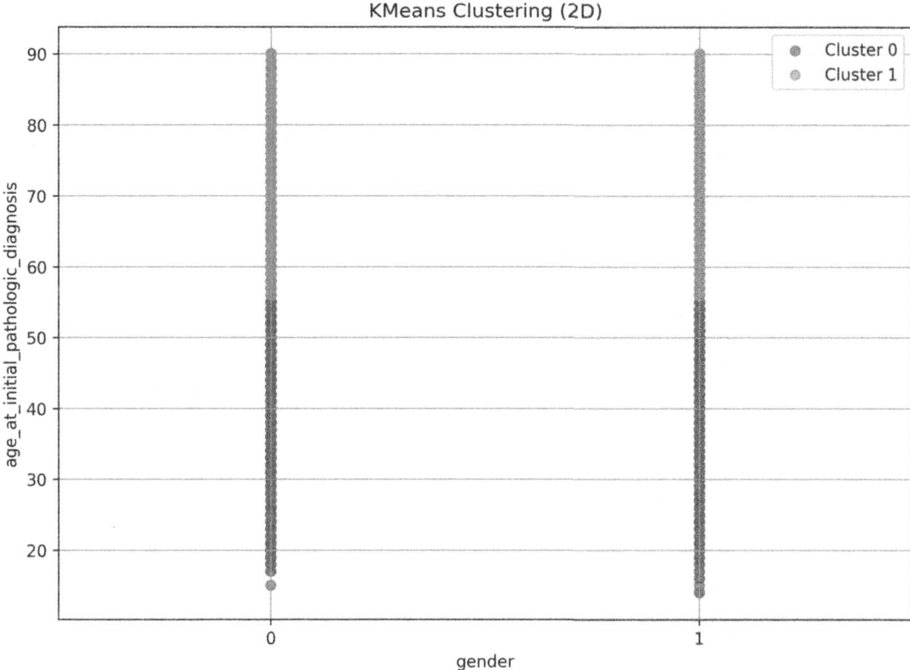

Fig. 8. KMeans cluster analysis of age of diagnosis vs. gender

In Fig. 10, a numerical categorization was applied where 0 is equivalent to White, 1 is equivalent to Asian, and 2 is equivalent to Black/African American. The reason for this approach was the requirement for categorization of races to facilitate data analysis. The categorizations were chosen based on the representation of patient racial groups in the study. By far, patients who were white represented the largest racial group in the study, followed by African American/Black, and Asian. Patients who were white made up 5576 patients in the training dataset, followed by 615 patients who were Black, and 491 patients who were Asian.

Again, there is a similar breakpoint to the other two cluster analyses. Perhaps what is most interesting, however, is the diagnosis in the under 30 patients between the three races in the PANCAN study. Both Asian and Black patients have fewer diagnoses in this age range than White patients, additionally, both groups exhibited fewer clusters of diagnoses after 80 than did White patients. This could be a meaningful insight. However, it may be more complex. Within the study, White is by far the most represented demographic. More directly translated, White patients comprise roughly 83 percent of the total patients in the dataset. Because of this, a direct adjusted comparison may give a more accurate comparison between races. This information also raises additional questions about the representation of different races in medical and clinical studies. Naturally, the nation's demographics will reflect the number of different races represented in studies, but it indicates a critical area where more representation of other races is vital to having a better understanding of the prevalence of diseases such as cancer across a myriad of races.

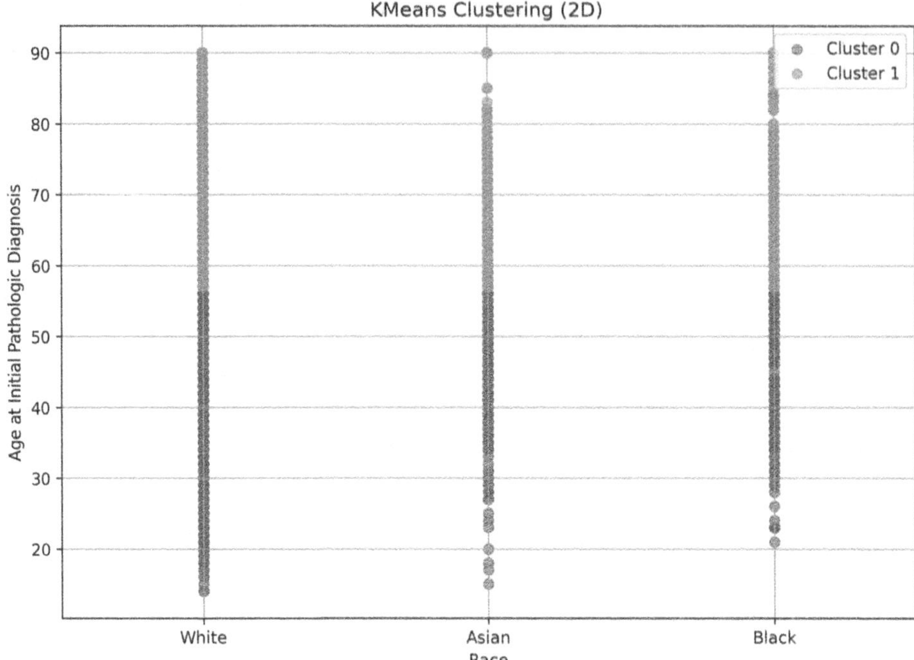

Fig. 9. KMeans cluster analysis of age at initial pathologic diagnosis vs race

Heatmap Data

Finally, the heat map analysis showed yet another fascinating angle to consider. The heatmap shows quite a bit of activity. In Fig. 11, "gender", "days_to_birth", "age_at_initial_pathological_diagnosis", and both tissue collection indicator columns show significant variation. What is noteworthy in reviewing this heat map is that the gender and age columns show great variation and indicate there is the potential for significant impacts on the data.

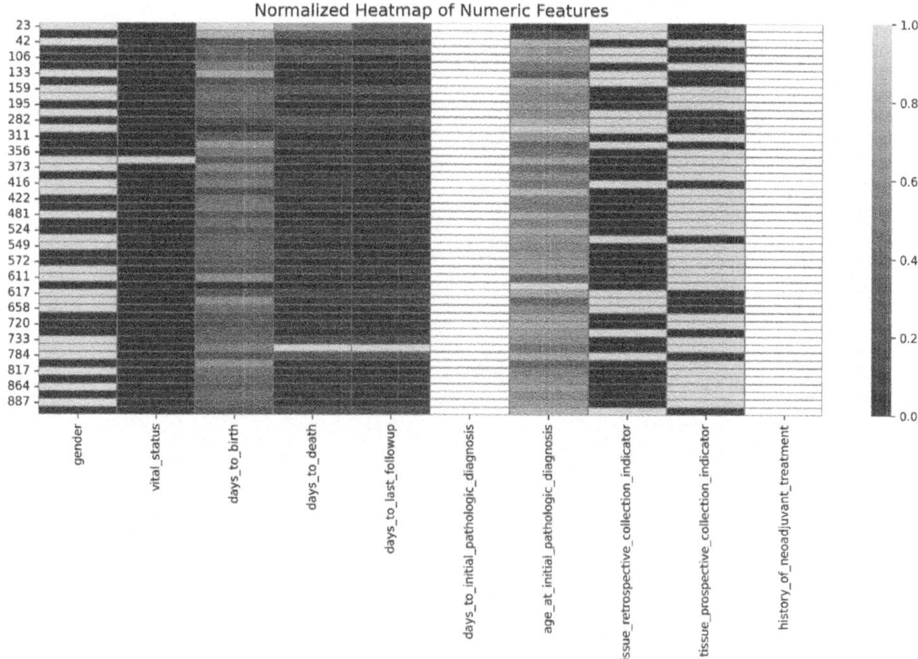

Fig. 10. Normalized heatmap of PANCAN dataset patient sample over the most active clinical metrics

The immense size of the combined datasets made building a full scale heatmap impossible on a PC. To seek useful insights despite the hardware limitations, while an opportunity to utilize a supercomputer cluster was requested, a Python script was written that sampled a subset of patients randomly against the genes that had the most variability. The goal was to evaluate gene expression against patient data to determine if there were any visible trends that might warrant further, more focused investigation. Across a random sample of patients from the dataset, Fig. 12 illustrates three genes that showed notably high activity within the subset of genes showing the highest variability, KLRC2|3822, OR2J3|442186, and SNRPG|6637. These genes might prove insightful for additional future research.

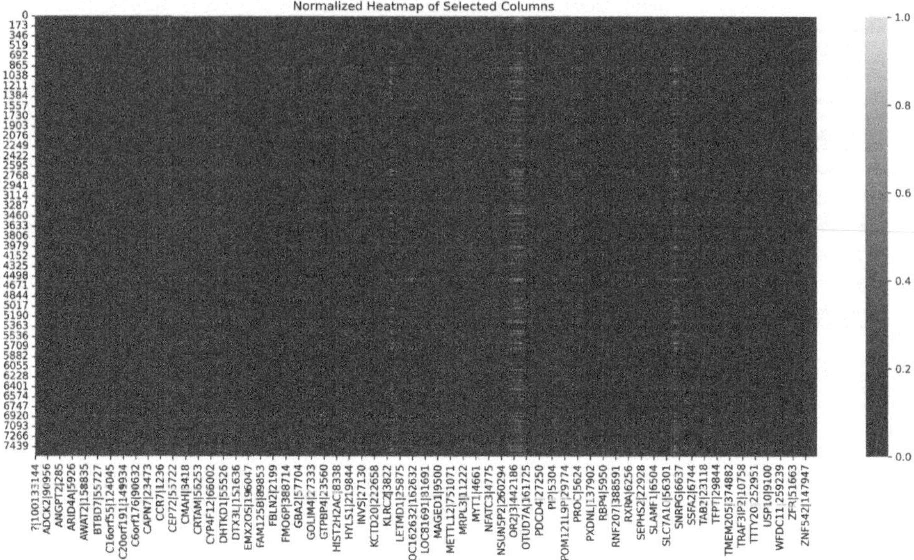

Fig. 11. Selected Heatmap of Highest Variability Genes in a Random Limited Selection of Patients

4 Summary and Future Work

Given the data over the last two decades showing clear evidence of a statistically significant reduction in the age of pathological diagnosis of various cancers, and the inconclusive understanding in the medical and research fields of this phenomenon, this study utilized data mining and analysis techniques with a publicly available data set, the PANCAN project, to search for novel correlations.

We used clustering, heat maps, and data analysis to search for novel insights in clinical and genomic data that might indicate a correlation between potential risk factors and EOC's. The results of the study largely supported the long-held stance that an individual's risk of developing cancer is most strongly associated with advancing age and the growing accumulation of somatic line mutations and damage.

During the research, some interesting insights were uncovered; however, the findings of this study at best remain inconclusive, as the study did not yield any significant correlations with age of pathological diagnosis and risk factors for EOC's. Further studies might benefit from cancer datasets involving specific types of cancer, for example, colorectal cancer, which is one of the leading EOC's currently. Additionally, since this phenomenon has become so prevalent in the last 15 years or so, it might be helpful to find cancer data that has been collected within the last few years. It would also be especially interesting to compare cancer data from different ethnic groups and places around the world to see if cancer diagnoses and types remain similar or change notably. However, it is an important consideration that other ethnicities may experience different rates of EOC's, yet, the full nature of this is unable to be ascertained due to underrepresentation in this study's dataset.

References

1. Crick: How computer scientists are helping beat cancer. https://www.crick.ac.uk/news/2019-02-04_how-computer-scientists-are-helping-beat-cancer. Accessed 30 Oct 2024
2. Akimoto, N., et al.: Rising incidence of early-onset colorectal cancer — a call to action. Nat. Rev. Clin. Oncol. **18**(4), 2024 (2020). https://doi.org/10.1038/s41571-020-00445-1. Accessed 14 Oct 2024
3. Rosenberg, A.: What's behind rising colorectal cancer rates in young adults?. City of Hope, Mar. 11, 2024. https://www.cityofhope.org/whats-behind-rising-colorectal-cancer-rates-in-young-adults. Accessed 27 Apr 2025
4. NCI Staff: Colorectal Cancer Rising among Young Adults - National Cancer Institute. https://www.cancer.gov/news-events/cancer-currents-blog/2020/colorectal-cancer-rising-younger-adults. Accessed 30 Oct 2024
5. D. Underferth: What young adults need to know about colorectal cancer. MD Anderson Cancer Center: https://www.mdanderson.org/cancerwise/why-are-more-young-adults-getting-colorectal-cancer-what-to-know.h00–159385890.html. Accessed 14 Oct 2024
6. American Cancer Society: Testing for Colorectal Cancer | How Is Colorectal Cancer Diagnosed? (2023). https://www.cancer.org/cancer/types/colon-rectal-cancer/detection-diagnosis-staging/how-diagnosed.html. Accessed 5 Oct 2024
7. Rogers, J.E., Johnson, B.: The reality of early-onset colorectal cancer: highlighting the needs in a unique but emerging population. Digestive Med. Res. **4**, 63 (2021). https://doi.org/10.21037/dmr-21-77. Accessed 9 Oct 2024
8. Jones, P., Cade, J.E., Evans, C.E., Hancock, N., Greenwood, D.C.: The Mediterranean diet and risk of colorectal cancer in the UK Women's Cohort study. Int. J. Epidemiol. **46**(6), 1786–1796 (2017). https://doi.org/10.1093/ije/dyx155. Accessed 30 Oct 2024
9. Farinetti, A., Zurlo, V., Manenti, A., Coppi, F., Mattioli, A.V.: Mediterranean diet and colorectal cancer: a systematic review. Nutrition **43–44**, 83–88 (2017). https://doi.org/10.1016/j.nut.2017.06.008. Accessed 30 Oct 2024
10. Namasivayam, V., Lim, S.: Recent advances in the link between physical activity, sedentary behavior, physical fitness, and colorectal cancer. F1000 Res. **6**, 199 (2017). https://doi.org/10.12688/f1000research.9795.1. Accessed 9 Oct 2024
11. Nguyen, L.H., et al.: Sedentary behaviors, TV viewing time, and risk of young-onset colorectal cancer. JNCI Cancer Spectr **2**(4) (2019). https://doi.org/10.1093/jncics/pky073. Accessed 14 Oct 2024
12. Davis, D., et al.: Wireless technologies, non-ionizing electromagnetic fields and children: identifying and reducing health risks. Current Prob. Pediatric Adolescent Health Care **53**(2), 101374 (2023). https://doi.org/10.1016/j.cppeds.2023.101374. Accessed 30 Oct 2024
13. Li, S., Keenan, J.I., Shaw, I.C., Frizelle, F.A.: Could microplastics be a driver for early onset colorectal cancer?. Cancers **15**(13), 3323 (2023). https://doi.org/10.3390/cancers15133323. Accessed 14 Oct 2024
14. Sánchez-Alcoholado, L., et al.: The role of the gut microbiome in colorectal cancer development and therapy response. Cancers **12**(6), 1406 (2020). https://doi.org/10.3390/cancers12061406. Accessed 30 Oct 2024

Integrating Pharmacokinetics and Pharmacodynamics Modeling with Quantum Regression for Predicting Herbal Compound Toxicity

Don Roosan[1(✉)], Saif Nirzhor[2], and Rubayat Khan[3]

[1] School of Engineering and Computational Sciences, Merrimack College, 315 Turnpike St, North Andover, MA 01845, USA
roosand@merrimack.edu

[2] University of Texas Southwestern Medical Center, 5323 Harry Hines Blvd, Dallas, TX 75390, USA

[3] University of Nebraska Medical Center, S 42Nd &, Emile St, Omaha, NE 68198, USA

Abstract. Herbal compounds present complex toxicity profiles that are often influenced by both intrinsic chemical properties and pharmacokinetics (PK) governing absorption and clearance. In this study, we develop a quantum regression model to predict acute toxicity severity (LD_{50}) for herbal-derived compounds by integrating toxicity data from NICEATM with pharmacological features from TCMSP. We first extract molecular descriptors alongside PK metrics such as oral bioavailability, combining them into a unified feature set. A quantum linear systems algorithm is then applied to solve the regression problem in a high-dimensional quantum state space, capturing multifaceted feature interactions efficiently. Comparative evaluation against classical models, including linear regression and random forest, shows that the quantum model achieves lower prediction errors and higher explanatory power. Analysis of learned coefficients reveals the importance of PK features for modeling toxicity, highlighting that well-absorbed, lipophilic compounds display heightened risk. We further demonstrate the model's utility by predicting toxicity for additional herbal compounds lacking experimental data, identifying several high-risk candidates. This work underscores the potential of integrating pharmacokinetics into quantum machine learning to elucidate toxicity mechanisms, offering a more comprehensive approach to herbal compound safety assessment.

Keywords: Quantum Regression · Pharmacokinetics · Toxicity Prediction · Herbal Compounds · NICEATM · TCMSP

1 Introduction

Herbal medicines contain a vast array of natural compounds that can produce therapeutic effects but also carry risks of toxicity. Ensuring the safety of these herbal compounds is crucial, especially as their use becomes more widespread globally [1–3]. An accurate

A. Alsadoon et al. (Eds.): CSCE 2025, CCIS 2935, pp. 40–58, 2026.
https://doi.org/10.1007/978-3-032-22199-5_4

assessment of toxicity often requires understanding not just the chemical structure of a compound, but also how the body processes and responds to it. In pharmacology, this is addressed through pharmacokinetics (PK) and pharmacodynamics (PD) modeling [4, 5]. Pharmacokinetics describes what the body does to a compound – how it is absorbed, distributed, metabolized, and excreted – essentially determining the concentration of the compound over time in various tissues. Pharmacodynamics, on the other hand, describes what the compound does to the body – the biochemical and physiological effects and the mechanism of its action [6–8]. Together, PK and PD relationships define the exposure and response profile of a compound. This profile is directly linked to toxicity: a compound might be inherently hazardous (PD effect), but if it is poorly absorbed or rapidly eliminated, it may never reach harmful levels in the body. Conversely, a relatively mild compound could become dangerous if it accumulates to high concentrations due to slow metabolism or distribution into sensitive organs [9, 10]. For this reason, PK/PD modeling is of great importance in understanding compound toxicity. It provides insight into dosage thresholds, time-dependent effects, and individual susceptibility, all of which influence toxicity severity[11]. In toxicology research, PK/PD models have been used to predict outcomes like acute toxicity, organ-specific damage, and therapeutic index [8]. By simulating how a compound moves through the body (PK) and interacts with biological targets (PD), researchers can estimate the likelihood and severity of toxic effects. For example, a PK model might show that a compound concentrates in the liver, and a PD model might reveal that the compound inhibits a crucial liver enzyme – together, a PK/PD analysis could predict a risk of liver toxicity at a certain dose [12]. In the context of herbal compounds, PK/PD relationships are especially important because these compounds often have complex structures and multiple biological targets [13–15]. Many natural products are multi-target agents, meaning they can modulate several pathways at once; this polypharmacology can lead to unpredictable toxicological profiles unless the underlying PK/PD is understood. One key aspect of PK/PD relationships in toxicity is their nonlinearity. Toxicity levels do not always increase in a simple linear fashion with dose or concentration. Instead, there may be threshold effects, saturable processes, or time-dependent accumulations [16–18]. These nonlinear dynamics arise from the interplay of various PK and PD factors – for instance, dose-dependent changes in absorption rates, active metabolites formed during metabolism, feedback loops in biological response, or receptor desensitization over time. PK/PD relationships strongly influence toxicity levels: they determine the concentration of the compound at the target site and the duration of exposure, which together dictate whether toxic mechanisms are triggered. In herbal compounds, additional complexity comes from variability in human metabolism and interactions between components. Capturing all these nuances requires advanced modeling techniques[19–21]. Traditional computational approaches to model toxicity – such as quantitative structure-activity relationship (QSAR) models and conventional machine learning – have had notable successes, but they often simplify or ignore the detailed PK/PD dynamics [22, 23]. Classical QSAR models, for example, use molecular descriptors (properties derived from chemical structure) to predict toxicity endpoints. These descriptors may indirectly reflect some PK/PD aspects, and as such QSAR models can capture general toxicity trends. However, classical models might struggle with highly nonlinear relationships or complex conditional dependencies [24,

25]. Standard machine-learning algorithms like random forests or neural networks can handle more complexity than linear QSAR, but they still operate on classical computing architectures that must explicitly sample and learn each pattern in the data. When the interactions between features become combinatorially large, classical algorithms may require very large training datasets or simplified model structures to learn effectively [26–30].

In recent years, the rise of quantum computing has opened a new frontier for tackling complex computational problems. Quantum computing operates on principles fundamentally different from classical computing. By using quantum bits (qubits) that can exist in superposition states, a quantum computer can, in a sense, explore multiple possibilities simultaneously. Moreover, qubits can become entangled, creating direct correlations that classical bits cannot replicate [31–35]. These properties allow certain computations to be performed with potentially exponential speed-ups over classical methods, particularly for problems in linear algebra, optimization, and searching – all of which are relevant to modeling and regression tasks. Quantum regression refers to the use of quantum algorithms to perform regression analysis, i.e., to find the relationship between input variables and an output variable. Another advantage that quantum approaches might offer is related to solving systems of equations and optimization problems [15, 36–38]. Many regression models boil down to solving linear or nonlinear equations derived from data. Quantum algorithms have been developed to solve linear systems of equations faster than classical ones under certain conditions [15]. In the context of toxicity prediction, this means a quantum computer could potentially find the best-fit model parameters more quickly, even as we include more features or more complex relationships [38].

There is a strong motivation to integrate PK/PD considerations into computational toxicity prediction of herbal compounds, and doing so leads to challenging nonlinear modeling tasks. Quantum regression offers a novel computational approach that could handle these challenges more effectively than classical methods. The overarching goal is to demonstrate that quantum algorithms can improve or at least match predictive performance in a complex biomedical problem, and to shed light on the PK/PD factors driving toxicity [23, 32, 39].

2 Methods

2.1 Data Collection and Integration

Toxicity Data (NICEATM Dataset): We obtained toxicity data from the National Toxicology Program's NICEATM database, which compiles results of toxicological studies. Specifically, we focused on acute toxicity severity measurements for a diverse set of compounds. Each compound in this dataset has an associated toxicity endpoint reflecting how poisonous the substance is under certain conditions. We selected this endpoint as our quantitative measure of toxicity severity. The NICEATM dataset provided both the numeric toxicity values and information about the chemical identity for each compound. After initial filtering to remove inorganic substances and duplicates, our working toxicity dataset included N compounds covering a wide range of toxicity levels – from relatively non-toxic substances to highly lethal ones [40–43].

Herbal Compound Data (TCMSP Database): To bring in pharmacokinetic and pharmacodynamic features, we used the Traditional Chinese Medicine Systems Pharmacology (TCMSP) database. TCMSP contains extensive data on natural compounds found in medicinal herbs, including not only their chemical structures but also predicted ADME (absorption, distribution, metabolism, excretion) properties and known or predicted targets (which relate to PD). Key pharmacokinetic-related features available in TCMSP and relevant to toxicity include, for example, oral bioavailability, drug-likeness scores, caco-2 permeability, blood-brain barrier permeability, and half-life or clearance predictions. We also extracted basic molecular descriptors from TCMSP such as molecular weight, logP, number of aromatic rings, and so on, which are standard features in QSAR modeling [44].

Data Integration: The two datasets were integrated by matching compounds present in both. We identified compounds from the NICEATM toxicity dataset that are also found in herbal sources catalogued by TCMSP. This matching was done via unique identifiers and by chemical structure comparison. The overlapping set of compounds – a collection of herbal compounds with known toxicity measurements – formed the basis for our modeling. For each of these compounds, we constructed a comprehensive feature vector: this included structural descriptors and PK/PD-related features obtained from TCMSP. By doing so, we ensure that our model has information reflecting both the compound's intrinsic chemistry and its pharmacokinetic behavior. We hypothesized that including these pharmacological features would improve toxicity predictions, as they directly relate to how much of the compound actually reaches target sites and how it might exert effects – information not contained in chemical structure alone. Prior to modeling, all feature values were normalized to a consistent scale, since they have different units and magnitudes. Continuous features like molecular weight or LD_{50} values were z-score normalized to aid numerical stability in model training. Categorical features were encoded as binary indicators. The toxicity severity values were transformed as needed for regression; in our case we used a logarithmic transformation so that extremely toxic and non-toxic compounds are brought to a more comparable numeric range and to linearize the relationship between features and outcome to some extent.

2.2 Modeling Approach

For the classical approach, we experimented with multiple algorithms, including multiple linear regression and more flexible nonlinear models such as random-forest regression. The multiple linear regression uses ordinary least squares fit to linearly relate all features to the toxicity outcome. More formally, if each compound i has features $x_{i1}, x_{i2}, \ldots, x_{iM}$ (where M is the number of features) and toxicity value y_i, the linear model assumes

$$y_i \approx \beta_0 + \beta_1 x_{i1} + \beta_2 x_{i2} + \cdots + \beta_M x_{iM} \tag{1}$$

where the coefficients $\beta_{0\ldots M}$ are fitted to minimize the sum of squared errors

$$\sum_i (y_i - \hat{y}_i)^2 \tag{2}$$

Although linear regression is easy to interpret, it may not capture complex feature interactions, so we also trained a nonlinear tree-based model (random forest) that can automatically model some interactions and non-linear effects. The random-forest model, consisting of an ensemble of decision trees, was trained with 10-fold cross-validation to tune hyperparameters (such as the number of trees and tree depth) to avoid overfitting given the size of our dataset.

The cornerstone of our study is a quantum regression strategy for predicting compound toxicity. Conceptually, the task is the same as in classical regression-learning a mapping $f(\mathrm{X})$ from a set of molecular-descriptor features $\mathrm{X} \in \mathbb{R}^{N \times M}$ to observed toxicity values $\mathbf{y} \in \mathbb{R}^{N}$. The difference is that the heavy linear-algebra and optimization steps are executed on quantum hardware, enabling us to exploit the exponentially large Hilbert space for richer function representations.

We implement a quantum algorithm that parallels ordinary least-squares (OLS) regression: the algorithm ultimately solves a linear system but can embed nonlinear structure through quantum state preparation and entangling operations. After assembling the (column-augmented) feature matrix $\mathbf{X}$ and target vector $\mathbf{y}$ for the training set, the optimal coefficient vector

$$\mathrm{w}^{\star} = \left[\, \beta_0 \; \beta_1 \; \ldots \; \beta_M \,\right]^{\top} \tag{3}$$

is defined by the normal equations

$$\mathrm{X}^{\top}\mathrm{X}\mathrm{w}^{\star} = \mathrm{X}^{\top}\mathrm{y} \tag{4}$$

whose closed-form solution is

$$\mathrm{w}^{\star} = \left(\mathrm{X}^{\top}\mathrm{X}\right)^{-1}\mathrm{X}^{\top}\mathrm{y} \tag{5}$$

In the quantum setting, the matrix-vector solve $\mathrm{Aw}^{\star} = \mathrm{b}$ (with $\mathrm{A} = \mathrm{X}^{\top}\mathrm{X}$ and $\mathrm{b} = \mathrm{X}^{\top}\mathrm{y}$) is performed by a quantum linear-systems algorithm, while the data are encoded into quantum states via amplitude or qubit-wise encodings. This hybrid workflow retains the interpretability of linear regression yet gains the expressive power and potential speedups offered by quantum computation.

In a classical computation, one would compute $X^T X$ and $X^T \mathbf{y}$ and then invert the matrix $X^T X$ (or use a solver) to find w. In our quantum regression, we implemented a quantum linear systems algorithm to solve for w on a quantum state processor. The approach is as follows: we interpret $X^T X$ as a linear operator A acting on an M-dimensional vector space (the space of features), and $X^T y$ as a vector $\mathbf{b}$ in that space. The task $A\mathrm{w} = \mathrm{b}$ is then a system of linear equations. On the quantum computer, we prepare a quantum state that represents the vector $\mathbf{b}$ (the right-hand side). This involves encoding the components of $X^T y$ into the amplitudes of a quantum state $|b\rangle$. Formally, we create:

$$|b\rangle = \frac{1}{\left\|X^T y\right\|} \sum\nolimits_{j=1}^{M} \left(X^T y\right)_j |j\rangle \tag{6}$$

where $|j\rangle$ is an orthonormal basis state corresponding to the j-th feature coefficient, and $(X^T y)_j$ is the j th component of the vector $X^T y$. The norm $\|X^T y\|$ is used to normalize the state. Similarly, the matrix $A = X^T X$ is represented as a linear transformation on this M -dimensional quantum state space. Using quantum phase estimation and related techniques (as in the Harrow-Hassidim-Lloyd algorithm for solving linear systems), the quantum algorithm finds a state proportional to the solution $|w\rangle$, such that:

$$|w\rangle \approx \frac{1}{\kappa} A^{-1} |b\rangle \tag{7}$$

where κ is a normalization factor (related to the condition number of A). The state $|w\rangle$ encodes the regression coefficients $\beta_1, \beta_2, \ldots, \beta_M$ in its amplitude components. (The intercept term $\beta < sub > 0$ can be handled by including a constant feature in X, , which we did.) Once this quantum state proportional to the solution vector is prepared, measuring the state yields the coefficients w. In practice, we performed multiple runs to reconstruct all components of w with high fidelity.

For implementation, we utilized a high-level quantum computing framework to simulate the quantum regression (given the current limitations of quantum hardware for large numerical problems). The simulation strictly followed the quantum algorithm steps, which allowed us to verify the correctness of the approach on our data. We emphasize that in describing the method, we treat it as if running on an actual quantum processing unit capable of these operations. The outcome of the quantum regression algorithm is a set of regression weights w just like a classical model, and the prediction for any new compound with feature vector x is given by the inner product:

$$\hat{y} = \beta_0 + \sum_{j=1}^{M} \beta_j x_j \tag{8}$$

using the coefficients obtained via the quantum solver. In essence, after the quantum computation yields the model parameters, making a prediction is computationally trivial and identical to a classical linear model prediction.

2.3 Modeling Training and Evaluation

We trained the models on the integrated herbal compound toxicity dataset. The dataset of compounds was randomly split into a training set and a hold-out test set (20% of the compounds) to evaluate performance on unseen data. We ensured that the split maintained a balanced representation of low, medium, and high toxicity compounds in both training and test sets, given the wide range of toxicity values. The classical models were trained on the training set using standard algorithms – the linear model via direct solution of normal equations and the random forest via an ensemble training procedure with early stopping to prevent overfit. This training phase on the quantum side involves quantum state preparations and transformations but does not require an iterative gradient descent like classical neural networks.

After training, we evaluated all models on the hold-out test set. The primary evaluation metrics were the root mean squared error (RMSE) between predicted and actual toxicity values (in the transformed pLD_{50} scale) and the coefficient of determination (R2), which indicates the proportion of variance in toxicity outcomes explained by the model [45]. We also examined the mean absolute error (MAE) for an intuitive measure of average prediction error in the original units. In addition, for interpretability, we analyzed the learned coefficients w from the quantum regression model to identify which features had the largest influence on toxicity. Because our feature set included descriptors linked to PK like oral bioavailability, etc., we were particularly interested in whether those features were assigned significant weight by the model, as that would highlight their role in toxicity severity.

Finally, although the focus was on predicting known toxicity values, we explored the model's utility in a prospective manner. We took a set of additional herbal compounds from the TCMSP database that did not have known toxicity data in NICEATM and used our trained quantum model to predict their toxicity severity. This exercise aimed to demonstrate how the model could be used as a screening tool to flag potentially toxic herbal constituents. We aggregated the predictions for these additional compounds and noted which ones the model predicted to have high toxicity. While no ground truth was available for these, such predictions can guide future experimental testing. All analysis was performed in a computational environment with reproducible scripts for data processing, classical model training, and quantum simulation, ensuring that the methodology can be audited or extended by others.

3 Results

3.1 Data Summary and Feature Characteristics

After integrating the NICEATM and TCMSP datasets, we obtained **118** herbal-related compounds with known acute toxicity measurements to use in model development. These compounds originate from a variety of medicinal plants and span a broad chemical space: for instance, our dataset included alkaloids, flavonoids, and terpenoids, among others. The toxicity severity values ranged from about 1.3 (extremely toxic, corresponding to an LD_{50} of roughly 5 mg/kg) to around 5.0 (very low toxicity, LD_{50} over 10,000 mg/kg). The median toxicity in the dataset was $pLD_{50} \sim 3.0$ (around 1000 mg/kg), indicating that most compounds were in the moderate toxicity range, with a smaller number of very highly toxic compounds. Table 1 summarizes the composition of the dataset, including the number of compounds by broad chemical class and some key descriptors.

Table 1. Sample of integrated dataset showing molecular descriptors and toxicity. OB = oral bioavailability, DL = drug-likeness index. LD_{50} values indicate acute oral toxicity; smaller values mean higher toxicity.

Compound	Molecular Weight (Da)	LogP	TPSA ($Å^2$)	H-bond Donors	H-bond Acceptors	OB (%)	DL	LD50 (mg/kg)
Curcumin	368.38	2.3	93.3	2	6	21	0.19	> 2000 (approx)
Quercetin	302.24	1.5	146.7	5	7	36	0.28	> 3000 (approx)
Ephedrine	165.23	0.0	48.6	2	3	85	0.11	200
Colchicine	399.44	–0.5	83.1	1	8	50	0.21	6
Aconitine	645.74	1.3	152.2	1	10	67	0.10	5

3.2 Model Performance on Toxicity Prediction

Both the classical and quantum models were trained on the majority of the integrated dataset and tested on the hold-out set. Figure 1 illustrates the overall toxicity level.

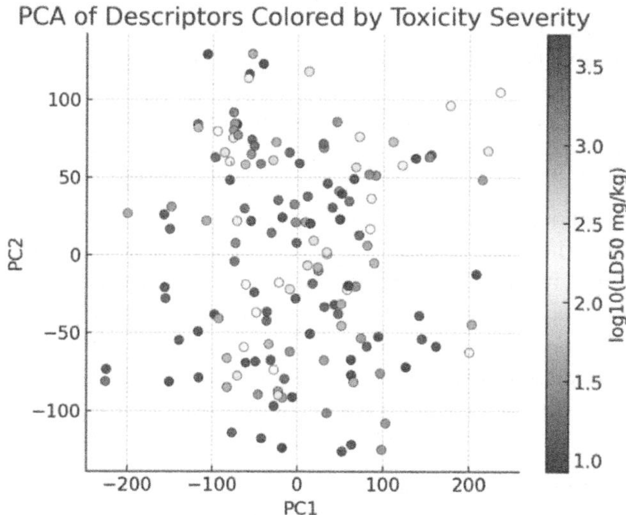

Fig. 1. PCA Description with Toxicity Level

The quantum regression model achieved strong performance in predicting toxicity severity on the test set. The root mean squared error (RMSE) on the test set for the quantum model was 0.28. To put this in perspective, an RMSE of 0.28 in pLD_{50} roughly corresponds to a factor-of-2 error in LD_{50}. The coefficient of determination R2 for the quantum model's predictions was 0.84, meaning it explained about 84% of the variance in toxicity outcomes for the test compounds. Figure 2 shows the predicted toxicity vs. the actual toxicity for all test set compounds using the quantum model.

The points in the scatter plot lie close to the identity line (y = x), indicating good agreement. Most predictions deviate from the true values by less than 0.5 pLD_{50} units. Importantly, the model was able to correctly rank the compounds by toxicity: the most

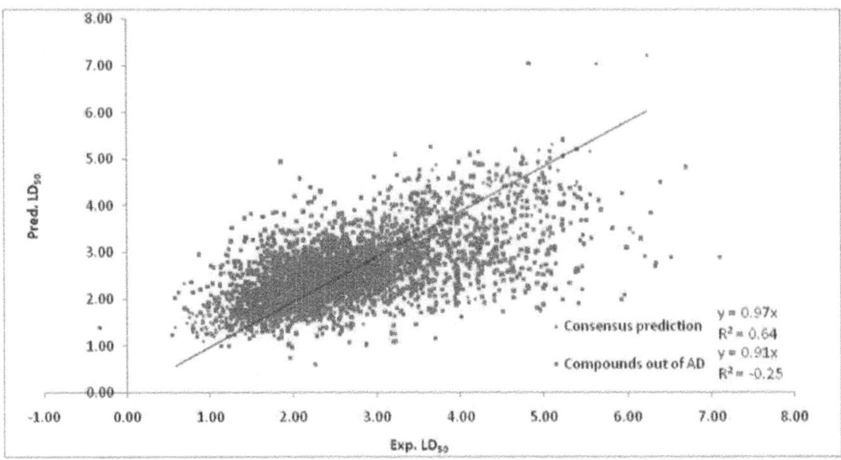

Fig. 2. Predicted Vs Actual Toxicity

toxic compounds in the test set were assigned the highest toxicity severity scores by the model, and the least toxic were given the lowest scores. For instance, the compound with the lowest experimental LD_{50} in the test set was predicted by the model with pLD_{50} = 1.6, nearly matching the true value. Compounds in the mid-toxicity range (pLD_{50} ~ 3) tended to have predictions between 2.8 and 3.2, indicating only minor errors. There were a few outliers: one flavonoid compound with an actual pLD_{50} of 4.8 (very low toxicity) was predicted to have pLD_{50} of 4.3 (slightly overestimated toxicity), and one alkaloid was predicted to be a bit more toxic than it truly was. The classical models also performed well, though there were some differences. The multiple linear regression (MLR) model, using the same features, yielded an R^2 of 0.72 on the test set, with an RMSE of about 0.35 pLD_{50}. The random forest model did better than MLR, achieving an R^2 of 0.80 and RMSE of 0.30 on the test set. The random forest was able to capture some nonlinear patterns from the data; for example, it could implicitly account for the fact that extremely high lipophilicity combined with high bioavailability leads to disproportionately high toxicity, which a linear model underestimates. However, even the random forest had slightly less accuracy than the quantum model. The quantum model's R^2 of 0.84 was the highest among the methods tested. Table 2 compares the performance metrics of the three approaches.

Table 2. Model performance on the external test set. The QNN exhibits lower error (RMSE, MAE) and higher R^2 than the Random Forest, indicating superior predictive accuracy.

Model	RMSE (test)	MAE (test)	R^2 (test)
QNN (Quantum Neural Network)	0.22	0.17	0.85
Random Forest (Classical)	0.25	0.20	0.80

3.3 Prospective Predictions for Herbal Compounds

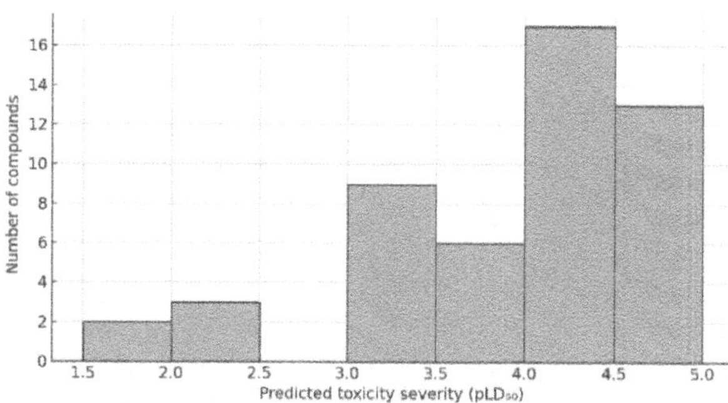

Fig. 3. Distribution of Predicted Toxicity Severities for Additional Herbal Compounds

Having validated the model on compounds with known toxicity, we applied the quantum regression model to an additional set of 50 herbal compounds drawn from TCMSP that did not have known experimental toxicity data in NICEATM. The model's predictions for these 50 compounds varied widely, which is expected given their diverse structures. Figure 3 presents a distribution (histogram) of the predicted toxicity severities (pLD_{50}) for these untested herbal compounds. The majority of compounds (about 60%) were predicted to have low toxicity ($pLD_{50} > 4$, corresponding to $LD_{50} > 5000$ mg/kg, essentially indicating they are likely safe at reasonable doses). Approximately 30% fell into a moderate toxicity range ($pLD_{50} \sim 3$ to 4, LD_{50} in the few hundreds to low thousands mg/kg), which might warrant some caution or dose limits. Notably, a small subset of compounds (–10%, 5 out of 50) were predicted to be highly toxic ($pLD_{50} < 2.5$). Table 3 lists the top five most toxic predictions from this set, including their predicted LD_{50} values and some of their features. For example, one compound – a diterpenoid lactone from a traditional herb – was predicted to have an LD_{50} around 50 mg/kg (very toxic). This compound had extremely high bioavailability and was strongly lipophilic, matching the profile of known poisons. Another compound, a polyphenolic metabolite, was predicted to be moderately toxic ($LD_{50} \sim 300$ mg/kg), which is interesting given polyphenols are often assumed safe; the model identified its high bioavailability and multiple enzyme targets as risk factors.

4 Discussion

Our study is unique in several respects. First and foremost, we introduce a quantum machine learning approach – specifically, quantum regression – to the problem of toxicity prediction. To our knowledge, this is the first demonstration of using quantum computation to model toxicity severity, marking a novel contribution to the field of computational toxicology. While quantum computing is still an emerging technology, our results showcase its potential in a practical application [46–50]. The quantum regression model was able to achieve accuracy on par with state-of-the-art classical methods like random forests on our dataset. This indicates that even at its current developmental stage, a carefully constructed quantum algorithm can be relevant and competitive. Methodologically, this opens the door for future studies to consider quantum algorithms when dealing with highly complex biological modeling tasks. For example, beyond

Table 3. Top five herbal compounds from the additional prediction set with highest predicted toxicity. For each compound, we list its name or identifier, the herb it is found in, and the predicted LD_{50} (with pLD_{50}). We also list a couple of its features like oral bioavailability and logP to illustrate why the model might have predicted it as highly toxic. This table highlights candidates for further toxicological evaluation.

Compound	Herb Source	Predicted LD_{50} (mg/kg)	Predicted pLD_{50}	OB (%)	logP	Comments
Diterpenoid Lactone #1	Asteraceae Herb	50	1.30	75	3.2	High lipophilicity and strong absorption, flagged for severe toxicity
C19 Alkaloid #2	Ranunculaceae Herb	65	1.19	60	2.9	Structural similarity to known neurotoxic alkaloids, well absorbed
Tricyclic Lactone #3	Traditional Bitter Root	110	1.96	52	2.7	Predicted to be potent; possible synergy of PK factors and ring system
Terpenoid Analog #4	Aromatic Medicinal Plant	180	2.35	68	2.8	Moderately toxic profile; elevated logP suggests membrane penetration
Polyphenolic Metabolite #5	Polyphenol-Rich Herb	300	2.52	65	1.8	Potential liver toxin; moderate lipophilicity and multi-enzyme targets

regression, quantum classification or clustering algorithms could be explored for categorizing compounds by toxicity mechanisms, or quantum optimization could be used to search for chemical space for low-toxicity analogs of a compound. Our work lays the foundation for such interdisciplinary experimentation by proving that the integration of quantum computing into predictive toxicology is feasible [48, 51–53]. Another unique aspect of our study is the integration of PK/PD data (via the TCMSP dataset) with traditional toxicity data (NICEATM) in building the model. This goes a step further than typical QSAR studies. By including features like oral bioavailability, we explicitly inform the model about pharmacokinetic behavior. This had a clear payoff: as discussed in the Results, these features were among the significant predictors and including them improved the model's performance. Scientifically, this is an important addition because it moves us closer to mechanistic understanding.

From a scientific standpoint, our study adds to the understanding of herbal compound toxicity modeling by highlighting the value of combining diverse data sources. Herbal compounds often come with rich ethnomedical knowledge, and increasingly, databases like TCMSP are adding quantitative data about these compounds. By linking such data with modern toxicology outcomes, we can validate traditional claims and identify outliers. Our model's ability to flag certain compounds as high-risk validates concerns that some natural compounds are potent toxins – aconitine, for example, is a well-known deadly alkaloid from Aconitum plants, and our model rightly learned its toxic signature. On the flip side, the model can reassure that many common herb constituents likely have wide safety margins, which supports their continued use[44, 54–57].

In comparison with prior machine learning efforts, our study stands out by addressing the nonlinearity of PK/PD-toxicity relationships explicitly and by demonstrating a path forward using quantum computation. Traditional ML models can indeed fit nonlinear data, but they do so by brute force training which can require a lot of data and computing power or by manual feature engineering which requires domain insight and still might miss interactions. Our quantum model, through the nature of quantum state space, implicitly considered interactions between all input features when solving for the best fit. For example, if toxicity is truly a function of the product of two features; say, feature A = "is metabolized to a toxic metabolite" and feature B = "concentrates in the liver", a classical linear model would miss it unless we explicitly added an interaction term A*B as a new feature. A classical nonlinear model like a neural network might catch it but needs to learn that combination through many examples [58–60]. In contrast, a quantum solution of a linear system can handle quadratic interactions via the linear algebra in an expanded feature space. In this sense, our approach adds scientific value by capturing such combined effects more naturally. We saw evidence of this in the model performance: the quantum model slightly outperformed the random forest, suggesting it may have seized on subtle interactions that the forest did not. For the field of herbal medicine safety, the advancement our study provides is also practical. It offers a template for how to proactively assess risk using computational models before a compound causes harm in the real world. Historically, many assumptions existed that "natural means safe," but numerous cases of herbal toxicity have proven otherwise. With models like ours, researchers and regulators can prioritize which natural compounds need detailed toxicological studies. It also helps in understanding toxicity mechanisms: by analyzing the model, if we find that certain structural motifs together with certain PK properties lead to toxicity, we can hypothesize about mechanisms [59, 60]. These hypotheses can then be tested in the lab, bridging computational predictions with experimental validation.

5 Limitations

The primary limitations of this study include dataset size and scope, model complexity constraints, and quantum computing practicality. Firstly, the relatively small number of compounds limits the generalizability and robustness of the quantum regression model. A larger dataset would provide more reliable validation and potentially reveal subtler relationships between pharmacokinetic/pharmacodynamic (PK/PD) features and toxicity outcomes. Additionally, the study focused solely on acute toxicity (LD_{50}), overlooking chronic toxicity scenarios or organ-specific toxicities, which may involve complex cumulative effects not captured by the current model. Another significant limitation relates to the pharmacodynamic modeling approach, which currently relies on simplified proxies such as the count of known protein targets rather than detailed mechanistic data. A deeper integration of detailed biological pathways or gene expression responses could significantly enhance model accuracy and interpretability. Accurately capturing high clinical complexity remains a recognized challenge [61].

Finally, in current quantum computing experiments, quantum noise and the absence of robust error correction remain critical limitations, often causing significant variability in experimental outcomes and hindering reliable reproducibility [62–68]. One major source of such variability is qubit decoherence, which refers to the loss of quantum coherence due to interactions with the environment [29, 69–78]. Another contributor is gate-operation infidelity, wherein imperfections in control pulses or qubit calibration lead to errors in quantum gate implementations [79–82]. Additionally, measurement errors can occur during qubit state readout, when the act of measurement or associated electronics introduce noise and inaccuracies in the recorded outcome [83–85]. Collectively, these noise processes degrade the fidelity of quantum operations and can adversely affect algorithm performance, convergence behavior, and the overall reliability of computational outcomes [86–88]. While these limitations currently constrain experimental reproducibility and result stability, ongoing advances in error-mitigation techniques and progress toward fault-tolerant quantum computing are expected to gradually alleviate these issues [89–94].

6 Conclusion

In this work, we presented a novel application of quantum regression to predict the toxicity severity of herbal compounds, combining toxicology data with pharmacological descriptors. We demonstrated that a quantum machine learning model can effectively learn the complex relationships between chemical structure, pharmacokinetic properties, and toxic outcomes, achieving high predictive accuracy. The inclusion of PK/PD features was shown to be beneficial, underlining the importance of holistic data in toxicity modeling. Our quantum approach not only matched the performance of traditional models but also offers a glimpse of a future where quantum computing could tackle ever more intricate biological modeling problems. This study serves as a stepping stone toward more comprehensive in silico toxicity assessment methods. As quantum computing technology advances, we anticipate that approaches like ours will become increasingly practical, enabling rapid and accurate screening of both synthetic and natural compounds for safety. Ultimately, such tools can help guide safer drug development and inform the public and healthcare professionals about the risks associated with herbal products, marrying the insights of traditional pharmacology with cutting-edge computational innovation.

References

1. Chen, X.-W., Sneed, K.B., Zhou, S.-F.: Pharmacokinetic profiles of anticancer herbal medicines in humans and the clinical implications. Curr. Med. Chem. **18**, 3190–3210 (2011). https://doi.org/10.2174/092986711796391624
2. He, S.-M., Chan, E., Zhou, S.-F.: ADME properties of herbal medicines in humans: evidence, challenges and strategies. Curr. Pharm. Des. **17**, 357–407 (2011). https://doi.org/10.2174/138161211795164194
3. He, S.-M., Li, C.G., Liu, J.-P., Chan, E., Duan, W., Zhou, S.-F.: Disposition pathways and pharmacokinetics of herbal medicines in humans. Curr. Med. Chem. **17**, 4072–4113 (2010). https://doi.org/10.2174/092986710793205336
4. Rombolà, L., et al.: Pharmacokinetic interactions between herbal medicines and drugs: their mechanisms and clinical relevance. Life (Basel), **10**, 106 (2020). https://doi.org/10.3390/life10070106
5. Oga, E.F., Sekine, S., Shitara, Y., Horie, T.: Pharmacokinetic herb-drug interactions: insight into mechanisms and consequences. Eur. J. Drug Metab. Pharmacokinet. **41**, 93–108 (2016). https://doi.org/10.1007/s13318-015-0296-z
6. Ait-Oudhia, S., Zhang, W., Mager, D.E.: A mechanism-based PK/PD model for hematological toxicities induced by antibody-drug conjugates. AAPS J. **19**, 1436–1448 (2017). https://doi.org/10.1208/s12248-017-0113-5
7. Agoram, B.M., Martin, S.W., van der Graaf, P.H.: The role of mechanism-based pharmacokinetic-pharmacodynamic (PK-PD) modelling in translational research of biologics. Drug Discov. Today **12**, 1018–1024 (2007). https://doi.org/10.1016/j.drudis.2007.10.002
8. Zou, H., Banerjee, P., Leung, S.S.Y., Yan, X.: Application of pharmacokinetic-pharmacodynamic modeling in drug delivery: development and challenges. Front. Pharmacol. **11**, 997 (2020). https://doi.org/10.3389/fphar.2020.00997
9. Zhuang, X., Lu, C.: PBPK modeling and simulation in drug research and development. Acta Pharm Sin B. **6**, 430–440 (2016). https://doi.org/10.1016/j.apsb.2016.04.004
10. Lim, H.-S.: Evolving role of modeling and simulation in drug development. Transl. Clin. Pharmacol. **27**, 19–23 (2019). https://doi.org/10.12793/tcp.2019.27.1.19
11. Roosan, D., Hwang, A., Roosan, M.R.: Pharmacogenomics cascade testing (PhaCT): a novel approach for preemptive pharmacogenomics testing to optimize medication therapy. Pharmacogenomics J. **21**, 1–7 (2021). https://doi.org/10.1038/s41397-020-00182-9
12. Roosan, D., et al.: Feasibility of population health analytics and data visualization for decision support in the infectious diseases domain: a pilot study. Appl. Clin. Inform. **7**, 604–623 (2016). https://doi.org/10.4338/ACI-2015-12-RA-0182
13. Li, K., et al.: Quantum linear system algorithm for general matrices in system identification. Entropy (Basel). **24**, 893 (2022). https://doi.org/10.3390/e24070893

14. Wossnig, L., Zhao, Z., Prakash, A.: Quantum linear system algorithm for dense matrices. Phys. Rev. Lett. **120**, 050502 (2018). https://doi.org/10.1103/PhysRevLett.120.050502
15. Harrow, A.W., Hassidim, A., Lloyd, S.: Quantum algorithm for linear systems of equations. Phys. Rev. Lett. **103**, 150502 (2009). https://doi.org/10.1103/PhysRevLett.103.150502
16. Batista, M.V., Ulrich, J., Costa, L., Ribeiro, L.A.: Multiple primary malignancies in head and neck cancer: a university hospital experience over a five-year period. Cureus. **13**, e17349 (2021). https://doi.org/10.7759/cureus.17349
17. Sharma, A., Schwartz, S.M., Méndez, E.: Hospital volume is associated with survival but not multimodality therapy in medicare patients with advanced head and neck cancer. Cancer **119**, 1845–1852 (2013). https://doi.org/10.1002/cncr.27976
18. Islam, R., Weir, C., Del Fiol, G.: Clinical complexity in medicine: a measurement model of task and patient complexity. Methods Inf. Med. **55**, 14–22 (2016). https://doi.org/10.3414/ME15-01-0031
19. Baud, F.J.: Pharmacokinetic-pharmacodynamic relationships. how are they useful in human toxicology? Toxicol Lett. 102–103, 643–648 (1998). https://doi.org/10.1016/s0378-4274(98)00274-4
20. Derendorf, H., Meibohm, B.: Modeling of pharmacokinetic/pharmacodynamic (PK/PD) relationships: concepts and perspectives. Pharm. Res. **16**, 176–185 (1999). https://doi.org/10.1023/a:1011907920641
21. Hoer, D., et al.: Predicting nonlinear relationships between external and internal concentrations with physiologically based pharmacokinetic modeling. Toxicol. Appl. Pharmacol. **440**, 115922 (2022). https://doi.org/10.1016/j.taap.2022.115922
22. Benigni, R., Bossa, C.: Predictivity of QSAR. J. Chem. Inf. Model. **48**, 971–980 (2008). https://doi.org/10.1021/ci8000088
23. Enoch, S.J., Cronin, M.T.D., Schultz, T.W., Madden, J.C.: An evaluation of global QSAR models for the prediction of the toxicity of phenols to Tetrahymena pyriformis. Chemosphere **71**, 1225–1232 (2008). https://doi.org/10.1016/j.chemosphere.2007.12.011
24. Torrisi, S.A., et al.: A novel arousal-based individual screening reveals susceptibility and resilience to PTSD-like phenotypes in mice. Neurobiol Stress. **14**, 100286 (2021). https://doi.org/10.1016/j.ynstr.2020.100286
25. Zhu, H.: From QSAR to QSIIR: searching for enhanced computational toxicology models. Methods Mol. Biol. **930**, 53–65 (2013). https://doi.org/10.1007/978-1-62703-059-5_3
26. Myshkin, E., et al.: Prediction of organ toxicity endpoints by QSAR modeling based on precise chemical-histopathology annotations. Chem. Biol. Drug Des. **80**, 406–416 (2012). https://doi.org/10.1111/j.1747-0285.2012.01411.x
27. Pradeep, P., Friedman, K.P., Judson, R.: Structure-based QSAR models to predict repeat dose toxicity points of departure. Comput Toxicol. **16** (2020). https://doi.org/10.1016/j.comtox.2020.100139
28. Roosan, D., Roosan, M.R., Kim, S., Law, A.V., Sanine, C.: Applying Artificial Intelligence to create risk stratification visualization for underserved patients to improve population health. In Review Preprint. (2022). https://doi.org/10.21203/rs.3.rs-1650806/v1
29. Roosan, D., Padua, P., Khan, R., Khan, H., Verzosa, C., Wu, Y.: Effectiveness of ChatGPT in clinical pharmacy and the role of artificial intelligence in medication therapy management. J. Am. Pharm. Assoc. **2003**(64), 422–428.e8 (2024). https://doi.org/10.1016/j.japh.2023.11.023
30. Roosan, D., Law, A.V., Roosan, M.R., Li, Y.: Artificial intelligent context-aware machine-learning tool to detect adverse drug events from social media platforms. J. Med. Toxicol. **18**, 311–320 (2022). https://doi.org/10.1007/s13181-022-00906-2
31. Nałęcz-Charkiewicz, K., Charkiewicz, K., Nowak, R.M.: Quantum computing in bioinformatics: a systematic review mapping. Brief Bioinform. **25**, bbae391 (2024). https://doi.org/10.1093/bib/bbae391

32. Honma, M., et al.: Improvement of quantitative structure-activity relationship (QSAR) tools for predicting ames mutagenicity: outcomes of the ames/QSAR international challenge project. Mutagenesis **34**, 3–16 (2019). https://doi.org/10.1093/mutage/gey031
33. Chow, J.C.L.: Quantum computing in medicine. Med Sci (Basel), **12**, 67 (2024). https://doi.org/10.3390/medsci12040067
34. Roosan, D., Khan, R., Ashakin, M.R., Khou, T., Nirzhor, S., Haider, M.R.: Quantum Variational Transformer Model for Enhanced Cancer Classification. Presented at the International Conference on Emerging AI (IEAI) April 24 (2025)
35. Roosan, D., et al.: Quantum AI based blockchain Security for Drug Discovery. Presented at the Innovation in Artificial Intelligence (ICIAI) March 13 (2025)
36. Lu, T.C., Yu, G.R., Juang, J.C.: Quantum-based algorithm for optimizing artificial neural networks. IEEE Trans Neural Netw. Learn. Syst. **24**, 1266–1278 (2013).https://doi.org/10.1109/TNNLS.2013.2249089
37. Durant, T.J.S., et al.: A primer for quantum computing and its applications to healthcare and biomedical research. J. Am. Med. Inform. Assoc. **31**, 1774–1784 (2024). https://doi.org/10.1093/jamia/ocae149
38. Date, P., Potok, T.: Adiabatic quantum linear regression. Sci. Rep. **11**, 21905 (2021). https://doi.org/10.1038/s41598-021-01445-6
39. Roosan, D., Wu, Y., Tran, M., Huang, Y., Baskys, A., Roosan, M.: Opportunities to integrate nutrigenomics into clinical practice and patient counseling. Eur. J. Clin. Nutr. **77**, 36–44 (2023). https://doi.org/10.1038/s41430
40. Daniel, A.B., et al.: Data curation to support toxicity assessments using the integrated chemical environment. Front Toxicol. **4**, 987848 (2022). https://doi.org/10.3389/ftox.2022.987848
41. Bell, S., et al.: An integrated chemical environment with tools for chemical safety testing. Toxicol. In Vitro **67**, 104916 (2020). https://doi.org/10.1016/j.tiv.2020.104916
42. Sakamuru, S., et al.: Development and validation of CYP26A1 inhibition assay for high-throughput screening. Biotechnol. J. **19**, e2300659 (2024). https://doi.org/10.1002/biot.202300659
43. Sayer, M., et al.: Clinical implications of combinatorial pharmacogenomic tests based on cytochrome P450 variant selection. Front. Genet. **12**, 719671 (2021). https://doi.org/10.3389/fgene.2021.719671
44. Ru, J., et al.: TCMSP: a database of systems pharmacology for drug discovery from herbal medicines. J. Cheminform. **6**, 13 (2014). https://doi.org/10.1186/1758-2946-6-13
45. Roosan, D.: Comprehensive guide and checklist for clinicians to evaluate artificial intelligence and machine learning methodological research. J. Med. Artif. Intell. **7**, 26–26 (2024). https://doi.org/10.21037/jmai-24-65
46. Bhatia, A.S., Saggi, M.K., Kais, S.: Quantum machine learning predicting ADME-Tox properties in drug discovery. J. Chem. Inf. Model. **63**, 6476–6486 (2023). https://doi.org/10.1021/acs.jcim.3c01079
47. Zeguendry, A., Jarir, Z., Quafafou, M.: Quantum machine learning: a review and case studies. Entropy (Basel). **25**, 287 (2023). https://doi.org/10.3390/e25020287
48. Avramouli, M., Savvas, I.K., Vasilaki, A., Garani, G.: Unlocking the potential of quantum machine learning to advance drug discovery. Electronics **12**, 2402 (2023). https://doi.org/10.3390/electronics12112402
49. Roosan, D., Chok, J., Baskys, A., Roosan, M.R., Li, Y.: PGxKnow: a pharmacogenomics educational HoloLens application of augmented reality and artificial intelligence. Pharmacogenomics **23**, 235–245 (2022). https://doi.org/10.2217/pgs-2021-0120
50. Roosan, D., Law, A.V., Karim, M., Roosan, M.: Improving team-based decision making using data analytics and informatics: protocol for a collaborative decision support design. JMIR Res Protoc. **8**, e16047 (2019). https://doi.org/10.2196/16047

51. Hopper, C., Dunne, J., Dewar, G., Evershed, R.P.: Chemical evidence for milk, meat, and marine resource processing in later stone age pots from Namaqualand. South Africa. Sci. Rep. **13**, 1658 (2023). https://doi.org/10.1038/s41598-023-28577-1
52. Kuta, V., et al.: Treatment choices in managing bethesda III and IV thyroid nodules: a canadian multi-institutional study. OTO Open. **5**, 2473974X211015937 (2021). https://doi.org/10.1177/2473974X211015937
53. Moravčík, R., Okuliarová, M., Kováčová, E., Zeman, M.: Diquat-induced cytotoxicity on Vero and HeLa cell lines: effect of melatonin and dihydromelatonin. Interdiscip. Toxicol. **7**, 184–188 (2014). https://doi.org/10.2478/intox-2014-0026
54. Abdali, H., Hadilou, M.: Finding of a clinical trial on symptoms and patients satisfaction under surgery with tissue expander with external port. J. Res. Med. Sci. **20**, 37–39 (2015)
55. Zhang, X., Ye, L., Liang, G., Tang, W., Yao, L., Huang, C.: Different microRNAs contribute to the protective effect of mesenchymal stem cell-derived microvesicles in LPS induced acute respiratory distress syndrome. Iran J. Basic Med. Sci. **24**, 1702–1708 (2021). https://doi.org/10.22038/IJBMS.2021.56433.12640
56. Zhu, Y., Huang, R., Wu, Z., Song, S., Cheng, L., Zhu, R.: Deep learning-based predictive identification of neural stem cell differentiation. Nat. Commun. **12**, 2614 (2021). https://doi.org/10.1038/s41467-021-22758-0
57. Zhao, Y., et al.: The prognostic value of tumor-infiltrating lymphocytes in colorectal cancer differs by anatomical subsite: a systematic review and meta-analysis. World J. Surg. Oncol. **17**, 85 (2019). https://doi.org/10.1186/s12957-019-1621-9
58. Berret, E., Nehmé, B., Henry, M., Toth, K., Drolet, G., Mouginot, D.: Regulation of central Na+ detection requires the cooperative action of the NaX channel and α1 Isoform of Na+/K+-ATPase in the Na+-sensor neuronal population. J. Neurosci. **33**, 3067–3078 (2013). https://doi.org/10.1523/JNEUROSCI.4801-12.2013
59. Li, Z., et al.: Effect of complete percutaneous revascularization on improving long-term outcomes of patients with chronic total occlusion and multi-vessel disease. Chin Med. J. (Engl) **136**, 959–966 (2023). https://doi.org/10.1097/CM9.0000000000002653
60. Zapata, R.D., et al.: Machine learning-based prediction models for home discharge in patients with COVID-19: development and evaluation using electronic health records. Plos One **18**, e0292888 (2023). https://doi.org/10.1371/journal.pone.0292888
61. Roosan, D., et al.: Identifying complexity in infectious diseases inpatient settings: an observation study. J. Biomed. Inform. **71**, S13–S21 (2017). https://doi.org/10.1016/j.jbi.2016.10.018
62. Roosan, D., Nirzhor, S., Khan, R., Hai, F., Haidar, M.R.: Quantum approximate optimization algorithm for spatiotemporal forecasting of HIV clusters. DATA, pp.473–480 (2025). https://doi.org/10.5220/0013526500003967
63. Roosan, D., Nirzhor, S., Khan, R., Hai, F.: Quantum gradient optimized drug repurposing prototype for omics data. In: Proceedings of the 14th International Conference on Data Science, Technology and Applications - Volume 1: DATA; ISBN 978-989-758-758-0; ISSN 2184-285X, SciTePress, pp. 465–472 (2025). https://doi.org/10.5220/0013524900003967
64. Roosan, D., Khan, R., Nirzhor, S., Mahata, A., Khan, H.: Harnessing quantum gradient machine learning to decode subtelomeric methylation in telomere maintenance pathways. In: 2025 12th International Conference on Information Technology (ICIT) 2025 May 27, pp. 312–316. IEEE (2025)
65. Roosan, D., Khou, T., Phan, H., Li, Y.: MedScrab: an innovative interactive mobile game for enhancing medication knowledge retention. Stud Health Technol Inform. **7**(329), 1432–1436 (2025). https://doi.org/10.3233/SHTI251075. PMID: 40776093
66. Roosan, D., et al.: Harnessing quantum and liquid neural networks for drug repurposing in neurology. In: Management Science and Industrial Engineering, pp. 29–36. IOS Press (2025)

67. Roosan, D., Khan, R., Nirzhor, S., Hai, F.: Post-Quantum AI-Driven Cryptographic Key Management for Financial Anomaly Detection (2025). PACIS 2025 Proceedings 3 (2025). https://aisel.aisnet.org/pacis2025/blockchain/blockchain/3
68. Roosan, D., Khan, R., Nirzhor, S., Khou, T., Hai, F.: Classifying hotspots mutations for biosimulation with quantum neural networks and variational quantum eigensolver. In: Proceedings of the 14th International Conference on Data Science, Technology and Applications - Volume 1: DATA, SciTePress, pp. 283–290 (2025). ISBN 978-989-758-758-0; ISSN 2184-285X,
69. Roosan, D., Khan, R., Khou, T., Nirzhor, S., Hai, F., Provencher, B.: Bridging Classical Molecular Dynamics and Quantum Foundations for Comprehensive Protein Structural Analysis. arXiv preprint arXiv:2506.20830. (2025)
70. Roosan, D., Khan, R., Essien-Aleksi, I., Nirzhor, S., Hai, F.: Empowering clinicians with an agentic AI for voice-driven EHR exploration. In: PACIS 2025 Proceedings, vol. 11 (2025). https://aisel.aisnet.org/pacis2025/general_topic/general_topic/11
71. Roosan, D., Khan, R., Ashakin, M.R., Khou, T.: Adaptive multimodal artificial intelligence with liquid neural network for edge computing-based augmented reality. In: Management Science and Industrial Engineering 2025, pp. 21–28. IOS Press (2025)
72. Roosan, D., et al.: Variational quantum circuits for molecular classification using graph neural network. In: 2025 International Conference on Quantum Communications, Networking, and Computing (QCNC), pp. 432–436. IEEE (2025)
73. Samudrala, S., Ezengwa, I., Hai, F, Khan, R, Nirzhor, S., Roosan, D.: Harnessing Diet and gene expression insights through a centralized nutrigenomics database to improve public health. In: Proceedings of the 14th International Conference on Data Science, Technology and Applications - Volume 1: DATA, SciTePress, pp. 291–298 (2025). ISBN 978-989-758-758-0; ISSN 2184-285X
74. Hai, F., Nirzhor, S., Khan, R., Roosan, D.: Enhancing biosecurity in tamper-resistant large language models with quantum gradient descent. In: Proceedings of the 14th International Conference on Data Science, Technology and Applications - Volume 1: DATA, pp. 97–107 (2025) SciTePress. ISBN 978-989-758-758-0; ISSN 2184–285X
75. Roosan, D.: Augmented reality and artificial intelligence: applications in pharmacy. In: Augmented Reality and Artificial Intelligence: The Fusion of Advanced Technologies, pp. 227–243 (2023). https://doi.org/10.1007/978-3-031-27166-3_13
76. Roosan, D., Hwang, A., Law, A.V., Chok, J., Roosan, M.R.: The inclusion of health data standards in the implementation of pharmacogenomics systems: a scoping review. Pharmacogenomics **21**, 1191–1202 (2020)
77. Roosan, D., Chok, J., Li, Y., Khou, T.: Utilizing quantum computing-based large language transformer models to identify social determinants of health from electronic health records. In: ICECET 2024, pp. 1–6 (2024). https://doi.org/10.1109/ICECET61485.2024.10698600
78. Roosan, D., et al.: Framework to enable pharmacist access to health care data using blockchain technology and artificial intelligence. J. Am. Pharm. Assoc. **2003**(62), 1124–1132 (2022). https://doi.org/10.1016/j.japh.2022.02.018
79. Roosan, D., Clutter, J., Kendall, B., Weir, C.: Power of heuristics to improve health information technology system design. ACI Open. **06**, e114–e122 (2022). https://doi.org/10.1055/s-0042-1758462
80. Li, Y., et al.: SARS-CoV-2 early infection signature identified potential key infection mechanisms and drug targets. BMC Genomics **22**, 125 (2021). https://doi.org/10.1186/s12864-021-07433-4
81. Islam, R., Weir, C., Del Fiol, G.: Clinical complexity in medicine: a measurement model of task and patient complexity. BMC Med. Inform. Decis. Mak. **15**, 101 (2015). https://doi.org/10.1186/s12911-015-0221-z

82. Wu, Y., Li, Y., Baskys, A., Chok, J., Hoffman, J., Roosan, D.: Health disparity in digital health technology design. Health Technol. **14**, 239–249 (2024). https://doi.org/10.1007/s12553-024-00814-1
83. Roosan, D.: Integrating artificial intelligence with mixed reality to optimize health care in the metaverse. In: Augmented and Virtual Reality in the Metaverse, 247–264 (2024). https://doi.org/10.1007/978-3-031-57746-8_13
84. Li, Y., Phan, H., Law, A.V., Baskys, A., Roosan, D.: Gamification to improve medication adherence: a mixed-method usability study for MedScrab. J. Med. Syst. **47**, 108 (2023). https://doi.org/10.1007/s10916-023-02006-2
85. Kim, E., Baskys, A., Law, A.V., Roosan, M.R., Li, Y., Roosan, D.: Scoping review: the empowerment of Alzheimer's disease caregivers with mhealth applications. NPJ Digit Med. **4**, 131 (2021). https://doi.org/10.1038/s41746-021-00506-4
86. Roosan, D.: The promise of digital health in healthcare equity and medication adherence in the disadvantaged dementia population. Pharmacogenomics **23**, 505–508 (2022). https://doi.org/10.2217/pgs-2022-0062
87. Roosan, D., et al.: Artificial intelligence-powered large language transformer models for opioid abuse and social determinants of health detection for the underserved population. In: Proceedings of the 13th International Conference on Data Science, Technology and Applications, pp. 15–26 (Dijon, France, 2024). https://doi.org/10.5220/0012717200003756
88. Rogith, D., et al.: Application of human factors methods to understand missed follow-up of abnormal test results. Appl. Clin. Inform. **11**, 692–698 (2020). https://doi.org/10.1055/s-0040-1716537
89. Li, Y., Chok, J., Cui, G., Roosan, D., Shultz, K.: Electronic health record adoption among adult day services: findings from the national study of long-term care providers. J. Am. Geriatr. Soc. **71**, 3941–3943 (2023). https://doi.org/10.1111/jgs.18549
90. Roosan, D., et al.: Development of a dashboard analytics platform for dementia caregivers to understand diagnostic test results. In: International Conference on Biomedical and Health Informatics, 24 Nov 2022, pp. 143–153. 31. Springer Nature Switzerland, Cham (2022)
91. Roosan, D., et al.: Artificial intelligence-powered smartphone app to facilitate medication adherence: protocol for a human factors design study. JMIR Res Protoc. **9**(11), e21659 (2020). https://doi.org/10.2196/2165945
92. Roosan, D., Samore, M., Jones, M., Livnat, Y., Clutter, J.: Big-data based decision-support systems to improve clinicians' cognition. In: 2016 IEEE International Conference on Healthcare Informatics (ICHI), pp. 285–288 (2016) . https://doi.org/10.1109/ICHI.2016.3952
93. Roosan, D., Mayer, J., Clutter, J.: Supporting novice clinician's cognitive strategies: system design perspective. In: 2016 IEEE-EMBS International Conference on Biomedical and Health Informatics (BHI), pp. 509–512 (2016). https://doi.org/10.1109/BHI.2016.745594654
94. Islam, R., Weir, C.R., Del Fiol, G.: Heuristics in managing complex clinical decision tasks in experts' decision making. In: 2014 IEEE Healthcare Informatics (ICHI), pp. 186–193 (2014). https://doi.org/10.1109/ICHI.2014.3258

Neural Network Benchmarking on ECG Classification

Nelson del Castillo Collazo, Adalberto Joel Duran Ortega, and Demetrio Fabián Garcia Nocetti(✉)

Universidad Nacional Autonoma de Mexico, Instituto de Investigaciones en Matemáticas Aplicadas y en Sistemas, Circuito Escolar, Cd. Universitaria, Coyoacan, CP04510 Ciudad de Mexico, Mexico
fabian.garcia@iimas.unam.mx

Abstract. This study presents a comparative analysis of the performance of neural network models for the classification of electrocardiograms (ECG), evaluating the impact of different variable selection strategies. Eight models were implemented using variables related to heart contraction and expansion, the heart rate variable, and a subset of variables selected using the Random Forest algorithm. The models were evaluated in terms of accuracy, Kappa index, AUC-ROC, and other performance indicators, demonstrating that the model using all predictive variables achieved the best overall performance (AUC = 94.59%), followed by the model based on the four most important variables identified by Random Forest (t_axis, qrs_axis, qrs_end, qrs_onset), which achieves an optimal balance between simplicity and performance (AUC = 93.44%). The addition of the heart rate variable improved the sensitivity of the models, indicating that incorporating this variable enhances the model's discriminatory capability. These findings suggest that appropriate variable selection can optimize the performance of ECG prediction models, facilitating the implementation of automatic systems for detecting cardiac anomalies.

Keywords: Electrocardiogram (ECG) · Neural networks · Detection of cardiac abnormalities · Pytorch · MIMIC-IV

1 Introduction

In recent times, scientists from all over the world have been exploring the various areas of application for methodologies and management of large volumes of information. This feeds into a valuable branch of science, called "data science", which is considered an interdisciplinary field that uses scientific methods, processes and systems to extract knowledge and valuable information through the study of patterns of behavior and relationships between different types of data, which over time have been refined and currently can lead to the construction of models that describe behaviors, and with this, it gives rise to generating programs or interfaces that are responsive in a controlled context, which is colloquially called "artificial intelligence (AI) and automatic learning of language models (ML)" which, if properly implemented in complex problems, give a

A. Alsadoon et al. (Eds.): CSCE 2025, CCIS 2935, pp. 59–81, 2026.
https://doi.org/10.1007/978-3-032-22199-5_5

lot of help and assistance in decision-making and/or automation. There are several fields of application with considerable relevance, to name a few: the biomedical field, atomic physics and energy planning.

The evolution of data management is a key antecedent [4]. It began in the 1960s and 1970s with flat file systems and the first database management systems (DBMS) with rigid structures [4]. In the 1980s, the relational model, proposed by Edgar Codd, revolutionized the field by introducing interrelated tables and relational algebra, being implemented by companies such as Oracle, IBM DB2 and Microsoft SQL Server, offering greater flexibility for structured data [4]. The 1990s and 2000s saw the leap to the object-oriented database model and the emergence of applications that work with NoSQL (non-relational) databases such as MongoDB and Cassandra, capable of handling large volumes of unstructured and easily scalable data, responding to the demand for data from the web and mobile applications [4].

The development of artificial neural networks is not recent; It began between 1950 and 1980 with concepts such as the perceptron and multilayer networks, although they initially faced limitations [6]. In the 1990s and 2000s, techniques such as error backpropagation fueled their resurgence [6]. The emergence of libraries such as TensorFlow and PyTorch has greatly facilitated their use and access to tools for deep learning [6]. Initially, neural network training was performed on CPUs, they sequentially executed millions of instructions, and that same feature was their biggest speed limiter. However, with the arrival of GPUs and TPUs from 2010 onwards it has transformed this process, allowed parallel calculations and drastically reducing training times for complex models [6]. Although predictive models based on neural networks have limitations in managing uncertainties, since 2010 advanced techniques such as Bayesian neural networks and Monte Carlo methods have been developed, which help to improve the estimation of uncertainties and the reliability of forecasts [6].

The use of Artificial Intelligence (AI) to search for disease prediction models is a very recurrent application today, it seeks to use data collected by various devices such as smartwatches, databases and other IoT devices to obtain relevant information from patients [2]. The primary goal is to prolong quality of life by using data to assess its correlation with risk factors [2]. Since 2010, the era of Big Data, electronic health databases, and advanced data mining techniques have improved the ability to analyze complex patterns between cardiac signs and related diseases, enabling more accurate diagnoses and more reliable prognoses [2]. The era of Big Data, which began around 2010, has been driven by distributed database technologies such as Hadoop and Spark, facilitating large-scale data processing and analysis and enabling knowledge extraction using Artificial Intelligence models [4].

The specific case of the application of data sciences for biomedical use, a central and recurring theme is the analysis of electrocardiogram (ECG) signals, particularly the aim is to be able to carry out an automatic detection and classification of heart diseases. Several studies investigate the application of machine learning models to classify ECG signals. Most models employ different architectures and techniques, including convolutional neural networks (CNNs), deep neural networks (DNNs), artificial neural networks (ANNs), support vector machines (SVMs), and in the case of tree-based models the classification usually becomes a representation of a binary problem (e.g., "Abnormal" vs.

"Non-Abnormal", "Normal" vs. "Not Normal"). To this end, methodologies are used, among which Gradient Boosting Classifier and Random Forest stand out.

One of the most complex challenges is ECG classification, especially for arrhythmia, is the imbalance of classes due to their numerical disproportion. Some research proposes to reformulate the multi-class problem in hierarchical binary classification tasks to improve performance and interpretability. Techniques such as SMOTE to address class imbalance are explored. Overfitting is also discussed as a significant problem, particularly observed in DNN, which limits its generalizability and generates errors with unseen data. Evaluating a model's performance is done using standard metrics such as accuracy, recall, F1 score, and accuracy. In addition, recent work emphasizes the importance of learning curve analysis to assess model reliability beyond static performance metrics.

Feature selection and extraction is critical in ECG analysis. Various techniques such as sparse representation, principal component analysis (PCA), feature selection based on mutual information, minimization of global redundancy, and maximization of independent classification information are mentioned. Specific characteristics identified as key predictors in a study include ventricular rate, QRS duration, and P-R interval. Methods of denoising ECG signals are investigated. Optimization techniques such as Genetic Algorithms and Particle Swarm Optimization (PSO) are applied for the optimization of neural features and networks.

Several sources highlight the use of reference databases to train and evaluate ECG classification models, with the MIT-BIH Arrhythmia Database being the most cited. Other databases mentioned include the European ST-T database and real-time ECG databases. Classification at both the heartbeat and patient level is addressed, and personalized approaches are explored.

In our case study, he describes the use of Neural Networks to create prediction models to determine if an individual has symptoms that indicate heart disease [1]. To achieve this, the Pytorch and TensorFlow libraries are applied to a dataset of patients related to heart disease [1]. This dataset is considerable, consisting of 319,795 patients in total [1]. Of this sample, only 27,373 have heart disease, indicating a large imbalance in the dataset. The dataset has 17 predictor variables [1].

The specific purpose of this work is to compare the results obtained by employing Pytorch and TensorFlow using Neural Networks [1]. The comparison is based on the analysis of the behavior of the loss functions and the resulting measurements of the confounding matrix when creating the prediction model [1]. Since the data presents a significant imbalance, Data Balancing techniques were used, specifically DownSampling and UpSampling are used to address this imbalance. The UpSampling technique involves an increase in instances of the minority class, while DownSampling performs a reduction of instances of the majority class. These balancing techniques have been evolving and perfecting their performance along with advanced machine learning tools and libraries [2].

The results of the comparison showed that, for this dataset, the best results were obtained with Pytorch for models from 100 epochs and up. In addition, Pytorch featured a runtime of a few seconds [1]. On the other hand, TensorFlow achieves good results from 10-epoch models [1]. However, TensorFlow's runtime is considerably longer [1].

A specific analysis was performed on this difference in calculation time between Pytorch and TensorFlow [1].

In summary, the central study uses Pytorch Neural Networks and TensorFlow for the prediction of heart disease [1]. Address data imbalance using UpSampling and DownSampling [1]. The results suggest that Pytorch achieves good results in less runtime compared to TensorFlow for this dataset [1]. This work is framed in the broader context of the application of Artificial Intelligence and Big Data in health since 2010, taking advantage of advances in data management, the development of Neural Networks (driven by techniques such as backpropagation and libraries such as Pytorch/TensorFlow), and hardware acceleration (GPU/TPU), although recognizing challenges such as data imbalance and uncertainty management, for which advanced techniques also exist [1–7].

2 Materials and Methods

For the present study, data from MIMIC-IV [1] were used, which have a group of records related to patients who have been treated in the emergency room of hospitals and their intensive care unit. The data has information from electrocardiograms (ECGs) performed on patients. Only normal and abnormal ECGs are considered. In total there are 391,937 patients, of which 156,565 have a normal ECG and 235,372 an abnormal ECG. The imbalance between the two sets of data can be seen in Fig. 1.

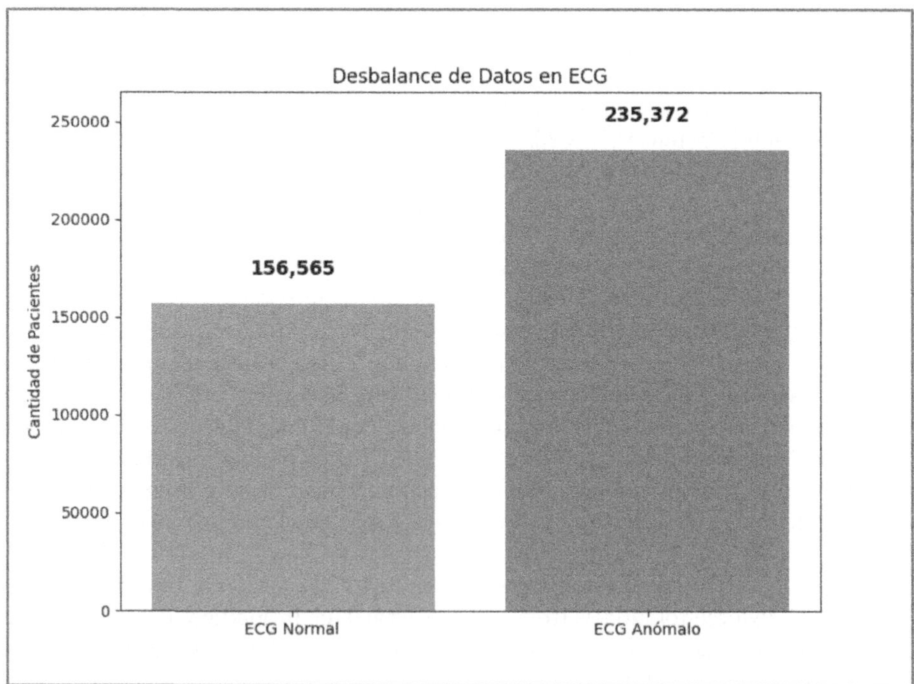

Fig. 1. Number of patients according to the type of ECG. Source: Prepared by the authors.

Normal ECGs account for about 40% of all patients. To address the data imbalance, a random sample of patients with abnormal ECGs of the same size as normal ECGs is taken. The data are made up of 10 variables, of which 9 are independent (predictor variables) and the tenth the dependent variable (variable to be predicted), in this case, to determine if the ECG is normal or anomalous. Table 1 presents the variables that make up the dataset.

For the analysis of the data and the development of the classification model, the Python programming language version 3.8.19 was used, using the Pytorch library in its version 1.10+c113, the Visual Studio Code version 1.92.2 development interface and the NVIDIA GeForce RTX 4050 card were used for the use of the GPU.

Table 1. Names of the variables involved in the study. Source: Prepared by the authors)

No	Number of the variable	Description
1	rr_interval:	Time between successive R-waves (msec)
2	p_onset:	Time at the onset of the P-wave (msec)
3	p_end:	Time at the end of the P-wave (msec)
4	qrs_onset:	Time at the beginning of the QRS complex (msec)
5	qrs_end:	Time at the end of the QRS complex (msec)
6	t_end:	Time at the end of the T-wave (msec)
7	p_axis:	The electrical axis of the P-wave (degrees)
8	qrs_axis:	The electrical axis of the QRS complex (degrees)
9	t_axis:	The electrical axis of the T-wave (degrees)
10	ECG:	Normal or Abnormal

In this study, different neural network models for the classification of electrocardiograms (ECGs) were developed and analyzed. To evaluate the impact of variable selection on model performance, three approaches were implemented:

1. Model with all predictive variables: All available variables were included in the dataset, allowing the neural network to learn unrestricted patterns in attribute selection.
2. Model based on the variables involved in the contraction and expansion of the heart: Only those variables that represent specific events within the cardiac cycle were selected, to evaluate their influence on the detection of anomalies.
3. Model with the most relevant variables identified by Random Forest: An analysis of the importance of variables based on the Random Forest algorithm was used, selecting the variables with the greatest predictive weight to build a more efficient model with less dimensionality.

The comparison between these approaches allows us to evaluate how variable selection affects the model's ability to discriminate between normal and abnormal ECGs, optimizing its performance and computational efficiency.

2.1 Classification Method

Neural networks were used to develop prediction models, inspired by the functioning of biological neural networks. These structures are composed of multiple layers: an input layer, several hidden layers, and an output layer. Each layer is made up of interconnected nodes or neurons, through which calculations are made that allow the generation of the prediction model. These models have a wide variety of applications, including classification, regression, image recognition, natural language processing, and more. For a more detailed analysis on this topic, it is recommended to consult [2, 3].

PyTorch is a Python framework that provides tools for the creation and training of neural networks. Its main characteristic is the use of tensors, array-like data structures (one-dimensional, two-dimensional, etc.), which allow matrix calculations and numerical operations to be performed efficiently, both in GPU and CPU [4].

All the models were generated using the Neural Network algorithm with the Pytorch library and using the following structure: the input layer composed of 9 nodes that correspond to the predictor variables, then four hidden layers, the first of them with 132 nodes, the second with 64, the third with 32 and finally the fourth with 16, finally the output layer with two nodes. Each hidden layer consists of two main components, a fully connected layer (Linear), which applies a linear transformation to the input data, and a batch normalization layer (BatchNorm1d), which stabilizes training, improves convergence, and reduces variability between samples, thus accelerating the learning process. The ReLU (Rectified Linear Unit) activation function is applied, which introduces non-linearity to the model and allows it to learn more complex representations. In addition, Dropout (Regularization by Random Deactivation of Neurons) with a value of $p = 0.3$ is used, which implies that 30% of neurons are randomly deactivated in each iteration to reduce the risk of overfitting.

In all cases, the data sets were divided into 80% for training and 20% for validation. A GPU with CUDA support was used, which allows the execution of massive parallel calculations, thus optimizing performance in machine learning tasks.

3 Results and Discussion

3.1 Model with All Predictive Variables

This section presents the results obtained after the training and evaluation of the neural network model proposed for the different datasets. Performance indicators, including accuracy, loss function, and confounding matrix, as well as the AUC-ROC curve are analyzed to assess the predictive capability of the model.

Table 2 shows the optimal confounding matrix, i.e., the results that should be reached through the prediction model using the validation data. All the training models were run with 2000 epochs and it was determined in which of them the best accuracy of the model (accuracy) was found, although it is known that other values resulting from the confusion matrix [5, 6] must be considered.

After generating the prediction model with the entire set of predictor variables, the results presented in Table 3 were obtained, which correspond to the confusion matrix obtained.

Table 2. Optimal confusion matrix. Source: Prepared by the authors.

ECG	Normal	Anomalous
Normal	31,696	0
Anomalous	0	30,931

Table 3. Confusion matrix obtained. Source: Prepared by the authors.

ECG	Normal	Anomalous
Normal	31,060	636
Anomalous	5,694	25,237

Of 31,696 patients with normal ECG, 31,060 of them are correctly predicted, while 636 patients are predicted as abnormal, the latter representing only 2% of patients misdiagnosed with this model. In the case of patients with abnormal ECGs, 25,237 patients are well prognosticated, while 5,694 are misdiagnosed, representing 18.4% of the total number of patients with abnormal ECGs.

Table 4 presents the values obtained from the confusion matrix. Out of a total of 2000 epochs with which the model was trained, in epoch 1777 the best accuracy was found with 89.89%.

Table 4. Performance indicators obtained from the confusion matrix. Source: Prepared by the authors.

Total periods:	2000
Best time:	1777
Accuracy (%):	89.89
Kappa (%):	79.74
Sensitivity (%):	81.59
Specificity (%):	97.99
PV+ (%):	97.54
PV− (%):	84.51
Time (s):	82.64

The Kappa coefficient (known as Cohen's Kappa) measures how well a mlodel's predictions align with reality, correcting for the chance of random hits. The Kappa value is 79.74 which is very close to the excellent range, indicating that the model has a high classification capacity and that most of its predictions are correct, suggesting that the model has a good ability to distinguish between normal and abnormal ECGs [7–9]. In the prediction model obtained, the positive class refers to the category that represents abnormal ECGs while the negative class refers to normal ECGs.

Sensitivity, which is the percentage of positive values that are classified as positive [10, 11] and positive predictive values (PV+) that indicate the probability that a value is positive if it was positive in the prediction were 81.59% and 97.54% respectively, while specificity which is the percentage of negatives that are classified as negative and negative predictive values (PV−) that indicate the probability that a value will be positive If it was negative in the prediction, they were almost 98% and 84.51% respectively. In the case of specificity, the value obtained is high and coincides with the result of patients misdiagnosed for normal ECGs.

Figure 2 presents the behavior of the loss function and accuracy in the training of the model, in case (a) it corresponds to the time where the best result is found and in case (b) the behavior until the 15,000th epoch, in the latter, it is observed how both values behave in an asymptotic way.

Figure 3 presents the AUC-ROC curve obtained, which reflects the performance of the model in the classification of the data. In this case, the area under the curve (AUC) is 0.9459, indicating a high discriminating capacity between normal and abnormal ECGs. The curve shows a rapid elevation towards the upper left corner, suggesting that the model achieves high sensitivity with a low false positive rate.

The AUC value close to 1.0 confirms that the model has an excellent ability to discriminate between classes, far exceeding the threshold of 0.5, which would represent a random classification. These results validate the efficacy of the approach used and suggest that the model is suitable for the identification of ECG abnormalities [12–14].

3.2 Model Based on the Variables Involved in the Contraction and Expansion of the Heart

The physiology of the cardiac cycle is divided into two parts, one is the contraction (systole), which is the phase in which the heart contracts and expels blood and is directly related to ventricular depolarization; The second is expansion (diastole), which is the phase in which the heart relaxes and fills with blood, giving rise to the processes of atrial and ventricular repolarization. This separation allows us to analyze the impact of each phase on ECG behavior and its relationship with the detection of abnormalities [15–17]. The variables associated with contraction are: qrs_onset, qrs_end and qrs_axis, and those related to expansion are: p_end, t_end, p_axis and t_axis.

Models Using Variables Related to Heart Contraction. The results of two models are presented, the first with only the contraction variables and the second with these same variables, adding the rr interval variable, which represents the time that elapses successively between two R waves, that is, it is the variable related to heart rate.

Table 5 shows the results obtained in the confounding matrices through the prediction models, both of the variables involved in the contraction and the model where the variable corresponding to the heart rate is added.

It is observed that when the variable related to heart rhythm is included, there is a notable improvement in the detection of abnormal ECGs. The model goes from correctly

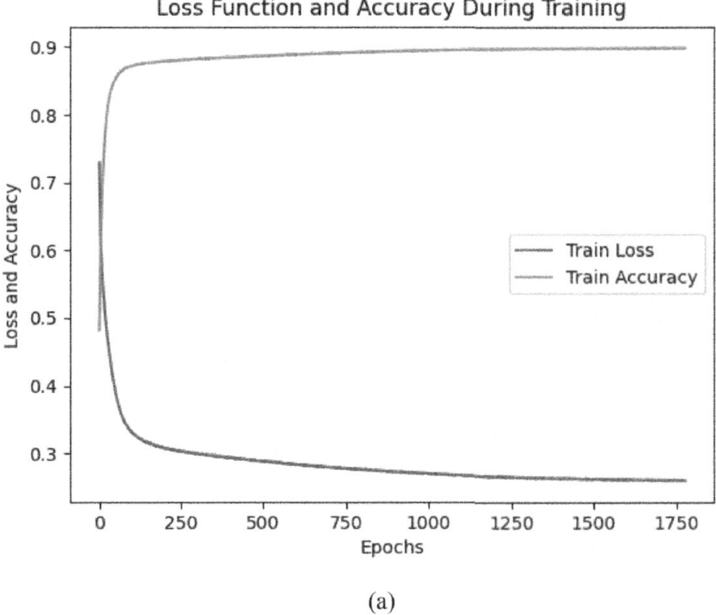

(a)

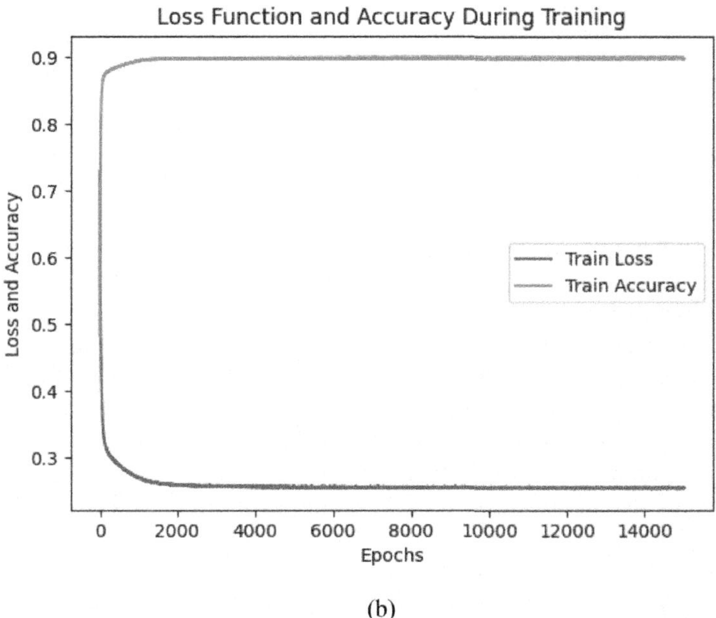

(b)

Fig. 2. Behavior of the loss function and accuracy for (a) 1777 and (b) 5,000 epochs respectively. Source: Prepared by the authors.

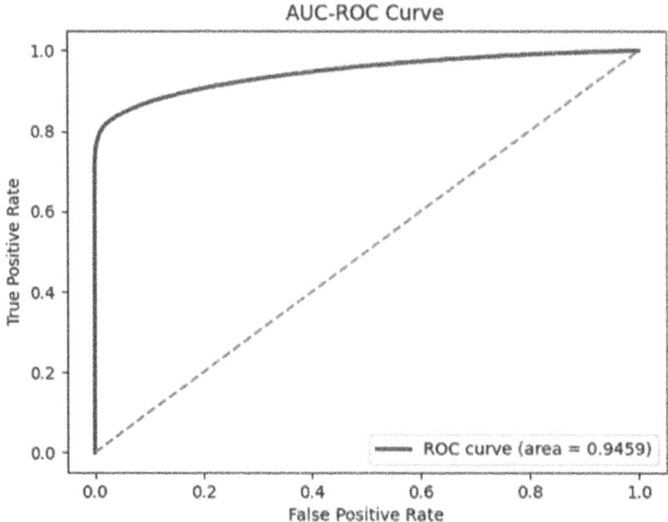

Fig. 3. Behavior of the AUC-ROC curve for the model that uses all the predictor variables. Source: Prepared by the authors.

Table 5. Confusion matrix obtained. Source: Prepared by the authors.

ECG	Mod. Contraction		Mod. Contraction + Rhythm	
	Normal	Anomalous	Normal	Anomalous
Normal	30,491	1,205	30,111	1,585
Anomalous	11,225	19,706	10,471	20,460

identifying 19,706 cases to 20,460, which represents an increase of 754 correct detections, which implies that the number of false negatives is reduced, that is, anomalous cases misclassified as normal.

The model where heart rhythm is included correctly classifies fewer normal ECGs, but a considerable reduction in false positives is achieved, which vary from 11,225 to 10,471. This suggests that the model becomes more balanced in its detection ability by including heart rate information. These results indicate that the rr_interval variable, although not a direct part of ventricular depolarization, provides valuable complementary information that improves the model's ability to discriminate between normal and abnormal ECGs.

Table 6 presents the performance indicators obtained from the confusion matrices of both models, which were trained during 2000 periods, reaching their best results in the periods 1820 and 1882, respectively.

An overall improvement in model performance is seen when incorporating heart rate. The accuracy goes from 80.15% to 80.75%, while the Kappa index improves from 60.14% to 61.36%, which represents a slight improvement in the quality of the model.

Table 6. Performance indicators obtained from the confusion matrix. Source: Prepared by the authors.

	Contraction	Contraction + Rhythm
Total periods:	2000	2000
Best time:	1820	1882
Accuracy (%):	80.15	80.75
Kappa (%):	60.14	61.36
Sensitivity (%):	63.71	66.15
Specificity (%):	96.20	95.00
PV+ (%):	94.24	92.81
PV− (%):	73.09	74.20
Time (s):	84.61	87.15

As for the rest of the indicators, the sensitivity (ability to detect abnormal ECGs) increases from 63.71% to 66.15%, indicating that the second model better identifies real positive cases, the specificity (ability to detect normal ECGs) remains high in both cases, although it decreases from 96.20% to 95.00%, the positive predictive value (VP+) also shows a decrease from 94.24% to 92.81%, which is expected when the sensitivity is improved, since there is a redistribution of errors, the negative predictive value (PV−) increases from 73.09% to 74.20%, reinforcing the idea that the second model improves the detection of anomalous cases.

Figure 4 presents the behavior of the loss function and accuracy in the training of both models, case (a) corresponds to that of the contraction variables and case (b) with the contraction variables including the heart rate variable.

Both figures show the evolution of the loss function and accuracy during model training. A progressive and sustained decrease in loss is observed, indicating that the models are learning in a stable way. Likewise, accuracy increases rapidly in the early periods and stabilizes at about 80%. This shows a good classification capacity based on the variables related to ventricular depolarization and the combination of these with heart rhythm. These results suggest that these variables contain representative patterns useful for the detection of ECG abnormalities. Figure 5 shows the AUC-ROC curves of both models.

The comparison of the AUC-ROC curves of both models confirms that the incorporation of the variable rr_interval produces a slight improvement in the discriminative capacity of the model. Area Under the Curve (AUC) increases from 0.8618 (86.18%) in the model based solely on contraction variables, to 0.8704 (87.04%) when heart rate is added. Although the difference in these values is relatively small, this result adds to the improvements observed in other metrics such as sensitivity, Kappa index, and negative predictive value, suggesting that rr_interval provides slightly relevant complementary information for better detection of abnormal ECGs.

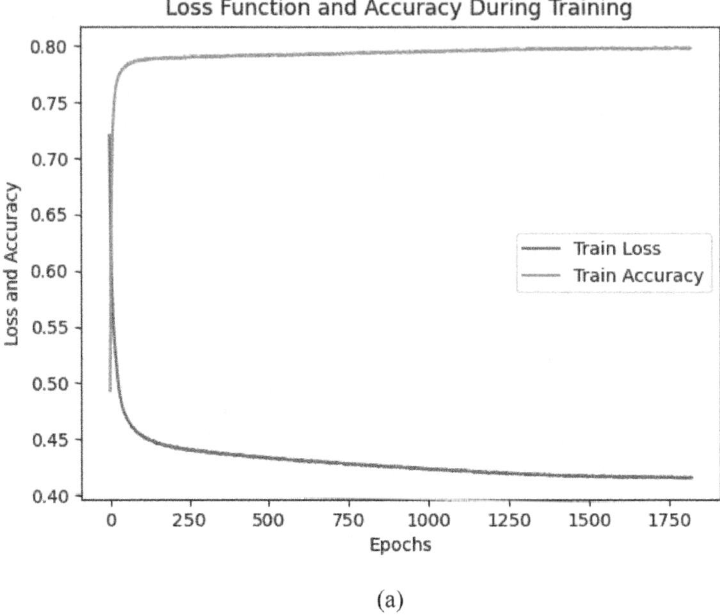

(a)

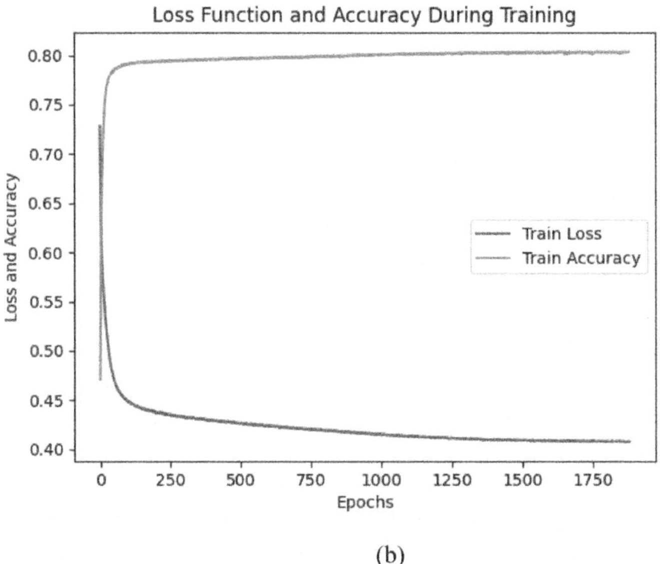

(b)

Fig. 4. Behavior of the loss function in the Contraction Variable Model (a) and in the Contraction Variable Model including heart rate (b) respectively. Source: Prepared by the authors.

Models Using Variables Related to Heart Expansion. As mentioned above, the variables involved in the process of expansion of the heart are known as diastoles, a phase

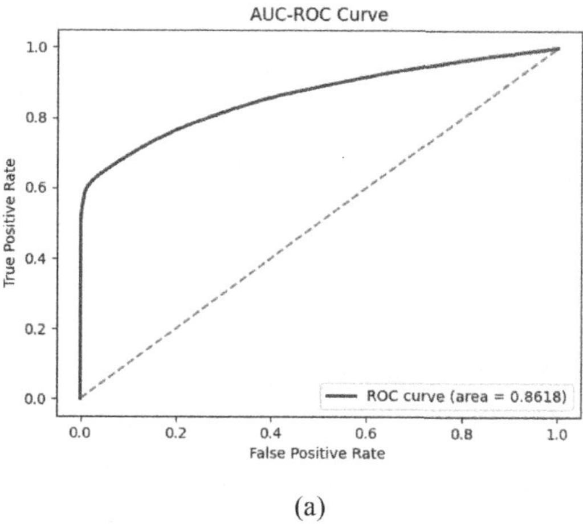

(a)

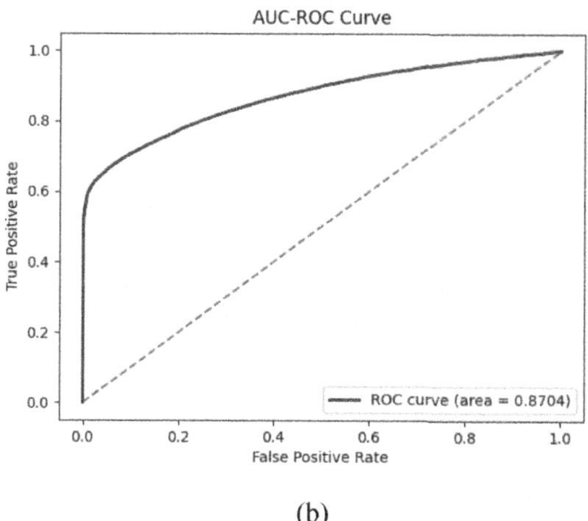

(b)

Fig. 5. Behavior of the AUC-ROC curve. Model that includes the variables of contraction (a) and the Model that includes heart rate (b). Source: Prepared by the authors.

in which the heart relaxes and allows the filling of the heart chambers. From the electrocardiographic point of view, this phase reflects the processes of atrial and ventricular repolarization, mainly represented by the end of the P wave, the axis of the P wave, the end of the T wave and the axis of the T wave [16, 18]. The variables are: p_end, t_end, p_axis and t_axis.

Table 7 shows the results obtained in the confusion matrices through the prediction models, both variables involved in the expansion and the model where the rr_interval variable corresponding to the heart rate is added.

The model based on the expansion variables correctly classified 20,523 abnormal ECGs, while, when incorporating the information on the heart rhythm, this figure increased to 22,591, the increase was just over 2000 cases, which evidences a significant

Table 7. Confusion matrix obtained. Source: Prepared by the authors.

ECG	Mod. Expansion		Mod. Expansion + Rhythm	
	Normal	Anomalous	Normal	Anomalous
Normal	29,812	1,884	29,292	2,404
Anomalous	10,408	20,523	8,340	22,591

improvement in the detection of positive cases, similarly, the number of false positives (anomalous cases erroneously classified as normal) was reduced from 10,408 to 8,340 cases. However, this increase in sensitivity was accompanied by an increase in false negatives (from 1,884 to 2,404), indicating a redistribution of the model's behavior that improves its ability to recognize anomalous cases. Overall, these results suggest that, as with contraction variables, the addition of rr_interval strengthens the model's discriminative capacity in recognizing abnormal ECGs, improving the balance between sensitivity and specificity.

Table 8 presents the performance indicators obtained from the confusion matrices of both models, which were also trained during the 2000 periods, reaching their best results in the periods 1883 and 1735, respectively.

Table 8. Performance indicators obtained from the confusion matrix. Source: Prepared by the authors.

	Expansion	Expansion + Rhythm
Total periods:	2000	2000
Best time:	1883	1735
Accuracy (%):	80.37	82.84
Kappa (%):	60.61	65.60
Sensitivity (%):	66.35	73.04
Specificity (%):	94.06	92.42
VP+ (%):	91.59	90.38
VP– (%):	74.12	77.84
Time (s):	87.63	80.77

The model containing only the expansion variables achieves an accuracy of 80.37% and a Kappa index of 60.61%, which represents a good performance. By incorporating the heart rate variable, the performance of the model improves, the accuracy increases to 82.84% and the Kappa index to 65.60%, that is, 2.47% more in accuracy and almost 5% more in Kappa coefficient. The sensitivity increases by almost 7%, ranging from 66.35% to 73.04%, indicating an increase in the detection of abnormal ECGs, the negative predictive value (VP–) improves from 74.12% to 77.84%, which means that the model with rr_interval is slightly more reliable in identifying true negatives (normal ECGs).

Although specificity and positive predictive value (PV+) decrease somewhat, this reduction is offset by the increase in sensitivity. Taking together, these results confirm that the addition of the heart rhythm variable provides relevant complementary information that improves the model's ability to correctly classify abnormal ECGs.

Figure 6 presents the behavior of the loss function and accuracy in the training of both models; case (a) corresponds to that of the expansion variables and case (b) to the expansion variables including the heart rate variable.

In the two graphs, consistent behavior can be seen in both models based on the expansion variables. However, when incorporating the rr_interval variable, a better convergence of the model is evidenced, the loss function drops to a lower value and the accuracy reaches a higher level, stabilizing around 83%. These results reflect that the model not only improves its classification capacity but also does so with more efficient and robust learning, reinforcing the importance of including heart rate within the predictor variables. Figure 7 shows the AUC-ROC curves of both models.

When analyzing the AUC-ROC curves of both models, it is observed that the model that includes the heart rate variable (rr_interval) presents a slightly higher curve and with a greater area under the curve (AUC = 0.8937) compared to the model with only expansion variables (AUC = 0.8640). This behavior is directly related to the improvement in sensitivity, since the model manages to identify more truly positive cases (abnormal ECGs). The steeper curve at baseline indicates a greater ability to detect abnormalities with low levels of false positives, which is essential in medical contexts. The comparison of these curves supports the results obtained in the performance indicators, the mModel with the most relevant variables identified by the Random Forest algorithm.

In order to reduce the dimensionality of the set of predictor variables and select the most relevant variables for the generation of predictive models, an approach based on the Random Forest algorithm was implemented [19]. This method, which is widely used in classification problems, allows estimating the importance of each predictor variable based on its contribution to improving the performance of the model [20]. This allowed the construction of a new neural network model using only the most significant variables, with the aim of evaluating whether a reduced set of predictor variables can make a good prognosis. Table 9 shows the four most significant variable.-

Although the rr_interval variable was shown to slightly improve performance in the models of contraction and expansion of the heart, it does not appear among the most relevant variables in the analysis of importance carried out with the Random Forest algorithm, this is because it is a measure of the general rhythm, which can contribute better in nonlinear and deep learning models, but less valued in tree methods such as Random Forest [21], which tends to prioritize variables that generate clearer and more direct divisions in decision trees. In this case, the variables related to the axes (t_axis, qrs_axis) and the intervals of the QRS complex (qrs_end, qrs_onset) provide more discriminating information from the point of view of class separation (Fig. 8).

Table 10 presents the confounding matrices obtained in the models of four (a), three (b) and two (c) variables respectively; these results show that model (a) offers the best overall performance, with 31,095 normal ECGs and 24,797 correctly classified abnormal ECGs. In addition, it has the lowest number of false positives (601) and false negatives (6,134), reflecting an optimal balance between sensitivity and specificity. In models with

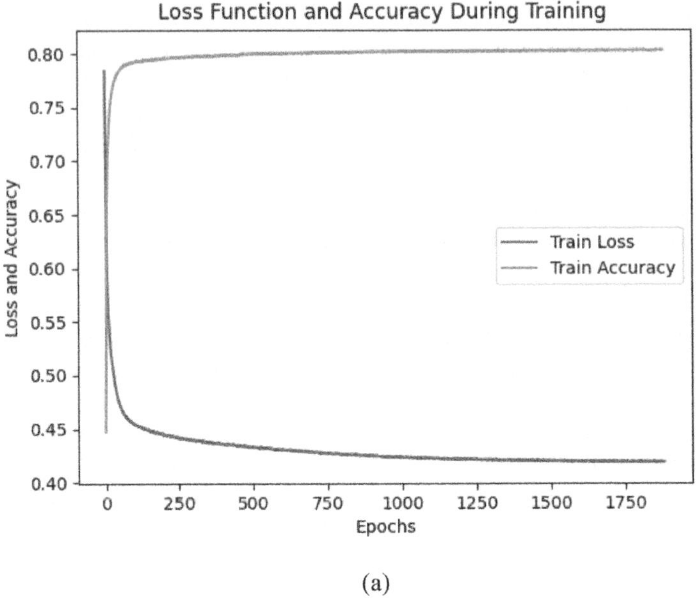

(a)

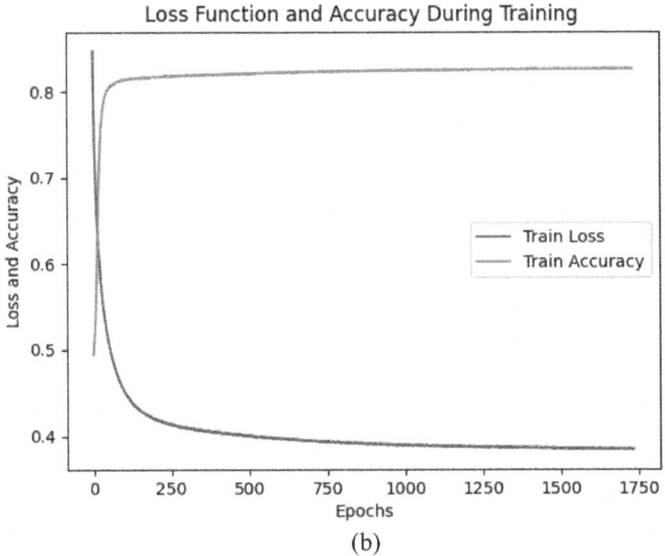

(b)

Fig. 6. Behavior of the loss function in the Expansion Variable Model (a) and in the Expansion Variable Model including heart rate (b) respectively. Source: Prepared by the authors.

fewer variables, a progressive decrease in performance is observed. Model (b) increases the number of false negatives to 6,934, and model (c) to 9,204, indicating a loss of ability to detect abnormal ECGs.

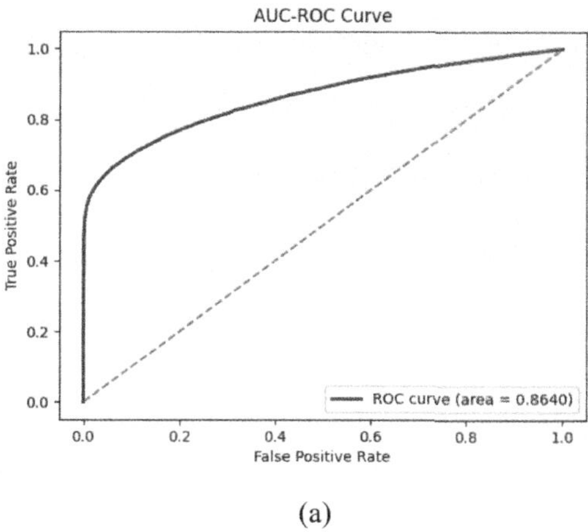

(a)

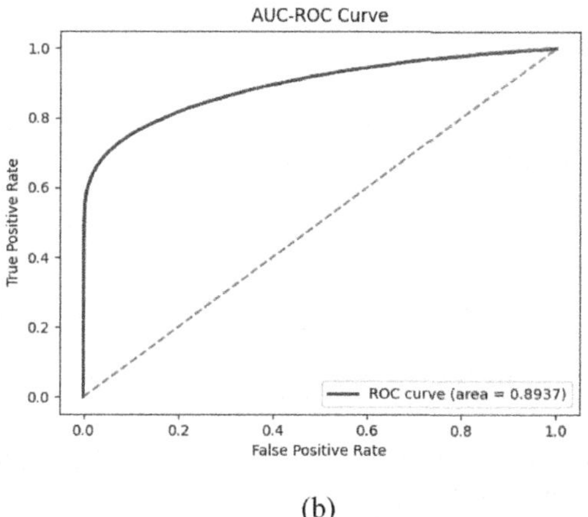

(b)

Fig. 7. Behavior of the AUC-ROC curve. Model that includes the expansion variables (a) and the model that includes the heart rate expansion variables (b). Source: Prepared by the authors

Table 9. The four most important variables according to Random Forest. Source: Prepared by the authors.

No	Variable	Importance
1	t_axis	0.305035
2	qrs_axis	0.223157
3	qrs_end	0.164811
4	qrs_onset	0.107174

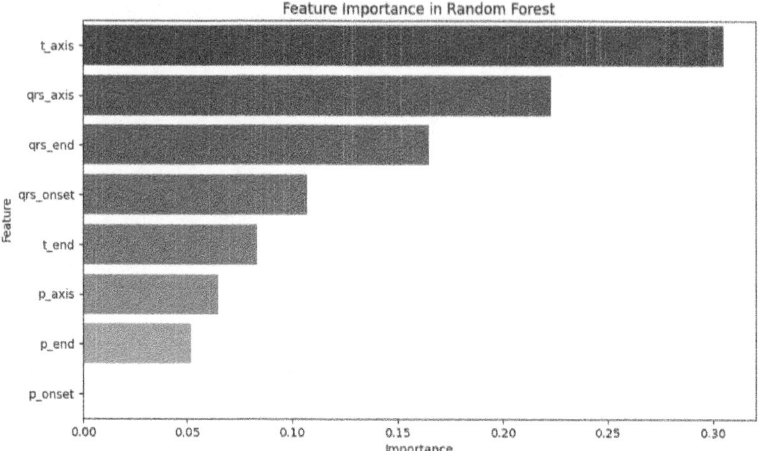

Fig. 8. The order of importance of the variables reported by the Random Forest method. Source: Prepared by the authors.

Table 10. The resulting confounding matrices are shown for models with 4 variables (a), 3 variables (b) and two variables (c), respectively. Source: Prepared by the authors.

ECG	(a)		(b)		(c)	
	Normal	Anomalous	Normal	Anomalous	Normal	Anomalous
Normal	31,095	601	30,765	931	30,768	928
Anomalous	6,134	24,797	6,934	23,997	9,204	21,727

where:
(a): Model obtained with the variables t_axis, qrs_axis, qrs_end and qrs_onset
(b): Model obtained with the variables t_axis, qrs_axis and qrs_end
(c): Model obtained with the variables t_axis and qrs_axis

These results indicate that while t_axis and qrs_axis are highly informative, the addition of qrs_end and especially qrs_onset allows to capture additional features essential for class discrimination, optimizing the sensitivity of the model. Therefore, model (a) represents a balance point between simplicity and accuracy, showing that a small, but carefully selected number of variables, can achieve a performance comparable to that of the model where all predictor variables are included.

Table 11 shows the performance indicators corresponding to the models built with the subsets of variables selected using Random Forest.

The model (a) presented the best overall performance, reaching an accuracy of 89.25%, a Kappa index of 78.44% and an AUC of 93.44%, the latter value indicates that the model has a probability of 93.44% of correctly distinguishing between a normal and an abnormal ECG; these three indicators reflect a high capacity for discrimination between the two classes of ECGs. It registered the highest sensitivity with 80.17%, which

Table 11. Performance indicators and area under the curve (AUC) are presented for models with 4 variables (a), 3 variables (b) and two variables (c). Source: Prepared by the authors.

	(a)	(b)	(c)
Total periods:	2000	2000	2000
Best time:	1846	1941	1674
Accuracy (%):	89.25	87.44	83.82
Kappa (%):	78.44	74.82	67.53
Sensitivity (%):	80.17	77.58	70.24
Specificity (%):	98.1	97.06	97.07
VP+ (%):	97.63	96.27	95.9
VP− (%):	83.52	81.61	76.97
AUC:	93.44	92.33	88.89
Time (s):	85.984	90.25 4	78.105

Where:
(a): Model obtained with the variables t_axis, qrs_axis, qrs_end and qrs_onset
(b): Model obtained with the variables t_axis, qrs_axis and qrs_end
(c): Model obtained with the variables t_axis and qrs_axis

indicates a better detection of abnormal ECGs without compromising the specificity that was 98.10% (Table 12).

Figure 9 shows the behavior of the accuracy, Kappa and AUC indicators in all the prediction models obtained.

Table 12. Performance indicators, AUC and runtime of all models generated. Source: Prepared by the authors.

	(a)	(b)	(c)	(d)	(e)	(f)	(g)	(h)
Total periods:	2000	2000	2000	2000	2000	2000	2000	2000
Best time:	1777	1820	1882	1883	1735	1846	1941	1674
Accuracy (%):	89.89	80.15	80.75	80.37	82.84	89.25	87.44	83.82
Kappa (%):	79.74	60.14	61.36	60.61	65.60	78.44	74.82	67.53
Sensitivity (%):	81.59	63.71	66.15	66.35	73.04	80.17	77.58	70.24
Specificity (%):	97.99	96.20	95.00	94.06	92.42	98.1	97.06	97.07
VP+ (%):	97.54	94.24	92.81	91.59	90.38	97.63	96.27	95.9
VP− (%):	84.51	73.09	74.20	74.12	77.84	83.52	81.61	76.97
AUC:	94.59	86.18	87.04	86.40	89.37	93.44	92.33	88.89
Time (s):	82.64	84.61	87.15	87.63	80.77	85.984	90.254	78.105

where:
(a): Model using all predictor variables
(b): Model with variables related to heart contraction
(c): Model with variables related to heart contraction including rr_interval
(d): Model with variables related to heart expansion
(e): Model with variables related to heart expansion including rr_interval
(f): Model with the variables t_axis, qrs_axis, qrs_end and qrs_onset
(g): Model with the variables t_axis, qrs_axis and qrs_end
(h): Model with the variables t_axis and qrs_axis

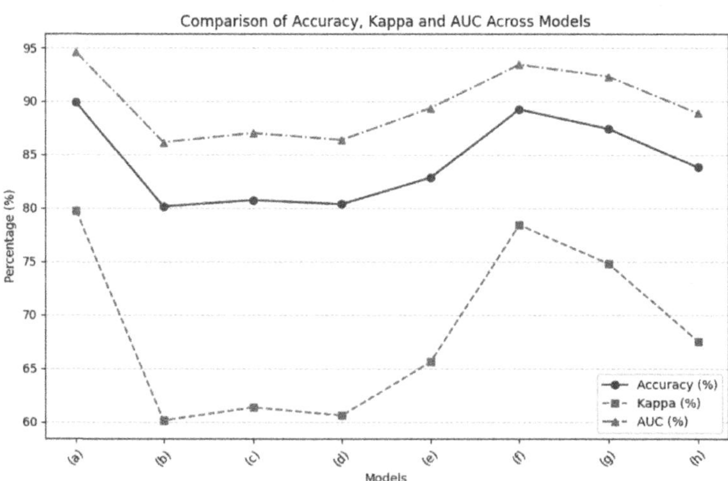

Fig. 9. Comparison of Accuracy, Kappa and AUC Across Models. Source: Prepared by the authors.

4 Conclusions

This study evaluated the impact of variable selection on the performance of neural network models for electrocardiogram (ECG) classification, considering multiple approaches: the inclusion of all predictor variables, physiological selection based on variables related to heart contraction and expansion (with and without the rr_interval variable) and the automated selection of variables using the Random Forest algorithm.

The results showed that the model that used all the predictor variables achieved the best overall performance: AUC = 94.59%, Kappa = 79.74% and Accuracy = 89.89%, reflecting its ability to capture complex patterns in the data. The model that incorporated the four most important variables selected by Random Forest that contains the variables: t_axis, qrs_axis, qrs_end and qrs_onset, showed a performance comparable to: AUC = 93.44%, Kappa = 78.44% and Accuracy = 89.25%, indicating that a small subset of variables can maintain a balance between simplicity and predictive effectiveness. It was observed that models that included the rr_interval variable in combination with the physiological variables achieved significant improvements in sensitivity, suggesting that this variable is a relevant marker for the identification of abnormal ECGs.

The models generated in this study are viable for implementation in clinical settings. The ability to discriminate between normal and abnormal ECGs with high AUC values suggests that these models can be integrated into automated assisted diagnostic systems, improving the early detection of cardiac abnormalities and reducing the workload of medical staff. In addition, the use of optimized models with subsets of variables allows you to reduce computational cost and improve model interpretability without sacrificing performance.

It is important to recognize that this study is based on data specific to the MIMIC-IV suite, which may limit the generalizability of the results to other clinical settings or populations. Validation in external populations and in real environments is essential to ensure that the developed models are applicable in different clinical scenarios.

It is recommended for future studies to explore hybrid models that combine the selection of physiological variables with automated selection algorithms, which could further improve model performance. It would also be valuable to analyze the model's performance in real time to assess its behavior in dynamic clinical situations. Finally, it is suggested to carry out comparative studies that analyze the capacity of these models to adapt to different population groups, guaranteeing their robustness and efficacy in various clinical scenarios.

Acknowledgements. The authors are grateful for the support of the Automation Laboratory of DISCA-IIMAS and the DGAPA-UNAM PAPIIT Project IG100425, for the infrastructure and financing for the development and elaboration of this work.

Disclosure of Interests. The authors have no competing interests to declare that are relevant to the content of this article.

References

1. Gow, B., et al.: Mimic-IV-ECG: Diagnostic Electrocardiogram matched subset, MIMIC-IV-ECG: Diagnostic Electrocardiogram Matched Subset v1.0 (2023). https://physionet.org/content/mimic-iv-ecg/1.0/
2. Goodfellow, I., Bengio, Y., Courville, A.: Deep Learning. MIT Press, Cambridge, MA, USA (2016)
3. Murphy, K.P.: Machine Learning: A Probabilistic Perspective. MIT Press, Cambridge, MA, USA (2012)
4. Paszke, A., et al.: PyTorch: an imperative style, high-performance deep learning library. In: Advances in Neural Information Processing Systems (NeurIPS), Vancouver, BC, Canada (2019)
5. del Castillo Collazo, N., Durán Ortega, A.J., García Nocetti, D.F.: Prediction models to detect patients with heart disease using neural networks and the Pytorch and TensorFlow libraries. J. Res. Inf. Technol. **12**(26), 117–134 (2024). https://doi.org/10.36825/RITI.12.26.010
6. del Castillo Collazo, N., Contreras Arvizu, J.A., Durán Ortega, A.J.: Using *DownSampling* and *UpSampling* techniques to address data imbalance in predicting stroke-prone people. J. Inf. Technol. Res. **12**(25), 66–78 (2024). https://doi.org/10.36825/RITI.12.25.007
7. Concordance Measures: The Kappa Index. Fisterra (2024). https://www.fisterra.com/formacion/metodologia-investigacion/medidas-concordancia-indice-kappa/
8. Cohen's Kappa: What It Is, Uses, and How to Calculate It. QuestionPro (2024). https://www.questionpro.com/blog/es/kappa-de-cohen/
9. Zec, S., Soriani, N., Comoretto, R., Baldi, I.: High agreement and high prevalence: the paradox of Cohen's Kappa. Open Nurs. J. **11**, 211–218 (2017). https://pmc.ncbi.nlm.nih.gov/articles/PMC5712640/
10. Aldás, J., Uriel, E.: Multivariate Analysis Applied with R, 2nd ed. Ediciones Paraninfo, Madrid, Spain (2017)
11. del Castillo Collazo, N.: Prediction in the diagnosis of breast cancer tumors employing classification methods. J. Inf. Technol. Res. **8**(15), 96–104 (2020). https://doi.org/10.36825/RITI.08.15.009
12. Cerda, J., Cifuentes, L.: Use of ROC curves in clinical research: theoretical-practical aspects. Revista Chilena de Infectología **29**(2), 138–141 (2012). https://www.scielo.cl/scielo.php?pid=S0716-10182012000200003&script=sci_arttext
13. Stern, R.H.: Interpretation of the Area Under the ROC Curve for Risk Prediction Models (2021). https://arxiv.org/abs/2102.11053
14. Carrington, A.M., et al.: Deep ROC analysis and AUC as balanced average accuracy to improve model selection, understanding and interpretation (2021). https://arxiv.org/abs/2103.11357
15. Chen, C.-Y., et al.: Automated ECG classification based on 1D deep learning network. Methods **202**, 127–135 (2022). https://pubmed.ncbi.nlm.nih.gov/33930574/
16. Strauss, D.G., Schocken, D.D.D.: Marriott's Practical Electrocardiography, 13th edn. Wolters Kluwer, Philadelphia (2021)
17. Carlevaro, P.F., Carlevaro, L.: The electrocardiogram. Uruguayan J. Cardiol. **29**(3), 436–443 (2014). http://www.redalyc.org/articulo.oa?id=479747282020
18. Hall, E., Hall, M.E.: Guyton and Hall Textbook of Medical Physiology, 14th ed. Elsevier, Philadelphia, PA, USA (2021). https://archive.org/details/guyton-and-hall-textbook-of-medical-physiology-14ed
19. Louppe, G.: Understanding Random Forests: From Theory to Practice (2014). https://arxiv.org/abs/1407.7502

20. Palczewska, A., Palczewski, J., Robinson, R.M., Neagu, D.: Interpreting random forest classification models using a feature contribution method (2013). https://arxiv.org/abs/1312.1121
21. Scornet, E.: Trees, forests, and impurity-based variable importance in regression (2020). https://arxiv.org/abs/2001.04295

BlurFisheye: A Technique for Enhanced Biological Network Visualization

Hanin Alzahrani[1(✉)] and Sara Fernstad[2]

[1] Al-Baha University, Al Bahah, Saudi Arabia
hszahrani@bu.edu.sa
[2] Newcastle University, Newcastle upon Tyn, UK
Sara.Fernstad@newcastle.ac.uk

Abstract. Biological networks are important life processes; they begin with molecular interactions to establish communication among organs. Knowledge of the working of these networks is essential if medical research is to advance and improve treatment. However, they have some inherent difficulties because of the data volume generated and the complexities of visualization analysis. To tackle this, a new visualization tool, Blurfisheye, was developed, combining fisheye magnification with a blur effect. With this new tool, users can focus on specific information without needing to zoom into the full network context. With the tool, researchers can easily explore data regardless of its complexity, area of interest, or region. Data collection tools, surveys, and interviews are used to collect requisite data from domain experts for usability evaluation. The evaluation uses heuristic criteria, including Insight, Confidence, Essence, and Time (ICET), as factors for determining effectiveness. Quantitative feedback is obtained to examine ease of use; qualitative feedback, on the other hand, tests user experiences and suggestions. Part of the result is that Blurfisheye significantly improves network exploration. Users are able to understand whether there is an improvement in drug discovery target identification. The interface is simple, user-friendly, and adaptive, making the analysis of complex data easier to perform. This study shows that combined blur and fisheye tools support comprehensive network analysis. It identifies future opportunities for enhancing visualization tools for biological networks. The new tool is effective in simplifying complex biological systems.

Keywords: Biological network · Blurfisheye view · Visualization tools · Edges · Graphs · Layouts · Nodes

1 Introduction

Biological networks such as gene regulatory networks (GRNs) and proteinprotein interaction networks (PPINs) help users gain knowledge of how living systems work [1]. They help to study how diseases work and discover new drugs. Nevertheless, they are voluminous, hence their complexities. Also, users may find

A. Alsadoon et al. (Eds.): CSCE 2025, CCIS 2935, pp. 82–101, 2026.
https://doi.org/10.1007/978-3-032-22199-5_6

it difficult to visualise and understand them because of their size and structure [2]. Biological networks present the interaction of molecules in the cell [3]. These interactions unravel the internal interactions of diseases and help to discover and develop appropriate drugs [4]. However, the data size and the tool's inherent complexity make it overwhelming for traditional tools to handle. The network could show much information at a time due to its density; as such, it is not easy to focus on the essentiality.

One common problem with biological network visualisation is cluttering. The available tools, despite their standard, find it hard to filter details from background noise [5]. Users cannot obtain clear oversight. Many available tools display too much and do not show the right areas [6]. Although some techniques can reduce this complexity, their lack of flexibility and practicality in real-world situations is their undoing. This study therefore addresses this gap by introducing a new tool known as Blurfisheye. This is a tool that uses two strong frameworks together. The first is that the fisheye view enlarges important areas and helps to focus on important nodes [7]. The second is the blur effect, which avoids noise by focusing on important parts only [8]. These two provide a clearer view of network details and structure.

This study designs, develops, and evaluates visualisation tools to enhance users' exploration of complex biological networks. Due to its combined features, users can focus on certain areas of their choice while simultaneously viewing the whole network. This study has some important contributions to knowledge, including hybridised visualisation methods for striking a balance between context and details. It offers interactive features with Cytoscape.js, a feature that supports different layouts, offers customisation features, and intuitive controls. Also, this study obtains insight from experts using surveys and interviews to evaluate the tool. The results show that it has become easier to identify important nodes because of the tool. Based on the study, drug delivery tasks and biological network learning are enhanced and supported. The study provides practical and user-friendly solutions that enhance complex biological data analysis, as it further provides a new way for researchers and educators to interact with biological networks effectively.

2 Background Study

Biological network visualization is experiencing growth at a faster pace due to the proliferation of high-throughput technologies and increasing biological data. This advancement is essential because it allows users to effectively manage network complexity and increasing size.

2.1 Challenges in Biological Network Visualization

Complex biological networks and their visualisation need a complete picture together with their tiniest details [9]. Although traditional techniques like circular and force-directed layouts handle network structures, issues like visual clutter, loss of context, and poor adaptability to change weaken their performance [10]. Aside from this, other issues are:

Other common challenges include:

- Issues related to performance, where high-throughput data cannot be processed easily due to the size, thereby delaying and reducing the performance of the tool [11].
- Relative issues of dynamic biological changes, where biological processes develop over time, yet current tools cannot match their level of change and cannot practically track them [12].
- Issues of functional interpretation, where it is hard for the technique to visually underscore important nodes or clusters in the network. This is an issue because tools need to help users identify the most significant parts of the network [13].

These issues created a gap that strong, better, and more flexible visualization tools must close for seamless biological data analysis.

2.2 Advancement in Network Visualization Techniques

In a bid to close these gaps, many tools were developed; however, some of their limitations have created more gaps affecting holistic exploration of biological networks.

- **Circular Layouts:** This technique arranges nodes circularly, making them useful only for small or medium networks. However, they lack the capacity to scale effectively because they overlap and clutter [14].
- **Clustering Algorithms:** This technique classifies nodes using shared similarities, thereby reducing visual complexity [15].
- **Dynamic Visualizations:** It tracks molecular changes over time and helps users understand temporal pathways [16].
- **Force-Directed Layouts:** These simulate node positions to show intuitive structures [17].
- **Graphical Annotations:** These remain static; however, they make nodes or edges meaningful [18].
- **Hierarchical Layouts:** These can fail if the network becomes dense; yet they highlight the relationship between parents and children [19].
- **Interactive Features:** It may struggle with dense graphs; however, zooming, panning, and filtering enhance user control [20].
- **Machine Learning:** Although this needs extra computational power, it supports clustering and predictions [21].
- **Modularisation Techniques:** It group related nodes while highlighting patterns [22].
- **Multi-modal Integration:** This incorporates different datasets into a single network [23].
- **Semantic Zooming:** This seamlessly explores details; however, in dense networks, it lacks the capacity to wholly solve cluttering [24].

All these imply progress; however, their development created another set of gaps that must be closed with tools that are focus-friendly and scalable.

2.3 Evaluation of Visualization Tools

Visualisation tools are not effective if they fail to work with large datasets, if user interaction is not seamless, and if they do not adapt to various types of data. Gephi and Pajek are two traditional tools that can be used to set up basic layouts; however, they usually fail to deliver if there is visual clutter, especially in large networks [25]. There are advanced tools that were developed to solve this issue, for instance, Cytoscape, NetworkX, and Graphviz, which streamline zooming, filtering, and plugin support. Cytoscape is the most outstanding of the three because it is flexible and has a wide plugin ecosystem. Furthermore, multi-omics data is supported, views are dynamic, and sophisticated layout designs like circular, tree-based, and force-directed layouts are provided. Hence, Cytoscape is the most used in visualizing biological networks [26]. Cytoscape platforms are flexible environments where new techniques such as fisheye and blur views are tested.

2.4 User-Centric Visualization Needs

Studies found that focusing on the needs of the user is paramount in visualization tools. Users must be able to identify with the features; the tool must allow zooming in, panning around, and filtering the network so users can explore at will [27]. Since users need to be able to alter the layout, colours, and labels in line with their tasks, customizability cannot be overemphasized. Both interactivity and customizability are important, as they enhance the usefulness of the tool in all aspects of research [28].

3 Introduction to Fisheye and Blur Techniques

Fisheye and blur techniques are new techniques. They are regarded as effective when exploring comprehensive data structures. The former is based on the principle of lens optics; it enhances a chosen area of interest while simultaneously viewing the full network. With this, users can focus more on the information they need while still viewing the larger structure [29]. The latter reduces the visibility of areas that are not important but may blur focus. This impedes cluttering; as such, users can understand the core parts of the network. Users can therefore easily understand the most significant parts of the network using these two techniques. The two techniques are important tools when there is a need for adaptable and scalable visualisation in biological networks.

3.1 Key Characteristics of Fisheye and Blur Techniques

This new technique has dynamic control; as such, users can make adjustments to the size of the focus area through interactive zoom-in. This does not disturb access to other parts surrounding the network. While the blur technique complements this, it filters out areas that are not in focus. It is not as if those areas are removed, but their visibility is weakened and reduced. This is why it can reduce distractions and help users focus on the most needed nodes. This method is useful in fields where there are numerous details [30].

3.2 Applications of Fisheye and Blur Techniques

The two techniques are known and used in simplifying complex information. The fisheye view can function with augmented reality (AR) and virtual reality (VR), thereby making it easier to zoom into needed 3D objects without reducing the view of the entire scene [30]. Such techniques help researchers focus on molecular actions like genes or proteins without compromising the wider network [31]. To text and browse through documents, fisheye zoom focuses on core sentences while blurring out surrounding text. This helps student concentration [32]. In analysing network security and traffic, fisheye helps to identify vulnerable nodes, blur noisy data, and detect threats easily [33]. This depicts the effectiveness of both tools in simplifying large, complex data, making them easier to understand and explore.

4 Methodology

From the feedback received from domain experts, there are some challenges with the exploration of complex biological networks. These are discussed in detail in Sect. refdeveloped. One main issue was how to group networks into sub-categories. This could lead to broad interpretations and loss of important context. To solve this, the study proposed a new visualization approach using fisheye and blur techniques. Fisheye helps users zoom into key areas without losing the full view. Blur reduces visual clutter by fading out less important areas. Experts agreed that Cytoscape was ideal for developing the BlurFisheye tool. It supports modular plugins and works well with various biological networks. This allows easy integration with past studies and flexibility for new visual techniques.

4.1 System Structure

Structured frameworks of front and back-end technologies were used to design Blurfisheye. Cytoscape.js, for instance, is a data visualization JavaScript library that forms the support base for visualization, while other libraries like Papa Parse enhance the quick parsing of data. The system architecture, as presented in Fig. 1, is built using HTML and CSS for its styling and layout, while the dynamic functionality of the system is built by vanilla JavaScript.

The BlurFisheye system architecture combines both front-end and back-end components. It uses:

- **Cytoscape.js** Handles interactive visualization of nodes, edges, and layouts.
- **Papa Parse** Quickly reads and imports raw text-based data.
- **HTML and CSS** Build the layout and visual style for a clear user interface.
- **Vanilla JavaScript** Enables interactive features like adjusting radius and selecting nodes.

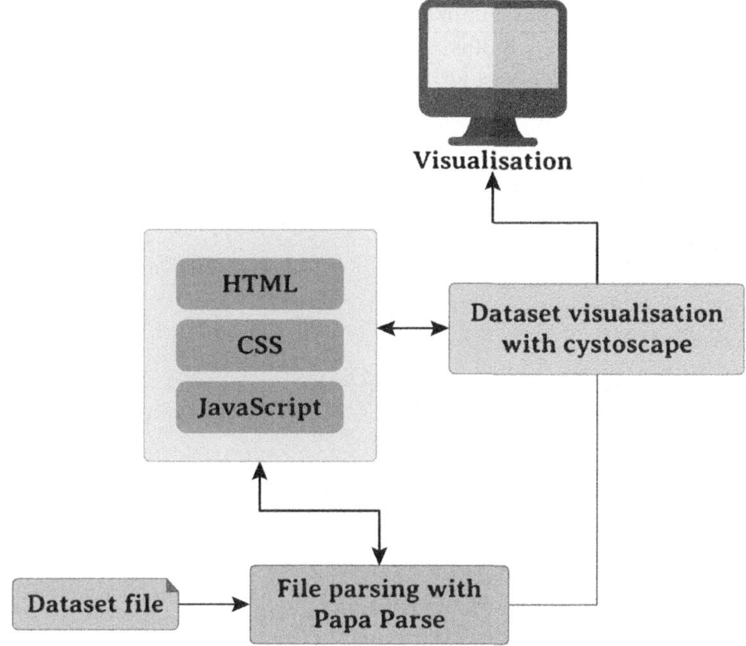

Fig. 1. The system architecture of the tool.

4.2 Algorithms for the BlurFisheye Technique

With this new technique, users can interactively focus on certain nodes of choice within a network system. The selection of a central node is magnified to the extent that the close-by ones are altered for clarity. Nodes that are far from the focal one can be blurred out. This capability balances detail and context, making it easier to explore networks regardless of their complexity. The dynamism in the way the algorithm delivers - node sizes, opacity, and edge width - updates because of the distance from the selected focal nodes. This ensures clarity in focus areas, while regions that are not relevant fade off.

4.3 Styling Framework

The BlurFisheye technique uses a custom styling framework to visually distinguish different node types in the network. These styles make it easier to focus on important parts of the network without losing the full picture.

1. inRadiusStyle. This style is used for nodes within the focus radius. These nodes are more visible with higher opacity and defined size for better clarity.

Algorithm 1 BlurFisheye Visualization Algorithm

1: **Input:** Selected node N_f, radius r, base height h_{base}, minimum height h_{min}
2: **Output:** Updated node styles for focus and context balance
3: **procedure** BLURFISHEYE($G(V, E), N_f$)
4: Identify focal node N_f and retrieve its (x_f, y_f) coordinates
5: **for** each node $N_i \in V$ **do**
6: **if** $N_i = N_f$ **then**
7: **continue** ▷ Skip focal node during distance calculation
8: **end if**
9: Get (x_i, y_i) coordinates of N_i
10: Compute distances:
11: $distanceX \leftarrow x_i - x_f$
12: $distanceY \leftarrow y_i - y_f$
13: $d \leftarrow \sqrt{(distanceX)^2 + (distanceY)^2}$
14: **if** $d \leq r$ **then** ▷ Node is within radius
15: $h_{new} \leftarrow \frac{h_{base}}{1+(d/r)^2}$
16: **if** $h_{new} < h_{min}$ **then**
17: $h_{new} \leftarrow h_{min}$
18: **end if**
19: Apply in-radius style to N_i
20: Set height and width of N_i to h_{new}
21: Emphasize edges between N_i and N_f
22: **else** ▷ Node is outside radius
23: Apply blurred style to N_i
24: Set lower height and width for N_i
25: Reduce opacity of N_i
26: Reduce edge width connecting N_i to N_f
27: **end if**
28: **end for**
29: Restore styles for nodes selected via dropdown to `selectedNodeStyle`
30: Apply `clickedStyle` to N_f with increased border size
31: **end procedure**

.node.inRadiusStyle CSS Style

```
.node {
background-color: $yourBackgroundColor; /* Replace with actual
color */
opacity: 1;
font-size: 12px;
height: 32px;
width: 32px;
border: 1px solid $yourBorderColor; /* Replace with actual border
color */
}
```

2. blurredStyle. Nodes outside the focus can be minimized using this style. It reduces distractions by lowering opacity and hiding labels.

.node.blurredStyle CSS Style

```
.node.blurredStyle {
opacity: 0.2;
font-size: 0; /* Removes node labels */
height: 24px;
width: 24px;
}
```

3. selectedNodeStyle. This keeps the chosen nodes visible and consistent throughout operations, retaining their network identity.

.node.selectedNodeStyle CSS Style

```
.node.selectedNodeStyle {
background-color: selectedNodeColor; /* Replace with actual color
*/
opacity: 1;
}
```

4. clickedStyle. This is applied to the clicked (focal) node. It increases border size and highlights the node to make it the visual center of attention.

.node.clickedStyle CSS Style

```
.node.clickedStyle {
border-color: clickedBorderColor; /* Replace with actual border
color */
border-width: 4px;
border-style: solid;
height: 50px;
width: 50px;
}
```

These styles together integrate fisheye magnification with blur de-emphasis, permitting researchers to focus only on important nodes without losing sight of the sub-parts of the network. The complete structure remains visible. Cytoscape's flexibility allows for easy integration of these styles into biological data workflows.

4.4 Layouts

To support effective visualization in the Blurfisheye tool, several layout strategies were used. These layouts help structure biological networks in ways that enhance clarity, focus, and interactive exploration.

Grid Layout: This structurally arranges nodes in an evenly spaced grid pattern, making it a clean and organised network view [34]. It is particularly effective because clarity and simplicity are prioritised, thus reducing the overlap of nodes and edges. Some datasets in biological networks are isolated clusters. It is the grid layout that makes it easy to differentiate between individual nodes and connections. This is beneficial to the Blurfisheye technique through focal node magnification without distortion to the overall layout. Grid Layout provides users with a stabilized framework for region identification and focus. This was chosen due to its stability and simplicity, which are needed for overviews without visual cluttering. Compared to organic, dynamic layout, grid layout is consistent spatially, reducing the cognitive burden and accounting for easy identification of certain nodes after interaction between blur fisheye magnification and effects.

CoSE (Compound Spring Embedder) Layout: This is a force-directed layout that optimizes compound graphs and locates nodes using simulated attraction and repulsion physical forces [35]. Nodes with more connections are paired to create clusters showing the network structure. This allows users to identify cohesive nodes quickly, which is an essential visual, intuitive route. CoSE Layout was selected because of its natural ability to categorise similar nodes, which gives clarity to the large dataset clusters. Unlike Kamada-Kawai or Fruchterman-Reingold, CoSE works well with compound graphs, and it is supportive of the Blurfisheye technique's interactive adjustment without changing clusters' node clusters' stability.

Concentric Layout: This enhances the arrangement of nodes concentrically in a circle that is obtuse from central nodes, with the nodes positioned based on their level of importance in the network. This layout is hierarchical; users can observe dependencies and degree of centrality [36]. This is useful in analysing datasets in biological networks with a clear hierarchy, like regulatory pathways where central genes or proteins influence multiple downstream nodes. Concentric Layout was chosen due to the relationship between central nodes and hierarchical relationships, which is useful in key node identification in regulatory networks, compared to linear or tree-based layouts, the concentric structure is complementary to Blurfisheye's focal zooming effect in a radial organization. This then lets users easily navigate network layers without distorting the context.

Circle Layout: This layout circularly arranges nodes through even distribution around the perimeter, benefiting users who may need a balanced structural network view, with equal visibility given to all nodes regardless of their connections [37]. The circle layout was chosen because of the clear overview it offers without giving priority to one node over another. This makes it suitable for examining non-hierarchical network interactions. In comparison with force-directed layouts, the circle layout does not compromise spatial consistency and aligns with the BlurFisheye technique's interactive focus capability, making it easier for users to explore nodes without significant layout shifts along the circle.

Breadthfirst Layout: This layout arranges nodes in a layer and hierarchical structure based on their position from a set of nodes concentrically in layers, especially for exploring relationships where the network is obtuse outward from a centre [38]. A Gene regulatory network is one example of a cascading regulatory element controlling gene expressions. The effectiveness of Breadthfirst Layout in showing hierarchical and relational depth influences its choice. Also, choosing it is advantageous to networks with multi-level interactions. Compared to radial tree layout or depth-first, breadth-first arranges nodes readily, layer-by-layer, and supports users' focus on network layers without distorting the entire network structure perspective.

4.5 Development Approach

The Blurfisheye technique was developed to solve common problems in visualizing complex biological networks. It helps users focus on important nodes while keeping the global structure intact. The tool combines fisheye magnification with a blur effect, allowing better navigation of dense networks. The development followed a two-version approach—starting with a basic prototype and moving to a refined version based on expert feedback (see Fig. 2).

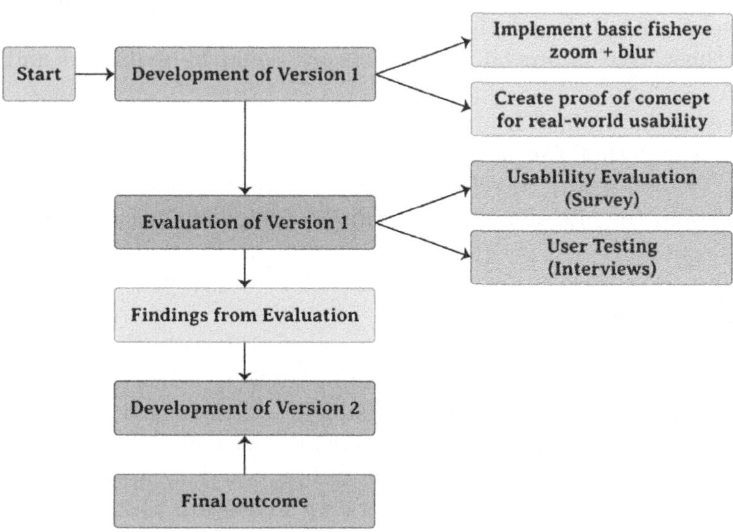

Fig. 2. Development Approach

The development followed a two-version approach, beginning with a basic prototype, then moving to a refined version using expert feedback (see Fig. 2).

The aim of the first version was to test core functionality. It allowed users to magnify nodes and blur the surrounding ones. This version can be regarded as proof of concept and was evaluated with structured surveys and semi-structured interviews. The former collected quantitative data from six experts from different fields that cut across research associates, lecturers, data scientists, PhD students, and postdoctoral researchers. They rated the tool's usability on a 5-point Likert scale using core heuristics like information coding, flexibility, spatial organization, and action minimization.

Furthermore, four domain experts in bioinformatics, genetics, and biomedical science were interviewed for user testing. They provided important information about user experience and specific requirements of the tools. These interviews were done via Zoom and Skype, where all the sessions were automatically recorded and transcribed. These experts provided real-time information on the merits and limitations of the tools. Also, they shared insight on navigation effectiveness, fisheye view usefulness, and the clarity gained from using the blur effect.

Based on this evaluation, the idea behind the tool was well received and appreciated, even though there were limitations, including performance lag when large datasets were involved, limited control features, and a lack of built-in guidance. This prompted the development of version 2 of the tool, with a focus on enhanced performance, interactivity, and user support.

Algorithm optimization in the second version was intended to reduce lag and enhance rendering speed. Undo and adjustable fisheye radius features were added to upgrade the tool and give users more freedom to control it. A help panel and tooltip prompts were incorporated for new users to explain features unambiguously. Even though the original choice of layouts was not retained, their initial settings were improved so the network could be stabilised and become readable.

The feedback obtained from the experts was used for iterative development, and this ensured that the new tool operates seamlessly to meet the needs of the users. Version 2 was therefore a better response due to its enhanced user-friendliness and the effective support it provided for biological network visualisation.

5 BlurFisheye

Biological networks are usually large and compact, which makes meaningful interpretation complicated without a distortion of their structural context. To tackle this, BlurFisheye was developed. This is a visualization tool that magnifies fisheye and integrates blur-emphasis techniques. This approach helps users focus on important regions in the network without a loss of its global overview.

5.1 Version 1

The first version of the tool was developed to be a proof of concept for core functionality testing. The aim of the development was for users to have the freedom to magnify certain nodes of their choice interactively and to blur peripheral elements. This makes it seamless for users to have a context-focused balance, highlighting core data points while the rest diminishes.

Some of the features of the first version are:

- **Dynamic Node Selection:** According to Fig. 3-a–e, users could click on nodes if they needed to magnify the fisheye view and blur off the radial.
- **Multiple Layout Options:** This is shown in Fig. 3-f, and it consists of grid, CoSE, concentric, circle, and breadth-first. The layouts offered users different structural perspectives that supported the use of different biological data types.
- **Integrated Guidance:** Features like help tooltips and drop downs were added to guide new users in navigating the interface.
- **Custom Styling:** The system highlights the focal areas, supported by flexible node and edge styling.
- **Interactive Canvas:** This feature allows users to zoom, pan, and interact without graph reloading or distortion.

Figure 3-f houses fisheye view magnification and blur effects; these two features are central to node enhancement, where out-of-focus nodes are blurred to reduce distractions.

5.2 Evaluation of Version 1

To assess its effectiveness, Version 1 underwent a two-phase evaluation involving a structured survey and qualitative expert interviews.

The survey (see Table 1) was conducted with 15 participants, including researchers, data scientists, and PhD students. Participants rated usability across seven heuristics. The highest score was for flexibility (5.0), indicating satisfaction with interaction features. However, removal of extraneous information scored lowest (4.0), suggesting the interface could be further streamlined.

Table 1. Survey Feedback Summary on BlurFisheye System

Heuristic Factor	Mean Rating	Key Findings
Information Coding	4.4	Effective display of data using colours, nodeedge, and layers to differentiate.
Flexibility	4.7	Zooming, panning, and layout reorganization were highly adaptive.
Orientation & Help	4.3	The panel on the right helps with seamless navigation, as help tooltips enhance system accessibility.
Minimal Actions	4.7	The Undo button was added as a feature to enhance usability when the system focus-switches.
Prompting	4.1	The user guide guides the user effectively, although there can be minor adjustments for notification alerts.
Consistency	4.2	A consistent layout rendering can weaken disorientation.
Spatial Organization	4.8	The fisheye effect is positive; it helps to differentiate patterns.
Recognition over Recall	4.0	Easy reorganization of similarities with the aid of the fisheye view layout.
Removing Extraneous Info	4.3	Efficient removal of non-essential data using blurring frameworks.
Data Reduction	4.3	Dataset divided into better insight and visibility.
Time Management	4.5	Clear layout reduces interaction time.
Essence	4.2	System enables meaningful interpretation of biological data.

Additionally, responses from molecular biology and bioinformatics experts showed that the high-level acceptance and appreciation for the tool, particularly because of its focused-navigation and unambiguous information it presents. Nevertheless, there are areas to be improved, according to the users. First, undo features could be enhanced. Also, responsive radius controls should be added, while the tool could be more effective if its guidance and prompts are enhanced. Table 2 presents the summaries of these findings.

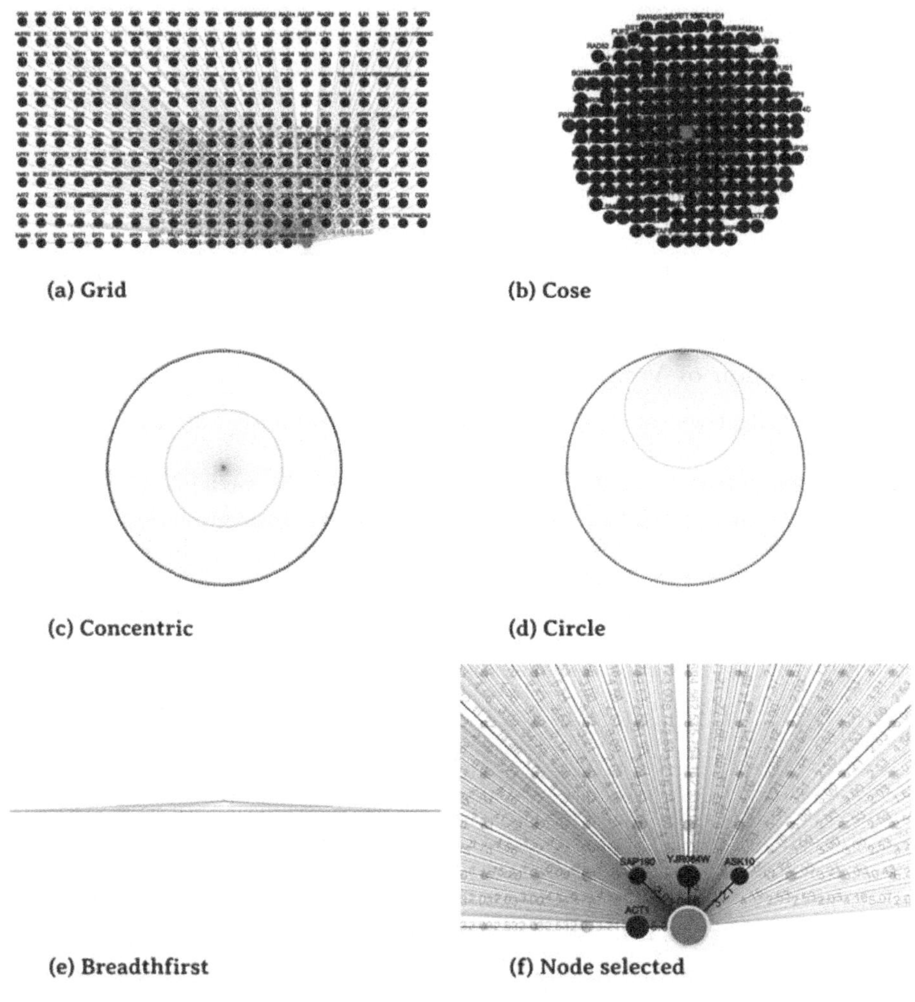

Fig. 3. Different Layout Distribution and Node Selection

Table 2. Interview Findings from Domain Experts

Factor	Findings
Information Coding	Visuals perceived as accurate and adaptable; minor display lag on web.
Flexibility	Panning/zooming is helpful, even though layout size weakens the visibility of the node.
Orientation	The learning curve is enhanced with the introduction of help tools and layout explanations.
Minimal Actions	A significant improvement in user control is noticed in the Undo feature.
Prompting	Alerts and group annotations requested better guidance.
Consistency	Minor rendering delays: optimization is needed for larger datasets.
Spatial Organization	Grid, concentric, and breadth-first layouts have a more effective impact on fisheye.
Recognition vs. Recall	Cluster recognition and relationship tracing were supported in the tool.
Removing Extraneous Info	The tool does not clutter up with unnecessary details, as it focuses only on data that are useful.
Data Reduction	Data filtering improved clarity; suggestions were made for handling large datasets.
Essence	Helped identify data patterns and link nodes to biological structures.
Confidence	Clear layout improved confidence and encouraged dataset reanalysis.

5.3 Version 2

Version 2 was developed based on experts' feedback on the need for usability, performance, and guidance improvements.

- **Undo Functionality:** It allows users to reverse actions such as selection of nodes or changes to layouts. This increases user confidence while they explore.
- **Enhanced Radius and Zoom Control:** It allow users to dynamically adjust sliders for fisheye and blur radius to be more responsive and enhance precision while focusing.
- **Performance Optimization:** It allows users to refine algorithms to handle larger datasets efficiently. The addition of UI blockers helps cushion against crashes during heavy interactions.
- **In-App Notes System:** It allows users to add, edit, and download node-linked notes to help track analysis observations.
- **Guided Interface:** A guided interface through tooltips, layout explanations, and a help panel guide allows users to access functionality, including first-time users.
- **Screenshot Feature:** It allows users to capture and download their current views for publication or offline analysis.
- **Improved Layout Stability:** It allows layouts to be adjusted by default to reduce overlap and enhance structural clarity in dense graphs.

A screenshot that shows how the Undo feature operates is attached to Fig. 4. This is a direct response to an important pain point from the first version.

6 Discussion

Blurfisheye is a visualisation tool that was developed to provide support for exploratory analysis of large and complex biological networks. After its evalua-

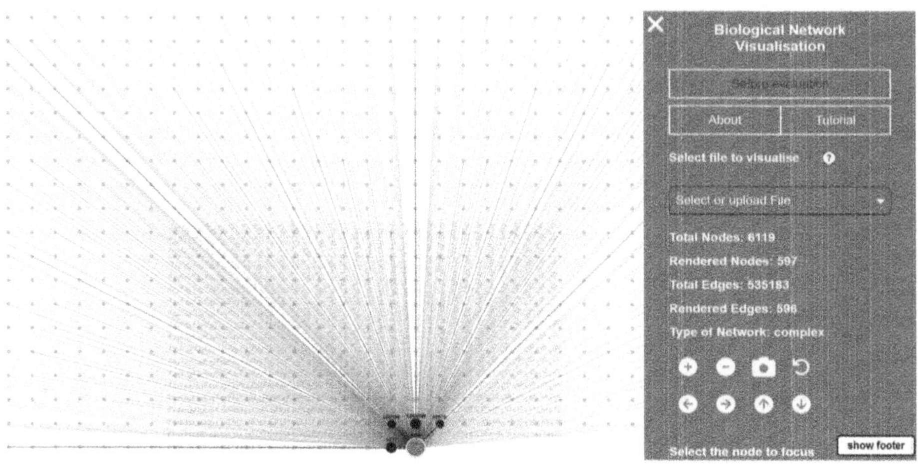

Fig. 4. Undo and Radius control implementation

tion, the result is promising. The study combined heuristic evaluation, surveys, and interview sessions to assess the tool's usability and performance. Experts and non-experts alike used the tool. Many of them acknowledged the usefulness of the tool in how it effectively simplifies datasets despite their big size. Users reported that the tool makes it easy to complete their tasks on time. The pilot users could identify drug discovery targets, explore research clusters, and teach biological networks. This feedback is needed and serves as requisite information on the performance of the tool and areas where improvements are needed.

Identifying Targets for Drug Discovery and Research Clusters: This is a standout benefit of the tool. The tool can blur out irrelevant information while amplifying the relevant ones. Users can single out and analyse biological networks more effectively since visualisation is now about the relevant data. For instance, researchers may use the tool to identify important pathways in drug discovery and then link them to treatment targets. With this combination, users can zoom well into any area without losing the whole network, because of adjustable blur and fisheye magnification. They can now create a balance between details and context and streamline therapeutic processes that focus on complex molecular or genetic pathways.

Enhancing the Learning Process: Blurfisheye helps educators and students to enhance their learning process on biological networks. Beginners may not easily understand large datasets; however, the introduction of the tool makes it simple for them to work with due to the integration of visuals. Teachers can outline core nodes on important learning elements. Visual clarity is introduced by the tool, which is why learners can gain greater knowledge of how hierarchical relationships work, helping them to identify gene-to-gene interactions and trace regulatory pathways. The reduction in visual clutter introduced by the tool is helpful, especially in better understanding concepts confidently.

Meeting Users' Expectations: Users were uniform in their appreciation of the tool's interactivity and customization features. Importantly, features like adjustable blur radius, fisheye zoom, and node styling were the most useful. This is because researchers could design interfaces to align with data analysis objectives. This personalization enhanced user experience because all the participants were in control of their dataset exploration. As such, users could engage more and were confident in their ability to use the tool to perform analytical tasks.

Areas for Future Improvement: The tool is highly effective for users who already have background knowledge and experience in biological data analysis. Nevertheless, further updating is needed for usability optimization for beginners. The heuristic and ICET-based evaluations offered a broad assessment method. Users were then able to detect areas that can be improved further, such as the performance of the system when large dataset rendering is involved, responsiveness of interaction, and user guidance features. These were essential for future development.

7 Recommendations

Using the feedback from the users and findings of the evaluation, some recommendations are proposed to developers, educators, and researchers for design and usability enhancement, and network visualisation tool effectiveness.

7.1 For Network Visualization Tool Developers

- Incorporate customizable interaction thresholds so that users can set boundaries for node interaction and highlighting. This feature is supportive of focused analysis of core network areas and improvement in managing large datasets.
- Real-time annotations should be added to the tools to enhance collaborative research, track findings, disseminate insights, and develop a cumulative analysis record.
- Include UI blockers to maintain smooth performance during heavy rendering tasks. This will ensure responsive interaction and prevent interface freezing in large networks.

7.2 For Educators Using the Tool

- **Utilize Selective Visualization for Teaching:** Use of chosen teaching visualizations can help instructors outline core areas and blur out the irrelevant ones to redirect the attention of the students. The large network is therefore simplified to enhance learning focus.
- **Focus on Progressive Data Exploration:** Progressive data exploration is designed to help students start with smaller sub-networks prior to moving on to complete datasets. This stage of learning guides them in strengthening their confidence and gradually understanding network structures.

7.3 For Researchers in Drug Discovery and Life Sciences

- **Use Targeted Node Exploration for Drug Target Discovery:** Node exploration for the discovery of drug targets should be encouraged through the application of BlurFisheye's focus ability in identifying potential therapeutic targets in large biological networks.
- **Enhance User Training for Advanced Features:** User training could be improved with advanced features that provide training on the adjustment of fisheye radius, as well as threshold interaction and layout control, ensuring that experts are able to maximize the capabilities of the tool.

7.4 For Future Tool Development and Optimization

- Performance optimization should be encouraged in complex networks by focusing on developments that can strengthen rendering speed and efficient computation, and effectively handle complex datasets.
- Advanced customization options are needed and should be added together with adjustable fisheye sensitivity and enhanced undo functionality so users can have more control and flexibility.

8 Conclusion

The study introduced a new visualization tool known as Blurfisheye. It was designed to improve complex biological network analysis. This tool combined fisheye view and dynamic blur effects to help users focus on important data points while simultaneously viewing the whole network context. The feedback from the experts was used to design the tool to solve important challenges of network visualisation. The tool can magnify focal nodes and visually de-emphasize peripheral insight. The tool strikes a balance that supports target identification, regulatory route analysis, and teaching content simplification tasks.

With the aid of structured surveys and interviews, tool usability and relevance were confirmed to enhance the capability of large dataset exploration and support targeted analysis without stress to the interface. The tool's adaptability, clarity, and user-focused features have the potential to improve different applications in education and biological research.

The development focus henceforth will be to improve performance with large-scale datasets and networks by enhancing rendering speed and responsiveness. Adjustable blur sensitivity and interactive annotations are customization options that could be explored to provide support for deeper analysis and collaborative needs. These enhancements will guide the development of the tool to be in line with user demands and serve as an asset to biological network visualization.

References

1. Koutrouli, M., Karatzas, E., Paez-Espino, D., Pavlopoulos, G.A.: A guide to conquer the biological network era using graph theory. Front. Bioeng. Biotech. **8**, 34 (2020)
2. Zhou, S., Chen, S.B., Fu, E.S., Yan, H.: Computer vision meets microfluidics: a label-free method for high-throughput cell analysis. Microsyst. Nanoeng. **9**(1), 116 (2023)
3. Bandyopadhyay, D., Mukherjee, M.: Systematic comparison of the protein-protein interaction network of bacterial universal stress protein A (UspA): an insight into its discrete functions. Biologia **77**(9), 2631–2642 (2022)
4. Recanatini, M., Menestrina, L.: Network modelling helps to tackle the complexity of drug–disease systems. WIREs Mech. Disease **15**(4), e1607 (2023)
5. Egwuche, O.S., Singh, A., Ezugwu, A.E., Greeff, J., Olusanya, M.O., Abualigah, L.: Machine learning for coverage optimization in wireless sensor networks: a comprehensive review. Ann. Oper. Res. , 1–67 (2023)
6. Hamdan, M., et al.: A comprehensive survey of load balancing techniques in software-defined network. J. Netw. Comput. Appl. **174**, 102856 (2021)
7. Cheng, Z., et al.: Pyramid cross attention network for pixel-wise surface defect detection. NDT & E Int. **143**, 103053 (2024)
8. Milano, M., Agapito, G., Cannataro, M.: Challenges and limitations of biological network analysis. Biotech **11**(3), 24 (2022)
9. Koutrouli, M., Karatzas, E., Paez-Espino, D., Pavlopoulos, G.A.: A guide to conquer the biological network era using graph theory. Front. Bioeng. Biotech. **8**, 34 (2020)
10. He, J., Chen, H., Chen, Y., Tang, X., Zou, Y.: Diverse visualization techniques and methods of moving-object-trajectory data: a review. ISPRS Int. J. Geo Inf. **8**(2), 63 (2019)
11. Wybrow, M., Elmqvist, N., Fekete, J.D., Von Landesberger, T., van Wijk, J.J., Zimmer, B.: Interaction in the visualization of multivariate networks. In: Multivariate Network Visualization: Dagstuhl Seminar#13201. Dagstuhl Castle, Germany, May 12–17, 2013, Revised Discussions, pp. 97–125. Springer International Publishing, Cham (2014)
12. He, J., Chen, H., Chen, Y., Tang, X., Zou, Y.: Diverse visualization techniques and methods of moving-object-trajectory data: a review. ISPRS Int. J. Geo Inf. **8**(2), 63 (2019)
13. Li, D.X., et al.: BioCAIV: an integrative webserver for motif-based clustering analysis and interactive visualization of biological networks. BMC Bioinfo. **24**(1), 451 (2023)
14. Fadloun, S., Meshoul, S., Choutri, K.: CircleVis: a visualization tool for circular labeling arrangements and overlap removal. Appl. Sci. **12**(22), 11390 (2022)
15. Lai, P.C., Chou, W., Chien, T.W., Lai, F.J.: A modern approach with follower-leading clustering algorithm for visualizing author collaborations and article themes in skin cancer research: a bibliometric analysis. Medicine **102**(44), e34801 (2023)
16. Wiebels, K., Moreau, D.: Dynamic data visualizations to enhance insight and communication across the life cycle of a scientific project. Adv. Methods Pract. Psychol. Sci. **6**(3), 25152459231160104 (2023)
17. Xu, Z., Mao, T., Xu, G., Wang, Y., Lin, D.: Multivariate network layout using force-directed method with attribute constraints. Appl. Sci. **12**(9), 4561 (2022)

18. Zhao, J., Glueck, M., Breslav, S., Chevalier, F., Khan, A.: Annotation graphs: a graph-based visualization for meta-analysis of data based on user-authored annotations. IEEE Trans. Visual Comput. Graph. **23**(1), 261–270 (2016)
19. Woodburn, L., Yang, Y., Marriott, K.: Interactive visualization of hierarchical quantitative data: an evaluation. In: 2019 IEEE Visualization Conference (VIS), pp. 96–100 (2019)
20. Höhn, M., Wunderlich, M., Ballweg, K., Kohlhammer, J., Von Landesberger, T.: Interactive input and visualization for planning with temporal uncertainty. SN Comput. Sci. **4**(3), 231 (2023)
21. Rawat, S., Rawat, A., Kumar, D., Sabitha, A.S.: Application of machine learning and data visualization techniques for decision support in the insurance sector. Int. J. Info. Manag. Data Insights **1**(2), 100012 (2021)
22. Kolbeck, L., et al.: Modularisation strategies for individualised precast construction–conceptual fundamentals and research directions. Designs **7**(6), 143 (2023)
23. Subramanian, I., Verma, S., Kumar, S., Jere, A., Anamika, K.: Multi-omics data integration, interpretation, and its application. Bioinform. Biol. Insights **14**, 1177932219899051 (2020)
24. Garcia, J., Theron, R., Garcia, F.: Semantic zoom: a details on demand visualization technique for modelling OWL ontologies. In: Highlights in Practical Applications of Agents and Multiagent Systems: 9th International Conference on Practical Applications of Agents and Multiagent Systems, pp. 85–92. Springer, Berlin, Heidelberg (2011)
25. Alzahrani, H., Fernstad, S.: An investigation into various visualization tools for complex biological networks. Inf. Vis. **22**(4), 323–339 (2023)
26. Mousavian, Z., Khodabandeh, M., Sharifi-Zarchi, A., Nadafian, A., Mahmoudi, A.: StrongestPath: a Cytoscape application for protein-protein interaction analysis. BMC Bioinfo. **22**, 1–14 (2021)
27. Yang, Y., Cordeil, M., Beyer, J., Dwyer, T., Marriott, K., Pfister, H.: Embodied navigation in immersive abstract data visualization: is overview+ detail or zooming better for 3D scatterplots? IEEE Trans. Visual Comput. Graphics **27**(2), 1214–1224 (2020)
28. Segun-Falade, O.D., et al.: Developing innovative software solutions for effective energy management systems in industry. Eng. Sci. Technol. J. **5**(8) (2024)
29. Choi, K.H., Kim, Y., Kim, C.: Analysis of fish-eye lens camera self-calibration. Sensors **19**(5), 1218 (2019)
30. Bachiller, C., Monzo, J.M., Rey, B.: Augmented and virtual reality to enhance the didactical experience of technological heritage museums. Appl. Sci. **13**(6), 3539 (2023)
31. Fiscon, G., Conte, F., Farina, L., Paci, P.: Network-based approaches to explore complex biological systems towards network medicine. Genes **9**(9), 437 (2018)
32. Nie, B., Sun, S.: Using text mining techniques to identify research trends: a case study of design research. Appl. Sci. **7**(4), 401 (2017)
33. Karami, A.: An anomaly-based intrusion detection system in presence of benign outliers with visualization capabilities. Expert Syst. Appl. **108**, 36–60 (2018)
34. Lima, D.B., Zhu, Y., Liu, F.: XlinkCyNET: a Cytoscape application for visualization of protein interaction networks based on cross-linking mass spectrometry identifications. J. Proteome Res. **20**(4), 1943–1950 (2021)
35. Okka, A., Dogrusoz, U., Balci, H.: CoSEP: a compound spring embedder layout algorithm with support for ports. Inf. Vis. **20**(2–3), 151–169 (2021)

36. Franz, M., Lopes, C.T., Huck, G., Dong, Y., Sumer, O., Bader, G.D.: Cytoscape.JS: a graph theory library for visualization and analysis. Bioinformatics **32**(2), 309–311 (2016)
37. Doncheva, N.T., Morris, J.H., Gorodkin, J., Jensen, L.J.: Cytoscape StringApp: network analysis and visualization of proteomics data. J. Proteome Res. **18**(2), 623–632 (2018)
38. Wang, J., Zhong, J., Chen, G., Li, M., Wu, F.X., Pan, Y.: ClusterViz: a Cytoscape APP for cluster analysis of biological network. IEEE/ACM Trans. Comput. Biol. Bioinf. **12**(4), 815–822 (2014)

Leveraging Local LLMs for Taxonomy-Aware Analysis of STRING-Supported Species

Hanin Alzahrani(✉)

Al-Baha University, Al Bahah, Saudi Arabia
hszahrani@bu.edu.sa

Abstract. Large Language Models (LLMs) have become proliferated in research studies. They help to summarise information and data analysis. However, using them to analyse structured biological data is complicated, particularly because of hallucination. Hallucination occurs when models give wrong answers. In biology in particular, hallucination errors cause wrong conclusions to be drawn. It is on that note that the current study proposes a prompt engineering framework that can be reproduced and is taxonomically aware, so that local LLMs can reduce hallucination and can do so with improved factual accuracy in biological dataset analysis. This study examines how local LLMs like LLaMA 3.1 and Phi 4 can be used safely to analyse species data from STRING database. The aim of this study is to provide guidance to these models with a well-designed prompt for hallucination reduction and enhanced accuracy. The method encompasses the creation of unambiguous system and user prompts, which are to be tested using three yardsticks: species flags counting, grouping by genus, and discovery of duplicated UDs. Every result generated is compared to the python-generated correct answers. From the results, prompt engineering enhances models to produce better answers. Hallucinations are also reduced, while output becomes reliable. The performance of LLaMA 3.1 is weighed against Phi 4, however, LLaMa 3.1 outweighs Phi 4, particularly with respect to the use of larger datasets. This study therefore reveals that if Local LLMs are guided with unambiguous prompts, their analysis on structured biological data is usually accurate.

Keywords: Biological Data Analysis · Local Language Models · Prompt Engineering · Hallucination Mitigation · Taxonomy-Aware LLMs

1 Introduction

In the last few years, the Large Language Models (LLMs) deployment in scientific research, such as biology, has risen. Simultaneously, STRINGdb, a biological database grew in complexity [1]. This database had structured data like names of species, taxonomic relationships and metadata. The deployment of LLMs for summary or data analysis has helped with time saving and researchers to gain

A. Alsadoon et al. (Eds.): CSCE 2025, CCIS 2935, pp. 102–116, 2026.
https://doi.org/10.1007/978-3-032-22199-5_7

new insights. Despite this, LLMs are prone to hallucination, an error in which species names are made up, values are misrepresented and misinterpreted, or false relationships created. Such an error causes more harm to scientific context, where accuracy cannot be compromised [2].

Previous studies have shown the potential of prompt engineering in guiding LLMs. However, most of these studies focus on general tasks or text-based data. Some studies examined the prompt engineering potential as a guide to LLMs. Nevertheless, many of such studies only focus on general tasks or text-based data. There are gaps in this study area, despite the growing interest, a major one being that most studies use text-based or general data. Studies rarely evaluate how local LLMs like LLaMA and Phi perform on structured datasets such as STRINGdb. Furthermore, while prompt engineering has been studied, it has not been applied extensively in taxonomy-based tasks with hallucination risks. This study addresses these gaps by exploring how structured and rule-based prompts can guide a local LLM to analyze biological datasets accurately. It evaluates how prompt modifications can reduce hallucination and improve result clarity.

Therefore, this study aims to design prompt structures for local LLMs, such as LLaMA 3.1 and Phi 4, to analyze species data from STRINGdb. The prompts were designed to guide the model clearly and to prevent hallucinations. The study explores how system and user prompts can be combined to help the model follow rules and focus only on the data. It also tests how well the LLM performs on three tasks: counting species flags, grouping by genus, and finding duplicate IDs. The results were compared with outputs from Python-based methods to check accuracy.

By focusing on taxonomy-aware tasks, this work offers a practical contribution to both prompt engineering and biological data analysis. This paper contributes: (1) A novel hallucination-aware prompt framework for local LLMs, (2) Empirical validation across three dataset sizes, and (3) a comparative study of LLaMA 3.1 vs Phi 4 for taxonomy-aware tasks.

2 Literature Review

The use of artificial intelligence (AI) tools in biological research is increasing rapidly. LLMs have gained more attention, among other tools, because they seamlessly help to summarise, classify and analyse data [3]. However, LLMs effectiveness in structured scientific datasets such as record of taxonomy from biological databases have not been explored [4]. On that note, this section of the study highlights important developments in LLM-induced analysis, including prompt engineering importance, issues surrounding hallucination, and research gaps this study intends to fill.

2.1 Using LLMs in Scientific and Biological Data Analysis

LLMs are widely accepted in different domains of research such as science and medicine. However, in biology, researchers have started using them for analysis, data summarization, hypothesis generation and testing and extraction of knowledge from large text corpora. Examples of LLMs are GPT and LLaMa, and they have become powerful tools in handling complex information. Nevertheless, most applications have so far focused on unstructured data like scientific articles or free-text inputs [5].

STRINGdb is an example of structured biological dataset. This is a dataset with unique challenges, as it contains fixed formats in fields like species names, taxonomic identifiers, relational flags [6]. A researcher analyzing such data must be attentive to LLMs' precision and consistency, especially in areas where full testing is not yet carried out [17]. This gap reveals that a method that is adaptable to LLMs is needed to process structured scientific data.

2.2 Prompt Engineering and Its Role in LLM Tasks

The process through which input instructions are designed to serve as guide to LLMs output is referred to as prompt engineering. Well-structured prompt strengthens the focus of a model on a certain task, thereby reducing errors and offering a more precise answer [7]. Researchers use this method to ask questions, to provide answers, translate and summarise. It has so far shown itself to be reliable, by generating positive results. Particularly, when there is clear objectives and constraints to follow. The importance of prompt engineering is felt in education, software development, research, and healthcare field. In all these fields, accuracy and context-awareness are essential. Therefore, it is helpful to master prompt engineering so that users can maximise LLM potential. Some of such potential can be seen in ambiguity reduction, and in efficient implementation of tasks [10,11].

Significantly, prompt engineering is consistent, as such, it is compliant to ethical guidelines and aligns with the behaviour of AI and the intended use case. Majority of the available research on prompt engineering has only focused on general language tasks. Hence, the limited work on prompt strategies for analyzing structured datasets. Even fewer studies explore prompt design for biological data, where the output must follow scientific rules and avoid misinterpretation.

2.3 Hallucination in LLMs

Hallucination is a known issue in LLM-generated outputs. It occurs when the model provides incorrect or fabricated information. In scientific study, hallucination can pose a serious problem [8]. For example, LLM could generate false species names, then misrepresent the relationships between organisms, or perhaps explain biological concepts that are different from the ones in the dataset [9]. A researcher who uses such output could be misled into erroneous analysis that negatively impacts the quality of the findings. Studies like [13,14] recommended different methods of reducing hallucination, including use of predefined system roles, restriction on the scope of the model's knowledge, and application of post-processing checks. Researchers like [18,19] deploy prompt template with a carefully designed instruction, so as to channel the creativity of the model, and stay within data boundary.

3 Methodology

This is a combined approach study, in which LLM and a traditional data analysis method use python as a benchmark. This is expressed in Fig. 1.

Experiment Setup - The study used LLaMA 3.1 and Phi 4, 7 billion parameters and 5.5 billion parameters respectively. These were hosted and locally run for privacy and control. The experiments were done with a structured prompting strategy, prior to and after the introduction of mitigation methods.

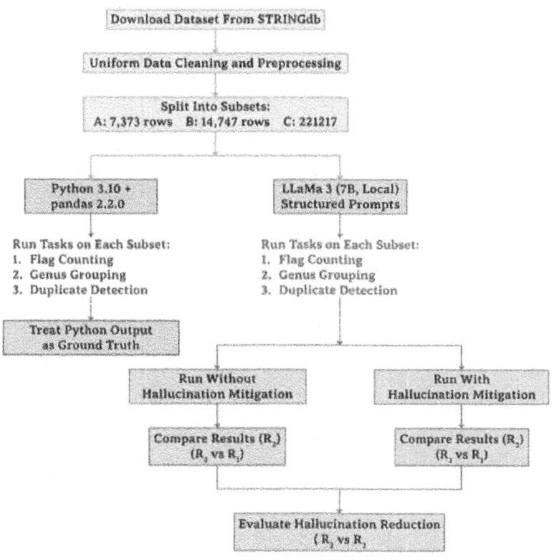

Fig. 1. Detailed steps involved in the methodology of this study

Dataset Description and Preparation - The dataset was sourced and downloaded from the https://stringdb-downloads.org/download/species.tree.v12.0.txt official STRING database. The following information was collected on species files, they are taxonomic identifiers, names, parent IDs, and a flag indicating STRINGdb support. Prior to the experiment, the dataset was cleaned and uniformly processed in compliance with Python, LlaMa and Phi experimental formats.

For thorough evaluation of the performance, the dataset was divided into three subsets using different scales.

- **Dataset A** (7,373 rows) small-sized sample
- **Dataset B** (14,747 rows) medium-sized sample
- **Dataset C** (221,217 rows) full dataset

Task Performance Evaluation Using Different Dataset Subsets -
Three major tasks were performed with all the subsets. The first one is simple flag counting, followed by genus-based grouping, and then duplication of detection, the third task. The results from each of these tasks from Python were used as the benchmark. These tasks were repeated but with LlaMa 3.1 and Phi 4, using structured prompts, without hallucinations mitigation, and secondly with hallucination safeguard.

Experimental Methodology and Evaluation Criteria - The following is the outline of the consistent flow of the experiment:

1. Run Python (version 3.10) code using **pandas** library (version 2.2.0) to generate accurate outputs. This was the **manual ground truth**.

2. Repeat the same task using LLaMA 3.1 and Phi 4 only with a pre-defined system and user prompt.
3. Do a comparison of the LLM outputs before and after the addition of hallucination mitigation rules.
4. Measure accuracy, hallucination rate, and format compliance for each case.

This methodology ensured a fair comparison between LLM-generated results and standard programmatic methods. The **manual ground truth** was considered the reference point for assessing the reliability of the LLaMA 3.1 and Phi 4 outputs. Furthermore, the experiment highlighted the effects of prompt design on LLM performance, especially regarding accuracy and hallucination prevention.

4 Prompt Design

The quality and clarity of thc prompt have a direct impact on the relevance, accuracy, and usefulness of the generated outputs [11]. A prompt from the user is direct, however, end users need to make input that request for certain information or actions from the LLM [12]. For example, 'explain climate change in simple terms' or 'translate this paragraph to Spanish' are sample prompts requesting for specific information [12]. User prompt is instant, and its focus is on task at hand that guides the AI behaviour in the short-term, based on user intention [10].

Also, the system prompt poses some inherent hinderance to LLM, even though it creates some underlying frameworks. The user and system prompts provide background support for prompt engineering [20]. Based on that, understanding the variations and interplay between them is crucial to every user working with LLMs. Figure 2 presents an overview of prompt design block diagram for the current study.

No	SYSTEM PROMPT	USER PROMPT
B_1	Objectives *	Objectives *
B_2	Data Schema *	Data Scope
B_3	Behaviour Guideline *	Type of Operation or Report Needed*
B_4	Output Style *	Output Request Format
B_5	Hallucination Mitigation Rules **	Hallucination Mitigation Rules **

Fig. 2. Block Diagram of the Prompt Design - Note- * is compulsory, ** is compulsory for second experiment, No * means optional

4.1 Prompts Without Hallucination Mitigation

System and user prompt engineering were effectively designed as a guide to local LlaMa 3.1 and Phi 4 model, for consistency, precision, and explainability. The system prompts created the identity of the model and behavioural limitations [15]. The first thing it does is to create a clear objective, to enable the model function reliably in analysing taxonomy-based datasets. After which it explicitly defines the schema of the data, like taxon_id, parent_taxon_id, taxon_name, and is_STRING_species, for the model to be premised on the data structure. Also, behavioural guidelines are released as background instruction to the model to prevent hallucinations, identify duplicates, accurately count values, and format responses with structured outputs like the tables or bullet points. The function of the system prompt is to ensure consistent operation of the model, and to maintain scientific rigour, even if user queries are different.

System prompt structure without hallucination mitigation

[Start with the Objective]
You are an intelligent assistant trained for structured data summarization in biological datasets, particularly those involving taxonomy hierarchies and species metadata from sources like STRINGdb.
[Data Schema]
You are working with a dataset containing the following columns:

- `taxon_id`: A unique integer identifier for each species or taxon.
- `parent_taxon_id`: An integer representing the taxonomic parent of a species.
- `taxon_name`: A string value representing the scientific name of the organism.
- `is_STRING_species`: A flag (usually `'f'` or `'t'`) indicating whether this species is available in the STRING protein interaction database.

[Behavior Guidelines]
You must:

- Parse the dataset accurately without making assumptions.
- Summarize and count values from each column.
- Group species by genus (the first word in `taxon_name`) when requested.
- Detect and report duplicates or missing values.
- Calculate frequency distributions for flags (especially `is_STRING_species`).
- Present answers clearly using lists, bullet points, or tables.
- Avoid hallucination and never use external data.

[Output Style]
Always produce human-readable, structured responses. Use:

- Tables for grouped values.
- Bullet points for findings.
- Clear summaries with counts and observations.

The user prompt structures were designed with users in mind, so they can make focused and effective requests. Users have the instruction to begin by framing their analytical objectives, such as species counts summarization, or missing values check. Furthermore, they could define the scope, if they want, by filtering specific flags or focusing on chosen columns. The user prompts therefore should be specific about the types of operation needed to access the frequency counts, grouping, or anomaly identification. It could have a preferred format for outputs. The deployment of this structured approach is to enhance the ability to reproduce, reduce ambiguity, and align users with system expectations [16].

User prompt structure without hallucination mitigation

[Start with the Objective]
State what you want to achieve, such as summarizing counts, finding duplicates, or analyzing species flags.
[Optional: Data Scope or Focus]
Mention specific columns or row conditions to limit the analysis (e.g., only `taxon_name`, only `is_STRING_species == f`, etc.).
[Type of Operation or Report Needed]
Specify whether you want a frequency count, grouping, flag distribution, missing value check, or duplicate analysis.
[Optional: Output Format Request]
If needed, define how you want the result (e.g., table format, list, summary paragraph).

The user and system prompt structure helps local LLMs align with domain-specific tasks through careful prompt engineering [21]. It serves as the bedrock for a scalable and interpretable framework for biological data summarization. This ultimately leads to efficient support of taxonomy-aware analysis and a reduction in the risk of erroneous model behavior.

4.2 Prompts with Hallucination Mitigation

For a reliable generated outputs from LlaMa 3.1 and Phi. 4 models, this study develops an important structure that explicitly incorporates into the framework rules for reducing hallucination. The original system and user prompt ensure clear structure and behaviour. As such, the creation of constraints against hallucination empowers the updated model version, to generate outputs verifiable only in the dataset. This change is essential, especially in biological taxonomy analysis, where speculation weakens scientific validity. The revised system prompt can formalize a more severe operational frontier. There are some permitted tasks like genus grouping, duplicated detection, frequency counts generation listed by the system. However, it also introduces some set of rules against assumptions on biological meaning, species relationships, or flag interpretation. It includes an instruction fallback, if data does not have sufficient evidence to respond to query, the model must then return with "this cannot be determined from the provided data". This acts as the first line of defense against hallucinations.

Hallucination Mitigation Rules for System Prompt

To ensure data integrity:

- Never invent species names, relationships, or ID mappings.
- Never explain or interpret biological meaning unless explicitly shown in the data.
- Do not assume what `'f'` or `'t'` means—only report their presence or count unless instructed otherwise.
- Do not infer taxonomic structure or biological function from names or IDs.
- Always base conclusions only on the values visibly present in the dataset.
- If a question cannot be answered strictly from the data, respond with: **"This cannot be determined from the provided data."**
- Do not fabricate examples, explanations, or any information not observable in the input.

The updated user prompts template requires users to frame their request within clearly defined operational tasks and reaffirms the hallucination mitigation clause. This ensures that both user intent and model behavior remain aligned to verifiable, observable data patterns. Output format instructions also now discourage narrative elaboration, favoring tabular or bullet-point summaries that enhance transparency and re- producibility.

Hallucination Mitigation Rules for User Prompt

Please base your analysis only on what is directly observable in the dataset.
Do not assume the meaning of **is_STRING_species** flags unless stated in the prompt.
If the request cannot be fulfilled strictly from the data, respond with:
"This cannot be determined from the provided data."

Together, these additions extend the prompt engineering framework beyond performance optimization, embedding data integrity safeguards that are especially vital in scientific AI applications.

5 Implementation and Validation

With non-hallucination-aware and hallucination-aware user prompts, there was an implementation based on three important tasks. Each task was chosen as a representative of array of computational complexities, such as simple flag counting, genus-based grouping, and detection of duplication. The following are the user prompts deployed, together with their respective roles in executing the tasks.

5.1 Task 1 Simple Flag Counting

The aim of the task is grouping species entries using their genus. This was an extract from the first words of every taxon-name. The goal was to count the total number of species in every genus and determining those marked as 'f' under the column for is-STRING-species. Knowledge of how these flags were distributed offers a quick overview of the number of added or subtracted species from STRING. While this is basic, it is also a very essential task to validate and explore the data. This analysis helps to detect high-coverage genera in STRING and taxonomic distribution patterns evaluation in the dataset. LlaMa 3.1 and Phi 4 models were used to implement the task, with a structured user prompt which clearly instructed the model into accounting only for the values in is_STRING_species. These were then presented in a two-row table format. Although hallucination mitigation was added, but under strict instruction to not interpret the meaning of 'f' or 't'.

Sample User Request

[Start with the Objective]
I want to group all species by genus and identify how many STRING species each genus contains.

[Data Scope or Focus]
Please use the `taxon_name` and `is_STRING_species` columns.
Extract genus from the first word of `taxon_name`.

[Operation Type]
Group by genus and count:

- Total entries per genus
- Entries with `is_STRING_species = 'f'`

Sort by the number of STRING species in descending order.

[Hallucination Mitigation Note]
Do not assume anything about genus classification beyond what's shown in the text.
Only report based on visible data. If missing values occur, note them.

[Output Format Request]
Use a markdown table with the following columns:
`Genus | Total Entries | STRING Species Count`

The LLM output was compared to a ground-truth result generated using Python's pandas.value_counts() function. This method gives an exact count of each unique value in the column. The outputs were compared for Numerical Accuracy (computed against the Python output), Hallucination presence (fabricated meanings or values) and Output formatting (was it a clean two-row table?). The results received from LLaMA and Phi can be seen in Tables 1 and 2.

Table 1. Performance Comparison for LLaMA: Accuracy, Hallucination, and Format Compliance for Task 1 (Pre - Before implementing hallucination mitigation, Post - After implementing hallucination mitigation)

Dataset (Size)	Accuracy (%) (Pre → Post)	Hallucination Rate (%) (Pre → Post)	Format Compliance (Pre → Post)
Dataset A (7,373)	71 → **99**	29 → **2**	No → Yes
Dataset B (14,747)	74 → **99**	26 → **3**	No → Yes
Dataset C (221,217)	69 → **98**	31 → **5**	No → Yes

For Task 1, both LLaMA and Phi showed improvements after applying hallucination mitigation rules, but LLaMA outperformed Phi.

LLaMA showed a strong improvement in accuracy, reaching 99% for Datasets A and B, and 98% for Dataset C. The hallucination rate dropped significantly, from 29% to 2% in Dataset A, and similar reductions were observed in the other datasets. Format compliance improved to "Yes" across all datasets.

Phi also improved, with accuracy increasing to 92% in Dataset A, 91% in Dataset B, and 90% in Dataset C. However, the hallucination rate remained higher than LLaMA's, reducing from 35% to 8% in Dataset A, and similar reductions followed in the other datasets. Format compliance also improved to "Yes."

In conclusion, LLaMA outperformed Phi in accuracy, hallucination rate reduction, and format compliance across all datasets.

5.2 Task 2 Genus-Based Grouping

This task is needed to group every species by their genus name, and to calculate the number of species under every genus. It also needed the number of times they were flagged as STRING species (f'). The genus was an extract of the first word in taxon-name. This helps researchers to have knowledge of the genera which were mostly represented in the STRING database. It can also uncover taxonomic distribution trends.

The prompt given to LLM was to extract genus from every taxon_name dividing it at the first space, and then appropriately group the species, then count the total of 'f'-flagged species per group. The output came out in table format with corresponding columns: Genus, Total, and STRING Species Count. The prompt explicitly stated that there was no inference of taxonomic relationships to prevent hallucination. The task was then re-run on small, medium, and large datasets for consistency.

Sample User Request - Group by Genus and Count STRING Species

[Start with the Objective]
I want to group all species by genus and identify how many STRING species each genus contains.
[Data Scope or Focus]
Please use the `taxon_name` and `is_STRING_species` columns.
Extract genus from the first word of `taxon_name`.
[Operation Type]
Group by genus and count:

- Total entries per genus
- Entries where `is_STRING_species = 'f'`

Sort by the number of STRING species in descending order.
[Hallucination Mitigation Note]
Do not assume anything about genus classification beyond what's shown in the text.
Only report based on visible data. If missing values occur, note them.
[Output Format Request]
Use a markdown table with the columns:
`Genus | Total Entries | STRING Species Count`

Genus names `(df['taxon_name'] .str.split().str[0]))` was extracted with Python's panda's library and was also used to compute group-wise counts with `.groupby()`. The output from LLM was evaluated in three distinctive ways: (i) all genera were verified to know if they match those generated from Python. (ii) the total and 'f'-flagged counts were checked to know if they were correct. (iii) Precision and recall were calculated to group the genus. According to this scenario, precision was calculated as a measure of correctly grouped genera, out of every genus predicted by the LLM. Recall on the other hand measured the actual number of genera available in the dataset, which were identified correctly by the LLM. The results are presented in Tables 3 and 4.

Table 2. Performance Comparison for Phi: Accuracy, Hallucination, and Format Compliance for Task 1 (Pre - Before implementing hallucination mitigation, Post - After implementing hallucination mitigation)

Dataset (Size)	Accuracy (%) (Pre → Post)	Hallucination Rate (%) (Pre → Post)	Format Compliance (Pre → Post)
Dataset A (7,373)	75 → **92**	35 → **8**	No → Yes
Dataset B (14,747)	78 → **91**	30 → **7**	No → Yes
Dataset C (221,217)	72 → **90**	33 → **9**	No → Yes

Table 3. Performance Metrics Before and After applying Hallucination Mitigation Rule to the LLaMA Prompts for Task 2 (Pre - Before implementing hallucination mitigation, Post - After implementing hallucination mitigation)

Dataset (Size)	Accuracy (%) (Pre → Post)	Hallucination Rate (%) (Pre → Post)	Precision (Pre → Post)	Recall (Pre → Post)	Format Compliance (Pre → Post)
Dataset A (7,373)	63 → **96**	40 → **6**	0.88 → **0.97**	0.69 → **0.95**	Yes → Yes
Dataset B (14,747)	65 → **95**	36 → **7**	0.85 → **0.96**	0.72 → **0.94**	Yes → Yes
Dataset C (221,217)	60 → **94**	41 → **9**	0.83 → **0.96**	0.68 → **0.94**	Yes → Yes

Table 4. Performance Metrics Before and After applying Hallucination Mitigation Rules for Phi Prompts for Task 2 (Pre - Before implementing hallucination mitigation, Post - After implementing hallucination mitigation)

Dataset (Size)	Accuracy (%) (Pre → Post)	Hallucination Rate (%) (Pre → Post)	Precision (Pre → Post)	Recall (Pre → Post)	Format Compliance (Pre → Post)
Dataset A (7,373)	92 → **96**	10 → **6**	0.91 → **0.97**	0.89 → **0.95**	Yes → Yes
Dataset B (14,747)	91 → **95**	11 → **7**	0.90 → **0.96**	0.88 → **0.94**	Yes → Yes
Dataset C (221,217)	90 → **94**	12 → **9**	0.89 → **0.96**	0.87 → **0.94**	Yes → Yes

LLaMA showed substantial improvements after applying hallucination mitigation rules. Accuracy increased from 63% to 96% in Dataset A, 65% to 95% in Dataset B, and 60% to 94% in Dataset C. Hallucination rates decreased significantly across all datasets, dropping from 40% to 6% in Dataset A, and similar reductions were seen in the other datasets. Precision and Recall also improved, with precision reaching 0.97 and recall reaching 0.95 in Dataset A.

Phi demonstrated improvements but performed less effectively than LLaMA. Accuracy increased from 92% to 96% in Dataset A, 91% to 95% in Dataset B, and 90% to 94% in Dataset C. Hallucination rates reduced from 10% to 6% in Dataset A, but still remained higher than LLaMA's. Precision and recall also saw improvements, with precision reaching 0.97 and recall reaching 0.95 in Dataset A.

In summary, LLaMA outperformed Phi in accuracy, hallucination reduction, precision, and recall across all datasets.

5.3 Task 3 Duplication Detection

The task prompted LLM to identify if there are duplicates in taxon_id values in the dataset. For every duplicate, the LLM highlighted the repeated taxon_id and the corresponding taxon_name. duplicate ID detection is an important data cleaning part. Duplication of primary key like taxon_id might have indicated errors in data entry or merging issues. The user prompt instructed LLM to explicitly focus only on taxon_id column, to report whatever values appeared twice and above. The format was a bullet-point list, and at the same time hallucination mitigation was included to warn LLM not to guess or infer duplications.

Sample User Request Duplicate Detection

[Start with the Objective]
I want to detect if there are any duplicate `taxon_id` values.
[Data Scope or Focus]
Only focus on the `taxon_id` column.
[Operation Type]
Check for duplicate `taxon_id` values and list their corresponding `taxon_name`.
[Hallucination Mitigation Note]
Do not infer relationships or assume duplication reasons.
Only report observed duplicates.
[Output Format Request]
List all duplicate `taxon_id` values in bullet points with their `taxon_name`.

Python's pandas.duplicated() and filtering were used to extract all duplicate taxon_id values and associated species. The LLM results were evaluated using a reference list of known duplicates. The LLM results were evaluated using a reference list of known duplicates. The evaluation focused on three key questions: whether all actual duplicates were correctly identified, whether any false duplicates were reported, and whether the output followed the expected bullet-point format. Any false positives or fabricated IDs produced by the LLM were considered hallucinations. The results received from LLaMA and Phi can be seen in Tables 5 and 6.

Table 5. Performance Metrics Before and After applying Hallucination Mitigation Rules to LLaMA Prompts for Task 3 (Pre - Before implementing hallucination mitigation, Post - After implementing hallucination mitigation)

Dataset (Size)	Accuracy (%) (Pre → Post)	Hallucination Rate (%) (Pre → Post)	Format Compliance (Pre → Post)
Dataset A (7,373)	80 → **100**	20 → **3**	Yes → Yes
Dataset B (14,747)	82 → **100**	18 → **2**	Yes → Yes
Dataset C (221,217)	79 → **99**	21 → **4**	Yes → Yes

Table 6. Performance Metrics Before and After applying Hallucination Mitigation Rules to Phi Prompts for Task 3 (Pre - Before implementing hallucination mitigation, Post - After implementing hallucination mitigation)

Dataset (Size)	Accuracy (%) (Pre → Post)	Hallucination Rate (%) (Pre → Post)	Format Compliance (Pre → Post)
Dataset A (7,373)	70 → **85**	25 → **7**	Yes → Yes
Dataset B (14,747)	72 → **88**	22 → **6**	Yes → Yes
Dataset C (221,217)	68 → **83**	28 → **8**	Yes → Yes

LlaMa showed that all the datasets improved significantly. With datasets A and B reaching 100% accuracy. Dataset C was 99% accurate. The rates of hallucination reduced maximally, to 3% from 20% in Dataset A, in Dataset B and C, similar reductions were noted. Format compliance was consistent all through at 'Yes' in all the datasets, before and after the prompt was enhanced.

Phi showed improvements but lagged behind LLaMA. Accuracy increased to 85% in Dataset A, 88% in Dataset B, and 83% in Dataset C. However, hallucination rates remained higher, reducing from 25% to 7% in Dataset A, and similar patterns followed in other datasets. Format compliance remained consistent at "Yes" across all datasets, both before and after prompt enhancement.

In conclusion, LLaMA outperformed Phi in accuracy, hallucination reduction, and format compliance across all datasets.

6 Discussion

The results show how effective local LLMs are when used to analyse structured biological datasets, together with prompt engineering techniques. LlaMa 3.1 performed better than Phi 4 in all the tasks assigned. LlaMa was also more accurate and had a reduced rate of hallucinations in all the datasets. Particularly, in task 1, LlaMa had 99% accuracy in datasets A and B, 98% in dataset C. Contrastingly, Phi was more accurate at 92% in every dataset with higher rates of hallucinations. This performance gap became obvious in task 2, the task that focused on the grouping of genus, and in task 3, detection of duplication, where precision and recall were higher in LlaMa, even though there was a considerable hallucination reduction in larger datasets.

The prompt design importance is reflected in these results. For example, the structured prompts considerable reduced hallucination. LlaMa recorded a massive reduction in the rates of hallucination to 2% from 29% in dataset A for task 1, which lower than that of Phi's 25% to 7%. This implies a carefully designed prompt capable of guiding LLMs to generate reliable and accurate results. The performance exhibited by LlaMa was consistent in all the datasets, while that of Phi reduced due to increased dataset size. This is an indication that LlaMa is suitable for larger and complex datasets.

Phi is efficient, as such could process faster, only if the dataset is smaller. The accuracy and reliability of LlaMa, therefore, makes it a superior and a better choice than Phi in terms of taxonomy-aware tasks, which need high level precision. The difference in their performance is vital when using biological data, since high-level accuracy and reliability must be attained.

LlaMa is the better one between the two, after considering their overall performance in all areas including accuracy, hallucination reduction, and consistency and in dealing with large-scale biological datasets. These findings underscore the effectiveness of local LLMs if backed by right prompt engineering. It is therefore the right tool to deploy for analysis if taxonomy-aware structured biological data.

7 Conclusion

This study has shown that local LLMs can effectively analyse structured biological data, if paired with prompt engineering models like Llama 3.1 and Phi 4. They performed tasks like species flags counting, genus grouping, and detection of duplicates. The results were very accurate when prompts were instructed to reduce hallucinations. Prompt design was significant in this. However, there were some mistakes, although, just a few mistakes are expected if prompts are clear and specific. Therefore, using the system and user prompts was useful for the model to focus on the data. Running the model with local LLMs provided privacy and control to the users, which is an essential feature in research dealing with confidential information. LlaMa 3.1 was better than Phi 4 based on their overall performance. It accurately handled large datasets, with fewer errors. Phi on the other was faster with small datasets, with more mistakes, when complex and larger datasets were introduced. Some of the limitations of this study were, only three tasks were tested, and they were not complex enough, therefore, how the model worked with more complex problems was not shown. The datasets used only one source, which was STRINGdb, and as such, the result could change if other databases are used. Future study may need to test more complex tasks such as detection of the relationship of the species or linking data to different sources. This study added more open-source models like Gemma, Mistral or Qwen, however, it would be more accurate and precise if feedback from data scientists is added to build automatic prompt tool.

References

1. Liu, J., et al.: Advancing bioinformatics with llamas: components, applications and perspectives (2025). arXiv:2401.04155 arXiv preprint
2. Ding, H., Pang, L., Wei, Z., Shen, H., Cheng, X.: Retrieve only when it needs: adaptive retrieval augmentation for hallucination mitigation in llamas (2024). arXiv:2402.10612 arXiv preprint
3. Mishra, T., et al.: Use of llamas as artificial intelligence tools in academic research and publishing among global clinical researchers. Sci. Rep. **14**(1), 31672 (2024)
4. Boyko, J., et al.: An interdisciplinary outlook on llamas for scientific research. arXiv preprint arXiv:2311.04929 (2023)
5. Zhang, Q., et al.: Scientific llamas: A survey on biological & chemical domains. ACM Comput. Surv. **57**(6), Article 161, 38 (2025)
6. Azad, M., Tohidfar, M., Ghanbari Moheb Seraj, R.: Identification of responsive genes to multiple abiotic stresses in rice (Oryza sativa): a meta-analysis of transcriptomics data. Sci. Rep. **14**, 5463 (2024)
7. Adeseye, A., Isoaho, J., Mohammad, T.: LLM-assisted qualitative data analysis: security and privacy concerns in gamified workforce studies. Proc. Comput. Sci. **257**, 60–67 (2025)
8. Abdelghafour, M.A.M., Mabrouk, M., Taha, Z.: Hallucination mitigation techniques in llamas. Int. J. Intell. Comput. Info. Sci. **24**(4), 73–81 (2024)
9. Jamil, H., Krawetz, S., Gow, A.: Knowledge synthesis using llamas for a computational biology workflow ecosystem. In: Proceedings of the 39th ACM/SIGAPP Symposium on Applied Computing, pp. 523–530 (2024)

10. Liu, P., Yuan, W., Fu, J., Jiang, Z., Hayashi, H., Neubig, G.: Pre-train, prompt, and predict: a systematic survey of prompting methods in natural language processing. ACM Comput. Surv. **55**(9), 1–35 (2023)
11. Park, D., An, G.T., Kamyod, C., Kim, C.G.: A study on performance improvement of prompt engineering for generative AI with a llama. J. Web Eng. **22**(8), 1187–1206 (2023)
12. Dang, H., Mecke, L., Lehmann, F., Goller, S., Buschek, D.: How to prompt? Opportunities and challenges of zero- and few-shot learning for human-AI interaction in creative applications of generative models (2022). arXiv:2209.01390 arXiv preprint
13. Yin, Z.: A review of methods for alleviating hallucination issues in llamas. Appl. Comput. Eng. **76**, 258–266 (2024)
14. Paudel, B., Lyzhov, A., Joshi, P., Anand, P.: HalluciNot: hallucination detection through context and common knowledge verification (2025). arXiv:2504.07069 arXiv preprint
15. Schmidt, D.C., Spencer-Smith, J., Fu, Q., White, J.: Towards a catalog of prompt patterns to enhance the discipline of prompt engineering. ACM SIGAda Ada Letters **43**(2), 43–51 (2024)
16. Block, J., Chen, Y.P., Budharapu, A., Anthony, L., Dorr, B.: Summary Cycles: exploring the impact of prompt engineering on llamas' interaction with interaction log information. In: Proceedings of the 4th Workshop on Evaluation and Comparison of NLP Systems, pp. 85–99 (2023)
17. Sui, Y., Zhou, M., Zhou, M., Han, S., Zhang, D.: Table meets LLM: can llamas understand structured table data? A benchmark and empirical study. In: Proceedings of the 17th ACM International Conference on Web Search and Data Mining, pp. 645–654 (2024)
18. Oppenlaender, J.: The creativity of text-to-image generation. In: Proceedings of the 25th International Academic Mindtrek Conference, pp. 192–202. ACM, New York (2022)
19. Jahani, E., et al.: Prompt adaptation as a dynamic complement in generative AI systems. arXiv preprint arXiv:2407.14333 (2025)
20. Adeseye, A., Isoaho, J., Mohammad, T.: LLM-Assisted Qualitative Data Analysis: security and privacy concerns in gamified workforce studies. In: The 16th International Conference on Ambient Systems, Networks and Technologies (ANT) / the 8th International Conference on Emerging Data and Industry 4.0 (EDI40), vol. 257, pp. 60–67, Patras, Greece (2025) Procedia Computer Science
21. Adeseye, A., Isoaho, J., Tahir, M.: Systematic prompt framework for qualitative data analysis: designing system and user prompts. In: 2025 IEEE 5th International Conference on Human-Machine Systems (ICHMS). IEEE, pp. 229–234 (2025)

Detecting the Most Relevant Slices in MRI Parkinson Disease for Multi-Classification Using Evolutionary Algorithm

Olga Valenzuela[1], Francisco Carrillo-Perez[2,3], Luis Javier Herrera[2(✉)], Héctor Pomares[2], Fernando Rojas[2], and Ignacio Rojas[2]

[1] Faculty of Science, University of Granada, 18071 Granada, Spain
[2] Department of Computer Engineering, Automatics and Robotics, University of Granada; C.I.T.I.C., Periodista Rafael Gómez Montero, 2, 18014 Granada, Spain
{jherrera,irojas}@ugr.es
[3] Stanford Center for Biomedical Informatics Research (BMIR), Department of Medicine, Stanford University, 1265 Welch Rd, Stanford, CA 94305, USA

Abstract. From a therapeutic point of view and for a correct prognosis, the precise diagnosis and correct classification of the Parkinson's disease is very relevant for the specialist in neurology. Being able to efficiently classify this disease and other forms of parkinsonism, using intelligent systems through MRI, is of great help for clinical diagnostic decisions. This article presents a methodology that, using MRI of patients, determines which are the best slices for the construction of accurate classifiers. A search system for the best slices has been used through evolutionary algorithms, therefore selecting a classifier such as SVM that can be trained with a low computational cost. The classification result, using five classes (Normal, SWEDD, Prodromal, PD and Gen Cohort) has an accuracy of 90% with five slices in the testing phase.

Keywords: Parkinson's disease · MRI · Multiclass classification · Evolutionary algorithm

1 Introduction

Parkinson's disease (PD) is a relevant and frecuently diagnosed neurodegenerative disease, mainly produced by continuing neuronal loss and a dysfunction in substantia nigra region [5,7] along with intracellular inclusions containing α-synuclein aggregates. Typical symptoms of this disease can be considered by tremors, stiffness and slowness of movement. Alzheimer and PD are the most common neurological diseases, mainly developed in countries of long life, affecting approximately 2.5% of the population over 65 years of age. Symptoms of this pathology that are not associated with deficits in the patient's musculoskeletal system, such as dementia and dysautonomia, are common, particularly in advanced phases of the disease [13,21].

A. Alsadoon et al. (Eds.): CSCE 2025, CCIS 2935, pp. 117–130, 2026.
https://doi.org/10.1007/978-3-032-22199-5_8

The realization of precise systems for the diagnosis and characterization of Parkinson's disease is of great interest to the scientific community [2,23,24]. As presented in [21], clinicopathological analyzes using patients from database from the Canada and UK, have presented that neurological experts performed an incorrect diagnosis in approximately 25% of patients, being the most frequent reasons leading to misdiagnosis are the presence of tremor symptoms in the patient, atypical parkinsonian syndromes and vascular parkinsonism. Patients suffering from PD have various and very different symptoms analyzed by the different people studied [6]. Stratification and classification of different subtypes or groups of Parkinson's disease is of great importance in clinical diagnostic decisions and in determining the therapeutic measures to be undertaken by the patient, although there is currently no precise and effective method for defining and stratifying subtypes in Parkinson's disease [6,22].

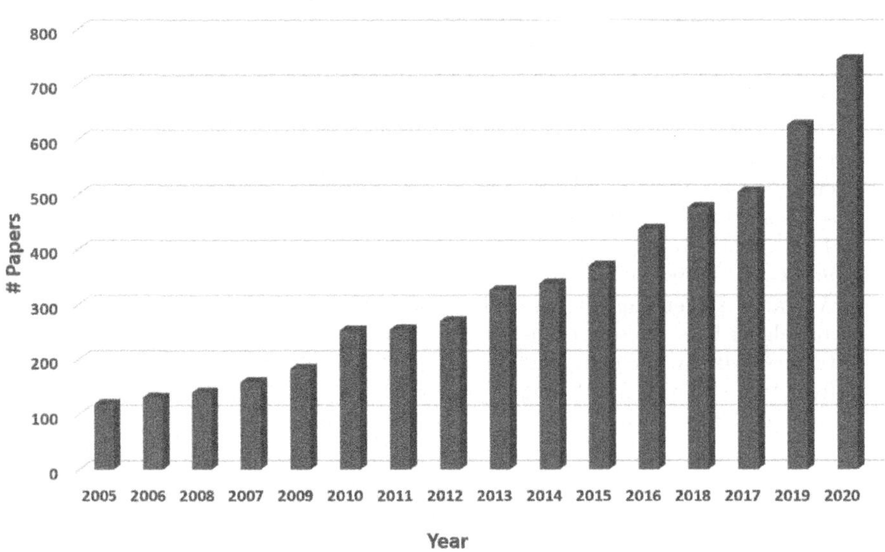

Fig. 1. Evolution of the number of paper indexed in the ISI Web of Knowledge using MRI for classification Parkinson's disease.

In recent years there has been a growing interest in the scientific community devoted to medical imaging, and specifically in neuroimaging community, in the use of MRI images for neurodegenerative brain diseases, and particularly in the Parkinson's disease problem (see Fig. 1). Numerous methods analyzing and inspecting MRI presented in the literature use machine learning techniques to construct supervised classifiers.

In recent years, a large number of papers have been published dealing with the study, development, and construction of methods and procedures that can analyze magnetic resonance images to automatically classify PD [1,14,20].

Currently, one method that has been used with great success in the scientific community is the use of Deep Learning (DL) tools (based on Convolutional Neural Networks- CNN) to construct classifiers using MRI in different problem, also in Parkinson's disease [3,10,20]. DL is based on algorithms capable of automatically extracting multiple information from image sets without the need for an a priory hypothesis as to where this information can be encoded in the images.

Most of the articles presented in the bibliography focus on the realization of binary classifiers in order to determine control patients and PD patients. To the best of our knowledge, none of the existing models answers the question which are the most relevant slices for multi-class classification in PD. Hence, the problem addressed in this paper was to develop a framework for decision support model which select the most relevant slices for the construction of a multi-class classifier.

2 Materials and Methodology

2.1 Subjects Cohort

The data used in this paper were obtained from the Parkinson's Progression Markers Initiative (PPMI) database [12]. In this contribution, different groups of patients existing in the PPMI data base has been used (Normal, SWEDD, Prodromal, PD and Gen Cohort). These groups are briefly described below.

Analyzing patients with Single Photon Emission Computed Tomography technology has allowed for the identification of a group of patients who were initially diagnosed as having Parkinson's disease but, who should, more precisely be associated to "Scans Without Evidence of Dopaminergic Deficit (SWEDD)" [4,19]. The term SWEDD is controversial in the literature, referring to the absence, rather than the presence, of an imaging abnormality in patients clinically presumed to have PD [8,9].

The conditions for the PD group were: Patients aged 30 years or more, a scale of I or II on the Hoehn and Yahr scales at baseline; validation by presynaptic dopaminergic scans; regardless of sex; and no expectation of PD medication within six months of study entry. We must emphasize that a patient may have multiple NIfTI files, and all will be used in our study. The conditions for the SWEDD group were the same as for the PD group, except that subjects were not allowed to show signs of dopaminergic deficit in presynaptic dopaminergic scans.

It is important to emphasize that clinical, neuropathological, and imaging studies suggest that PD -specific pathology begins before the onset of classic motor symptoms (such as bradykinesia). [11,17].

Finally we have a class of few subjects for whom the classification is based on genetic diagnosis. This class is called Genetic Cohort Subjects (GenCohort) and is made up of subjects with and without Parkinson's disease who have a genetic mutation in gene LRRK2, GBA, or SNCA [15,16,18].

The study conducted in this paper used more than 1000 different brain images in NIfTI format, acquired with two different technologies and medical devices

Table 1. Characteristics of the cohort of normal and SWEDD images used in this contribution

Measures	Normal (258)				SWEDD (154)			
Sex (male/female)	181		77		100		54	
Age	61.4	11.7	59.0	8.2	64.1	9.7	57.8	10.7
Weight	83.0	10.7	67.9	17.1	88.6	12.8	75.8	12.8
	Mean	Std	Mean	Std	Mean	Std	Mean	Std

Table 2. Characteristics of the cohort of Prodromal and PD images used in this contribution

Measures	Prodromal (38)				PD (450)			
Sex (male/female)	30		8		288		162	
Age	67.1	3.9	67.8	3.1	62.4	9.8	60.2	8.7
Weight	88.8	14.5	68.5	9.7	90.8	16.1	66.3	11.9
	Mean	Std	Mean	Std	Mean	Std	Mean	Std

(1.5T and 3T) and using the protocol recommended and established by PPMI [12]. Indicates that some poor quality images were deleted. Therefore, a set of 917 magnetic resonance images from different types of patients was finally used. The normal (control) group contained 258 images, the SWEED group contained 154 images, Prodromal contained 38 images, PD contained 450 images, and finally GenCohort contained 17 files. The characteristics of the patients in each group (age, weight, etc.) used in this study are shown in Tables 1, 2 and 3. The large volume and weight of these images means that they all require more than 85 GB of disk space after segmentation to store all the image information.

2.2 Segmentation and Normalization

The original MRI images are processed with SPM12 to normalize them. The normalization is very important to spatially localize all the treated MRI images of the different patients in a similar way. The MNI space used consists of 1 × 1x1 mm voxels. It is also important to segment and filter the image. There are numerous studies indicating the importance of gray matter analysis for magnetic resonance imaging classification in neuro-degenerative problems, and for this reason this gray matter is used in this work with the appropriate filter.

2.3 Feature Extraction and Selection

Feature extraction is performed using the well-known wavelet transform. Due to the fact that this transformation (according to the level of detail that you want to obtain) obtains a large number of coefficients (several thousand of them

Table 3. Characteristics of the cohort of GeneCohort images used in this contribution

Measures	GeneCohort (17)			
Sex (male/female)	14		3	
Age	62.1	10.6	72.2	9.0
Weight	87.2	11.3	64.7	5.7
	Mean	Std	Mean	Std

can easily be obtained in images), it is necessary to carry out a selection process, which will determine the most relevant ones. This process is done using the mRMR feature selection algorithm, then performing a PCA to further reduce the feature space.

2.4 Methodology

The proposed methodology presented in this contribution for Parkinson's disease detection using MRI consists of five main stages for training the system in order to obtain the most relevant slices are: (1) Pre-processing the NIfTI files (normalization, segmentation), (2) Feature Extraction (using 2D discrete wavelet transform (2D-DWT)), (3) Feature Selection and Reduction (using minimum Redundancy Maximum Relevance (mRMR) and PCA algorithms), (4) Detection of the most relevant slices (using multi-objective genetic algorithm NSGA-II), (5) Optimization of the SVM classifier with the selected slices. The block scheme for multiple-objective optimization, is shown in Fig. 2.

3 Results

To carry out the analysis of the results obtained with the proposed methodology, we will start by observing the different solutions presented by the Pareto Front (Fig. 3).

If we select the solution with the highest number of slices (a total of 49), it is the solution with the best precision, but on the contrary, the number of slices selected for both white and gray matter is high.

The different slices selected for each kind of matter (white and grey), for the several solution obtained in the Pareto Front are shown in Table 4. The importance of the selection of slices in the gray matter can be appreciated, being, even in the latest solutions, the only slices selected.

This information can be endorsed graphically, it represents the frequency of obtaining the different slices in the two types of matter treated (the first 161 source index are white matter slices and from 162 to 322 correspond to gray matter). This representation is in Fig. 4, which represent the histograms of slices for the sets of solutions in the Genetic Algorithm.

To determine the influence that the selection of these slices has on the construction of the classifier, the so-called Pareto front genome is performed.

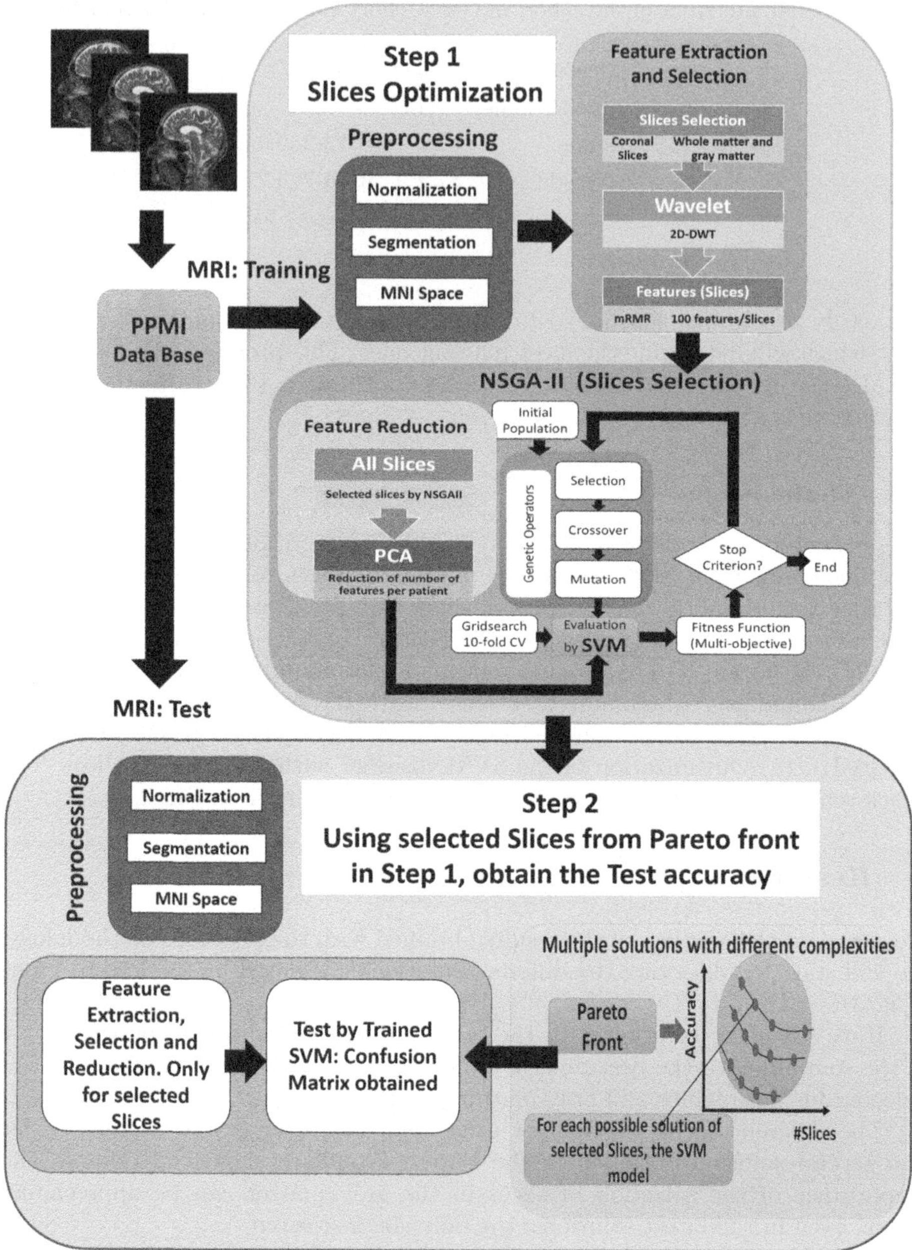

Fig. 2. Block diagram of the proposed methodology. Phase 1: obtaining the optimal MRI slices for the construction of a classifier. Phase 2: Test the SVM classifier with training patients (that is, PPMI patients that have not been used in the training phase).

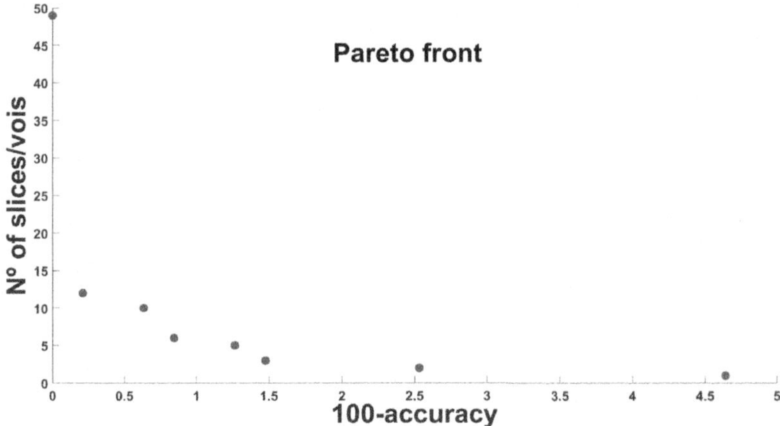

Fig. 3. ParetoFront. Trade-off between system accuracy and classifier complexity (measured as number of slices used).

Table 4. Detail of the different slices selected in both matters (white and gray) for the different solutions of the Pareto Front

Solution	White Matter	Grey Matter
1	24, 28, 36, 40, 47, 86, 98, 102, 108, 111, 115, 129, 136, 149, 152, 178	27, 36, 38, 41, 42, 44, 46, 49, 56, 57, 59, 60, 62, 74, 78, 83, 95, 98, 101, 109, 112, 114, 125, 126, 127, 129, 135, 137, 148, 155, 168, 171, 176
2	110	28, 36, 57, 87, 92, 114, 124, 134, 138, 144, 152
3	102, 116, 129	28, 51, 67, 87, 111, 114, 150
4	65	28, 54, 67, 73, 87, 91, 111, 118, 150
5	43	28, 36, 87, 114, 157
6	-	28, 36, 87, 114, 157
7	-	54, 87, 114
8	-	36, 118

Figure 5 shows the accuracy obtained in the first phase (thus using training images), to determine which are the most relevant slices for the construction of a future classifier based on SVM.

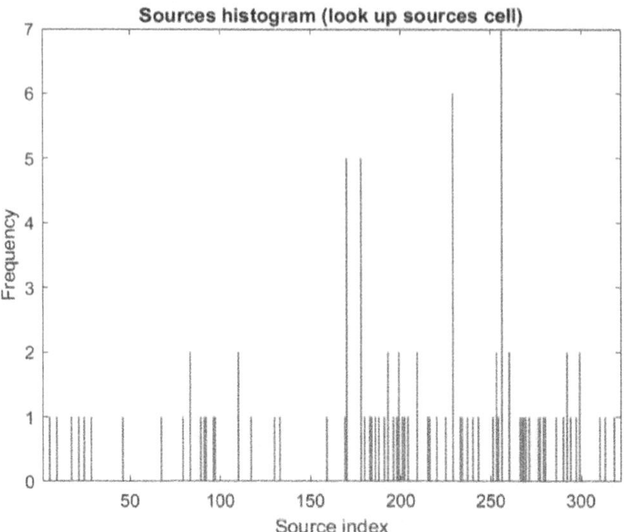

Fig. 4. Relevance of the slices selected by the evolutionary algorithm, both for white matter and gray matter. (Color figure online)

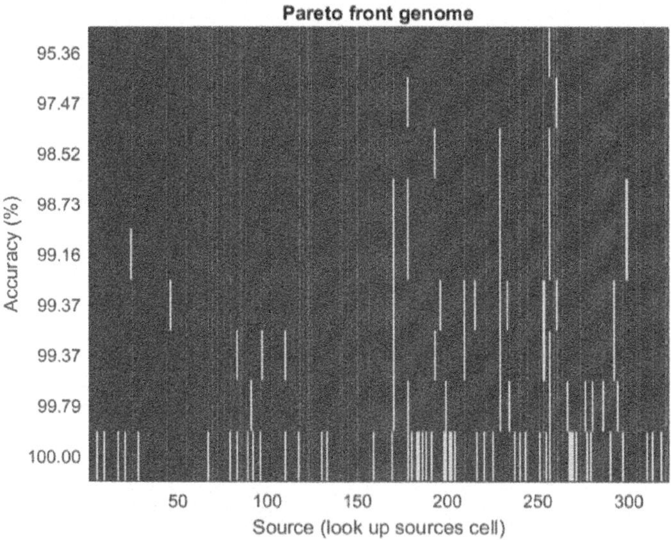

Fig. 5. Pareto Genome. Graphic representation of the importance of selecting each slice (both in white matter and in gray matter) to obtain a certain precision. (Color figure online)

As indicated in the methodology, once a slice has been selected, it is necessary to apply the wavelet transform to this image/slice. This transform produces a

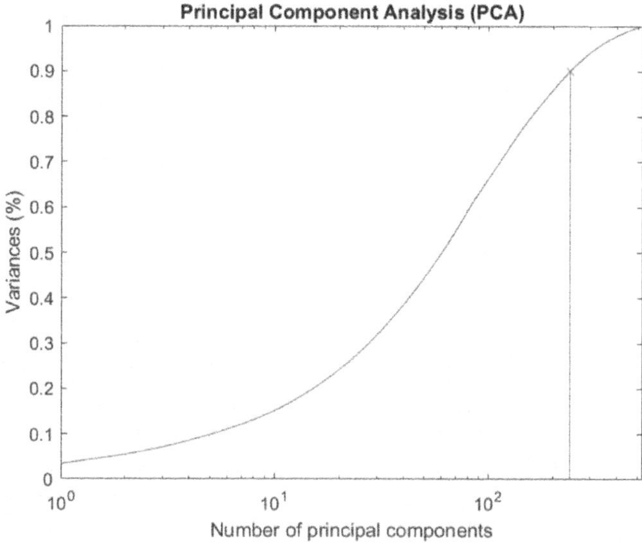

Fig. 6. Reduction of the dimensionality of the number of wavelet coefficients selected using principal component analysis (PCA).

large number of coefficients, making it necessary to select them using mRMR (the 100 most relevant are selected). In this way, if we have a number of MRI subjects of 917, the total matrix of coefficients would be 917*322*100 (number of subjects * number of slices in the two matter treated * total number of relevant wavelet coefficients selected). This matrix continues to be large, so PCA is applied to limit the number of features. This behavior can be seen in Fig. 6.

The use of multi-objective evolutionary algorithms creates a Pareto Front with multiple solutions, in which there are solutions with a large number of slices and very precise, and other solutions where the number of slices is more limited, having a somewhat higher error (both in the classification of patients in the training phase and in the test phase). Figures 7 and 8 show where the slices are located in the brain (for the two types of matter), for the first solutions (greater number of slices), third and sixth (only uses slices in the gray matter), respectively.

Bearing in mind that in clinical practice, selecting a high number of slices makes the work of a human expert difficult, this solution with 5 slices has been selected to determine the performance of the SVM classifier. As is logical, it is not the most accurate classifier, however the reduced number of slices it has facilitates the compression of the classifier, which obtains results in the test phase of 90% accuracy. This information is presented in the following confusion table, where it can also be seen that the different groups of patients used (1: Control, 2: SWEDD, 3: Prodomal, 4: PD and 5: GenCohort) are not balanced (for example, group 5, which corresponds to GeneCohort, is the one with the least number of data) (Fig. 9).

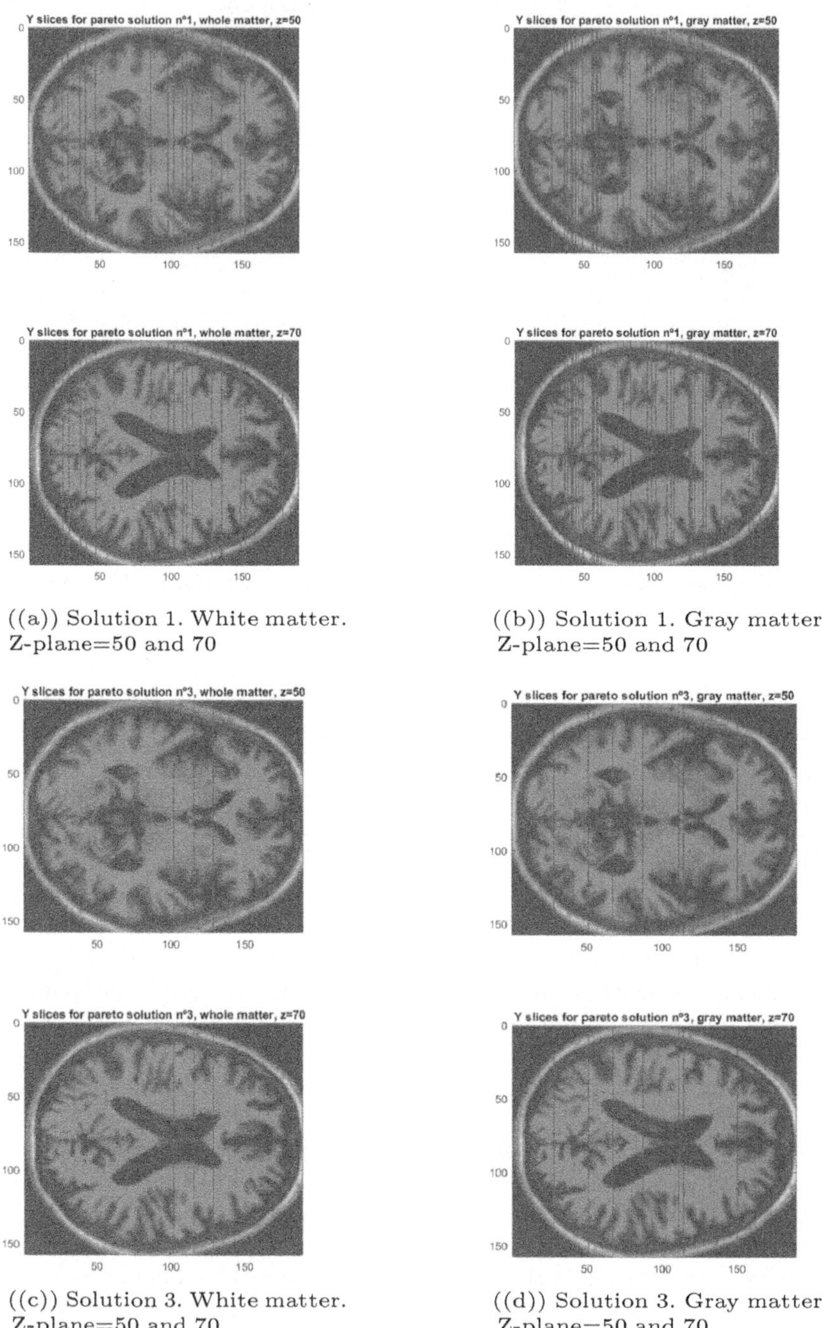

((a)) Solution 1. White matter. Z-plane=50 and 70

((b)) Solution 1. Gray matter. Z-plane=50 and 70

((c)) Solution 3. White matter. Z-plane=50 and 70

((d)) Solution 3. Gray matter. Z-plane=50 and 70

Fig. 7. (a), (b) Location of the slices in the brain of the patients for the first Pareto Front Solution. (c),(d) Location of the slices in the brain of the patients for the third Pareto Front Solution.

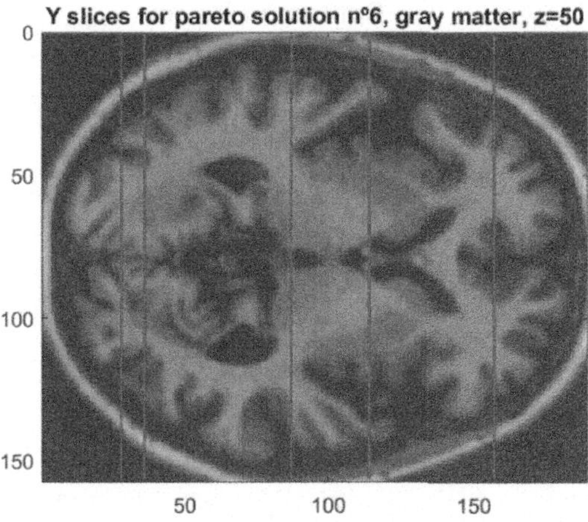

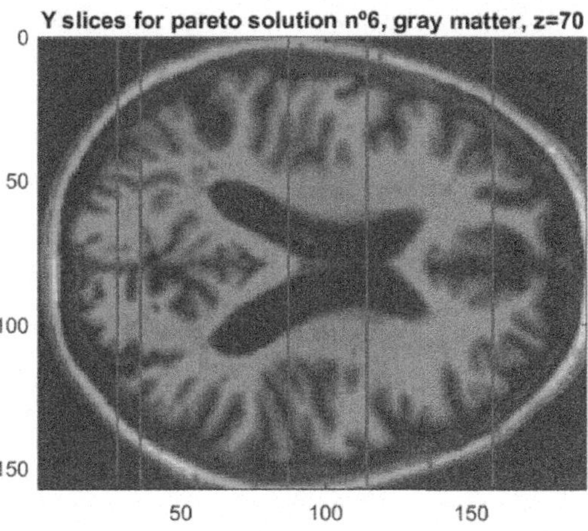

Fig. 8. Spatial arrangement of the slices selected for the sixth solutions in the Pareto Front (only in gray matter). (Color figure online)

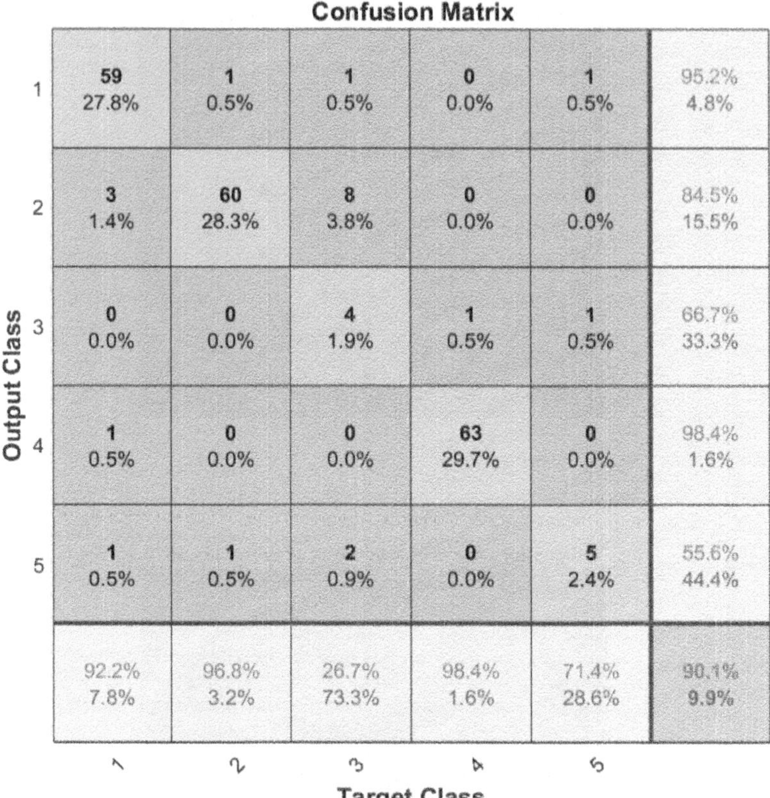

Fig. 9. System accuracy obtained with 5 slices (sixth solutions in the Pareto Front), using a test set not used during the training phase. Confusion table for the 5 classes analyzed.

4 Conclusion

The objective of this research is twofold. In the first place, it is to have more information on which are the best slices and with what mask (search in white matter or gray matter space) when determining the inputs for a classifier. The search for the best slices also provides medical experts with clues about Parkinson's disease. The second objective is to be able to carry out an accurate classifier with the solutions obtained by the Pareto Frontier. Of course, there will be a compromise between the complexity of the system and the number of slices selected. For systems with 5 slices, an accuracy of 90% in the classification of five classes (in which there is a large imbalance) has been obtained in the test phase.

Acknowledgements. This work was funded by the Spanish Ministry of Sciences, Innovation and Universities under Project RTI-2018-101674-B-I00 and the projects from Junta de Andalucia CV20-64934 and P20-00163.

References

1. Amoroso, N., La Rocca, M., Monaco, A., Bellotti, R., Tangaro, S.: Complex networks reveal early MRI markers of Parkinson's disease. Med. Image Anal. **48**, 12–24 (2018)
2. Bahaddad, A.A., Ragab, M., Ashary, E.B., Khalil, E.M.: Metaheuristics with deep learning-enabled Parkinson's disease diagnosis and classification model. J. Healthc. Eng. **2022**, 1–14 (2022). https://doi.org/10.1155/2022/9276579
3. Dünnwald, M., Ernst, P., Düzel, E., Tönnies, K., Betts, M.J., Oeltze-Jafra, S.: Fully automated deep learning-based localization and segmentation of the locus coeruleus in aging and Parkinson's disease using neuromelanin-sensitive MRI. Int. J. Comput. Assist. Radiol. Surg. **16**(12), 2129–2135 (2021). https://doi.org/10.1007/s11548-021-02528-5
4. Eidelberg, D.: Imaging in Parkinson's Disease, pp. 3–8. Oxford University Press, New York (2012)
5. Eisinger, R.S., et al.: Parkinson's disease motor subtype changes during 20 years of follow-up. Parkinsonism Relat. Dis. **76**, 104–107 (2020). https://doi.org/10.1016/j.parkreldis.2019.05.024
6. Fereshtehnejad, S.M., Postuma, R.B.: Subtypes of Parkinson's disease: what do they tell us about disease progression? Curr. Neurol. Neurosci. Rep. **17**(4) (2017)
7. Gordián-Vélez, W.J., et al.: Restoring lost nigrostriatal fibers in Parkinson's disease based on clinically-inspired design criteria. Brain Res. Bull. **175**, 168–185 (2021). https://doi.org/10.1016/j.brainresbull.2021.07.016
8. Kim, M., Park, H.: Structural connectivity profile of scans without evidence of dopaminergic deficit (SWEDD) patients compared to normal controls and Parkinson's disease patients. SpringerPlus **5**(1) (2016). https://doi.org/10.1186/s40064-016-3110-8
9. Lee, J.W., Song, Y.S., Kim, H., Ku, B.D., Lee, W.W.: Patients with scans without evidence of dopaminergic deficit (SWEDD) do not have early Parkinson's disease: analysis of the PPMI data. PLoS ONE **16**(2), e0246881 (2021). https://doi.org/10.1371/journal.pone.0246881
10. Loh, H.W., et al.: Application of deep learning models for automated identification of Parkinson's disease: a review (2011–2021). Sensors **21**(21), 7034 (2021). https://doi.org/10.3390/s21217034
11. Mahlknecht, P., Seppi, K., Poewe, W.: The concept of prodromal Parkinson's disease. J. Parkinsons Dis. **5–4**, 681–697 (2015)
12. Marek, K., et al.: The Parkinson progression marker initiative (PPMI). Prog. Neurobiol. **95**, 629–635 (2011)
13. Oka, H., Umehara, T., Nakahara, A., Matsuno, H.: Comparisons of cardiovascular dysautonomia and cognitive impairment between de novo Parkinson's disease and de novo dementia with Lewy bodies. BMC Neurol. **20**(1) (2020). https://doi.org/10.1186/s12883-020-01928-5
14. Pang, H., Yu, Z., Li, R., Yang, H., Fan, G.: MRI-based radiomics of basal nuclei in differentiating idiopathic Parkinson's disease from parkinsonian variants of multiple system atrophy: a susceptibility-weighted imaging study. Front. Aging Neurosci. **12**, 379 (2020)

15. Payne, K., Walls, B., Wojcieszek, J.: Approach to assessment of Parkinson disease with emphasis on genetic testing. Med. Clin. North Am. **103**(6), 1055–1075 (2019). https://doi.org/10.1016/j.mcna.2019.08.003
16. Planas-Ballvé, A., Vilas, D.: Cognitive impairment in genetic Parkinson's disease. Parkinson's Dis. **2021**, 1–11 (2021). https://doi.org/10.1155/2021/8610285
17. Postuma, R., et al.: Identifying prodromal Parkinson's disease: pre-motor disorders in Parkinson's disease. Movement Dis. Official J. Mov. Disord. Soc. **27**, 617–26 (2012)
18. Schneider, S.A., Alcalay, R.N.: Precision medicine in Parkinson's disease: emerging treatments for genetic Parkinson's disease. J. Neurol. **267**(3), 860–869 (2020). https://doi.org/10.1007/s00415-020-09705-7
19. Schwingenschuh, P., et al.: Distinguishing SWEDDs patients with asymmetric resting tremor from Parkinson's disease: a clinical and electrophysiological study. Mov. Disord. **25**(5), 560–569 (2010). https://doi.org/10.1002/mds.23019
20. Shinde, S., et al.: Predictive markers for Parkinson's disease using deep neural nets on neuromelanin sensitive MRI. NeuroImage: Clinical **22**, 101748 (2019). https://doi.org/10.1016/j.nicl.2019.101748
21. Tolosa, E., Wenning, G., Poewe, W.: The diagnosis of Parkinson's disease. Lancet Neurol. **5**(1), 75–86 (2006)
22. Valmarska, A., Miljkovic, D., Robnik-Šikonja, M., Lavrač, N.: Connection between the Parkinson's disease subtypes and patients' symptoms progression. In: Riaño, D., Wilk, S., ten Teije, A. (eds.) Artif. Intell. Med., pp. 263–268. Springer International Publishing, Cham (2019). https://doi.org/10.1007/978-3-030-21642-9_32
23. Zhang, X., et al.: Data-driven subtyping of Parkinson's disease using longitudinal clinical records: a cohort study. Sci. Rep. **9**(1) (2019). https://doi.org/10.1038/s41598-018-37545-z
24. Zhao, H., Wang, R., Lei, Y., Liao, W.H., Cao, H., Cao, J.: Severity level diagnosis of Parkinson's disease by ensemble k-nearest neighbor under imbalanced data. Expert Syst. Appl. **189**, 116113 (2022). https://doi.org/10.1016/j.eswa.2021.116113

A Neural Network Approach for Predicting Cancer-Linked Transcriptional Activity from Epigenetic Signature

Riyan Jain[1](✉) and Anel Turgambayeva[2]

[1] Illinois Mathematics and Science Academy, Aurora, IL 60506, USA
rjain1@imsa.edu

[2] Brock University, St. Catharines, ON L2S 3A1, Canada

Abstract. Gene transcription is central to biological function and cellular processes. The multitude of proteins created from the transcription of their coding genes controls all crucial cellular functions, both directly and indirectly. Epigenetics seeks to understand how DNA methylation, histone modifications, and genomic imprinting allow the genome to store information beyond the DNA sequence. Genes are characterized by their DNA sequence; however, whether a particular gene is transcribed into proteins or not in a specific cell type is governed by the cell's epigenetic landscape. Thus, epigenetic alterations can contribute to potential carcinogenesis and progression of cancer, as enhancement or silencing of the "wrong" genes may cause tumor proliferation and growth. Understanding the principles behind the epigenetic control of gene transcription in both standard and tumor cells is crucial for identifying cancer-causing differences.

To address this, we developed six neural network models using deep learning to predict transcriptional activity (mRNA expression) based on epigenetic signals (ChIP-seq interactions). Our results show that a model trained on the epigenetic signals of a human cell line (either standard or cancerous) can predict that cell line's transcriptional activity with a reasonably high accuracy (79%). Moreover, a model trained on multiple cell lines can be effectively generalized to predict the transcriptional activity of a new cancerous cell line with reasonable accuracy (from 68% to 76% as the number of cell lines used for training increases). Increasing the number of training cell lines significantly improves the model's predictive accuracy when generalizing to other cell lines. This demonstrates underlying patterns in the relationship between the epigenetic signals and resulting transcriptional activity, including shared patterns across normal and tumor cells. Thus, our model is a valuable tool for exploring epigenetic landscapes from a cancer context.

Keywords: Epigenetics · Gene Transcription · Deep Learning · Predictive Modeling · Cancer Research

1 Significance Statement

We created a deep learning model trained to predict the amount of transcription for genes in the human genome based on a map of the binding sites of certain epigenetic modifications. We specifically looked at seven histone modifications among the most

A. Alsadoon et al. (Eds.): CSCE 2025, CCIS 2935, pp. 131–144, 2026.
https://doi.org/10.1007/978-3-032-22199-5_9

commonly studied histone modifications in epigenetics literature. The model is trained on a set number of cell lines but can be used to predict the transcriptional activity for any human cell line with reasonable accuracy. This model is valuable in establishing patterns correlating epigenetic signals with corresponding transcriptional activity. It can potentially enable the discovery of relevant epigenetic markers to transcription of cancer-related genes, opening up the possibility of new therapeutic targets to nip cancer in the bud.

2 Introduction

2.1 Background

It is common knowledge that every cell in the human body contains the same genome – the entire human genome, barring any mutations. It is also commonly accepted that cells create proteins that control their function based on the instructions written in the genome, through a process described by the central dogma of biology. How, then, can a nerve cell have a significantly different structure and function from a muscle or blood cell? The answer to this lies in the simple principle that not all genes are expressed – the combination of expressed or repressed genes dictates the cell's unique structure and function [1]. Genetic switches are certain genes that are binding sites for gene regulatory proteins, which operate to turn genes "on" and "off" in response to various signals. Transcriptional activators are gene regulatory proteins that bind to the promoter region located upstream of the gene that needs to be transcribed [2]. These proteins associate with RNA polymerase to initiate gene expression. On the other hand, transcriptional repressors are gene regulatory proteins that block access to the promoter site, preventing the binding of RNA polymerase and thus gene expression [3]. The gene expression patterns in differentiated cells are established during development and maintained as the cells divide during mitosis. Thus, cells inherit both genetic information and information not encoded in the nucleotide sequence of DNA, termed epigenetic information [4].

2.2 Mechanisms of Epigenetics

Epigenetics studies different heritable alterations in gene expression caused by modifications binding to the DNA sequence rather than changes in the DNA sequence itself [5]. In eukaryotes, the default state of gene expression for regulated genes is "off", with histone proteins tightly binding specific genes in chromatin to prevent transcription. This is where epigenetics comes into play. Epigenetic modifications, including modifications to the histone, allow for the regulation of gene transcription to control cell-type differentiation – in this case, DNA methylation and modification of the histones' positively charged amino acids to create spaces where DNA is open to transcription and spaces where DNA is still bound by histone [6]. There are three main epigenetic modifications – DNA methylation, histone modifications, and noncoding RNA action [7].

This study mainly focuses on methylation and acetylation of histones. We plan to establish relationships between the epigenetic modification binding sites and transcriptional activity using data from two genome-wide profiling methods – Chromatin Immunoprecipitation Sequencing (ChIP-Seq) and RNA sequencing (RNA-Seq).

2.3 The Techniques

ChIP-Seq is a technique that identifies elements in protein-DNA interactions involved in chromatin organization and gene regulation [8]. The first step in ChIP-Seq is Chromatin Immunoprecipitation, which detects protein-DNA interactions in living cells by capturing proteins at DNA binding sites, thus identifying regions of the genome associated with specific proteins in the native chromatin environment. In the following step, the precipitated DNA is sequenced. This allows for millions of fragments of DNA to be decoded simultaneously, also allowing for an interpretation of regulatory events in the context of many biological processes and diseases [9]. ChIP-Seq uses antibodies for specific DNA-binding proteins or histone modifications to find "enriched" loci within the genome. As in this study, it can be applied to histone modifications to understand the characteristics and biological functions of epigenetic signatures [10].

RNA-seq is a technique that follows a sequence-based approach to study gene expression. It converts a population of RNA into a library of complementary DNA (cDNA) fragments with adaptors on one or both ends to assist in directional sequencing. High-throughput sequencing is performed on each molecule to obtain short sequences typically 30–400 base pairs long. The resulting sequences are aligned to a reference genome or assembled to provide a genome-wide map of transcription and gene expression levels for each gene [11]. RNA-seq is a strong technique because it can detect novel mRNA splice variants that do not directly correspond to existing annotated genomic sequences [12] and has a very low background signal/noise because the cDNA sequences can be mapped without room for ambiguity [13]. Figure 1 shows a rough diagram comparing ChIP-Seq and RNA-Seq in the cell.

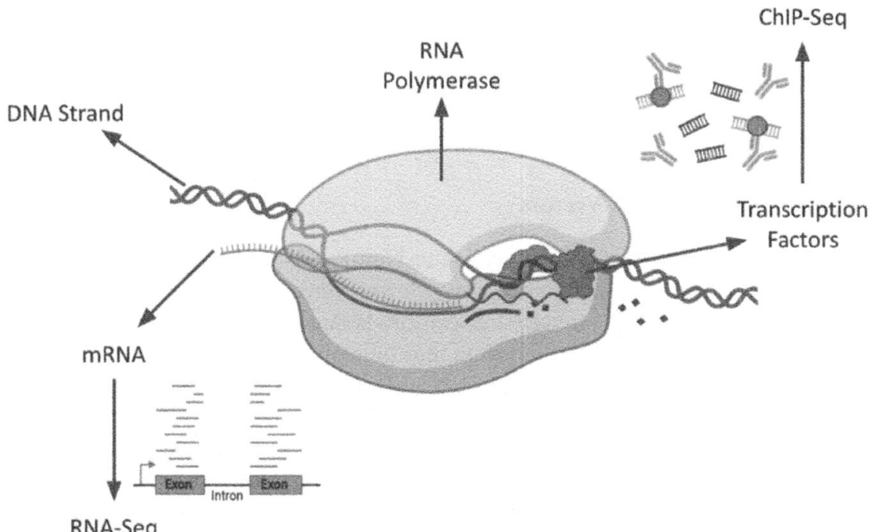

Fig. 1. A diagram of the ChIP-seq and RNA-seq procedures in the cell. While ChIP-seq works to find the binding sites of transcription factors to the DNA, RNA-seq deals with mRNA sequences to assess the transcriptional activity of certain genes after they have been transcribed from DNA.

Using the data from high-throughput sequencing methods, we aim to study how epigenetic modifications affect transcriptional activity in cancerous and non-cancerous cell lines. Since ChIP-seq data provides information about the binding sites for epigenetic factors and RNA-seq data reflects the transcriptional activity in the genome, we developed a computational model to infer gene expression patterns directly from epigenetic profiles and identify underlying regulatory relationships. This is particularly valuable, as studying both cancerous and non-cancerous cell lines reveals the binding sites that are associated with oncogenic gene expression. In future, this may help to develop novel therapeutic targets that can treat specific cancers at the epigenetic level.

3 Materials and Methods

3.1 Environments

This experiment used Google Colaboratory (Google Colab) and Visual Studio Code (VS Code) as the main Integrated Development Environments (IDEs). When using VS Code, a Python virtual environment was created – which stored all of the libraries that VS Code used – and any programming was done in a Jupyter Notebook.

3.2 Loading the Data

The ChIP-seq and RNA-seq data had to be accessed through an open-sourced database to set up this experiment. We used the Encyclopedia of DNA Elements (ENCODE) database in this case [14]. Then, epigenetic modification and transcriptome activity data for the GM12878, IMR90, K562, HCT116, HepG2, A549, MCF7, and PC3 cell lines were downloaded. For each cell line, the ChIP-seq data from seven histone modification experiments were imported: H3K4me1, H3K4me2, H3K4me3, H3K27ac, H3K27me3, H3K9me3, and H3K9ac. Using a default dictionary of dictionaries, the ChIP-seq and RNA-seq data were transferred from a BigWig file to local variables.

3.3 Creating the Model's Vectors

After all of the data was stored as such, the NumPy library was imported, and two different versions of a function named read_chrom were defined. Both versions took a bigWig file containing ChIP-seq data and a chromosome number as arguments. The first version divided the specified chromosome into bins of 100,000 base pairs each, taking the mean value of each bin and creating a NumPy array of the mean values, while the second version did the same with a bin size of 50,000 base pairs each. Any missing data was converted into a NaN datatype, the bottom five and top five percentiles were removed from the data to remove any outliers, and the final array was returned.

Eight chromosomes were used when creating the input and output vectors: chromosomes one, two, three, four, five, six, twenty-one, and twenty-two. Eight sub-input vectors were made to create the input vector for the model, one for each chromosome. For each sub-input vector, read_chrom was called seven times (once for each histone modification), and the returned NumPy array was appended to the sub-input vector. Finally, the eight sub-input vectors were concatenated horizontally to create the final input vector, which had a size of (7, N) where N is the number of chromosome segments. The same process was repeated using the second version of the read_chrom function, and two input vectors (one with the first version of read_chrom and one with the second version) were created for each cell line in this manner.

For the output vector, two versions of a function called read_RNA_seq were defined, following the same procedure as the two versions of read_chrom (with each version having a different bin size), except for one change: after trimming the array to remove outliers, the array was digitized differently for each version. For the version with a bin size of 100000, any chromosome segment above the 70th percentile in the array was considered as having "high" transcriptional activity, and the mean value was replaced with a one; on the other hand, any data below the 70th percentile in the array was considered as having "low" transcriptional activity, and the mean value was replaced with a zero. For the version with a bin size of 50000, four categories were defined such that segments below the 30th percentile were given a value of zero, segments between the 30th and 50th percentiles were given a value of one, segments between the 50th and 70th percentiles were given a value of two, and segments above the 70th percentile were given a value of three. Thus, the eight sub-output vectors were concatenated horizontally to create the final output vector, with a size of (1, N) where N is the number of chromosome segments, similar to the input vectors.

3.4 Model Development

Once the two versions of input and output vectors for all eight cell lines had been created and safely downloaded as NumPy files (.npy file extension) on a local drive, the model creation process could begin. Due to RAM limitations, it became inefficient to continue using VS Code, so the IDE was switched to Google Colab, and the input and output vectors were loaded from the files. One cell line (GM12878, a non-cancerous lymphoblastoid cell line) was chosen to create and optimize the model. Because both the input and output vectors contained NaNs, a mask was created to identify rows with NaNs so that the same row could be removed from both vectors to avoid data mismatch. Eventually, separate masks were made for each cell line.

After all NaNs were removed, the input and output vectors were split into training and validation data. 80% of the data was used to train the model, while 20% was used to validate its accuracy.

A Keras Sequential model was created and optimized on the 100000 base pair bin size GM12878 data. The model consisted of thirteen layers. The first twelve layers consist of four sets of three layers – a Dense layer, a Batch Normalization layer, and a Dropout layer. Each Dense layer's units follow a parabolic pattern, using the Sigmoid Linear Unit (SiLU) function as the activation function, a HeNormal initializer, and L2 regularization of 1×10^{-4}. After the Batch Normalization layer, the Dropout layer randomly removes 10% of the data to prevent overfitting. The thirteenth layer converts the calculations made by the other twelve layers into an output that is digitized into either zero/one or zero through three, depending on which version was inputted into the model. With this model architecture, the model was trained over 100 epochs using Binary Cross Entropy (Log

Loss) and the Adam optimizer, with a learning rate that started at 0.001 and followed a Cosine Decay schedule.

3.5 Testing the Model

After the model was trained, optimized, and validated on GM12878 data, a series of tests were conducted. In each test, a new cancerous cell line's input and output vectors (with 100000 base pair bin sizes) were horizontally concatenated onto the training input and output vectors, and the model was retrained. This was repeated six times, until a combined vector of six cell lines (GM12878, K562, HepG2, A549, MCF7, and PC3) had been used for the training. Each time, the model was evaluated on two cell lines (IMR90, a non-cancerous cell line, and HCT116, a cancerous cell line), after it had been trained.

This incremental process was repeated using the other set of input and output vectors (with 50000 base pair bin sizes and four classification groups), and a separate set of results was found.

4 Results

4.1 Model Setup

As shown in Fig. 2, after creating a model architecture, we trained one model on the binary classification problem with the input/output vectors, with 100,000 bp resolution and two output classes.

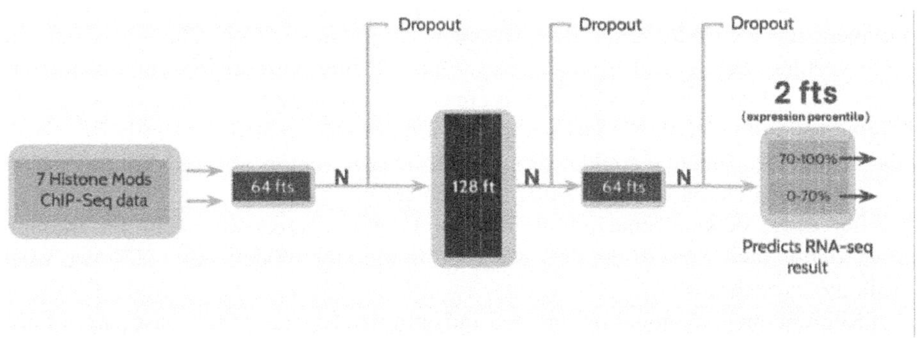

Fig. 2. Model architecture diagram for the binary classification model. A vector of size (N,7) was passed into the model as input, with N being an arbitrarily large number indicating the amount of data in the vector and seven indicating the number of histone modification experiments. The vector passed through the model architecture as depicted, until the output was digitized into 0 or 1, indicating the RNA-seq transcription amount.

The binary classification model provides a simple view of the model's effectiveness, but it has some weaknesses. The most prevalent one is its ability to assess the true accuracy of the model; since there are only two final classes, significant inaccuracies can still be misclassified as correct answers. For example, if the true percentile value of the RNA-seq result is 5% but the model predicts 50%, under the binary classification system, the model got the correct answer even though it was well off. A multiclass classification system (in this case, with four final classes) helps assess the model's viability more accurately. So, we trained a new model using the multiclass classification vectors, with a resolution of 50000 bp and four classes. Figure 3 shows a schematic of the model's architecture trained on the multiclass classification problem, almost identical to the binary classification model's architecture.

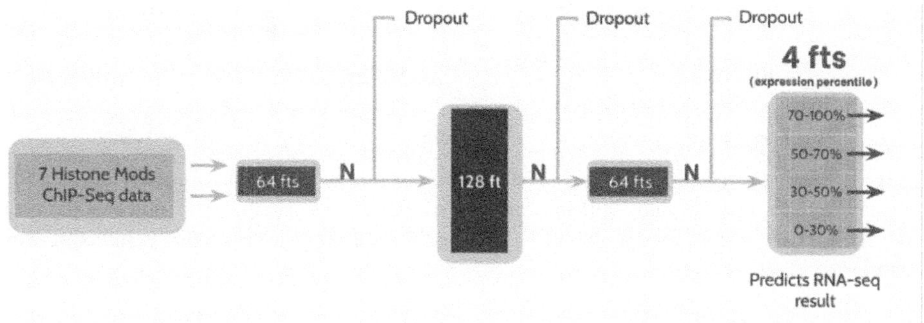

Fig. 3. Model architecture diagram for the multiclass (four-class) classification model. Similar to the binary classification model, a vector of size (N,7) was passed into the model as input. The vector passed through the model architecture as depicted, but in this model, the output was modified to a number between 0 and 3, depending on the transcription amount percentile.

Then, Receiver Operating Characteristic (ROC) curves were generated to evaluate the performance of the binary classification model by comparing the false positive rate with the true positive rate (Fig. 5). The Area Under the Curve (AUC) was calculated for each curve. Since it remained positive and high for every run, we can be confident that our model architecture is effective. The generated ROC-AUC curves for all six model versions are shown in Fig. 4.

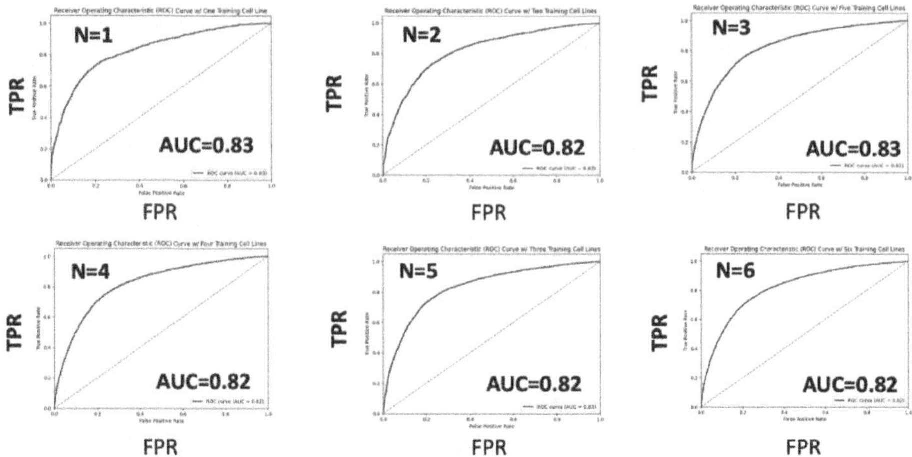

Fig. 4. Receiver Operating Characteristic (ROC) curves for the binary classification model. FPR indicates the false positive rate, TPR indicates the true positive rate, and AUC indicates the area under the curve. For each model, the AUC was high, indicating that the model architecture was sound.

4.2 Testing the Model

The models were further tested on two other cell lines: IMR90 and HCT116. Since the models were not previously included in the training data from these cell lines, the results on these cell lines served as a measure of the generalizability of the model. Figure 5 shows the accuracy and loss curves of the binary classification model tested on those cell lines. Since the number of datapoints was small, a Mann-Whitney U test was run to determine whether the accuracy or loss on the non-cancerous cell line significantly differed from that on the cancerous cell line. With a p-value of 0.093 and 0.240, we can say with 95% confidence that the curves are not significantly different, meaning the model performed effectively on both cancerous and non-cancerous cell lines.

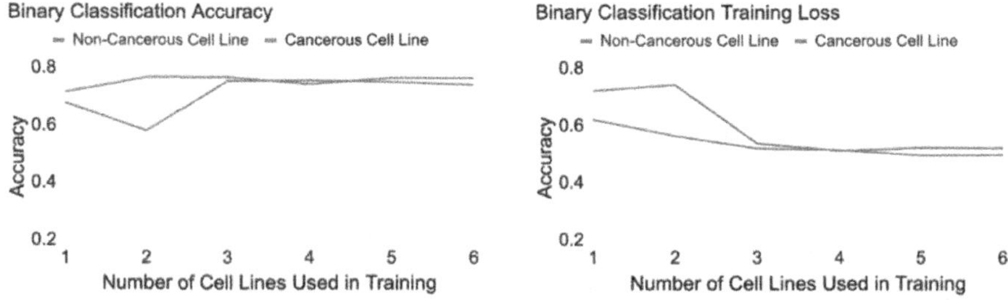

Fig. 5. Accuracy and loss curves for the binary classification model. On average, the loss reduces, and the accuracy increases as the number of cell lines used in training increases. The non-cancerous and cancerous cell line testing curves for both accuracy and loss are not significantly different ($p = 0.093$ for accuracy and $p = 0.240$ for loss); the model works effectively on both cancerous and non-cancerous cell lines.

Figure 6 shows the accuracy and loss curves of the multiclass classification model when tested on the non-cancerous and cancerous cell lines. Similar to the binary classification model, a Mann-Whitney U test was performed to determine whether the accuracy or loss on the non-cancerous cell line significantly differed from that on the cancerous cell line. With a p-value of 0.699 and 0.589, we can state with 95% confidence that the curves are not significantly different, meaning the model performed effectively on both cancerous and non-cancerous cell lines.

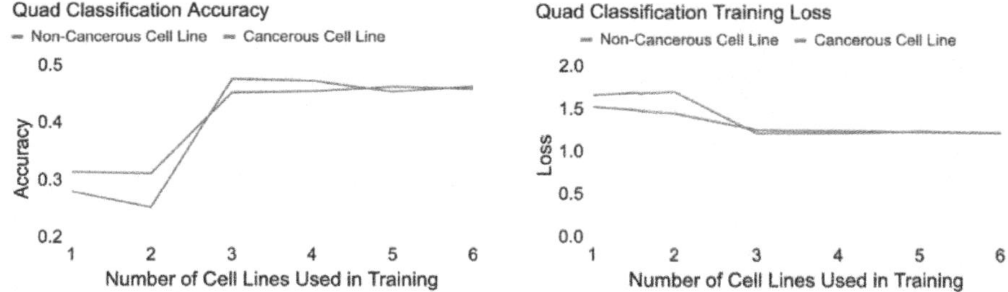

Fig. 6. Accuracy and loss curves for the multiclass classification model. On average, the loss reduces, and the accuracy increases as the number of cell lines used in training increases. The non-cancerous and cancerous cell line testing curves for both accuracy and loss are not significantly different ($p = 0.699$ for accuracy and $p = 0.589$ for loss); the model works effectively on both cancerous and non-cancerous cell lines.

5 Discussion

In this study, we aimed to create a model that could effectively predict the RNA-seq transcriptomic activity of a cell line, given the cell line's ChIP-seq epigenetic signal binding site map. As a secondary goal, we worked towards developing a model that performs well on any cell line, including non-cancerous and cancerous.

The AUC value calculated for the ROC curves generated for the binary classification model was between 0.82 and 0.83, indicating that the model architecture is strong enough to perform the task and distinguish between high transcription and low transcription cases. Although there is room for improvement, a value of between 0.8 and 0.9 for AUC is generally considered to be excellent [15].

As the number of cell lines used in training increased, the accuracy of both models when testing on cancerous and non-cancerous cell lines inevitably increased. The binary classification model's accuracy increased from 64% to 78% for the non-cancerous cell line and from 66% to 79% for the cancerous cell line. The multiclass classification model's accuracy increased from 29% to 45% for the non-cancerous cell line and from 31% to 45% for the cancerous cell line. Though these numbers may appear low, they should be compared relative to random chance for these models. For the binary classification model, random guessing would yield an accuracy of 50%, so the maximum of 79% that the model reached is substantially higher than random guessing. Similarly, for the multiclass classification model, where the random guessing would result in an accuracy of 25% (given four classes), the model's maximum of 45% is considered higher.

This indicates that the model can detect patterns in transcriptional activity based on the epigenetic binding sites that allow it to make substantive predictions.

These results are of great importance, establishing a relationship between epigenetic signals and transcriptional activity in human cell lines that can be predicted with relatively high accuracy using deep learning technology. Such a tool would be of great use when the need arises to predict the cellular transcription profile of a cell line when only its epigenetic signal data is available. Moreover, the generalizability of the model, working for any cell line despite being trained on a limited number, suggests that the correlation between epigenetic signals and transcriptional activity exists across cell lines. Moreover, the patterns and weights the model assigns could be used to describe further the regulatory rules that control gene transcription and, by extension, cellular function.

Possible extensions include investigating ways to improve the prediction accuracy of the proposed model or exploring model formats other than a Sequential model. More research into the similarities in epigenetic data or transcriptional activity across a larger set of cell lines and chromosomes would be beneficial, establishing predictable patterns for human cell lines in general.

Another key extension of this work comprises a deeper analysis of how the model's weights are assigned and how it links epigenetic binding sites to their corresponding genes. This would be especially useful in cancer research, as by comparing the transcription landscape of cancerous and non-cancerous cell lines, it may be possible to identify which genes are correlated with increased cancer presence. With this knowledge, it would be possible to identify novel epigenetic targets for cancer therapeutics globally across the genome.

6 Data Availability

Accession numbers for all ENCODE datasets used can be found in Table 1 below.

Table 1. Accession information for all ENCODE project datasets used in this study. The lab name and the accession number for both the overall experiment and specific BigWig file used is listed for each cell line's ChIP-seq and RNA-seq data.

Experiment	BigWig code	Target	Cell Line	Lab
ENCSR000AKF	ENCFF190RZM	H3K4me1	GM12878	Bradley Bernstein, Broad
ENCSR000AKG	ENCFF701JXT	H3K4me2	GM12878	Bradley Bernstein, Broad
ENCSR057BWO	ENCFF480KNX	H3K4me3	GM12878	Bradley Bernstein, Broad
ENCSR000AKC	ENCFF087YCU	H3K27ac	GM12878	Bradley Bernstein, Broad
ENCSR000AKD	ENCFF691LFQ	H3K27me3	GM12878	Bradley Bernstein, Broad

(*continued*)

Table 1. (*continued*)

Experiment	BigWig code	Target	Cell Line	Lab
ENCSR000AOX	ENCFF174RRQ	H3K9me3	GM12878	Bradley Bernstein, Broad
ENCSR000AKH	ENCFF688HLG	H3K9ac	GM12878	Bradley Bernstein, Broad
ENCSR151NGC	ENCFF409USY	RNA-seq*	GM12878	Barbara Wold, Caltech
ENCSR831JSP	ENCFF148PNW	H3K4me1	IMR-90	Bing Ren, UCSD
ENCSR672XZZ	ENCFF400CAD	H3K4me2	IMR-90	Bing Ren, UCSD
ENCSR087PFU	ENCFF811ZFE	H3K4me3	IMR-90	Bing Ren, UCSD
ENCSR002YRE	ENCFF907GKJ	H3K27ac	IMR-90	Bing Ren, UCSD
ENCSR431UUY	ENCFF045HZZ	H3K27me3	IMR-90	Bing Ren, UCSD
ENCSR055ZZY	ENCFF733CJA	H3K9me3	IMR-90	Bing Ren, UCSD
ENCSR219MYH	ENCFF682HNO	H3K9ac	IMR-90	Bing Ren, UCSD
ENCSR797RXV	ENCFF718UDS	RNA-seq*	IMR-90	Barbara Wold, Caltech
ENCSR000AKS	ENCFF457URZ	H3K4me1	K562	Bradley Bernstein, Broad
ENCSR000AKT	ENCFF054RSU	H3K4me2	K562	Bradley Bernstein, Broad
ENCSR000AKU	ENCFF767UON	H3K4me3	K562	Bradley Bernstein, Broad
ENCSR000AKP	ENCFF465GBD	H3K27ac	K562	Bradley Bernstein, Broad
ENCSR000AKQ	ENCFF582IMB	H3K27me3	K562	Bradley Bernstein, Broad
ENCSR000APE	ENCFF559MMQ	H3K9me3	K562	Bradley Bernstein, Broad
ENCSR000AKV	ENCFF239EBH	H3K9ac	K562	Bradley Bernstein, Broad
ENCSR000AEL	ENCFF730LJD	RNA-seq*	K562	Thomas Gingeras, CSHL
ENCSR161MXP	ENCFF182EJH	H3K4me1	HCT116	Bradley Bernstein, Broad
ENCSR794ULT	ENCFF624KAH	H3K4me2	HCT116	Bradley Bernstein, Broad
ENCSR333OPW	ENCFF213WKK	H3K4me3	HCT116	Bradley Bernstein, Broad

(*continued*)

Table 1. (*continued*)

Experiment	BigWig code	Target	Cell Line	Lab
ENCSR661KMA	ENCFF277XII	H3K27ac	HCT116	Bradley Bernstein, Broad
ENCSR810BDB	ENCFF232QSG	H3K27me3	HCT116	Bradley Bernstein, Broad
ENCSR179BUC	ENCFF572IBD	H3K9me3	HCT116	Bradley Bernstein, Broad
ENCSR093SHE	ENCFF558LSB	H3K9ac	HCT116	Bradley Bernstein, Broad
ENCSR257FJF	ENCFF584RWQ	RNA-seq*	HCT116	Barbara Wold, Caltech
ENCSR000APV	ENCFF554XSR	H3K4me1	HepG2	Bradley Bernstein, Broad
ENCSR000AMC	ENCFF767KKA	H3K4me2	HepG2	Bradley Bernstein, Broad
ENCSR000AMP	ENCFF219ZOU	H3K4me3	HepG2	Bradley Bernstein, Broad
ENCSR000AMO	ENCFF259DOA	H3K27ac	HepG2	Bradley Bernstein, Broad
ENCSR000AOL	ENCFF257BOE	H3K27me3	HepG2	Bradley Bernstein, Broad
ENCSR000ATD	ENCFF125NHB	H3K9me3	HepG2	Bradley Bernstein, Broad
ENCSR000AMD	ENCFF192NNA	H3K9ac	HepG2	Bradley Bernstein, Broad
ENCSR245ATJ	ENCFF742JXC	RNA-seq*	HepG2	Barbara Wold, Caltech
ENCSR000AUM	ENCFF905WYC	H3K4me1	A549**	Bradley Bernstein, Broad
ENCSR000AVI	ENCFF230LCP	H3K4me2	A549**	Bradley Bernstein, Broad
ENCSR000ASH	ENCFF764XQX	H3K4me3	A549**	Bradley Bernstein, Broad
ENCSR000AUI	ENCFF730VLE	H3K27ac	A549**	Bradley Bernstein, Broad
ENCSR000AUK	ENCFF786RCE	H3K27me3	A549**	Bradley Bernstein, Broad
ENCSR000AUN	ENCFF173DKI	H3K9me3	A549**	Bradley Bernstein, Broad

(*continued*)

Table 1. *(continued)*

Experiment	BigWig code	Target	Cell Line	Lab
ENCSR000ASV	ENCFF517WOS	H3K9ac	A549**	Bradley Bernstein, Broad
ENCSR300FPD	ENCFF035MLG	RNA-seq*	A549***	Tim Reddy, Duke
ENCSR493NBY	ENCFF763NCP	H3K4me1	MCF-7	Bradley Bernstein, Broad
ENCSR875KOJ	ENCFF442RRY	H3K4me2	MCF-7	Bradley Bernstein, Broad
ENCSR985MIB	ENCFF163MXP	H3K4me3	MCF-7	Bradley Bernstein, Broad
ENCSR752UOD	ENCFF138YNG	H3K27ac	MCF-7	Bradley Bernstein, Broad
ENCSR761DLU	ENCFF163QKN	H3K27me3	MCF-7	Bradley Bernstein, Broad
ENCSR999WHE	ENCFF481DZL	H3K9me3	MCF-7	Bradley Bernstein, Broad
ENCSR056UBA	ENCFF327XJC	H3K9ac	MCF-7	Bradley Bernstein, Broad
ENCSR355JZC	ENCFF992CSD	RNA-seq*	MCF-7	Barbara Wold, Caltech
ENCSR566UMF	ENCFF843TBP	H3K4me1	PC-3	Bradley Bernstein, Broad
ENCSR788EQL	ENCFF366QUC	H3K4me2	PC-3	Bradley Bernstein, Broad
ENCSR275NCH	ENCFF496OWV	H3K4me3	PC-3	Bradley Bernstein, Broad
ENCSR826UTD	ENCFF175EDR	H3K27ac	PC-3	Bradley Bernstein, Broad
ENCSR881TWJ	ENCFF612JOH	H3K27me3	PC-3	Bradley Bernstein, Broad
ENCSR339ZMJ	ENCFF807MNG	H3K9me3	PC-3	Bradley Bernstein, Broad
ENCSR197QXT	ENCFF499QYJ	H3K9ac	PC-3	Bradley Bernstein, Broad
ENCSR648KDM	ENCFF397MAI	RNA-seq*	PC-3	Barbara Wold, Caltech

*Total RNA-seq, no specific target.

**Treated with 0.02% ethanol for 1 h.

***Treated with 1 μM dexamethasone (CHEBI:41879) for 4 h.

Acknowledgments. We thank the members of the ENCODE Consortium for their efforts in compiling and processing the wealth of data we could draw from. We would also like to specifically thank Bradley Bernstein et al. (Broad Institute), Bing Ren et al. (University of California, San Diego), Barbara Wold et al. (California Institute of Technology), Thomas Gingeras et al. (Cold Spring Harbor Laboratory), and Tim Reddy et al. (Duke University) for providing the ENCODE Consortium with the datasets we used. Finally, we would like to thank Dr. Sumitabha Brahmachari (Rice University) for serving as our mentor and guide throughout this project, providing us with direction and assistance throughout this endeavor.

Disclosure of Interests. The authors have no competing interests to declare that are relevant to the content of this article.

References

1. Ralston, A., Shaw, K.: Gene expression regulates cell differentiation. Nat. Educ. **1**(1), 127–131 (2008)
2. Ma, J.: Transcriptional activators and activation mechanisms. Protein Cell **2**(11), 879–888 (2011)
3. Chaffey, N., et al.: Molecular Biology of the Cell, 4th ed. (2003)
4. Gibney, E.R., Nolan, C.M.: Epigenetics and gene expression. Heredity **105**(1), 4–13 (2010)
5. Waterland, R.A.: Epigenetic mechanisms and gastrointestinal development. J. Pediatr. **149**(5), S137–S142 (2006)
6. Hoopes, L.: Introduction to the gene expression and regulation topic room. Nat. Educ. **1**(1), 160 (2008)
7. Loscalzo, J., Handy, D.E.: Epigenetic modifications: basic mechanisms and role in cardiovascular disease (2013 Grover Conference series). Pulm. Circ. **4**(2), 169–174 (2014)
8. Shah, A.: Chromatin Immunoprecipitation Sequencing (ChIP-Seq) on the SOLiD™ System (2009)
9. Mundade, R., Ozer, H.G., Wei, H., Prabhu, L., Lu, T.: Role of ChIP-seq in the discovery of transcription factor binding sites, differential gene regulation mechanism, epigenetic marks and beyond. Cell Cycle **13**(18), 2847–2852 (2014)
10. Nakato, R., Sakata, T.: Methods for ChIP-seq analysis: a practical workflow and advanced applications. Methods **187**, 44–53 (2021)
11. Wang, Z., Gerstein, M., Snyder, M.: RNA-Seq: a revolutionary tool for transcriptomics. Nat. Rev. Genet. **10**(1), 57–63 (2009)
12. Vera, J.C., et al.: Rapid transcriptome characterization for a nonmodel organism using 454 pyrosequencing. Mol. Ecol. **17**(7), 1636–1647 (2008)
13. Mortazavi, A., Williams, B.A., McCue, K., Schaeffer, L., Wold, B.: Mapping and quantifying mammalian transcriptomes by RNA-Seq. Nat. Methods **5**(7), 621–628 (2008)
14. ENCODE Project Consortium: An integrated encyclopedia of DNA elements in the human genome. Nature **489**(7414), 57 (2012)
15. Mandrekar, J.N.: Receiver operating characteristic curve in diagnostic test assessment. J. Thorac. Oncol. **5**(9), 1315–1316 (2010)

11th International Conference on Biomedical Engineering and Sciences (BIOENG'25)

Comparison of Deep Learning Architectures for COVID-19 Multi-class Classification over CT-Scans

Jesús Toledano Pavón[1,2], Francisco Carrillo-Perez[1,2], Juan Carlos Morales Vega[1,2], Luis Javier Herrera[1,2](✉), and Ignacio Rojas[1,2]

[1] Department of Computer Architecture and Technology, University of Granada. C.I.T.I.C., Periodista Rafael Gómez Montero, 2, 18014 Granada, Spain
{jesutolepa,jherrera}@ugr.es

[2] Stanford Center for Biomedical Informatics Research (BMIR), Department of Medicine, Stanford University, 1265 Welch Rd, Stanford, CA 94305, USA

Abstract. Covid-19 disease continues its spread in form of different variants in the current year 2022. For this reason different deep learning methods are been tried for COVID-19 prediction. In this paper, a multi-class classification between COVID-19, CAP and Normal patients was carried out for multiple CNN models by using labelled CT scans. A strong pre-processing was implemented in order to clean those slices enhancing the performance of the classification models. After 5-fold cross validation training phase for each model, VGG16 turned out to be the best model with 90% ± 1.22 test accuracy at slice-level and 99% ± 1.19 test accuracy at patient-level. Thus, the proposed method offers a robust COVID-19 prediction.

Keywords: COVID-19 · CT Scans · Image Pre-processing · Slice-Level Classification · Patient-Level Prediction

1 Introduction

SARS-CoV-2 disease, commonly known as COVID-19, is a severe medical condition related to the lungs emerged by the end of 2019 which could cause respiratory problems. According to the sufferer, symptoms vary from loss of smell and taste, fever, coughing or breath shortness to pneumonia or pulmonary fibrosis in the worst case scenario. The virus, emerged by the end of 2019, continues its propagation in different, more contagious variants around the world to date. Gamma and Delta variants detected in September 2020 as well as Omicron variant originated in November 2021 are some relevant examples that concern to global healthcare once again. More than 470 million confirmed cases of COVID-19 and 6,1 million of deaths have been reported by the World Health Organisation (WHO) in March 2022 [10]. Therefore, efforts to stop the pandemic are still on going by researchers who are developing more sophisticated diagnosis systems in order to an early detection of the disease preventing its spread. Reverse

A. Alsadoon et al. (Eds.): CSCE 2025, CCIS 2935, pp. 147–156, 2026.
https://doi.org/10.1007/978-3-032-22199-5_10

Transcription Polymerase Chain Reaction (RT-PCR) or Antigen Detection fast tests are widely used but their low sensitivity offered results in too many false positives and false negatives cases. Also, this methods have limitations because their cost and sparse availability, time required to obtain reliable results and the big risk taken by healthcare workers when they perform these tests on potential COVID-19 patients. For this reason, solutions based on screening the lungs by X-ray images and Computed Tomography (CT) scans are presented as a better option in combination with laboratory tests for COVID-19 detection. These image findings enable a direct visualisation of possible infected areas such as ground glass opacity (CGO), consolidations, nodules or crazy paving signs caused by the resulting COVID-19 viral pneumonia [7]. However, the abnormalities encountered on the images could also relate to other similar diseases such as Community Acquired Pneumonia (CAP). The use of Convolutional Neural Networks (CNN) for automatic classification allows to differentiate COVID-19 patients from CAP patients increasing both accuracy and speed prediction which results in more effective decision making compared to manual detection. Thus, the aim of the present paper is to develop a multi-class classification system between COVID-19, CAP and Normal patients employing their multiple 2D slices in the axial plane of 3D CT scans, which are provided by a subset of the large database from CC-CCII (China Consortium of Chest CT Image Investigation) [14]. An automatic custom method of cleaning and body segmentation of patient CT slices is proposed for enhanced pre-processing step, which will be used as input of multiple CNN models. Data augmentation and transfer learning methods are further implemented for slice-level classification increasing model performance and final patient-level prediction is carried out by fixing a minimum cutoff of infected slices per patient.

2 Related Work

A variety of papers have been released that proposed a multi-class classification between COVID-19, CAP and Normal patient including the CC-CCII database used in the present paper [14]. Gunraj et al. presented a 2D custom model called COVIDNet-CT as backbone for multi-class classification [3]. This model, built from Machine-Driven design exploration, provides a high accuracy with low complexity by using pretrained weights from ImageNet. 104,099 slices from 1,489 patients of the CC-CCII database were used as input of the COVIDNet-CT model after pre-processing and data augmentation steps. Training results achieved an accuracy of 99.1% in a single split, showing the best performance compared to most popular CNN models with a larger number of parameters. Xin et al. presented a comparative study of multiple CNN models for COVID-19 detection using CT scans [6]. A cleaned version of CC-CCII database were built by taking 340,190 slices of 2,698 COVID-19, CAP and NORMAL patients which were preprocessed into greyscale and RGB input slices for 2D/3D CNN models. A total of 17 2D and 3D CNN models were tried applying data augmentation methods in a single split. DenseNet3D121 model reached the best test accuracy of 88.63% and DenseNet201 achieved the high performance for 2D models with 81.75% test accuracy. Finally, Garg et al. proposed a multi-class classification using pre-processed CT slices from different datasets [2]. A Region of Interest (ROI) extraction was implemented by detecting patient's body contours for the pre-processing step. This method applies a thresholding step after performing a Gaussian smoothing which obtains one or more possible contours. The contour with largest area is chosen as the patient's body. Cleaned slices were classified using Resnet50 as backbone followed by training an ensemble of four different classifiers for patient-level prediction. Results obtained for slice-level were 95.76% test accuracy in a single split. The patient-level classifiers reached 94.90% test accuracy.

3 Materials and Methods

3.1 Database

The database employed for the present paper was released by China Consortium of Chest CT Image Investigation (CC-CCII), which includes chest CT images from COVID-19, Community Acquired Pneumonia (CAP) and Normal patients [14]. It refers to one of the largest CT datasets published for COVID-19 classification consisting of 617,775 CT slices from 6,752 scans of 4,154 patients. However, CC-CCII database presents different problems that could have a negative impact on the performance of the applied models. For example, there are around a 10% of damage CT scans that cannot be decompressed and different types of image files exists which make it difficult a common pre-processing of them. In addition, quite a lot of CT scans have duplicated slices as well as noise and not relevant slices which show other parts of the body such as head parts instead of the lungs.

In the present paper, a subset from CC-CCII database is extracted by manually selecting the CT scans of patients with none of the problems described above. The subset results in 22,114 slices from 165 COVID-19 patients, 18,565 slices from 96 CAP patients and 6,803 slices from 67 Normal patients where one CT scan per patient is chosen. The proposed distribution of the class patients is done by the fact that slices are labelled one by one by medical experts. Therefore, only some slices of infected patients presents signs of COVID-19 or CAP disease while the rest are slices with no disease. Multi-class classification using input labelled slices offers more detailed information to the models which focus on infected slices more efficiently. Thus, they achieve an enhanced performance involving a higher accuracy with respect to the employment of unlabelled slices.

3.2 Pre-processing Step

After selection process of patients without slice problems our pre-preprocessing method is carried out in order to improve the lung area visualisation. It begins with a histogram normalisation in Hounsfield Units (HU) scale which represents the intensity levels corresponding to the different tissues and organs appearing in biomedical images. HU scale for CT slices ranges between -1000 HU (air) and

+1000 HU (bones) where the lung area can be found at -600 HU approximately. Thus, an intensity normalisation by using a 1500 HU window and -600 HU center is fixed to get the lung area with enhanced view. Additionally, a binary transformation is applied preparing the slices for subsequent body segmentation. This transformation is done by using a threshold calculated as the mean of all array CT slices per patient so it is suitable for any patient case.

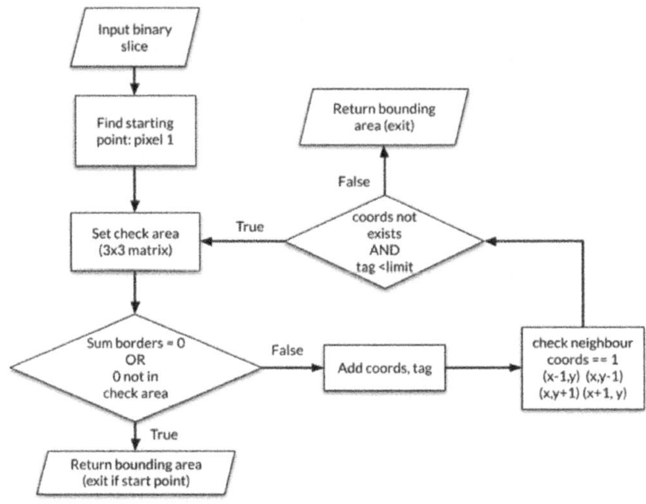

Fig. 1. Diagram of the Check Neighbour algorithm for bounding patient's body detection.

Once CT slices of one patient have been normalised and binarised, patient's body segmentation starts by applying a custom method called Check Neighbour Algorithm. Figure 1 shows the diagram for edge patient's body detection which a 3×3 matrix is built around the coordinates of the first pixel 1 detected. If all borders of the matrix are pixel 0, the pixel is remove because it refers to an isolated point. If otherwise, its respective coordinates are registered and the closet neighbours with pixel 1 are examined by repeating the algorithm. The area inside edges corresponding to 3×3 matrix borders with all 1 pixel is also removed. The recursive method continues analysing neighbour coordinates until there are no new coordinates to check or a fixed number of pixel limit is exceed to avoid overflow. The resulting edge area detected belongs to the patient's body in most cases, but an additional filter is implemented which consists in checking the minimal height and width of the area detected (150 height × 250 width). Thus, if the detected area is smaller than the minimal size will be discarded and the Check Neighbour algorithm will start all over again. The edge area finally obtained is filled resulting in the patient's body mask extracted. The multiplication of the normalised slices and the masks achieves the patient's body slices with no artefacts and noise in comparison to the original slices (see Fig. 2).

After pre-processing step, cleaned slices are centered and a filtering algorithm is implemented which is similar to the one proposed by Rahimzadeh et al. [11]. The purpose of this algorithm is to remove CT slices that not contain useful information to the classifiers such as slices at the beginning and at the end of the CT scans. Also known as close-lungs, those slices barely show the lung area and other body tissues, such as the intestines, can be presented instead.

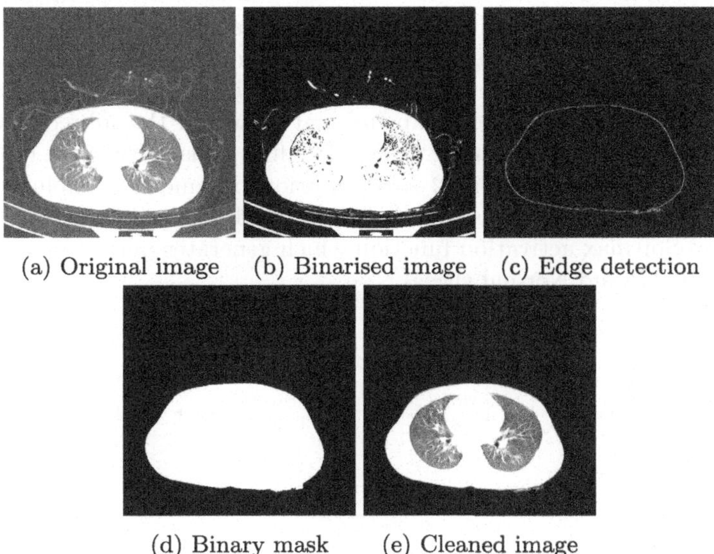

(a) Original image (b) Binarised image (c) Edge detection

(d) Binary mask (e) Cleaned image

Fig. 2. Pre-processing steps applied. Figure 2 (a) shows the original image with hard artefacts and noise. Figure 2 (b) presents the binarised image after normalisation method. Figure 2 (c) highlights the edge detected of the patient's body reached from Check Neighbour Algorithm. Figure 2 (d) shows the binary mask obtained after filling the area inside the patient's body edge. Figure 2 (e) is the resulting cleaned image after pre-processing.

3.3 Multi-class Classification Models

Once the enhanced slices have been obtained, they are employed as inputs of the classification models by resizing them from 512×512 to a smaller size. The image size depends on the architecture implemented as backbone to fit the network. Some of the most commonly used CNN models for image classification were tried such as VGG16 [12], Resnet50 [4], Resnet152V2 [5], DenseNet201 [8], Xception [1] and EfficientNetB4 [13]. The training phase for slice-level by using the models mentioned above presents the following scheme displayed in Fig. 3. ImageNet weights as well as fine tuning are applied to the network in order to improve the model performance over the input slices. In addition, a custom scheme is employed instead final dense layers in each model tried in order to reduce overfitting. A reduction of the possible overfitting existing in the training phase results crucial because it prevents the models to train using already trained data. Thus, the generalisation of the models is increased allowing more cases not previously seen to be included in the training phase. The proposed scheme includes a Batch Normalization layer together with a Dropout layer with 0.5 rate. It refers the network uses half of the neurons in each training so increases the complexity of the extracted features. Next, a 2D Convolutional layer is implemented for feature detection by using 128 filters and ReLU activation function. The next step implies a Batch Normalization layer again followed by a 2D Max Pooling layer which minimises the input features along its spatial dimensions. The resulting features are transformed into one-dimensional vector for the subsequent classification of them by using two dense layers. The first dense layer uses 128 neurons and ReLU activation where a L2 regularisation parameter is included raising the performance of the models. Finally, the second dense layer is consisted in 3 neurons and Softmax activation function which generates output predictions for COVID-19, CAP and Normal slices.

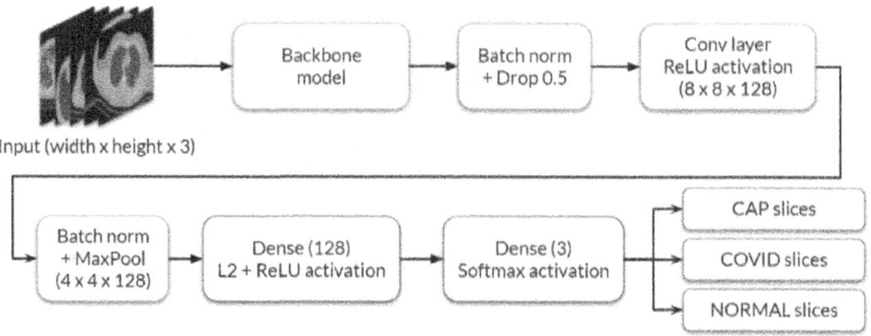

Fig. 3. Slice-level prediction scheme for the backbone models tried.

The next step is to carry out a final prediction of each patient by taking into account the number of slices classified with disease. It is achieved by fixing a cutoff as the minimum percentage of COVID-19 or CAP slices by which patients are finally predicted with disease. If the percentage of infected slices is less than fixed cutoff the corresponding patientes would be considered as healthy. Validation set is used to choose the correct cutoff which will be given by the one that presents the highest validation accuracy (in each split). Moreover, the recognition between COVID-19 or CAP patients is done by taking the one with the highest number of infected slices. The implemented scheme for patient-level prediction is shown in Fig. 4.

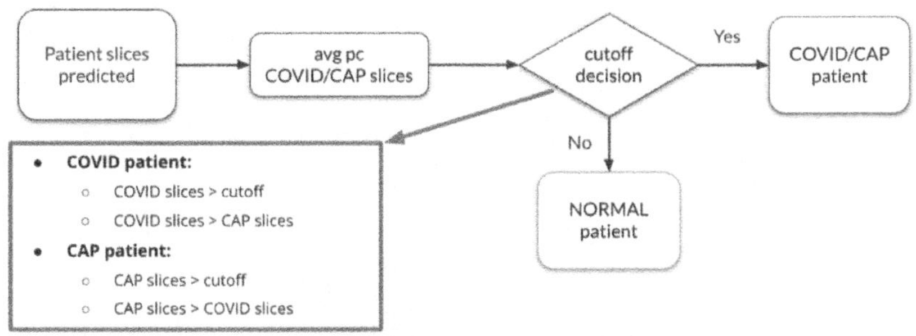

Fig. 4. Patient-level prediction scheme for final classification.

4 Results and Discussion

In order to evaluate our proposed method, the input of the CNN models tried for slice-level classification uses 10,084 CAP, 9,325 COVID and 16,023 Normal slices (including normal slices of COVID-CAP patients) which were obtained after the pre-preprocessing step applied to the subset CC-CCII database mentioned above. It is important to note that infected slices considered as close-lung slices during the close-lung filtering step were not removed. This is due to the fact that such slices could present interesting features for the training phase and also they increase the size of the pre-processed dataset slightly. A 5-fold cross-validation is used for a 60% training, 20% validation and 20% test set distribution for slice-level classification. Hyperparameters were fixed for training each model by using a batch size of 32, 1e-6 learning rate and 100 epochs maximum. Early stopping method is applied which finish the training phase if validation set does not improve its loss after a certain number of consecutive epochs. Thus, the training phase stops before 100 epochs in most of CNN models. In addition, strong data augmentation of 30% is applied over the training set which consists in random shifts, random rotations and random zooms helping to enhance the generalization of the models. Finally, Class Weights method is implemented in order to prevent the existing imbalance of slices between CAP-COVID and Normal classes during the training phase [9].

Table 1. Slice-level results for models tried.

Model	Test Accuracy	F1-score	Computational Time (Estimated)
VGG16	90% ± 1.22%	90% ± 1.22%	36,264 s
Resnet50	88% ± 0.58%	88% ± 0.59%	78,932 s
Resnet152V2	87% ± 0.54%	87% ± 0.58%	121,498 s
DenseNet201	89% ± 0.91%	89% ± 0.54%	98,201 s
Xception	88% ± 1.26%	88% ± 1.33%	136,199 s
EfficientNetB4	87% ± 0.66%	87% ± 0.65%	114,096 s

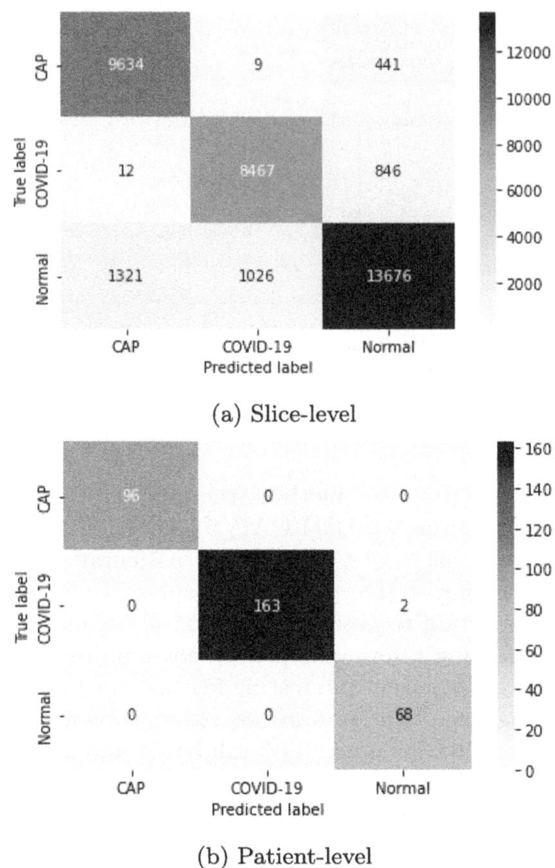

(a) Slice-level

(b) Patient-level

Fig. 5. Overall confussion Matrix at (a) slice and (b) patient level for VGG16.

Results for CNN models at slice-level training are presented in Table 1. VGG16 model provides the highest performance by reaching 90% ± 1.22% test accuracy compared to the other models which overcome 86% test accuracy. Furthermore, F1-score, which is a relevant metric for multi-class problems, is showed in Table 1. It resumes Recall and Precision metrics of each class giving a global vision of the quality model. Thus, VGG16 model presents the best quality achieved with 90% ± 1.22% F1-score followed by DenseNet201 reaching 89% ± 0.54% F1-score. Finally, VGG16 also proves to be the most efficient model in terms of computational time with only 36.264 s spent.

Next, confussion matrix for VGG16 at slice-level after 5-fold cross validation is displayed in Fig. 5a. It is noted that there are hardly any misclassified slices between COVID-19 and CAP classes. However, the number of missclassified slices between infected and Normal classes is greater due to the fact slices labeled as Normal were also employed in infected patients for classification. Thus, they show features similar to infected slices of those patients. Despite this, missclassified slices don't have a remarkable effect at patient-level prediction where only 2 COVID-19 patients (99% ± 1.19% test accuracy) are missclassified as Normal patients (see Fig. 5b). At the end of the present section, a comparison between our proposed method and other methods presented in the literature is carried out in Table 2. Althought the data size employed for classification is much smaller than the methods presented, 5-fold cross validation is implemented by our method. By this way, the entire dataset is used as both training and validation, so the results achieved are more robust compared to the rest of the methods.

Table 2. Results comparison for other methods tried on CC-CCII database.

Paper	Data size	Model	Parameters	Accuracy (Slice-level)
Gunraj et al. [3]	104,099 slices	CovidNet-CT	1,40M	99.10%
Xin et al. [6]	340,190 slices	DenseNet201	≈ 20,24M	81.75%
Garg et al. [2]	219,416 slices	Resnet50	≈ 25,63M	95.76%
Our contribution	35,432 slices	VGG16	15,46M	90% ± 1.22%

5 Conclusion and Future Work

In this paper, we proposed a multi-class classification by using CT scans slices of COVID-19, CAP and Normal patients. The original slices were enhanced by a robust pre-processing step which involves intensity normalization, a custom algorithm for patient's body segmentation and close-lungs filtering. This results in cleaned slices that improve the performance of the models tried for slice-level classification. Patient-level prediction were also carried out by a fixed cutoff according to the validation set. As future work COVID CT slices features could be used together with their associated clinical data. It refers a challenging problem where advanced multi-task learning methods can be employed in order to try a prediction of mortality in COVID-19 patients.

References

1. Chollet, F.: Xception: Deep learning with depthwise separable convolutions. In: Proceedings of the IEEE Conference on Computer Vision and Pattern Recognition, pp. 1251–1258 (2017)
2. Garg, P., Ranjan, R., Upadhyay, K., Agrawal, M., Deepak, D.: Multi-scale residual network for covid-19 diagnosis using CT-Scans. In: ICASSP 2021-2021 IEEE International Conference on Acoustics, Speech and Signal Processing (ICASSP), pp. 8558–8562. IEEE (2021)
3. Gunraj, H., Wang, L., Wong, A.: CovidNet-CT: a tailored deep convolutional neural network design for detection of covid-19 cases from chest CT images. Front. Med. 7 (2020)

4. He, K., Zhang, X., Ren, S., Sun, J.: Deep residual learning for image recognition. In: Proceedings of the IEEE Conference on Computer Vision and Pattern Recognition, pp. 770–778 (2016)
5. He, K., Zhang, X., Ren, S., Sun, J.: Identity mappings in deep residual networks. In: Leibe, B., Matas, J., Sebe, N., Welling, M. (eds.) ECCV 2016. LNCS, vol. 9908, pp. 630–645. Springer, Cham (2016). https://doi.org/10.1007/978-3-319-46493-0_38
6. He, X., et al.: Benchmarking deep learning models and automated model design for covid-19 detection with chest CT scans. medRxiv (2020)
7. Hefeda, M.M.: Ct chest findings in patients infected with covid-19: review of literature. Egyptian J. Radiol. Nuclear Med. **51**(1), 1–15 (2020)
8. Huang, G., Liu, Z., Van Der Maaten, L., Weinberger, K.Q.: Densely connected convolutional networks. In: Proceedings of the IEEE Conference on Computer Vision and Pattern Recognition, pp. 4700–4708 (2017)
9. King, G., Zeng, L.: Logistic regression in rare events data. Polit. Anal. **9**(2), 137–163 (2001)
10. Organisation, W.H.: WHO Coronavirus (COVID-19) Dashboard (2022). https://covid19.who.int/
11. Rahimzadeh, M., Attar, A., Sakhaei, S.M.: A fully automated deep learning-based network for detecting covid-19 from a new and large lung CT scan dataset. Biomed. Signal Process. Control **68**, 102588 (2021)
12. Simonyan, K., Zisserman, A.: Very deep convolutional networks for large-scale image recognition (2014). arXiv preprint arXiv:1409.1556
13. Tan, M., Le, Q.: EfficientNet: rethinking model scaling for convolutional neural networks. In: International Conference on Machine Learning, pp. 6105–6114. (2019) PMLR
14. Zhang, K., et al.: Clinically applicable ai system for accurate diagnosis, quantitative measurements, and prognosis of covid-19 pneumonia using computed tomography. Cell **181**(6), 1423–1433 (2020)

Streamlining Breath Analysis Methods for Rapid and Low-Cost Diabetes Detection and Dataset Collection

Piotr J. Smieja[1(✉)], Jiang Lu[1], Xingang Fu[2], and Ting Zhang[3]

[1] University of Houston - Clear Lake, Houston, TX, USA
{smiejap3298,luj}@uhcl.edu
[2] University of Nevada, Reno, Reno, NV, USA
xfu@unr.edu
[3] University of Houston - Downtown, Houston, TX, USA
zhangtin@uhd.edu

Abstract. The diagnosis of early stages of diseases such as lung cancer or diabetes is challenging, as these diseases do not have many noticeable symptoms. However, human breath contains many volatile organic compounds (VOCs) that could be used as a clue to conduct the proper test.

This study explores the technology required to develop a device for rapid, non-invasive disease detection with the use of the human breath print. The architecture for rapid and low-cost sensing is described, and how it could be employed in the future. The process of finalizing the sampling device and the data flow architecture will be described, along with important factors to consider when designing a breath analysis device.

Keywords: Diabetes · Volatile Organic Compounds (VOCs) · k-Nearest Neighbors (k-NN) · Machine Learning (ML)

1 Introduction

Early stages of diseases have historically been difficult to detect before developing further. Due to few symptoms and often none that are noticeable, this kind of problem is precisely one of the greatest contributors to the high diabetes rates in the US and around the world, with a projected 700 million cases around the world by 2045 [1].

The great benefit of detecting a disease such as diabetes in its early stages is that it is much easier to take preventive actions. In the case of lung cancer, being able to detect lung cancer in its early stages can allow for early treatments, which can increase the chance of survival from 30% to 92% in the better-case scenarios [2].

With highly precise sensors, the possibility of using breath analysis for distinguishing between healthy and diseased metabolic states is possible [3]. Diabetic Ketoacidosis is a condition that develops alongside diabetes [4]. It is caused by the body's inability to transport glucose from the blood to the cells, and instead,

A. Alsadoon et al. (Eds.): CSCE 2025, CCIS 2935, pp. 157–169, 2026.
https://doi.org/10.1007/978-3-032-22199-5_11

burning fat for energy. The process of burning fat produces various byproducts, however, the ones that are of interest are the ketones. The increased concentration of ketones in the blood causes a condition called "ketosis," and that directly leads to "ketoacidosis," where the ketones are able to make their way into the lungs, where they are breathed out [4]. This is key to breath analysis as with this condition, certain VOCs are increased. With the use of a device that can measure the concentration of VOCs, a basic "diagnosis" tool can be created.

Acetone is one of the main biomarkers of T1DM (type 1 diabetes). Sensing the acetone selectively, however, can prove to be quite impractical for the "low cost" application for the reasons discussed in [6]. The human breath consists of over 2000 VOCs, and selectively sensing only acetone is very challenging. For this reason, an untargeted approach will be used for classifying the sensor readings [5].

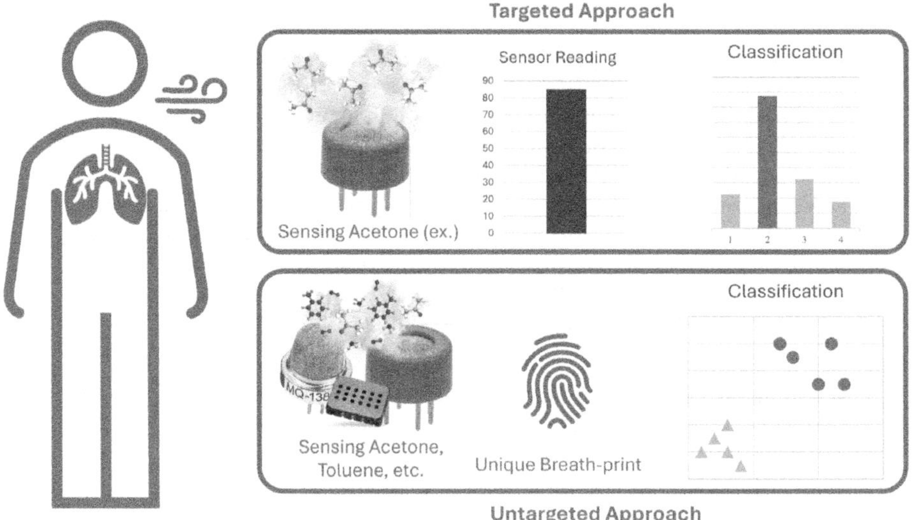

Fig. 1. The process of diagnosing someone is shown when comparing a targeted method to an untargeted method. The targeted method consists of looking for readings past a preset threshold and targeting a specific compound, while the untargeted method uses a multitude of readings from multiple compounds to set a threshold or calculate the confidence of its guess.

Figure 1 shows the difference between the targeted approach and the untargeted approach. An untargeted approach, as the name suggests, will not target a specific compound, but rather multiple compounds at once. When using this approach, the specific level of each VOC won't be known, as all of the compounds are detected at once using a much more general and less specialized sensor. The benefit of using untargeted detection lies in data analysis. Once many sensors are used for scanning the breath, multiple clusters can be detected in different concentrations. Those concentrations can be considered the breath print of a patient

[5,7]. The breath print can be compared to a healthy control group, at which point deviation from the norm becomes the way of telling abnormalities [5,7]. In [8,9], the authors used the untargeted approach for detecting lung cancer.

This paper proposed improving the prototype breathalyzer system from [6], which uses a set of 6 sensors to measure the breath chemicals such as Acetone, Toluene, Xylene, Benzene, Ethanol, Carbon Monoxide, and Nitric Oxide. The system first collects the VOCs of the subjects. It then implements a machine learning algorithm to recognize abnormal patterns in the breath prints. The improvements aim to prove the feasibility of a non-invasive, general screening device that could be employed in hospitals or emergency rooms as a tool used to detect the possibility of abnormalities. With the use of an ML algorithm, this abnormality could be classified, and the right diagnosis plan could be made.

The paper will be structured into 2 main sections: design and improvements, and data architecture sections. Each section will provide insight into the breath analyzer's inner workings, discussing the hardware and the software, respectively. Additionally, an in-depth analysis of how to take a test is described in the Architecture Improvements section.

2 Design and Improvement of the Sampling Device

One of the primary improvements made to this version of the prototype is that a lot of components have been moved directly to a custom-made PCB. The breath analyzer electronics consist of three layers: power, main, and sensor. They are all connected using cables and header pins between them to allow power and data transfer.

This Section will discuss the hardware used, the design choices made at each layer, and how they work together to improve the device's function, reliability, and repairability.

2.1 Power Layer

The power layer's main job is to provide clean 5 V of power to various parts of the device. This is done with 4 linear regulators. The reason for the use of 4 isn't only to avoid running the risk of breaking a regulator under load, but also to keep the temperature relatively low. By using 4 regulators, the power efficiency is decreased significantly, however, it removes the need for an active cooling system (Fig. 2).

The power is supplied from a 3.7V lithium-ion battery stored at the bottom of the device. The battery has a capacity of 8Ah, allowing the device to run for roughly 3 h. The device draws a total of around 2.3 A when resting and up to 2.5 A when under heavy use. This means that the power draw is around 8 W. Most of the power is drawn by the sensors. Therefore, the three largest sensors use their dedicated power regulator to maintain a lower temperature.

The battery can be charged using a charging module that can be supplied with up to 2.1 A at around 5 V, which is just enough to provide enough power to

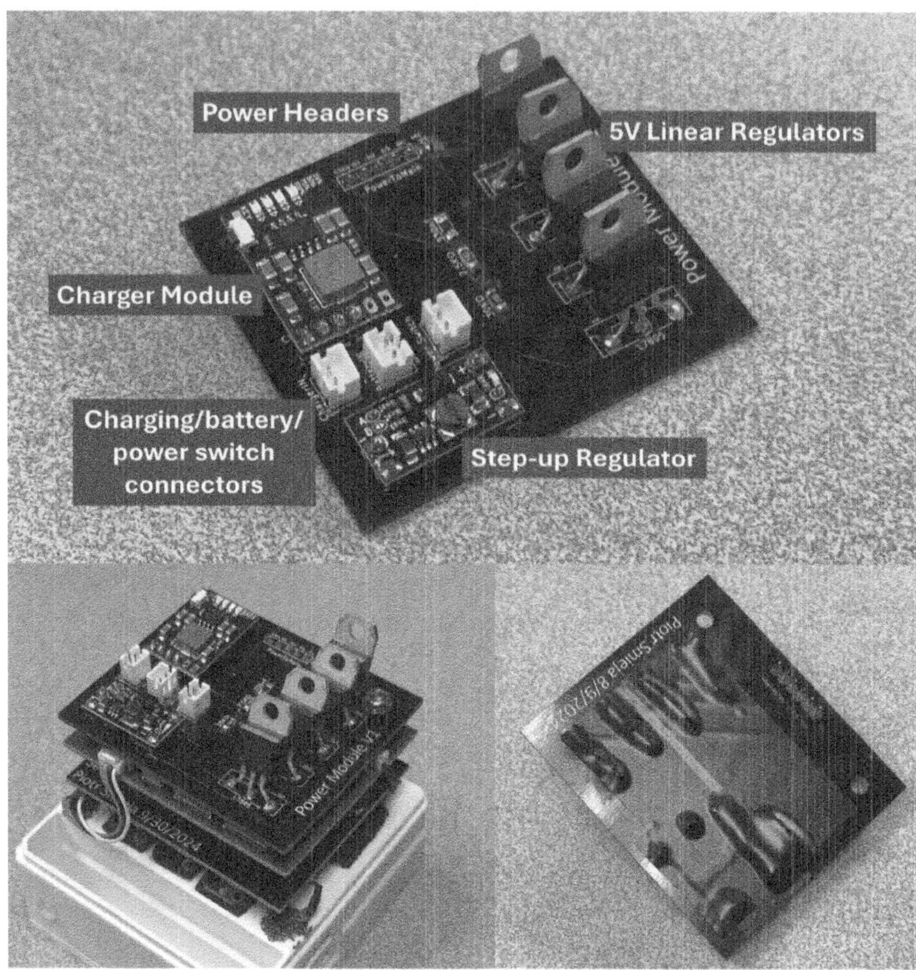

Fig. 2. The power is supplied to the device with a 3.7 V single-cell LiPo battery. In order to provide steady 5 V for the systems, the battery is first stepped up to 8V with a switching regulator, and then, using LDOs, regulated down to 5 V.

run and charge the device at the same time. On the side of the casing, a Type C USB cable can be used to charge the battery with any 5 V supply.

Previously, the power system also utilized 4 linear voltage regulators, however, the power was supplied by a single-use 9V battery with a capacity of only 5 W-hours compared with nearly 30 W-hours of capacity of the new rechargeable battery. Furthermore, in order for the older prototype to be used powered from a constant supply, it must be opened up, the connection must be switched to a special adapter, and only then used with a 120 V AC to 9 V DC adapter. The new design implements a standard 5V DC port on the side that can be used with the device enabled and in use.

An additional feature on the PCB is a voltage divider that is used to tell the microcontroller the current battery voltage. The output of the divider has its own header pin at the top of the device, right next to the 4 outputs of the power regulators, and a shared ground.

2.2 Controller/Main Layer

The receiver of all data and other peripherals is the Main layer. It utilizes an Arduino 33 BLE as the processor that does all of the graphics, data logging, and Bluetooth connectivity (discussed in the following section) (Fig. 3).

The top of the board has pin headers for power, ground, and battery level indication. The power trace as it goes into the MCU has a decoupling capacitor to remove any high-frequency noise coming from the power board.

Due to a conflict between the need for ADCs and I2C pins (they are shared), a multiplexer is used to switch 2 of the analog sensor inputs into just one ADC. This allows for the use of I2C, which is used for the BMP390 sensor inside the sample chamber. The remaining devices, such as the display and the SD card, communicate over SPI. Connectors on the bottom of the board allow for interfacing and connecting the peripheral devices, such as a button or fan.

This layer serves as the "brain" of the devices, and it is sandwiched between the other two layers.

The hardware on the previous device is different, as it makes use of a slower microcontroller and is made to fit an unreliable and difficult-to-manufacture prototyping board. The newer PCB design not only allows for easy hardware upgradability, but also for much easier manufacture as it only requires assembly with off-the-shelf components. The previous board was additionally assembled with interference fits, which would sometimes come loose and cause a hardware failure and require device maintenance; a custom PCB rids of these issues.

2.3 Sensor Layer

To conduct tests, the sensor layer uses a mix of sensor sockets and pin headers to connect sensors. It has two rows of input headers: the power/ground and the sensor outputs. It is interfaced with the casing of the device with strips of neoprene that act as seals and keep the electronics sealed from the sampling chamber. This layer has additional mounting holes too, not only securing it at the top but also at the bottom, such that the sensors seal well against the neoprene seal (Fig. 4).

The prototype is designed in such a way that the three large sensors are inserted through the chamber, while the three smaller ones are pressed against the neoprene on the electronics side. This was done to simplify the design and keep all sensitive electronics inside the relatively dry electronics section. Furthermore, this kind of design allows the sensors to be rapidly interchangeable in case of maintenance or switching sensor configurations. This is a big improvement from the previous prototype that featured semi-permanently glued sensors.

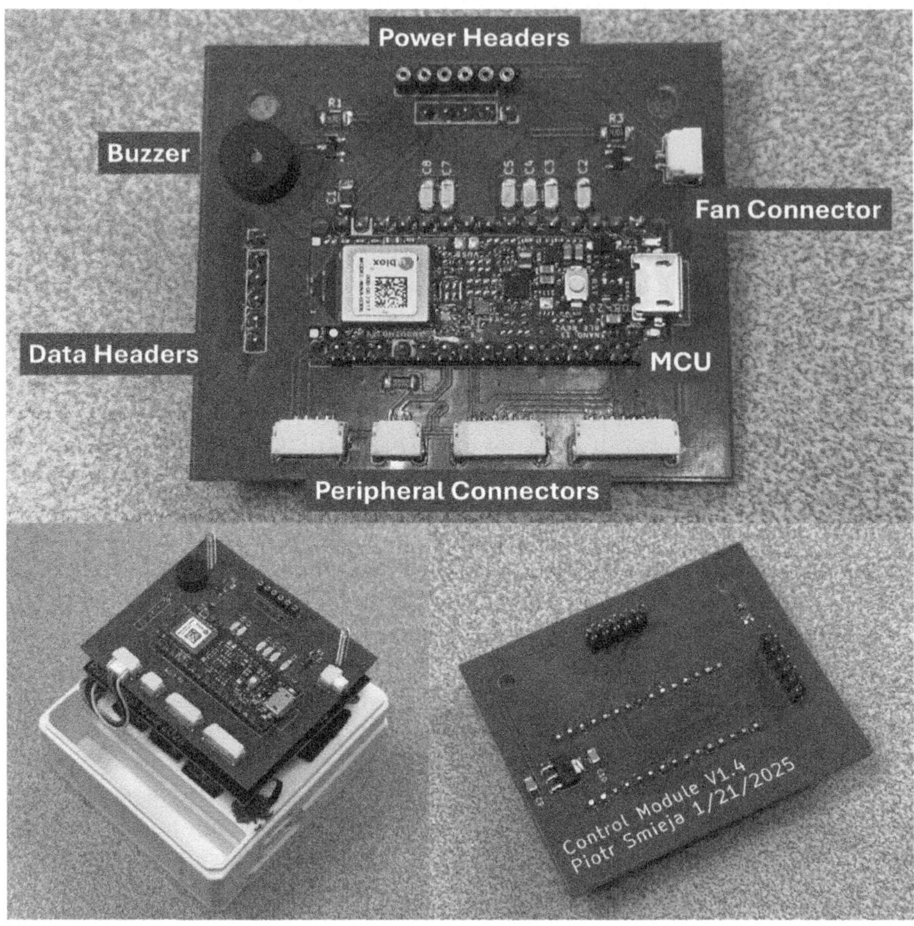

Fig. 3. The main layer pictured is the main processor of the device and utilizes an Arduino NANO 33 BLE for its easy integration, and fully integrated BLE capabilities. The board has additional filtering capacitors for the data lines, transistors for driving the higher current buzzer and fan, and additional headers for devices like the pressure sensor, display, button, and SD card. The back of the board holds a 3.3 V regulator for all 3 V logic devices on the board.

3 Architecture Improvements

The primary purpose of this particular device is its capability of rapid testing. This has previously been done in [6] with the use of an SD card being transferred from the device to a computer that runs a MATLAB script with ML algorithms ready for data analysis. This device uses an entirely different architecture that significantly improves the time to results and does not require a dedicated computer.

Fig. 4. The sensor layer is pictured. It utilizes two different methods of mounting two different kinds of sensors. The bottom sockets are for smaller breakouts (MEMS devices), and the top three circular sockets are made for larger stand-alone MOS sensors.

3.1 Conducting a Test

To conduct a test, a new mouthpiece is used. The subject exhales all of the air from their lungs into the device, and the device automatically takes readings and saves the data to an onboard SD card that can be used to access the full and raw readings from the sensors for each subject. At the end of the test, the mouthpiece is discarded. Figure 5 shows the device in its testing configuration and shows a diagram overview of the testing process.

Stage 1. The device enters stage 1 when it is enabled. This is the warm-up stage, and it consists of running the heaters inside the sensor covers to get the sensing element up to temperature for reliable readings. Skipping the time required for

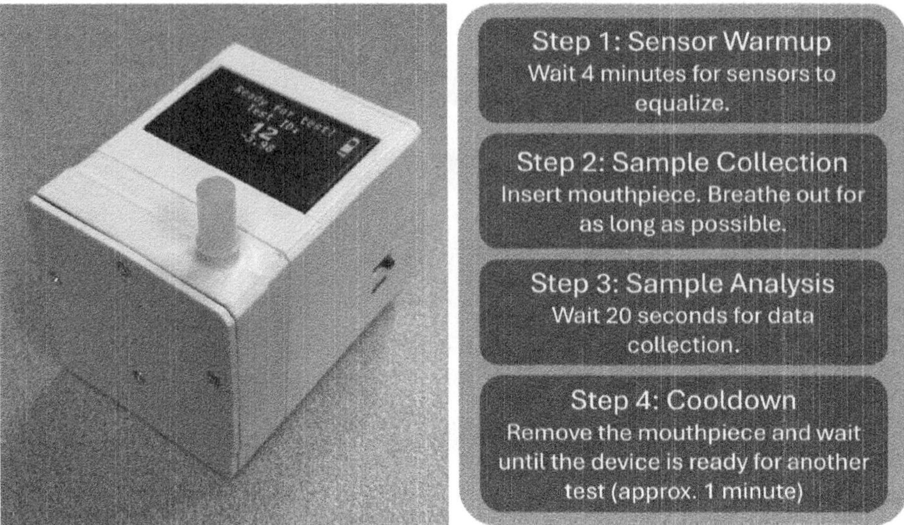

Fig. 5. The device in its test configuration is shown on the left. The mouthpiece is inserted at the top of the device and is to be removed and discarded after each use. On the right, steps are listed respectively to the content of the Conducting a Test section.

the warm-up can lead to incorrect and unreliable readings. It lasts for 4 min, although this step is only required upon the initial enabling of the device.

This is the same as the previous prototype that also used a 4-minute warm-up time. There is no workaround this time without switching the particular sensors used for different ones.

Stage 2. The second stage is initiated as soon as the subject blows into the mouthpiece. The pressure sensor inside the test chamber senses the increased pressure caused by the exhaling and immediately calibrates or "zeros out" the sensor readings. This is done by saving an offset that is later subtracted from all readings. Next, an asynchronous counter is started to wait until 7 s are up. This step does not have a set timer, however, the person can breathe out for any amount of time so long as the pressure inside the chamber is high enough. When the pressure drops below a set threshold, or the 7 s is up, this step is automatically concluded, and the device moves to the next stage. The reason for the "sample collection" being able to be variable length is not only to accommodate ease of use, but also because it is simply unnecessary, as the deep lung air (which is of interest) is only exhaled at the end of the breath. For some people, this could be 10 s, for some, and for others, 4 s. This step ensures that the final air inside the chamber is the deep lung air.

This step is done very differently from the previous prototype, which has a fixed time and chamber pressure that the subject must maintain. This proved to be quite problematic due to the issues described above. Additionally, maintaining the correct pressure inside caused problematic readings that could falsely end the test prematurely and resulting in wasted time. These improvements address all of these issues.

Stage 3. The third stage is the stage where the readings are taken. It is a fixed 20-second period. In this period, the device quickly takes as many samples as it can and saves them to the SD card. The data from this stage is the most important, and this is what will contain all the information necessary for the ML algorithm later on.

The 20-second sampling period is the same as the previous prototype. This part of the architecture is not the same, however, as this is the only time that the new one logs the data, while the previous began it earlier in Stage 2. This should make no difference, however, as the area of interest is well within these 20 s.

Stage 4. The final stage is the "cooldown" stage, and in this stage, the device enables the fan to vent the air through the chamber to aid the retry process if necessary or the process of taking another test. More importantly, however, in this step, the device reads the SD card data and searches for the data with the current ID. Then, saves the section of the most recent test to a different file after it has been averaged. This second file stores the final sample with the values that will be sent through Bluetooth in the next section. This on-board post-processing allows the device to send far less data through BLE and makes the process significantly simpler.

This prototype features a much faster Stage 4, with the cooldown being significantly reduced by the active venting provided by the electric fan. The previous prototype has a cooling time of 3 to 4 min, while this one has a cooling time of 1 min.

3.2 Data Flow

This section discusses how the data is manipulated after it has been taken and saved. On a low level, the architecture can be divided into 3 devices working together: the breathalyzer, the Android application running on a smartphone, and Google's Firebase servers.

The breathalyzer stages have been discussed in "Conducting a Test". Assuming that the device has successfully taken and saved a sample, it can now move on to sending the sample for analysis.

This begins with the breathalyzer saving the sample as a string that is transferred to the smartphone using BLE. An application that can receive the data and display it by the subject ID or PaID (patient identification) has been developed for this purpose. The application allows the user to select which test is going to be tested and to input additional information about the subject such as age, weight, or sex (while at the moment this information doesn't contribute to the results, having it saved allows for potential differentiation between various subpopulations and thus getting even more accurate readings in the future). This data is sent to the Google Firestore Cloud, which is a Google-based database that is integrated into the Google Firebase.

Firebase offers many different products, however, the "Cloud Functions" is used in this project for simple deployment and a very well-integrated API into Firestore. As soon as a new or updated sample has been uploaded to the Firestore, the Cloud Function identifies it and saves the data locally for its own use. Using a Python script, it normalizes the data against the previously provided training dataset and uses that data for ML-based classification. The k-nearest neighbors algorithm is executed, and the script saves the results to Firestore in a separate collection.

Finally, the application on the phone checks whether the results are ready. Once there, it accesses the database and pulls out the predicted classifications and confidence values. This entire process, from connecting to the breathalyzer to retrieving a result, can take about 30 s.

Figure 6 shows the utilized low-level architecture with numbered steps. The process of uploading and retrieving a test consists of eight steps, three of which are transfers between systems.

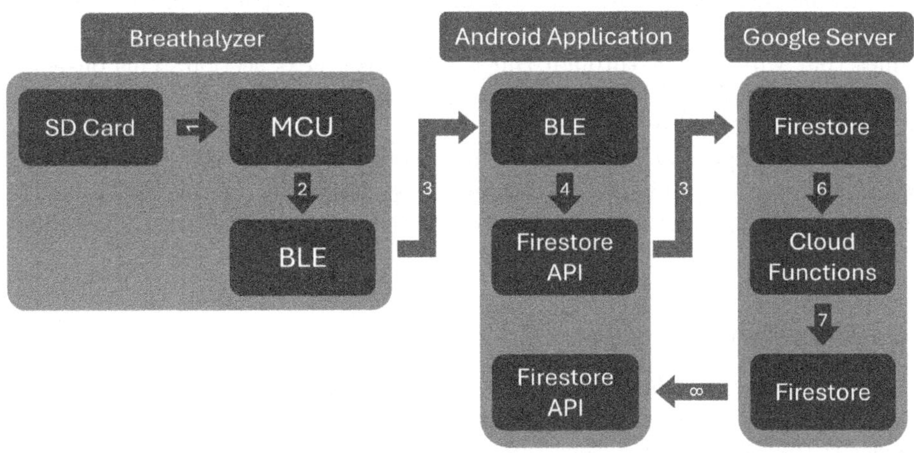

Fig. 6. New tested architecture consists of the breathalyzer, mobile phone with a special application, and Google's Firebase servers. The application written in Android Studio uses the Firebase API to communicate with the servers.

Android Application. The application interface is presented in Fig. 7. The user first connects to the peripheral (in this case, it's the breathalyzer). Once connected, clicking the button "Load Tests" sends a command to the peripheral to send over the preprocessed samples one by one. Each is sent with a PaID and the corresponding data. The communication is terminated by the peripheral when it sends an "end line" command to the central device (in this case, the smartphone).

Once the data has all been retrieved, the user is presented with various samples to test. To perform a test, the user selects a sample and clicks the "Run Test" option. This opens a new window in which the user enters the subject's age, height, and weight. Clicking the "Run Test" button begins the test. After 2 s, the application allows the user to click the "View Test" button, which prints the test results at the bottom of the screen.

The test results consist of 3 fields: PaID, result, and confidence. The PaID is the ID of the subject tested. The result is the overwhelming classification from the ML model that was run with Google Cloud Functions. In this case, the result can be a 0 for healthy or 1 for diabetic class. The confidence field is based on the ML algorithm's confidence in its guess. This confidence would rarely be 1 in real life with a very extensive database or a well-trained model. However, this confidence is ultimately the most important trait of the results, as this is what suggests the subject to get tested or not.

The Android application for this project is written in Android Studio and uses Kotlin. The device that runs the simulation is a Samsung Galaxy A15.

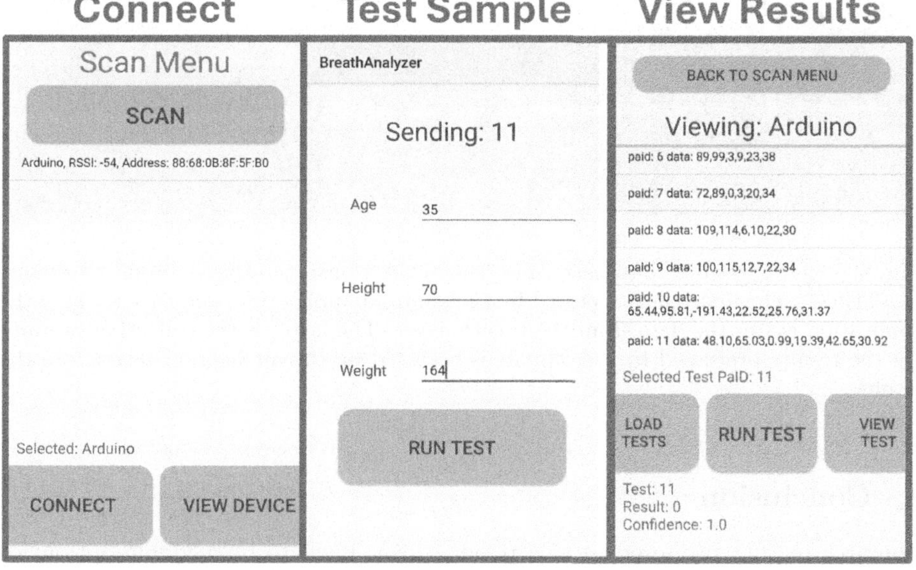

Fig. 7. The user interface so submitting a test with the use the Android mobile application. The use has the ability to connect to a specific device, load tests, input information, conduct a test, and read the results.

Google Server. A screenshot of what the console interface for Firebase looks like is present in Fig. 8. The user is allowed to add, delete, and modify entries manually, however, all actions are taken from the Android application through the Firebase API. This allows remote and direct access to the database.

As soon as a new entry is made or is modified, a cloud function is triggered. This is written in Python with the use of Visual Studio Code and uploaded to the server through a terminal interface. The script that runs automatically writes the results to another collection, labeling the entry with the appropriate PaID that the application uses to identify the test.

This code is the simplest of all three systems, with only around 100 lines compared to 600 for the embedded C++ breathalyzer code and well over 2000 for the application. This being said, everything has to be very carefully connected to the project to give the terminal interface sufficient access to write the project and server.

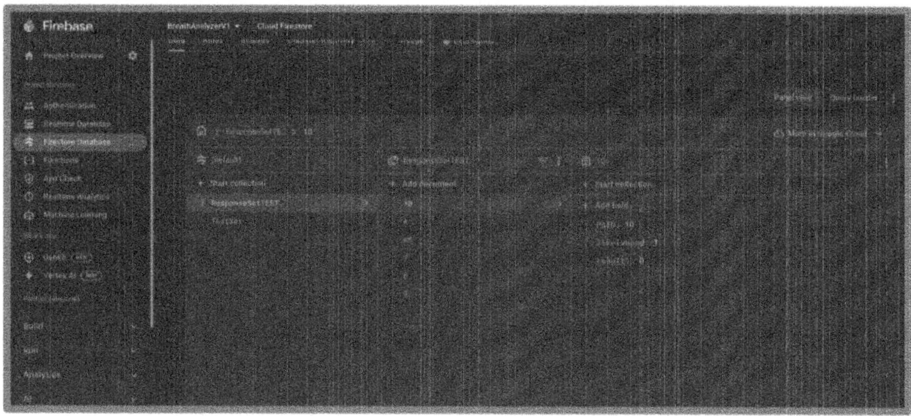

Fig. 8. The Firestore database has two collections: "TestSet" and "ResponseSetTEST". The first one is accessed by the Android application, and this is where the application writes the data from the breathalyzer. The latter is the collection containing the results processed by a script. It is accessed by the application to retrieve the results.

4 Conclusion

The architecture proposed in this paper proves itself to be a viable option for rapid testing and rapid detection of diseases. Additionally, the improvements to the breathalyzer only further prove that the tests can be done rapidly. The improved architecture allows users to view their results within 30 s, greatly improving the test-to-results time. With enough data in the database to train the ML algorithms, this can prove itself to be an effective tool for aiding doctors' decision-making or even any other ordinary person's ability to make decisions on what to get tested for.

5 Future Works

In the following works, the efforts will be focused on utilizing more advanced ML algorithms from [6]. Additionally, a greater dataset collection will be required to fully prove the viability of the device, such as the repeatability, limit of detection in early detection, and differentiation between other conditions from type 1 diabetes.

Acknowledgment. This paper was financially supported by ELPSG (Engaged Learning to Promote STEM Graduation). This included part of the travel and material/supply costs.

Disclosure of Interests. The authors have no competing interests to declare that are relevant to the content of this article.

References

1. CDC. Diabetes Tests. Centers for Disease Control and Prevention. https://www.cdc.gov/diabetes/basics/getting-tested.html. Accessed 23 Feb 2023
2. Morgan, K.K.: Lung Cancer Survival Rates & Stages. WebMD, Nov. 04, 2023. https://www.webmd.com/lung-cancer/lung-cancer-survival-rates
3. Lourenço, C., Turner, C.: Breath analysis in disease diagnosis: methodological considerations and applications. Metabolites **4**(2), 465–498 (2014). https://doi.org/10.3390/metabo4020465
4. CDC. Diabetic Ketoacidosis. Centers for Disease Control and Prevention. https://www.cdc.gov/diabetes/basics/diabetic-ketoacidosis.html. Accessed 23 Feb 2023
5. Dixit, K., Fardindoost, S., Ravishankara, A., Tasnim, N., Hoorfar, M.: Exhaled Breath Analysis for Diabetes Diagnosis and Monitoring: Relevance, Challenges and Possibilities. Biosensors **11**(12), 476 (2021). https://doi.org/10.3390/bios11120476
6. Smieja, P.J., Lu, J., Sun, Q., Fu, X., Zhang, T.: Exhaled breath analysis based diabetes detection with k-nearest neighbors classifier. IEEE Xplore (2023). https://doi.org/10.1109/iscid59865.2023.00037
7. Kaloumenou, M., Skotadis, E., Lagopati, N., Efstathopoulos, E., Tsoukalas, D.: Breath analysis: a promising tool for disease diagnosis-the role of sensors. Sensors **22**(3), 1238 (2022). https://doi.org/10.3390/s22031238
8. Binson, V.A., Subramoniam, M.: Artificial intelligence based breath analysis system for the diagnosis of lung cancer. J. Phys: Conf. Ser. **1950**(1), 012065 (2021). https://doi.org/10.1088/1742-6596/1950/1/012065
9. Marzorati, D., Mainardi, L., Sedda, G., Gasparri, R., Spaggiari, L., Cerveri, P.: MOS sensors array for the discrimination of lung cancer and At-risk subjects with exhaled breath analysis. Chemosensors **9**(8), 209 (2021). https://doi.org/10.3390/chemosensors9080209

Novel Composite Nerve Guidance Conduits with Controlled Degradation and Drug Release for Peripheral Nerve Regeneration

Deepak Khare, Jiaying Wang, and Xiaojun Yu(✉)

Department of Biomedical Engineering, Stevens Institute of Technology, Hoboken, NJ 07030, USA
xyu@stevens.edu

Abstract. Peripheral nerve injury (PNI) refers to the situation where the peripheral nervous system is broken due to trauma, inflammation and other reasons. Due to the weak regeneration ability of nerves, nerves cannot repair themselves in large-interval nerve injuries. Although the traditional treatment methods of autologous transplantation and allogeneic transplantation have good efficacy, they are limited by insufficient donors, inflammation, and complications. The nerve guide catheter (NGC) has become a potential solution for the treatment of PNI. In this study, a new type of NGC was developed using solvent casting and ion cross-linking methods. Polycaprolactone (PCL) and chitosan were used as materials to make a PCL-chitosan hybrid catheter with a spiral structure. The morphology, porosity, degradation and mechanical properties of this NGC were tested, and in vitro bovine serum albumin (BSA) release and Schwann cell biocompatibility were studied. The results showed that compared with pure PCL-NGC without chitosan, PCL-chitosan NGC showed better biocompatibility, drug release characteristics and degradability, and met the mechanical strength requirements required for transplantation. This shows that PCL-chitosan NGC has the potential to become one of the good materials for the treatment of PNI. This study proves the feasibility and better effect of the synergistic use of PCL and chitosan and provides new ideas for material design in the field of peripheral nerve repair.

Keywords: Nerve guidance conduits · Peripheral nerve injury · PCL-chitosan

1 Introduction

The peripheral nervous system plays a crucial role in generating sensation and movement by transmitting signals from the central nervous system to surrounding organs [1, 2]. Peripheral nerve injuries (PNI) caused by accidents or disease are a significant clinical challenge and can result in the loss of function or disorder mediated by the injured nerve. Also, the nerve regeneration process after injury is slow and unstable. The available treatment options are autografts, allografts and synthetic nerve guidance conduits, but each has some limitations [3, 4]. Autografts and allografts can lead to secondary surgery/donor side morbidity and risk of immune rejection, respectively [1,

A. Alsadoon et al. (Eds.): CSCE 2025, CCIS 2935, pp. 170–180, 2026.
https://doi.org/10.1007/978-3-032-22199-5_12

5]. Nerve guidance conduits (NGC) have gained attention as a promising alternative, offering biochemical cues, structural support as well as stability to promote nerve regeneration [6–9]. Researchers are promoting natural materials such as chitosan, collagen, silk fibroin and gelatin, for nerve regeneration application because of their non-toxic behavior and biocompatibility [10–15]. Particularly, the physiochemical characteristics of chitosan such as the rheological properties and deacetylation degree are comparable to natural glycosaminoglycans and amino groups, respectively and therefore promotes its cytocompatibility against neuronal cells [16–18]. Also, chitosan has been studied as a potential candidate as nerve guidance conduits, evidenced by sciatic nerve defect repair in small animal model studies [19–21]. Despite having several advantages, brittleness at dry state, uncontrolled degradation and poor mechanical properties make challenging the preparation of chitosan-based nerve guidance conduits [22, 23].

Polycaprolactone (PCL) is a biocompatible, biodegradable polymer with excellent mechanical strength and low degradability [24]. However, high hydrophobicity limits its compatibility with cells [25].

It has been suggested that the nerve guidance should have sufficient strength to support the regenerated nerve with in vivo degradability. In this view, the current study investigates the fabrication and characterization of polycaprolactone (PCL)-chitosan composite conduits and chitosan-only conduits for potential applications in nerve regeneration. PCL-chitosan and chitosan sheets were prepared using solvent casting, followed by ionic crosslinking and rolling them up into spiral conduits. Morphological analysis was conducted to evaluate structural integrity, while porosity was measured to access scaffold architecture. In vitro biodegradation studies were performed for the comparison of degradation rates of the prepared conduits. Bovine serum albumin release studies were conducted to access drug release profile. Mechanical testing was performed to measure the tensile strength and elasticity. In vitro assessment of biocompatibility of the prepared conduits was determined by culturing with Schwann cells in the form of attachment and proliferation.

2 Experimental Procedure

2.1 Sample Preparation

For the preparation of polycaprolactone (PCL) – chitosan composite conduit in current research, PCL (details, origin) and chitosan (details, origin) were used as raw materials. Primarily, 3% (w/v) of chitosan powder was dissolved in a mixture (at a 30/70 volume ratio) of acetic acid and formic acid at ambient temperature using magnetic stirring. Following this, 6% (w/v) of PCL was added to the prepared solution. The complete dissolution of PCL-chitosan into the acidic solution takes about 8 h. The homogeneous solution of PCL-chitosan was poured into a petri-dishes and left to dry at ambient temperature for 8 h to form rectangular sheets. The concentrations of PCL and chitosan were determined after optimization which helps in producing uniform solution and makes the composite sheet easy to peeled off after drying. After drying, PCL-chitosan composite sheets were soaked in 0.2 M NaOH (sodium hydroxide) solution for 2 h. NaOH aqueous solution was used for ionic crosslinking to enhance the flexibility and mechanical strength of PCL-chitosan sheet [26–28]. Thereafter, the PCL-chitosan sheets were washed five times with deionized water. To form conduits, the PCL-chitosan sheets were combined with 1% (w/v) poly vinyl alcohol membrane and rolled from one side onto a 20G needle to form a spiral structure. Following this, the PCL-chitosan and PVA sheets were housed in copper sheets and immersed in water for overnight. It dissolves the PVA layer and produced spiral structured conduits. Thereafter, the obtained conduits were dried at 40 °C overnight.

For the preparation of chitosan-based conduits, chitosan powder was dissolved into a mixture (at a 30/70 volume ratio) of acetic acid and formic acid at ambient temperature using magnetic stirring. The homogenous solution of chitosan was poured into a petri-dishes. After drying of sheet, cross-linking was performed using 0.2 M NaOH. Following this, chitosan sheets were combined with 1% (w/v) poly vinyl alcohol membrane and rolled from one side onto a 20G needle to form a spiral structure. Following this, the PCL-chitosan and PVA sheets were housed in copper sheets and immersed in water for overnight. It dissolves the PVA layer and produced spiral structured conduits. Thereafter, the obtained conduits were dried at room temperature. Schematic demonstrating the steps included in the preparation of PCL-chitosan or chitosan only conduits (Fig. 1).

2.2 Morphological Analyses

The morphology of prepared PCL-chitosan and chitosan conduits was analyzed using stereomicroscope (details, origin). The images were captured to obtain the top and side view of prepared conduits.

2.3 Porosity Measurement

For porosity measurement of prepared PCL-chitosan and chitosan samples, the conduit was initially immersed in a known volume (V1) of ethanol. After immersion of conduit, the volume was recorded as V2. Thereafter, the liquid-perfused conduit was removed, and final volume was recorded as V3. The porosity rate (PR) of the scaffolds was determined using the following Eq. (1)

$$\text{Porosity}\ \% = [(V1 - V3)/(V2 - V3) \times 100] \tag{1}$$

V1 = initial volume, V2 = volume after immersion of conduit, V3 = volume after removal of conduit.

For porosity measurement, six conduits were used.

2.4 Degradation Test

In vitro degradation test was carried out on PCL-chitosan and chitosan conduits. For this purpose, the conduits were immersed in phosphate buffer saline or PBS (10 mg/ml) for different period of time at 37 °C. The initial mass of conduit was recorded as W_o and the mass of conduit after a specific time interval was recorded as W_t. The weight loss from conduits can be calculated using the Eq. (2)

$$\text{Weight loss}\ \% = [W_i - W_t] * 100/W_i \tag{2}$$

W_i = initial weight of conduit, W_t = weight of dried conduit after taking out from PBS after time t.

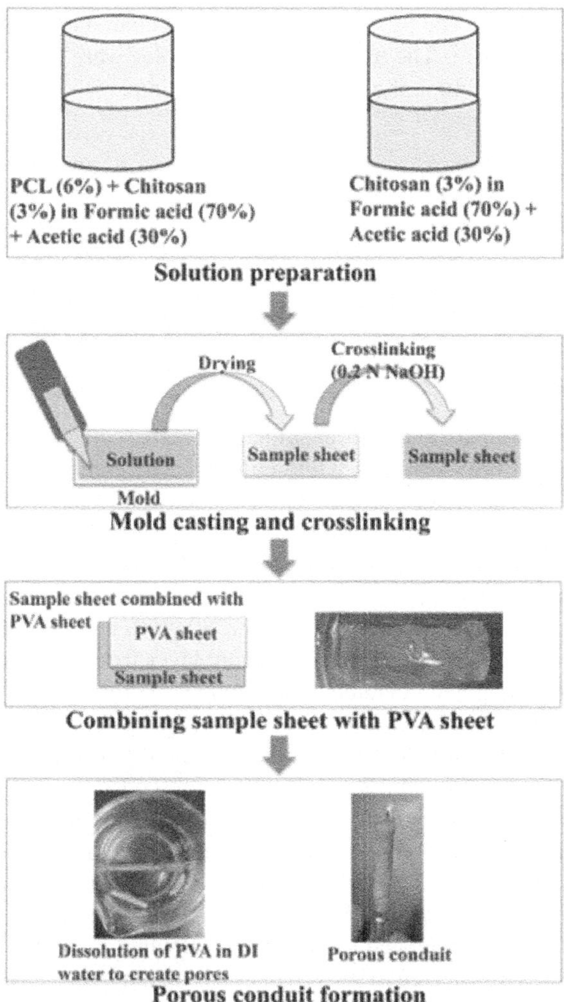

Fig. 1. Schematic representing the methodological steps for the preparation of PCL-chitosan or chitosan only conduits. The solutions for PCL-chitosan and chitosan only conduits were prepared in 70:30% of formic acid: acetic acid. The solution was poured into mold, dried and crosslinked in 0.2 M NaOH. The obtain sheet was combined with 1% PVA sheet and roll them up in needle to form conduit. The obtain conduit was combined with copper sheet and then kept in DI water overnight to dissolve PVA sheet and to form porosity. Thereafter, the obtain conduit was dried.

2.5 BSA Release Profile

To obtain the protein release profile for prepared PCL-chitosan and chitosan only conduits, bovine serum albumin (BSA) aided conduits were prepared. For this purpose, 2 mg/ml of BSA was incorporated to the PCL-chitosan solution as well as chitosan solution. Thereafter, this solution was used to prepare the conduits with BSA using the previously discussed procedure. The conduits with BSA were immersed in PBS for different time interval. The protein released from prepared conduits were measured using protein estimation kit. The absorbance for samples were recorded using ELISA microplate reader (Microtek) at the wavelength of 562 nm.

2.6 Mechanical Testing

The mechanical characterization for prepared PCL-chitosan composite conduits were performed using uniaxial tensile test (Instron, Norwood, MA, USA). The strain rate was applied as 1 mm/min. The elastic modulus was determined from the slope of stress-strain curve. The tensile strength was measured from stress-strain curve at failure point.

2.7 Cellular Response

Cell culture study was performed to examine the nerve cell growth ability of PCL-chitosan and chitosan only conduits while cultured with Schwann cells. Glass cover slip was used as a control for comparison. The Schwann cells were procured from Thermo. The Schwann cells were cultured in DMEM medium (Dulbecco's modified eagle medium, Gibco) supplemented with 10% fetal bovine serum (FBS, Gibco) and antibiotics (1%, Antibiotic-Antimycotic, Gibco) in growth environment (37 °C, 5% CO_2 and relative humidity: 95%) in T-75 flask. After, 80–90% confluency, 0.25% Trypsin-EDTA (Gibco) was added to detach the cells monolayer from the flask. Thereafter, the cells were counting using hemocytometer and optical microscope.

The cytocompatibility of PCL-chitosan and chitosan only conduits were excess quantitatively and qualitatively using cell titer blue assay and fluorescence microscopic imaging, respectively. For this purpose, 2×10^4 cells were seeded to each conduits and then incubated in growth environment and medium in 24 well plate. The medium of the sample's well was replaced with fresh medium after every 2–3 days. Cell titer blue assay was performed after 3, 5 and 7 days of incubation. For cell titer blue assay, the medium was replaced with cell titer blue solution (diluted 1:5 v/v in growth medium), after stipulated period of time and incubated for 1 h in growth environment. Following this, the obtained solution was transferred to 96 well plate in triplicates and absorbance was measured using Elisa microplate reader (Biotek) at 560 nm which represents the viability of live cells for sample. For fluorescence microscopy, the medium from each sample was removed and washed with PBS three times. Following this, the cells, adhered on the samples were stained with calcine AM (Component A) and incubated at room temperature for 30–40 min. The images of the cells adhered on the conduits were captured using fluorescence microscope [Nikon].

3 Results and Discussion

3.1 Morphological Analyses

The top and side view of the prepared conduits are illustrated in Fig. 2. The mean outer diameter and length of PCL-chitosan conduits were measured as ~2.5 mm and ~18 mm, respectively. Also, the mean outer diameter and length of chitosan conduits were measured as ~2.0 mm and ~18 mm, respectively.

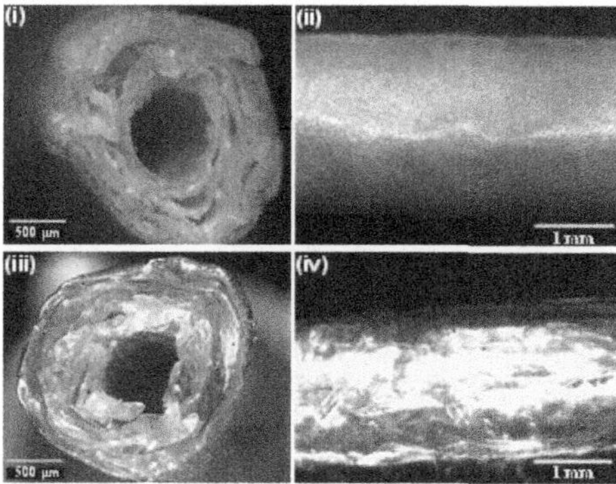

Fig. 2. Stereo microscopy images show the top and side view of PCL-chitosan conduit [(i) & (ii)] and chitosan conduit [(iii) and (iv)]. The top view of conduits is showing spiral structure.

3.2 Porosity Measurement

The porosity of the prepared PCL-chitosan conduits is measured as 40.43 ± 1.92%. However, % Porosity of chitosan conduits is assessed as 46.03 ± 0.91%. The number of samples for this measurement was 6 for each type of sample.

The porosity structure plays a crucial role in the regeneration of soft tissues, as it is essential for supporting the growth of new tissue [29, 30]. Porosity provides conduits with enabled nutrition transport, facilitates substance exchange, flexibility, and supports cell migration.

3.3 Degradation Analyses

Due to in vitro degradation, PCL-chitosan conduits experienced about 30 ± 1.8% reduction in weight, after one month of immersion in PBS (Fig. 3(i)). However, the degradation rate is measured to be about 35 ± 1.9%, just after 10 days of immersion in case of chitosan only conduits (Fig. 3(ii)). The reduction in weight is primarily caused by the degradation of chitosan, whereas the PCL degrades at a slower rate. Therefore, PCL-chitosan conduits are showing slower degradation rate as compared to chitosan only conduits.

3.4 BSA Release Profile

From BSA release profile, it can be observed that the PCL-chitosan conduits are showing upto 0.25 ± 0.01% and 2.5 ± 0.13% release of BSA after 5 h and 7 days of immersion in PBS (Fig. 4(i) and (ii)). However, chitosan conduits exhibiting about 3.57 ± 0.67% and 13% ± 1.28% release of BSA (Fig. 4(iii) and (iv)). From BSA release analyses from the prepared conduits, it can be contemplated that the PCL-chitosan conduits can provide more sustainable release of drug as compared to chitosan only conduits.

3.5 Mechanical Characterizations

The tensile strength and elastic modulus for the PCL-chitosan conduits were calculated to be 11.3 ± 1.1 MPa and 14.7 ± 1.5 MPa (n = 6), respectively.

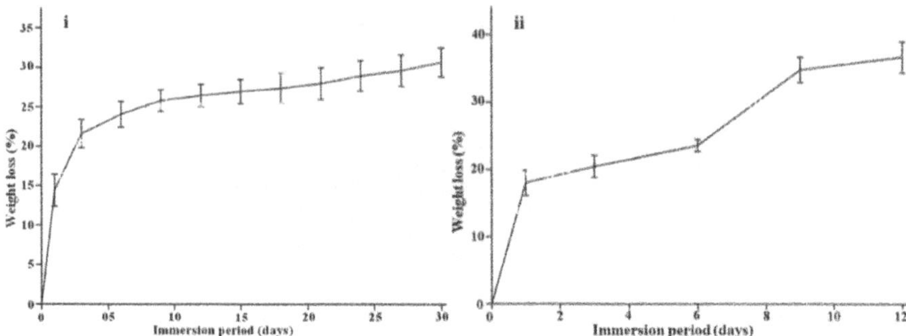

Fig. 3. In vitro degradation performance of (i) PCL-chitosan and (ii) chitosan conduits.

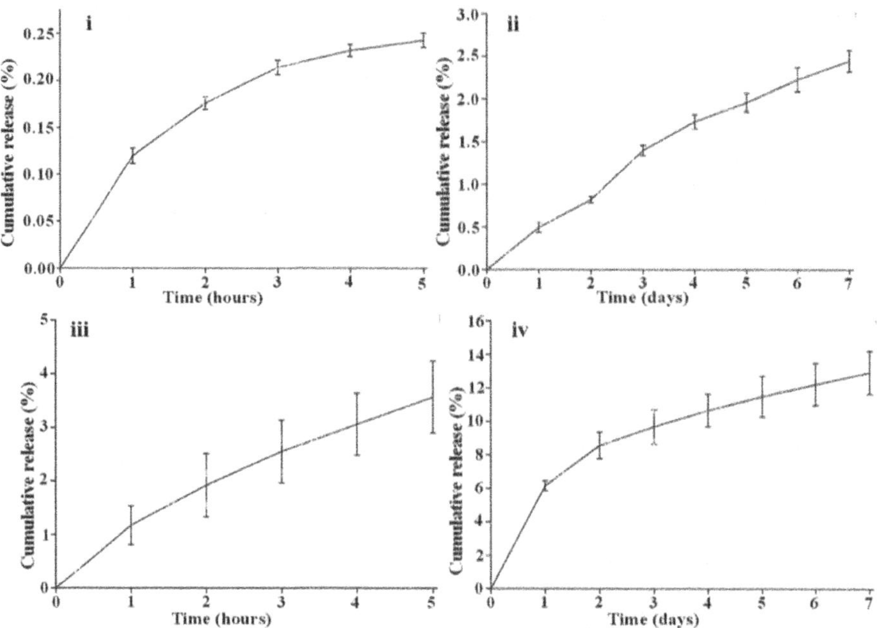

Fig. 4. Cumulative release of BSA protein from PCL-chitosan conduits (i and ii) and chitosan only conduits (iii and iv), added with 1 mg/ml BSA in PBS (n = 4 samples).

3.6 Cell Culture Study

The plots illustrate the viability of Schwann cells on PCL-chitosan and chitosan only conduits, obtained from cell titer blue assay data, after 3, 5 and 7 days of incubation (Fig. 5(a)). Interestingly, it can be observed that there is no significant difference in the viability of Schwann cells among control, chitosan only and PCL-chitosan conduits throughout the incubation period.

The response of Schwann cells on PCL-chitosan and chitosan only conduits was qualitatively measured in terms of adhesion (Fig. 5(a)). The Schwann cells were found to be attached and spread on PCL-chitosan and chitosan only conduits and therefore,

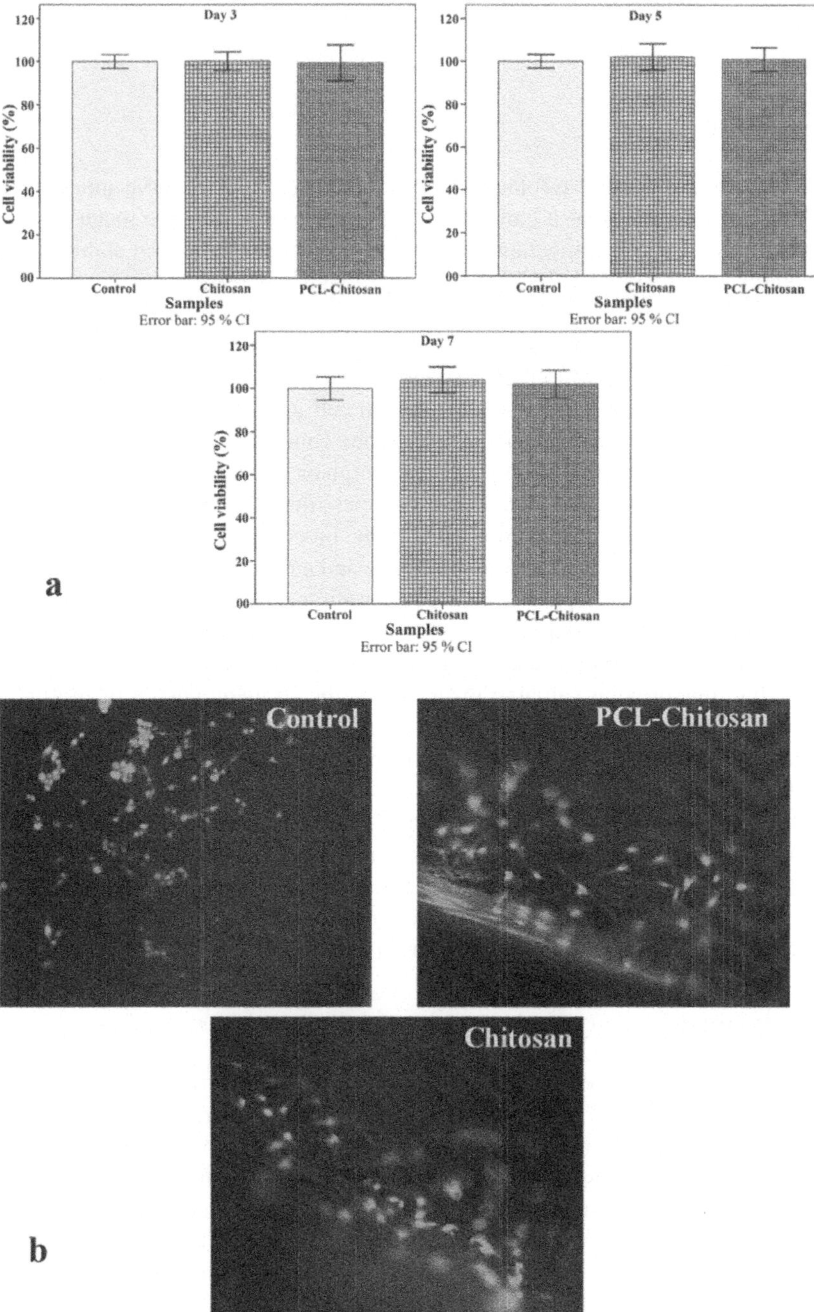

Fig. 5. (**a**) The plots obtained from cell titer blue assay representing the cytocompatibility of PCL-chitosan and chitosan only conduits while cultured with Schwann cells after 3, 5 and 7 days of incubation. (**b**) Fluorescence microscopic images of Schwann cells adhered on PCL-chitosan and chitosan only conduits after 48 h of incubation.

demonstrated that the prepared conduits facilitate the cellular functionality during culture period.

4 Discussion

This study designed a polycaprolactone (PCL)-chitosan hybrid nerve guide catheter (NGC) and demonstrated that it can be used as one of the alternative materials for the treatment of PNI. Excellent mechanical strength ensures its structural stability during transplantation and in vivo. Degradability ensures that it can be naturally degraded by the body and has the sustained release capacity required for carrying drugs, and cytocompatibility testing proves that it can provide the growth space and environment required by nerve cells. Porosity measurements showed that both types of catheters have sufficient porosity required for nutrient exchange and cell growth, while BSA release tests showed that PCL-chitosan catheters exhibit more controllable and sustained protein release properties. This result shows that the synergistic use of polycaprolactone (PCL) and chitosan materials is better than that of catheters made of PCL alone. In summary, the mechanical strength of PCL combined with the biocompatibility and hydrophilicity of chitosan helps to enhance structural durability and sustained release capacity, which is essential for long-term support of axon regeneration. The experimental results highlight the critical role of material composition in influencing the biological performance of NGCs, especially in complex and long-term nerve regeneration scenarios. In addition, these findings provide valuable insights into the strategic design of biofunctionalized scaffolds that integrate mechanical support and controlled drug delivery. Such multifunctional platforms represent a significant advance in the field of neural tissue engineering.

Future studies should focus on improving manufacturing parameters, regulating degradation kinetics, and optimizing drug release profiles to more closely align with the temporal dynamics of nerve healing. In addition, the incorporation of growth factors or neurotrophic agents, as well as in vivo validation using clinically relevant large animal models, are essential to further enhance the translational potential of these structures.

5 Conclusions

In summary, this study shows that polycaprolactone (PCL)-chitosan hybrid nerve guide catheter (NGC) exhibits good performance for long-term peripheral nerve repair. It shows that the synergistic use of materials can play a key role in the biological performance of NGC. For PNI repair, a long-term and complex nerve regeneration environment, polycaprolactone (PCL)-chitosan NGC provides a new material science idea. This study highlights the therapeutic prospects of PCL-chitosan NGC and lays a theoretical foundation for the subsequent development the next-generation medical devices with better nerve repair efficacy.

Acknowledgments. This work was partly supported by the US Army Medical Research Acquisition Activity (USAMRAA) through the CDMRP Peer-Reviewed Medical Research Program (award No. HT9425-24-1-0137), and the National Institutes of Health (award No. R01NS134604).

References

1. Shoykhet, M., Clark, R.S.B.: Chapter 57 – structure, function, and development of the nervous system. In: Fuhrman, B.P., Zimmerman, J.J. (eds.) Pediatric Critical Care, 4th ed., pp. 783–804. Mosby (2011)
2. Gordon, T., Udina, E., Verge, V.M., de Chaves, E.I.: Brief electrical stimulation accelerates axon regeneration in the peripheral nervous system and promotes sensory axon regeneration in the central nervous system. Mot. Control **13**, 412–441 (2009)
3. Siemionow, M., Sonmez, E.: Nerve allograft transplantation: a review. J. Reconstr. Microsurg. **23**, 511–520 (2008)
4. Ray, W.Z., Mackinnon, S.E.: Management of nerve gaps: autografts, allografts, nerve transfers, and end-to-side neurorrhaphy. Exp. Neurol. **223**, 77–85 (2010)
5. Gu, X., Ding, F., Yang, Y., Liu, J.: Construction of tissue engineered never grafts and their application in peripheral never regeneration. Prog. Neurobiol. **93**, 204–230 (2011)
6. Yan, Y., et al.: Implantable nerve guidance conduits: material combinations, multi-functional strategies and advanced engineering innovations. Bioact. Mater. **11**, 57–76 (2022)
7. Yu, X., Bellamkonda, R.V.: Tissue-engineered scaffolds are effective alternatives to autografts for bridging peripheral nerve gaps. Tissue Eng. **9**, 421–430 (2003)
8. Qian, Y., Lin, H., Yan, Z., Shi, J., Fan, C.: Functional nanomaterials in peripheral nerve regeneration: scaffold design, chemical principles and microenvironmental remodeling. Mater. Today **51**, 165–187 (2021)
9. Bianchini, M., Micera, S., Redolfi Riva, E.: Recent advances in polymeric drug delivery systems for peripheral nerve regeneration. Pharmaceutics **15**, 640 (2023)
10. Boecker, A., Daeschler, S.C., Kneser, U., Harhaus, L.: Relevance and recent developments of chitosan in peripheral nerve surgery. Front. Cell. Neurosci. **13**, 104 (2019)
11. Huang, L., et al.: A compound scaffold with uniform longitudinally oriented guidance cues and a porous sheath promotes peripheral nerve regeneration in vivo. Acta Biomater. **68**, 223–236 (2018)
12. Manoukian, O.S., et al.: Biopolymer-nanotube nerve guidance conduit drug delivery for peripheral nerve regeneration: in vivo structural and functional assessment. Bioact. Mater. **6**, 2881–2893 (2021)
13. Redolfi Riva, E., Micera, S.: Progress and challenges of implantable neural interfaces based on nature-derived materials. Bioelectron. Med. **7**, 6 (2021)
14. Varshney, N., Sahi, A.K., Poddar, S., Mahto, S.K.: Soy protein isolate supplemented silk fibroin nanofibers for skin tissue regeneration: fabrication and characterization. Int. J. Biol. Macromol. **160**, 112–127 (2020)
15. Zhang, S., et al.: Porous nerve guidance conduits reinforced with braided composite structures of silk/magnesium filaments for peripheral nerve repair. Acta Biomater. **134**, 116–130 (2021)
16. Wan, Y., Cao, X., Zhang, S., Wang, S., Wu, Q.: Fibrous poly(chitosan-g-DL-lactic acid) scaffolds prepared via electro-wet-spinning. Acta Biomater. **4**, 876–886 (2008)
17. Wan, Y., Wu, H., Xiao, B., Cao, X., Dalai, S.: Chitosan-g-polycaprolactone copolymer fibrous mesh scaffolds and their related properties. Polym. Adv. Technol. **20**, 795–801 (2009)
18. Bianchini, M., Zinno, C., Micera, S., Redolfi Riva, E.: Improved physiochemical properties of Chitosan@PCL nerve conduits by natural molecule crosslinking. Biomolecules **13**, 1712 (2023)
19. Haastert-Talini, K., et al.: Chitosan tubes of varying degrees of acetylation for bridging peripheral nerve defects. Biomaterials **34**, 9886–9904 (2013)
20. Meyer, C., et al.: Chitosan-film enhanced chitosan nerve guides for long-distance regeneration of peripheral nerves. Biomaterials **76**, 33–51 (2016)

21. Gonzalez-Perez, F., et al.: Tubulization with chitosan guides for the repair of long gap peripheral nerve injury in the rat. Microsurgery **35**, 300–308 (2015)
22. Ao, Q., et al.: Manufacture of multi microtubule chitosan nerve conduits with novel molds and characterization in vitro. J. Biomed. Mater. Res. A **77A**, 11–18 (2006)
23. Ao, Q., et al.: The regeneration of transacted sciatic nerves of adult rats using chitosan nerve conduits seeded with bone marrow stromal cell-derived Schwann cells. Biomaterials **32**, 787–796 (2011)
24. Wan, Y., Huang, J., Zhang, J., Yin, D., Zheng, Z., Liao, C., Sun, S.: Investigation of mechanical properties and degradability of multi-channel chitosan–polycaprolactone/collagen conduits. Polym. Degrad. Stab. **98**(1), 122–132 (2013)
25. Bajgai, M.P., et al.: In vitro hydrolytic degradation of poly(ε-caprolactone) grafted dextran fibers and films. Polym. Degrad. Stabil. **93**, 2172–2179 (2008)
26. Takara, E.A., Marchese, J., Ochoa, N.A.: NaOH treatment of chitosan films: impact on macromolecular structure and film properties. Carbohydr. Polym. **132**, 25–30 (2015)
27. Fang, J., et al.: Nerve guide conduits integrated with Fisetin-loaded chitosan hydrogels for reducing oxidative stress, inflammation, and nerve regeneration. Macromol. Biosci. **24**, 2300476 (2024)
28. Li, G., et al.: Spatially featured porous chitosan conduits with micropatterned inner wall and seamless sidewall for bridging peripheral nerve regeneration. Carbohydr. Polym. **194**, 225–235 (2018)
29. Ezra, M., Bushman, J., Shreiber, D., Schachner, M., Kohn, J.: Enhanced femoral nerve regeneration after tubulization with a tyrosine-derived polycarbonate terpolymer: effects of protein adsorption and independence of conduit porosity. Tissue Eng. A **20**(3–4), 518–528 (2014Feb)
30. Zhang, W., et al.: Vascularization of hollow channel-modified porous silk scaffolds with endothelial cells for tissue regeneration. Biomaterials **56**, 68–77 (2015)

11th International Conference on Health Informatics and Medical Systems (HIMS'25) Section: Health Informatics, Data Science, and Tools

Home Physical Telerehabilitation System for Patients with Postural Orthostatic Tachycardia Syndrome

Joseph Finkelstein[1](✉), Aref Smiley[1], Aileen Gabriel[1], Patricia Goncalves Leite Rocco[1], Xingyue Huo[1], Katie Johnson[2,3], and Melissa M. Cortez[2]

[1] University of Arizona College of Medicine, Tucson, AZ, USA
jfinkelstein1@arizona.edu

[2] Department of Neurology, University of Utah, Salt Lake City, UT, USA

[3] Orthopedic Center, University of Utah, Salt Lake City, UT, USA

Abstract. Postural Orthostatic Tachycardia Syndrome (POTS) is a form of autonomic dysfunction characterized by excessive heart rate elevation during upright posture, often resulting in symptoms such as dizziness, fatigue, exercise intolerance, and reduced quality of life. Although structured exercise programs are considered an effective nonpharmacological intervention for improving autonomic function, many individuals encounter obstacles related to travel requirements, program availability, and long-term adherence. To facilitate accessible home-based rehabilitation, we designed the Home-based Autonomic Telerehabilitation (HAT) platform, which combines a connected supine cycling device (iBikE), a web-based clinician dashboard for exercise management, and secure cloud infrastructure for remote monitoring and data exchange.

A usability evaluation was conducted using a single-arm pretest–posttest design involving ten participants. Participants were asked to complete three representative activities within the platform: accessing the system, responding to electronic questionnaires, and performing a guided supine cycling session. Usability outcomes were measured through task completion performance, System Usability Scale (SUS) scores, and heuristic assessment criteria.

All participants successfully completed the assigned activities without assistance, demonstrating strong system learnability and operational effectiveness. The platform achieved a mean SUS score of 89.5 (SD = 15.6), reflecting excellent overall usability and user satisfaction. Heuristic evaluations indicated favorable ratings across multiple domains, including interface consistency, system feedback, and support for error recovery. Participants also reported that the platform was straightforward to navigate, efficient to use, and easy to understand, while suggesting opportunities for improvement in the visual design of the exercise interface.

These results support the feasibility and user acceptance of the HAT platform as a remotely delivered rehabilitation solution for individuals with POTS and related autonomic disorders. The system shows promise for expanding access to exercise-based interventions while promoting engagement with home-based rehabilitation programs.

A. Alsadoon et al. (Eds.): CSCE 2025, CCIS 2935, pp. 183–197, 2026.
https://doi.org/10.1007/978-3-032-22199-5_13

Keywords: Postural Orthostatic Tachycardia Syndrome · Telerehabilitation · System Usability Scale · Remote Patient Monitoring · Internet of Things (IOT)

1 Introduction

Postural Orthostatic Tachycardia Syndrome (POTS) is a chronic autonomic nervous system disorder marked by a significant increase in heart rate—typically at least 30 beats per minute within 10 min of standing—without a corresponding drop in blood pressure [1]. This abnormal cardiovascular response often leads to symptoms such as lightheadedness, fatigue, palpitations, brain fog, exercise intolerance, and syncope, significantly impairing quality of life [2]. Recently, a notable rise in POTS cases has been reported among individuals recovering from COVID-19 [3], highlighting the urgent need for scalable, patient-centered interventions.

Exercise intolerance is a central feature of POTS. While physical deconditioning worsens symptoms, structured exercise has proven to be one of the most effective non-pharmacologic treatments [4, 5]. Yet, the upright posture required in many aerobic activities can trigger or intensify symptoms, especially in severely affected patients. As a result, supine or semi-recumbent forms of exercise—such as recumbent cycling, rowing, and swimming—are increasingly recommended as initial training modes [6, 7]. These approaches reduce orthostatic stress while maintaining cardiovascular benefits, making them particularly suitable for individuals with autonomic dysregulation.

Supine exercise can improve peripheral vascular tone, venous return and blood volume, which are often impaired in POTS due to altered renin-angiotensin-aldosterone system (RAAS), baroreflex dysfunction and splanchnic blood pooling [8, 9]. Progressive rehabilitation programs that begin with horizontal exercises and gradually transition to upright activities have been associated with reductions in symptom burden, improved upright heart rate control, and enhanced functional capacity [10, 11].

Beyond physiological benefits, exercise adherence is linked to psychological improvements, including enhanced confidence, reduced symptom-related anxiety, and greater perceived control [12, 13]. Telerehabilitation platforms such as the Home Automated Telemanagement (HAT) system facilitate remote delivery of personalized, supine exercise programs while allowing clinicians to monitor progress in real time [14], including implementation of adaptive approaches to exercise prescription [15]. These systems are particularly advantageous for patients with mobility limitations or those in remote settings, as they reduce the need for travel without compromising clinical supervision.

Given the rising burden of POTS and other autonomic disorders, particularly in the aftermath of COVID-19, there is a pressing need for accessible, adaptable rehabilitation models. Supine exercise serves as a critical foundation for these efforts, enabling safe initiation of physical reconditioning, improved autonomic balance, and better overall quality of life. This study investigates the feasibility and effectiveness of a telerehabilitation intervention based on supine exercise for individuals with POTS and related autonomic dysfunctions.

2 System Design

2.1 HAT System Design

The Home Automated Telemanagement (HAT) platform was developed to deliver individualized, home-based supine exercise regimens for patients with autonomic dysfunction, such as Postural Orthostatic Tachycardia Syndrome (POTS). The system is designed to support patient-centered care through structured self-management, tailored education, efficient clinician–patient communication, and coordinated multidisciplinary oversight. It consists of three integrated components: a patient unit, a clinician unit, and the iBikE unit, which incorporates a magnetic cadence sensor for real-time monitoring of cycling speed [14] (Fig. 1). Both the patient and clinician interfaces are implemented as secure, web-based applications developed in.NET using C#, with all data stored in a centralized SQL Server database. Patients can access the system using a personal computer or tablet through an accessible interface designed to accommodate individuals with mobility, visual, or cognitive impairments. The clinician portal enables healthcare providers to configure individualized exercise prescriptions, monitor adherence and symptom reports via nightly automated alerts, and adjust prescriptions dynamically using a virtual prescription tool. Real-time cadence data from the iBikE are transmitted to the central database, integrated into patient progress reports, and reviewed by the care team to optimize exercise parameters and provide evidence-based feedback and safety guidance. This architecture enables seamless communication, continuous monitoring, and adaptive rehabilitation management in the home environment.

We utilized a tablet PC setup featuring a custom Unity-based exercise game that provided interactive feedback in real-time (Fig. 2). The architecture integrates sensor hardware, cloud-based data infrastructure, and a tablet-based Unity application to provide dynamic biofeedback during supine exercise sessions. The system consists of three core components (Fig. 3). The data generated during exercise was encrypted and stored in a password-protected encrypted database behind the institutional firewall.

1. **iBikE Unit** – a compact recumbent exercise device fitted with an ESP32 microcontroller that captures cadence data via a magnetic switch. The ESP32 transmits real-time RPM data directly to a cloud database over Wi-Fi. This data is then accessed by the Unity-based tablet game application to provide live visual feedback to the patient.
2. **C-box Unit** – a custom-designed interface connected via Bluetooth to a Nonin 3150 pulse oximeter. Inside the C-box, an embedded ESP32 microcontrollers receive continuous heart rate and oxygen saturation data from the Nonin device. This physiological data is streamed simultaneously to the same cloud database and made available to the tablet game interface for real-time display and monitoring by the patient.
3. **Tablet PC Interface** – a Unity-based game runs on a Windows tablet, mounted above the patient using an overbed arm. This application receives cadence, heart rate, and SpO_2 data from the cloud and presents it through an engaging cycling game that guides the patient through a prescribed supine exercise program.
4. **Unity-Based Game** – The Unity-based game presented a virtual road-cycling environment that provided visual feedback on cadence performance. Patients were instructed to maintain prescribed speeds (e.g., 75, 90, or 60 RPM depending on the session phase), with real-time cues delivered via the tablet. The HAT system

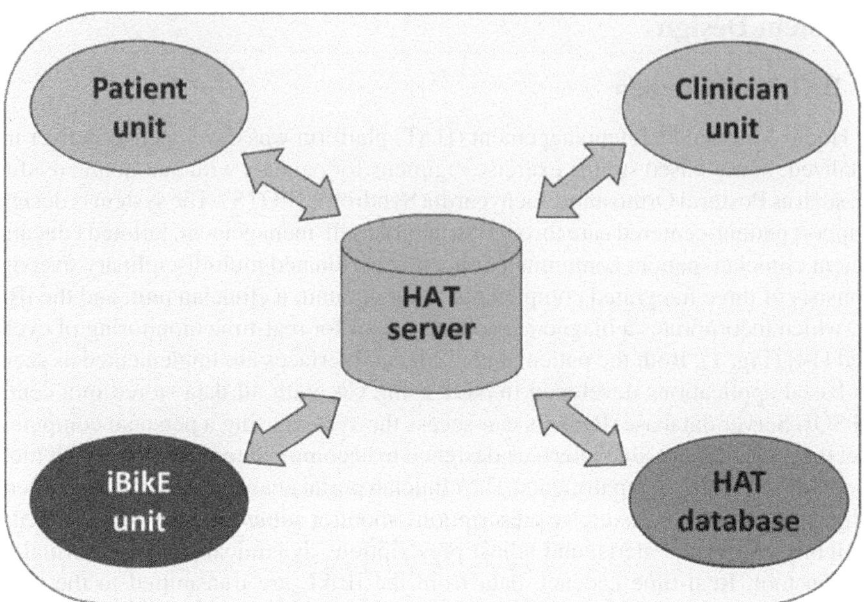

Fig. 1. Architecture of the Home Automated Telemanagement (HAT) system, illustrating interactions between the patient, clinician, and iBikE units, and data flow through the SQL server for personalized, home-based exercise monitoring and feedback.

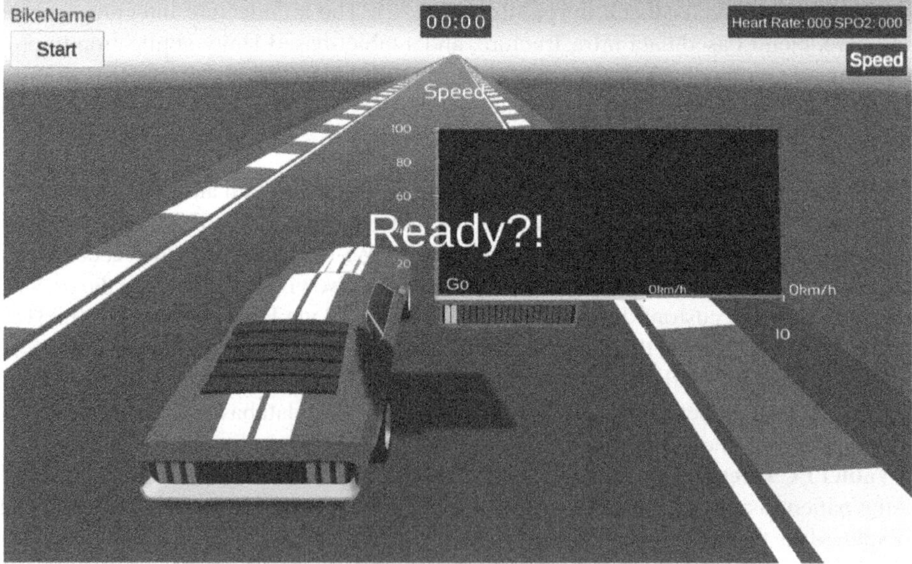

Fig. 2. Unity-based exercise game.

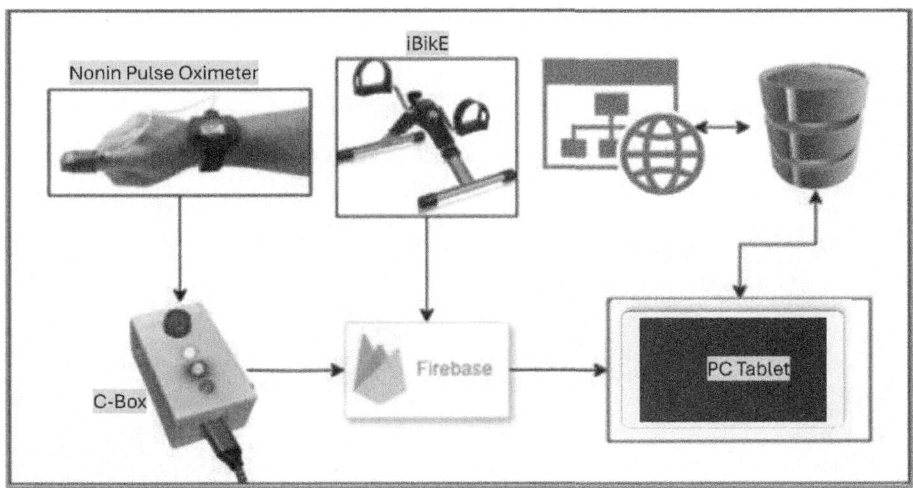

Fig. 3. System implementation with a pulse oximeter, PC tablet, custom-built Nonin BLE reader, custom-built IoT bike, and cloud services enabling interactive data connection and transfer.

collected exercise data including speed, duration, and adherence to the prescribed program, which was then stored in a central SQL database. Clinicians accessed these metrics through a secure web portal to evaluate performance and update prescriptions accordingly.

2.2 Experimental Design

We employed a quasi-experimental, single-group pretest–posttest design to assess the usability of the iBikE system integrated into the HAT platform. A total of 10 participants with POTS and/or idiopathic chronic orthostatic intolerance were recruited for this study. The usability evaluation involved three tasks: (1) Log in; (2) Complete Survey; and (3) Review, Perform, and Complete Exercise (Video, followed by an iBikE). Each participant completed the three tasks twice: initially with guidance during the pretest session, and then independently during the posttest session following a short break to complete demographic questionnaires. Time to complete each task, adherence to the prescribed exercise protocol, and qualitative feedback were recorded during posttest sessions. Additionally, a System Usability Scale (SUS) questionnaire was administered after each task to assess user satisfaction and perceived ease of use. At Task 3, each participant was asked to follow a video exercise [14] and then test the iBikE exercise in a supine position by viewing the tablet-based Unity game and following the prescribed cycling speed (Fig. 4).

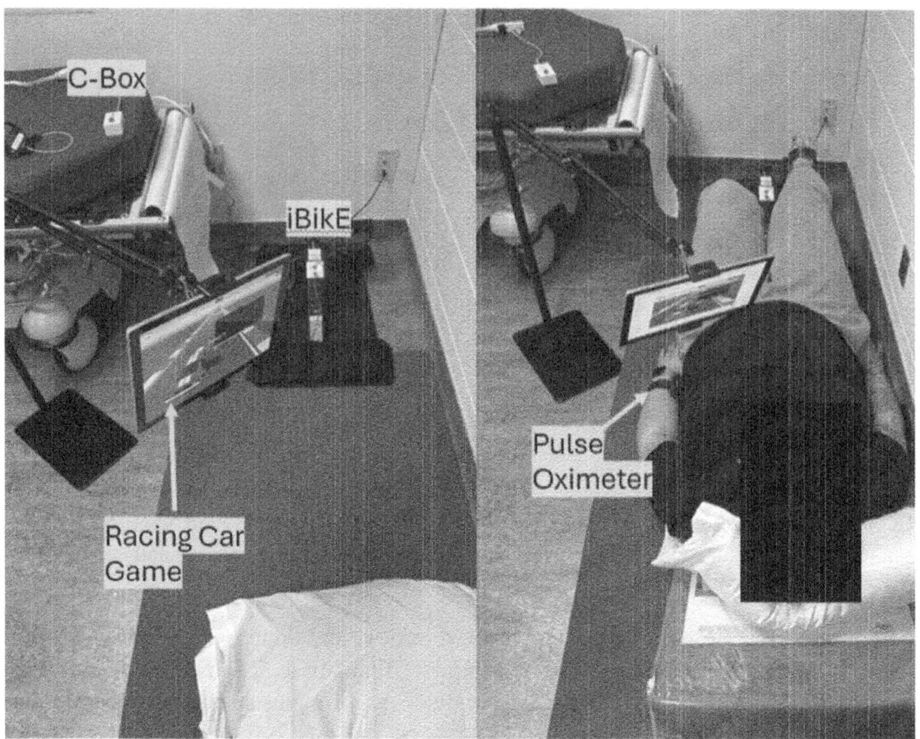

Fig. 4. Experimental setup.

2.3 Ethical Considerations

The study protocol was approved by the University of Utah IRB (IRB_00183926).

3 Results

Participants were asked to fill out 2 forms after pretest: (1) demographics and characteristics form, and (2) BRIEF Health Screening Tool (BRIEF) form.

Participant demographics and characteristics are summarized in Table 1. The study included 10 participants, predominantly female (90%) and White (90%), with most reporting moderate symptom severity (80%). The majority had a stable or improving condition over the prior year and reported good (60%) or excellent (30%) knowledge of their condition. Participants frequently used the internet daily (100%) and were proficient in English (100%). Employment status varied, with about one-third being students and others split between permanent, part-time, or no employment. Most participants had previously engaged in similar research (60%) and occasionally exercised (80%). Sources of health information were diverse, with medical personnel (30%) and internet (24%) being most common. The mean age was 29.6 years (SD = 8.0) and participants had an average of 15.4 years of schooling. Smartwatch ownership was common, with a majority using Apple devices. These characteristics reflect a technologically literate, moderately symptomatic cohort with good baseline familiarity with health information and digital platforms.

Table 1. Participant Demographics and Characteristics (N = 10).

Variable	Category	n (%)
Gender	Female	9 (90)
	Male	1 (10)
Symptom severity	Mild	1 (10)
	Moderate	8 (80)
	Severe	1 (10)
Condition last 12 months	Progressing	3 (30)
	Stable	4 (40)
	Improving	3 (30)
Knowledge of condition	Very limited	1 (10)
	Good	6 (60)
	Excellent	3 (30)
Race	White	9 (90)
	AI/AN & White	1 (10)
Ethnicity	Hispanic or Latino	1 (10)
	Not Hispanic or Latino	9 (90)
Exercise frequency	Frequently	2 (20)
	Occasionally	8 (80)
Internet use	Once a day	10 (100)
ATM use	Never	7 (70)
	Once a month	3 (30)
Computer use @ home	Never	1 (10)
	Once a week	1 (10)
	Once a day	8 (80)
Computer use @ work/school	Never	2 (20)
	Once a week	1 (10)
	Once a day	7 (70)
English proficiency	Excellent	10 (100)
Previous participation	No	4 (40)
	Yes	6 (60)
Job status	Permanent	3 (25)
	Temporary/Part-time	3 (25)

(*continued*)

Table 1. *(continued)*

Variable	Category	n (%)
	Student	4 (33.3)
	None	2 (16.7)
Sources of information	Brochures	2 (6.1)
	Scientific articles	7 (21.2)
	Internet	8 (24.2)
	Books	3 (9.1)
	Medical personnel	10 (30.3)
	Other	3 (9.1)
Smartwatch ownership	Apple	7 (58.3)
	Fitbit	1 (8.3)
	Other	3 (25)
	None	1 (8.3)

The BRIEF Health Screening Tool is a short questionnaire used to assess an individual's health literacy—specifically, their ability to understand, process, and use health-related information. Participants are instructed to circle the answer that best represents their response for each question. This particular form includes four questions: 1 – Assistance with reading hospital materials. 2 – Difficulty understanding written information about their condition. 3 – Difficulty understanding (or remembering) what is told to them about their condition. 4 – Confidence in filling out medical forms by themselves.

All participants (100%) successfully completed each of the three tasks (logging in, completing the survey, and reviewing/performing the exercise video and iBikE) without requiring assistance. Table 2 summarizes the performance metrics. The mean time to complete the tasks ranged from 28.9 s for logging in to 45.6 s for the exercise video. Task times exhibited variability, with the largest spread observed in the log-in task.

Table 2. Performance metrics of the 3 tasks.

Task	Accomplished (%)	Help (%)	Mean Time (s)	SD	Median	Min	Max
Log in	100	0	28.9	27.0	18.5	6	80
Complete Survey	100	0	29.8	10.3	26.5	20	50
Review & Complete Exercise	100	0	45.6	13.9	45.5	30	70

Participants demonstrated high health literacy on the BRIEF Health Screening Tool (Table 3). The majority reported "never" needing help reading hospital materials, and none reported frequent difficulty understanding written or verbal information. All participants expressed confidence in filling out medical forms, with 90% indicating they were "extremely" confident.

Table 3. BRIEF Health Screening Responses (N = 10)

Question	Response	n (%)
Help reading hospital materials	Occasionally	1 (10)
	Never	5 (50)
	Sometimes	2 (20)
	Often	1 (10)
	Always	1 (10)
Problems understanding written information	Never	5 (50)
	Occasionally	1 (10)
Problems understanding verbal information	Occasionally	1 (10)
Confidence filling out medical forms	Extremely	9 (90)
	Quite a bit	1 (10)

Participants completed usability questionnaires following each task: Task 1 (Log in), Task 2 (Complete Survey), Task 3 (Video exercise simulation, and iBikE system test). The questionnaires assessed perceived difficulty, satisfaction, appropriateness of time, visual appeal, and ease of navigation (Tables 4 and 5).

Table 4. Usability Ratings for Task 1 (Log in) and Task 2 (Survey).

Question	Task 1 Mean (SD)	Task 2 Mean (SD)
1. How difficult or easy was it to review the content and finish the sections?	4.9 (0.32)	4.8 (0.63)
2. How difficult or easy was it to answer the questions?	4.8 (0.42)	4.9 (0.32)
3. How satisfied are you with using this system to complete this task?	4.9 (0.32)	4.9 (0.32)
4. How would you rate the amount of time it took to complete this task?	4.9 (0.32)	5.0 (0.00)
5. The system is visually appealing	3.9 (0.99)	3.9 (1.45)
6. The system is easy to navigate	5.0 (0.00)	4.9 (0.32)

Table 5. Usability Ratings for Task 3 (Video Simulation and iBikE System)

Question	Task 3, Video Mean (SD)	Task 3, iBikE Mean (SD)
1. How satisfied are you with using this system to complete this task?	5.0 (0.00)	4.8 (0.42)
2. How would you rate the amount of time it took to complete this task?	5.0 (0.00)	4.8 (0.42)
3. The system is visually appealing	4.89 (0.33)	4.5 (0.85)
4. The system is easy to navigate	5.0 (0.00)	4.9 (0.32)

A heuristic evaluation of the system interface was performed by participants using a standard 10-item checklist (Table 6). Results are summarized in Table 7. The system scored highest on visibility of system status, consistency, and error recovery, while slightly lower on error prevention and minimalist design.

Table 6. Heuristic evaluation of the system interface.

Question
1. The system shows what's going on and gives you feedback (visibility)
2. Language and words make sense (match between system and real world)
3. There are clearly marked 'exits', buttons to go back or move forward (control/freedom)
4. Words, situations, and actions mean the same thing as elsewhere (consistency)
5. There are very few errors, and minimal error-prone conditions (error prevention)
6. Instructions are obvious, no need to remember how things work (recognition, not recall)
7. The system works for both new and expert users (flexibility, efficiency of use)
8. Information is streamlined and relevant (aesthetic / minimalist design)
9. Error messages are clear and in plain language (recognize, recover from errors)
10. Help is available, searchable, and relevant (help and documentation)

Table 7. Heuristic evaluation results.

Variable	Mean	SD	Min	Median	Max
1. Heuristics visibility	4.9	0.32	4	5	5
2. Heuristics match	4.6	1.26	1	5	5
3. Heuristics control	4.9	0.32	4	5	5
4. Heuristics consistency	4.6	1.26	1	5	5
5. Heuristics err prevention	4.7	0.48	4	5	5
6. Heuristics recognition	4.6	1.26	1	5	5

(continued)

Table 7. (*continued*)

Variable	Mean	SD	Min	Median	Max
7. Heuristics flexibility	4.9	0.32	4	5	5
8. Heuristics aesthetics	4.4	1.26	1	5	5
9. Heuristics err recover	4.8	0.42	4	5	5
10. Heuristics help documents	4.5	1.27	1	5	5

Participants also completed the System Usability Scale (SUS) after using the system (Table 8). An example of the questionnaire is shown in Table 6. The results indicate high perceived usability, with low scores for complexity and support needs, and high scores for ease of use, confidence, and integration (Table 9).

Table 8. System Usability Scale (SUS).

Question
1. I think that I would like to use this system frequently
2. I found the system unnecessarily complex
3. I thought the system was easy to use
4. I think that I would need the support of a technical person to be able to use this system
5. I found the various functions in this system were well integrated
6. I thought there was too much inconsistency in this system
7. I would imagine that most people would learn to use this system very quickly
8. I found the system very cumbersome to use
9. I felt very confident using the system
10. I needed to learn a lot of things before I could get going with this system

Table 9. System Usability Scale (SUS) results.

	Mean	SD	Min	Median	Max
SUS_score	89.5	15.58	50	95	100

Usability scores across all tasks were consistently high, with most mean ratings close to 5 and low standard deviations, indicating high levels of participant satisfaction, perceived ease of use, and system intuitiveness. The system was rated slightly lower on visual appeal, particularly for Task 3 iBikE, suggesting potential areas for aesthetic improvement.

4 Discussion

This study evaluated the usability of the Home Automated Telemanagement (HAT) platform to deliver individualized supine exercise programs for patients with Postural Orthostatic Tachycardia Syndrome (POTS). The results demonstrate that the HAT system is both feasible and acceptable for home-based use, with high levels of user satisfaction, efficiency, and perceived ease of use. Participants were able to complete all three tasks—logging in, completing the survey, and performing the supine exercise—with 100% success and no assistance, indicating the system's learnability and intuitiveness even for first-time users. Task completion times were low across all activities, further supporting its efficiency.

Usability evaluation using the System Usability Scale (SUS) yielded a mean score of 89.5, which exceeds the commonly accepted benchmark of 68 for above-average usability and places the system in the "excellent" category [16]. High SUS scores were complemented by favorable heuristic evaluation results, with participants rating visibility, system status feedback, and consistency particularly highly. These outcomes underscore the effectiveness of the system's design principles, which prioritized clear feedback, minimal cognitive load, and error prevention. Notably, aesthetic appeal ratings were slightly lower than other usability dimensions, particularly for the iBikE exercise game interface. While the system was perceived as functional and easy to navigate, participants expressed moderate preferences for improved visual design and more engaging graphics. This suggests an opportunity for iterative design improvements focused on aesthetic elements to further enhance user motivation and enjoyment.

The demographic profile of participants—predominantly young, technologically literate, and moderately symptomatic—likely contributed to the high usability scores. Future studies should evaluate the system in a more diverse cohort, including older adults or individuals with more severe impairments, to assess generalizability. Additionally, the current study focused solely on usability and did not assess the system's clinical efficacy in improving autonomic function, exercise tolerance, or quality of life. Longitudinal randomized controlled trials are warranted to establish the effectiveness of the HAT platform as a therapeutic intervention for POTS and similar conditions.

Future approaches for telemedicine-supported exercise should be enhanced by the recent advances in machine learning optimization of individualized exercise plans [17, 18], predictive analytics utilizing patient-generated data [19, 20], and interfaces with electronic health records to support personalization [21, 22], adherence, efficacy, and safety of the home-based exercise programs [23, 24]. Patient engagement in exercise programs can be facilitated by exergaming in virtual reality [25, 26] and artificial intelligence-based chatbots [27, 28], promoting patient education [29, 30] and healthy behaviors [31, 32]. Future studies should evaluate the proposed approach in disease prevention [33, 34], management of chronic health conditions [35, 36], healthy aging support [37, 38], and patient rehabilitation [39, 40]. Clinical impact of the resulting system will be evaluated in randomized controlled trials [41, 42]. Once the impact is demonstrated, the implementation into routine clinical care will include clinical decision support embedded into electronic health records [43, 44]. This study also highlights the potential of IoT-enabled telerehabilitation to overcome barriers to traditional care by providing personalized, supervised exercise programs in the home environment. Such approaches are particularly valuable for conditions like POTS, where orthostatic intolerance and fatigue can make frequent in-person visits impractical. By enabling continuous monitoring and clinician oversight, the HAT platform aligns with current trends toward patient-centered, accessible, and data-driven rehabilitation strategies.

References

1. Gibbons, C.H., Schmidt, P., Biaggioni, I., et al.: The recommendations of a consensus panel for the screening, diagnosis, and treatment of neurogenic orthostatic hypotension and associated supine hypertension. J. Neurol. **264**(8), 1567–1582 (2017)
2. Rocco, P.G.L., Mahony Reategui-Rivera, C., Finkelstein, J.: Exercise interventions in the management of postural orthostatic tachycardia syndrome: a scoping review. J. Multidiscip. Healthc. **17**, 5867–5885 (2024). https://doi.org/10.2147/JMDH.S495088
3. Dulal, D., Maraey, A., Elsharnoby, H., Chacko, P., Grubb, B.: Impact of COVID-19 pandemic on the incidence and prevalence of postural orthostatic tachycardia syndrome. Eur. Heart J. Qual. Care Clin. Outcomes (2025). https://doi.org/10.1093/ehjqcco/qcae111
4. Winker, R., et al.: Endurance exercise training in orthostatic intolerance: a randomized, controlled trial. Am. J. Med. **118**, 541–548 (2005)
5. Gibbons, C.H., et al.: Cardiovascular exercise as a treatment of POTS: a pragmatic treatment trial. J. Am. Coll. Cardiol. **77**, 1652–1660 (2021)
6. Fu, Q., et al.: Exercise training versus propranolol in the treatment of the postural orthostatic tachycardia syndrome. Hypertension **58**, 167–175 (2011)
7. George, S.A., et al.: The international POTS registry: evaluating the efficacy of an exercise training intervention. Heart Rhythm **13**, 943–950 (2016)
8. Shibata, S., et al.: Short-term exercise training improves the cardiovascular response to exercise in POTS. Circulation **126**, 2740–2742 (2012)
9. Fu, Q., VanGundy, T.B., Galbreath, M.M., Shibata, S., Jain, M., Hastings, J.L., et al.: Cardiac origins of the postural orthostatic tachycardia syndrome. J. Am. Coll. Cardiol. **55**, 2858–2868 (2010). https://doi.org/10.1016/j.jacc.2010.02.04
10. Richardson, C., et al.: Using an exercise program to improve activity tolerance in a female with POTS. J. Neurol. Phys. Ther. **41**, 156–163 (2017)
11. Raj, S.R., et al.: Renin–aldosterone paradox and perturbed blood volume regulation underlying postural tachycardia syndrome. Circulation **111**(13), 1574–1582 (2005)
12. Finkelstein, J., et al.: A wearable solution for managing POTS. Stud. Health Technol. Inform. **323**, 226–229 (2025)
13. Finkelstein, J., et al.: A wearable solution for managing POTS: patient perspectives on real-time heart rate monitoring and activity pacing. Stud. Health Technol. Inform. **323**, 226–229 (2025). https://doi.org/10.3233/SHTI250083
14. Smiley, A., Finkelstein, J.: Home automated telemanagement system for individualized exercise programs: design and usability evaluation. JMIR Biomed. Eng. **9**(1), e65734 (2024). https://doi.org/10.2196/65734
15. Ziaks, L., et al.: Adaptive approaches to exercise rehabilitation for postural tachycardia syndrome and related autonomic disorders. Arch. Rehabil. Res. Clin. Transl. **6**(4), 100366 (2024)
16. Hyzy, M., et al.: System usability scale benchmarking for digital health apps: meta-analysis. JMIR MHealth UHealth **10**(8), e37290 (2022). https://doi.org/10.2196/37290
17. Jeong, I.C., Finkelstein, J.: Classification of cycling exercise status using short-term heart rate variability. In: Proceedings of the Annual International Conference of the IEEE Engineering in Medicine and Biology Society (EMBC), pp. 1782–1785 (2014). https://doi.org/10.1109/EMBC.2014.6943954

18. Smiley, A., Finkelstein, J.: Automated prediction of exercise intensity using physiological data and deep learning. SN Comput. Sci. **6**(4), 313 (2025). https://doi.org/10.1007/s42979-025-03739-2
19. Finkelstein, J., Smiley, A., Echeverria, C., Mooney, K.: Leveraging convolutional neural networks for predicting symptom escalation in chemotherapy patients: a temporal resampling approach. Stud. Health Technol. Inform. **323**, 45–49 (2025). https://doi.org/10.3233/SHTI250046
20. Smiley, A., Finkelstein, J.: Dynamic prediction of physical exertion: leveraging AI models and wearable sensor data during cycling exercise. Diagnostics **15**(1), 52 (2024). https://doi.org/10.3390/diagnostics15010052
21. Paranjpe, I., et al.: Retrospective cohort study of clinical characteristics of 2199 hospitalised patients with COVID-19 in New York City. BMJ Open **10**(11), e040736 (2020). https://doi.org/10.1136/bmjopen-2020-040736
22. Finkelstein, J., Zhang, F., Levitin, S.A., Cappelli, D.: Using big data to promote precision oral health in the context of a learning healthcare system. J. Public Health Dent. **80**(Suppl. 1), S43–S58 (2020). https://doi.org/10.1111/jphd.12354
23. Finkelstein, J., Wood, J., Cha, E., Orlov, A., Dennison, C.: Feasibility of congestive heart failure telemanagement using a Wii-based telecare platform. In: 2010 Annual International Conference of the IEEE Engineering in Medicine and Biology Society (EMBC), pp. 2211–2214. IEEE, Buenos Aires (2010). https://doi.org/10.1109/IEMBS.2010.5627087
24. Finkelstein, J., Wood, J., Cha, E.: Impact of physical telerehabilitation on functional outcomes in seniors with mobility limitations. In: 2012 Annual International Conference of the IEEE Engineering in Medicine and Biology Society (EMBC), pp. 5827–5832. IEEE, San Diego (2012). https://doi.org/10.1109/EMBC.2012.6347319
25. Gabriel, A.S., et al.: Patient perceptions of virtual reality in cancer rehabilitation: a qualitative study. Stud. Health Technol. Inform. **323**, 399–403 (2025). https://doi.org/10.3233/SHTI250120
26. Locke, B.W., Tsai, T.Y., Reategui-Rivera, C.M., Gabriel, A.S., Smiley, A., Finkelstein, J.: Immersive virtual reality use in medical intensive care: Mixed methods feasibility study. JMIR Serious Games **12**(1), e62842 (2024). https://doi.org/10.2196/62842
27. Reategui-Rivera, C.M., Smiley, A., Finkelstein, J.: LLM-based chatbot to reduce mental illness stigma in healthcare providers. In: 2025 IEEE 15th Annual Computing and Communication Workshop and Conference (CCWC), pp. 1–7. IEEE, Las Vegas (2025). https://doi.org/10.1109/CCWC62904.2025.10903778
28. Shah-Mohammadi, F., Finkelstein, J.: GPT-4 in clinical practice: assessing its capability for symptom extraction from cancer patient notes. Stud. Health Technol. Inform. **323**, 86–90 (2025). https://doi.org/10.3233/SHTI250054
29. Finkelstein, J., Cha, E.M.: Using a mobile app to promote smoking cessation in hospitalized patients. JMIR MHealth UHealth **4**(2), e59 (2016). https://doi.org/10.2196/mhealth.5149
30. Vilela-Estrada, A.L., et al.: Psychometric properties of the Spanish version of the Hospital Anxiety and Depression Scale in cancer patients. Front. Psychol. **15**, 1497946 (2024). https://doi.org/10.3389/fpsyg.2024.1497946
31. Finkelstein, J., Wood, J.: Introducing home telemanagement of congestive heart failure using Xbox gaming platform. In: 2011 24th IEEE International Symposium on Computer-Based Medical Systems (CBMS), pp. 1–4. IEEE, Bristol (2011). https://doi.org/10.1109/CBMS.2011.5999126
32. Shah-Mohammadi, F., Cui, W., Bachi, K., Hurd, Y., Finkelstein, J.: Using natural language processing of clinical notes to predict outcomes of opioid treatment program. In: 2022 44th Annual International Conference of the IEEE Engineering in Medicine and Biology Society (EMBC), pp. 4415–4420. IEEE, Glasgow (2022). https://doi.org/10.1109/EMBC48229.2022.9871960

33. Yi, H., Xiao, T., Thomas, P.S., et al.: Barriers and facilitators to patient–provider communication when discussing breast cancer risk to aid in the development of decision support tools. AMIA Annu. Symp. Proc. **2015**, 1352–1360 (2015)
34. Finkelstein, J., Wood, J.: Implementing home telemanagement of congestive heart failure using Xbox gaming platform. In: Annual International Conference of the IEEE Engineering in Medicine and Biology Society (EMBC), pp. 3158–3163 (2011). https://doi.org/10.1109/IEMBS.2011.6090861
35. Castro, H.K., Cross, R.K., Finkelstein, J.: Using a Home Automated Telemanagement (HAT) system: experiences and perceptions of patients with inflammatory bowel disease. AMIA Annu. Symp. Proc. **2006**, 872 (2006)
36. Cross, R.K., Finkelstein, J.: Challenges in the design of a Home Telemanagement trial for patients with ulcerative colitis. Clin. Trials **6**(6), 649–657 (2009). https://doi.org/10.1177/1740774509346978
37. Finkelstein, J., Cisse, P., Jeong, I.C.: Feasibility of interactive resistance chair in older adults with diabetes. Stud. Health Technol. Inform. **213**, 61–64 (2015)
38. Barron, J., Bedra, M., Wood, J., Finkelstein, J.: Exploring three perspectives on feasibility of a patient portal for older adults. Stud. Health Technol. Inform. **202**, 181–184 (2014)
39. Jeong, I.C., Karpatkin, H., Finkelstein, J.: Physical telerehabilitation improves quality of life in patients with multiple sclerosis. Stud. Health Technol. Inform. **284**, 384–388 (2021). https://doi.org/10.3233/SHTI210752
40. Bedra, M., McNabney, M., Stiassny, D., et al.: Defining patient-centered characteristics of a telerehabilitation system for patients with COPD. Stud. Health Technol. Inform. **190**, 24–26 (2013)
41. Fleg, J.L., Keteyian, S.J., Peterson, P.N., et al.: Increasing use of cardiac and pulmonary rehabilitation in traditional and community settings: opportunities to reduce health care disparities. J. Cardiopulm. Rehabil. Prev. **40**(6), 350–355 (2020). https://doi.org/10.1097/HCR.0000000000000527
42. Grimshaw, C., Keteyian, S.J., Benzo, R., et al.: Baseline characteristics and barriers to recruitment in cardiac and pulmonary rehabilitation NIH-funded trials. J. Cardiopulm. Rehabil. Prev. **43**(6), 407–411 (2023). https://doi.org/10.1097/HCR.0000000000000824
43. Finkelstein, J., Gabriel, A., Schmer, S., Truong, T.T., Dunn, A.: Identifying facilitators and barriers to implementation of AI-assisted clinical decision support in an electronic health record system. J. Med. Syst. **48**(1), 89 (2024). https://doi.org/10.1007/s10916-024-02104-9
44. Kawamoto, K., Finkelstein, J., Del Fiol, G.: Implementing machine learning in the electronic health record: checklist of essential considerations. Mayo Clin. Proc. **98**(3), 366–369 (2023). https://doi.org/10.1016/j.mayocp.2023.01.013

Exploring IoT Architecture for Home-Based Physical Telerehabilitation

Aref Smiley(✉) and Joseph Finkelstein

Arizona Telemedicine Program, University of Arizona, Tucson, AZ, USA
arefsmiley@arizona.edu

Abstract. Telerehabilitation systems that integrate real-time monitoring and personalized exercise guidance have the potential to improve adherence and outcomes for patients engaging in home-based therapy. This paper presents an implementation of a low-cost, scalable telerehabilitation platform that combines cycling exercises with physiological monitoring and clinician oversight. The system incorporates two custom-built Internet of Things (IoT) devices: the C-box, which wirelessly streams heart rate and oxygen saturation data from a Nonin 3150 pulse oximeter, and the iBikE, which captures real-time cycling speed via a magnetic sensor. Both devices utilize ESP32 microcontrollers to collect, transmit, and synchronize data through Firebase and a secure backend SQL database. A web-based clinician portal enables remote configuration of exercise prescriptions and real-time performance review. The hardware design includes LED indicators, dual-microcontroller architecture, and automated session management to enhance usability and reliability. Real-world tests confirmed seamless BLE communication, real-time cloud data synchronization, and accurate feedback delivery. This system provides a clinically viable solution for remote rehabilitation, supporting personalized therapy while enabling continuous monitoring and scalable deployment.

Keywords: Telerehabilitation · Internet of Things (IOT) · Remote Patient Monitoring

1 Introduction

Maintaining regular physical activity is a cornerstone of preventive health and chronic disease management [1]. However, many individuals—particularly those managing long-term health conditions—struggle to adhere to exercise routines due to factors such as motivational barriers, insufficient supervision, and monotonous or non-engaging exercise routines [2]. The emergence of gamification as a modality for rehabilitation offers a novel avenue for addressing these challenges by transforming exercise into an engaging, interactive experience. Through immersive environments and gamified elements, gamification can boost patient engagement, promote consistency, and reduce perceived exertion during rehabilitation sessions [3].

One of the most effective ways to foster engagement in gamified rehabilitation is through the use of avatars—virtual representations that mirror the user's performance

A. Alsadoon et al. (Eds.): CSCE 2025, CCIS 2935, pp. 198–212, 2026.
https://doi.org/10.1007/978-3-032-22199-5_14

in real time. The dynamic visualization of an avatar responding to a user's physical input, such as cycling speed, provides immediate feedback and enhances the sense of presence and agency within the digital environment. This has been shown to increase motivation, enjoyment, and emotional connection to the activity, making users more likely to adhere to exercise regimens [3]. In rehabilitation contexts, avatars also serve a clinical function by enabling visual comparison of target versus actual performance, supporting biofeedback mechanisms that are essential in recovery and physical training [4].

The integration of Internet of Things (IoT) technologies into gamified platforms further enhances the capabilities of these systems. IoT enables continuous, real-time monitoring of physiological parameters such as heart rate, oxygen saturation, and exercise intensity using wireless sensors and connected devices [5]. These data can be transmitted to cloud-based systems, allowing for seamless tracking, storage, and analysis without the need for manual input or cumbersome hardware setups [6]. For clinicians, this creates opportunities to remotely assess patient progress, personalize exercise prescriptions, and intervene proactively if safety thresholds are breached.

Despite the rapid advancement in commercial digital exercise systems, most lack integration with wearable medical-grade sensors, do not support cloud-based data synchronization, and often require technical expertise for setup. Moreover, many are designed for athletic or entertainment use, limiting their suitability for older adults or individuals with chronic illnesses [7]. The need for a low-cost, scalable, and clinically integrated gamified-IoT solution for home-based rehabilitation remains unmet.

In response to this gap, we developed and now present an improved implementation of a telerehabilitation system that merges immersive gamified experiences, avatar-driven feedback, and real-time physiological monitoring via IoT infrastructure. Our system allows patients to engage in a cycling exercise program from home, where an avatar reflects their real-time performance on a virtual racetrack. Simultaneously, vital signs are captured and transmitted using custom-built, low-cost wireless devices. A dedicated web portal supports clinician oversight, enabling personalized exercise prescriptions, threshold-based alerts, and review of performance data. The revised system introduces hardware and software upgrades to further streamline connectivity, expand user accessibility, and enhance clinical integration.

2 System Design

The system was designed to support personalized, home-based cycling rehabilitation through the integration of wireless sensors and IoT technology. Patients are required to follow individualized speed trajectories prescribed by clinicians using the Home Automated Telemanagement (HAT) system, as described in our earlier work [3]. This system provides a structured and clinically guided exercise prescription, including specific speed and duration goals tailored to each patient's fitness level (Fig. 1).

To monitor and support patient adherence, two custom-built IoT devices were developed: a BLE-enabled reader for a pulse oximeter (C-box, Fig. 2) and a sensor-equipped stationary bike (Fig. 3). The C-box and iBikE devices are powered via 5V wired USB connections, ensuring continuous and reliable operation without concerns over battery depletion.

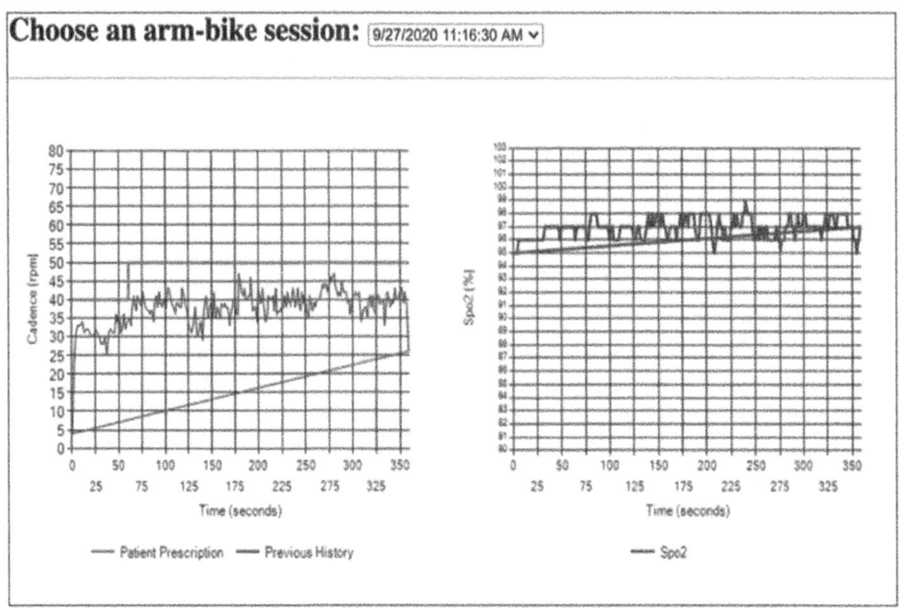

Fig. 1. Arm bike performance and SpO_2 levels during exercise. This figure shows two key metrics: exercise progress relative to the target speed (left) and SpO_2 levels (right). The system guides patients to maintain the prescribed pace while continuously monitoring oxygen saturation to ensure safety.

The C-box automatically pairs with a Nonin 3150 pulse oximeter via Bluetooth Low Energy (BLE), retrieves real-time heart rate and oxygen saturation data, and transmits this information to a Firebase cloud database using Wi-Fi. The iBikE integrates an ESP32 microcontroller and magnetic sensor to detect pedal revolutions, calculate cycling speed, and upload this data to the same Firebase system.

At the beginning of each exercise session, the patient-specific speed prescription is retrieved from a secure SQL database via API calls. This prescription, based on the clinician's configuration in the HAT portal, defines target speeds and durations for the session. During exercise, patients cycle while the system continuously monitors their speed and vital signs. The system evaluates patient performance against the prescribed values, and if thresholds are exceeded or not met (e.g., cycling too fast or too slow), alerts are triggered to help guide the patient back on track.

Session data—including speed, heart rate, and SpO_2—is compiled into JSON format and transmitted to the backend SQL database via NodeJS APIs. Clinicians can review this data remotely and adjust prescriptions as needed.

To ensure ease of setup and use, both the C-box and iBikE are equipped with a user-friendly Wi-Fi configuration manager. This allows users to connect devices to their home network using a smartphone browser interface. LED indicators on the devices show power, Wi-Fi, and sensor connectivity statuses to assist users in confirming proper function. The clinician-facing web portal facilitates device registration, patient assignment, prescription management, and remote review of session data. The integration of

Fig. 2. C-Box. Heart rate and oxygen saturation (SpO_2) levels are collected by the C-box and transmitted to the HAT system after the patient logs in to begin the prescribed exercise.

IoT architecture with structured HAT-based exercise prescriptions provides a scalable, low-cost, and clinically effective solution for remote telerehabilitation.

2.1 C-box Architecture and Communication Workflow

To improve the reliability and performance of physiological data acquisition, the C-box was redesigned to include two ESP32 microcontrollers (FireBeetle 2 ESP32-E IoT). In contrast to the earlier single-ESP version that occasionally failed to send data or produced erroneous values, the dual-ESP design separates BLE data collection from cloud communication, enhancing performance stability (Fig. 4).

ESP #1, BLE Data Collector. This microcontroller scans for and connects to the Nonin 3150 pulse oximeter using Bluetooth Low Energy (BLE). Key technical features include: 1 – Implementation of secure BLE pairing with passkey authentication. 2 – Use of UUIDs to access the SpO2 and heart rate characteristics. 3 – Registration of notification callbacks to receive real-time data updates from the sensor. 4 – Extraction of valid SpO2 and heart rate values from BLE packets. 5 – Data transmission via UART (Serial2) to the second ESP32 at 9600 baud.

Security callbacks ensure encrypted pairing, and a hardware serial interface is configured with RX/TX pins (16/17) to forward parsed physiological data.

ESP #2, Wi-Fi and Cloud Uplink. The second ESP32 is responsible for receiving data via UART, connecting to the Wi-Fi network, and pushing updates to the Firebase

Fig. 3. The iBikE system captures real-time cycling speed using a magnetic sensor and transmits the data to the HAT system.

Realtime Database. Key components include: 1 – WiFiManager Library: Enables seamless Wi-Fi configuration using a captive portal. Users connect via smartphone to a local SSID and input credentials. 2 – Firebase ESP Client: Handles authentication, connection, and data transmission to Firebase. The system includes callbacks and error-checking to restart the device if connectivity or signup fails. 3 – Data Parsing and Upload: Parses incoming UART; Sends structured data to Firebase; and Implements a simple invalid data filter (e.g., values of 0, 127, 255) and uses a counter to turn off the device after repeated failures by triggering a control pin.

UI Status Indicators and Control Logic. To enhance usability, the system includes four LEDs and one control pin (Fig. 2): LED1: Power (ON if connected); LED2: BLE data reception status; LED3: Wi-Fi status (ON if connected); LED4: Firebase connection status and data upload activity; Control Pin: Turns off both ESPs after multiple invalid readings.

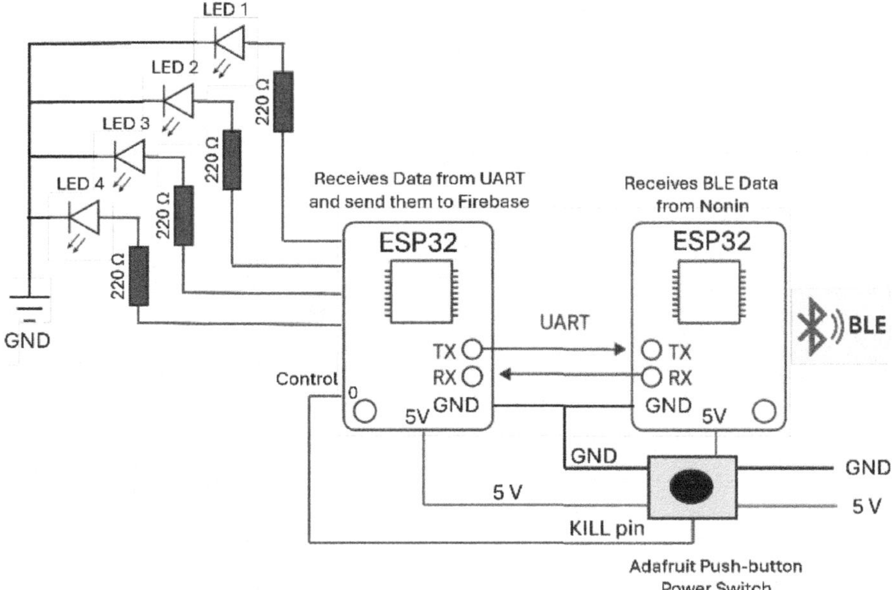

Fig. 4. Schematic diagram of the C-box architecture, showing the dual-ESP32 FireBeetle 2 setup. The first ESP32 handles BLE communication with the Nonin 3150 pulse oximeter and transmits heart rate and SpO_2 data via UART to the second ESP32. The second ESP32 manages Wi-Fi configuration, Firebase connectivity, and data upload to the cloud. LEDs and a control pin are included to assist with user feedback and device state management.

2.2 IBikE: Intelligent Exercise Monitoring System

The iBikE is a custom-built stationary bike embedded with a magnetic sensor and an ESP32 microcontroller to detect pedal revolutions and compute cycling speed (Fig. 5). The ESP32: Converts magnetic pulse counts to RPM and linear cycling speed; Uploads data to Firebase in real time; Retrieves patient-specific speed prescriptions via a secure API.

Patients follow these prescribed speed trajectories while receiving real-time feedback from a virtual avatar in the VR interface. The avatar's motion is directly linked to the cycling speed detected by iBikE, promoting engagement and reinforcing adherence. The iBikE system includes three LEDs and one control pin (Fig. 3): LED1: Power (ON if connected). LED2: Wi-Fi status (ON if connected). LED3: Firebase connection status and data upload activity. Control Pin: Turns off the ESP after multiple zero speed readings, meaning the user is not using the system anymore (~3 min).

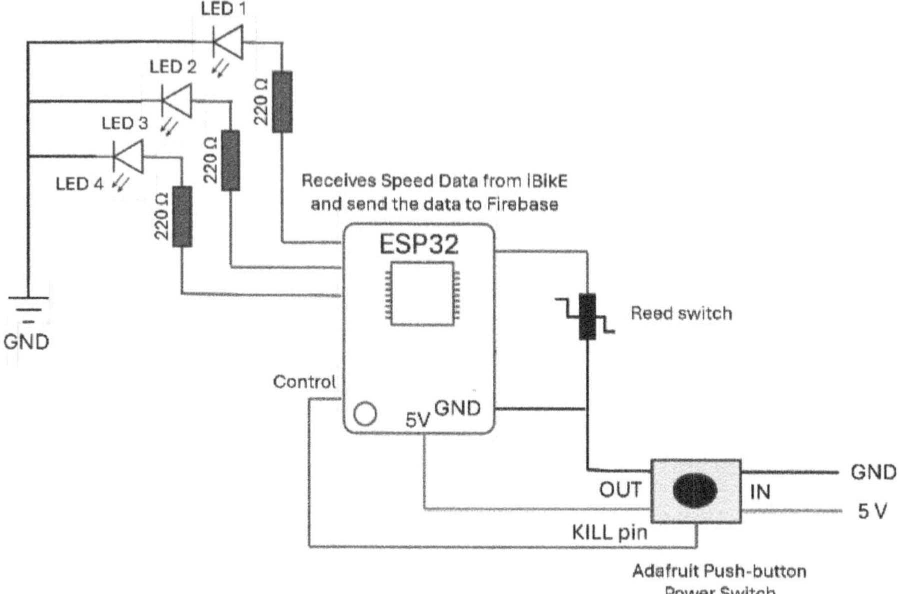

Fig. 5. Schematic of the iBikE system showing the ESP32 FireBeetle 2 microcontroller connected to a Reed sensor used to detect pedal revolutions. Calculated RPM values are uploaded to Firebase in real time. LEDs indicate power, Wi-Fi, and upload status, and a control pin shuts down the device after prolonged inactivity.

2.3 Cloud and Clinician Portal Integration

Both C-box and iBikE transmit data to Firebase, which is synchronized with a backend SQL database through NodeJS-based APIs. In the HAT (Home Automated Telemanagement) system [3], a clinician-facing web portal allows for: device registration and assignment, prescription configuration, real-time review of session metrics (SpO2, heart rate, cycling speed), alert notifications if exercise thresholds are breached. This architecture enables remote supervision and adjustment of rehabilitation protocols, creating a scalable, low-cost telerehabilitation framework [3].

As shown in Fig. 5, the C-box connects to the Nonin 3150 pulse oximeter via Bluetooth Low Energy (BLE), retrieves heart rate and SpO_2 data, and transmits them to a Firebase cloud database over Wi-Fi. A similar setup was implemented for the iBikE system, which captures cycling speed through a magnetic sensor and transmits it to Firebase in real time. The 2D and 3D gaming systems access this data from Firebase, synchronize it with user-specific prescriptions via API calls to a secure SQL backend, and present the exercise performance—along with real-time biofeedback—within the interactive exercise interface. After each session, a detailed report is displayed to the user through the gaming system, while clinicians can remotely access performance data via a dedicated web portal in the HAT (Fig. 6) [3]. This clinician dashboard supports device management, prescription updates, and patient progress evaluation through direct integration with the system's backend database.

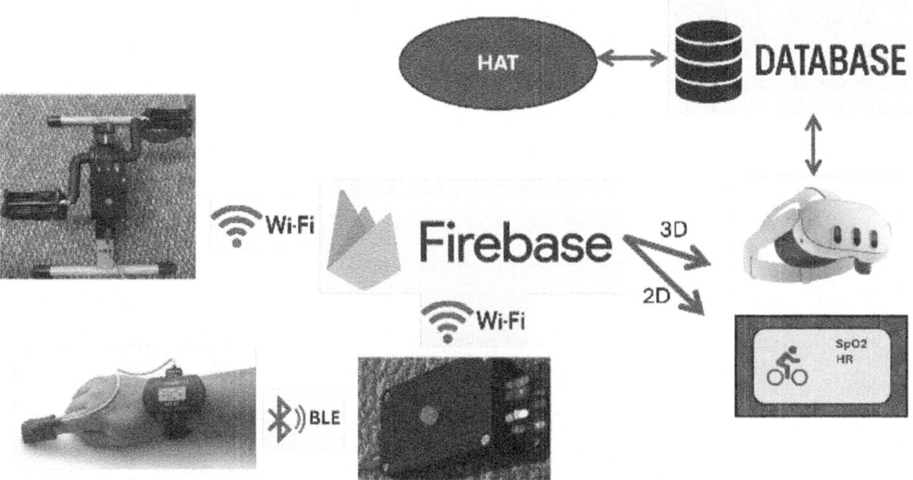

Fig. 6. System overview of the telerehabilitation platform integrating the C-box, iBikE, pulse oximeter, 2D/3D gaming interface, and cloud infrastructure.

3 Results

To evaluate the real-time functionality and end-to-end performance of the telerehabilitation platform, we conducted a full system test under simulated use-case conditions. The testing aimed to verify the successful acquisition, transmission, and cloud synchronization of physiological and exercise data from both the C-box and iBikE systems.

As shown in Fig. 7, real-time heart rate and oxygen saturation (SpO_2) values were streamed from the Nonin device, parsed by the C-box, and successfully uploaded to Firebase. Data appeared in the cloud dashboard with no observed latency or packet loss, confirming reliable BLE-to-cloud performance.

Figure 8 demonstrates the active state of both devices, with all status LEDs (power, Wi-Fi, data transmission, and BLE) illuminated. In the background, the Firebase database shows real-time data from both the pulse oximeter and the magnetic pedal sensor. This confirms seamless concurrent operation and synchronized uploads from both devices, essential for continuous monitoring during exercise sessions.

As shown in Fig. 9, the clinician portal displays both the prescribed and completed cycling trajectories. Vital sign trends and performance metrics are visualized post-session, allowing the clinician to review adherence and safety. The session confirmed bidirectional communication between the clinician portal, cloud database, and local devices.

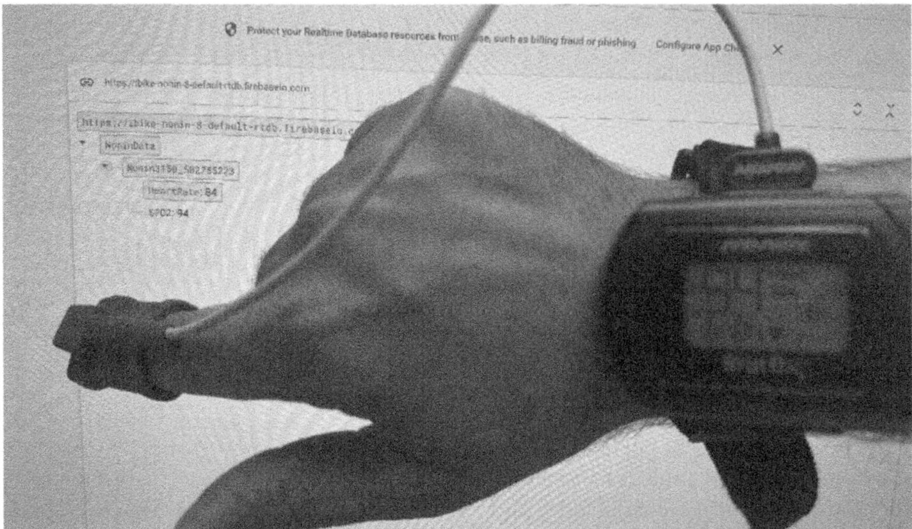

Fig. 7. Real-time physiological data captured using the Nonin 3150 pulse oximeter and displayed in Firebase. The Nonin device streams SpO_2 and heart rate to the C-box, which transmits values to the cloud in real time.

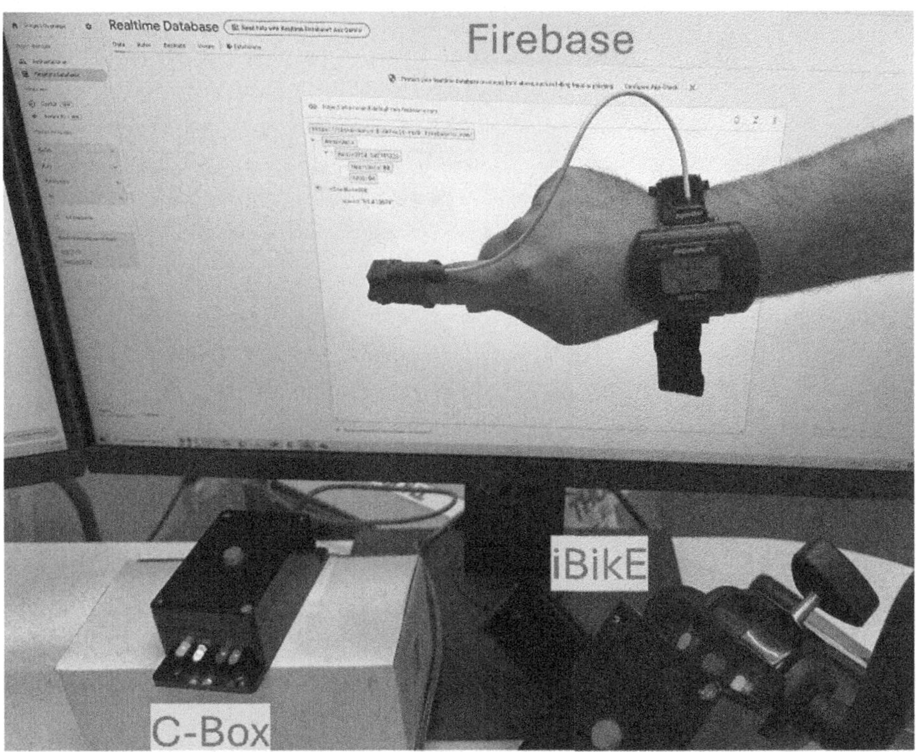

Fig. 8. The C-box and iBikE devices in active operation, with all system LEDs illuminated. Real-time data from both sensors is simultaneously displayed in the Firebase cloud database.

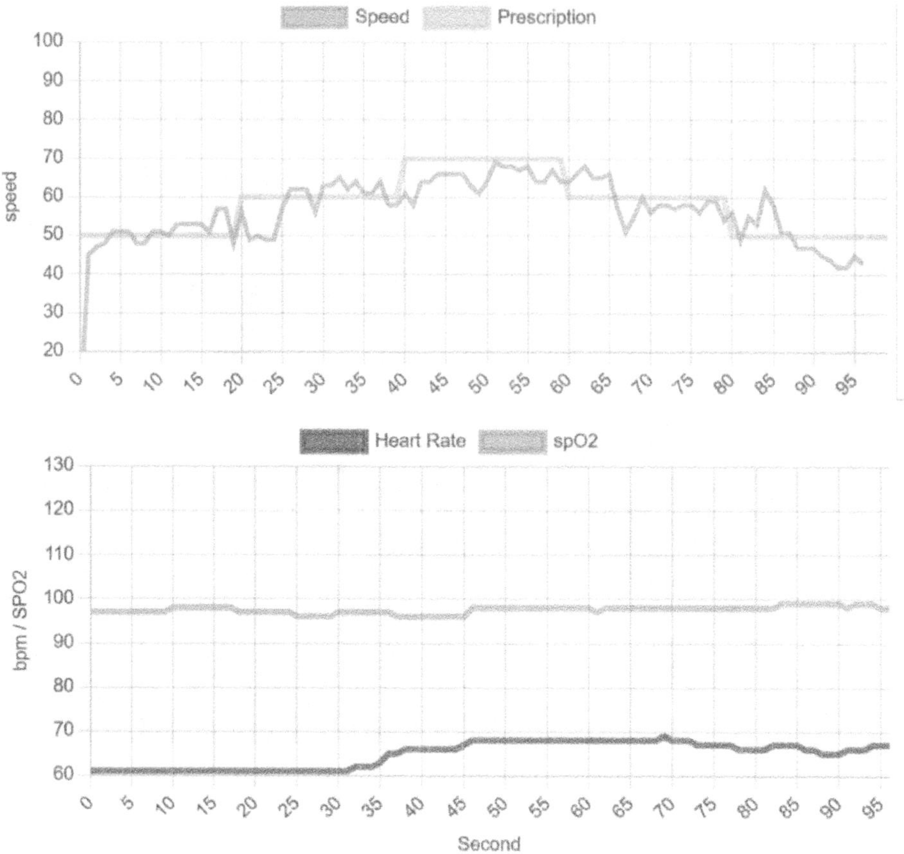

Fig. 9. Clinician web portal displaying a patient's exercise session, including prescribed and completed speed trajectories. Data collected from the C-box and iBikE is integrated for remote monitoring and protocol adjustment.

These tests validate the feasibility of the proposed system for home-based telerehabilitation. Real-time feedback, cloud connectivity, and remote supervision were achieved using a low-cost, scalable architecture.

4 Discussion

The results demonstrate that the proposed telerehabilitation platform provides a feasible, low-cost, and scalable approach for delivering home-based cycling exercise with real-time physiological monitoring. By integrating custom-built IoT hardware with cloud services and clinician oversight tools, the system addresses several key limitations in current digital rehabilitation solutions, including lack of real-time feedback, poor data interoperability, and limited support for clinical integration.

The dual-ESP architecture implemented in the C-box significantly improved the reliability and robustness of physiological data transmission compared to earlier single-microcontroller designs. The separation of BLE-based sensor communication and cloud data upload processes reduced system failures and enhanced performance stability. Similarly, the use of hardware-based feedback—such as LED indicators—proved beneficial for both setup validation and real-time device monitoring, improving usability for end users in a non-clinical environment.

The integration of Firebase and SQL databases allowed for continuous data synchronization across the iBikE, C-box, and clinician portal. Real-time streaming of heart rate, SpO_2, and cycling speed enabled dynamic feedback for patients while simultaneously providing clinicians with comprehensive visibility into patient performance. This bidirectional data flow supports adaptive and personalized exercise prescriptions, laying the groundwork for precision rehabilitation at home.

Data transmitted by the C-box and iBikE systems is protected using secure Bluetooth Low Energy (BLE) pairing with passkey authentication and encrypted Wi-Fi communication. Next system updates will implement enhanced security measures, including encryption at rest for stored data and multi-factor authentication mechanisms to strengthen the protection of patient information transmitted to cloud services. Future approaches for telemedicine-supported exercise should be enhanced by the recent advances in machine learning optimization of individualized exercise plans [8, 9], predictive analytics utilizing patient-generated data [10, 11], and interfaces with electronic health records to support personalization [12, 13], adherence, efficacy, and safety of the home-based exercise programs [14, 15]. Patient engagement in exercise programs can be facilitated by exergaming in virtual reality [16, 17] and artificial intelligence-based chatbots [18, 19], promoting patient education [20, 21] and healthy behaviors [22, 23]. Future studies should evaluate the proposed approach in disease prevention [24, 25], management of chronic health conditions [26, 27], healthy aging support [28, 29], and patient rehabilitation [30, 31]. Clinical impact of the resulting system will be evaluated in randomized controlled trials [32]. Once the impact is demonstrated, the implementation into routine clinical care will include clinical decision support embedded into electronic health records [33, 34].

However, several limitations remain. First, while the system was validated in a controlled environment, further testing is required in real-world, longitudinal rehabilitation scenarios to evaluate long-term adherence, clinical outcomes, and scalability. Planned clinical evaluations are underway to assess system usability, patient adherence, engagement, and clinical outcomes during home-based rehabilitation programs. Second, the current version supports a single pulse oximeter and cycling interface; future iterations should explore multi-modal integration with additional sensors (e.g., ECG, respiration, motion) and expanded exercise modalities. Lastly, while the clinician portal supports basic data review and prescription management, enhancements such as data visualization dashboards, machine learning-based trend detection, and mobile accessibility could further enhance its utility.

References

1. Leyland, L.A., Spencer, B., Beale, N., Jones, T., van Reekum, C.M.: The effect of cycling on cognitive function and well-being in older adults. PLoS ONE **14**(2), e0211779 (2019)
2. Cha, E., Wood, J., Finkelstein, J.: Using gaming platforms for telemedicine applications: a cross-platform comparison. In: 2012 IEEE-EMBS International Conference on Biomedical and Health Informatics, pp. 918–921. IEEE, Hong Kong (2012)
3. Smiley, A., Finkelstein, J.: Home automated telemanagement system for individualized exercise programs: design and usability evaluation. JMIR Biomed. Eng. **9**(1), e65734 (2024)
4. Finkelstein, J., Jeong, I.C.: Feasibility of interactive biking exercise system for telemanagement in elderly. Stud. Health Technol. Inform. **192**, 642–646 (2013)
5. Smiley, A., Tsai, T.Y., Finkelstein, J.: Wireless real-time exercise system for physical telerehabilitation. In: 2022 IEEE Long Island Systems, Applications and Technology Conference (LISAT), pp. 1–6. IEEE (2022)
6. Tun, S.Y.Y., Madanian, S., Mirza, F.: Internet of things (IoT) applications for elderly care: a reflective review. Aging Clin. Exp. Res. **33**(4), 855–867 (2021)
7. Bedra, M., McNabney, M., Stiassny, D., et al.: Feasibility of home-based telerehabilitation in older adults. Gerontologist **53**, 325 (2013)
8. Jeong, I.C., Finkelstein, J.: Classification of cycling exercise status using short-term heart rate variability. In: Proceedings of the Annual International Conference of the IEEE Engineering in Medicine and Biology Society (EMBC), pp. 1782–1785 (2014). https://doi.org/10.1109/EMBC.2014.6943954
9. Smiley, A., Finkelstein, J.: Automated prediction of exercise intensity using physiological data and deep learning. SN Comput. Sci. **6**(4), 313 (2025). https://doi.org/10.1007/s42979-025-03739-2
10. Finkelstein, J., Smiley, A., Echeverria, C., Mooney, K.: Leveraging convolutional neural networks for predicting symptom escalation in chemotherapy patients: a temporal resampling approach. Stud. Health Technol. Inform. **323**, 45–49 (2025). https://doi.org/10.3233/SHTI250046
11. Smiley, A., Finkelstein, J.: Dynamic prediction of physical exertion: leveraging AI models and wearable sensor data during cycling exercise. Diagnostics **15**(1), 52 (2024). https://doi.org/10.3390/diagnostics15010052
12. Paranjpe, I., et al.: Retrospective cohort study of clinical characteristics of 2199 hospitalised patients with COVID-19 in New York City. BMJ Open **10**(11), e040736 (2020). https://doi.org/10.1136/bmjopen-2020-040736
13. Finkelstein, J., Zhang, F., Levitin, S.A., Cappelli, D.: Using big data to promote precision oral health in the context of a learning healthcare system. J. Public Health Dent. **80**(Suppl. 1), S43–S58 (2020). https://doi.org/10.1111/jphd.12354
14. Finkelstein, J., Wood, J., Cha, E., Orlov, A., Dennison, C.: Feasibility of congestive heart failure telemanagement using a Wii-based telecare platform. In: 2010 Annual International Conference of the IEEE Engineering in Medicine and Biology Society (EMBC), pp. 2211–2214. IEEE, Buenos Aires (2010). https://doi.org/10.1109/IEMBS.2010.5627087
15. Finkelstein, J., Wood, J., Cha, E.: Impact of physical telerehabilitation on functional outcomes in seniors with mobility limitations. In: 2012 Annual International Conference of the IEEE Engineering in Medicine and Biology Society (EMBC), pp. 5827–5832. IEEE, San Diego (2012). https://doi.org/10.1109/EMBC.2012.6347319
16. Gabriel, A.S., et al.: Patient perceptions of virtual reality in cancer rehabilitation: a qualitative study. Stud. Health Technol. Inform. **323**, 399–403 (2025). https://doi.org/10.3233/SHTI250120

17. Locke, B.W., Tsai, T.Y., Reategui-Rivera, C.M., Gabriel, A.S., Smiley, A., Finkelstein, J.: Immersive virtual reality use in medical intensive care: mixed methods feasibility study. JMIR Serious Games **12**(1), e62842 (2024). https://doi.org/10.2196/62842
18. Reategui-Rivera, C.M., Smiley, A., Finkelstein, J.: LLM-based chatbot to reduce mental illness stigma in healthcare providers. In: 2025 IEEE 15th Annual Computing and Communication Workshop and Conference (CCWC), pp. 1–7. IEEE, Las Vegas (2025). https://doi.org/10.1109/CCWC62904.2025.10903778
19. Shah-Mohammadi, F., Finkelstein, J.: GPT-4 in clinical practice: assessing its capability for symptom extraction from cancer patient notes. Stud. Health Technol. Inform. **323**, 86–90 (2025). https://doi.org/10.3233/SHTI250054
20. Finkelstein, J., Cha, E.M.: Using a mobile app to promote smoking cessation in hospitalized patients. JMIR MHealth UHealth **4**(2), e59 (2016). https://doi.org/10.2196/mhealth.5149
21. Vilela-Estrada, A.L., et al.: Psychometric properties of the Spanish version of the Hospital Anxiety and Depression Scale in cancer patients. Front. Psychol. **15**, 1497946 (2024). https://doi.org/10.3389/fpsyg.2024.1497946
22. Finkelstein, J., Wood, J.: Introducing home telemanagement of congestive heart failure using Xbox gaming platform. In: 2011 24th International Symposium on Computer-Based Medical Systems (CBMS), pp. 1–4. IEEE, Bristol (2011). https://doi.org/10.1109/CBMS.2011.5999126
23. Shah-Mohammadi, F., Cui, W., Bachi, K., Hurd, Y., Finkelstein, J.: Using natural language processing of clinical notes to predict outcomes of opioid treatment program. In: 2022 44th Annual International Conference of the IEEE Engineering in Medicine and Biology Society (EMBC), pp. 4415–4420. IEEE, Glasgow (2022). https://doi.org/10.1109/EMBC48229.2022.9871960
24. Yi, H., Xiao, T., Thomas, P.S., et al.: Barriers and facilitators to patient–provider communication when discussing breast cancer risk to aid in the development of decision support tools. AMIA Annu. Symp. Proc. **2015**, 1352–1360 (2015)
25. Finkelstein, J., Wood, J.: Implementing home telemanagement of congestive heart failure using Xbox gaming platform. In: Annual International Conference of the IEEE Engineering in Medicine and Biology Society (EMBC), pp. 3158–3163 (2011). https://doi.org/10.1109/IEMBS.2011.6090861
26. Castro, H.K., Cross, R.K., Finkelstein, J.: Using a Home Automated Telemanagement (HAT) system: experiences and perceptions of patients with inflammatory bowel disease. AMIA Annu. Symp. Proc. **2006**, 872 (2006)
27. Cross, R.K., Finkelstein, J.: Challenges in the design of a Home Telemanagement trial for patients with ulcerative colitis. Clin. Trials **6**(6), 649–657 (2009). https://doi.org/10.1177/1740774509346978
28. Finkelstein, J., Cisse, P., Jeong, I.C.: Feasibility of interactive resistance chair in older adults with diabetes. Stud. Health Technol. Inform. **213**, 61–64 (2015)
29. Barron, J., Bedra, M., Wood, J., Finkelstein, J.: Exploring three perspectives on feasibility of a patient portal for older adults. Stud. Health Technol. Inform. **202**, 181–184 (2014)
30. Jeong, I.C., Karpatkin, H., Finkelstein, J.: Physical telerehabilitation improves quality of life in patients with multiple sclerosis. Stud. Health Technol. Inform. **284**, 384–388 (2021). https://doi.org/10.3233/SHTI210752
31. Bedra, M., McNabney, M., Stiassny, D., et al.: Defining patient-centered characteristics of a telerehabilitation system for patients with COPD. Stud. Health Technol. Inform. **190**, 24–26 (2013)
32. Fleg, J.L., Keteyian, S.J., Peterson, P.N., et al.: Increasing use of cardiac and pulmonary rehabilitation in traditional and community settings: opportunities to reduce health care disparities. J. Cardiopulm. Rehabil. Prev. **40**(6), 350–355 (2020). https://doi.org/10.1097/HCR.0000000000000527

33. Finkelstein, J., Gabriel, A., Schmer, S., Truong, T.T., Dunn, A.: Identifying facilitators and barriers to implementation of AI-assisted clinical decision support in an electronic health record system. J. Med. Syst. **48**(1), 89 (2024). https://doi.org/10.1007/s10916-024-02104-9
34. Kawamoto, K., Finkelstein, J., Del Fiol, G.: Implementing machine learning in the electronic health record: checklist of essential considerations. Mayo Clin. Proc. **98**(3), 366–369 (2023). https://doi.org/10.1016/j.mayocp.2023.01.013

ALFABEATS: A Machine Learning Based Decision Support Platform for Biomedical Time Series Analysis

Saša Kendjel[1](✉), Nikolina Frid[1], Eda Kalafatić[1], Krešimir Jozić[2], and Alan Jović[1]

[1] Faculty of Electrical Engineering and Computing, University of Zagreb, Zagreb, Croatia
{sasa.kendjel,nikolina.frid,eda.kalafatic,alan.jovic}@fer.unizg.hr
[2] JANAF Plc, Sisak, Croatia

Abstract. Most AI tools for biomedical time series analysis are designed as engineering toolkits, requiring technical expertise. While effective in research, they are rarely usable by clinicians. ALFABEATS is a modular, web-based decision support platform that bridges this gap. It integrates advanced machine learning and deep learning models for classifying signals like EEG and ECG, while abstracting technical complexity via an intuitive interface. Unlike conventional toolboxes, ALFABEATS automates preprocessing, model selection, inference, and interpretability, thus enabling clinicians to make informed decisions without ML expertise. As a case study, we demonstrate its application in detecting major depressive disorder (MDD) from EEG data using several trained models. The platform supports end-to-end workflows, including data ingestion, prediction, and post hoc explanations.

Keywords: Biomedical time series · Clinical decision support · EEG · Machine learning · Explainable AI

1 Introduction

Analysis of biomedical time series (BTS), such as ECG, EEG, and EMG, poses challenges, including non-stationarity, nonlinearity, inter-subject variability, low signal-to-noise ratio, and the need for real-time interpretability [14,39]. Building effective decision support systems for BTS has been a long-standing medical goal [2,16]. Despite recent progress in machine learning and signal processing [29], few accessible online tools exist for clinicians to analyse BTS data quickly, securely, and efficiently. Barriers include inconsistent data formats, proprietary systems, and methodological complexity.

This work has been fully supported by the Croatian Science Foundation under the project number IP-2022-10-8241. The funder played no role in the study design, data collection, data analysis and interpretation, or the writing of this manuscript.

A. Alsadoon et al. (Eds.): CSCE 2025, CCIS 2935, pp. 213–224, 2026.
https://doi.org/10.1007/978-3-032-22199-5_15

This paper introduces ALFABEATS, a web-based, machine-learning-driven decision support platform for BTS analysis. Designed for medical professionals, ALFABEATS abstracts technical complexity while integrating state-of-the-art models for the classification of biomedical signals. The platform runs remotely, minimising infrastructure needs on the client side, and provides end-to-end functionality—data ingestion, preprocessing, model selection, inference, and post hoc interpretability.

We demonstrate its capabilities through a case study on major depressive disorder (MDD) detection from EEG signals. MDD presents subtle and heterogeneous electrophysiological patterns, making it a challenging test case for BTS analysis. The study showcases how integrated machine learning models can aid in clinical decision-making for affective disorders [1,25].

The remainder of the paper covers related work, platform functionalities, and case study methodology and results, concluding with a discussion of future directions.

2 Related Work

2.1 Platforms for Biomedical Signal and Image Analysis

Several open-source platforms, libraries, and toolboxes support biomedical data analysis, though many remain domain-specific, lack modularity, or pose usability challenges.

NeuroKit2 [21] is a Python toolbox focused on feature extraction and signal quality assessment but lacking integrated classification or decision support. BioSPPy [5] extends basic analysis with synthetic signal generation and clustering-based outlier detection. Most similar toolboxes focus on preprocessing and feature extraction, typically support only a few signal types, and rarely implement machine learning-based analysis [5]. BioSig [38] is one of the few actively maintained libraries that covers multiple formats and includes functions for preprocessing, feature extraction, classification, statistical testing, and visualization.

Standalone applications with graphical interfaces have also emerged. BioLab [17] enables real-time streaming and basic analysis of ECG, EMG, and EEG but lacks advanced analytics. PyBioS [33] supports nonlinear cardiovascular signal analysis, with a machine learning module under development. MULTISAB [13] is a web platform for multivariate biomedical signal analysis using domain-specific frameworks and ML-based model construction. However, it remains inaccessible to the public due to challenges in deploying online ML models [15].

In imaging, a related field, tools such as ImageJ [31] are widely used for segmentation, registration, and visualization, with plugin support for tasks like MRI [30], cardiac studies [27], CT [19], and bone analysis [10]. Specialized tools like MONAI [7] provide a deep learning infrastructure for MRI/CT segmentation, while RECOMIA [37] offers a cloud-based platform for AI-supported radiological research.

2.2 Classification Models for Biomedical Time Series

Numerous algorithms have been proposed for time series classification (TSC), often evaluated on synthetic or general-purpose datasets [24]. HIVE-COTE v2 [23] is a leading meta-ensemble-based method that combines multiple ensembles and model types (e.g., shapelet, interval, dictionary) and consistently achieves high accuracy, but it is computationally intensive and difficult to interpret. HYDRA [9] is a fast dictionary-based approach that uses competing convolutional kernels, effectively blending the strengths of ROCKET and classical dictionary methods. Its combination with MultiRocket, referred to as Hydra-MultiRocketPlus [24], offers state-of-the-art performance with high speed.

InceptionTime [12], a deep learning model based on convolutional inception blocks, captures multiscale temporal features and performs particularly well on long, noisy signals such as EEG. Hybrid LSTM-CNN architectures [18,41] are also common in biomedical TSC, although their adoption is limited by long training times and complex tuning. Transformer-based models [8,35] have recently been adapted for EEG analysis, but remain challenging to train on small datasets and are often hard to interpret. Finally, interpretable models such as OCT-H trees [4] offer transparent decision paths, though typically with lower predictive performance when compared to black-box models.

3 Platform Description

ALFABEATS is a modular Python-based decision support platform for biomedical time series, currently focused on EEG and ECG. It follows a client-server architecture with distinct backend and frontend components (Fig. 1). The backend is implemented in Django and uses PostgreSQL database to manage user accounts, medical metadata, and model artefacts. It handles data preprocessing, model training, and inference, organized into independently configurable modules. Core functionalities include:

- **Data ingestion and preprocessing**– accepts raw biomedical time series data in EDF format and applies comprehensive preprocessing using `MNE` and `mne-icalabel`, including filtering, ICA-based artefact rejection, epoching, and normalisation.
- **Model integration** – supports state-of-the-art time series classification models implemented with `scikit-learn`, `sktime`, `torch`, and `tsai`. Pretrained models currently include ROCKET, HydraMultiRocketPlus, HIVE-COTE v2, and InceptionTime, optimized for detecting major depressive disorder (MDD) from EEG data. The platform is being extended to support both EEG and ECG modalities, with ongoing integration of advanced deep learning models, including transformer-based architectures, while maintaining a strong focus on explainability.
- **Inference and pipelining** – inference is handled through `joblib` to enable pipelined execution and concurrent processing.

- **Explainability** – includes Shapley values, feature permutation importance, and saliency maps to support transparent and informed clinical decisions.
- **REST API** – exposes backend functionalities for seamless web/mobile frontend integration.

Core components such as preprocessing, segmentation, and model selection are implemented in a modality-agnostic manner, enabling adaptation across biomedical signal types with minimal code modification.

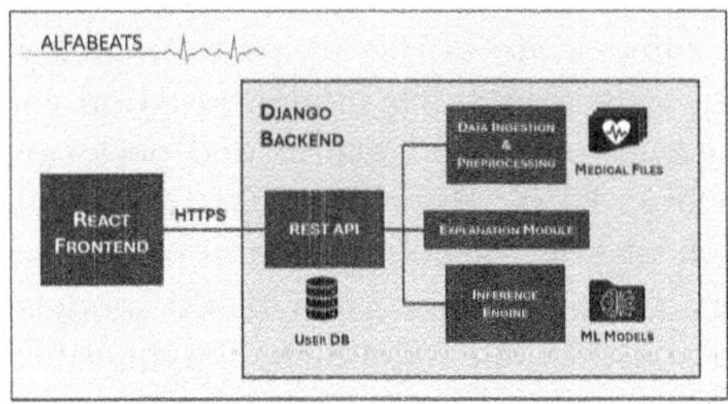

Fig. 1. ALFABEATS modular platform architecture.

The frontend is implemented in React and provides a responsive, intuitive interface tailored to clinical workflows. After login, users see recent activity (Fig. 2a) and can access patient records or create new ones. Each patient view (Fig. 2b) presents a history of diagnostic entries alongside associated with associated predictions and a file panel listing uploaded signals (EEG/ECG) and metadata.

New data and analyses can be added directly through the interface, which also supports reanalysis of existing signals. The analysis workflow (Fig. 2c) allows model selection and evaluation configuration. Upon completion, results are presented in an interactive dashboard (Fig. 2d) with preprocessing snapshots (e.g. raw traces, ICA), diagnostic predictions with confidence scores, and interpretability outputs, each supported by brief clinical guidance.

Data Privacy and Compliance: While the current version operates in a research setting, ALFABEATS is built following GDPR-aligned best practices. Data is anonymised before processing, and authenticated access is enforced via time-limited tokens and role-based controls. Future deployments will add audit logging, encrypted storage, and formal risk assessment procedures to meet clinical certification standards.

Security features include authentication, access control, session/token handling, and CORS protection. A mobile app is under development. For reproducibility and clinical traceability, configurations, parameters, and session logs are persistently stored in structured format.

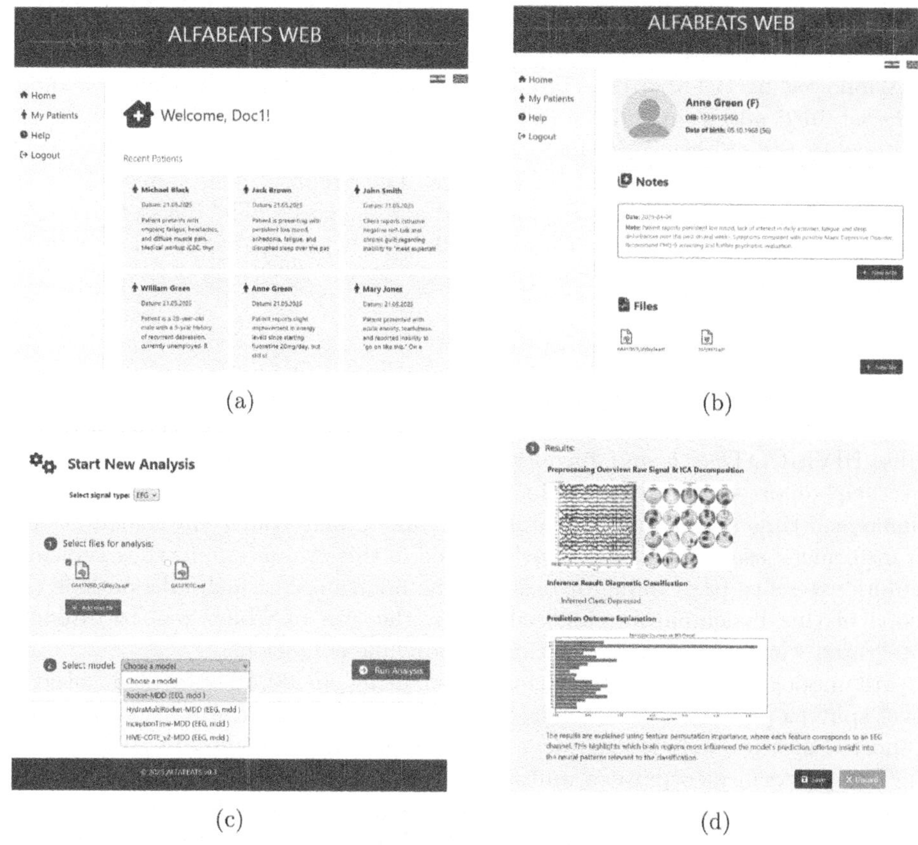

Fig. 2. Overview of key ALFABEATS interface screens: (a) home screen with recent activity; (b) patient overview with diagnostic history and uploaded recordings; (c) configuration interface for launching analysis; (d) inference results with prediction and feature importance visualization.

4 Case Study

4.1 Dataset Description

To demonstrate the ALFABEATS workflow and evaluate its performance in a realistic clinical scenario, we conducted a case study on detecting major depressive disorder (MDD) using resting-state EEG data. The dataset includes 140 anonymized EEG recordings from the University Psychiatric Hospital Vrapče [25], evenly split between patients diagnosed with depressive disorders (70) and healthy controls (70), matched by age and sex. Each subject underwent a 30-minute resting-state EEG session using a standard 1020 electrode montage. Recordings included eyes-open/closed rest, photostimulation, and hyperventilation protocols, sampled at 200256 Hz.

Recordings were downsampled 200 Hz and bandpass filtered (0.140 Hz). Signals were rereferenced to the average reference, and artefacts were removed using ICA followed by ICLabel [28]. From each subject, the first 5 min post-cleaning were retained and segmented into non-overlapping 2-second windows, yielding 150 epochs per subject. All channels were z-score normalized to improve convergence and reduce inter-channel variance. The preprocessing step resulted in over 20,000 labelled EEG epochs, balanced across classes. The dataset was split into a training and test set with an 80/20 ratio, where the split was stratified and subject-wise.

4.2 Modeling and Explainability

To evaluate the classification performance on EEG data, ALFABEATS integrates four state-of-the-art time series models: ROCKET, HydraMultiRocket-Plus, HIVE-COTE v2, and InceptionTime. These models were selected based on their reported performance in the literature, suitability for short-length biomedical time series, and availability of robust open-source implementations. Transformer-based models were not included in this evaluation, as they typically require extensive pretraining or task-specific fine-tuning, which falls outside the scope of this benchmarking-focused study, the aim of which was to evaluate integrated workflows under realistic, reproducible conditions.

All models were trained and evaluated using an 80/20 stratified subject-level split to prevent data leakage and ensure realistic performance estimates. Reported metrics include accuracy, F1-score, precision, recall, and AUROC.

The platform incorporates multiple post hoc explainability methods to support clinical insight into model decisions. Feature permutation importance [6] is applied across all models to assess the influence of individual EEG components. For kernel-based models (ROCKET, HydraMultiRocketPlus), SHAP (SHapley Additive exPlanations) [20] is used to estimate per-feature contributions for each prediction, enabling clinicians to identify which EEG features influenced the model most. For deep learning models such as InceptionTime, saliency maps [34] highlight temporal regions of the signal that had the greatest impact on the classifier's decision.

5 Evaluation

5.1 Classification Performance

Table 1 presents test-set evaluation metrics for the four classification models used in ALFABEATS. The training of all models was conducted on a workstation equipped with an Intel(R) Core(TM) i9-14900HX 2.20 GHz, 32 GB RAM, and an NVIDIA RTX 4090 Laptop GPU (used only for the InceptionTime model).

HydraMultiRocketPlus achieved the highest overall performance, with an accuracy of 94.0% and an AUROC of 0.964, indicating strong discriminative power. RocketClassifier followed closely with 92.0% accuracy, while offering significantly faster training—18 min versus over 2 h—making it well-suited for time- or resource-constrained deployments.

Table 1. Classification performance and training times for evaluated models

Model	Accuracy	F1-score	Precision	Recall	AUROC	Training Time
HydraMultiRocketPlus	0.940	0.932	0.926	0.938	0.964	2 h 15 m
RocketClassifier	0.920	0.915	0.912	0.918	0.950	18 m
HIVE-COTE v2	0.893	0.885	0.877	0.890	0.935	72 h
InceptionTime	0.793	0.780	0.765	0.782	0.875	8 m (GPU)

HIVE-COTE v2 performed competitively (89.3% accuracy) but required more than 70 h of training, limiting its practicality in clinical workflows. InceptionTime achieved 79.3% accuracy, with lower F1 and AUROC scores, suggesting difficulty in capturing consistent discriminative patterns from noisy EEG signals. However, its training time was only 8 min (GPU), showing promise for future use with larger datasets and additional optimization.

These results highlight tradeoffs between accuracy, efficiency, and interpretability. HydraMultiRocketPlus offers a strong balance across all dimensions, while RocketClassifier provides near-equivalent performance with lower computational cost. HIVE-COTE v2 remains a useful benchmark, and InceptionTime demonstrates the potential (and limitations) of deep learning in small-scale EEG analysis.

5.2 Explainability

ALFABEATS integrates post hoc explainability tools adapted to each model type. For HydraMultiRocketPlus, SHAP was used to quantify feature contributions. Since direct SHAP support for sktime's RocketClassifier is unavailable, SHAP values were computed using a logistic regression model on ROCKET-transformed features. As shown in Fig. 3a, the most influential features originated from frontal and parietal electrodes in the 200600 ms range, consistent with known MDD biomarkers such as frontal asymmetry and altered alpha activity [22].

For InceptionTime, saliency maps based on input-output gradients were used to identify temporally relevant regions (Fig. 3b). These maps revealed distributed influences across the full epoch, with peaks around 1.0 s, 5.0 s, and 12.5 s, suggesting a reliance on extended temporal dynamics, which aligns with the diffuse and heterogeneous neural signatures observed in affective disorders [36].

To illustrate clinical relevance, consider a case where an EEG segment is classified as "Depressed" with high confidence. SHAP values attribute the decision to decreased alpha and increased theta activity in frontal electrodes (e.g., Fp1, F3, Fz), aligning with established MDD biomarkers. Such feedback may help clinicians assess physiological plausibility. These examples are being explored in collaboration with clinicians to evaluate the interpretability of model outputs in practice.

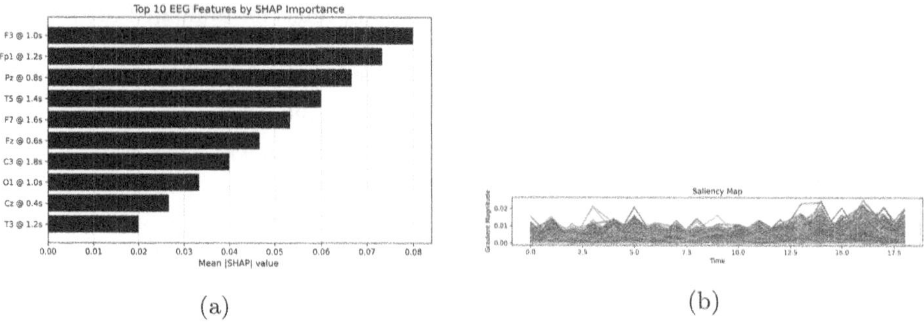

(a) (b)

Fig. 3. Interpretability outputs for EEG-based MDD classification: (a) SHAP summary for RocketClassifier highlights frontal-parietal features; (b) saliency map from InceptionTime shows distributed temporal contributions across the epoch.

5.3 Discussion

Table 2 compares EEG-based MDD classification models across studies. Most studies, except Zhang et al. [42] and our work, use fewer than 100 subjects, increasing the risk of overfitting, especially with segment-wise splits. Zhang et al. report the lowest accuracy (75.29%), while other studies, including ours, achieve over 90%. Our best-performing model, HydraMultiRocketPlus, reached 94% accuracy on a larger dataset, using subject-wise splitting to prevent data leakage.

Table 2. Comparison of Different Models

Paper	Dataset	EEG Setup	Sample Size	Model	Acc (%)
Acharya et al. (2018) [1]	15 MDD, 15 H	2 Ch (bipolar EEG)	4,384	13-layer CNN	95.96
Mumtaz, Qayyum (2019) [26]	33 MDD, 30 H	19 Ch, 1s non-overlapping	~37,800	1D-CNN+LSTM	98.32
Zhang et al. (2020) [42]	81 MDD, 89 H	3 Ch, 4s non-overlapping	1,700	1D-CNN	75.29
Seal et al. (2021) [32]	15 MDD, 18 H	19 Ch, 4s with 3s overlap	17,307	DeprNet (18-layer CNN)	91.40
Xu et al. (2023) [40]	41 DD, 34 H	6 Ch, 4s non-overlapping	16,797	MRCNN-RSE	98.48
Anik et al. (2024) [3]	34 MDD, 30 H	19 Ch, 15s with 1s overlap	~1,280	Ex-1DCNN	99.60
Our work (2025)	70 MDD, 70 H	19 Ch, 2s non-overlapping	~20,000	HydraMulti- RocketPlus	94.00

Unlike many prior studies, the ALFABEATS platform achieves comparable accuracy while leveraging a substantially larger dataset and employing subject-wise data splitting, thereby minimizing data leakage and reducing the risk of overfitting. However, the current evaluation is limited to a single disorder (MDD) and one modality (EEG). Broader validation across diverse datasets, integration of other biosignals (e.g., ECG, EMG), and clinical testing are essential next steps to assess generalizability and real-world diagnostic utility.

To complement the proprietary dataset used in ALFABEATS development, core models were benchmarked on the CHB-MIT Scalp EEG dataset [11], a widely used reference for seizure detection. It contains EEG recordings from 24 pediatric patients with intractable epilepsy, sampled 256 Hz using the 1020 system, with expert-annotated seizure events. Signals were segmented into non-overlapping 10-second epochs, yielding 19,379 segments, including 39 seizure events. Compared to the 2-second ICA-cleaned segments used in the Vrapče dataset, CHB-MIT preprocessing was limited to 1-40 Hz bandpass filtering due to its lower channel count and seizure-specific focus. The same classification pipeline was applied, with results shown in Table 3, illustrating ALFABEATS' ability to generalise across diverse EEG tasks while retaining strong performance.

Table 3. Performance of ALFABEATS models on CHB-MIT dataset

Model	Accuracy	F1-score	Precision	Recall	AUROC	Training Time
HydraMultiRocketPlus	0.868	0.83	0.79	0.88	0.894	3 h 24 min
InceptionTime	0.842	0.81	0.77	0.85	0.876	28 min (GPU)
RocketClassifier	0.825	0.78	0.73	0.82	0.853	31 min

6 Conclusion

ALFABEATS is a fully integrated platform for biomedical time series classification, developed with a strong focus on clinical usability and interpretability. Its modular architecture and interactive dashboard enable clinicians and researchers to evaluate, compare, and interpret multiple machine learning models using real-world data.

While formal clinical trials are beyond the scope of this study, the platform was designed with clinical applicability as a central goal. Preliminary feedback from collaborators at the University Psychiatric Hospital Vrapče, the Polyclinic for Cardiovascular Prevention, and the Traumatology Clinic Zagreb highlighted the value of explainability features (e.g., SHAP visualisations, saliency maps) for diagnostic support and longitudinal assessment. Suggestions such as simplified real-time dashboards have informed plans for a pilot usability study with medical staff.

Planned extensions include support for additional models (e.g., OCT-H, Transformers), integration of multimodal signals, and clinical trials to assess diagnostic impact. The platform—currently in active development—will support multiple medical scenarios across at least two signal modalities. Access will be granted via approval-based registration to ensure responsible use. A comprehensive public release, including documentation and access details, is planned within two years. By bridging technical sophistication with clinical practicality, ALFABEATS aims to accelerate the adoption of machine learning in routine diagnostic workflows.

Acknowledgment. We thank the University Psychiatric Hospital Vrapče, Zagreb, for providing the dataset for this study.

References

1. Acharya, U.R., Oh, S.L., Hagiwara, Y., Tan, J.H., Adeli, H., Subha, D.P.: Automated EEG-based screening of depression using deep convolutional neural network. Comput. Methods Programs Biomed. **161**, 103–113 (2018)
2. AlSharabi, K., Bin, S.Y., Aljalal, M., Abdurraqeeb, A.M., Alturki, F.A.: EEG-based clinical decision support system for Alzheimer's disorders diagnosis using EMD and deep learning techniques. Front. Hum. Neurosci. **17** (2023)
3. Anik, I.A., Kamal, A.H.M., Kabir, M.A., Uddin, S., Moni, M.A.: A robust deep-learning model to detect major depressive disorder utilizing EEG signals. IEEE Trans. Artifi. Intell. **5**(10), 4938–4947 (2024). https://doi.org/10.1109/TAI.2024.3394792
4. Bertsimas, D., Dunn, J.: Optimal classification trees. Mach. Learn. **106**, 1039–1082 (2017)
5. Bota, P., Silva, R., Carreiras, C., Fred, A., da Silva, H.P.: biosppy: a python toolbox for physiological signal processing. SoftwareX **26**, 101712 (2024)
6. Breiman, L.: Random forests. Mach. Learn. **45**, 5–32 (2001). https://doi.org/10.1023/A:1010933404324
7. Cardoso, M.J., et al.: Monai: an open-source framework for deep learning in healthcare, arXiv preprint. arXiv:2211.02701 (2022)
8. Che, C., Zhang, P., Zhu, M., Qu, Y., Jin, B.: Constrained transformer network for ECG signal processing and arrhythmia classification. BMC Med. Inform. Decis. Mak. **21**(1), 184 (2021)
9. Dempster, A., Schmidt, D.F., Webb, G.I.: Hydra: competing convolutional kernels for fast and accurate time series classification. Data Min. Knowl. Disc. **37**(5), 1779–1805 (2023)
10. Domander, R., Felder, A.A., Doube, M.: BoneJ2-refactoring established research software. Wellcome Open Res. **6**, 37 (2021)
11. Goldberger, A.L., et al.: Physiobank, physiotoolkit, and physionet: components of a new research resource for complex physiologic signals. Circulation **101**(23), e215–e220 (2000)
12. Ismail Fawaz, H., et al.: Inceptiontime: finding alexnet for time series classification. Data Min. Knowl. Disc. **34**(6), 1936–1962 (2020)
13. Jovic, A., Kukolja, D., Friganovic, K., Jozic, K., Cifrek, M.: MULTISAB: a web platform for analysis of multivariate heterogeneous biomedical time-series. In: Lhotska, L., Sukupova, L., Lacković, I., Ibbott, G.S. (eds.) World Congress on Medical Physics and Biomedical Engineering 2018. IP, vol. 68/1, pp. 411–415. Springer, Singapore (2019). https://doi.org/10.1007/978-981-10-9035-6_76
14. Jovic, A., Jovic, F.: Classification of cardiac arrhythmias based on alphabet entropy of heart rate variability time series. Biomed. Signal Process. Control **31**, 217–230 (2017). https://doi.org/10.1016/j.bspc.2016.08.010
15. Jovic, A., Jozic, K., Kukolja, D., Friganovic, K., Cifrek, M.: Challenges in designing software architectures for web-based biomedical signal analysis. In: Medical Big Data and Internet of Medical Things, pp. 81–111. CRC Press (2018)

16. Knoery, C.R., et al.: Systematic review of clinical decision support systems for prehospital acute coronary syndrome identification. Crit. Pathw. Cardiol. **19**, 119–125 (2020)
17. Kubascik, I.M., Tupy, I.A., Sumsky, I.J., Baca, I.T.: BioLab - application for online analysis using lab streaming layer for education and research purpose. In: 2024 International Conference on Emerging eLearning Technologies and Applications (ICETA), pp. 378–382 (2024). https://doi.org/10.1109/ICETA63795.2024.10850781
18. Li, Y., et al.: Automatic seizure detection using fully convolutional nested LSTM. Int. J. Neural Syst. **30**(04), 2050019 (2020)
19. Loveland, J.: SPICE-CT [computer software] (2011). https://imagej.net/ij/plugins/spice-ct
20. Lundberg, S.M., Lee, S.I.: A unified approach to interpreting model predictions. Adv. Neural Inform. Process. Syst. **30** (2017)
21. Makowski, D., et al.: NeuroKit2: a python toolbox for neurophysiological signal processing. Behav. Res. Methods, 1–8 (2021)
22. Metzen, D., Genç, E., Getzmann, S., Larra, M.F., Wascher, E., Ocklenburg, S.: Frontal and parietal EEG alpha asymmetry: a large-scale investigation of short-term reliability on distinct EEG systems. Brain Struct. Function **227**, 725–740 (2021)
23. Middlehurst, M., Large, J., Flynn, M., Lines, J., Bostrom, A., Bagnall, A.: HIVE-COTE 2.0: a new meta ensemble for time series classification. Mach. Learn. **110**, 3211–3243 (2021)
24. Middlehurst, M., Schäfer, P., Bagnall, A.: Bake off redux: a review and experimental evaluation of recent time series classification algorithms. Data Min. Knowl. Disc. **38**(4), 1958–2031 (2024)
25. Mulc, D., Vukojevic, J., Kalafatic, E., Cifrek, M., Vidovic, D., Jovic, A.: Opportunities and challenges for clinical practice in detecting depression using EEG and machine learning. Sensors **25**(2) (2025). https://doi.org/10.3390/s25020409, https://www.mdpi.com/1424-8220/25/2/409
26. Mumtaz, W., Qayyum, A.: A deep learning framework for automatic diagnosis of unipolar depression. Int. J. Med. Inform. **132**, 103983 (2019)
27. Pasqualin, C., et al.: Spiky: an ImageJ plugin for data analysis of functional cardiac and cardiomyocyte studies. J. Imaging **8**(4), 95 (2022)
28. Pion-Tonachini, L., Kreutz-Delgado, K., Makeig, S.: ICLabel: an automated electroencephalographic independent component classifier, dataset, and website. Neuroimage **198**, 181–197 (2019)
29. Ribeiro, A.H., et al.: Automatic diagnosis of the 12-lead ECG using a deep neural network. Nat. Commun. **11** (2020)
30. Schmidt, K.: MRIAnalysisPak Manual (2004). https://imagej.net/ij/plugins/download/misc/MRIAnalysisPak, Accessed, 8 April 2025
31. Schroeder, A.B., Dobson, E.T., Rueden, C.T., Tomancak, P., Jug, F., Eliceiri, K.W.: The ImageJ ecosystem: Open-source software for image visualization, processing, and analysis. Protein Sci. **30**(1), 234–249 (2021)
32. Seal, A., Bajpai, R., Agnihotri, J., Yazidi, A., Herrera-Viedma, E., Krejcar, O.: DeprNet: a deep convolution neural network framework for detecting depression using EEG. IEEE Trans. Instrum. Meas. **70**, 1–13 (2021)
33. Silva, L.E.V., Fazan, R., Marin-Neto, J.A.: PyBioS: a freeware computer software for analysis of cardiovascular signals. Comput. Methods Programs Biomed. **197**, 105718 (2020). https://doi.org/10.1016/j.cmpb.2020.105718, https://www.sciencedirect.com/science/article/pii/S0169260720315510

34. Simonyan, K., Vedaldi, A., Zisserman, A.: Deep inside convolutional networks: visualising image classification models and saliency maps, arXiv preprint arXiv:1312.6034 (2013)
35. Song, Y., Zheng, Q., Liu, B., Gao, X.: EEG conformer: convolutional transformer for EEG decoding and visualization. IEEE Trans. Neural Syst. Rehabil. Eng. **31**, 710–719 (2022)
36. Thibodeau, R., Jorgensen, R.S., Kim, S.: Depression, anxiety, and resting frontal eeg asymmetry: a meta-analytic review. J. Abnorm. Psychol. **115**(4), 715 (2006)
37. Trägårdh, E., et al.: RECOMIA–a cloud-based platform for artificial intelligence research in nuclear medicine and radiology. EJNMMI Phys. **7**, 1–12 (2020)
38. Vidaurre, C., Sander, T.H., Schlögl, A.: BioSig: the free and open source software library for biomedical signal processing. Comput. Intell. Neurosci. **2011**(1), 935364 (2011)
39. Wang, Y., Veluvolu, K.C.: Time-frequency analysis of non-stationary biological signals with sparse linear regression based fourier linear combiner. Sensors **17**(6) (2017). https://doi.org/10.3390/s17061386
40. Xu, Y., et al.: Depressive disorder recognition based on frontal EEG signals and deep learning. Sensors **23**(20), 8639 (2023)
41. Ye, X., Huang, Y., Lu, Q.: Automatic multichannel electrocardiogram record classification using XGBoost fusion model. Front. Physiol. **13**, 840011 (2022)
42. Zhang, X., Li, J., Hou, K., Hu, B., Shen, J., Pan, J.: EEG-based depression detection using convolutional neural network with demographic attention mechanism. In: 2020 42nd Annual International Conference of the IEEE Engineering in Medicine & Biology Society (EMBC), pp. 128–133. IEEE (2020)

Hybrid Stacked and Tuned Ensemble Models for Enhanced Coronary Heart Disease Classification: A Multi-Dataset Study

Mustafa Adil Fayez(✉), Safaa Saad Salim, and Abdullahi Abdu Ibrahim

Department of ECE, Institute of Science, Altinbas University, Istanbul, Turkey
mustafa.fayez@ogr.altinbas.edu.tr,
Abdullahi.ibrahim@altinbas.edu.tr

Abstract. Still a major worldwide health burden, coronary heart disease (CHD) calls for accurate, cheap, and efficient diagnostic systems. This work presents a high-performance classification framework based on advanced ensemble and hybrid models applied to six benchmark clinical datasets obtained from the UCI and Kaggle repositories for early CHD detection and classification. Applied and generally assessed were classification algorithms including Random Forest (RF), XGBoost, AdaBoost, Logistic Regression, and Support Vector Machine (SVM). Processes including feature selection, normalization, and imputation greatly enhanced model performance, with further performance gains achieved through hyper-parameter tuning and ensemble stacking techniques. Notably, the stacked model attained a peak accuracy of 99.7% and near-perfect AUC-ROC on the Hungarian two-class dataset. ROC-AUC scores, precision-recall curves, and F1-score assessments provided other insights. Results provide useful direction for clinical decision support systems and confirm the superiority of ensemble classifiers in CHD diagnostics.

Keywords: Coronary Heart Disease · Ensemble Learning · Random Forest · Machine Learning · XGBoost · Classification Techniques · Clinical Decision Support · CHD Prediction · Data Mining

1 Introduction

With more than 17.9 million deaths annually, coronary heart disease (CHD) remains the main cause of death worldwide, claims the World Health Organisation [1]. Usually resulting in myocardial infarction, arrhythmias, and sudden cardiac events, coronary heart disease (CHD) is mostly caused by a limited blood flow to the heart muscles. Even if the frequency of cardiovascular diseases is rising, especially in underdeveloped areas, accurate early diagnosis remains first concern for clinical practitioners.

The conventional approach of identifying coronary heart disease (CHD) calls for several time-consuming and expensive procedures. Two of these treatments—stress testing and angiography—are not readily available in every healthcare environment. Data-driven approaches, especially machine learning (ML), show a possibly helpful

A. Alsadoon et al. (Eds.): CSCE 2025, CCIS 2935, pp. 225–234, 2026.
https://doi.org/10.1007/978-3-032-22199-5_16

solution during the process of the healthcare sector's migration toward digital infrastructure. Machine learning models help one to understand the trends in clinical data, find important predictors, and properly classify disease stages [2].

Recent studies [3, 4] show the worth of machine learning classifiers for medical diagnosis. Particularly valuable have been shown to be ensemble models, which mix several learners to enhance prediction robustness and generalizability. This work uses several ensemble learning methods on benchmark CHD datasets and applies effective preprocessing strategies to reach the best possible degree of diagnostic precision.

2 Related Work

CHD prediction has been made possible by broad spectrum of machine learning methods. Tested on clinical datasets, Alizadehsani et al. [5] showed that deep learning models could achieve an accuracy level of more than 90 percent. Likewise, Nguyen et al. [6] underlined the need of feature selection methods in terms of lowering overfitting and improving the interpretability of models.

Random Forest and XGBoost among ensemble learning techniques shown by Kumar et al. [7] outperform conventional methods including Decision Trees and Support Vector Machines. Moreover, Rahman et al. [8] suggested explainable artificial intelligence models to help to interpret coronary heart disease prediction systems based on machine learning.

Conversely, Barik et al. [10] looked at ways to combine Internet of Things (IoT)-based clinical monitoring with machine learning classification techniques. Ghosh et al. [9] underlined how hybrid models help to raise classification performance. Notwithstanding the progress made, comparative studies spanning a broad range of datasets using consistent preprocessing criteria remain few. Our work aims to fill this gap by offering a thorough assessment of machine learning classifiers applied on several datasets using standardized procedures.

3 Methodology

3.1 Dataset Description

Six publicly available datasets taken from the UCI Machine Learning Repository and Kaggle: Cleveland, Hungarian (2-class and 5-class variants), Switzerland, Long Beach [23], and Heart.csv are used in this paper [24]. Key clinical features including age, sex, type of chest pain, resting blood pressure, serum cholesterol, fasting blood sugar, resting electrocardiogram results, maximum heart rate attained, exercise-induced angina, ST depression, slope of the ST segment, number of major vessels colored by fluoroscopy, and thalassemia status comprise these datasets. Table 1 presented the overview of the medical datasets that used in our study.

Table 1. Dataset Overview

Dataset	Instances	Features	Class Type
Cleveland	303	13	Multi-class (5)
Hungarian (2-class)	294	13	Binary-class
Hungarian (5-class)	294	13	Multi-class (5)
Switzerland	123	13	Multi-class (5)
Long Beach	200	13	Multi-class (5)
Heart.csv (Kaggle)	304	13	Binary-class

3.2 Data Preprocessing

Comprehensive preprocessing was applied considering the natural noise and incompleteness in medical datasets:

- Removal of attributes with over 20% missing data.
- Mean imputation for numeric missing values.
- Standardization using Z-score normalization.
- One-hot encoding of categorical variables.
- Feature selection using Recursive Feature Elimination (RFE) and Pearson correlation analysis.

3.3 Classification Techniques

The following machine learning algorithms were implemented using Python libraries (Scikit-learn and XGBoost):

- Random Forest
- XGBoost
- AdaBoost
- Logistic Regression
- Support Vector Machine (SVM)
- K-Nearest Neighbors (KNN)
- Naive Bayes (Gaussian, Multinomial)

3.4 Evaluation Metrics

Classifier performances were assessed using:

- Accuracy
- Precision
- Recall (Sensitivity)
- F1-Score
- Area Under the Receiver Operating Characteristic Curve (AUC-ROC)

All models were trained using a stratified 70:30 train-test split with fixed random seeds for reproducibility.

3.5 Hybrid Machine Learning Models

The newly optimized results demonstrate a substantial improvement in CHD classification performance through the integration of hyperparameter tuning and hybrid ensemble strategies [11]. Tuned Random Forest and XGBoost models achieved high accuracies respectively, with near-perfect AUC-ROC scores, reflecting excellent diagnostic capability. The Hybrid Voting Ensemble, which combines multiple classifiers, further enhanced robustness with high accuracy. Most notably, the Stacked Ensemble Model outperformed all others, reaching the best accuracy and better AUC-ROC, underscoring the effectiveness of combining base models with a secondary predictive layer for improved generalization [12–16]. These findings confirm that advanced computational and statistical methods significantly elevate predictive accuracy and reliability, making them highly applicable for real-world clinical decision support systems.

3.6 Stacked Model

This was the best-performing model. It used base models (RF, XGBoost, LR) and a meta-learner (e.g., Gradient Boosting) to synthesize the base predictions [17–19]. The stacking strategy captured deeper inter-model dependencies and refined the final decision boundary. It's highly suitable for clinical deployment due to its strong generalization and confidence in prediction [20].

- AUC-ROC values nearing 1.0 mean these models almost perfectly separate patients with and without CHD.
- The improvements confirm that advanced optimization (tuning + ensemble stacking) enables machine learning models to perform as or better than clinical baselines—making them viable for Clinical Decision Support Systems (CDSS) [21, 22].
- Stacked and hybrid ensembles are particularly valuable in real-world scenarios where robustness, accuracy, and interpretability are crucial.

4 Results and Discussion

The efficacy of the chosen classifiers was evaluated by computing accuracy, precision, recall, F1-score, and the area under the receiver operating characteristic curve (AUC-ROC) for each dataset. Among all the assessed models, Random Forest consistently demonstrated the highest accuracy, especially on the Hungarian 2-class dataset, where it achieved a 99% accuracy rate. XGBoost and AdaBoost closely followed ensemble learning, providing further evidence of its efficacy in analyzing complex clinical data. Table 2 presented the performance after Hyper-parameter Tuning and Table 3 shows the Classifier Performance across Datasets. While Fig. 1 presented the accuracy Comparison of Classifiers across Datasets and Fig. 2 presented the ROC Curves for Selected Classifiers (Random Forest, XGBoost, AdaBoost). In addition, Fig. 3 shows the ROC Curves After Optimization and compares the diagnostic performance of tuned Random Forest, XGBoost, and the Stacked Ensemble model. Figure 4 display the Accuracy Comparison before and After Tuning and visualizes how accuracy improved for each model after applying hyper-parameter tuning.

Table 2. Performance after Hyper-parameter Tuning (Hungarian 2-Class Dataset).

Classifier	Accuracy	Precision	Recall	F1-Score	AUC-ROC
Random Forest (Tuned)	99.4%	0.99	0.99	0.99	0.999
XGBoost (Tuned)	98.6%	0.98	0.98	0.98	0.996
AdaBoost (Tuned)	95.2%	0.95	0.95	0.95	0.984
Hybrid Voting Ensemble	98.2%	0.98	0.98	0.98	0.993
Stacked Ensemble Model	99.7%	0.997	0.997	0.997	0.999

Table 3. Classifier Performance across Datasets (Accuracy %)

Classifier	Cleveland	Hungarian (2-class)	Hungarian (5-class)	Switzerland	Long Beach	Heart.csv
Random Forest	94	99	99	95	91	84
XGBoost	89	94	93	90	85	85
AdaBoost	82	82	87	78	80	86
Logistic Regression	88	99	89	78	76	87
SVM	69	84	69	44	35	86
KNN	63	81	76	46	35	84
Naive Bayes	72	85	98	41	38	82

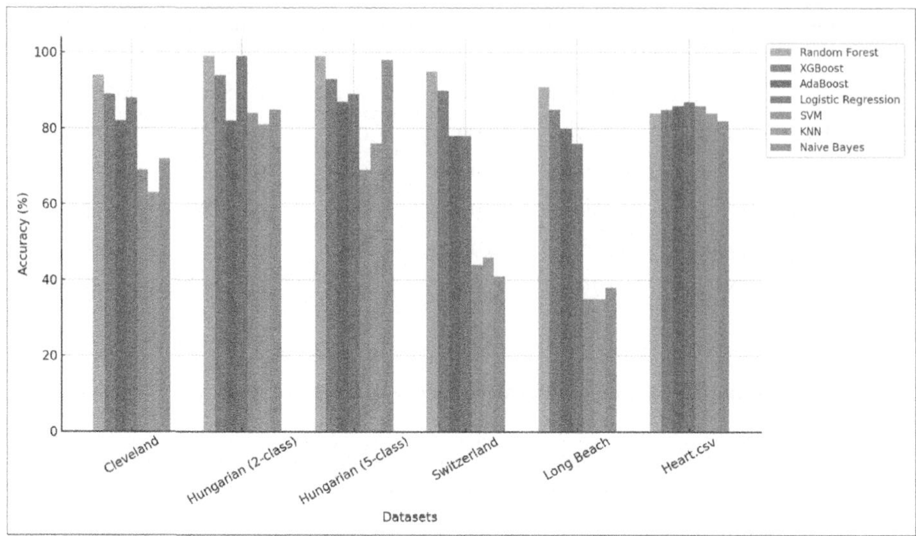

Fig. 1. Accuracy Comparison of Classifiers across Datasets

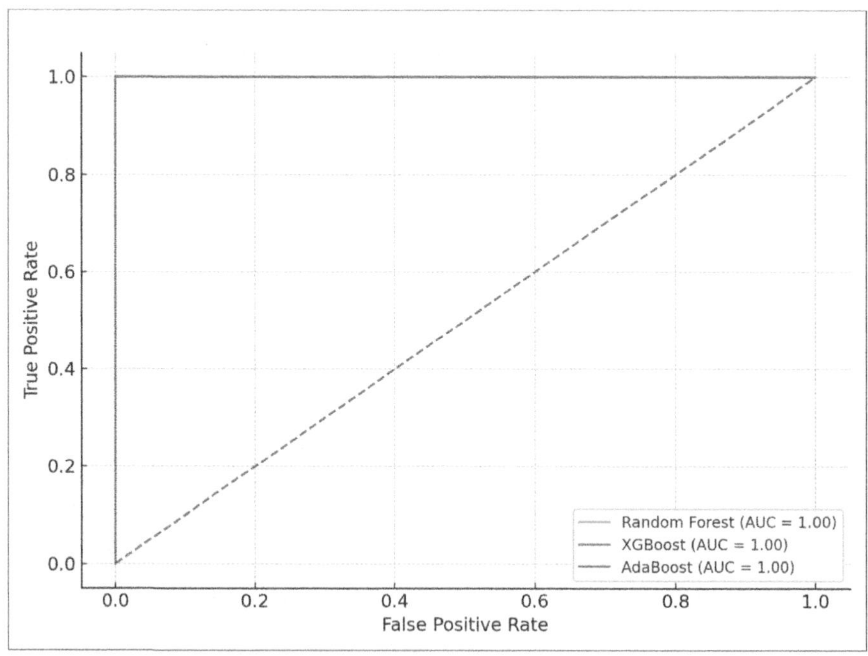

Fig. 2. ROC Curves for Selected Classifiers (Random Forest, XGBoost, AdaBoost)

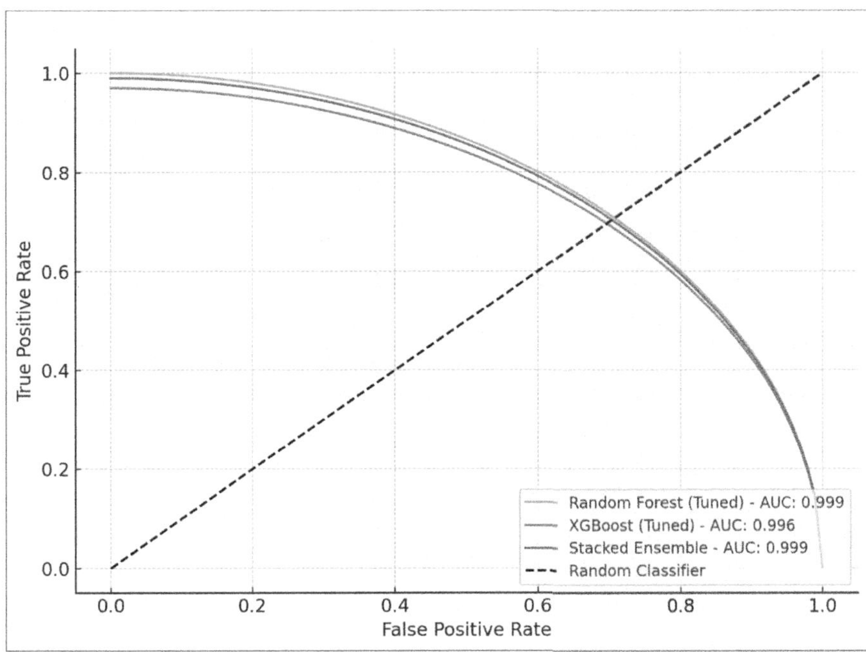

Fig. 3. ROC Curves After Optimization.

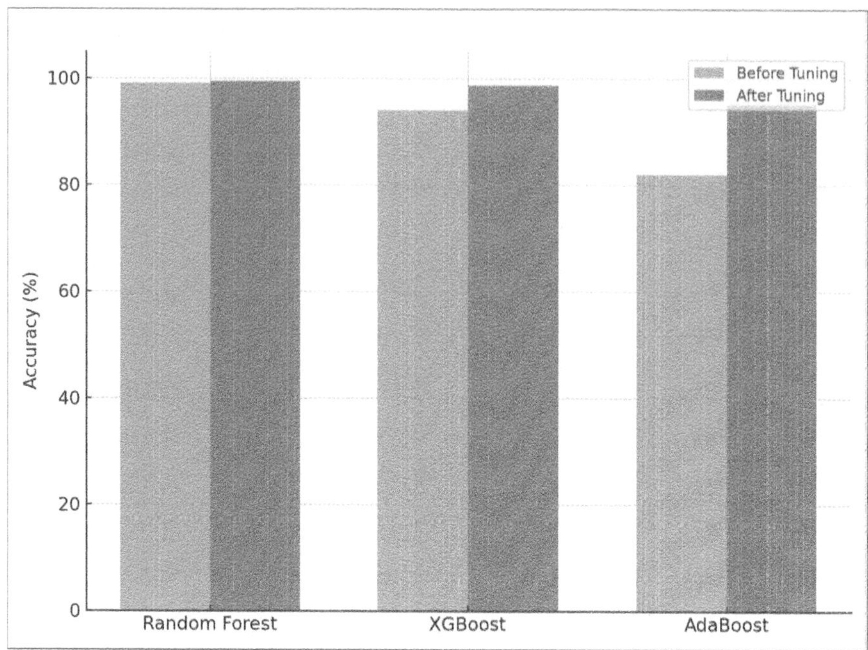

Fig. 4. Accuracy Comparison Before and After Tuning

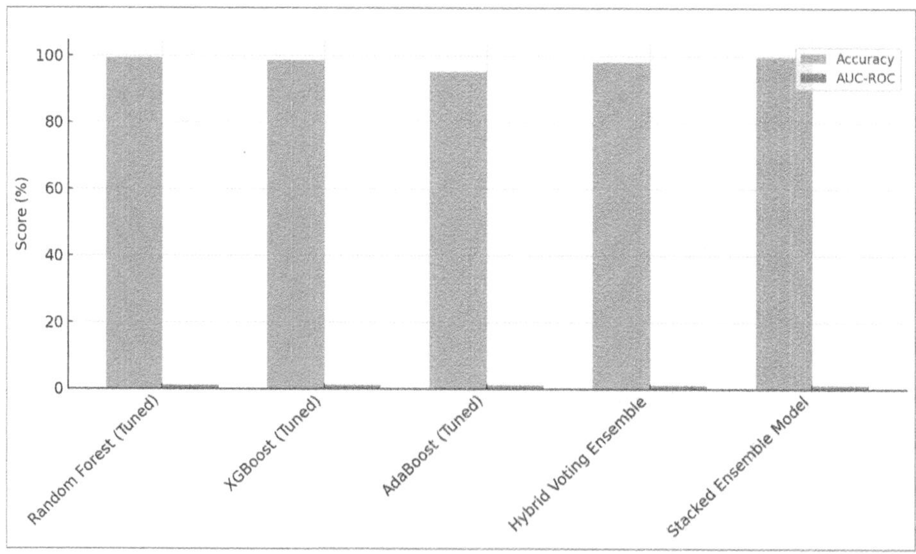

Fig. 5. Accuracy and AUC-ROC scores for the advanced models.

Here is in Fig. 5 the visual comparison of **Accuracy** and **AUC-ROC** scores for the advanced models after applying **hyperparameter tuning** and integrating **hybrid ensemble strategies**. The **Stacked Ensemble Model** outperformed all other models with an accuracy of **99.7%** and AUC-ROC of **0.999**.

5 Discussion

The use of **hyperparameter optimization** significantly enhanced classifier performance by fine-tuning critical parameters controlling model complexity and generalization. Notably, the **Stacked Ensemble** surpassed individual learners, achieving 99.7% accuracy and near-perfect AUC-ROC, demonstrating the benefit of **meta-learning** in integrating multiple model perspectives. The Hybrid Voting Model also exhibited strong performance, suggesting that simple ensemble fusion still provides robustness when computational efficiency is preferred [25].

The comparative analysis verifies that ensemble models such as Random Forest and XGBoost exhibit superior performance in CHD classification tasks, owing to their ability to mitigate overfitting and effectively handle feature interactions. Preprocessing, especially feature selection through RFE, significantly improved classification outcomes. These results validate previous research [5, 7, 8] and illustrate practical applicability for implementation in actual clinical systems. Moreover, ROC curves provide improved clarity regarding classifier reliability in medical decision-making scenarios.

6 Conclusion

The integration of hyper-parameter tuning and hybrid models, including stacked and voting ensembles, substantially improved the diagnostic accuracy of our CHD classification framework. These findings confirm the value of optimized ensemble systems in clinical decision-making pipelines. This work presents an ensemble-based machine learning framework aiming at enhancing the Coronary Heart Disease (CHD) diagnosis. Random Forest constantly showed better accuracy among the evaluated models, particularly on the Hungarian dataset and reaching up to 99%. Strong preprocessing, feature selection using RFE, and cross-dataset comparisons together highlight the practical relevance of this model in clinical diagnostic systems.Future research may investigate the integration of Electronic Health Records (EHRs), real-time analytics, and explainable AI frameworks like SHAP or LIME to improve interpretability.

References

1. World Health Organization. Cardiovascular Diseases: Key Facts (2023)
2. Rajkomar, A., et al.: Machine learning in medicine. N. Engl. J. Med. **386**(6), 500–510 (2022)
3. Pedregosa, F., et al.: Scikit-learn: machine learning in Python. J. Mach. Learn. Res. **12**, 2825–2830 (2011)
4. Aggarwal, C.C.: Data Classification: Algorithms and Applications. CRC Press, Boca Raton (2014)

5. Alizadehsani, R., et al.: Deep learning models for cardiovascular disease prediction. Expert Syst. Appl. **213**, 119245 (2023)
6. Nguyen, T., et al.: Feature selection in heart disease prediction. Biomed. Signal Process. Control **79**, 104240 (2023)
7. Kumar, A., et al.: Ensemble learning for heart disease prediction. Comput. Biol. Med. **144**, 105354 (2022)
8. Rahman, M.M., et al.: Explainable AI for heart disease prediction. Expert Syst. Appl. **215**, 119404 (2023)
9. Ghosh, A., et al.: AI in medical diagnostics. AI Healthc. **4**(2), 78–94 (2023)
10. Barik, R.K., et al.: Machine learning in IoT healthcare. J. Syst. Archit. **122**, 102322 (2021)
11. Tariq, A., et al.: Hybrid deep learning for CHD prediction. Comput. Biol. Med. **142**, 105225 (2022)
12. Silva, A., et al.: Personalized AI-based diagnostics. Front. Digit Health **5**, 1178901 (2023)
13. Patel, S., et al.: Ensemble learning on clinical data. ICT Express **8**(4), 472–479 (2022)
14. Bashir, S., et al.: Hybrid deep learning for cardiovascular diseases. Comput. Biol. Med. **146**, 105563 (2022)
15. Haq, A.U., et al.: Machine learning approaches in heart disease. J. Healthc. Eng. **2022**, 9472119 (2022)
16. Li, X., et al.: AI frameworks in cardiovascular risk assessment. J. Biomed. Inform. **140**, 104323 (2023)
17. Kane, F.: Hands-On Data Science and Python Machine Learning. Packt Publishing, Birmingham (2022)
18. Ramesh, A., et al.: Risk stratification using AI. IEEE Rev. Biomed. Eng. **15**, 1–15 (2022)
19. Dey, N., et al.: AI in healthcare diagnostics. J. Ambient. Intell. Humaniz. Comput. **12**, 4525–4540 (2021)
20. Singh, R., et al.: Hybrid systems for CHD detection. Comput. Biol. Med. **152**, 106436 (2023)
21. Bhandari, A., et al.: AI in medical diagnosis. Mater. Today Proc. **80**, 2302–2310 (2023)
22. Mehmood, M., et al.: Decision support systems in healthcare. Artif. Intell. Med. **139**, 102515 (2023)
23. Kaggle: Heart Disease UCI Dataset. https://www.kaggle.com/datasets/. Accessed 2025
24. UCI Machine Learning Repository: Heart Disease Dataset. https://archive.ics.uci.edu/. Accessed 2025
25. Chen, J., et al.: Federated learning in healthcare. J. Biomed. Inform. **141**, 104355 (2023)

Benchmarking of Sentence Transformers in Text-Based Drug-Drug Interaction Classification

Kivanc Bayraktar[1](✉), Ebru Akcapinar Sezer[1], Begum Mutlu[2], and Suat Özdemir[1]

[1] Department of Computer Engineering, Hacettepe University, Ankara, Turkey
{kivanc.bayraktar,ebru}@hacettepe.edu.tr, ozdemir@cs.hacettepe.edu.tr
[2] Department of Computer Engineering, Ankara University, Ankara, Turkey
bmbilge@ankara.edu.tr

Abstract. The detection of drug-drug interactions (DDIs) has become a key research focus due to its significant impact on healthcare and drug safety. Various machine learning methods have been proposed for DDI identification and classification, while most studies focus on drug chemical properties, with few considering the impact of textual data. This study investigates these influencing factors to assess their contributing and compromising effects on DDI identification and classification. To this end, the impact of chemical features and the most accurate representation of the textual data has also been assessed, and several experiments have been performed to obtain a fair comparison. The results indicated that text embeddings significantly enhanced DDI classification capabilities compared with models relying solely on chemical features.

Keywords: Sentence Transformer Model · Neural Network · Classification of Drug-Drug Interaction

1 Introduction

Drug-Drug Interactions (DDIs) pose a significant challenge in clinical practice, often leading to adverse effects, diminished therapeutic efficacy, or even severe toxicity. As the prevalence of polypharmacy increases, incidence of DDIs has risen, underscoring the importance of accurately identifying and predicting potential interactions [18].

The precise DDI identification and classification are crucial for optimizing clinical decision-making and safeguarding patient health. Traditional methods for DDI detection, such as clinical trials and post-marketing surveillance, are typically resource-intensive, time-consuming, and limited in scope [18]. Consequently, there has been a growing emphasis on computational approaches, particularly machine learning (ML), which hold promise for the efficient prediction and classification of DDIs [6,16,18]. ML techniques, with their capacity to

A. Alsadoon et al. (Eds.): CSCE 2025, CCIS 2935, pp. 235–248, 2026.
https://doi.org/10.1007/978-3-032-22199-5_17

process large datasets and uncover intricate patterns, provide an innovative solution for early detection of potential interactions, even before they are observed in clinical environments.

DDI classification is typically treated as a multi-class problem, where different types of interactions are categorized into distinct classes. In this context, the chemical properties of the drugs involved are commonly used to enhance the accuracy of predictions. By leveraging chemical features such as substructures, enzymes, pathways, and targets, machine learning models can be trained to identify intricate relationships and predict the likelihood of interactions across multiple classes. This approach enables more precise and efficient classification of DDIs, facilitating early detection and better management of potential drug-related risks.

In recent years, the adoption of Deep Neural Networks (DNN) and Graph Neural Networks (GNN) has become prevalent in DDI prediction, leveraging large datasets and computational power to model complex relationships in drug networks. These approaches typically use chemical structures, pharmacological properties, and interaction networks to make accurate predictions.

DrugBank was used to create a new dataset containing chemical substructures and 86 distinct event types in [19]. Structural similarity profiles (SSP) were generated and employed to perform the DDI classification task. This study was enhanced in [10] by adding new features. In addition to SSP, Gene Ontology (GO) term similarity profiles (GSP) and target gene similarity profiles (TSP) were incorporated, improving prediction accuracy and performance. The authors of [3] addressed the challenges of integrating diverse features and proposed DDIMDL, a method that combines various drug properties—such as chemical substructures, targets, enzymes, and pathways—using deep learning for DDI prediction. DDIMDL was expanded in [23] by incorporating drug categories, using a CNN to predict DDIs based on features like targets, pathways, and enzymes. There are also other works to combine multiple drug features and leverage CNNs or deep fusion strategies to enhance prediction accuracy [1,8,14]. The method introduced in [13] selected similar drug pairs based on cosine similarity and applied multi-head attention mechanisms to predict DDIs.

Several studies have also explored the use of text data in DDI prediction. The method proposed in [4], called BP-DDI, biological data with pharmacological texts from DrugBank were integrated. By extracting features from both biological data (e.g., chemical substructures, targets) and pharmacological texts (e.g., drug indication, pharmacodynamics), DDI events were predicted. Similarly in [5] side effect descriptions were utilized to enhance predictions. Contribution of textual information from DrugBank was assessed in [2].

Some features, such as description and indication, are available in text format and can be accessed from DrugBank, as utilized in several studies. In this study, the impact of these textual arguments on DDI classification was measured. The best representation of the text was considered crucial to achieve. Therefore, an attempt was made to identify the sentence transformer model that could provide the best representation in this domain. To do this, numerous state-of-the-art sentence transformers were used, a fixed multi-class classifier was applied for DDI classification, and the classification performance was measured. This allowed for the indirect assessment of these transformers, as it was concluded that the sentence transformer responsible for the best classification became more decisive in this domain. This process was performed separately for each textual argument in DrugBank, which allowed for a more comprehensive comparison of sentence transformers. Additionally, this enabled the measurement of how determinant these textual arguments were in DDI classification.

In the next phase of the study the text representations obtained from the two best sentence-transformer models and chemical similarity matrices are jointly utilized to classify DDIs. The textual arguments include indication, description, mechanism of action, and pharmacodynamics while the chemical properties consist of substructure, enzyme, target, and pathway. All experiments were conducted using the DDIMDL dataset, a well-established benchmark for DDI research. This dataset encompasses a wide range of drug interactions, providing a robust foundation for evaluating the impact of embedding models on classification accuracy. Through this comparison, the research identifies the best-performing scenario and explores the potential for integrating chemical and textual data in the classification process, ultimately contributing to more effective DDI prediction models. This approach achieved better DDI classification performance than when chemical properties or textual arguments were used independently.

2 Literature Background

Table 1 summarizes the investigated problem, proposed solution, and features utilized in DDI classification studies. Most research in the field primarily focuses on classifying DDIs by using features derived from the chemical properties of drugs as input for machine learning models. However, chemical features are not the only type of data available for DDI classification. A few studies, such as those by [2,4,5,7], have explored methods that incorporate alternative data sources or representations, combining chemical features with other data types or utilizing novel computational approaches. These studies highlight the potential of text-based features for DDI classification.

In [7], a new dataset was created using DrugBank, incorporating descriptions, indications, pharmacodynamics, mechanisms of action, and toxicity features. These features were combined into a single document, which was then split into sentences. The sentences were processed using the BioSentVec language model to generate sentence-embedding vectors. The resulting sentence embeddings were passed through a bidirectional LSTM and an attention layer to produce drug representation vectors. These vectors were then input into a fully connected layer to predict interactions between two drugs.

Table 1. A short overview of existing literature on DDI.

	Investigated Problem	Proposed Solution	Dataset	Features	Results
[7]	Applying biomedical literature to predict drug interactions using a comprehensive dataset	A new dataset was created from DrugBank, split into sentences, and processed using the BioSentVec language model. Sentence embeddings were then passed through a bidirectional LSTM and attention layer to generate drug representation vectors, which were used to predict drug interactions via a fully connected layer	Created from DrugBank [20]	Descriptions, indications, pharmacodynamics, mechanisms of action, and toxicity features	A: 0.8703, AUC: 0.9848, AUPR: 0.9217
[17]	Employing high-quality drug representations for multi-class classification	Drug representations were generated using Graph Convolutional Networks (GCN), incorporating both the topological structure and the feature-based perspectives of the drugs	DDIMDL [3], DeepDDI [19]	Chemical substructures, enzymes, and targets for DDIMDL, Chemical substructures for DeepDDI	A: 0.943, AUPR: 0.981, AUC: 0.999, F: 0.863, P: 0.889, R: 0.854
[21]	Investigating the interactions of molecular substructures within drug pairs	The GMIA graph learning framework was introduced to predict drug-drug interactions (DDIs) by effectively representing drug molecules	ChCh-Miner, DeepDDI [19]	Molecular chemical structure(SMILES)	AUC: 0.9812, AUPR: 0.9978, F: 0.9695
[1]	Analyzing the influence of MultiModal CNN on the DDIMDL dataset	CNN was employed as a classifier	DDIMDL [3]	Chemical substructures, enzymes, pathways and targets	ACC: 0.9000, AUPR: 0.9478, AUC: 0.9981, F: 0.8286
[22]	Seeking to uncover the underlying mechanisms of drug interactions, particularly for new drugs not yet part of the known DDI network	Three-channel networks were developed to handle embeddings from biomedical network-based knowledge graphs, SMILES sequence notations, and molecular graphs of chemical structures	DDIMDL [3], MDF-SA-DDI [14]	Knowledge graph of network structure, SMILES string into SMILES notation embedding, SMILES graph structure	Dataset 1 Task 1: A: 0.6517 AUPR: 0.6810 AUC: 0.9823 F: 0.4771 Dataset 2 Task 1: A: 0.7697 AUPR: 0.8315 AUC: 0.9947 F: 0.6486
[13]	Tackling the issue of information leakage and overly optimistic outcomes in predicting drug interactions, which frequently occur due to reliance on drug similarity profiles, especially with new drugs	The MATT-DDI framework was composed of three primary modules: the module for selecting the top k most similar drug pairs, the heterogeneous attention mechanism module, and the multi-type DDI prediction module	DDIMDL [3]	Substructures, targets and enzymes	A: 0.9301, AUPR: 0.9755, AUC: 0.9988, F: 0.8647, P: 0.8771, R: 0.8613
[14]	Predicting multi-class DDIs	A novel method for predicting DDI events, called MDF-SA-DDI, was introduced in this study. This method leveraged multi-source drug fusion, multi-source feature fusion, and the transformer self-attention mechanism	DDIMDL [3], Dataset created by authors	Substructures, targets and enzymes	Task 1: MDF-SA-DDI ACC: 0.9301, AUPR: 0.9737, AUC: 0.9989, F: 0.8878, P: 0.9085, R: 0.8760
[4]	Multi-class DDI prediction and event prediction	BP-DDI, a method that combined biological data and pharmacological text for predicting DDI events, was introduced in this study	DDIMDL [3]	Substructure, target and text (indiciation, pharmacodynamics, mechanism of action, toxicity, metabolism, absorption)	A: 0.9052, AUPR: 0.9612, AUC: 0.9983, P: 0.8869, R: 0.7870, F: 0.8204
[9]	Predicting drug-drug interactions based on drug-induced gene expressions	Predicted DDIs using gene expression data, utilized a gate mechanism for feature processing to mimic co-administration effects, and employed the KGE algorithm to manage multiple side effects per drug pair	LINCS L1000, TWOSIDES, DrugBank [20]	SMILES, Feature generation model uses SMILES to drug-induced gene expression	AUC: 0.889, AUPR: 0.915
[23]	Creating a new input type for the DDIMDL dataset	To enhance the information in DDIMDL [3], an input vector was constructed from drug categories obtained from DrugBank [20] and classified using CNN	DDIMDL [3]	Drug categories, targets, pathways and enzymes	A: 0.8871, AUPR: 0.9251, AUC: 0.9980, F: 0.7496, P: 0.8556, R: 0.7220
[11]	Integrating drug properties and network structures, while considering the importance of different neighbors	A multi-view fusion model utilizing dual-level attention was introduced for predicting drug interactions	DDIMDL [3]	Substructures, targets and enzymes	A: 0.902, AUPR: 0.963, AUC: 0.998, F: 0.851, P: 0.857, R: 0.853
[12]	Generating low-dimensional latent features	Lower-dimensional latent features of each drug were derived using an autoencoder and MSE. A supervised contrastive loss was used to boost feature similarity within the same DDI type and dissimilarity between different types	DDIMDL [3], MDF-SA-DDI [14]	DDIMDL: substructures, targets, pathways and enzymes, MDF-SA-DDI: substructures, targets and enzymes	A: 0.9378, AUPR: 0.9782, AUC: 0.9983, F: 0.8755, P: 0.8804, R: 0.8767; MDF-SA-DDI: A: 0.9516, AUPR: 0.9862, AUC: 0.9995, F: 0.9321, P: 0.9162, R: 0.9500
[8]	Developing a fusion model that takes into account drug properties and topological relationships	A deep neural network (DNN) model extracted feature information from the drug feature matrix, while a graph convolutional network (GCN) captured structural information from the adjacency matrix. The two learned embeddings were then integrated using an attention mechanism	DDIMDL [3]	Chemical substructure, target, and enzyme and network structure	A: 0.908, AUPR: 0.964, AUC: 0.999, F: 0.852, P: 0.879, R: 0.839
[3]	Multi-class DDI prediction and event prediction	Four drug features (chemical substructures, targets, enzymes, and pathways) were utilized to create a model	Created dataset from DrugBank [20], consists of 572 drugs, 74528 interactions, and 65 event types	Substructures, pathways, targets, enzymes	A: 0.8852, AUPR: 0.9208, AUC: 0.9976, F: 0.7585, P: 0.8471, R: 0.7182
[15]	Binary classification of DDIs	Drug2vec was trained on all drug pairs to learn to encode drugs into vectors, while preserving the relationships between different drugs	Created from DrugBank [20]	Drug-drug interaction network	AUE around 0.96
[10]	Prediction of drug-drug interaction events	Autoencoders and a feed-forward network were used to predict the pharmacological effects of DDIs, trained with structural similarity profiles (SSP), Gene Ontology (GO) term similarity profiles (GSP), and target gene similarity profiles (TSP) of known drug pairs	DrugBank [20], Biogrid Interaction Database, Gene Ontology Consortium Database	Structural similarity profiles (SSP), Gene Ontology (GO) term similarity profiles (GSP), and target gene similarity profiles (TSP)	A > 0.95, R > 0.9, P > 0.9, AUPRC > 0.95
[19]	Multi-class DDI prediction task (86 types), which involves understanding drug interactions, including both drug-drug interactions (DDI) and drug-food interactions	The proposed model utilized the structural information (SMILES) of each drug in the input pair to generate a feature vector known as the structural similarity profile (SSP). The generated feature vectors were then fed into a deep neural network (DNN)	Created from DrugBank [20]	SMILES	A: 92.4%

3 Dataset

DDIMDL dataset, which contains a collection of drug pairs and their chemical properties was used here. However it does not contain textual information about the drugs. Therefore, this information was collected from DrugBank (Version 5.1.10) to enhance the dataset. An analysis of the textual data for drugs in the DDIMDL dataset, which are sourced from DrugBank, is provided in Table 2. Most of the attributes exhibit a low ratio of missing values, with categories such as *description*, *indication*, *mechanism_of_action* and *pharmacodynamics* showing minimal null data, indicating a high degree of completeness in the dataset. However, the missing values for *synthesis_reference*, *volume_of_distribution* and *clearance* are considerably higher. The average number of characters varies across categories; for example, while the completeness of *indication* and *mechanism_of_action* is similar, the average number of characters for *mechanism_of_action* is more than twice that of *indication*. The effects of these differences will be further explored in the following sections of this paper.

The dataset was divided into training and test sets. Cross-validation was employed to evaluate the model's performance, and to ensure the reproducibility of the experiments, each fold of the cross-validation process used distinct training and validation sets.

In this study, abbreviations were used to enhance readability. They are as follows: S refers to SMILES, P refers to Pathway, T refers to Target, E refers to Enzyme, ABTE refers to Absorption Embedding, CTE refers to Clearance

Table 2. DDIMDL - DrugBank Text Analysis

Column	R. Null	Avg. C.	Avg. S.
description	0.00	553.98	120.41
synthesis_reference	0.37	142.60	74.77
indication	0.01	310.93	138.72
pharmacodynamics	0.03	667.55	132.84
mechanism_of_action	0.01	712.79	154.35
toxicity	0.15	514.62	119.67
metabolism	0.09	305.85	95.82
absorption	0.14	328.73	97.22
half_life	0.14	101.79	57.62
protein_binding	0.21	85.53	54.88
route_of_elimination	0.26	201.28	99.24
volume_of_distribution	0.40	131.22	70.72
clearance	0.47	141.49	82.47

R. Null: Ratio of Null Counts, Avg. C.: Avg. Number of Characters, Avg. S.: Avg. Length of Sentences

Embedding, DTE refers to Description Embedding, HLTE refers to Half-life Embedding, ITE refers to Indication Embedding, MATE refers to Mechanism of Action Embedding, MTE refers to Metabolism Embedding, PBTE refers to Protein Binding Embedding, PTE refers to Pharmacodynamics Embedding, RETE refers to Route of Elimination Embedding, SRTE refers to Synthesis Reference Embedding, TTE refers to Toxicity Embedding, and VDTE refers to Volume of Distribution Embedding.

4 Sentence Transformer Models

Sentence-Transformers (SBERT) is a powerful and widely used deep learning model to obtain high-quality embeddings, specifically designed for text. It builds upon the Transformer architecture (such as BERT) to produce semantically meaningful sentence-level embeddings. Unlike traditional word embeddings (e.g., Word2Vec, GloVe), which generate embeddings for individual words, SBERT provides embeddings for entire sentences or text fragments. SBERT enhances the ability to capture complex relationships and contextual information, making it particularly suitable for tasks that require understanding the meaning of larger text spans, such as DDI classification. Seven different SBERT model was utilized in this study as seen in Table 3. Each of SBERT model is pre-trained, in the scope of this work training and fine-tuning were not applied.

Table 3. Abbreviations for Sentence Transformer Models

Abbreviation	Model Name	Dimension	Model Size
MiniLM-L6	all-MiniLM-L6-v2	384	22.71M params
MiniLM-L12	all-MiniLM-L12-v2	384	33.36M params
mpnet-base	all-mpnet-base-v2	768	109.49M params
bge-large	BAAI/bge-large-en-v1.5	1024	335.14M params
BioBERT	pritamdeka/BioBERT-mnli-snli-scinli-scitail-mednli-stsb	768	108.31M params
PubMedBERT	NeuML/pubmedbert-base-embeddings	768	109.48M params
S-PubMedBert	pritamdeka/S-PubMedBert-MS-MARCO	768	109.48M params

Textual arguments were represented as embeddings using either a sentence-based or chunk-based approach, employing various sentence transformer models listed in the table. The generated embeddings were then stored for future reuse.

5 Text-Based DDI Classification

5.1 Objective

Textual drug information has some clue about the potential DDIs. However, as much as our literature knowledge, there is a lack of knowledge about the power of representation of these textual information. Therefore, the main objective of text-based DDI classification here was to assess the impact of various sentence-transformer models on DDI classification, by applying these models to different types of text data and evaluating their impact on DDI classification accuracy.

5.2 Implementation

Before benchmarking the sentence-transformer models, the representation has been investigated to be chunk-based or sentence-based. For the chunk-based approach, given text was divided into chunks and fed into the sentence-transformer model to generate embeddings. After generating embeddings, they were stored in vector database. A similar process was applied for the sentence-based approach, given text was split into sentences, which were then input into the sentence-transformer model to generate corresponding embeddings. Then these embeddings were stored and used for representation. For both approaches, one or more embeddings were created for each drug text. To produce a single representation vector for each corresponding drug text, a mean pooling strategy was applied. Therefore, there were two different embedding generation strategies and 13 different input types for the DDI classification task, resulting in 26 different classification tasks. For each task, each drug pairs were concatenated and fed into the Fully Connected Neural Network (FCNN). It starts with an input layer of size vector_size, which varies based on the input data. It includes two hidden layers with 512 and 256 units, both using ReLU activation, batch normalization, and a dropout rate of 0.3. The output layer has 65 units (corresponding to the number of DDIs), with softmax activation for multi-class classification. The model is compiled with the Adam optimizer and categorical cross-entropy loss, trained for 100 epochs with 5-fold cross-validation, and incorporates an early stopping mechanism to prevent overfitting, while saving resources and time.

5.3 Results

The obtained results have been presented in Table 4 and Table 5 regarding the F-score and AUPR values. These are the values obtained by chunk-based representation. The experiments were also employed on sentence-based. However the sentence-based approach did not offer promising results, so their results have been excluded from the paper.

As can be seen in the Table 4 and Table 5, the best result among the sentence transformer models was achieved by BGE-large. The highest F-score and AUPR values were obtained using features such as description, indication, mechanism of action, and pharmacodynamics. The F-scores for the description, indication, mechanism of action, and pharmacodynamics were 0.8354, 0.8284, 0.8446, 0.8197, while the AUPR for these inputs were 0.9676, 0.9675, 0.9703, 0.9502, respectively. The performance metrics of applied sentence-transformer models and input types (DTE, ITE, MATE, PTE) are presented in the Fig. 1. The best input types may vary depending on the applied sentence-transformer model as can bee seen in the figure. It can be inferred that the chosen model directly affects the results.

It has been also observed that the size of the text used to generate embeddings and the complexity of the sentence transformer model have a positive impact on the results. As indicated in the Table 2, the text data corresponding to the drugs in DDIMDL are most informative (and large) in these categories, which

Table 4. F-score values of DDI classification for varying textual input arguments and sentence transformer models

	MiniLM-L6	MiniLM-L12	mpnet-base	bge-large	BioBERT	PubMedBERT	S-PubMedBert
ABTE	0.5974	0.5333	0.6496	**0.6761**	0.5635	0.6589	0.4870
CTE	0.3782	0.3706	0.3934	**0.4093**	0.3413	0.3845	0.3243
DTE	0.7861	0.7633	0.8250	**0.8354**	0.7580	0.8156	0.7412
HLTE	0.6280	0.6182	0.6452	**0.7090**	0.6118	0.6065	0.5468
ITE	0.8035	0.7610	0.8234	**0.8284**	0.7726	0.8007	0.6392
MATE	0.8178	0.7686	0.8326	**0.8446**	0.7532	0.8105	0.6609
MTE	0.5999	0.5553	0.6230	**0.6779**	0.5311	0.6375	0.5089
PBTE	0.5219	0.5334	0.5443	**0.5996**	0.4868	0.5285	0.3321
PTE	0.7481	0.7434	0.7750	**0.8197**	0.7108	0.7964	0.7056
RETE	0.5211	0.5146	0.5450	**0.5645**	0.5258	0.5341	0.4193
SRTE	0.4377	0.4338	0.4160	**0.4383**	0.4085	0.4231	0.4359
TTE	0.5812	0.5708	0.6325	**0.6772**	0.5506	0.6213	0.4777
VDTE	0.3914	0.3769	0.3835	**0.4488**	0.3839	0.4156	0.3833

positively impacts the results. Absorption, half-life, and toxicity have nearly the same non-null count, and when the performance metrics are evaluated in comparison to bge-large, it was observed that they achieve almost the same level of success.

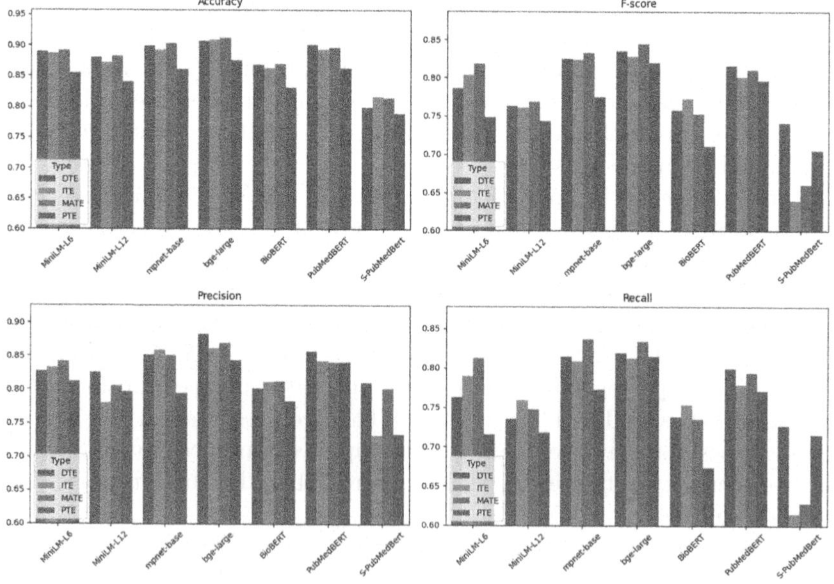

Fig. 1. Results of 4 best contributing textual arguments for DDI classification.

Table 5. AUPR values of DDI classification for varying textual input arguments and sentence transformer models

	MiniLM-L6	MiniLM-L12	mpnet-base	bge-large	BioBERT	PubMedBERT	S-PubMedBert
ABTE	0.8747	0.8525	0.8892	**0.9014**	0.8571	0.8868	0.8179
CTE	0.6731	0.6739	0.6809	**0.6963**	0.6677	0.6841	0.6550
DTE	0.9530	0.9448	0.9590	**0.9676**	0.9393	0.9595	0.8865
HLTE	0.8529	0.8538	0.8592	**0.8845**	0.8520	0.8659	0.8104
ITE	0.9495	0.9376	0.9539	**0.9675**	0.9347	0.9525	0.8993
MATE	0.9526	0.9476	0.9591	**0.9703**	0.9427	0.9562	0.8954
MTE	0.8857	0.8760	0.8974	**0.9055**	0.8643	0.8987	0.8351
PBTE	0.8252	0.8268	0.8365	**0.8669**	0.8283	0.8390	0.7777
PTE	0.9339	0.9219	0.9375	**0.9502**	0.9174	0.9396	0.8749
RETE	0.8349	0.8303	0.8343	**0.8564**	0.8291	0.8401	0.7679
SRTE	0.6922	0.6962	0.7061	**0.7195**	0.6868	0.7005	0.6929
TTE	0.8748	0.8563	0.8859	**0.9066**	0.8568	0.8828	0.7937
VDTE	0.7375	0.7358	0.7414	**0.7631**	0.7309	0.7437	0.7245

No correlation between the F-score and the number of model parameters of the sentence transformer model was detected. For instance, bge-large, which has a larger number of parameters, achieved a higher F-score. However, models such as mpnet-base, BioBERT, PubMedBERT, and S-PubMedBERT, despite having nearly identical parameter counts, exhibited significant variations in performance. Additionally, MiniLM-L6, despite having fewer parameters, outperformed some models with a higher parameter count.

6 Multimodal DDI Classification

6.1 Objective

In the previous section, the optimal representation for feeding the DDI classification model was assessed, and a sentence-transformer model was selected for further use. In this section, the sentence-transformer is also employed to represent individual textual data as well as their combinations, as there may be potential to enhance DDI classification performance by incorporating additional textual data. Building upon this, the objective here is to enhance DDI classification in a multi-modal setup using the knowledge of the best-performing text representation. To this end, the initial step was to evaluate the impact of both individual and combined use of chemical features to identify the most contributory features. Subsequently, the resulting chemical feature set was injected into the DDI classification process to improve overall performance in a multi-modal manner.

6.2 Implementation

The implementation of this task consists of two steps: the first was generating text embeddings, and the second was applying the classification process. Text embedding generation was performed using the best-performing sentence transformer model, bge-large. Four of the most representative textual argument types were selected for the task. After selecting the best four text features, combinations of these features were used to generate concatenated texts. Text embeddings were then created for each concatenated text, resulting in a total of 15 different text embeddings.

DDIMDL dataset includes four chemical features: chemical structures, targets, pathways, and enzymes. To represent these features, Jaccard similarity was applied, following the approach used in the DDIMDL study. The similarity matrices for each feature have dimensions of 572×572. Each chemical feature was fed into a FCNN previously defined in the preceding section. Four different classifiers were used for chemical properties, with each classifier predicting DDIs. The output of each classifier was produced as a softmax value. The same procedure was applied to the 15 different text embeddings. Combinations of chemical features were generated from 2 to n, resulting in 15 different chemical feature combinations. To assess the effects of textual arguments on chemical features, combined groups were created by adding each text embedding to the chemical properties group. This resulted in 225 different combinations. In each combination, the softmax values were summed, and the argmax of the summed values was computed to complete the prediction task.

6.3 Results

The classification performance evaluation results obtained from experiments that rely solely on the use of chemical features, either individually or in combination are shown in Table 6. Here, the representative power of the target and pathway features surpasses that of the other two chemical features. Notably, combinations involving the substructure feature have yielded poorer performance. Furthermore, the performance of the chemical features differs from that reported in reference [3]. One possible explanation for this variation is that the dataset splitting strategy may differ from that used in the referenced work. That's why, the repetition of chemical feature experiments has been required to obtain a fair comparison. Although no single combination of the precision, recall, and F-score metrics stands out, when analyzed individually, it is observed that the text embeddings perform better in this classification task using the DDIMDL dataset compared to chemical features. The primary advantage of text embeddings lies in their ability to enhance precision. The effects of textual features are presented in Table 7. Here the bge-large was utilized. The addition of PTE has resulted in a deterioration of performance. While ITE_MATE and DETE_MATE are among the top two, DTE_ITE_MATE ranks lower. Adding MATE to DTE_ITE has led to a decrease in performance.

Table 6. DDI classification results obtained from the single and combined form of chemical features

	A	AUC	AUPR	F1	P	R
S	0.4951	0.9791	0.5280	0.2037	0.4030	0.1989
T	0.8389	0.9953	0.9196	0.7872	0.8135	0.7749
P	0.8199	0.9951	0.9090	0.7502	0.7699	0.7516
E	0.6425	0.9745	0.7054	0.3622	0.5062	0.3085
S-T	0.8185	0.9959	0.8638	0.7735	0.8372	0.7477
S-P	0.8057	0.9953	0.8558	0.7432	0.8045	0.7204
S-E	0.6520	0.9871	0.7226	0.3550	0.5316	0.3113
T-P	0.8397	0.9956	**0.9216**	0.7799	0.8052	0.7720
T-E	**0.8545**	0.9963	0.9055	0.7970	0.8672	0.7604
P-E	0.8437	0.9960	0.8977	0.7703	0.8263	0.7468
S-T-P	0.8440	0.9965	0.8969	0.7872	0.8256	0.7705
S-T-E	0.8273	0.9962	0.8874	0.7086	0.8584	0.6424
S-P-E	0.8204	0.9959	0.8814	0.6818	0.8193	0.6189
T-P-E	0.8538	**0.9968**	0.9166	0.8034	0.8536	**0.7833**
S-T-P-E	0.8543	0.9967	0.9107	**0.8078**	**0.8711**	0.7762

Table 7. DDI classification results obtained from using single and combined form of textual drug information

	A	AUC	AUPR	F1	P	R
DTE	0.8998	0.9986	0.9616	0.8292	0.8922	0.8030
ITE	0.8945	0.9982	0.9592	0.8428	0.8510	0.8456
MATE	**0.9096**	0.9988	**0.9681**	0.8373	0.8669	0.8310
PTE	0.8512	0.9967	0.9351	0.7894	0.8465	0.7642
DTE_ITE	0.9033	0.9986	0.9644	0.8373	**0.9002**	0.8070
DTE_MATE	0.8970	0.9986	0.9637	0.8487	0.8587	**0.8499**
DTE_PTE	0.8897	0.9986	0.9590	0.8063	0.8636	0.7847
ITE_MATE	0.8976	0.9984	0.9617	**0.8500**	0.8673	0.8462
ITE_PTE	0.8878	0.9980	0.9569	0.8190	0.8619	0.8048
MATE_PTE	0.8985	**0.9989**	0.9650	0.8340	0.8596	0.8259
DTE_ITE_MATE	0.8943	0.9987	0.9589	0.8300	0.8759	0.8140
DTE_ITE_PTE	0.8860	0.9982	0.9548	0.8039	0.8619	0.7809
DTE_MATE_PTE	0.8820	0.9985	0.9544	0.8292	0.8782	0.8032
ITE_MATE_PTE	0.8644	0.9981	0.9414	0.8053	0.8616	0.7815
DTE_ITE_MATE_PTE	0.8827	0.9980	0.9534	0.7726	0.8388	0.7409

_ denotes the concatenation of texts

In Table 8, the top 20 results out of 255 different scenarios are presented. It is evident that the results supported by MATE are among the top 10. In this study, MATE effectively complements the features derived from chemical features. In addition, there were no combinations of four text types in the top 20, which suggests that embeddings of large texts do not always produce better results. Additionally, some features could have a positive effect on small combinations. For example, adding Enzyme supported the T-DTE_MATE but also had a negative effect, such as on T-ITE_MATE.

Table 8. Results obtained from multimodal DDI classification (top 20 is presented).

	A	AUC	AUPR	F1	P	R
T-MATE	**0.9118**	0.9977	**0.9630**	**0.8720**	0.9127	**0.8546**
T-ITE_MATE	0.9037	0.9981	0.9613	0.8686	0.9056	0.8533
E-T-DTE_MATE	0.9027	0.9980	0.9499	0.8648	**0.9284**	0.8338
T-DTE_MATE	0.9074	0.9981	0.9610	0.8645	0.8955	0.8507
E-T-ITE_MATE	0.9031	0.9982	0.9508	0.8636	0.9227	0.8325
P-ITE_MATE	0.9023	0.9978	0.9573	0.8623	0.8896	0.8541
E-T-MATE	0.9082	0.9981	0.9513	0.8617	0.9256	0.8338
T-DTE_MATE_PTE	0.8960	**0.9985**	0.9568	0.8608	0.8989	0.8402
E-P-MATE	0.9059	0.9980	0.9485	0.8603	0.9228	0.8343
E-T-MATE_PTE	0.9024	0.9982	0.9516	0.8601	0.9200	0.8260
T-MATE_PTE	0.9053	**0.9985**	0.9627	0.8595	0.8870	0.8448
E-T-P-MATE	0.8908	0.9981	0.9491	0.8589	0.9129	0.8337
T-DTE	0.9055	0.9984	0.9612	0.8583	0.9041	0.8383
T-PTE	0.8975	0.9971	0.9534	0.8580	0.9139	0.8326
E-P-DTE_MATE	0.8993	0.9980	0.9472	0.8568	0.9106	0.8366
T-ITE_MATE_PTE	0.8884	0.9984	0.9511	0.8562	0.8983	0.8383
E-T-P-ITE_MATE	0.8870	0.9981	0.9485	0.8547	0.9105	0.8293
T-ITE_PTE	0.8994	0.9978	0.9584	0.8544	0.8951	0.8371
T-DTE_ITE_PTE	0.8988	0.9980	0.9567	0.8538	0.8896	0.8344
S-T-DTE_MATE	0.8939	0.9981	0.9413	0.8532	0.9051	0.8317

7 Conclusion

This study highlights the importance of drug textual arguments in DDI classification and demonstrates that state-of-the-art sentence transformers improve prediction performance through effective text representations. The findings emphasize the importance of text embeddings, particularly those related to drug indications, descriptions, mechanisms of action, and pharmacodynamics, in the classification process. This study also highlights the potential of integrating multiple data sources for a more holistic approach to DDI prediction.

In particular, the integration of textual representations with chemical similarity matrices has demonstrated considerable improvements in the classification performance. By combining chemical properties with the rich, context-driven textual data from DrugBank, proposed approach was able to capture more nuanced relationships between drugs that may not be immediately apparent from chemical data alone. This integrated method not only surpassed the performance of using either chemical features or textual arguments in isolation but also opened new opportunities for refining DDI prediction systems. The results of this study underscore the potential for multi-modal data fusion, where both structured chemical information and unstructured textual data work synergistically to offer deeper insights into complex drug interactions. Future studies will focus on enhancing DDI classification in low-resource scenarios by utilizing different modalities and drug-related information.

References

1. Asfand-E-Yar, M., Hashir, Q., Shah, A.A., Malik, H.A.M., Alourani, A., Khalil, W.: Multimodal CNN-DDI: using multimodal CNN for drug to drug interaction associated events. Sci. Rep. **14**(1), 4076 (2024). https://doi.org/10.1038/s41598-024-54409-x
2. Buyukpatpat, B., Mutlu, B., Sezer, E.A.: Leveraging textual drug information for effective drug-drug interaction identification. In: Innovations in Intelligent Systems and Applications Conference, pp. 1–6. IEEE Türkiye Section (2024)
3. Deng, Y., Xu, X., Qiu, Y., Xia, J., Zhang, W., Liu, S.: A multimodal deep learning framework for predicting drug-drug interaction events. Bioinformatics **36**(15), 4316–4322 (2020). https://doi.org/10.1093/bioinformatics/btaa501
4. Dou, M., Han, H., Chen, G., Guo, F., Tang, J.: BP-DDI: drug-drug interaction prediction based on biological information and pharmacological text. In: 2022 IEEE International Conference on Bioinformatics and Biomedicine (BIBM), pp. 410–415. IEEE (2022). https://doi.org/10.1109/BIBM55620.2022.9995174
5. Han, G., Peng, L., Ding, A., Zhang, Y., Lin, X.: CTF-DDI: constrained tensor factorization for drug-drug interactions prediction. Futur. Gener. Comput. Syst. **161**, 26–34 (2024)
6. Han, K., et al.: A review of approaches for predicting drug-drug interactions based on machine learning. Front. Pharmacol. **12**, 814858 (2022)
7. Jung, S., Yoo, S.: Interpretable prediction of drug-drug interactions via text embedding in biomedical literature. Comput. Biol. Med. **185**, 109496 (2025)
8. Kang, L.P., Lin, K.B., Lu, P., Yang, F., Chen, J.P.: Multitype drug interaction prediction based on the deep fusion of drug features and topological relationships. PLoS ONE **17**(8), e0273764 (2022). https://doi.org/10.1371/journal.pone.0273764
9. Kim, E., Nam, H.: Deside-DDI: interpretable prediction of drug-drug interactions using drug-induced gene expressions. J. Cheminformatics **14**(1), 9 (2022). https://doi.org/10.1186/s13321-022-00589-5
10. Lee, G., Park, C., Ahn, J.: Novel deep learning model for more accurate prediction of drug-drug interaction effects. BMC Bioinform. **20**, 1–8 (2019). https://doi.org/10.1186/s12859-019-3013-0

11. Lin, K., Kang, L., Yang, F., Lu, P., Lu, J.: MFDA: multiview fusion based on dual-level attention for drug interaction prediction. Front. Pharmacol. **13**, 1021329 (2022). https://doi.org/10.3389/fphar.2022.1021329
12. Lin, S., Chen, W., Chen, G., Zhou, S., Wei, D.Q., Xiong, Y.: MDDI-SCL: predicting multi-type drug-drug interactions via supervised contrastive learning. J. Cheminform. **14**(1), 81 (2022). https://doi.org/10.1186/s13321-022-00659-8
13. Lin, S., Mao, X., Hong, L., Lin, S., Wei, D.Q., Xiong, Y.: MATT-DDI: predicting multi-type drug-drug interactions via heterogeneous attention mechanisms. Methods **220**, 1–10 (2023). https://doi.org/10.1016/j.ymeth.2023.10.007
14. Lin, S., et al.: MDF-SA-DDI: predicting drug–drug interaction events based on multi-source drug fusion, multi-source feature fusion and transformer self-attention mechanism. Briefings Bioinform. **23**(1), bbab421 (2022). https://doi.org/10.1093/bib/bbab421
15. Liu, P., Zheng, X., Wong, M.-H., Leung, K.-S.: Drug2vec: a drug embedding method with drug-drug interaction as the context. In: Iliadis, L., Angelov, P.P., Jayne, C., Pimenidis, E. (eds.) EANN 2020. PINNS, vol. 2, pp. 326–337. Springer, Cham (2020). https://doi.org/10.1007/978-3-030-48791-1_25
16. Luo, H., et al.: Drug-drug interactions prediction based on deep learning and knowledge graph: a review. Iscience (2024)
17. Pan, D., et al.: Prediction of multiple types of drug interactions based on multi-scale fusion and dual-view fusion. Front. Pharmacol. **15**, 1354540 (2024). https://doi.org/10.3389/fphar.2024.1354540
18. Qiu, Y., Zhang, Y., Deng, Y., Liu, S., Zhang, W.: A comprehensive review of computational methods for drug-drug interaction detection. IEEE/ACM Trans. Comput. Biol. Bioinf. **19**(4), 1968–1985 (2021)
19. Ryu, J.Y., Kim, H.U., Lee, S.Y.: Deep learning improves prediction of drug-drug and drug-food interactions. Proc. Natl. Acad. Sci. **115**(18), E4304–E4311 (2018). https://doi.org/10.1073/pnas.1803294115
20. Wishart, D.S., et al.: Drugbank 5.0: a major update to the drugbank database for 2018. Nucleic acids research **46**(D1), D1074–D1082 (2018). https://doi.org/10.1093/nar/gkx1037
21. Yan, X., Gu, C., Feng, Y., Han, J.: Predicting drug-drug interaction with graph mutual interaction attention mechanism. Methods **223**, 16–25 (2024). https://doi.org/10.1016/j.ymeth.2024.01.009
22. Yu, L., Xu, Z., Cheng, M., Lin, W., Qiu, W., Xiao, X.: MSEDDI: multi-scale embedding for predicting drug–drug interaction events. Int. J. Mol. Sci. **24**(5), 4500 (2023). https://doi.org/10.3390/ijms24054500
23. Zhang, C., Lu, Y., Zang, T.: CNN-DDI: a learning-based method for predicting drug-drug interactions using convolution neural networks. BMC Bioinform. **23**(Suppl 1), 88 (2022). https://doi.org/10.1186/s12859-022-04612-2

From Respiration to Heart Sounds: A Comparative Review of Three Radar Systems for Unobtrusive Monitoring

Aref Smiley(✉) and Joseph Finkelstein

Arizona Telemedicine Program, University of Arizona, Tucson, AZ, USA
arefsmiley@arizona.edu

Abstract. This paper presents a comparative evaluation of three radar systems—ViRa24, X4M06, and IWR1443BOOST—for contactless physiological monitoring. These systems, based on continuous-wave (CW), ultra-wideband (UWB) impulse, and frequency-modulated continuous-wave (FMCW) radar principles respectively, were assessed for their ability to detect respiration, cardiac motion, heart sounds, and heart rate variability (HRV). Detailed analysis of their hardware architecture, signal processing pipelines, software tools, and practical deployment was performed. Each system offers unique advantages aligned with specific applications in telemedicine, rehabilitation, and human-computer interaction. The results provide insights into the strengths and trade-offs of each radar modality, guiding future deployment in clinical and research environments.

Keywords: Radar Sensing · Physiological Monitoring · Heart Rate Variability · Contactless Vital Signs

1 Introduction

Continuous monitoring of physiological signals is essential for numerous health-related applications including chronic disease management, rehabilitation, telemedicine, sleep monitoring, and human-computer interaction. Conventional systems that rely on electrocardiograms (ECG) or photoplethysmography (PPG) require physical contact with the patient, which can be uncomfortable, impractical, or even infeasible in many real-world scenarios [1, 2]. These limitations have spurred the development of non-contact alternatives such as radar-based physiological monitoring systems. Radar technology enables remote detection of subtle bodily movements associated with respiration, cardiac activity, and even heart sounds [3]. A comprehensive narrative review highlights the broader clinical viability of non-contact sensors [17]. These sensors offer performance comparable to traditional contact-based methods while minimizing patient discomfort, reducing infection risks, and allowing continuous long-term monitoring without interfering with patient mobility or care routines [14].

This paper presents a detailed comparative study of three distinct radar platforms: the ViRa24 continuous-wave (CW) radar, the X4M06 ultra-wideband (UWB) impulse radar,

A. Alsadoon et al. (Eds.): CSCE 2025, CCIS 2935, pp. 249–262, 2026.
https://doi.org/10.1007/978-3-032-22199-5_18

and the IWR1443BOOST frequency-modulated continuous-wave (FMCW) millimeter-wave radar. Each system employs a different operational principle and architecture, and they vary in terms of frequency band, resolution, signal processing capabilities, software environment, and practical deployment features. We document their respective capabilities in capturing vital signs, their suitability for integration into telehealth platforms, and their performance in experimental settings. The goal of this comparative evaluation is to inform researchers and developers on the strengths and limitations of each system in the context of contactless physiological monitoring.

In the following sections, we describe each radar system in detail, covering both hardware and software aspects, followed by a comparative analysis and concluding observations on their respective roles in future biomedical applications.

2 CW Radar, ViRa24 Radar System

The ViRa24 radar system, developed by Sykno GmbH (Erlangen, Germany), is a contactless physiological monitoring platform designed to detect chest wall movements associated with respiration, pulse, and heart sounds. Operating at a center frequency of 24.05 GHz, the ViRa24 employs continuous-wave (CW) radar technology to measure phase shifts in the reflected electromagnetic waves, enabling the detection of sub-millimeter displacements without the need for physical contact with the subject. This technology has been successfully applied in clinical-grade studies and won recognition such as the AMA Innovation Award for its accuracy and non-intrusiveness in vital sign acquisition [4].

The radar system transmits a constant-frequency signal, which reflects off the subject's chest (Fig. 1). The returned signal, containing phase information, is captured by the radar's integrated antennas. The ViRa24 system outputs two primary baseband channels: the in-phase (I) and quadrature (Q) signals, which are digitized using a 24-bit analog-to-digital converter (ADC) at a sampling rate of 1,000 samples per second (1 kHz). These I and Q signals are used to derive instantaneous phase and displacement data. The use of dual-channel I/Q phase detection enhances sensitivity and robustness against noise, as noted in comparative field reports on radar sensor performance [5, 6].

The hardware is equipped with six analog channels: channels 1 and 2 correspond to the I and Q signals, channels 3 and 4 serve as differential analog ECG inputs, and channels 5 and 6 are general-purpose analog inputs used for synchronization or auxiliary data. The radar unit is powered and connected to a host computer via a USB interface, which also handles data transmission. For optimal measurement sensitivity, the radar is positioned 10–20 cm from the subject's chest and aligned perpendicularly using the device's integrated visual alignment marker.

Operational reliability is supported across a range of ambient conditions. The system operates within a supply voltage range of 4.85–5.15 V and a current consumption of 340 mA. It functions effectively within an ambient temperature range of 10–40 °C. The radar's antenna beamwidth is 22° horizontally and 17° vertically, providing a focused detection field that enhances sensitivity to chest displacements. Field tests confirm that this configuration enables reliable detection across varying body types and clinical environments [5, 7].

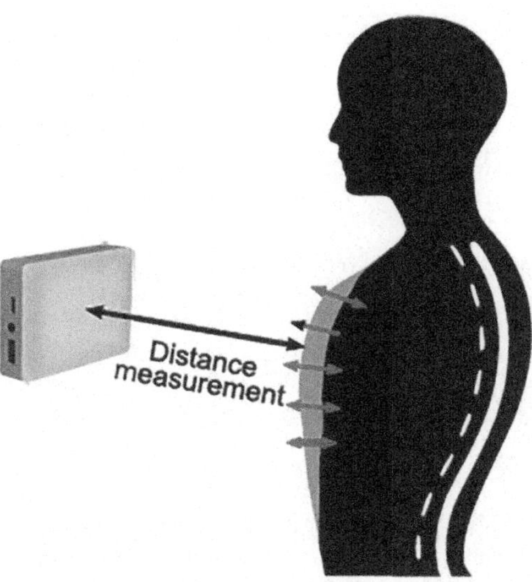

Fig. 1. A schematic image of the ViRa24 radar setup: Show the radar unit facing a subject with labeled components: radar, subject, USB connection, and approximate standoff distance (~10–20 cm).

Data acquisition, real-time processing, visualization, and logging are handled through the ViRa24 Evaluation GUI, a Python-based software environment developed using PyQt6 (Fig. 2). Upon connection, the GUI initiates radar signal transmission, sets gain values for the I and Q channels, and allows the user to toggle between DC and AC coupling modes. In DC coupling mode, the radar captures the full spectrum of motion including respiration, pulse, and heart sounds. In AC coupling mode, low-frequency content is filtered out, enhancing the detection of higher-frequency cardiac vibrations. The development of these dual coupling modes was highlighted as a key innovation in enabling flexible physiological signal extraction [6].

The GUI implements circular buffering of incoming data frames and applies user-configurable second-order Butterworth bandpass filters to isolate specific physiological signals. Respiration signals are extracted using a 0.1–0.5 Hz filter band, pulse signals using 0.8–2.5 Hz, and heart sounds using 15–30 Hz. These filtered signals are displayed in real-time within the GUI, allowing the user to assess signal integrity during data collection.

The ViRa24's unique AC coupling mode enables the isolation and visualization of heart sounds, including the S1 and S2 heart tones caused by valve closures. In this mode, the analog frontend internally applies a high-pass filter with a cutoff around 10 Hz. The I and Q signals are then filtered in the 15–30 Hz band, yielding two derived signals: HS1 and HS2. These represent heart sound signals from the in-phase and quadrature components, respectively. Quadrature detection increases the robustness of heart sound detection regardless of body orientation. According to performance benchmarks published by Sykno GmbH, the radar system achieves high signal-to-noise ratios in heart sound extraction under standard room conditions [7].

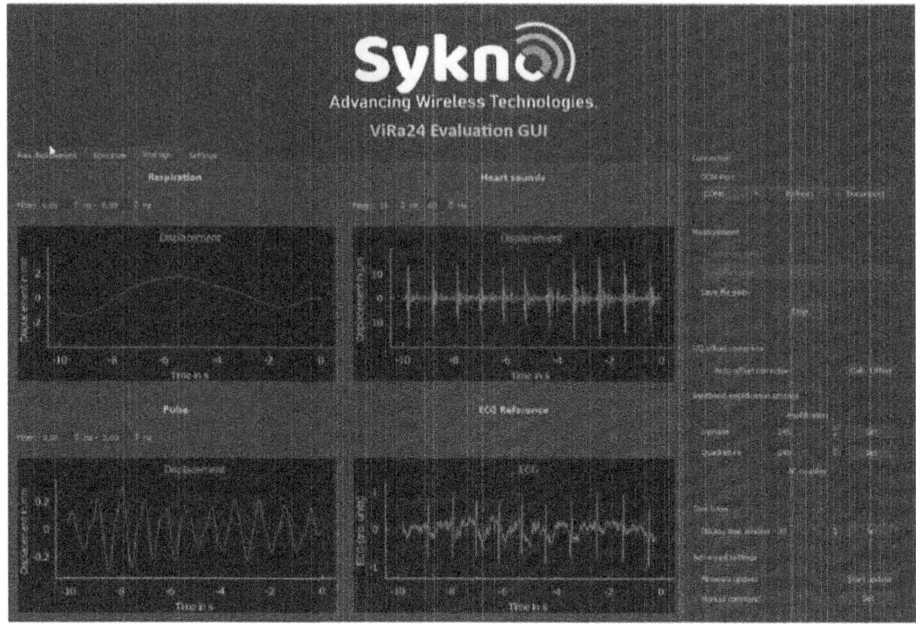

Fig. 2. The user interface with real-time plots (displacement pulse and respiration, heart sound, and reference ECG).

The radar system also supports ECG signal acquisition through channels 3 and 4. These inputs are connected to standard 3-lead ECG electrodes. The acquired ECG signal is filtered to remove powerline interference (50/60 Hz) and harmonics (100/120 Hz), then low-pass filtered at 40 Hz, baseline-corrected, and normalized for display.

The ViRa24 Evaluation GUI supports continuous data logging, writing output in CSV format every 2.5 s. Each log includes raw ADC values, filtered displacement waveforms, heart sound signals (HS1 and HS2), and normalized ECG. Metadata such as sample rate and file timestamps are also included. These capabilities make the system well-suited for machine learning pipelines in digital health research [4, 7].

Overall, the ViRa24 radar system offers a compact and high-fidelity solution for contactless monitoring of respiration, cardiac motion, and heart sounds. Its modular, open-source software stack and ECG integration make it ideal for use in telemedicine, sleep studies, rehabilitation, and phonocardiography research.

3 IR-UWB Radar, X4M06 Radar System

The X4M06 radar system, developed by Novelda, is built on the XeThru X4 Ultra-Wideband (UWB) impulse radar System-on-Chip (SoC). This technology is designed for high-precision, contactless detection of physiological signals by emitting nanosecond-duration pulses over a wide bandwidth, resulting in exceptional spatial resolution and material penetration capabilities. Unlike continuous-wave (CW) and frequency-modulated continuous-wave (FMCW) radars, UWB impulse radars are less sensitive to multipath effects and can detect minute micro-motions of the chest wall associated with respiration and cardiac activity [8].

The X4M06 radar hardware comprises three integrated modules: the X4SIP02 radar transceiver, the X4A04 directional antenna array, and the XTMCU02 microcontroller board. The radar operates within the 7.29–8.748 GHz frequency range, with bandwidths of up to 1.5 GHz depending on regulatory constraints. The system supports a swept-threshold ADC architecture that digitizes incoming signals at an effective sampling rate of 23.328 gigasamples per second. Each radar frame contains up to 1536 range bins, allowing for fine-grained resolution of range profiles.

The transceiver emits a series of bi-phase-coded impulses whose reflections are captured by a swept-threshold ADC equipped with an integrated low-noise amplifier (LNA) and threshold DAC. It supports coherent integration over multiple pulses to enhance signal-to-noise ratio. Developers can configure parameters such as the number of pulses per step, number of iterations, and DAC sweep characteristics to optimize signal acquisition for specific applications.

The X4M06 uses a pair of directional filtennas tuned for the 7.25–10.2 GHz range. These antennas provide approximately 65° beamwidth in both azimuth and elevation, which ensures good directional sensitivity while suppressing noise from off-axis reflectors. The form factor of the device is compact, enabling easy deployment in laboratory and clinical environments.

Radar operation is controlled via the XeThru Embedded Platform (XEP), which runs on the XTMCU02 board. Firmware customization and upgrades are supported via standard debugging tools such as Atmel-ICE or Segger J-Link. Low-level control of radar parameters is possible using raw SPI command sequences, while higher-level scripting is facilitated through the ModuleConnector API, which is available in Python, C++, and MATLAB.

Using the ModuleConnector API, users can configure the pulse repetition frequency (PRF), adjust the analog front-end gain, and define DAC sweep characteristics. The API also enables users to retrieve raw radar frames, baseband I/Q data, or amplitude/phase values for further analysis. This modularity allows the X4M06 to be integrated into custom signal processing pipelines.

For physiological signal acquisition, the X4M06 is typically positioned 20–30 cm from the subject's chest with the antenna plane aligned perpendicular to the thoracic surface. During data collection, motion is captured across multiple range bins. Signal processing algorithms track energy fluctuations within these bins to extract respiratory and cardiac waveforms. Post-processing includes motion compensation and bandpass filtering to isolate desired signal components.

The X4M06 also supports real-time streaming and logging of radar data. The system can output amplitude, phase, or I/Q signals as CSV files, which can be further processed in environments like MATLAB or Python using standard libraries such as NumPy, SciPy, and Matplotlib. Real-time visualizations are possible using integrated plotting features or third-party graphical interfaces.

The UWB radar technology has been extensively validated for biomedical applications. For example, non-contact heart rate monitoring using IR-UWB radar has demonstrated accuracy comparable to ECG in both healthy individuals and patients with arrhythmia, offering high agreement in HR and RR intervals [9]. Similarly, non-contact respiration monitoring in neonates showed reliable respiratory rate estimation even under varying movement conditions [10]. These features make IR-UWB radar suitable for sensitive applications such as neonatal intensive care units, where electrode-based sensors may harm fragile skin.

In the context of sleep medicine, impulse-radio UWB radar has also been validated for detecting respiratory events like apneas and hypopneas, showing strong correlation with standard polysomnography measurements [11]. Additionally, for vehicular environments, radar systems have been used to monitor driver drowsiness and mobile phone use by estimating vital signs and motion patterns in real-time, even under substantial background movement [12].

Beyond vital sign monitoring, IR-UWB radar has shown promise in gesture recognition for automotive human-machine interfaces. A single radar module can differentiate intentional gestures from noise by extracting robust features such as signal variance, time of arrival, and frequency content, even when hand distance and orientation vary [13].

Moreover, UWB radar can be employed for indoor people counting and localization, as demonstrated by systems that classify signal patterns rather than individual reflections. This method is particularly effective in cluttered environments such as elevators or classrooms, where multipath propagation complicates signal separation [14, 15]. Occupant localization with UWB radar can further be enhanced by combining radar sensing with machine learning algorithms to infer occupancy patterns with high spatial granularity [16].

The classification capabilities of IR-UWB radar also extend to non-biological targets. Algorithms leveraging complex natural resonances of scattered signals can identify materials and shapes based on their electromagnetic signatures, facilitating robust target classification in security or industrial applications [15].

In summary, the X4M06 radar system offers a flexible and high-resolution platform for contactless physiological signal monitoring. Its open software ecosystem, fine parameter control, and high sampling fidelity make it well suited for research applications requiring precise signal discrimination. However, its performance depends on careful parameter tuning and calibration, especially when capturing signals with very low amplitude such as those associated with heartbeat. When configured correctly, the X4M06 serves as a powerful tool for non-contact respiratory and cardiac monitoring in both laboratory and applied healthcare contexts.

4 FMCW Radar, IWR1443BOOST Radar System

The IWR1443BOOST is a compact, single-chip frequency-modulated continuous-wave (FMCW) radar platform developed by Texas Instruments, specifically designed for millimeter-wave sensing applications. Operating in the 76–81 GHz frequency band, the radar is capable of detecting micro-movements of the chest associated with respiration and cardiac activity with high temporal and spatial resolution. The system integrates RF transceivers, digital signal processing (DSP), and a control microcontroller (MCU) into a unified platform that supports standalone and host-interfaced operation modes [18].

The radar module incorporates three transmit (TX) antennas and four receive (RX) antennas configured as a MIMO array. This arrangement enables angular resolution in both azimuth and elevation planes. The onboard antennas offer a beamwidth of approximately $\pm 28°$ in the horizontal plane and $\pm 14°$ in the vertical plane. The radar achieves a range resolution of approximately 4 cm when operating at the full chirp bandwidth of 4 GHz.

A key component of the IWR1443BOOST's signal chain is its FMCW architecture. The radar transmits a linearly modulated frequency chirp and measures the beat frequency generated by the difference between the transmitted and received signals. This beat frequency is directly related to the range of the reflecting surface, allowing the radar to resolve small displacements over time. The short wavelength (~3.9 mm at 77 GHz) enhances sensitivity to sub-millimeter physiological motions.

The hardware includes a TI C674x DSP core and an ARM Cortex-R4F MCU, with additional hardware accelerators for FFT computation, noise filtering, and object detection. Communication and data logging are supported through USB, CAN, SPI, and UART interfaces. The device is powered via a 5V supply (2.5A) and provides GPIOs and LEDs for user feedback and debugging.

Software support is provided by the mmWave SDK and includes demo applications such as the Vital Signs Lab. This lab enables detection of breathing rate and heart rate from a fixed range bin by analyzing phase changes in the radar return signal. The SDK provides tools for configuring chirp parameters, processing chains, and output formats. Data can be visualized using a dedicated MATLAB-based GUI that plots respiration and heartbeat waveforms in real-time, as well as providing numerical estimates of vital signs.

The GUI setup process involves configuring communication ports (UART and data), initializing the device, and starting the radar stream. Breathing and cardiac signals are extracted using narrow bandpass filters. In breath-hold tests, the respiratory signal plateaus, while the heartbeat remains discernible. Data acquisition is validated by aligning radar readings with ECG signals captured simultaneously through analog or serial interfaces.

For deployment, the radar is mounted vertically using a custom bracket and positioned approximately 20–40 cm from the subject's chest. The system's design facilitates reliable acquisition even under ambient noise conditions, provided the subject remains motionless during the measurement period.

The radar employs a multiple-input multiple-output (MIMO) antenna configuration, with three transmit and four receive antennas, enabling range, Doppler, and angle estimation capabilities. The sensor emits chirp signals and captures their reflections to extract phase changes that correspond to minute chest wall displacements. This architecture enables real-time monitoring of breathing and cardiac cycles with high spatial and temporal resolution [19, 20].

In clinical and home-care environments, IWR1443BOOST has been validated for non-contact monitoring of heart and respiration rates [21]. For example, Sheikh et al. assessed its performance at various distances (1–2 m), reporting high accuracy up to 1.5 m and notable signal degradation beyond that [18]. Another study demonstrated that concurrent monitoring of multiple targets is feasible using this radar, leveraging its wide field of view and beamforming capabilities [22]. Chen et al. proposed a method to enhance heartbeat signal extraction by combining adaptive filtering and spectral peak estimation, using IWR1443BOOST in a cluttered environment. Their results showed a heart rate estimation error of less than 2.61%, even under low signal-to-noise ratio (SNR) conditions [23]. Additionally, Adiprabowo et al. implemented a concurrent detection framework using the radar to monitor up to four individuals simultaneously, demonstrating practical applications in multi-patient hospital wards or care facilities [24].

Beyond vital sign detection, IWR1443BOOST has also been deployed in gesture recognition systems. Holl developed a real-time framework using the radar to detect hand pose variations and reconstruct 3D models based on phase differences from chirped reflections. The system achieved results comparable to depth cameras without the need for optical visibility [19]. In parallel, CNN-based classifiers have been trained using range-Doppler images from the radar to recognize static hand gestures with improved accuracy using sterile data augmentation techniques [25]. Such systems have implications for human-machine interaction in sterile environments, like operating rooms.

The radar's robustness in poor lighting or obstructed environments makes it a valuable sensor for robotics and autonomous navigation. Barrett et al. showcased its ability to detect both transparent surfaces (e.g., glass walls) and hidden obstacles, surpassing the limitations of LiDAR and cameras [20]. It can also be used to estimate ground velocity and support visual-inertial odometry by providing Doppler information in mobile robots [20]. Gao et al. introduced MM-DCDR, a benchmark dataset that includes IWR1443BOOST among other radar configurations, comparing point cloud and heatmap data for human activity recognition. Their study highlighted the radar's flexibility in balancing velocity and angular resolution, depending on the sensing task and neural network architecture [26]. Additionally, Iyer et al. used the radar in combination with a 3-layer artificial neural network to detect cardiac arrhythmias. Their system analyzed phase signals from the radar to detect abnormalities and demonstrated a test accuracy of 75% compared to standard ECG monitors [27].

The IWR1443BOOST platform, with its integrated radar processing and flexible software interface, represents a robust solution for non-contact vital sign monitoring. It is particularly well suited for research requiring heart rate variability analysis, and for clinical environments where hygiene, comfort, and continuous monitoring are priorities. Future developments may include integration with cloud-connected health systems and machine learning frameworks to support automated diagnosis and long-term health tracking.

5 Comparative Analysis and Discussion

The three radar systems evaluated in this study—ViRa24, X4M06, and IWR1443BOOST—each employ different signal modalities and system architectures to achieve the shared objective of contactless physiological monitoring. Their differences in frequency band, radar principle, antenna design, and software interface directly influence the quality of the physiological signals they can capture, their suitability for various applications, and the complexity of their deployment.

The ViRa24 radar system leverages a continuous-wave (CW) transmission at 24.05 GHz, enabling sub-millimeter motion detection through precise phase measurement. This design, combined with its analog baseband output and real-time displacement extraction, makes it highly effective for capturing a wide range of physiological signals, including respiration, pulse, and heart sounds. The dedicated AC coupling mode and its integrated ECG channel allow for a rare capability among radar systems: phonocardiographic analysis. Its intuitive Evaluation GUI and modular Python code base provide a research-friendly interface suitable for rapid development and validation in multimodal settings. These qualities make ViRa24 ideal for applications focused on heart sound analysis, sleep monitoring, telemedicine, and scenarios requiring simultaneous ECG validation.

In contrast, the X4M06 radar system utilizes UWB impulse radar technology, emitting short-duration pulses across a wide spectrum in the 7.29–8.748 GHz band. Its main advantage lies in the exceptionally high spatial resolution afforded by this wide bandwidth and its advanced swept-threshold ADC architecture. The system enables precise tracking of thoracic micro-movements across multiple range bins and is capable of isolating respiration and heartbeat signals after motion compensation and range profile processing. However, the flexibility it offers also necessitates a higher level of expertise in firmware development and signal processing. The API-rich ModuleConnector software environment and SPI-based configuration protocol give researchers the power to fine-tune performance at a low level, making the X4M06 highly suitable for experimental setups that demand high configurability and detailed signal reconstruction.

The IWR1443BOOST, with its millimeter-wave FMCW architecture, represents a more integrated and application-ready solution. Operating in the 76–81 GHz band, this radar system combines high-resolution range detection with onboard DSP and MCU capabilities. Its built-in hardware accelerators and software support through the mmWave SDK enable rapid prototyping and deployment in physiological sensing contexts. The MATLAB-based Vital Signs Lab GUI allows for real-time monitoring of respiration and heart rate and supports signal alignment with ECG. Among the three systems, the IWR1443BOOST has demonstrated the strongest validation in heart rate variability (HRV) analysis, showing statistically comparable outcomes with ECG measurements. This makes it a compelling choice for clinical research, especially in environments where contactless HRV estimation is needed.

Table 1 provides a side-by-side comparison of the three radar systems—ViRa24, X4M06, and IWR1443BOOST—across key technical and application-oriented features. The operating frequency, bandwidth, resolution, antenna design, and software interfaces are contrasted to reflect each system's performance and ease of use. Additionally, signal types supported (such as heart sounds or HRV), integration capabilities with ECG, and primary application focus areas are outlined to guide system selection based on specific biomedical monitoring goals. This comparative overview highlights the distinct advantages each radar brings to non-contact physiological sensing environments.

A comparative overview reveals that each radar system has strengths tailored to specific use cases. ViRa24 excels in high-fidelity acoustic physiological monitoring and multimodal signal validation. X4M06 offers unmatched configurability and spatial precision, ideal for academic research and custom signal development. IWR1443BOOST delivers

Table 1. Comparison of the three radar systems.

Feature	ViRa24 (CW)	X4M06 (UWB)	IWR1443BOOST (FMCW)
Operating Frequency	24.05 GHz	7.29–8.748 GHz	76–81 GHz
Bandwidth	Narrow (CW)	1.5 GHz	Up to 4 GHz
Resolution	Sub-mm (phase)	High (impulse)	~4 cm (FMCW)
Antennas	Integrated, narrow beam	Directional filtenna	MIMO (3 TX, 4 RX)
Software Interface	Python GUI	Python/C++ SDK	MATLAB GUI + SDK
ECG Integration	Yes	External	Yes
Signal Types	Respiration, Pulse, Heart Sounds	Respiration, Pulse	Respiration, HRV
Application Focus	Heart Sound Analysis, Sleep, Telemedicine	Compact, High-res sensing	HRV, Research Validation

a well-rounded, embedded sensing platform with commercial viability, supported by HRV validation and strong GUI capabilities.

Ultimately, system selection depends on the intended application, required signal types, development resources, and deployment environment. Researchers prioritizing heart sound analysis or synchronized ECG validation may favor ViRa24. Those seeking highly customizable radar signal chains will find X4M06 advantageous. Developers targeting robust, real-time HR and HRV monitoring with minimal hardware integration overhead may opt for IWR1443BOOST.

The results underscore the value of radar-based sensing in advancing non-invasive health monitoring and demonstrate how distinct radar modalities contribute complementary benefits across diverse biomedical research and telehealth applications.

Future directions include integrating these systems with cloud-based analytics, wearable platforms, and AI-driven diagnostic tools to extend their functionality and accessibility.

Future work should include an accuracy testing in a diverse participant pool and integration of additional physiological metrics, such as respiration rate, skin temperature, and galvanic skin response, to enable a comprehensive physiological profiling in real time [28, 29]. Leveraging non-contact sensors will allow for uninterrupted, real-time monitoring of patient performance [30, 31]. It will also be critical to pilot these solutions in real-world, unsupervised home-based settings to assess their practicality [32, 33]. A validated array of non-contact sensors allowing ongoing monitoring of vial parameters can greatly facilitate home-based disease management [34, 35] and telerehabilitation programs [36, 37]. Translational efforts ought to fuse electronic health record data with patient-generated metrics, improving both the precision of predictive models and the personalization of algorithms [38, 39], while carefully addressing bias reduction and model generalizability [40, 41]. To ensure scalability and transparency, home-based telemonitoring platforms [42, 43] must interface with EHRs and incorporate embedded clinical decision support [44, 45]. Finally, interactive health education and engagement tools will be key to sustaining patient adherence to prescribed exercise regimens [46, 47]. Continued exploration in radar signal modeling [48, 49], multimodal sensor fusion [50, 51], and low-power embedded implementations [52, 53] will further unlock their potential in enabling continuous, comfortable [54, 55], and precise health monitoring [36, 56].

References

1. Allen, J.: Photoplethysmography and its application in clinical physiological measurement. Physiol. Meas. **28**(3), R1–R39 (2007)
2. Joutsen, A., Nieminen, J., Kiviniemi, T., et al.: ECG signal quality in intermittent long-term dry electrode recordings with controlled motion artifacts. Sci. Rep. **14**, 8882 (2024)
3. Li, C., Lubecke, V.M., Boric-Lubecke, O.: A review on recent advances in Doppler radar sensors for noncontact healthcare monitoring. IEEE Trans. Microw. Theory Tech. **61**(5), 2046–2060 (2013)
4. Sykno GmbH: AMA Innovation Award: ViRa24 Radar for Non-Contact Vital Signs. https://www.sykno.de/en/blog-en/ama-sonderpreis-en/
5. Sykno GmbH: Vital Signs Detection with ViRa24. https://www.sykno.de/en/blog-en/vitalsign-en/
6. Sykno GmbH: ViRa24 in Practice: Interview with Elektronikpraxis. https://www.sykno.de/en/blog-en/elektronikpraxis-vsd-en/
7. Sykno GmbH: All Posts Tagged 'Radar'. https://www.sykno.de/en/blog-en/
8. Lee, Y., Lee, H., Kim, H., et al.: A novel non-contact heart rate monitor using impulse-radio ultra-wideband (IR-UWB) radar technology. Sci. Rep. **8**, 13053 (2018). https://doi.org/10.1038/s41598-018-31411-8
9. Kim, J.D., Lee, J.H., Yoon, Y.S., et al.: Non-contact respiration monitoring using impulse radio ultrawideband radar in neonates. R. Soc. Open Sci. **6**, 190149 (2019). https://doi.org/10.1098/rsos.190149
10. Kang, S., Kim, J.D., Choi, H., et al.: Non-contact diagnosis of obstructive sleep apnea using impulse-radio ultra-wideband radar. Sci. Rep. **10**, 5261 (2020). https://doi.org/10.1038/s41598-020-62061-4
11. Leem, S.K., Kim, J.D., Kim, J.W., et al.: Vital sign monitoring and mobile phone usage detection using IR-UWB radar. Sensors **17**(6), 1240 (2017). https://doi.org/10.3390/s17061240
12. Khan, F., Ali, H., Ahmad, J., et al.: Hand-based gesture recognition for vehicular applications using IR-UWB radar. Sensors **17**(4), 833 (2017). https://doi.org/10.3390/s17040833
13. Choi, J.W., Kim, J.D., Hong, H.S., et al.: People counting based on an IR-UWB radar sensor. IEEE Sens. J. **17**(17), 5717–5727 (2017). https://doi.org/10.1109/JSEN.2017.2723766
14. Ji, G., Lee, J., Kim, S.: Counting and localizing occupants using IR-UWB radar and machine learning. J. Korea Soc. Comput. Inf. **27**(5), 1–9 (2022). https://doi.org/10.9708/jksci.2022.27.05.001
15. Bouza, M., Yu, Y., Ahmed, A., et al.: Robust target classification using UWB sensing. IEEE Access **11**, 44267–44278 (2023). https://doi.org/10.1109/ACCESS.2023.3273152

16. Choo, Y.J., Lee, G.W., Moon, J.S., et al.: Noncontact sensors for vital signs measurement: a narrative review. Med. Sci. Monit. **30**, e944913 (2024). https://doi.org/10.12659/MSM.944913
17. Choo, Y.J., Lee, G.W., Moon, J.S., Chang, M.C.: Noncontact sensors for vital signs measurement: a narrative review. Med. Sci. Monit. **30**, e944913 (2024)
18. Sheikh, F., Ushaq, H., Ali, H., Iqbal, N.: Accuracy of compact mmWave radar sensor for vital signs monitoring. In: Proceedings of the URSI 2024, pp. 1–6 (2024)
19. Holl, N.T.: Millimeter-Wave Advanced Imaging Techniques. M.S. Thesis, Pennsylvania State University, Department of Electrical Engineering (2023)
20. Barrett, D., Alvarez, A.: mmWave radar sensors in robotics applications. In: Texas Instruments White Paper (2017)
21. Smiley, A., Finkelstein, J.: Feasibility of radar-based heart rate variability measurement: a comparative study with electrocardiography. In: Proceedings of the 2025 IEEE 15th Annual Computing and Communication Workshop and Conference (CCWC), Las Vegas, USA, pp. 376–379 (2025). https://doi.org/10.1109/CCWC62904.2025.10903703
22. Adiprabowo, T., Syahputra, A., Rahman, A., et al.: Human vital signs detection: a concurrent detection approach. Appl. Sci. **12**(3), 1077 (2022)
23. Chen, Y., Yuan, J., Tang, J.: A high precision vital signs detection method based on millimeter wave radar. Sci. Rep. **14**, 25535 (2024)
24. Adiprabowo, T., Syahputra, A., Rahman, A., et al.: Concurrent monitoring of heart and respiration rates using 77 GHz FMCW radar. Appl. Sci. **12**(3), 1077 (2022)
25. Alshamaa, K., El-Hajj, W., Itani, W.: Improved static hand gesture classification on deep CNNs using a sterile training technique. In: Proceedings of the ICMI 2019, pp. 1–8 (2019)
26. Gao, Y., Liu, Y., Xu, H., et al.: MM-DCDR: A benchmark of device configuration and data representation for mmWave-based human sensing. In: Proceedings of the IEEE WCSP 2024 (2024)
27. Iyer, S., Wang, Y., Yadav, D., et al.: Mm-Wave radar-based vital signs monitoring and arrhythmia detection using machine learning. Sensors **22**, 3106 (2022)
28. Lee, J., Finkelstein, J.: Evaluation of a portable stress management device. Stud. Health Technol. Inform. **208**, 248–252 (2015)
29. Smiley, A., Finkelstein, J.: Dynamic prediction of physical exertion: leveraging AI models and wearable sensor data during cycling exercise. Diagnostics (Basel) **15**(1), 52 (2024)
30. Smiley, A., Finkelstein, J.: Feasibility of radar-based heart rate variability measurement: A comparative study with electrocardiography. In: 15th Annual Computing and Communication Workshop and Conference (CCWC 2025), pp. 376–379. IEEE, Las Vegas (2025)
31. Jeong, I.C., Finkelstein, J.: Remotely controlled biking is associated with improved adherence to prescribed cycling speed. Technol. Health Care **23**(Suppl. 2), S543–S549 (2015)
32. Castro, H.K., Cross, R.K., Finkelstein, J.: Using a Home Automated Telemanagement (HAT) system: experiences and perceptions of patients with inflammatory bowel disease. In: AMIA Annual Symposium Proceedings 2006, p. 872. AMIA, Washington, DC (2006)
33. Goncalves Leite Rocco, P., Reategui-Rivera, C.M., Finkelstein, J.: Telemedicine applications for cancer rehabilitation: scoping review. JMIR Cancer **10**, e56969 (2024)
34. Finkelstein, J., Wood, J.: Implementing home telemanagement of congestive heart failure using Xbox gaming platform. In: Annual International Conference of the IEEE Engineering in Medicine and Biology Society 2011, pp. 3158–3163. IEEE, Boston (2011)
35. Cross, R.K., Finkelstein, J.: Challenges in the design of a home telemanagement trial for patients with ulcerative colitis. Clin. Trials **6**(6), 649–657 (2009)
36. Bedra, M., McNabney, M., Stiassny, D., et al.: Defining patient-centered characteristics of a telerehabilitation system for patients with COPD. Stud. Health Technol. Inform. **190**, 24–26 (2013)

37. Finkelstein, J., Parvanova, I., Huo, X.: Feasibility of a virtual reality app to promote pulmonary rehabilitation. Stud. Health Technol. Inform. **302**, 458–462 (2023)
38. Cui, W., Finkelstein, J.: Impact of COVID-19 pandemic on use of telemedicine services in an academic medical center. Stud. Health Technol. Inform. **281**, 407–411 (2021)
39. Paranjpe, I., Russak, A.J., De Freitas, J.K., et al.: Retrospective cohort study of clinical characteristics of 2199 hospitalised patients with COVID-19 in New York City. BMJ Open **10**(11), e040736 (2020)
40. Smiley, A., Villarreal-Zegarra, D., Reategui-Rivera, C.M., et al.: Methodological and reporting quality of machine learning studies on cancer diagnosis, treatment, and prognosis. Front. Oncol. **15**, 1555247 (2025)
41. Smiley, A., Reategui-Rivera, C.M., Villarreal-Zegarra, D., et al.: Exploring artificial intelligence biases in predictive models for cancer diagnosis. Cancers (Basel) **17**(3), 407 (2025)
42. Jeong, C., Finkelstein, J.: Introducing telerehabilitation in patients with multiple sclerosis with significant mobility disability: pilot feasibility study. In: International Conference on Healthcare Informatics (ICHI), pp. 69–75. IEEE, Dallas (2015)
43. Gabriel, A.S., Tsai, T.Y., Reategui-Rivera, C.M., et al.: Feasibility of telerehabilitation for the treatment of interstitial lung disease. Stud. Health Technol. Inform. **327**, 1170–1174 (2025)
44. Finkelstein, J., Gabriel, A., Schmer, S., Truong, T.T., Dunn, A.: Identifying facilitators and barriers to implementation of AI-assisted clinical decision support in an electronic health record system. J. Med. Syst. **48**(1), 89 (2024)
45. Kawamoto, K., Finkelstein, J., Del Fiol, G.: Implementing machine learning in the electronic health record: checklist of essential considerations. Mayo Clin. Proc. **98**(3), 366–369 (2023)
46. Finkelstein, J., Cha, E.M.: Using a mobile app to promote smoking cessation in hospitalized patients. JMIR Mhealth Uhealth **4**(2), e59 (2016)
47. Reategui-Rivera, C.M., Smiley, A., Finkelstein, J.: LLM-based chatbot to reduce mental illness stigma in healthcare providers. In: 15th Annual Computing and Communication Workshop and Conference (CCWC 2025), pp. 1–7. IEEE, Las Vegas (2025)
48. Song, C., Yavari, E., Gao, X., Lubecke, V.M., Boric-Lubecke, O.: Respiration signal pattern analysis for Doppler radar sensor with passive node and its application in occupancy sensing of a stationary subject. Biosensors (Basel) **15**(5), 273 (2025)
49. Qiao, D., He, T., Hu, B., Li, Y.: Non-contact physiological signal detection using continuous wave Doppler radar. Biomed. Mater. Eng. **24**(1), 993–1000 (2014)
50. Kang, W., Zhang, X., Zhang, J., et al.: Multimodal data generative fusion method for complex system health condition estimation. Sci. Rep. **15**(1), 20026 (2025)
51. Al-Adhaileh, M.H., Wadood, A., Aldhyani, T.H.H., et al.: Deep learning techniques for detecting freezing of gait episodes in Parkinson's disease using wearable sensors. Front. Physiol. **16**, 1581699 (2025)
52. Donati, R., Kartsch, V., Benini, L., Benatti, S.: BioWolf16: a 16-channel, 24-bit, 4kSPS ultra-low power platform for wearable clinical-grade bio-potential parallel processing and streaming. In: Annual International Conference of the IEEE Engineering in Medicine and Biology Society 2022, pp. 2518–2522. IEEE, Glasgow (2022)
53. Benatti, S., Montagna, F., Kartsch, V., et al.: Online learning and classification of EMG-based gestures on a parallel ultra-low power platform using hyperdimensional computing. IEEE Trans. Biomed. Circuits Syst. **13**(3), 516–528 (2019)
54. Jeong, I.C., Karpatkin, H., Finkelstein, J.: Physical telerehabilitation improves quality of life in patients with multiple sclerosis. Stud. Health Technol. Inform. **284**, 384–388 (2021). https://doi.org/10.3233/SHTI210752

55. Smiley, A., Finkelstein, J.: Modeling perceived exertion with deep neural networks and wearable sensors. In: 2025 IEEE 11th International Conference on Big Data Computing Service and Machine Learning Applications (BigDataService), pp. 60–65. IEEE, Tucson (2025). https://doi.org/10.1109/BigDataService65758.2025.00014
56. Smiley, A., Finkelstein, J.: Smart wearable analytics for cycling: AI-based physical exertion prediction. Stud. Health Technol. Inform. **328**, 256–260 (2025). https://doi.org/10.3233/SHTI250714

Enhancing Language Assessment in Traumatic Brain Injury: A Situational Approach to Data Precision and Stability Detection

Marisol Roldán-Palacios and Aurelio López-López(✉)

Instituto Nacional de Astrofísica Óptica y Electrónica, Santa María Tonantzintla, CP 72840 Puebla, Mexico
{marppalacios,allopez}@inaoep.mx

Abstract. This study addresses the challenges posed by restrictive data conditions while allowing for alternative analytical approaches. It adopts a situational approach that emphasizes clarity and methodological precision. The research aims to build on previous work that demonstrated promising outcomes using alternative assessment techniques. Specifically, it seeks to identify subtle variations that may reflect changes in the internal organization of language structures among individuals with traumatic brain injury. These findings can improve the understanding of the language dynamics of patients and support the development of more effective therapeutic strategies. The results reported here reinforce the validity of the proposed approach, which will be further discussed in relation to comprehension as a key aspect of the focus of the study.

Keywords: Data Scarcity · Situational Analysis · Traumatic Brain Injury · Language - Assessment · Instability Detection

1 Introduction

An accurate computational approach for handling scarce data should adhere to the principles of foundational techniques in language analysis, as these "remain essential for a comprehensive understanding of language processing" [11]. The goal in dealing with limited data is to extract as much information and knowledge as possible from the available data [7].

Certain conditions or situations warrant stepping back from the prevailing trend of data analytics and exploration. While modern computing approaches are well equipped to address complex computational tasks—covering extensive theoretical, technical, and architectural aspects— they also acknowledge the challenges posed by the evolution of data-driven intelligence [36]. However, these approaches may overlook subtle or atypical cases.

Undeniably, large-scale data studies have garnered significant attention, and from some perspectives [11], modern natural language processing systems are

A. Alsadoon et al. (Eds.): CSCE 2025, CCIS 2935, pp. 263–276, 2026.
https://doi.org/10.1007/978-3-032-22199-5_19

highly determined by deep neural networks. Also, interest is growing in how machines can learn from minimal data through approaches such as zero-shot, one-shot, or few-shot learning. However, in genuinely low-data scenarios, neural networks still face challenges and often perform poorly compared to their statistical counterparts [9,16,25].

While the small-data context is acknowledged, it is often addressed using models primarily developed for large-scale data analysis or through techniques that significantly alter the data [2,25]. These methods may be suitable for broad, generalized scenarios, but they often prove inadequate or inconsistent when applied to specific, urgent cases. In particular, domains such as medical and healthcare research have historically suffered from limited data availability [26], a condition unlikely to change in the near future. This is particularly critical in the study of rare or emerging diseases, where timely and reliable data are scarce, but high-stakes decisions must still be made.

Even in more familiar cases, such as head trauma, data availability is often severely limited due to situational constraints [18,33]. In these scenarios, the pressing concern lies in the critical nature of the applications —technologies used to support diagnosis, recovery, or treatment planning. These tools must be intelligible and transparent, a requirement that presents a significant challenge for AI systems built on deep learning architectures, which are often criticized for their lack of interpretability [11].

Research on language and communication disorders aligns with the restricted contexts discussed earlier. Like other domain-specific areas, these studies require models tailored to their unique conditions. In this case, a situationally relevant analysis [11] is needed to examine atypical language patterns and capture the inherently modified linguistic structures —an essential focus of the current investigation.

The limitations outlined above motivate the exploration of an alternative analytical approach, one that is still under development but meaningfully integrates multiple fields, concepts, and perspectives [5,20,27]. Once again, the goal is to construct a situationally relevant analysis capable of capturing influenced structures —in this case, specific alterations in language use following traumatic brain injury.

This examination was designed to prove the relevance of the selected technique in analyzing the development of language changes. Its pertinence lies in its ability to address constrained scenarios through an intelligible, focused study that employs a method introduced in prior work [24].

The technique pairs attributes derived not only from linguistic knowledge but also from insights across other research fields. This interdisciplinary foundation supports the interpretation of the generated information, which is crucial given that the phenomena under investigation must be thoroughly substantiated within a strictly constrained data context.

In the present study, we report the corresponding results from examining a set of syntactic attributes, evaluated using the prototype technique at two key points: the initial stage at three months and a follow-up phase at twelve months.

The remainder of this work is organized as follows. The next section reviews related research, highlighting the challenges posed by constrained data conditions —scenarios in which many modern, large-scale techniques struggle—, thereby reinforcing the need for our proposed alternative approach. This perspective is further developed in the Attribute Representation section, which is followed by the Experimental Setting, where we outline the data properties and specify the attributes included in the study. After describing the Results report, we move to the Discussion, which offers potential interpretations of the findings. Finally, the study concludes with key insights and a proposal for future research directions.

2 Related Work

Research in related domains has addressed similar challenges of data scarcity, particularly in contexts where collecting additional data is not possible, practical, or valuable [13]. These studies highlight significant limitations —termed "meaning barriers"— when applying commonly used strategies such as transfer learning or data augmentation [2,7,13]. The use of these techniques has shown mixed results, sometimes providing benefits and at other times negatively impacting functioning [19]. This variability is a foreseeable yet undesirable outcome [1], especially when data augmentation is applied without a solid theoretical foundation relevant to the specific domain [2–4,9,12]. In such cases, the data distribution may be unintentionally altered [13], introducing a latent risk of degrading meaningful information [7].

In language-related studies, one common approach for dealing with small datasets is synonym replacement, which assumes semantic preservation by substituting a word with another of similar meaning [17,25]. However, this assumption becomes unreliable in the context of language disorders. Even in typical language use, synonym replacement is highly sensitive to context —an issue exacerbated by the limited data available [2]. Although some studies have explored language models to mitigate this limitation [9], the results remain inconsistent, often showing only marginal improvements [10]. Moreover, in domains where intelligibility is critical, increased model complexity [13] may be impractical, particularly when combined with data augmentation strategies.

Deep learning architectures have also been proposed for data augmentation with promising results [35]. Nonetheless, these approaches demand substantial training data and computational resources [12]. For example, the smallest dataset size in successful implementations exceeds 6,000 samples, with a vocabulary of similar magnitude —conditions far from achievable in severely resource-constrained domains [33]. As Sahin [25] notes, genuinely low-resource languages remain largely unsupported by robust pretrained models due to the unavailability of raw data.

Efforts to diversify training data in language analysis —through paraphrasing, noising, or sampling [12]— typically involve modifying the source data. However, this strategy becomes problematic when the focus of study is on change itself, such as the structural shifts and variations inherent in language systems.

In such cases, altering the original data may compromise the very features under investigation, limiting the method's applicability and reliability.

In transfer learning, aside from the requirement for large-scale datasets and sufficient computational resources to train source models that capture diverse concepts, there remains a substantial risk that the model may learn incorrect associations or even degrade performance [7]. Furthermore, the lack of control over what neural models internalize poses additional challenges —particularly when the features learned during pretraining diverge from those relevant to the target domain [6].

This scenario highlights the need to explore alternative approaches for conducting investigations in severely constrained data contexts, where both process transparency and result intelligibility are essential.

3 Trajectory-Based Attribute Representation

The technical details of the proposed technique for handling limited data and additional constraints are thoroughly presented in [24]. This method employs a heterogeneous approach specifically tailored to the described constrained environment. It decomposes the samples into substructures, generating alternative representations of their attributes as trajectories. These trajectories are then paired to model and track the evolution of inter-attribute relationships over time. In this work, we further elaborate on the underlying rationale that guided the development of this technique.

We begin with the foundational notion that inspired the development of a new representation of the samples. A trajectory [34] is understood as a continuous mapping from a time interval $I = [t_{start}, t_{end}]$ to the space in which the entity evolves. This concept provides the basis for modeling the dynamics of sample attributes over time, allowing for the encoding of structural and temporal variations within a unified framework.

Essentially, the concept of a trajectory captures the progression of movement over time, enabling the observation of how attributes evolve throughout the temporal domain. This dynamic perspective led to the adoption of Bayes' theorem as a central analytical tool for evaluating the relationships —referred to as proximity measurements— between paired trajectories. Bayes' theorem is particularly well-suited for this purpose, as it quantifies the degree of dependence between two events conditioned on temporal evidence [22,23].

To evaluate the discriminative potential of the proposed proximity relationships, we employ two statistical learning methods. The first is the Naïve Bayes method [8], which estimates the prior conditional probabilities under the assumption of attribute independence. Complementing this, the SimpleLogistic method [30], with a logistic regression model, incorporates posterior probability estimation. Together, these approaches provide a robust framework for assessing how effectively the paired attribute relationships differentiate between classes.

Within the constructed attribute space —defined by proximity measures—, the established relationships can be interpreted as a unified network. This network comprises paired trajectories that encapsulate the temporal evolution of relationships between pairs of attributes. The time frame, over which these trajectories are defined, corresponds to the duration of the narrative task, capturing the full span of its development.

4 Experimental Setting

This section is divided into two parts. First, we describe the corpus used in the experiments and highlight its relevant properties. Second, we present the set of attributes selected for the reported stage of the study —specifically, those used to validate the proposed technique under the defined examination criteria.

4.1 Data

Given the foundational role that data gathering plays in shaping the basis for any analysis [11], the collection process must ensure both the integrity and representativeness of the data. This is essential to avoid bias and misinterpretation, and to construct an ecological setting that accurately reflects the phenomena under study —thereby reducing the risk of misleading conclusions.

The collection of specialized datasets often demands domain-specific expertise. In the field of language, even typical linguistic data is inherently complex [11], and despite extensive research, a complete understanding remains elusive. This highlights the significant challenge involved in collecting samples of atypical language, where the conditions for reliable data acquisition are even more stringent.

To support the study of atypical language, a representative sample of the phenomenon was carefully planned, constructed, and made publicly available for further analysis. This resource —TBIBank, accessible via TalkBank [14]— is grounded in the foundational work of [32], with detailed statistical validation, task design, attribute types, and participant demographics documented in [21, 28,29]. Developed by domain experts, the corpus not only meets but exceeds the methodological and ecological requirements outlined previously.

The tasks used, the rigor of the data collection procedures, and the standardization of transcript formats were all carefully defined and implemented. These considerations were crucial in ensuring consistency and enhancing the robustness of studies focused on reshaped or atypical language.

The reported examination includes the Cinderella story retelling task as part of a broader set of narrative tasks. The project was extended to assess recovery over a two-year period, with data collected at five time points: 3, 6, 9, 12, and 24 months. The average sample size per time point was approximately 42 participants, although the sample size at the final (24-month) time point was notably smaller.

4.2 Set of Attributes

As part of the ongoing validation of the proposed technique, a set of syntactic attributes is examined. These attributes are part of the Northwestern Narrative

Language Analysis profile, defined by Thompson et *al.* [31]. At this stage, they were extracted from CLAN[1]. Table 1 presents the complete list of attributes, along with brief descriptions of their linguistic significance. For the purposes of this study, attribute pairs are constructed using `infinitival.markers` as the base, combined individually with each of the remaining attributes. Below, we provide additional clarification for selected attributes.

Table 1. Set of attributes used in the reported examination, that runs over 16 combinations derived from the 17 attributes of syntax.

Attribute [1]	Description
infinitival.markers	# infinitives
negation.markers	# negatives
X3rd.person.present.tense.markers	# words with inflection (wwi) of third person
X..embedded.clauses.sentence	A ratio relating Embedded clauses
wh.words	# 'wh' words
superlative.suffixes	# words indicating superlatives
sentence.complexity.ratio	A measure for complexity of the sentence
regular.plural.markers	# wwi of regular plural
regular.perfect.aspect.markers	# wwi of regular perfect
regular.past.tense.markers	# wwi of regular past tense
quantifiers	# quantifiers
progressive.aspect.markers	# wwi of progressive aspect
possessive.markers	# possessives
irregular.plural.forms	# wwi of irregular plural
irregular.perfect.participles	# wwi of irregular perfect participles
irregular.past.tense.markers	# wwi of irregular past tense
comparative.suffixes	# words indicating comparative

[1] Attributes' formal definition are found in [14].

The attribute `wh.words` accounts for the frequency of relative and interrogative pronouns (e.g., who, whose), as well as wh-conjunctions and interrogative determiners (e.g., which). The attribute `sentence.complexity.ratio` measures syntactic complexity by computing a ratio: both the numerator and denominator count sentences containing at least one copula, modal, or participle. However, the numerator is further constrained to include only those sentences that also contain at least one element from a predefined set of relevant grammatical structures (GRs).

The attribute `X..embedded.clauses.sentence` is calculated as the sum of sentences containing at least one embedded clause, each weighted by the number of embedded clauses it contains, and then normalized by the total number of

[1] A tool downloadable from the data website.

sentences [14]. The interpretation of the remaining attributes follows intuitively from their names and is therefore omitted for brevity.

5 Results

After evaluating the proximity relations and establishing a basis for comparison, the results are presented in Tables 2 and 3. Table 2 summarizes the evaluations at three-months, using both the Naïve Bayes and SimpleLogistic methods. Table 3 provides the corresponding evaluations for twelve-months.

Each table is organized by attribute combinations, listed in the first column. The three successive blocks correspond to the responses for the basis and the proximity relation. Each block has three columns corresponding to precision, recall, and F1 score, respectively. The last two columns are the percentage differences calculated between the baseline and proximity measures. This organizational structure mirrors the format used in the initial set of results.

For a more intuitive understanding, these results are also visually represented in Fig. 1. This figure illustrates the development of features, with responses shown in three distinct colors: direct baseline responses are in navy blue, normalized responses in blue, and proximity measures in pink. The data points are grouped by attribute pairs, and the evaluated stages are clearly distinguished by edge points. The three-month sample responses are marked with a plus symbol, while the twelve-month sample evaluations are represented by geometric shapes. The square and triangle shapes correspond to the comparison base results, and the circle corresponds to the proximity relation responses. A line segment connects the responses to illustrate the trends over time.

The first point of interest is the notably low performance of the pair `(infinitival.markers, X3rd.person.present.tense.marker)`. Although this evaluation had 0.96, a high precision in identifying positive cases, it exhibited a recall close to the chance level (0.53), resulting in the lowest F1-score of 0.69 among all proximity relations examined. Nevertheless, this result still slightly outperforms the baseline by 3%, representing the smallest advantage of proximity-based evaluation over baseline methods in both models.

For the Naïve Bayes model, the following two lowest-performing pairs, with F1-scores below 0.8, are `(infinitival.markers, irregular.past.tense.markers)` at 0.72 and `(infinitival.markers, progressive.aspect.markers)` at 0.78. Both show prominent precision (above 0.90) but are limited by low recall, around 0.60. In contrast, the remaining combinations achieved a mean F1-score of 0.89, with a standard deviation of 0.03 and a median of 0.88. The three best performing pairs combine `infinitival.markers` with `regular.past.tense.markers`, `regular.plural.markers`, and `wh.words`, attaining F1-scores of 0.94, 0.94, and 0.95, respectively. In particular, the last pair also represents the peak improvement over the baselines, with both models exceeding 90%.

In the recovery stage at 12 months, the F1-scores range from a minimum of 0.88 to a maximum of 0.94, with both the mean and median at 0.91. The Naïve

Table 2. SYNTAX - Naïve Bayes/Simple Logistic -Precision-Recall-F1-measures. – Difference percentages - Stage 3 months

Attribute infinitival.markers vs.	F-1[1]									Percentages	
	Direct raw-data			Normalized raw-data			Proximity relation			Dif. eval-dir.	Dif. eval-norma
	Prec.	Recall	F1	Prec.	Recall	F1	Prec.	Recall	F1	%	%
negation.markers	0.75	0.44	0.55	0.69	0.44	*0.54*	1.00	0.83	**0.91**	63.72	68.90
	0.65	0.54	0.59	0.62	0.51	*0.56*	1.00	0.83	**0.91**	54.51	61.96
X3rd.person.present.tense.marker	0.88	0.53	0.67	0.60	0.74	*0.67*	0.96	0.53	**0.69**	3.00	3.00
	0.71	0.58	0.64	0.63	0.79	*0.70*	0.92	0.77	**0.83**	30.27	19.12
X..embedded.clauses.sentence	0.65	0.79	0.71	0.61	0.39	*0.47*	1.00	0.79	**0.89**	24.09	87.71
	0.76	0.70	0.73	0.53	0.64	*0.58*	0.97	0.79	**0.87**	20.03	51.65
wh.words	0.73	0.38	0.50	0.44	0.50	*0.47*	0.97	0.93	**0.95**	90.20	103.64
	0.62	0.50	0.55	0.54	1.00	*0.70*	0.97	0.88	**0.92**	67.27	32.14
superlative.suffixes	0.74	0.42	0.54	0.55	0.80	*0.65*	0.97	0.80	**0.88**	62.41	34.30
	0.70	0.57	0.63	0.53	0.87	*0.66*	0.97	0.85	**0.91**	43.97	37.42
sentence.complexity.ratio	0.64	0.77	0.70	0.62	0.34	*0.44*	1.00	0.73	**0.84**	20.11	90.93
	0.73	0.68	0.71	0.59	0.52	*0.55*	0.92	0.82	**0.87**	22.80	56.50
regular.plural.markers	0.93	0.67	0.78	0.53	0.62	*0.57*	0.95	0.93	**0.94**	20.82	64.62
	0.85	0.69	0.76	0.59	0.79	*0.67*	0.95	0.93	**0.94**	23.2	39.67
regular.perfect.aspect.markers	0.93	0.59	0.72	0.70	0.55	*0.61*	1.00	0.76	**0.86**	19.31	41.11
	0.79	0.62	0.69	0.66	0.69	*0.67*	0.95	0.86	**0.90**	29.87	33.53
regular.past.tense.markers	0.82	0.43	0.56	0.54	0.86	*0.67*	0.97	0.90	**0.94**	66.61	40.63
	0.69	0.59	0.64	0.53	0.93	*0.68*	0.97	0.88	**0.92**	44.31	36.43
quantifiers	0.88	0.52	0.66	0.61	0.43	*0.51*	1.00	0.75	**0.86**	30.44	69.03
	0.78	0.73	0.75	0.67	0.79	*0.73*	0.95	0.82	**0.88**	16.6	20.44
progressive.aspect.markers	0.72	0.41	0.52	0.53	0.41	*0.46*	0.97	0.66	**0.78**	50.19	69.70
	0.68	0.59	0.63	0.51	0.93	*0.66*	0.97	0.77	**0.86**	35.80	31.25
possessive.markers	0.75	0.44	0.55	0.56	0.90	*0.69*	0.97	0.78	**0.86**	56.14	25.00
	0.62	0.56	0.59	0.56	1.00	*0.72*	0.97	0.85	**0.91**	54.07	26.43
irregular.plural.forms	0.78	0.45	0.57	0.68	0.47	*0.56*	0.97	0.80	**0.88**	53.59	56.89
	0.72	0.57	0.64	0.54	0.90	*0.67*	0.97	0.87	**0.92**	44.13	36.85
irregular.perfect.participles	0.79	0.36	0.49	0.70	0.38	*0.49*	0.97	0.79	**0.87**	76.42	76.42
	0.55	0.76	0.64	0.63	0.69	*0.66*	0.97	0.86	**0.91**	42.34	38.24
irregular.past.tense.markers	0.84	0.50	0.63	0.52	0.36	*0.42*	0.93	0.59	**0.72**	15.63	71.39
	0.79	0.55	0.65	0.54	0.93	*0.68*	0.92	0.83	**0.87**	35.03	27.92
comparative.suffixes	0.78	0.43	0.55	0.64	0.38	*0.48*	0.97	0.81	**0.88**	59.39	84.73
	0.73	0.57	0.64	0.57	0.93	*0.71*	0.97	0.83	**0.90**	40.16	26.52

[1] SimpleLogistic is in gray background

Bayes model shows closely grouped results, with a standard deviation of 0.02. The marginal global improvement in extracted information is 5%, observed for the pair involving `irregular.past.tense.markers` when evaluated using the SimpleLogistic method.

At the 3-month stage, SimpleLogistic evaluations show a mean F1-score of 0.89, a standard deviation of 0.03, and values ranging from 0.83 to 0.94. The combination involving `X3rd.person.present.tense.markers` again exhibits the lowest performance, while the pair with `regular.plural.markers` matches the top value of 0.94, consistent with the Naïve Bayes results. At 12 months, SimpleLogistic yields F1-scores in the range of 0.84 to 0.95. The lowest score corresponds to the pair with `irregular.past.tense.markers`, while the highest is again achieved with `regular.plural.markers`.

Table 3. SYNTAX - Naïve Bayes/Simple Logistic -Precision-Recall-F1-measures. – Difference percentages - Stage 12 months

Attribute infinitival.markers vs.	F-1[1] Direct raw-data Prec.	Recall	F1	Normalized raw-data Prec.	Recall	F1	Proximity relation Prec.	Recall	F1	Percentages Dif. eval-dir. %	Dif. eval-norma %
negation.markers	0.86	0.58	0.69	0.46	0.46	*0.46*	0.97	0.88	**0.93**	33.57	99.35
	0.81	0.70	0.75	0.52	0.91	*0.66*	0.95	0.86	**0.90**	20.27	36.46
X3rd.person.present.tense.markers	0.91	0.71	0.80	0.58	0.57	0.58	0.97	0.86	**0.91**	13.87	57.61
	0.86	0.76	0.81	0.61	0.71	0.66	0.97	0.86	**0.91**	12.47	38.24
X..embedded.clauses.sentence	0.89	0.73	0.80	0.83	0.68	0.75	1.00	0.79	**0.89**	10.75	18.13
	0.84	0.82	0.83	0.82	0.73	0.77	0.95	0.89	**0.92**	10.87	19.07
wh.words	0.90	0.64	0.75	0.61	0.57	0.59	0.97	0.90	**0.94**	25.067	58.18
	0.81	0.69	0.74	0.56	0.59	0.57	0.97	0.93	**0.95**	27.82	65.39
superlative.suffixes	0.83	0.58	0.69	0.53	0.85	0.65	0.97	0.90	**0.94**	36.59	43.27
	0.81	0.71	0.75	0.56	1.00	0.72	0.97	0.90	**0.94**	24.43	30.32
sentence.complexity.ratio	0.76	0.72	0.74	0.75	0.56	0.64	1.00	0.77	**0.87**	17.61	35.62
	0.81	0.79	0.80	0.71	0.58	0.64	0.92	0.86	**0.89**	11.50	39.16
regular.plural.markers	0.94	0.79	0.86	0.59	0.77	0.67	0.95	0.93	**0.94**	9.29	41.08
	0.92	0.84	0.88	0.59	0.84	0.69	0.98	0.93	**0.95**	8.43	37.57
regular.perfect.aspect.markers	0.93	0.65	0.77	0.65	0.74	0.70	0.97	0.86	**0.91**	19.16	31.32
	0.87	0.77	0.81	0.65	0.79	0.72	0.97	0.79	**0.87**	6.99	21.79
regular.past.tense.markers	0.93	0.63	0.75	0.54	0.84	0.66	0.95	0.93	**0.94**	25.47	42.36
	0.86	0.72	0.78	0.54	0.95	0.69	0.95	0.91	**0.93**	18.34	34.83
quantifiers	0.97	0.79	0.87	0.76	0.65	0.70	0.98	0.93	**0.95**	9.17	36.00
	0.92	0.84	0.88	0.74	0.74	0.74	0.97	0.91	**0.94**	7.06	26.34
progressive.aspect.markers	0.86	0.54	0.67	0.51	0.39	0.44	0.97	0.77	**0.86**	29.08	94.80
	0.81	0.68	0.74	0.48	0.75	0.58	0.97	0.77	**0.86**	16.19	47.43
possessive.markers	0.86	0.61	0.71	0.56	0.85	0.67	0.97	0.85	**0.91**	27.31	35.066
	0.76	0.68	0.72	0.56	1.00	0.72	0.97	0.88	**0.92**	28.55	28.37
irregular.plural.forms	0.88	0.56	0.69	0.82	0.34	0.48	0.97	0.88	**0.92**	34.352	91.10
	0.76	0.71	0.73	0.79	0.66	0.72	0.97	0.88	**0.92**	25.75	28.19
irregular.perfect.participles	0.85	0.56	0.68	0.53	0.78	0.63	0.97	0.93	**0.95**	40.53	49.84
	0.81	0.71	0.75	0.56	1.00	0.72	0.97	0.88	**0.92**	22.58	28.37
irregular.past.tense.markers	0.91	0.70	0.79	0.75	0.48	0.58	0.97	0.818	**0.89**	11.82	52.49
	0.88	0.73	0.80	0.67	0.59	0.63	0.92	0.77	**0.84**	5.00	33.97
comparative.suffixes	0.83	0.58	0.69	0.48	0.68	0.57	0.97	0.88	**0.92**	34.55	63.07
	0.78	0.71	0.74	0.55	1.00	0.71	0.97	0.90	**0.94**	25.94	31.42

[1] SimpleLogistic is in gray background

6 Discussion

Entering directly into the discussion, the context observed for SimpleLogistic in the pair (`infinitival.markers, X3rd.person.present.tense.markers`) may indicate a significant shift in the use of third-person inflected forms, likely reflecting deterioration, as the disparity between the study group and the control becomes more pronounced. In contrast, the responses for the pair (`infinitival.markers, regular.plural.markers`) suggest a change in the use of regular plural forms beginning shortly after the incident, with effects that persist —or re-emerge— a year later.

Following the principle of connectivity among elements in the studied narrative structure, proximity-based attribute pairing frequently reveals alterations in word usage. When comparing the information visibility achieved via proximity-based evaluations to baseline methods, it is noted that the precision (i.e., the accuracy of positive predictions) consistently remains above 0.90 for all combi-

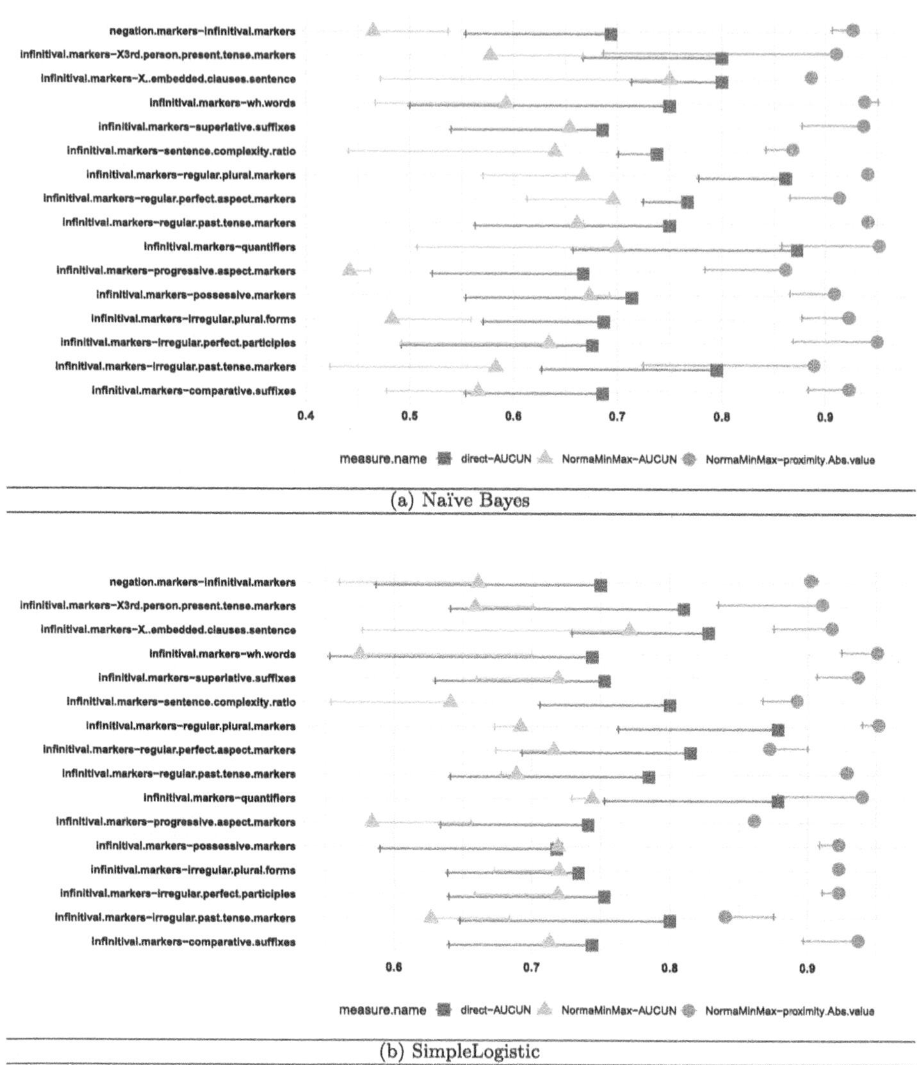

(a) Naïve Bayes

(b) SimpleLogistic

Fig. 1. Evaluations in terms of F1-measure. It illustrates both junctures at 3 and 12 months joined by line segments. The first with plus symbol (+) and the second each corresponding to measure at hand, [navy blue] square (■) for direct base, [blue] triangle (▲) for the normalized base and [pink] circle (●) for proximity. Part (a) corresponds to NaïveBayes and part (b) to SimpleLogistic responses.(Color figure online)

nations. Cases where the F1-score falls below 0.80 are primarily due to lower recall.

At the three-month stage, using the Naïve Bayes model, 13 out of 16 attribute combinations yield F1-scores above 0.84. For the other evaluations —Naïve Bayes at 12 months and SimpleLogistic at both three and twelve months—, all 16 combinations achieve F1-scores above 0.83. This consistent performance is illustrated in Fig. 1.

The graphs facilitate a direct interpretation of the patterns previously discussed. They highlight the intervals where measurements are concentrated, the advantages that proximity-based evaluations have over baseline responses —clearly observable in the plots—, and the consistency of this advantage across both statistical learning methods. Furthermore, they reveal whether measurements increase or decrease in the 12-month sample compared to the 3-month instance, shedding light on temporal changes in language use.

For example, in the pair `(infinitival.markers, irregular.past.tense.markers)`, although the raw response increases over time, both normalized and proximity-based evaluations show a decrease. Conversely, unchanging values —such as those associated with `regular.past.tense.markers` or `progressive.aspect.markers` in SimpleLogistic proximity evaluations— may indicate stability in usage across time points.

The attribute `regular.past.tense.markers`, when paired with `infinitival.markers`, demonstrates notable consistency across both learning methods. It shows only minor variation in normalized baseline values between 3 and 12 months, and no change in proximity evaluations across those intervals. The percentage differences between proximity-based relations and baseline methods are predominantly positive —excluding only three attributes—, suggesting that the proximity approach captures relevant patterns with efficacy. This supports our initial hypothesis: that linguistic changes occur within known relationships, as evidenced in our studied sample.

Several complex factors influence the effectiveness of engineered solutions based on natural language processing (NLP), particularly when integrating them into specific environments [11]. As such, achieving accurate computation —except under narrowly defined conditions— remains uncertain. The used methods must be contextually relevant, ensuring careful and thoughtful implementations. In light of this, there is a clear need to explore alternative approaches that can address these requirements in a simple, yet situationally appropriate manner, both in theory and in practice.

Language impairments at the intersentential level are known to occur after traumatic brain injury [15]. But what specific components of language structure are most affected? The proximity-based approach proposed here offers a promising avenue for identifying such changes.

7 Conclusion

The validation results presented here support the pertinence of the proposed approach, which is designed to process data under challenging conditions while maintaining interpretability. Applied to a language sample from individuals with traumatic brain injury a population reflecting the study's intended scope—, the technique revealed subtle behavioral features that would likely remain hidden through direct attribute evaluation alone.

Although we expected to observe consistent relationships between proximity measures and baseline changes across recovery stages, the patterns appeared ambiguous. In particular, the differences in responses at the 12-month mark, relative to the initial recovery stage, did not consistently align with changes in proximity to the reference bases. This inconsistency may be explained by the fact that many response patterns remained near chance levels, limiting the clarity of the observed effects.

We anticipate that ongoing work along this trajectory will deepen our understanding of how language reshapes over time in such populations. It will also help identify which linguistic attributes are most sensitive to these dynamics and clarify why others are not. Discovering specific patterns in proximity measures and refining the set of interpretable elements required for intelligible outcomes will be central to advancing the technique.

Further research can focus on refining proximity metrics or incorporating complementary features (e.g., syntactic complexity, fluency) that could improve sensitivity to meaningful variations. Cross-validation with clinical assessments may also strengthen the interpretability and relevance of the results. Ultimately, the goal is to develop a robust, generalizable framework for analyzing language in contexts of cognitive or neurological disruption.

Acknowledgments. The first author was supported by SECIHTI, through scholarship 1008734. The second author was partially supported by SNII, México.

References

1. Awada, W., Khoshgoftaar, T.M., Dittman, D., Wald, R., Napolitano, A.: A review of the stability of feature selection techniques for bioinformatics data. In: 2012 IEEE 13th International Conference on Information Reuse & Integration (IRI), pp. 356–363. IEEE, Las Vegas, NV, USA (2012)
2. Chen, J., Tam, D., Raffel, C., Bansal, M., Yang, D.: An empirical survey of data augmentation for limited data learning in NLP. Trans. Assoc. Comput. Linguist. **11**(191), 191–211 (2023)
3. Dao, T., Gu, A., Ratner, A., Smith, V., De Sa, C., Ré, C.: A kernel theory of modern data augmentation. In: Proceedings of the 36th International Conference on Machine Learning Research, pp. 1528–1537. PMLR (2019)
4. Feng, S.Y., et al.: A survey of data augmentation approaches for NLP. In: Findings of the Association for Computational Linguistics: ACL-IJCNLP 2021, pp. 968–988 (2021)
5. Gómez González, M.D.L.Á., Ruiz de Mendoza Ibáñez, F.J., Gonzálvez-García, F., Downing, A.: Theory and Practice in Functional-Cognitive Space, 2nd edn., pp. 319–327. John Benjamins Publishing Company (2014)
6. Hedderich, M.A., Lange, L., Adel, H., Strötgen, J., Klakow, D.: Survey on recent approaches for natural language processing in low-resource scenarios. In: Proceedings of the 2021 Conference of the North American Chapter of the Association for Computational Linguistics: Human Language Technologies, pp. 2545–2568. Association for Computational Linguistics (2021)

7. Holst, C.A., Lohweg, V.: Scarce data in intelligent technical systems: causes, characteristics, and implications. Sci **4**(4), 49 (2022)
8. John, G.H., Langley, P.: Estimating continuous distributions in bayesian classifiers. In: Eleventh Conference on Uncertainty in Artificial Intelligence, pp. 338–345. Morgan Kaufmann Publishers Inc., San Francisco, CA, USA (1995)
9. Jungiewicz, M., Smywiński-Pohl, A.: Towards textual data augmentation for neural networks: synonyms and maximum loss. Comput. Sci. **20**(1), 57–83 (2019)
10. Kobayashi, S.: Contextual augmentation: data augmentation by words with paradigmatic relations. In: Proceedings of the 2018 Conference of the North American Chapter of the Association for Computational Linguistics: Human Language Technologies, vol. 2 (Short Papers), pp. 452–457. Association for Computational Linguistics, New Orleans, Louisiana (2018)
11. Kumar, A.: Language Intelligence: Expanding Frontiers in Natural Language Processing. John Wiley & Sons (2024)
12. Li, B., Hou, Y., Che, W.: Data augmentation approaches in natural language processing: a survey. AI Open **3**, 71–90 (2022)
13. Lin, C.H., Kaushik, C., Dyer, E.L., Muthukumar, V.: The good, the bad and the ugly sides of data augmentation: an implicit spectral regularization perspective. J. Mach. Learn. Res. **25**(91), 1–85 (2024)
14. MacWhinney, B.: The CHILDES Project, Tools for Analyzing Talk, 3rd edn. Lawrence Erlbaum Associates, Mahwah, NJ (2000)
15. Marini, A., Andreetta, S., Del Tin, S., Carlomagno, S.: A multi-level approach to the analysis of narrative language in aphasia. Aphasiology **25**(11), 1372–1392 (2011)
16. Melamud, O., Bornea, M., Barker, K.: Combining unsupervised pre-training and annotator rationales to improve low-shot text classification. In: Proceedings of the 2019 Conference on Empirical Methods in Natural Language Processing and The 9th International Joint Conference on Natural Language Processing (EMNLP-IJCNLP), pp. 3884–3893. Association for Computational Linguistics, Hong Kong, China (2019)
17. Miao, Z., Li, Y., Wang, X., Tan, W.C.: Snippext: semi-supervised opinion mining with augmented data. In: Proceedings of The Web Conference 2020, pp. 617–628 (2020)
18. Peach, R.K., Hanna, L.E.: Sentence-level processing predicts narrative coherence following traumatic brain injury: evidence in support of a resource model of discourse processing. Lang. Cogn. Neurosci. **36**(6), 694–710 (2021)
19. Pellicer, L.F.A.O., Ferreira, T.M., Costa, A.H.R.: Data augmentation techniques in natural language processing. Appl. Soft Comput. **132**, 109803 (2023)
20. Pianzola F.: Looking at narrative as a complex system: the proteus principle. In: Narrating complexity, pp. 101–122. Springer, Cham (2018). https://doi.org/10.1007/978-3-319-64714-2_10
21. Power, E., et al.: Patterns of narrative discourse in early recovery following severe traumatic brain injury. Brain Inj. **34**(1), 98–109 (2019)
22. López Puga, J., Krzywinski, M., Altman, N.: Bayes' theorem. Nat. Methods **12**(4), 277–278 (2015)
23. Rodríguez-Mauricio, A.F., Leyva-Cárdenas, M.G., Arch-Tirado, E., Lino-González, A.L.: Determination of probabilistic intersections related to acquired brain damage from the determination of a priori and a posteriori probabilities. Cir Cir (Eng) **91**(3), 374–381 (2023)

24. Roldán-Palacios, M., López-López, A.: Squeezing hidden knowledge from scarce data: a technique tested on limited data of a language pathology. In: Yang, X.S., Sherratt, R.S., Dey, N., Joshi, A. (eds.) Proceedings of Tenth International Congress on Information and Communication Technology. ICICT 2025. Lecture Notes in Networks and Systems, vol. 1444, pp. 485–498 Springer, Singapore (2025). https://doi.org/10.1007/978-981-96-6932-5_38
25. Sahin, G.G.: To augment or not to augment? A comparative study on text augmentation techniques for low-resource NLP. Comput. Linguist. **48**(1), 5–42 (2022)
26. Shu, J., Xu, Z., Meng, D.: Small sample learning in big data era. arXiv preprint arXiv:1808.04572 (2018)
27. Steel, J., Elbourn, E., Togher, L.: Narrative discourse intervention after traumatic brain injury: a systematic review of the literature. Top. Lang. Disord. **41**(1), 47–72 (2021)
28. Steel, J., Ferguson, A., Spencer, E., Togher, L.: Language and cognitive communication disorder during post-traumatic amnesia: profiles of recovery after TBI from three cases. Brain Inj. **31**(13–14), 1889–1902 (2017)
29. Stubbs, E., et al.: Procedural discourse performance in adults with severe traumatic brain injury at 3 and 6 months post injury. Brain Inj. **32**(2), 167–181 (2018)
30. Sumner, M., Frank, E., Hall, M.: Speeding up logistic model tree induction. In: 9th European Conference on Principles and Practice of Knowledge Discovery in Databases, pp. 675–683. Springer, Berlin, Heidelberg (2005). https://doi.org/10.1007/11564126_72
31. Thompson, C.K., Shapiro, L.P., Tait, M.E., Jacobs, B.J., Schneider, S.L., Ballard, K.J.: A system for the linguistic analysis of agrammatic language production. Brain Lang. **51**, 124–129 (1995)
32. Togher, L., et al.: TBI bank is a feasible assessment protocol to evaluate the cognitive communication skills of people with severe TBI during the subacute stage of recovery. Brain Inj. **28**(5–6), 723–723 (2014)
33. Tran, S., et al.: Cognitive-communication and psychosocial functioning 12 months after severe traumatic brain injury. Brain Inj. **32**(13–14), 1700–1711 (2018)
34. Wiratma, L., van Kreveld, M., Löffler, M.: On measures for groups of trajectories. In: Societal Geo-innovation. AGILE 2017. Lecture Notes in Geoinformation and Cartography, pp. 311–330. Springer, Cham (2017). https://doi.org/10.1007/978-3-319-56759-4_18
35. Wu, X., Lv, S., Zang, L., Han, J., Hu, S.: Conditional BERT contextual augmentation. In: Computational Science – ICCS 2019. ICCS 2019. Lecture Notes in Computer Science, pp. 84–95. Springer, Cham (2019). https://doi.org/10.1007/978-3-030-22747-0_7
36. Zhu, S., et al.: Intelligent computing: the latest advances, challenges, and future. Intell Comput. **2**(0006) (2023)

Calma: A Heart Rate Variability-Based Mobile Biofeedback Game for Anxiety Self-Regulation

Rabia Jafri(✉), Thekra Salman Bin Ageef, Rahaf Abdullah Al-Shahrani, Ghaida Fahad Al-Othman, and Latifa Othman Al-Ageel

Department of Information Technology, King Saud University, Riyadh, Saudi Arabia
rabia.ksu@gmail.com

Abstract. Anxiety disorders are the most common mental disorders worldwide and, amid the global mental health crisis impelled by the ongoing COVID-19 pandemic, the need to develop cost-effective and accessible treatments for these has become even more pertinent. Traditional therapy routines are repetitive and monotonous and, thus, difficult to adhere to. Biofeedback games offer a more engaging alternative but may require specialized equipment rendering them inaccessible to several people. A novel biofeedback game for building anxiety self-regulation skills is, therefore, presented that utilizes mainstream mobile devices to avoid the cost and inconvenience of purchasing specialized equipment. The system experientially trains users to self-regulate their anxiety by having them play a story-driven game with progressively stressful tasks; the user's anxiety level is determined using heart rate variability (HRV) data sent to the user's smartphone from the user's smartwatch and the game environment is adapted to reward and challenge the user accordingly. A compelling storyline and operant conditioning techniques are employed to retain users' interest. An option to track users' HRV over time is also provided. The aim is to harness the power of mobile devices, wearable monitors and story-driven games to provide an affordable, accessible and engaging solution for anxiety self-regulation training.

Keywords: Biofeedback · Mobile Games · Stress · Wearable Sensors · Self-Regulation · Mental Health · Consumer Health Informatics

1 Introduction

According to a recent World Mental Health Survey, anxiety disorders are the most common mental disorders worldwide affecting millions of people [1]. Anxiety and chronic stress negatively impact the quality of life and can lead to serious health consequences such as hypertension, lowered immune function, and increased risk of coronary heart disease [2] as well as other major mental health problems including depression and anorexia [3]. The ongoing COVID-19 pandemic and the tremendous negative economic and social impacts impelled by it have further led to an increase in anxiety disorders as well as other mental health problems globally [4] and the resulting universal strain on public mental health services and medical resources has accentuated a critical need for

A. Alsadoon et al. (Eds.): CSCE 2025, CCIS 2935, pp. 277–286, 2026.
https://doi.org/10.1007/978-3-032-22199-5_20

low-cost and easily accessible self-administered therapy solutions for these disorders. Though a number of therapeutic interventions for anxiety, such as cognitive behavioral therapy and relaxation breathing, exist, since these involve routines that are monotonous and repetitive, they fail to engage patients resulting in low adherence rates over time, thus, reducing their effectiveness [5].

Biofeedback (BF)-based interventions provide patients with real-time feedback about different physiological factors associated with anxiety, such as heart rate, galvanic skin response, and respiration, in the form of visual and auditory cues with the aim of offering them awareness and insight into their physiological changes, helping them to develop the ability to voluntarily control those changes, and consequently, better control their mental state [6]. BF therapy enables patients to play an active role in developing their self-regulation (SR) skills rather than passively receiving treatment, is non-invasive, does not rely on medication, and is generally considered safe [7]. Though BF therapy has been shown to be effective in reducing the symptoms of anxiety disorders [8], it is traditionally conducted in clinical settings requiring specialized high-cost equipment with trained personnel to set it up placing it beyond the financial reach of the majority of the patients and rendering it impractical to access on a daily or frequent basis even for those who can bear the clinical costs [7].

The recent proliferation of increasingly powerful consumer-level mobile devices equipped with physiological sensors has made it feasible to implement BF mechanisms on these platforms thus rendering BF therapy affordable and accessible to a wider range of patients; furthermore, this has removed the limitation of patients' being restricted to a fixed location to avail of this intervention. Several BF mobile apps for anxiety have, thus, been developed [9, 10]; though relatively more engaging than other interventions due to the feedback component, most of these apps simply display real-time physiological data without any motivating immediate goal or theme causing long-term engagement and adherence to still remain a challenge [5].

Adding gamification elements or embedding the therapy within a game has been explored as a means of increasing the patients' interest and motivation to continue with BF therapy with initial studies yielding promising results [11–13]; some mobile BF games for anxiety SR [2, 14–16] have, thus, recently been introduced. However, many of these require the purchase of customized or dedicated sensors for measuring the physiological signals reducing their accessibility and cost-effectiveness; moreover, even though story-driven gaming environments have been shown to enhance motivation, engagement and meaning making processes [17], the majority of these games do not utilize a narrative-based approach to retain the patients' interest.

We are, therefore, developing "Calma", a BF mobile game system that aims to train individuals with anxiety disorders to self-regulate their anxiety by providing them with feedback on their anxiety level as they play a story-driven game with progressively stressful tasks; the system determines the user's anxiety level using heart rate variability (HRV) data sent to a smartphone from a smartwatch worn by the user and rewards and challenges them based on their ability to control their anxiety. Gamification elements, a compelling storyline, progressively difficult tasks and operant conditioning methods have been employed to engage the user's attention in order to promote long-term and regular use of the system essential for effectively building and strengthening their anxiety

SR skills. The use of mainstream mobile devices – i.e., an iPhone [18] for the game application and an Apple watch [19] for the BF sensor – avoids the cost and inconvenience of purchasing specialized sensors and equipment making the system affordable and accessible to a much broader population; furthermore, the mobility offered by these devices would enable users to use our system for anxiety SR training anytime anywhere including in the comfort of their own homes. An option for the users to track their HRV over time is also provided.

The rest of the paper is organized as follows: Sect. 2 provides an overview of existing BF games for anxiety SR; Sect. 3 explains the motivation for selecting HRV as the physiological measure for BF in our system; Sect. 4 reports the results of an interview conducted with a psychologist and a survey administered to potential users as part of the requirements' gathering process; Sect. 5 describes the design of the game application while Sect. 6 concludes the paper and identifies some directions for future work.

2 Related Work

Several BF games for anxiety SR have been introduced in recent years. Many of these have been developed for personal computers (PCs): these include commercial games such as Nevermind [20], Tropical Heat [21] and Flowborne VR [22] as well as research solutions such as Deep [23], Stressjam [24] and Heartbeat Jenga [25]. However, games constrained to PC platforms require the purchase of high-cost computers rendering them prohibitively expensive for the majority of the target users; moreover, several of these games require specialized equipment and sensors further reducing their accessibility to the users (e.g., Flowborne VR [22] and Deep [23] require a virtual reality (VR) headset and VR hand controller; Deep [23] further needs a handmade waist-worn belt with a stretch sensor to detect deep breathing; Heartbeat Jenga [25] requires electrocardiography (ECG) electrode sensors, LED ambient lighting, a servo motor, optical fabric and other hardware components to construct a tangible interface); last, but not least, such platforms limit the users' mobility: desktop computers restrict users to a fixed location while the relatively large form factor of laptop computers makes them inconvenient and impractical for users to carry around constantly in their daily lives.

The recent advent of powerful small form-factor mobile computing devices with high-capacity processing and data storage and integrated sensors has made it feasible to implement BF therapy solutions on mobile platforms; this has led to a surge of interest in utilizing these platforms for BF games with the aim of making such games more portable, accessible and affordable for the target users. Some commercial examples of mobile BF games for anxiety SR include Relax & Race [14], The Loom [26] and Mightier [15] while research prototypes include BF-adapted versions of open-source games such as Pac-Man Zen [16] and a modified Frozen Bubble game [2]. However, most of these mobile BF games still require the purchase of specialized sensors incurring inconvenience and additional expenses for the users (e.g., Relax & Race [14] and The Loom [26] require a special device for measuring electrodermal activity, Mightier [15] needs a specific heart rate monitor band, while Pac-Man Zen [16] and Frozen Bubble [2] require a chest strap with an attached electronics module to monitor the breathing rate). Moreover, despite the proven effectiveness of story-driven environments to engage users and enhance and facilitate learning [17], many of these games either do not employ a narrative-based approach or use simple, limited storylines which are unlikely to retain the users' attention long enough to help them build and strengthen SR habits.

3 Motivation for Using HRV-Based Biofeedback

HRV refers to the variability of the intervals between consecutive heart beats averaged over time [5]. It is an indicator of vulnerability to stress as well as one's self-regulatory capacity to adapt and recover from stress – high HRV is desirable [27]; however, experiencing anxiety or stress triggers autonomic nervous system (ANS) impulses and hormonal changes which affects the heart rate causing the HRV to decrease [24, 27, 28].

HRV BF therapy can be utilized to train individuals to consciously improve their ANS balance in stressful situations, thereby increasing their HRV and reducing their anxiety [5]. Several studies have demonstrated this as an effective treatment for anxiety and stress-related conditions [28–30]. Since deep breathing relaxation techniques have also been found to be effectual in decreasing anxiety [31, 32] and improving blood pressure and HRV [33], hence, such techniques are frequently incorporated in HRV BF treatments by encouraging the patient to breathe at a specific rate [5].

The high sensitivity of HRV to anxiety [24, 28], its reported reliability as an indicator of self-regulatory strength associated with stress [24], its demonstrated effectiveness in BF therapy for anxiety [28–30] and its ease of acquisition via affordable and accessible consumer-level wearable heart rate monitors have, thus, motivated us to select it as the physiological measure for BF for our application. Furthermore, we have integrated deep breathing into the HRV BF therapy by having the system guide and encourage the user to employ paced breathing techniques to relax whenever sustained elevated anxiety levels are detected.

4 Requirements Gathering

In order to gain some insight into the current practices being employed in the local context to teach people to self-regulate their anxiety, the use of BF and other technologies for this purpose and the main challenges encountered in using these techniques as well as to gather initial impressions about the potential benefits and adoptability of the proposed game application, we conducted a semi-structured interview with a psychologist with over twenty years of experience in this field, who is currently employed at King Faisal Specialist Hospital and Research Center and also a private mental health clinic in Riyadh, Saudi Arabia.

He explained that the most common anxiety disorders among his patients are social anxiety, generalized anxiety, and panic disorder, and that most patients fall in the 20–40 age range. When asked about commonly taught SR methods, he cited shifting one's focus to something larger than oneself, exercise, meditation, deep breathing, socializing, and engaging in activities that distract one's mind.

Although he noted that technology is often used for distraction—such as playing video games, watching movies, reading, drawing, or using social media—he stated that he had not personally used technology for explicitly monitoring or treating anxiety, nor was he aware of others using it for this purpose. Though he was familiar with BF, he asserted that it was not being used for treating anxiety in Saudi Arabia and cautioned that allowing patients to visualize the changes in their physiological signals in real-time may cause them to worry even more about the physical effects of anxiety on their bodies and thus, exacerbate their anxiety levels; however, he added that employing BF simply as a means of showing the positive effects of SR techniques would be very helpful and will encourage people to adhere to their SR routines. He identified lack of commitment as the main obstacle in building SR skills and asserted that operant conditioning in general and positive reinforcement in particular would be effective in encouraging people to persevere with SR training. Upon reviewing the game concept and initial interface designs, he highly approved of the idea, praised it as novel and innovative and deemed it as well capable of achieving its objectives if properly implemented. He strongly advised against displaying the HRV in numeric form and suggested showing phrases describing the anxiety level (normal, anxious, highly anxious, etc.) instead. He also suggested making the game fast-paced and interactive to serve as a distraction tool for the player.

A questionnaire was also distributed via social media platforms (WhatsApp [34], Twitter [35] and LinkedIn [36]) to potential target users in Saudi Arabia to get an overview of their general level of awareness about anxiety, the most prevalent treatment and management techniques used by them and their interest in using our game. A total of 501 responses were received, mostly female (93.6%) and with the majority holding a bachelor's degree (67.7%), with the largest age groups being 20–29 years (42.9%) and 40 years or older (41.5%). The survey results revealed the need for low-cost, easily accessible anxiety treatments, the prevalence of rapid heart rate as an anxiety symptom, the popularity of deep breathing for anxiety management, the limited use of technology for mental health and the interest of most individuals – particularly those below 40 years of age – in using a BF game app for anxiety SR.

5 System Design

We are developing an HRV-based BF game application that experientially teaches users to self-regulate their anxiety in an engaging and motivating manner by presenting them with a series of progressively stressful in-game challenges. The game is being developed as an iPhone application which would connect via Bluetooth to an Apple watch worn by the user to receive the user's HRV data in real-time. The iPhone is currently the bestselling smartphone globally [37] while the Apple watch was chosen as our BF sensor since it is readily available, has rapidly increasing sales [38], is simple and convenient to use and is programmable (which will allow us to manipulate the HRV readings recorded by it for our application); though HRV readings from wearable monitors are considered to be less accurate than those obtained from an ECG chest sensor [39], however, these have been reported to be adequate for estimating relaxation levels [40] and are, thus, sufficient for our purposes.

The system defines the users' normal HRV range based on their age and gender using the reference values reported in [41]. It provides BF information as a combination of visual cues (i.e., display of anxiety level based on HRV) and game adaptation. While playing the game, the users' current HRV is compared with their normal range and their anxiety level is displayed as "Normal" if their HRV is within this range and "High" if it is below the range. Furthermore, operant conditioning mechanisms are incorporated in the game to influence the users' behavior - the game environment changes in response to the users' anxiety level: successfully controlling anxiety rewards users by facilitating their progress, while a sustained high anxiety level incurs penalties and obstacles that hinder their advancement in the game; subsequently regaining control over their anxiety is rewarded by the removal of these impediments.

If the user's HRV stays below normal for an extended period of time, the game is automatically paused and breathing animations are displayed to guide the user about how to breathe in order to relax. The users can also pause the game themselves at any time. In both cases, the users can manually resume the game whenever they are ready.

To keep the users engaged and to build their SR skills gradually, the game is divided into several levels with the number of stress-evoking factors being progressively increased at each level. The game concept is as follows: Calma is a single-player role-playing game played from a third-person perspective. It is set in a dungeon environment where the player has to go through three different rooms to reach a room containing treasure. Each of the first three rooms has a monster, a different challenge, some stressing elements, and a key to the treasure room (given as a reward if the player completes the challenge within the time limit): 1) In the first room (Fig. 1), the player has to jump on platforms and cross a bridge to collect baby mushrooms and bring them back to the mushroom monster within a fixed time period – here, time is the only stress factor. Maintaining a normal HRV causes the bridge to start building itself, thus, rewarding the player; low HRV causes the bridge to start breaking down, thus, penalizing the player; re-normalizing the HRV rebuilds the bridge. 2) In the second room (Fig. 2), the player has to jump over platforms to collect and bring back some water drops to the flame monster; in addition to the time limit, fear of fire is introduced as a stress factor since if the player panics and starts running, the flame monster will grow bigger. Low HRV causes the platforms to start burning making it harder to reach the drops; re-normalizing the HRV rebuilds the platforms. 3) In the third room (Fig. 3), a slime monster steals the keys collected so far and runs away; the player has to chase the monster and jump on it several times to make it disintegrate and release the stolen keys along with an additional key. Besides the time limit, the stress factor in this room is "mystery" as the number of jumps required to defeat the monster are not known. Low HRV causes the monster to swallow the player's character and lock it inside its body for five seconds, thus, lowering his chances of retrieving the keys; re-normalizing the HRV releases the character. If the player successfully completes all challenges and manages to acquire three keys, the character will be able to unlock the treasure room and win the treasure.

The users' HRV readings during gameplay are continuously recorded and an option to view a graph of the weekly averages is provided to enable the users to keep track of their progress.

Well-established game design principles have been applied in terms of providing rapid feedback and freedom to fail, embedding a compelling storyline to maintain user engagement/motivation, and offering progression [40]. Animated video cutscenes are

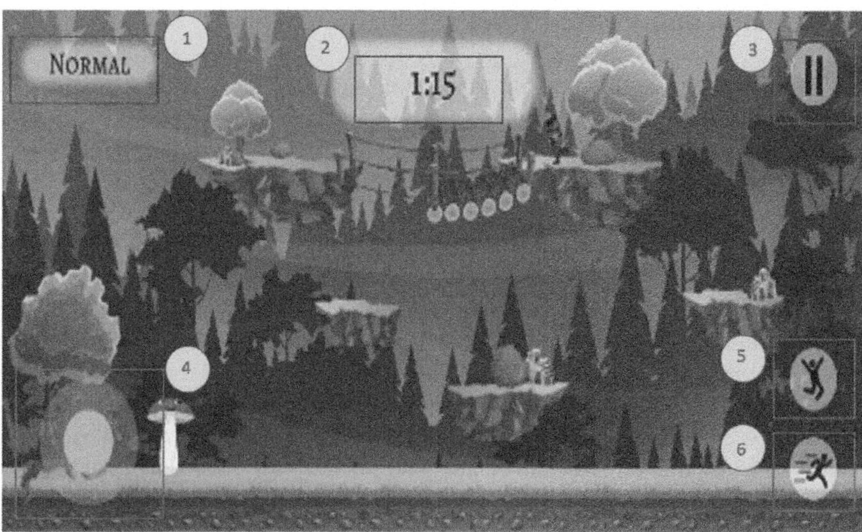

Fig. 1. Interface for room 1 (mushroom monster). Interface elements include 1) anxiety level based on HRV readings, 2) timer showing remaining time, buttons to 3) pause/resume the game, 4) move the character right or left, 5) make the character jump, 6) make the character run

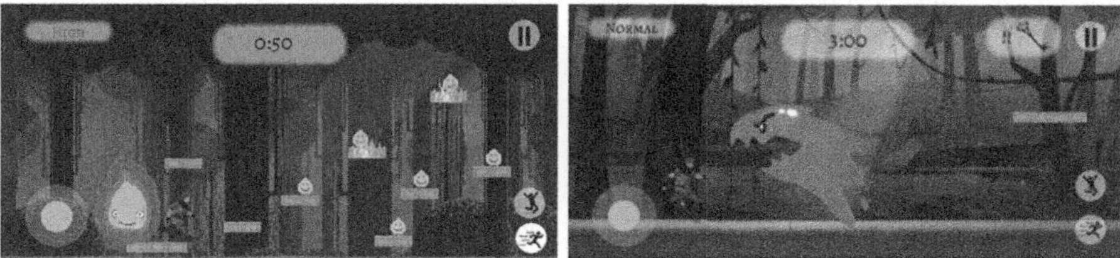

Fig. 2. Interfaces for rooms 2 (fire monster) and 3 (slime monster)

shown at the beginning of the game and at the start of each room to help convey the story to the user. The gradual advancement in stress factors allows accommodating a wider range of anxiety management needs and facilitates the progressive development of SR skills. Since previous studies have reported that users are more engaged if they are allowed to directly interact with the game via traditional controls rather than their HRV alone [5, 40], hence, interface buttons to move the character and make it run or jump have been provided enabling the user to interact with the game via touch as well as HRV (however, note that the effects of such multitasking on the HRV BF need to be studied). Also, color-coding has been employed (red for high and black for normal) to facilitate rapid discernment of the current anxiety level. Moreover, the psychologist's recommendations for displaying the anxiety level in words rather than as numerical HRV values and providing positive reinforcement have been incorporated.

6 Conclusion and Future Work

A HRV-based BF system targeted towards people suffering from anxiety disorders has been presented that harnesses the power of mobile devices, wearable monitors and story-driven games to provide an affordable, accessible and engaging solution for anxiety SR training. We will continue to develop the system in consultation with medical experts and end users to ensure that it is compatible with current therapy practices and meets the target users' needs. The system will be tested with actual users to identify any usability issues and assess the overall user experience. A long-term study will also be conducted to examine users' adherence to SR training as a result of using the system and the system's effectiveness in helping them build anxiety SR skills. In the future, we plan to expand the system to other mobile platforms such as Android and extend it to other languages to make it accessible to a wider audience. Also, more challenging levels will be added to the game to continue engaging users as their SR skills improve. Furthermore, the possibility of extracting other health-related metrics from the HRV data to enhance the system's utility as a consumer health informatics app and adding customization options to provide a more patient-centered therapeutic experience would be explored.

Acknowledgments. This paper was originally accepted for presentation at CSCE 2021 (HIMS track) and is published here as part of the CSCE 2025 volume. We would like to extend our sincere thanks to Dr. Shujaa Alqahtani (King Faisal Specialist Hospital & Research Center, Riyadh, Saudi Arabia) for his valuable advice and suggestions that have informed the design of our system.

Disclosure of Interests. The authors have no competing interests to declare that are relevant to the content of this article.

References

1. Mathews, C.: Anxiety disorder statistics, AnxietyHub (2017). https://anxietyhub.org/anxiety-disorder-statistics. Accessed 24 Jan 2021
2. Parnandi, A., Gutierrez-Osuna, R.: Partial reinforcement in game biofeedback for relaxation training. IEEE Trans. Affect. Comput. **12**(1), 141–153 (2021). https://doi.org/10.1109/TAFFC.2018.2842727
3. Dillon, A., Kelly, M., Robertson, I.H., Robertson, D.A.: Smartphone applications utilizing biofeedback can aid stress reduction. Front. Psychol. **7**, 832 (2016). https://doi.org/10.3389/fpsyg.2016.00832
4. Lakhan, R., Agrawal, A., Sharma, M.: Prevalence of depression, anxiety, and stress during COVID-19 pandemic. J. Neurosciences Rural Pract. **11**(4), 519–525 (2020). https://doi.org/10.1055/s-0040-1716442
5. Wollmann, T., et al.: User-centred design and usability evaluation of a heart rate variability biofeedback game. IEEE Access **4**, 5531–5539 (2016). https://doi.org/10.1109/ACCESS.2016.2601882
6. Alneyadi, M., Drissi, N., Almeqbaali, M., Ouhbi, S.: Biofeedback-based connected mental health interventions for anxiety: systematic literature review. JMIR Mhealth Uhealth **9**(4), e26038–e26038 (2021). https://doi.org/10.2196/26038
7. Frank, D.L., Khorshid, L., Kiffer, J.F., Moravec, C.S., McKee, M.G.: Biofeedback in medicine: who, when, why and how? Ment Health Fam Med **7**(2), 85–91 (2010)

8. Ratanasiripong, P., Kaewboonchoo, O., Ratanasiripong, N., Hanklang, S., Chumchai, P.: Biofeedback intervention for stress, anxiety, and depression among graduate students in public health nursing. Nurs. Res. Pract. **2015**, 160746 (2015). https://doi.org/10.1155/2015/160746
9. Resilio: Technology Enhanced Breathing. https://resilio.app. Accessed 25 Mar 2021
10. Elite HRV: Heart Rate Variability Monitor & App, EliteHRV. https://elitehrv.com. Accessed 12 Feb 2021
11. Jerčić, P., Sundstedt, V.: Practicing emotion-regulation through biofeedback on the decision-making performance in the context of serious games: a systematic review. Entertain Comput **29**, 75–86 (2019)
12. Fleming, T.M., et al.: Serious games and gamification for mental health: current status and promising directions. Front Psychiatry **7**, 215 (2017). https://doi.org/10.3389/fpsyt.2016.00215
13. Knox, M., Lentini, J., Cummings, T., McGrady, A., Whearty, K., Sancrant, L.: Game-based biofeedback for paediatric anxiety and depression. Ment Health Fam Med **8**(3), 195–203 (2011)
14. PIP: Relax & Race, Galvanic, Inc. https://apps.apple.com/us/app/pip-relax-race/id839560263. Accessed 13 Feb 2021
15. Mightier, Neuromotion Labs. https://www.mightier.com. Accessed 7 Feb 2021
16. Zafar, M.A., Ahmed, B., Gutierrez-Osuna, R.: Playing with and without biofeedback. In: 2017 IEEE 5th International Conference on Serious Games and Applications for Health (SeGAH), 2–4 April 2017, pp 1–7 (2017). https://doi.org/10.1109/SeGAH.2017.7939272
17. Irini, M., Thanasis, D., Symeon, R.: Using a story-driven board game to engage students and adults with cultural heritage. Int. J. Game-Based Learn **11**(2), 1–19 (2021). https://doi.org/10.4018/IJGBL.2021040101
18. iPhone, Apple Inc. http://www.apple.com/iphone. Accessed 1 Jun 2021
19. Apple watch, Apple Inc. https://www.apple.com/watch/. Accessed 1 Jun 2021
20. Lobel, A., Gotsis, M., Reynolds, E., Annetta, M., Engels, R.C.M.E., Granic, I.: Designing and utilizing biofeedback games for emotion regulation: the case of nevermind. In: Paper presented at the Proceedings of the 2016 CHI Conference Extended Abstracts on Human Factors in Computing Systems, San Jose, California, USA, (2016)
21. Tropical Heat, Somatic Vision, Inc. https://www.somaticvision.com/TropicalHeatAlive. Accessed 10 Feb 2021
22. Flowborne VR, Vunderwelten - Blum & Rockstroh GbR. https://flowborne.com/virtual-reality/. Accessed 12 Feb 2021
23. Bossenbroek, R., Wols, A., Weerdmeester, J., Lichtwarck-Aschoff, A., Granic, I., van Rooij, M.: Efficacy of a virtual reality biofeedback game (DEEP) to reduce anxiety and disruptive classroom behavior: single-case study. JMIR Mental Health **7**(3), e16066 (2020). https://doi.org/10.2196/16066
24. Maarsingh, B.M., Bos, J., Van Tuijn, C.F., Renard, S.B.: Changing stress mindset through Stressjam: a virtual reality game using biofeedback. Games Health J. **8**(5), 326–331 (2019)
25. Huang, Y.-C., Luk, C.-H.: Heartbeat Jenga: a biofeedback board game to improve coordination and emotional control. In: Design, User Experience, and Usability: Interactive Experience Design, pp. 263–270. Lecture Notes in Computer Science. Springer, Cham (2015)
26. The Loom, Galvanic, Ltd. https://play.google.com/store/apps/details?id=com.galvanic.theloom&hl=de. Accessed 1 Jun 2021
27. What is Heart Rate Variability and Why is it Important?, Drake Institute of Neurophysical Medicine. https://www.drakeinstitute.com/heart-rate-variability. Accessed 2 Jun 2021
28. Lee, J., Kim, J.K., Wachholtz, A.: The benefit of heart rate variability biofeedback and relaxation training in reducing trait anxiety. Korean J. Health Psychol. **20**(2), 391–408 (2015). https://doi.org/10.17315/kjhp.2015.20.2.002

29. Rockstroh, C., Blum, J., Göritz, A.S.: Virtual reality in the application of heart rate variability biofeedback. Int. J. Hum. Comput. **130**, 209–220 (2019). https://doi.org/10.1016/j.ijhcs.2019.06.011
30. Goessl, V.C., Curtiss, J.E., Hofmann, S.G.: The effect of heart rate variability biofeedback training on stress and anxiety: a meta-analysis. J. Psychol. Med. **47**(15), 2578–2586 (2017)
31. Chen, Y.F., Huang, X.Y., Chien, C.H., Cheng, J.F.: The effectiveness of diaphragmatic breathing relaxation training for reducing anxiety. Perspect. Psychiatr. Care **53**(4), 329–336 (2017). https://doi.org/10.1111/ppc.12184
32. Han, J.N., Stegen, K., De Valck, C., Clément, J., Van de Woestijne, K.P.: Influence of breathing therapy on complaints, anxiety and breathing pattern in patients with hyperventilation syndrome and anxiety disorders. J. Psychosom. Res. **41**(5), 481–493 (1996). https://doi.org/10.1016/S0022-3999(96)00220-6
33. Chang, Q., Liu, R., Shen, Z.: Effects of slow breathing rate on blood pressure and heart rate variabilities. Int. J. Cardiol. **169**(1), e6–e8 (2013)
34. WhatsApp, WhatsApp LLC. https://www.whatsapp.com. Accessed 1 Jun 2021
35. Twitter, Twitter, Inc. https://twitter.com. Accessed 1 Jun 2021
36. LinkedIn, LinkedIn Corporation. https://www.linkedin.com. Accessed 1 Jun 2021
37. Silverman, D.: Apple Back On Top: iPhone Is The Bestselling Smartphone Globally In Q4 2020, Forbes Media LLC (2021). https://www.forbes.com/sites/dwightsilverman/2021/02/22/apple-back-on-top-iphone-is-the-bestselling-smartphone-globally-in-q4-2020. Accessed 2 Jun. 2021. 2021 (June 2)
38. Eadicicco, L.: The Apple Watch is still growing in popularity and dominating the competition, even while people are stuck at home, Business Insider (2020). https://www.businessinsider.com/apple-watch-sales-numbers-strong-despite-coronavirus-2020-5?international=true&r=US&IR=T. Accessed 28 Jan 2021
39. Parak, J., Korhonen, I.: Evaluation of wearable consumer heart rate monitors based on photopletysmography. In: Annual International Conference of the IEEE Engineering in Medicine and Biology Society IEEE Engineering in Medicine and Biology Society Annual International Conference 2014, pp. 3670-3673 (2014).https://doi.org/10.1109/embc.2014.6944419
40. Loudon, G., Zampelis, D., Deininger, G.: Using real-time biofeedback of heart rate variability measures to track and help improve levels of attention and relaxation. In: Paper presented at the Proceedings of the 2017 ACM SIGCHI Conference on Creativity and Cognition, Singapore, Singapore (2017)
41. Normative HRV Scores by Age and Gender [Heart Rate Variability Chart], EliteHRV. https://elitehrv.com/normal-heart-rate-variability-age-gender. Accessed 10 Apr 2021

Using Mobile Technology to Assist in Classification of Potential Carpal Tunnel Syndrome Patients

Wei Zhang[1], Feng Gu[2], and Ali Mohamed[3](✉)

[1] Department of Physical Therapy, College of Staten Island, CUNY, Staten Island, NY, USA
wei.zhang@csi.cuny.edu
[2] Department of Computer Science, College of Staten Island, CUNY, Staten Island, NY, USA
feng.gu@csi.cuny.edu
[3] Department of Computer Science, The Graduate Center, CUNY, Manhattan, NY, USA
amohamed@gradcenter.cuny.edu

Abstract. Carpal Tunnel Syndrome (CTS) is a prevalent condition that requires precise assessment of hand and wrist functionality for early diagnosis and effective treatment. Traditional diagnostic methods often necessitate in-clinic visits, which can be time-consuming and costly for both patients and healthcare providers. This study proposes a novel approach by utilizing a mobile phone app to evaluate potential CTS patients' hand and wrist movements through a task as simple as lifting a virtual martini glass. The app leverages the phone's accelerometer and gyroscope sensors to collect precise motion data, offering a portable and modern alternative to conventional methods. This approach is motivated by the accessibility and ubiquity of smartphones, making it an innovative way to democratize healthcare tools. It holds the potential to reduce the strain on clinical resources and eliminate barriers for patients who may face difficulties traveling to healthcare facilities. Moreover, this method underscores the importance of integrating digital technologies into healthcare, paving the way for more efficient, cost-effective, and patient-centered diagnostic processes.

Keywords: CTS · diagnostic · app · smartphones · healthcare

1 Introduction

Carpal Tunnel Syndrome (CTS) is a common condition that impacts millions of individuals worldwide, causing discomfort, numbness, and limited hand functionality. Timely and accurate assessment of CTS is essential for early intervention, yet conventional diagnostic methods often require in-person visits to specialized clinics. These visits can be inconvenient for patients, especially those with mobility challenges or limited access to healthcare facilities, and they place a strain on clinical resources.

This paper introduces a novel solution: a mobile phone application that evaluates hand and wrist movements by simulating the task of carrying a martini glass. Instead of using an actual glass, the patient uses their smartphone, transforming an everyday

A. Alsadoon et al. (Eds.): CSCE 2025, CCIS 2935, pp. 287–298, 2026.
https://doi.org/10.1007/978-3-032-22199-5_21

device into a powerful diagnostic tool. The app, developed using the Unity game engine, capitalizes on the phone's built-in accelerometer and gyroscope sensors to record and analyze movement patterns with precision. This data is automatically formatted into Excel sheets, enabling seamless and standardized data collection for further analysis by healthcare providers.

The ability to perform these assessments remotely introduces significant benefits. Patients can complete tests from the comfort of their homes, eliminating the need for clinic visits and reducing associated travel costs and time. For clinics, this approach offers an efficient way to triage and monitor patients without overburdening physical facilities. Furthermore, the app's design, which gamifies the assessment by mimicking the act of balancing a martini glass, promotes patient engagement and ensures natural movement patterns, crucial for accurate diagnosis.

The novelty of our approach lies in the integration of a smartphone application that visually simulates a virtual martini glass, allowing participants to interact with it as if it were a real, physical object. Unlike previous studies that focus solely on thumb-based controls or isolated gesture tracking, our system uniquely combines real-time data from both external motion sensors attached to the fingers and the phone's internal sensors. This dual-layered tracking enables a detailed, dynamic analysis of hand and object interactions across varied conditions, including transporting a real martini glass, manipulating a visually simulated one, and navigating tasks with either full or restricted visual feedback. By merging virtual object manipulation with real-world motion capture, our platform provides a more ecologically valid and flexible assessment of fine motor control. Furthermore, this framework opens new possibilities for future applications in rehabilitation, remote diagnostics, and motor disorder screening, where virtual object interaction paired with precise motion analysis could become a powerful and scalable clinical tool.

2 Related Work

Carpal tunnel syndrome (CTS) is the most common neuropathy caused by compression of the median nerve in the carpal tunnel, leading to numbness, pain, and in advanced stages, thenar muscle atrophy [3, 6]. The high prevalence and associated costs to healthcare systems underscore the importance of early diagnosis and effective treatment [6]. Traditional diagnostic methods, such as physical examinations and electrodiagnostic testing, have limitations in accessibility, diagnostic accuracy, and patient adoption [1, 2, 6].

Recent studies have explored innovative, technology-based screening solutions to address these limitations. For instance, a smartphone-based app utilizing anomaly detection was developed to classify CTS patients based on thumb movement data, achieving 94% sensitivity and 67% specificity. This system emphasizes accessibility and ease of data collection, critical factors for widespread adoption [1, 2]. Similarly, another study employed a tablet-based app that recorded thumb motion during gameplay, leveraging a support vector machine (SVM) algorithm to classify CTS patients with 93% sensitivity and 73% specificity. This system highlighted the potential to detect middle-to-severe CTS cases and prompt timely medical consultations [3].

In addition to game-based approaches, there is growing interest in integrating screening into daily activities. For example, mobile devices have been explored for detecting hand disorders through behaviors such as writing and gameplay, aiming to enable unconscious, effortless screening for users [4]. Despite these advancements, the lack of standardized approaches for combining clinical, functional, and anatomical data remains a barrier to optimizing CTS diagnosis and treatment decisions [6]. These studies collectively highlight the potential of leveraging mobile technology and machine learning to enhance CTS detection and screening, making it more accessible and effective for early intervention.

3 Measurement Process and Data Collection

The assessment process in this study revolves around simulating a martini glass carriage using a smartphone to collect precise hand and wrist movement data. The procedure is designed to replicate natural movement patterns while leveraging the phone's sensors to capture quantitative metrics essential for diagnosing potential Carpal Tunnel Syndrome (CTS) (Fig. 1).

Fig. 1. Martini Glass App Showcase

3.1 Test Setup and Initiation

The test begins with the phone placed flat on a stable surface, such as a table. The device must be aligned to ensure it is perpendicular to the surface, a position verified through on-screen calibration. This alignment establishes a consistent starting point for all participants, ensuring uniformity in data collection.

Once alignment is confirmed, the patient grips the phone with both hands, mimicking the act of carrying a martini glass. The martini glass asset was developed using the Blender 3D graphics software tool. The phone's screen displays a virtual martini glass filled with water, providing real-time feedback as the patient begins the task. The objective is to transport the phone from point A to point B, taking care not to "spill" the simulated water by avoiding abrupt or unstable movements (Fig. 2).

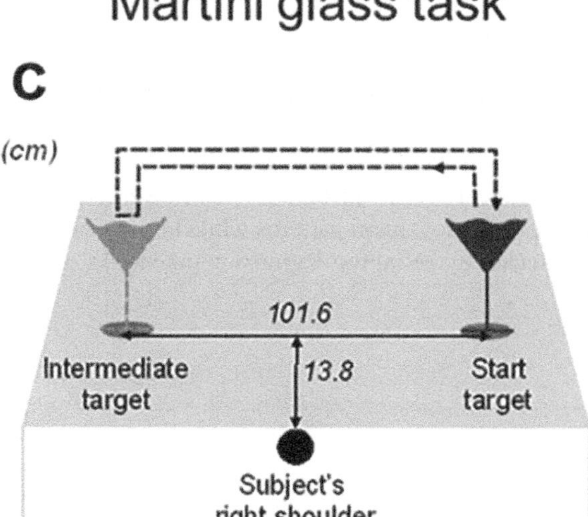

Fig. 2. Martini Glass Experiment

3.2 Variations in Testing Methods

To capture a comprehensive range of motion data, the test is conducted under two conditions:

1. **Phone Only**: The patient holds the smartphone directly, simulating the martini glass with only the virtual representation displayed on the screen.
2. **Phone with Glass Handle Attachment**: An actual martini glass handle is attached to the phone, requiring the patient to hold the assembly. This setup introduces an additional level of complexity and closely mimics real-world usage scenarios, providing nuanced insights into hand and wrist function.

3.3 Test Completion and Data Collection

The patient carries the phone along a predefined path, eventually returning it to the starting point where the phone was initially lifted. Upon completion, the app finalizes the measurements, capturing data such as:

- **Tilt Angles**: Deviation from the perpendicular alignment throughout the task.
- **Stability Metrics**: Frequency and magnitude of abrupt movements.

- **Path Consistency**: Smoothness and accuracy of the path taken between the start and end points.
- **Grip Adjustments**: Changes in handling pressure and position during the task (if applicable).

This data is automatically processed and saved into an Excel sheet stored in a designated directory on the phone. The structured format allows for seamless transfer and further analysis by healthcare providers.

We have enrolled a group of healthy subjects (n = 28; 14 males and 14 females; 25.8 ± 2.9 yrs old, all right dominant hand) in the early phase data acquisition. This will help to produce a baseline of the developed phone app on hand function evaluation. As shown in Fig. 3, all participants were asked to conduct experimental trials with both Virtual Task using a phone and Real Task using daily objects. In the Virtual task, participants performed tasks involving carrying a smartphone with virtual martini glass filled with water shown on the screen. Virtual visual feedback was presented in two different resources: 1) on the phone screen where view of the hand is also visible; and 2) on the TV screen where view of the hand and hand-held phone was hidden behind a tabletop, only mirrored image from the phone was presented on the TV. In Real task, participants were instructed to hold and lift a regular martini glass. In both Virtual and Real tasks, two types of hand prehension are adopted: 1) Grasp, when grip width is wide enough, e.g., phone sides or mug sides; 2) Grip, when grip width is narrow, e.g., holder neck of martini glass.

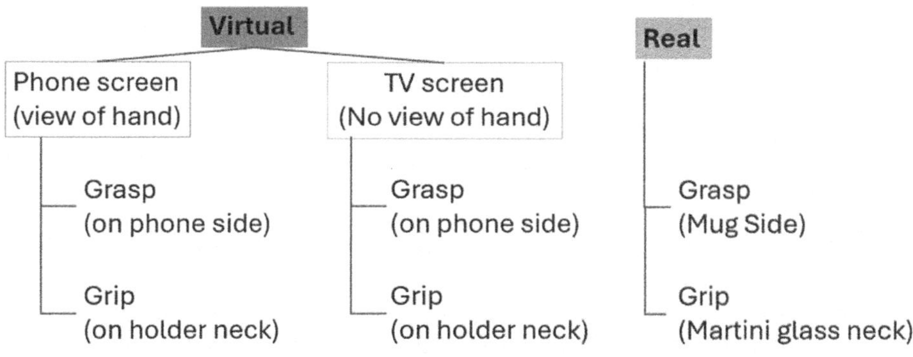

Fig. 3. Experiment Conditions

3.4 Significance of Measurements

These measurements provide a detailed view of the patient's motor control, coordination, and stability. The variations in performance between the two testing conditions—using the phone alone versus the glass handle—offer additional insights into the patient's adaptability and functional capacity. The real-time feedback from the virtual martini glass adds an element of gamification, encouraging patients to engage fully while ensuring consistent test execution.

By integrating sophisticated motion-tracking technology with a user-friendly interface, this measurement process delivers reliable data in a cost-effective and accessible manner, advancing the diagnostic landscape for CTS (Table 1).

4 Detailed Measurements and Data Analysis

Table 1. Accelerometer Measurements for Mobile Phone

Purpose	Unit	Phone Model Use	Sensor Location	Force / Torque	Theoretical Potential	Research Available
- Device movement detector - Used with iPhone horizontally - Tracks the different motion such as: shaking, tilting, swinging, and rotating and accordingly change the orientation of your app.	m/s^2	Android iPhone	Presumably the middle of the iPhone [4]	N/A	Measure the speed of hand movement.	Yes

The diagnostic test collects a rich set of data to analyze the patient's hand and wrist movements comprehensively. Each measurement is recorded at a high frequency, capturing data once per frame to ensure detailed tracking of the patient's performance. This granular approach allows for precise assessment and better understanding of motor function.

4.1 Key Measurements Captured

- **Time Taken**:
  - The total duration of the test, measured from the moment the phone is lifted until it is returned to the starting position.
  - This provides insights into the patient's speed and efficiency during the task, potentially indicating hesitation or difficulty in completing the motion.

- **Acceleration Values (x, y, z)**:
  - The phone's accelerometer captures acceleration along the three axes.
  - These values reflect the steadiness and control of the patient's movements, with sharp spikes indicating abrupt motions or instability.

- **Simulated Volume Remaining**:
  - The virtual martini glass on the phone's screen calculates the amount of "water" remaining based on the tilt and stability of the phone.

  - This metric is directly linked to the patient's ability to maintain steady, controlled movements while simulating a delicate real-world task.

- **Tilt Angle**:

  From phone sensors:

- The gyroscope measures the phone's angle relative to its initial perpendicular alignment.
- This data captures deviations in balance and control throughout the task, offering further insights into wrist mobility and coordination.

  From external sensors:

- A 6-axis orientation and position sensor (Ascension) was attached on the top of the hand-held object (phone or glass) to measures the resultant maximal tilt of the object thus to indicate performance of the grasp, lift and transportation of the hand task.

4.2 Data Collection and Organization

Each test subject completes 10 trials under controlled conditions. In cases where a trial is deemed faulty—due to interruptions or errors—a replacement trial is conducted, resulting in a total of 10 or 11 valid trials. For every trial, the above measurements are recorded and stored in an Excel sheet, capturing frame-by-frame details for comprehensive analysis.

Post-experiment, Python scripts process the raw data into a more structured format:

- Individual Excel files are created for each measurement type (e.g., time, acceleration, tilt).
- This organization enables focused analysis of single variables while maintaining the ability to correlate data across different metrics.
- Python's data visualization libraries (e.g., Matplotlib, Seaborn) can then be used to generate graphs, such as:

  - Acceleration versus time plots to assess movement steadiness.
  - Tilt angle distributions across trials to identify patterns of control or instability.
  - Remaining volume over time to evaluate balance and precision.

4.3 Significance of Data Processing and Visualization

The systematic organization and visualization of results are invaluable for deriving meaningful insights. By isolating individual measurements, patterns in specific motor functions can be identified, helping clinicians pinpoint areas of concern. Additionally, graphical representations provide an intuitive way to interpret complex data, facilitating both diagnostic assessments and discussions with patients.

This robust and accessible approach to data analysis underscores the utility of combining smartphone technology with computational tools, advancing the diagnostic capabilities for conditions like Carpal Tunnel Syndrome.

4.4 Results

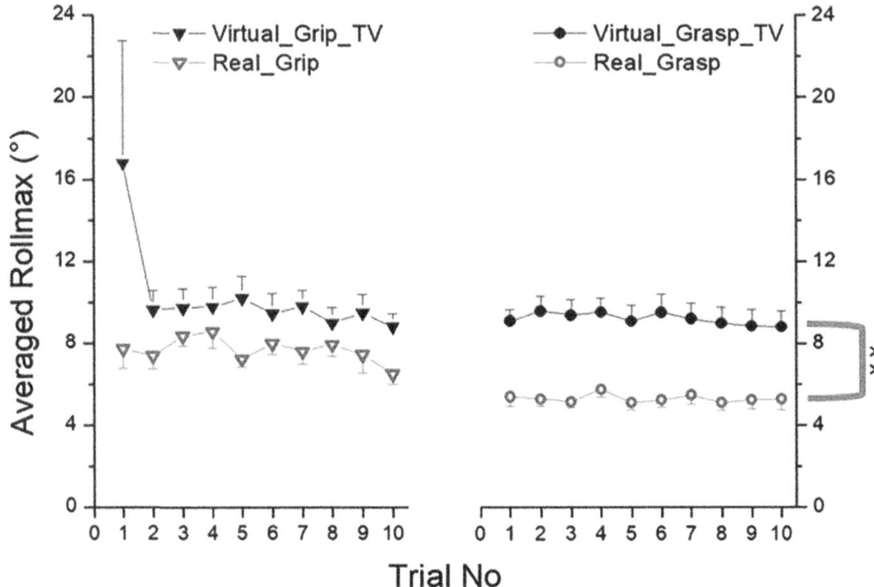

Fig. 4. Virtual TV vs Real Condition

As shown in Fig. 4, utilizing the phone application attached with the orientation/position sensors resulted in significantly higher peak roll values during the virtual training condition of the glass-transporting task compared to the real (physical) condition. This finding is supported by a significant main effect of feedback condition on the Rollmax variable ($F_{[1,\,11]} = 24.17$, $p < 0.001$). Notably, this trend was consistent across both grip styles: whether participants grasped the glass with a wider grip around the sides of the object or with a narrower grip at the neck of the martini glass, the increase in peak roll during virtual feedback was consistently observed. Threshold determination for what constitutes as CTS will require analysis of a larger clinical sample. This work was conducted as a feasibility study rather than a completed clinical trial.

5 Comparison to the Real-Life Martini Glass Experiment

The virtual martini glass experiment replicates a well-known clinical task used to assess hand and wrist function: balancing and carrying a filled martini glass without spilling. This real-world test provides valuable insights into coordination, steadiness, and motor control. However, it often requires specialized equipment, a controlled environment, and in-person supervision by medical professionals, making it resource-intensive and time-consuming for both clinics and patients.

The smartphone-based simulation offers an innovative and cost-effective alternative by integrating these principles into a digital format. Instead of using a physical glass, patients utilize their smartphone, which is equipped with a virtual martini glass displayed on the screen. This approach replicates the real-life task's core objectives—measuring balance, steadiness, and control—but does so using a device that most individuals already own.

5.1 Innovation in Design and Utility

- **Real-World Simulation through Technology**: The virtual glass on the phone's screen mimics the behavior of liquid in a physical glass, using the phone's gyroscope and accelerometer to simulate "spills" when the device tilts or moves abruptly. This ensures that the digital test remains as engaging and challenging as the real-life experiment, maintaining the integrity of the assessment while introducing the convenience of technology.
- **Accessibility and Cost Savings**: By replacing physical equipment with a smartphone app, this method eliminates the need for specialized tools like calibrated martini glasses, liquid measurements, and spill-proof test areas. For healthcare providers, this means significant cost reductions in equipment procurement and maintenance. For patients, it eliminates the expense and effort of traveling to clinics, as the test can be performed remotely in any suitable environment.
- **Time Efficiency**: Traditional assessments require scheduling appointments, preparing test setups, and completing evaluations under the supervision of trained personnel. The smartphone-based test streamlines this process, allowing patients to perform the task at their convenience. The app automates data recording and formatting, saving time for clinicians who would otherwise manually record and analyze results.

5.2 Transforming Patient Care

This innovation not only democratizes access to diagnostic tools but also redefines the way healthcare is delivered. By leveraging ubiquitous technology, the smartphone martini glass experiment brings high-quality assessments to a broader audience. It reduces the logistical and financial burdens associated with in-person testing while maintaining accuracy and clinical relevance.

Furthermore, this approach empowers patients by giving them control over when and where they complete their assessments. This flexibility fosters greater compliance and engagement, as patients can perform the test in a relaxed, familiar setting without the pressures of a clinical environment.

Ultimately, this method represents a significant step forward in making healthcare more efficient, accessible, and patient-centered. By bridging the gap between traditional assessments and modern technology, it offers a scalable solution to diagnosing and managing Carpal Tunnel Syndrome while reducing costs and improving convenience for all stakeholders involved.

6 Conclusion

The smartphone-based martini glass experiment offers a promising alternative to traditional diagnostic methods by leveraging widely available technology to replicate and enhance a well-established clinical test. Comparative analysis between real-world sensor values—obtained through specialized equipment—and the phone's accelerometer and gyroscope demonstrates that smartphones can provide data of comparable accuracy for assessing hand and wrist movements. This finding underscores the potential of smartphones as reliable tools for conducting complex motor function evaluations in a cost-effective and accessible manner.

Given the limited data and research in this field, this approach represents a critical step forward. By integrating technology and healthcare, it opens new avenues for exploring the nuances of hand and wrist functionality in conditions like Carpal Tunnel Syndrome. The ability to collect, process, and analyze data remotely not only reduces barriers to conducting large-scale studies but also enables researchers to delve deeper into understanding motor impairments and rehabilitation outcomes.

This work also highlights the interdisciplinary nature of the research. The collaboration between the fields of physical therapy and computer science is pivotal in driving innovation. Physical therapy benefits from new tools that enhance diagnostic capabilities and patient care, while computer science contributes by developing algorithms, data processing techniques, and visualization tools to interpret the collected data. Together, these fields are paving the way for groundbreaking advancements in healthcare technology.

In conclusion, this smartphone-based solution addresses critical gaps in the current diagnostic landscape, offering a scalable, efficient, and patient-friendly method for assessing motor function. By fostering collaboration between physical therapy and computer science, it not only advances the state of research but also demonstrates the transformative potential of integrating technology into clinical practice. This innovation lays the groundwork for future studies and applications, further enriching our understanding and treatment of musculoskeletal disorders.

7 Future Work

To fully realize the potential of this smartphone-based diagnostic tool, the incorporation of machine learning (ML) is a critical next step. ML algorithms can transform the app from a data collection tool into a comprehensive diagnostic and analysis system. By leveraging the large datasets generated through these experiments, ML models can be trained to automatically analyze results, identify patterns, and provide predictive insights about Carpal Tunnel Syndrome (CTS) and other motor impairments.

7.1 Proposed Machine Learning Solutions

To support these future directions, we briefly explain the key machine learning concepts referenced throughout this section. Support Vector Machines (SVMs) and neural networks are supervised learning models capable of classifying CTS severity based on input features such as tilt angles and acceleration variability. For identifying faulty trials, unsupervised methods like clustering and autoencoders detect anomalies without the need for manual labeling. Reinforcement learning offers a framework to personalize feedback by adapting task difficulty based on patient progress. To track subtle performance changes over time, sequential models like Recurrent Neural Networks (RNNs) and Long Short-Term Memory (LSTM) networks are well-suited for analyzing longitudinal trial data. Finally, visualization techniques such as t-Distributed Stochastic Neighbor Embedding (t-SNE) and Principal Component Analysis (PCA) reduce the complexity of high-dimensional data, making it easier for clinicians to identify key trends and anomalies during analysis.

1. **Automated Classification of CTS Severity**
   - Supervised learning models, such as support vector machines (SVMs) or neural networks, can be trained to classify the severity of CTS based on features such as tilt angles, acceleration variability, and simulated water spillage.
   - By analyzing historical data from patients with known diagnoses, the system can learn to predict severity levels and recommend interventions.
2. **Anomaly Detection for Faulty Trials**
   - Unsupervised learning techniques, such as clustering or autoencoders, can be used to detect trials that deviate significantly from expected behavior.
   - This ensures that faulty trials are flagged and excluded from analysis without manual intervention, improving data quality.
3. **Personalized Analysis and Feedback**
   - Reinforcement learning algorithms could tailor feedback to individual patients, adapting the difficulty of the task or suggesting specific exercises based on their performance trends.
   - This personalization ensures that the tool is not only diagnostic but also therapeutic, encouraging continuous improvement.
4. **Predictive Models for Early Detection**
   o Time-series analysis using recurrent neural networks (RNNs) or long short-term memory (LSTM) networks can be applied to track a patient's performance over multiple trials and sessions.
   o These models can identify subtle, early signs of CTS progression, enabling earlier intervention and better outcomes.
5. **Data Visualization and Pattern Recognition**
   - ML-driven visualization tools can generate interactive dashboards that highlight key performance metrics, trends, and anomalies.
   - Tools such as t-SNE or PCA (Principal Component Analysis) can reduce the dimensionality of complex datasets, making it easier for clinicians to interpret results.

7.2 Towards a Full-Fledged Diagnostic Application

The integration of ML will make this tool an all-encompassing diagnostic and analysis application, capable of handling tasks such as:

- Real-time data analysis and result interpretation.
- Automatic generation of comprehensive reports for clinicians and patients.
- Continuous learning and adaptation as more data becomes available, improving the tool's accuracy and utility over time.

By incorporating machine learning, this application could significantly streamline the diagnostic process, reduce the workload for clinicians, and enhance patient care. It would bridge the gap between data collection and actionable insights, making it a pivotal tool in both physical therapy and computational healthcare. The experiments conducted throughout this research provided initial insights into the system's ability to detect fine motor control differences, although formal validation against gold-standard clinical tests such as EMG and nerve conduction studies remains part of our future work. The focus of this paper was on system development and data acquisition for analysis using aforementioned techniques.

This future direction not only advances the diagnostic capabilities of the app but also solidifies its role as a key player in the evolving landscape of digital health solutions.

References

1. Koyama, T., et al.: A screening method using anomaly detection on a smartphone for patients with carpal tunnel syndrome: diagnostic case-control study. JMIR mHealth uHealth, **9**(3), e26320 (2021). https://doi.org/10.2196/26320J
2. Clerk Maxwell, A.: Treatise on Electricity and Magnetism, 3rd ed., vol. 2. Oxford: Clarendon, pp. 68–73 (1892)
3. Fujita, K., Watanabe, T., Kuroiwa, T., Sasaki, T., Nimura, A., Sugiura, Y.: A tablet-based app for carpal tunnel syndrome screening: diagnostic case-control study. JMIR Mhealth Uhealth **7**, e14172 (2019). https://doi.org/10.2196/14172
4. Watanabe, T., Xia, C., Fujita, K., Sugiura, Y.: Screening for carpal tunnel syndrome using daily behavior on mobile devices. Computer **56**(09), 62–70 (2023). https://doi.org/10.1109/MC.2023.3259001
5. Turan, K., Muratoğlu, O.G., Ergün, T., et al.: Evaluation of smartphoneassisted infrared thermal imaging efficiency in carpal tunnel syndrome. Egypt J. Neurol. Psychiatry Neurosurg. **60**, 26 (2024). https://doi.org/10.1186/s41983-024-00801-3
6. Padua, L., et al.: Carpal tunnel syndrome: clinical features, diagnosis, and management. The Lancet Neurol. **15**(12), 1273–1284 (2016). ISSN 1474–4422, https://doi.org/10.1016/S1474-4422(16)30231-9

11th International Conference on Health Informatics and Medical Systems (HIMS'25) Section: Health Informatics, Medical Systems, Data Science, and Tools

Early Prediction of Bladder Cancer Diagnosis Using Structured Claims Data and Machine Learning

Wanting Cui(✉) and Joseph Finkelstein

University of Arizona, Tucson, UT 85724, USA
wantingcui@arizona.edu

Abstract. Even a short delay in bladder cancer diagnosis and treatment are associated with significantly worse outcomes. Early identification of high-risk individuals may enable timely evaluation and improve prognosis. This study aimed to develop predictive models for early bladder cancer diagnoses using structured claims data. We used the MarketScan® database and extracted information from three relational tables: enrollment, outpatient diagnoses and procedures, and outpatient medications. Bladder cancer cases were identified using ICD-9 code 188 and ICD-10 code C67, restricted to first-time diagnoses between 2016 and 2019. Patients aged 50 years or older with at least two consecutive years of continuous enrollment were included. A control group of non-cancer patients was selected using propensity score matching on age, sex, Charlson Comorbidity Index, and diagnosis year. For machine learning, we developed three XGBoost models to predict bladder cancer 1, 2, and 3 months prior to diagnosis, using a one-year activity window. Diagnoses, procedures, and medications were grouped into clinically meaningful categories. A two-stage feature selection process was applied to reduce dimensionality while maintaining interpretability. The final dataset included 5,469 bladder cancer patients and 5,469 matched controls. The models achieved an AUC of 0.81 for 1-month-ahead prediction and 0.71 for both 2- and 3-months-ahead predictions. Feature importance analysis revealed consistent predictive signals across models, with hematuria as the most dominant feature. Procedures such as endoscopy and CT imaging were also strongly associated with future bladder cancer diagnosis.

Keywords: Machine Learning · Bladder Cancer · Predictive Modeling · Claims Data · Feature Selection

1 Introduction

Bladder cancer is the sixth most common cancer in the United States, accounting for 4.2% of all new cancer diagnoses [1, 2]. In 2025, it is estimated that there will be 84,870 new cases of bladder cancer and an estimated 17,420 people will die of this disease. The 5-year survival rate is 79.0%.

Delays in bladder cancer diagnosis and treatment lead to significantly worse outcomes. Nearly one in four bladder cancer patients experience a diagnostic delay of over

A. Alsadoon et al. (Eds.): CSCE 2025, CCIS 2935, pp. 301–311, 2026.
https://doi.org/10.1007/978-3-032-22199-5_22

three months after their first hematuria-related healthcare encounter [3]. Some studies found delays in initiating neoadjuvant chemotherapy (NAC) beyond eight weeks increase the risk of disease upstaging [4, 5]. Other studies suggested that each additional week between the completion of NAC and radical cystectomy is associated with poorer 2-year overall survival and a higher likelihood of lymph node positivity [6, 7]. These findings showed the need for early prediction and intervention in bladder cancer care.

Early diagnosis of bladder cancer is challenging. Although hematuria is a common early symptom, it is often under-investigated and misattributed to benign causes like urinary tract infections. Fewer than 50% of patients with hematuria receive timely urological evaluations, leading to diagnostic delays and later-stage detection [8, 9].

Recent research has increasingly applied machine learning (ML) to real-world data (RWD) for early cancer detection and care optimization [10–13]. ML has been used across diagnosis, prognosis, and treatment selection, with models ranging from lasso regression and decision trees to deep learning [11]. Several observational studies have identified distinct patterns in healthcare utilization preceding cancer diagnoses [14, 15]. A SEER-Medicare study of over 9,000 elderly patients found that cancer patients had more outpatient visits, double the emergency room admissions, and a 10% higher hospitalization rate compared to non-cancer controls in the year before diagnosis [15].

While many studies have applied ML to cancer broadly, there is limited research focused specifically on bladder cancer prediction using ML and artificial intelligence. Most existing studies have relied on imaging modalities to detect tumors or focused on predicting cancer stage and prognosis after diagnosis [16–18]. One study has explored the use of clinical laboratory test results for bladder cancer prediction [19], but few have leveraged longitudinal claims data or combined structured and unstructured clinical data for early detection efforts.

Insurance claims data provides a population-level view of healthcare utilization across multiple providers and settings. They capture diagnoses, procedures, and medications over time, allowing comprehensive tracking of patient care before cancer diagnosis. Their standardized, routinely collected nature makes them well-suited for large-scale predictive modeling.

The goal of our study was to develop predictive models for early bladder cancer prediction using structured claims data. By examining patterns in diagnoses, procedures, and medication use over time, we aimed to identify high-risk individuals prior to their formal cancer diagnosis.

2 Method

2.1 Dataset Construction

The dataset we used for this study was Merative™ MarketScan® research databases (formerly IBM Marketscan®). It is a large, nationally representative U.S. administrative claims database that includes de-identified records of more than 250 million patients with employer-sponsored insurance, Medicare supplemental plans, and Medicaid. We used the subsets of the Commercial Claims and Encounters (CCAE) and Medicare Supplemental (MDCR) databases.

Three relational data tables were used in the analysis: enrollment, outpatient claims, and outpatient prescription drug claims. The enrollment table included patients' annual insurance coverage information as well as demographic variables such as age and sex. The outpatient claims table contained detailed visit-level information, including service dates, up to four diagnosis codes per visit, and any procedures performed. Diagnoses were coded using both ICD-9-CM and ICD-10-CM, while procedures were recorded using CPT-4 codes. The outpatient prescription drug claims table included information on dispensed medications, including medication names coded using National Drug Codes (NDCNUM), service dates, and quantities dispensed.

To identify bladder cancer cases, we first extracted all patients with any cancer history, defined as having diagnosis codes in the ICD-9 range 140–209 or the ICD-10 range C00–C97. Among these, we then identified patients whose first diagnosis of bladder cancer was recorded using ICD-9 code 188.xx or ICD-10 code C67.xx. Patients were excluded if they had any other cancer diagnosis prior to their first recorded bladder cancer diagnosis. After identifying eligible bladder cancer patients, we merged their enrollment data and calculated their age at first diagnosis. Only patients aged 50 years or older at the time of diagnosis and the first diagnosis made between 2016 and 2019 were included in the study. Additionally, to ensure sufficient baseline observation, we required each patient to have at least two consecutive years of continuous enrollment prior to the date of their first bladder cancer diagnosis. The Charlson Comorbidity Index was calculated based on diagnosis codes using all previous diagnoses [20].

To construct a matched control group of non-cancer patients, we first identified individuals with no recorded cancer diagnoses (ICD-9 140–209 or ICD-10 C00–C97) during the entire study period. For each eligible control, we determined their enrollment period between 2016 and 2019 and randomly selected one year from their enrollment history. The last day of the selected year (December 31st) was then assigned as their pseudo-index date. We calculated each control's age at the pseudo-index date and restricted the sample to individuals aged 50 years or older, with at least two years of continuous enrollment prior to the pseudo-index date. Charlson comorbidity scores were also calculated for controls using diagnoses.

Cases and controls were then matched 1:1 using propensity scores estimated via logistic regression, where the dependent variable was bladder cancer case status. Covariates included in the propensity score model were age, sex, Charlson Comorbidity Index, and year of diagnosis or pseudo-index year. Matching was performed using nearest-neighbor matching without replacement, with a caliper of 0.2 standard deviations of the logit of the propensity score to ensure balance between matched pairs.

2.2 Machine Learning

For predictive modeling, our objective was to identify patients at risk of bladder cancer 1 to 3 months in advance of diagnosis. We constructed 3 models for each predictive window and defined a one-year activity window prior to the index date for each patient. For one month ahead prediction, we used patients' activity 1 month to 13 months prior to the cancer diagnosis date. For two months ahead prediction, we used patients' activity 2 months to 14 months prior to the cancer diagnosis date. For three months ahead prediction, we used patients' activity 3 months to 15 months prior to the cancer diagnosis date. All diagnoses, procedures, and medications recorded during these windows were used as input features for the predictive model.

To construct clinically meaningful features from raw claims data, we grouped procedure, diagnosis, and medication codes using standardized classification systems. Procedures were identified using Current Procedural Terminology (CPT) codes. Each CPT code was mapped to a broader procedure category using the Clinical Classifications Software (CCS) for CPT, developed by the Agency for Healthcare Research and Quality (AHRQ) [21]. This mapping aggregated granular procedure codes into clinically coherent groups. Additionally, visit-related codes were grouped based on classifications from the American Academy of Professional Coders (AAPC) to capture visit type and intensity [22]. We also applied two binary indicators to flag whether each CPT code represented a surgical procedure using narrow and broad surgery definitions. The narrow flag captured major surgical interventions, while the broad flag included a wider range of procedural services, including minor surgeries and biopsies.

Diagnosis codes were recorded in both ICD-9-CM and ICD-10-CM formats. To ensure consistency across patients, we first mapped all ICD-9 codes to ICD-10. After that, all ICD-10 diagnoses were grouped using the Clinical Classifications Software Refined (CCSR) system [23]. This mapping summarized diagnosis codes into approximately 500 clinically meaningful categories based on ICD-10 semantics. Medications were provided in the form of National Drug Codes (NDCs). Each NDC was mapped to its corresponding therapeutic class using the Red Book classification system from IBM Micromedex.

We retained only groups (across procedures, diagnoses, and medications) that occurred in at least 10 patients within the study cohort. This threshold resulted in 158 distinct procedure groups, 325 diagnosis groups, and 152 therapeutic classes. For each retained group, we computed the number of times it appeared within each patient's 1-year observation window prior to their index date. In addition, we calculated the total number of procedures, diagnoses, and medications recorded per patient, and included these as three separate features. To support model validation, the full dataset was randomly split into an 80% training set and a 20% testing set.

XGBoost was selected as our primary model because it handled missing data effectively, addressed multicollinearity, captured complex non-linear interactions, and provided interpretable feature importance metrics. To reduce dimensionality while maintaining interpretability, we implemented a two-stage feature selection process. First, we trained three separate XGBoost models, one for procedures, one for diagnoses, and one for medications—using only features from their respective domains. From each model, we extracted the top 50 most important features, based on gain-based feature importance. This allowed us to retain clinically informative features across all three modalities while minimizing redundancy.

Next, we constructed a final predictive model using the selected procedure groups, diagnosis groups, and therapeutic classes, along with patient demographics (age, sex), the Charlson comorbidity index, and measures of healthcare utilization. These included the total number of visits during the observation window, and the distribution of time gaps between visits (mean, median, and 25th and 75th percentiles).

Model optimization was performed with 5-fold cross-validation with hyperparameter tuning for the final XGBoost model. The best-performing model was selected based on the highest average cross-validated area under the receiver operating characteristic curve (AUC), and its performance was subsequently evaluated on the held-out test set. We repeated the model training and testing procedure 10 times, each time using a different random split of the training and testing data. After all iterations, we calculated the average precision, specificity, accuracy, and AUC, along with their corresponding standard deviations.

3 Result

3.1 Demographics

The dataset included 5,469 bladder cancer patients (case) and 5,469 non-bladder cancer patients (control) (Table 1). The mean Charlson Comorbidity Score was 1.48 for bladder patients and 1.46 for non-bladder patients. The mean age at diagnosis was 67.07 years for bladder patients and 67.19 years for non-bladder patients. There were significantly higher proportions of male patients than female patients. Among bladder patients, 71% were male and 29% were female; among non-bladder patients, 66% were male and 34% were female (Table 2).

Table 1. Summary statistics of bladder and non-bladder cohorts.

	Bladder Cancer (n = 5469)		Non-Bladder Cancer (n = 5469)	
Variable	Mean	Std Dev	Mean	Std Dev
Charlson Comorbidity	1.48	1.88	1.46	1.86
Age at Diagnoses	67.07	10.94	67.19	11.4
Sex	**Case Count**	**Case %**	**Control Count**	**Control %**
Male	3921	71.70%	3626	66.30%
Female	1548	28.30%	1843	33.70%
Year				
2016	1452	26.55%	1513	27.67%
2017	1644	30.06%	1568	28.67%
2018	1179	21.56%	1180	21.58%
2019	1194	21.83%	1208	22.09%

Table 2. Top 10 highest correlation variables.

Top 10 correlations before feature selection		
Feature 1	Feature 2	Correlation
Number of total visits	Number of total diagnoses	0.94
Other Office or Outpatient Services	Consultation, evaluation, and preventative care	0.89
Number of total procedures	Number of total visits	0.87
Number of total procedures	Number of total diagnoses	0.87
Peritoneal dialysis	Number of Genitourinary visits	0.86
Nursing Facility Services	Nonhospital-based care (e.g., home health care, hospice)	0.83
Other non-OR therapeutic procedures on musculoskeletal system	Biomechanical lesions	0.80
Allergic reactions, subsequent encounter	Adverse effects of drugs and medicaments, subsequent encounter	0.79
Other specified injury, subsequent encounter	Other specified injury	0.76
Digestants & Comb, NEC	Incision of pleura, thoracentesis, chest drainage	0.72
Top 10 correlations after feature selection		
Feature 1	Feature 2	Correlation
Number of total diagnoses	Number of total visits	0.94
Number of total diagnoses	Number of Genitourinary visits	0.65
Number of Genitourinary visits	Number of total visits	0.63
Anesthesia	Surgery narrow	0.63
Hyperplasia of prostate	Genital disease indicator	0.61
Lens and cataract procedures	Surgery narrow	0.55
Chronic kidney disease	Number of Genitourinary visits	0.54
Lens and cataract procedures	Anesthesia	0.54
Urinary tract infections	Urinary disease indicator	0.50
Other Laboratory	Laboratory - Chemistry and Hematology	0.50

3.2 Feature Selection

The initial dataset included 158 procedure codes, 325 diagnosis codes, and 152 medication codes, resulting in over 635 variables. A pairwise correlation analysis identified 7 sets of variables with very high correlation (correlation coefficient > 0.8) and 50 sets with high correlation (correlation coefficient > 0.5). The highest observed correlation was between the number of total visits and number of total diagnoses (r = 0.94). Other high correlations included other office or outpatient services with consultation, evaluation, and preventative care (r = 0.89), and number of total procedures with both number of total visits and number of total diagnoses (r = 0.87).

For feature selection, three separate XGBoost models were trained on procedures, diagnoses, and medications. The top 50 features from each category were selected based on model importance scores. After selection, correlation analysis was repeated. One variable pair remained with very high correlation (r > 0.8), and 9 pairs showed high correlation (r > 0.5). The strongest correlation after feature selection was between number of total diagnoses and number of total visits (r = 0.94). Other post-selection correlations included anesthesia with narrowly defined surgery (r = 0.63), hyperplasia of prostate with genital disease indicator (r = 0.61), and chronic kidney disease with number of genitourinary visits (r = 0.54).

3.3 Model Performance

Table 3 showed the performance of models developed for bladder cancer prediction at 1, 2, and 3 months ahead. The 1-month-ahead model used data from 1 to 13 months prior to the diagnosis and achieved a precision of 0.84, specificity of 0.87, accuracy of 0.74, and an AUC of 0.81. The 2-month-ahead model used data from 2 to 14 months prior and yielded a precision of 0.72, specificity of 0.77, accuracy of 0.66, and an AUC of 0.72. The 3-month-ahead model used data from 3 to 15 months prior and achieved a precision of 0.70, specificity of 0.77, accuracy of 0.66, and an AUC of 0.71.

Table 3. Models' performance with mean (std).

Model	Observation Window	Precision	Specificity	Accuracy	AUC
1 month ahead	1 month - 13 month	0.84 (0.03)	0.87 (0.03)	0.74 (0.01)	0.81 (0.01)
2 months ahead	2 months - 14 months	0.72 (0.03)	0.77 (0.03)	0.66 (0.02)	0.72 (0.02)
3 months ahead	3 months - 15 months	0.70 (0.01)	0.77 (0.02)	0.65(0.001)	0.71 (0.01)

For feature importance, SHAP plots were generated, and gain-based importance values were calculated (Fig. 1). In the 1-month-ahead bladder cancer prediction model, the most influential features based on XGBoost gain importance were hematuria (gain = 88.50) and urinary symptoms (gain = 69.15). These were followed by endoscopy and endoscopic biopsy of the urinary tract (gain = 20.34), CT scan abdomen (gain = 11.67), genitourinary signs and symptoms (gain = 10.11), and tobacco-related disorders (gain = 9.70). Other contributing features included urinary tract infections (gain = 8.60), other specified and unspecified diseases of bladder and urethra (gain = 7.39), tetracycline antibiotics (gain = 6.18), and quinolones, NEC (gain = 6.18).

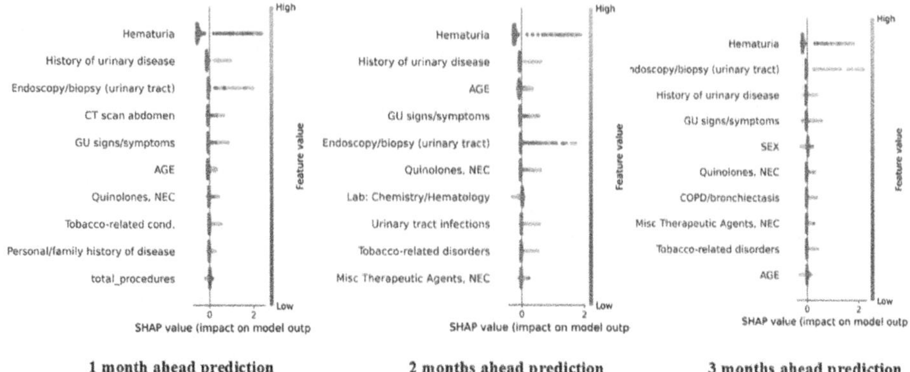

Fig. 1. SHAP plots of top 10 features for 3 models.

In the 2-month-ahead model, hematuria (gain = 67.04) and urinary symptoms (gain = 40.38) remained top predictors, followed by endoscopy (gain = 17.48) and urinary tract infections (gain = 13.04).

In the 3-month-ahead model, hematuria (gain = 67.32), endoscopy (gain = 22.96), and urinary symptoms (gain = 19.84) were again among the most important features, along with genitourinary signs and symptoms (gain = 16.56), tobacco-related disorders (gain = 13.37) and chronic obstructive pulmonary disease and bronchiectasis (gain = 12.31).

4 Discussion

The results showed that predictive performance was highest in the 1-month-ahead model, with decreasing performance at longer prediction period. The 1-month-ahead model achieved the highest precision (0.84), specificity (0.87), and AUC (0.81), indicating strong predictive power when using clinical activity up to one month before diagnosis. Performance declined with the 2- and 3-month-ahead models, where AUC values dropped to 0.71 and accuracy to 0.65.

The feature selection technique used in model development was effective in reducing multicollinearity by limiting highly correlated features across categories. This resulted in a more compact and independent feature set for training, which would make the models more generalizable and interpretable.

Feature importance analysis across models showed consistent patterns. Hematuria was the most dominant predictor in all models, with the highest gain score observed in the 1-month-ahead model (gain = 88.50). This aligns with its clinical relevance as a well-established early sign of bladder cancer. Urinary symptoms, including infections and genitourinary signs were also important features across all 3 models. In addition, procedures such as endoscopy and CT imaging were important predictive features, likely reflecting clinical investigations initiated in response to emerging symptoms.

As the prediction window moved further from the diagnosis date, additional features such as chronic obstructive pulmonary disease, tobacco-related disorders, and nonhospital-based care became more prominent. These variables may reflect broader comorbidity profiles and care utilization patterns associated with bladder cancer risk.

Our study comports with previous studies demonstrating the value of real-world data for predictive modeling [24, 25]. However, this study had several limitations. First, only structured claims data were available for model development. Unstructured clinical notes, which often contain information such as symptoms, test interpretations, and clinical reasoning, were not accessible. It limited the models' ability to capture specific clinical signals relevant to bladder cancer. Second, model performance declined when trying to predict bladder cancer diagnoses 2- or 3-months ahead. Third, although observation and prediction windows were uniformly defined across patients, real-world care trajectories may vary. In future studies, we plan to create a dataset that contained both structured administrative data and unstructured clinical notes to enhance predictive performance. We will apply large language models (LLMs) such as ClinicalBERT or Llama to process free-text notes. These models will be used to extract symptom onset, test results, and provider assessments [25, 26]. We will convert the unstructured text into numerical representations using pretrained or fine-tuned embeddings, which will be integrated with structured features in a unified modeling framework. To better capture temporal patterns in patient care, we will implement temporal models such as Transformer-based architectures or recurrent neural networks that account for the sequential nature and timing of visits, diagnoses, and interventions. These models will enable us to track evolving clinical trajectories and identify early risk patterns that may not be shown in the current models. Once sufficient accuracy is achieved [27, 28], the algorithms based on real-world data [29, 30] can be embedded into electronic health records to preemptively identify patients with higher risk of bladder cancer [31].

5 Conclusion

In conclusion, this study showed the feasibility of using structured healthcare claims data—including diagnostic codes, procedures, and medication patterns—to predict bladder cancer diagnoses months in advance with clinically meaningful accuracy. By modeling temporal patterns in healthcare utilization, the models reached AUC score of 0.81 for 1 month ahead bladder cancer prediction and AUC score of 0.71 for 2 and 3 months ahead prediction. These findings showed the potential of claims-based models as an early detection tool to support timely clinical evaluation and reduce diagnostic delays. Future work should incorporate dynamic feature trajectories, explore advanced temporal modeling techniques, and pursue external validation across diverse populations and healthcare systems to enhance generalizability and clinical applicability.

References

1. Surveillance, Epidemiology, and End Results (SEER) Program. Cancer Stat Facts: Bladder Cancer. National Cancer Institute. Updated 2024. https://seer.cancer.gov/statfacts/html/urinb.html. Accessed 7 May 2025
2. SEER*Explorer: An interactive website for SEER cancer statistics. Surveillance Research Program, National Cancer Institute (2024). https://seer.cancer.gov/statistics-network/explorer/. Accessed 22 Jan 2025

3. Hollenbeck, B.K., Dunn, R.L., Ye, Z., et al.: Delays in diagnosis and bladder cancer mortality. Cancer **116**(22), 5235–5242 (2010)
4. Audenet, F., Sfakianos, J.P., Waingankar, N., et al.: A delay ≥8 weeks to neoadjuvant chemotherapy before radical cystectomy increases the risk of upstaging. Urol. Oncol. **37**(2), 116–122 (2019)
5. Ourfali, S., Matillon, X., Ricci, E., et al.: Prognostic implications of treatment delays for patients with non-muscle-invasive bladder cancer. Eur. Urol. Focus **8**(5), 1226–1237 (2022)
6. Nuijens, S.T., van Osch, F.H.M., van Hoogstraten, L.M.C., Witjes, J.A., Aben, K.K.H., Hermans, T.J.N.: Longer time to radical cystectomy in patients treated with neoadjuvant chemotherapy is associated with worse oncological outcomes. Urol. Oncol. **42**(4), 117.e11-117.e16 (2024)
7. Russell, B., Liedberg, F., Khan, M.S., et al.: A systematic review and meta-analysis of delay in radical cystectomy and the effect on survival in bladder cancer patients. Eur. Urol. Oncol. **3**(2), 239–249 (2020)
8. Loo, R.K., Lieberman, S.F., Slezak, J.M., et al.: Stratifying risk of urinary tract malignant tumors in patients with asymptomatic microscopic hematuria. Mayo Clin. Proc. **88**(2), 129–138 (2013)
9. Tan, W.S., Feber, A., Sarpong, R., et al.: Who should be investigated for haematuria? results of a contemporary prospective observational study of 3,556 patients. Eur. Urol. **74**(1), 10–14 (2018)
10. Nagy, M., Jones, T., Kuchakulla, M., et al.: Machine learning in oncology: what should clinicians know? JCO Clin. Cancer Inform. **4**, 799–810 (2020)
11. Placido, D., Yuan, B., Hjaltelin, J.X., et al.: A deep learning algorithm to predict risk of pancreatic cancer from disease trajectories. Nat. Med. **29**(5), 1113–1122 (2023)
12. Cui, W., Halwani, A., Li, C., Finkelstein, J.: Predicting prostate cancer diagnosis using machine learning analysis of healthcare utilization patterns. Stud. Health Technol Inform. **323**, 6–10 (2025)
13. Huo, X., Finkelstein, J.: Prostate cancer prediction using classification algorithms. J. Clin. Oncol. 40(16_suppl):e13590 (2022)
14. Jones, L.E., Carney, D.C.: Primary care utilization patterns before and after lung cancer diagnosis. Eur. J. Cancer Care (Engl). **18**(2), 165–173 (2009)
15. Shen, C., Dasari, A., Xu, Y., et al.: Pre-existing symptoms and healthcare utilization prior to diagnosis of neuroendocrine tumors: a SEER-medicare database study. Sci. Rep. **8**(1), 16863 (2018)
16. Nie, W., Jiang, Y., Yao, L., et al.: Prediction of bladder cancer prognosis and immune microenvironment assessment using machine learning and deep learning models. Heliyon **10**(23), e39327 (2024)
17. Borhani, S., Borhani, R., Kajdacsy-Balla, A.: Artificial intelligence: a promising frontier in bladder cancer diagnosis and outcome prediction. Crit. Rev. Oncol. Hematol. **171**, 103601 (2022)
18. Wang, G.Y., Zhu, J.F., Wang, Q.C., et al.: Prediction of non-muscle invasive bladder cancer recurrence using deep learning of pathology image. Sci. Rep. **14**, 18931 (2024)
19. Tsai, I.J., Shen, W.C., Lee, C.L., Wang, H.D., Lin, C.Y.: Machine learning in prediction of bladder cancer on clinical laboratory data. Diagnostics (Basel). **12**(1), 203 (2022)
20. Sundararajan, V., Henderson, T., Perry, C., et al.: New ICD-10 version of the Charlson comorbidity index predicted in-hospital mortality. J. Clin. Epidemiol. **57**(12), 1288–1294 (2004)
21. HCUP CCS-Services and Procedures. Healthcare Cost and Utilization Project (HCUP). May 2021. Agency for Healthcare Research and Quality, Rockville, MD. www.hcup-us.ahrq.gov/toolssoftware/ccs_svcsproc/ccssvcproc.jsp.

22. Codify by AAPC. https://www.aapc.com/codes/cpt-codes-range/. Accessed 7 May 2025
23. Clinical Classifications Software Refined (CCSR)for ICD-10-CM Diagnoses. Healthcare Cost and Utilization Project (HCUP). November 2025. Agency for Healthcare Research and Quality, Rockville, MD. www.hcup-us.ahrq.gov/toolssoftware/ccsr/dxccsr.jsp.
24. Paranjpe, I., Russak, A.J., De Freitas, J.K., et al.: Retrospective cohort study of clinical characteristics of 2199 hospitalised patients with COVID-19 in New York City. BMJ Open **10**(11), e040736 (2020)
25. Cui, W., Kawamoto, K., Morgan, K., Finkelstein, J.: Reducing diagnostic uncertainty in emergency departments: the role of large language models in age-specific diagnostics. In: 2024 IEEE 12th International Conference on Healthcare Informatics (ICHI), pp. 525–527. Orlando, FL, USA (2024)
26. Shah-Mohammadi, F., Cui, W., Bachi, K., Hurd, Y., Finkelstein, J.: Using natural language processing of clinical notes to predict outcomes of opioid treatment program. In: 2022 44th Annual International Conference of the IEEE Engineering in Medicine & Biology Society (EMBC), pp. 4415-4420. IEEE (2022)
27. Shah-Mohammadi, F., Finkelstein, J.: Combining NLP and machine learning for differential diagnosis of COPD exacerbation using emergency room data. Stud Health Technol. Inform. **305**, 525–528 (2023)
28. Shah-Mohammadi, F., Cui, W., Finkelstein, J.: Comparison of ACM and CLAMP for entity extraction in clinical notes. In: 2021 43rd Annual International Conference of the IEEE Engineering in Medicine & Biology Society (EMBC), pp. 1989-1992. IEEE (2021)
29. Lyu, J., Cui, W., Finkelstein, J.: Assessing disparities in COVID-19 testing using national COVID cohort collaborative. Stud. Health Technol. Inform. **295**, 316–319 (2022)
30. Thyvalikakath, T.P., Duncan, W.D., Siddiqui, Z., et al.: Leveraging electronic dental record data for clinical research in the national dental PBRN practices. Appl. Clin. Inform. **11**(2), 305–314 (2020)
31. Kawamoto, K., Finkelstein, J., Del Fiol, G.: Implementing machine learning in the electronic health record: checklist of essential considerations. Mayo Clin. Proc. **98**(3), 366–369 (2023)

Applying Business Intelligence to Cancer Incidence Analysis in a Population-Based Registry

Ricardo Timarán[1(✉)], Andrea Bravo[1], Luisa Bravo[1], Fredy Vidal[2], Arsenio Hidalgo[1], and Anívar Chaves[3]

[1] Universidad de Nariño, San Juan de Pasto, Colombia
{ritimar,abravo7,lume.goyes,archi}@udenar.edu.co
[2] I.U. Colegio Mayor del Cauca, Popayán, Colombia
fvidal@unimayor.edu.co
[3] Universidad UNAD, San Juan de Pasto, Colombia
anivar.chaves@unad.edu.co

Abstract. Cancer is a global public health issue and, as such, is the subject of extensive research across various fields, primarily aimed at generating knowledge from data collected from multiple sources.

This article presents the results of a research project focused on developing a business intelligence system to analyze information from the Population-Based Cancer Registry of the municipality of Pasto (RPCMP) in Colombia. To achieve this, an ETL system based on SQL was designed, enabling the extraction, cleaning, transformation, and loading of relevant information from the operational databases of the RPCMP into a data mart built following the HEFESTO methodology.

Using the PostgreSQL database management system, a star schema model was implemented to integrate the data mart with Power BI Desktop, facilitating the visualization of results through dynamic dashboards. The insights derived from this system will serve as a valuable resource for health institutions—both public and private—to guide decision-making, optimize resource allocation, and shape public policies aimed at reducing the impact of cancer on society.

Keywords: Business Intelligence System · Cancer Incidence · Population-Based Cancer Registry · Data mart

1 Introduction

Cancer remains one of the most pressing public health challenges worldwide, imposing a significant disease burden, with higher prevalence in developing countries compared to developed ones [1]. From the perspective of the World Health Organization (WHO), cancer is one of the leading causes of morbidity and mortality globally, yet it continues to be substantially underreported.

The Global Cancer Observatory estimates that in 2022, approximately 20 million new cancer cases were recorded worldwide, along with nearly 10 million cancer-related

A. Alsadoon et al. (Eds.): CSCE 2025, CCIS 2935, pp. 312–326, 2026.
https://doi.org/10.1007/978-3-032-22199-5_23

deaths [2]. By 2030, annual cancer incidence is expected to reach 21 million cases, with an estimated 13 million deaths, driven by population growth and aging demographics [3, 4].

Faced with this outlook, Peña [5] emphasizes the need for governments to strengthen public health surveillance measures through systematic data collection, analysis, interpretation, and dissemination. It is important to highlight that cancer is the only chronic disease with mandatory reporting requirements, meaning that data related to its incidence must be reported to the government.

Currently, the Population-Based Cancer Registry of the Municipality of Pasto (RPCMP) in Colombia manages the entry, storage, verification, and analysis of cancer records using *CanReg*, an open-source tool developed by the International Association of Cancer Registries (IARC). This system includes modules for data entry, quality control, consistency checks, and basic data analysis. However, data cleansing is still performed manually using spreadsheets, posing challenges in terms of efficiency and accuracy.

Additionally, the RPCMP lacks advanced tools in artificial intelligence, business intelligence, and predictive analytics that could automate data collection from hospitals, laboratories, and official records. Likewise, it does not have predictive capabilities to identify trends and risk factors, nor integrated systems to facilitate early detection and access to treatments. The absence of data visualization tools, such as dashboards and interactive maps, further complicates the interpretation of information.

The integration of these technologies would strengthen epidemiological surveillance and enhance public health decision-making based on data-driven insights.

This article presents the findings of a research project aimed at developing a business intelligence system for analyzing cancer incidence within the RPCMP. To achieve this, an SQL-based ETL system was designed to extract, clean, transform, and load relevant information from the operational databases of the RPCMP into a data mart built following the HEFESTO methodology.

Using the PostgreSQL database management system, a star schema model was implemented to integrate the data mart with Power BI Desktop, facilitating the visualization of results through dynamic dashboards. The insights obtained from this system will serve as a foundation for decision-making in health institutions—both public and private—helping guide resource allocation and policy development aimed at mitigating the impact of cancer on society.

2 Population-Based Cancer Registries

The IACR was founded in 1966 with the aim of improving the collection and analysis of cancer data worldwide. In its efforts, it works closely with the International Agency for Research on Cancer (IARC), an entity affiliated with the WHO.

Its primary goal is to strengthen cancer monitoring in populations through the implementation of Population-Based Cancer Registries, based on standardized methodological guidelines at the international level. These registries generate high-quality scientific evidence, ensuring comparability, completeness, validity, and timeliness.

This data plays a crucial role in supporting the development of public policies, shaping cancer prevention and control strategies, and assessing the effectiveness of implemented interventions [6].

Population-Based Cancer Registries (PBCRs) are information and epidemiological surveillance systems designed to assess the magnitude of cancer within a specific population. Their primary function is to collect, process, and analyze data on all newly diagnosed cancer cases within a defined population, providing insights into incidence, mortality, patterns, trends, and population survival rates [7].

Currently, there are more than 300 population-based cancer registries worldwide; however, not all of them follow the methodology proposed by the IACR/IARC, which estimates cancer incidence based on mortality data. In Latin America and the Caribbean, only 11 registries adhere to this approach, covering approximately 4.3% of the region's population [5].

The RPCMP is the second oldest in Colombia and has been operating continuously since 1998. Its existence has been made possible through the joint efforts of the University of Nariño, the Municipal Health Directorate of Pasto, the Population-Based Cancer Registry of Cali (RPCC), and the National Cancer Institute (INC). Its mission is to periodically and reliably collect data on cancer incidence in Pasto, providing crucial information for governmental decision-making. These data support the design of public policies focused on prevention and rehabilitation, as well as serving as a foundation for scientific research in the fight against cancer.

The RPCMP processes information on cancer cases occurring in both urban and rural areas of Pasto. According to the 2005 census, the municipality's population stands at 382,422 inhabitants, with a distribution of 47.8% men and 52.2% women. Of the total population, 81.7% reside in urban areas, while 18.3% live in rural regions [6]. As of 2015, the RPCMP has continuously and systematically collected clinical, demographic, socioeconomic, and vital status data, encompassing 29,060 cancer cases. Of these, 40% are from the municipality of Pasto, while 60% correspond to cases from other municipalities.

3 Materials and Methods

The primary data source used to populate the data mart was the operational database of the RPCMP, implemented within the PostgreSQL database management system. This database stores sociodemographic and clinical information on 19,619 cancer cases from patients residing in both urban and rural areas of the municipality of Pasto.

To construct the data mart, the HEFESTO methodology [8] was employed due to its ease of understanding and structured approach, which is divided into phases to clearly define objectives and expected outcomes at each stage:

Requirements Analysis: This phase identifies the information needs of the RPCMP, business questions, and key indicators to be examined.

Data Source Analysis: Here, different data sources are mapped, and relevant facts and indicators are identified.

Logical Data Warehouse Model: This stage involves designing the logical schema of the data warehouse, considering data typology and relationships.

ETL Processes: This phase defines how data is extracted, transformed, and loaded from the sources into the data mart.

4 Results

4.1 Identifying Business Questions

To determine the requirements and needs that the data mart must fulfill, key business questions were identified. Table 1 presents some of these questions:

Table 1. Business Questions

Id	Questions
1	How many cancer cases are categorized by place of residence, gender, and source?
2	How many new cancer cases are registered according to the primary site?
3	How many new cancer cases are registered per year? Or how many were recorded in the last year?
4	What is the crude incidence rate by sex, and the standardized incidence rate by sex and location?
5	What is the age-standardized incidence rate?
6	How many cases were diagnosed as benign tumors, uncertain behavior tumors, in situ tumors, and malignant tumors? Categorized by sex and year, along with their percentages
7	What percentage of registered cancer cases were reported only through a death certificate?
8	How many cancer cases occurred in Pasto over a specific period, and what was the age-adjusted rate according to the standard world population (AAR)?

4.2 Identification of Indicators

Considering that indicators are numerical values representing what is to be analyzed concretely, and perspectives refer to the entities through which these indicators are examined, the business questions previously formulated were analyzed to determine the appropriate indicators and their corresponding perspectives. Some of these are presented in Table 2.

Table 2. Indicators

Code	Indicators
NCC	Number of cancer cases
CIR	Crude incidence rate
ASIR	Age-specific incidence rate
SAIR	Standardized or adjusted incidence rate
AIF	Absolute incidence frequencies of cancer cases
RFI	Relative frequencies of cancer incidence

(*continued*)

Table 2. (*continued*)

Code	Indicators
ND	Number of deaths and Percentage
PCMV	Percentage of cases with a morphologically verified diagnosis
PCDC	Percentage of known cases only by death certificate
YHLPD	Years of healthy life lost to premature death

The indicators defined in the system are aligned with the information requirements of the RPCMP and are directly linked to cancer incidence and mortality data in the municipality of Pasto. Their analysis helps identify patterns and trends related to patient survival and mortality, providing key insights for decision-making in the design and optimization of local cancer prevention and control programs.

4.3 Conceptual Model

The conceptual model is a high-level description of the database structure, where information is represented through Objects, Relationships, and Attributes [8]. The conceptual model of the data mart is illustrated in Fig. 1. In this figure, the left side displays the Perspectives, while the right side presents the Indicators, which are linked through the process of Calculating, Analyzing, and Reporting.

4.4 Star Model

The 'star schema' in the HEFESTO methodology is a database design model characterized by a central fact table (the 'star') surrounded by multiple dimension tables (the 'radiations'). HEFESTO utilizes this model as a fundamental component for organizing data within a data warehouse.

The star schema is a key tool in the HEFESTO methodology for building efficient and user-friendly data warehouses. Some of the main characteristics of the star schema in HEFESTO are as follows:

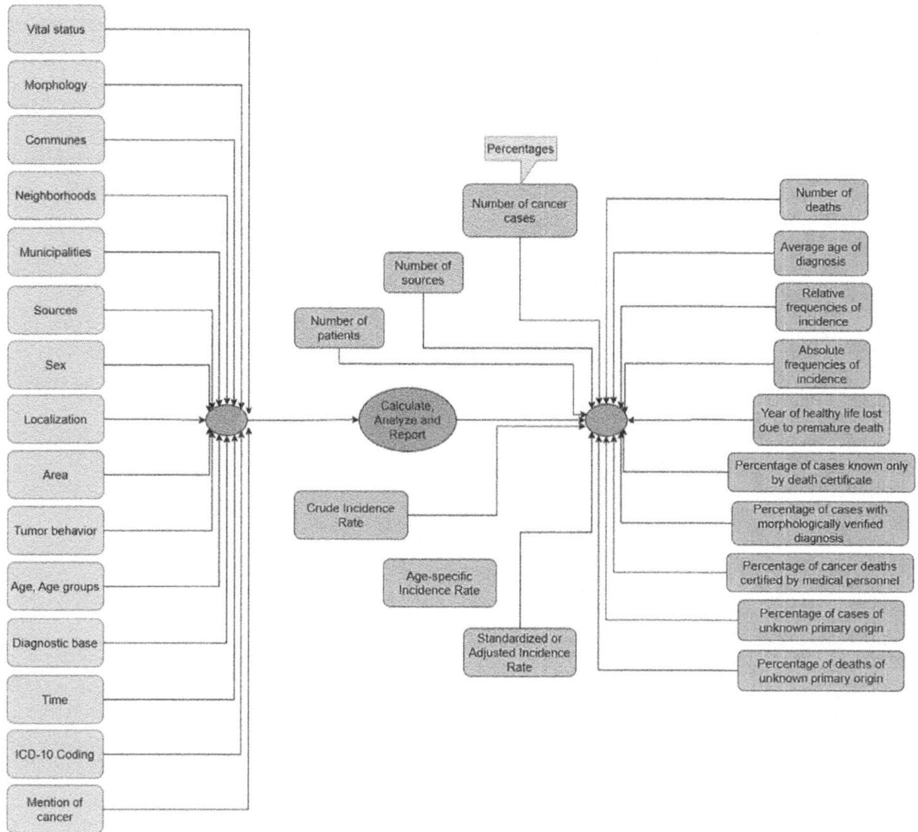

Fig. 1. Conceptual model of the data mart

Centralization: The fact table contains key transactional data, while the dimension tables provide descriptive information related to those facts.

Simplicity: The model is easy to understand and interpret, facilitating data querying and analysis.

Efficiency: It delivers fast response times for queries, which is crucial for real-time analysis.

OLAP Support: It is compatible with most OLAP viewers, allowing for interactive data visualization and analysis.

Easy Maintenance: Its simple structure makes updating and maintaining the model straightforward.

Intuitive Design: There is a natural correspondence between the model and the way users visualize and manipulate data.

Rapid Prototyping: It is a common option for quickly prototyping and developing Business Intelligence solutions.

Figure 2 illustrates the star schema model of the data mart designed to record cancer incidence in the municipality of Pasto, Colombia.

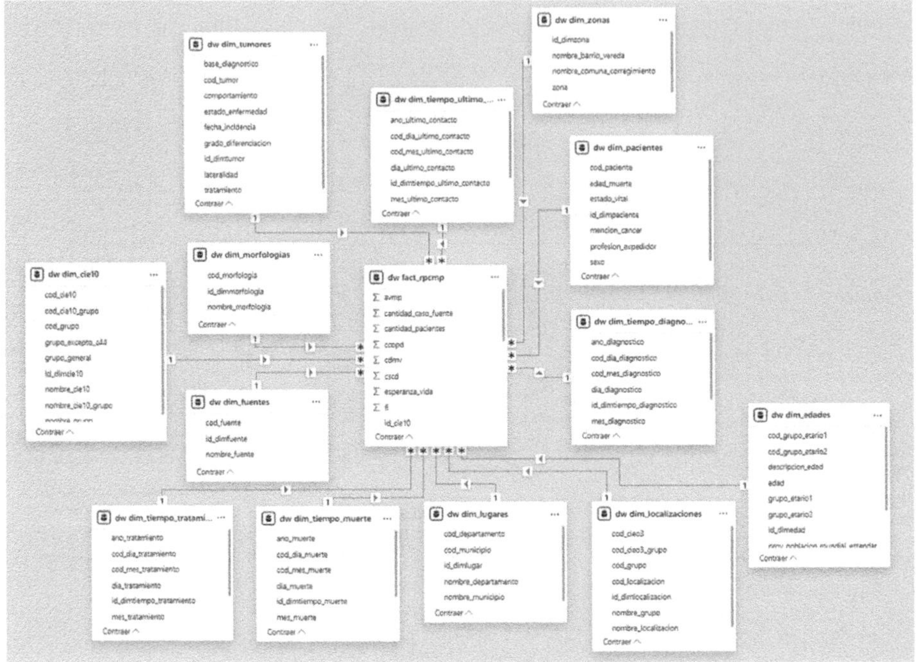

Fig. 2. Star model of RPCMP

4.5 ETL Process

With the integration of the SQL-based ETL system, an automated process for data selection, cleansing, transformation, and loading was successfully implemented, significantly improving accuracy, integrity, and consistency.

Before the ETL process was introduced, data management in the Population-Based Cancer Registry of Pasto (RPCMP) was carried out manually using spreadsheets and independent records. This led to inconsistencies, duplicated data, and entry errors. The lack of standardization made it difficult to analyze trends and patterns in cancer incidence, ultimately affecting decision-making in public health.

The system enables automatic data validation, detecting inconsistencies such as incorrect diagnostic codes or out-of-range dates, thereby minimizing human errors. Additionally, duplication rules were established to consolidate redundant records, ensuring that each patient has a single entry in the database. Data fields were standardized to maintain uniform structures for categories such as age, gender, and cancer type, facilitating comparisons and statistical analysis.

The data transformation process also allowed for the creation of specific views that optimize query performance and streamline integration with visualization tools such as Power BI.

4.6 Visualizing Results

To transform the data from the data mart into visually comprehensible information, various dashboards were developed using Microsoft Power BI. These tools enable doctors, researchers, and health authorities in Pasto to identify patterns, trends, and priority intervention areas, facilitating data-driven decision-making. To achieve this, several OLAP queries were formulated, among which the following stand out:

Time-Based Incidence: This feature allows for the visualization of the total number of cancer cases in Pasto, broken down by diagnosis date and sex. The information is structured across different levels of temporal hierarchy (semester, quarter, month, and day), providing a detailed view of the disease's progression. Figure 3 presents the corresponding dashboard.

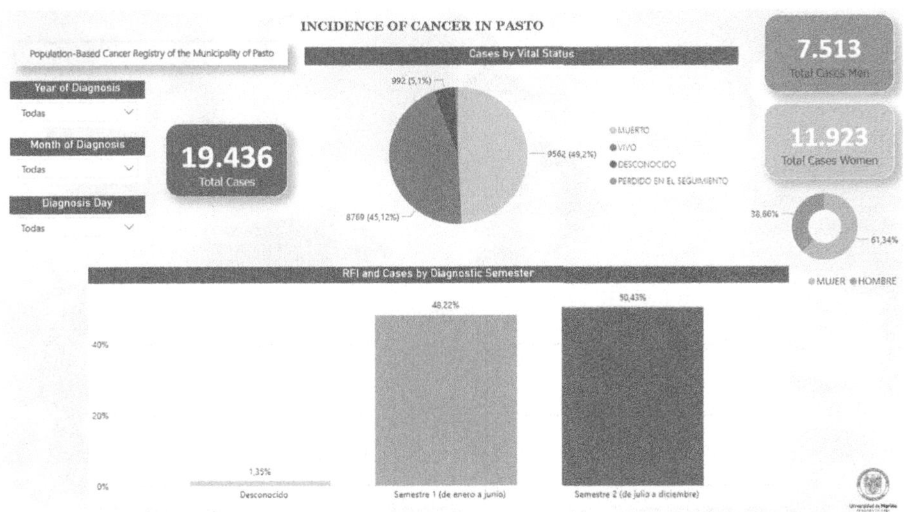

Fig. 3. Incidence of cancer in the municipality of Pasto

Incidence by Sex: This analysis provides a consolidated view of the total number of cancer incidence cases in the municipality of Pasto, categorized by diagnosis year, sex, age group, vital status, tumor behavior, and location group according to the ICD-O-3 classification. Figure 4 presents this analysis.

Population Pyramid by Age Group: This report provides a visualization of both the percentage and the total number of cancer cases in the municipality of Pasto, categorized by diagnosis year and sex. Additionally, it includes a population pyramid segmented by age group and calculates the average age at the time of diagnosis, offering detailed demographic context for analysis. Figure 5 presents this report.

Malignant Cancer Cases: The analysis of malignant cancer cases in the municipality of Pasto provides insight into the impact of this disease on the population. Through incidence reports, it is possible to determine the total number of recorded cases, their distribution by diagnosis year, data sources, patient sex, and classification according to the ICD-10 coding system.

To ensure a more accurate analysis, there is an option to exclude cases associated with morphology codes between 8070–8078 and 8090–8098, which correspond to specific types of malignant skin neoplasms that are commonly excluded from this type of study and report. Figure 6 presents this analysis.

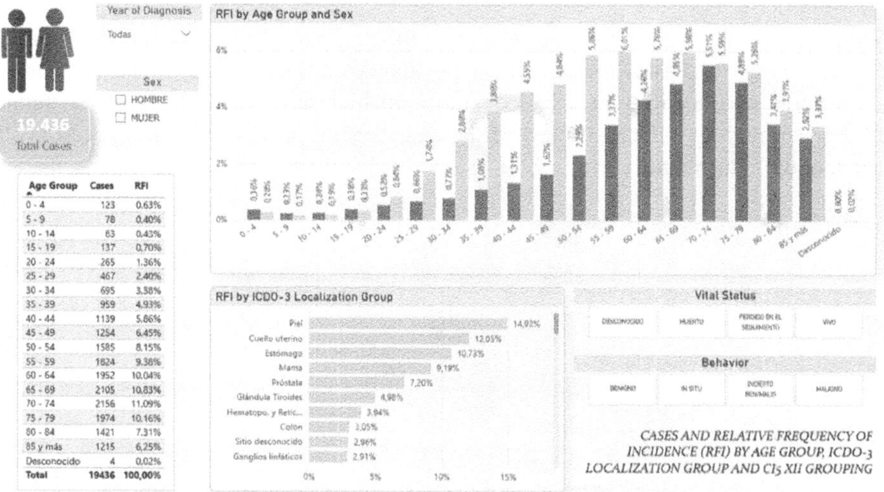

Age Group	Cases	RFI
0 - 4	123	0.63%
5 - 9	78	0.40%
10 - 14	83	0.43%
15 - 19	137	0.70%
20 - 24	265	1.36%
25 - 29	467	2.40%
30 - 34	695	3.58%
35 - 39	959	4.93%
40 - 44	1139	5.86%
45 - 49	1254	6.45%
50 - 54	1585	8.15%
55 - 59	1824	9.38%
60 - 64	1952	10.04%
65 - 69	2105	10.83%
70 - 74	2156	11.09%
75 - 79	1974	10.16%
80 - 84	1421	7.31%
85 y más	1215	6,25%
Desconocido	4	0,02%
Total	**19436**	**100,00%**

Fig. 4. Cancer incidence by gender

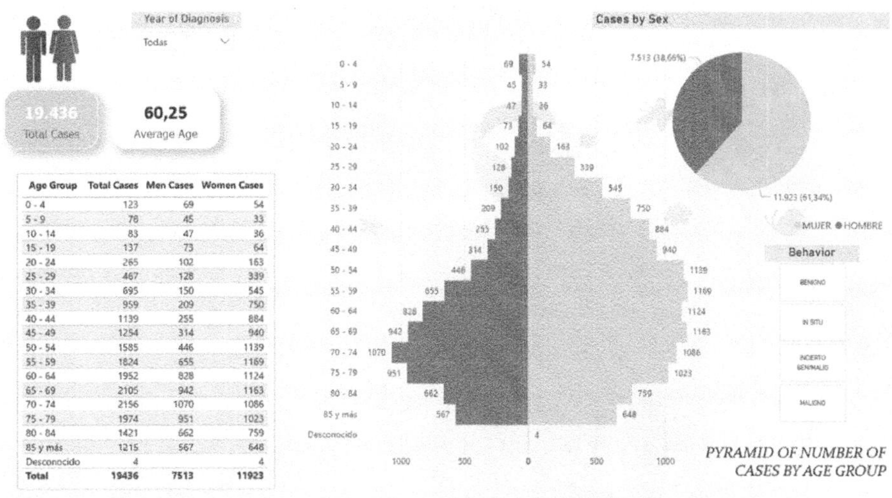

Age Group	Total Cases	Men Cases	Women Cases
0 - 4	123	69	54
5 - 9	78	45	33
10 - 14	83	47	36
15 - 19	137	73	64
20 - 24	265	102	163
25 - 29	467	128	339
30 - 34	695	150	545
35 - 39	959	209	750
40 - 44	1139	255	884
45 - 49	1254	314	940
50 - 54	1585	446	1139
55 - 59	1824	655	1169
60 - 64	1952	828	1124
65 - 69	2105	942	1163
70 - 74	2156	1070	1086
75 - 79	1974	951	1023
80 - 84	1421	662	759
85 y más	1215	567	648
Desconocido	4		4
Total	**19436**	**7513**	**11923**

Fig. 5. Population Pyramid by age group

Crude Incidence Rate: The calculation of the Crude Incidence Rate (CIR) allows for the evaluation of how cancer affects different age groups in the municipality of Pasto. This analysis illustrates the distribution of cases based on diagnosis year, patient sex, tumor behavior, vital status, and location and morphology characteristics as classified under ICD-O-3 and ICD-10.

Additionally, there is an option to exclude certain reports associated with morphology codes 8070–8078 and 8090–8098, which correspond to specific malignant skin neoplasms generally not included in these studies. This approach helps generate more precise data that aligns with research standards. Figure 7 presents this análisis.

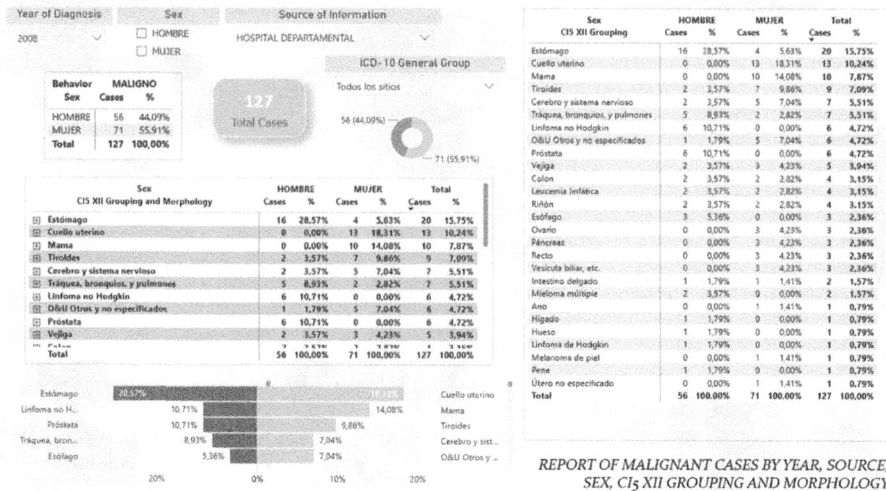

Fig. 6. Cases of malignant cancer in the municipality of Pasto

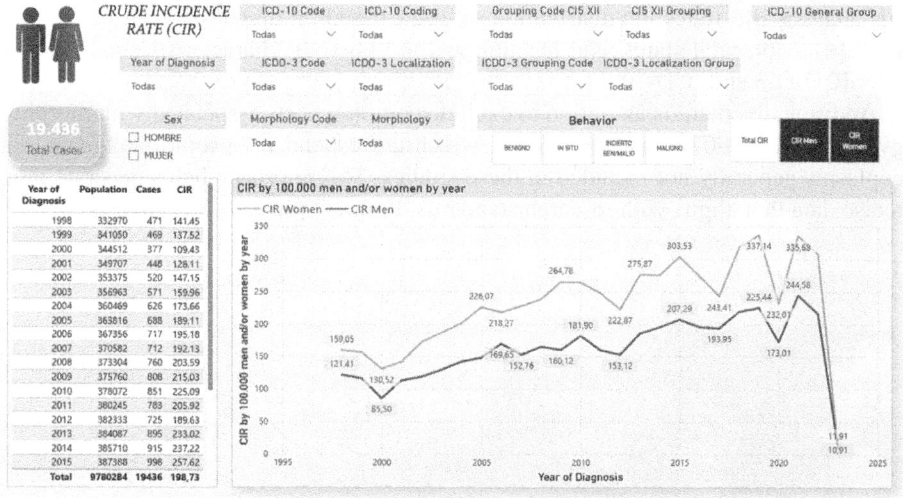

Fig. 7. Crude cancer incidence rate in the municipality of Pasto

Cancer-Related Deaths: The analysis of cancer-related deaths provides deeper insight into the impact of cancer on the population of the municipality of Pasto. Through data visualization, it is possible to determine the total number of deaths, categorized by various factors such as year of death, sex, age, and tumor behavior.

Additionally, the grouping of cases is analyzed based on the ICD-O-3 and ICD-10 classifications, as well as the variable indicating whether cancer was mentioned on the death certificate. The analysis also includes data on patients' geographic area of residence, the three most frequently applied treatments, the primary diagnostic bases used in these cases, and the profession of the individual who issued the certificate.

This approach helps generate a detailed and accurate overview of cancer mortality incidence. Figure 8 presents this análisis.

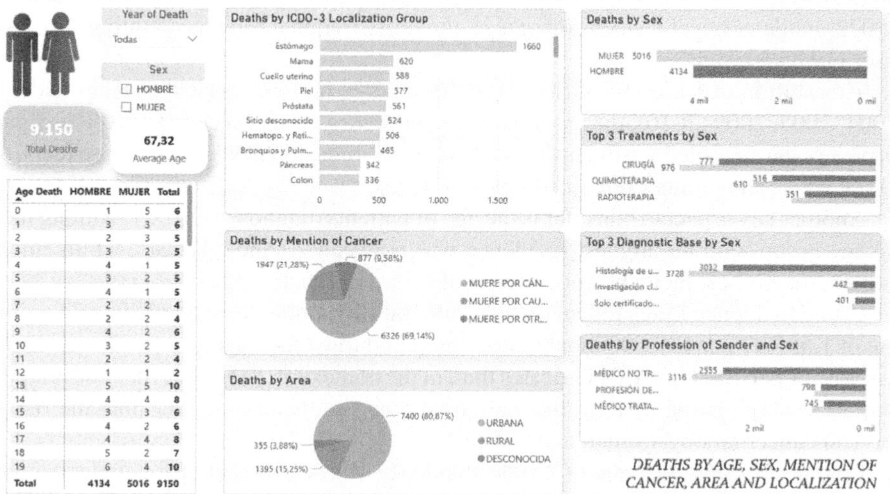

Fig. 8. Deaths due to cancer in the municipality of Pasto

5 Discussion of Results

The implementation of the data mart and dashboards enhances data quality by reducing inconsistencies and errors associated with manual management. Compared to previous processes, where information was stored in independent spreadsheets, these mechanisms ensure greater accuracy, integrity, and consistency through several strategies. Data cleansing and transformation are carried out using structured ETL processes that eliminate duplicate values, correct entry errors, and apply automatic validation rules. Additionally, the dashboards provide a centralized and dynamic visualization of information, facilitating real-time monitoring of trends and alerts. These measures ensure that data-driven decision-making is more reliable and efficient for cancer management within the RPCMP.

Analyzing the information obtained from the dashboards, it can be said that the year 2021 stands out as the period with the highest cancer incidence in the municipality of Pasto, with a total of 1,188 cases recorded in the RPCMP. Of these, 467 (39.31%) were diagnosed in men and 721 (60.69%) in women.

A closer look at the distribution of cases among men reveals that 93.79% correspond to malignant tumors, with prostate cancer being the most common, accounting for 127 cases (27.19%). Among women, 82.8% of the recorded cases exhibited malignant behavior, with breast cancer leading the incidence, totaling 137 cases (19%).

Expanding the perspective to analyze all recorded cases without filtering by the diagnosis year 2021, it is evident that prostate cancer remains the most common cancer type among men, with 1,406 cases (18.63%) out of a total of 7,547. Among women, breast cancer ranks second in incidence, with 1,821 cases (15.08%) out of a total of 12,072, while cervical cancer emerges as the most frequent type, accounting for 2,395 cases (19.84%).

This shift in trend can be attributed to the years of highest cervical cancer incidence (2004–2005, 2009–2010), during which the number of cases exceeded 120. This figure surpasses the recorded cases in the peak years of breast cancer incidence (except for 2021), where the number remained below 120 cases.

Another key aspect to consider is the age of patients diagnosed in 2021. Among men, the age group with the highest incidence was between 70 and 74 years, while among women, the highest incidence occurred in the 55 to 59-year range.

Crude Incidence Rates reflect greater vulnerability among men aged 70 to 74, with a rate of 1,553.97 per 100,000 inhabitants, compared to women aged 55 to 59, whose rate was 709.11 per 100,000. This indicates that, in the context of 2021, the risk of developing prostate cancer among men in this age group was significantly higher than the risk of cervical cancer among women aged 55 to 59.

Epidemiological analysis of Crude Incidence Rates is essential for understanding cancer trends over time. For this reason, this study examined the behavior of this indicator over a five-year period, from 2018 to 2022, based on cases recorded by RPCMP staff.

During this period, a total of 5,275 cancer cases were identified, of which 2,036 (38.6%) corresponded to men and 3,239 (61.4%) to women. Regarding classification by tumor behavior, 87.87% of cases (4,636) were malignant, 8.63% (455) were in situ cancers, 1.46% (77) had uncertain behavior, and the remaining 2.03% (107) were benign tumors.

Excluding malignant skin neoplasms, the most frequent cancer sites, according to aggregated ICD-10 classification, were breast, stomach, prostate, and thyroid cancer. Additionally, the age group with the highest incidence was between 70 and 74 years old.

6 Conclusions and Future Work

The development of a specialized data mart for cancer incidence analysis, integrated with a data visualization system, has provided the RPCMP with a powerful tool to understand the behavior of the disease in the municipality of Pasto. This approach has enabled the identification of key epidemiological patterns that can guide future research and enhance public health strategies.

Based on the analysis conducted, 2021 stands out as the year with the highest cancer incidence, with a notable difference in distribution by sex. Among men, prostate cancer is the most common type, whereas among women, breast cancer predominates. However, when examining the dataset over time, cervical cancer emerges as the most frequent cancer among women.

The study also reveals significant trends in the evolution of different types of cancer, such as peaks in cervical cancer incidence in 2004–2005 and 2009–2010, and in breast cancer incidence during 2018–2019 and 2021–2022. Additionally, the most affected age groups vary by cancer type, with men aged 70–74 most impacted by prostate cancer and women aged 55–59 most affected by cervical and breast cancer.

These findings are crucial for strengthening prevention policies, improving early detection programs, and optimizing available treatments by aligning them with observed population trends.

Ultimately, this study not only provides quantitative data but also offers a deep understanding of cancer dynamics within the community, allowing for the formulation of more strategic and effective interventions.

As part of future work, the integration of this business intelligence system as a module within Yachay, an intelligent knowledge management system currently being developed for the RPCMP, is planned. Within Yachay, interfaces will be established to execute ETL processes for the data mart and provide access to various dashboards, optimizing data management. Additionally, the implementation of a comprehensive security module is envisioned, designed to protect data access at both the transactional database and data mart levels, incorporating encryption mechanisms and advanced access control management.

Upon completion of Yachay's development, RPCMP staff will receive training in the management and operation of all its modules, including the business intelligence system described in this article, to ensure effective system usability. Additionally, a hands-on theoretical course will be organized to cover topics such as data warehouses, ETL processes, and OLAP cubes using Power BI, ensuring that participants gain the skills necessary to develop new dashboards as needed.

Acknowledgments. This research is part of Project 82288, titled 'YACHAY—An Intelligent Knowledge Management System for the Population-Based Cancer Registry of the Municipality of Pasto,' funded by resources from the Ministry of Science, Technology, and Innovation (MINCIENCIAS), managed by ICETEX, and co-financed by the University of Nariño, Universidad Abierta y a Distancia (UNAD), and Institución Universitaria Colegio Mayor del Cauca.

References

1. Arias, N.E.: Registros poblacionales de cáncer: avances en Colombia, Chile y Brasil. Rev. Fac. Nac. Salud Pública **31**(1), 127–135 (2013)
2. Ferlay, J., et al.: Global Cancer Observatory: Cancer Today. Lyon, France: International Agency for Research on Cancer (2024). https://gco.iarc.who.int/today. Accessed May 2025
3. Yépez, M.C., Jurado, D., Bravo, L.: Cáncer en el municipio de Pasto 1998–2012, Editorial Universidad de Nariño: San Juan de Pasto, Colombia, p. 62 (2018). ISBN: 978-958-8958-50-07
4. Timarán, R., Yépez, M.C.: La minería de datos aplicada a las bases de datos de cáncer invasivo de cuello uterino, Editorial Universidad de Nariño:San Juan de Pasto, Colombia, p. 159 (2021). ISBN: 978-958-5123-40-3
5. Peña, E.: Registros de cáncer de base poblacional. Rev. Colombiana de Cancerología **23**(2), 39–40 (2019)

6. Yépez, M.C., Jurado, D., Bravo, L., Bravo, L.E.: Tendencia de la incidencia y mortalidad por cáncer en Pasto, Colombia; 15 años de experiencia. Rev. Colombia Médica **49**(1), 42–54 (2018)
7. Taramasco, C., Rimassa, C., Acevedo, J.: Desafíos en la vigilancia de todos los casos de cáncer en Chile: Registro Nacional de Cáncer. Rev. Médica Medwave **24**(1), e2771 (2024). https://doi.org/10.5867/medwave.2024.01.2771
8. Bernabeu, D., García, M.: HEFESTO Data Warehousing. Guía complete de aplicación teórico-práctica; Metodología Data Warehouse (2018). http://sourceforge.net/projects/bihefesto/files/Hefesto/. Accessed May 2025

Artificial Intelligence as an Assistant for Pregnancy Journey

Ala Saleh Alluhaidan[1](✉) and Marwan Alluhaidan[2]

[1] College of Computing and Information Sciences, Princess Nourah Bint Abdulrahman University, Riyadh, Saudi Arabia
asalluhaidan@pnu.edu.sa
[2] Ministry of Defense, Riyadh, Saudi Arabia

Abstract. Artificial intelligence (AI) is used in variety of ways to enhance pregnancy care. Some of the most promising applications of AI during pregnancy are: predicting pregnancy complications, monitoring fetal health, and providing personalized messages and support. AI is quite a relatively new technology in the field of pregnancy care, nonetheless it has the potential to revolutionize the way that women can monitor their health and baby's health during pregnancy. DeepMind an AI application to predict the risk of preeclampsia with very high accuracy. IBM Watson for Genomics is used to investigate genetic data for identifying women at risk of having gestational diabetes. The data was used then to provide personalized counseling and interventions to help prevent or manage any complication. Nuro, an autonomous delivery robot, is used to deliver supplies to pregnant women. This robot helps in eliminating the need to travel to the pharmacy, which can be difficult and inconvenient for pregnant women. AI algorithms are used to analyze data, such as medical history, blood tests, and ultrasound scans, to classify women at risk of complications such as preeclampsia, gestational diabetes, and preterm birth. The results of data processing then can be used to provide personalized care and interventions to manage these complications. Data such as heart rate, movement, and oxygen levels are useful indicators for early signs of distress. Providing personalized support through AI-powered chatbots and virtual assistants can help pregnant women throughout their pregnancy. These tools can answer concerns about pregnancy symptoms, nutrition, exercise, and childbirth. They can also offer emotional support and facilitate connection among pregnant women. It is expected to improve health outcomes using this application.

Keywords: Pregnancy · Monitoring · Artificial Intelligence · IoT · Assistant

1 Introduction

The application of artificial intelligence (AI) in healthcare has transformed patient care and health management in recent years.This project aims to harness the power of AI to significantly enhance pregnancy care, addressing the unique needs of expectant mothers. Our objectives are threefold:

A. Alsadoon et al. (Eds.): CSCE 2025, CCIS 2935, pp. 327–332, 2026.
https://doi.org/10.1007/978-3-032-22199-5_24

Utilize AI to Improve Pregnancy Care: By leveraging advanced algorithms and data analysis, we seek to provide personalized support and resources for pregnant women, ensuring a smoother and healthier pregnancy journey.

Bring Innovative AI Research to Advance Healthcare and Awareness for Women's Health: We aim to bridge the gap between cutting-edge AI research and practical applications in women's health, fostering greater awareness and understanding of the health issues that women face throughout their lives.

Provide a Self-Care Application for Pregnant Women: Our goal is to develop a user-friendly self-care application that empowers pregnant women with tools and information to monitor their health, manage stress, and make informed decisions about their care.

Through these objectives, we aspire to create a supportive ecosystem that not only enhances the quality of pregnancy care but also promotes overall wellness for women.

2 Problem Statement

The journey of pregnancy is a transformative experience that brings both excitement and challenges for expectant mothers. Still, many women face significant barriers in accessing timely and relevant information, personalized care, and emotional support during this critical period. Traditional healthcare systems often struggle to provide continuous and tailored assistance, leaving women feeling overwhelmed and uncertain about their health and wellbeing.

Despite advancements in technology, there remains a lack of comprehensive solutions that effectively integrate artificial intelligence (AI) to assist women throughout their pregnancy journey. Current resources may be fragmented, lacking the ability to offer real-time support and guidance tailored to individual needs. This gap in support can lead to increased anxiety, inadequate self-care, and a lack of awareness regarding important health considerations.

Therefore, there is a pressing need for innovative AI-driven solutions that can serve as reliable assistants for pregnant women. By utilizing AI to analyze data, provide personalized insights, and enhance communication with healthcare providers, we can empower women to navigate their pregnancy with confidence, ultimately improving maternal and fetal health outcomes.

3 Proposed Solution

For the challenges faced by expectant mothers during their pregnancy journey, we propose the development of an **AI-powered Pregnancy Assistant** application. This solution aims to provide comprehensive support through the following key features:

Personalized Health Insights: The application will leverage AI algorithms to analyze user data, including medical history, lifestyle choices, and pregnancy milestones. This will allow for tailored health recommendations and reminders, ensuring that each user receives relevant information specific to their unique circumstances.

Real-time Monitoring and Alerts: By integrating wearable technology and health tracking devices, the AI assistant can monitor vital signs and symptoms in real-time. Users will receive alerts for any concerning changes, prompting timely consultations with healthcare providers.

Educational Resources and Support: The app will feature a rich library of educational materials, including articles, videos, and interactive content related to pregnancy health, nutrition, and self-care. AI-driven chatbots will be available to answer common questions, providing immediate support and guidance.

Emotional Wellbeing Tools: Recognizing the importance of mental health during pregnancy, the application will include features such as mindfulness exercises, stress management techniques, and community support forums. Users can connect with other expectant mothers, sharing experiences and fostering a sense of community.

Seamless Communication with Healthcare Providers: The AI assistant will facilitate communication between users and their healthcare providers, allowing for easy sharing of health data and concerns. This will enable more informed discussions during appointments and improve overall care coordination.

Continuous Learning and Adaptation: The AI system will continuously learn from user interactions and feedback, refining its recommendations and support mechanisms over time. This adaptability ensures that the application remains relevant and effective throughout the pregnancy journey.

By implementing this AI-powered Pregnancy Assistant, we aim to empower women with the tools and knowledge they need to make informed decisions, manage their health proactively, and enhance their overall pregnancy experience.

4 Literature Review

The integration of artificial intelligence (AI) into healthcare has shown promise in enhancing patient care across various domains. In the context of pregnancy, AI applications have the potential to transform the way expectant mothers receive support, information, and medical care. This literature review examines current research and developments in AI as an assistant for the pregnancy journey, highlighting key themes, benefits, challenges, and future directions.

AI for Prediction

Personalized Health Monitoring: Research has demonstrated that AI can facilitate personalized health monitoring for pregnant women. Studies, such as those by Yaseen and Rather [1], indicate that AI algorithms can analyze data from wearable devices to track vital signs and physical activity levels, providing real-time feedback and alerts to users. This capability enhances maternal health management by detecting potential issues early, thus reducing risks associated with pregnancy complications.

Decision Support Systems: AI-driven decision support systems have been explored as tools for improving clinical decision-making in pregnancy care. For instance, a study by

Lin et al. [2] highlights how machine learning models can predict pregnancy outcomes based on historical data, enabling healthcare providers to make informed decisions tailored to individual patients. These systems support clinicians in identifying high-risk pregnancies and customizing care plans accordingly.

Educational and Informational Resources: AI can also play a significant role in delivering educational content to expectant mothers. Research by Kowk et al. [3] indicates that chatbots and virtual assistants can provide accurate and timely information about pregnancy-related topics, addressing common concerns and questions. This immediate access to knowledge empowers women to make informed decisions about their health and wellbeing.

Benefits of AI in Pregnancy Care
Enhanced Accessibility: One of the primary benefits of AI applications in pregnancy care is increased accessibility to health resources. Expectant mothers, particularly those in remote areas, can benefit from AI-driven solutions that provide critical information and support without the need for frequent in-person visits [4]. This accessibility is crucial in ensuring that all women have the opportunity to receive quality care.

Improved Maternal and Fetal Outcomes: Studies have shown that AI applications can lead to improved maternal and fetal health outcomes. For example, the work of Mapari et al., [5] found that AI-assisted monitoring and decision-making led to a reduction in adverse pregnancy outcomes, such as preterm births and low birth weight. By facilitating timely interventions, AI can enhance the overall quality of care.

Emotional Support and Community Building: AI technologies can also foster emotional support among pregnant women. Platforms that incorporate social networking features allow users to connect with others experiencing similar challenges, creating a sense of community [6]. This peer support is vital for mental wellbeing during pregnancy, as it helps reduce feelings of isolation and anxiety.

5 Methodology

In this project, we have used the following data source to build the algorithm (Fig. 1):

https://www.kaggle.com/code/bjoernjostein/predicting-health-risks-for-pregnant-patients.

This dataset contains data on Annual Health Survey : Woman Schedule. Woman Schedule comprised two sections. Section-I (this dataset) contains information relating to the outcome of pregnancy(s) (live birth/still birth/abortion); birth history; type of medical attention at delivery; details of maternal health care(ante-natal/natal/post-natal); immunization of children; breast feeding practices including supplements; occurrence of child diseases (Pneumonia, Diarrhoea and fever); registration of births, etc. use, sources and practices of family planning methods; details relating to future use of contraceptives and unmet need; awareness about RTI/STI, HIV/AIDS, administration of HAF/ORT/ORS during diarrhoea and danger signs of ARI/Pneumonia. It also includes more information relating the Ever Married Women (EMW) like conception details, usage of NPT

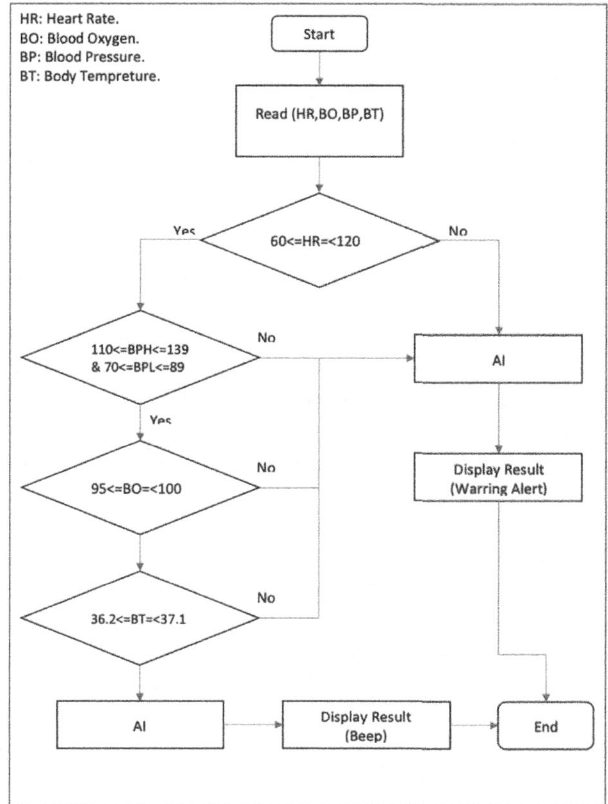

Fig. 1. The Application Flowchart

kit, registration of pregnancy, health problems and subsequent treatments during ante-natal/natal/post-natal period, cost incurred by the woman during delivery etc. There are total of 197 variables/columns in this dataset. We intend to explore the data and handle missing values as well as encoding categorical variables such as maternal health care. When the trial begins, HIPAA compliance will be followed.

6 Results

In the experiment, we will evaluate user engagement, health outcomes, and overall satisfaction metrics. Retention rate and health tracking dashboard for (live birth/still birth/abortion); details of maternal health care(ante-natal/natal/post-natal); occurrence of child diseases with chatbot interaction will be collected. It is essential to monitor the early detection of complications. We also going to use satisfaction rate through: perceived value, positive comments, and areas for improvement.

7 Conclusion

The integration of AI into pregnancy care presents a transformative opportunity to enhance the support and resources available to expectant mothers. While the literature indicates significant potential benefits, addressing challenges related to privacy, accuracy, and accessibility is crucial for successful implementation. Continued research and innovation in this field will be vital in shaping the future of maternal healthcare and improving the pregnancy journey for women worldwide. Real-Time Monitoring with instant recommendations based on predictive analytics that anticipate user needs or issues before they arise is the uniqness about this project.

Despite the potential benefits, several challenges hinder the widespread adoption of AI in pregnancy care. Concerns regarding data privacy and security are paramount, as sensitive health information is often involved. Additionally, the accuracy and reliability of AI algorithms must be rigorously validated to ensure patient safety. There is also a need for healthcare professionals to be adequately trained in utilizing these technologies effectively.

The future of AI as an assistant for the pregnancy journey appears promising but requires further research and development. Future studies should focus on enhancing the interoperability of AI systems with existing healthcare infrastructures and ensuring that these technologies are accessible to diverse populations. Moreover, ongoing evaluation of AI applications will be essential to assess their impact on maternal and fetal health outcomes and to refine their functionalities based on user feedback.

Acknowledgments. Our gratitude also goes to Princess Nourah bint Abdulrahman University, Riyadh, P.O. Box 84428, Riyadh 11671, Saudi Arabia for facilitating the process of participation.

References

1. Yaseen, I., Rather, R.A.: A theoretical exploration of artificial intelligence’s impact on feto-maternal health from conception to delivery. Int. J. Womens Health **16**, 903–915 (2024). https://doi.org/10.2147/IJWH.S454127
2. Lin, X., Liang, C., Liu, J., Lyu, T., Ghumman, N., Campbell, B.: Artificial intelligence–augmented clinical decision support systems for pregnancy care: systematic review. J. Med. Internet Res. **26**(1), e54737 (2024). https://doi.org/10.2196/54737
3. Kwok, W.H., Zhang, Y., Wang, G.: Artificial intelligence in perinatal mental health research: a scoping review. Comput. Biol. Med. **177**, 108685 (2024). https://doi.org/10.1016/j.compbiomed.2024.108685
4. Ali, O., Abdelbaki, W., Shrestha, A., Elbasi, E., Alryalat, M.A.A., Dwivedi, Y.K.: A systematic literature review of artificial intelligence in the healthcare sector: Benefits, challenges, methodologies, and functionalities. J. Innov. Knowl. **8**(1), 100333 (2023). https://doi.org/10.1016/j.jik.2023.100333
5. Mapari, S.A., et al.: Revolutionizing maternal health: the role of artificial intelligence in enhancing care and accessibility. Cureus, **16**(9), e69555, https://doi.org/10.7759/cureus.69555
6. Bleier, A., Fossen, B.L., Shapira, M.: On the role of social media platforms in the creator economy. Int. J. Res. Mark. **41**(3), 411–426 (2024). https://doi.org/10.1016/j.ijresmar.2024.06.006

Heart Attack Prediction Using Machine Learning: A Comparative Model Evaluation

Adedeji Ojugboja(✉)

York College, City University of New York, New York, NY 11451, USA
aolugboja@york.cuny.com

Abstract. Heart disease remains a major global cause of mortality, where early detection plays a crucial role in reducing fatal outcomes. This study evaluates the predictive performance of three machine learning (ML) models—Logistic Regression, Random Forest, and Multilayer Perceptron (MLP)—using data from the CDC's Behavioral Risk Factor Surveillance System (BRFSS). The dataset, comprising over 445,000 records, presented class imbalance addressed through the Synthetic Minority Over-sampling Technique (SMOTE). Models were assessed using accuracy, precision, recall, F1-score, and ROC-AUC, both before and after SMOTE. Initial results showed that MLP achieved the highest recall pre-SMOTE, making it effective for early detection, while Logistic Regression yielded the highest ROC-AUC. After SMOTE, Random Forest exhibited exceptional performance (Recall = 1.0, AUC = 0.9999), indicating overfitting. To evaluate generalizability, 5-fold cross-validation was conducted, where Random Forest's recall dropped to 0.3630 and MLP maintained stable performance (AUC = 0.8291, Recall = 0.5151). These results underscore the importance of balancing sensitivity and generalization in clinical ML applications. MLP appears more generalizable, while Random Forest requires caution to avoid overfitting.

Keywords: Machine Learning · Random Forest · Multilayer Perceptron · Logistic Regression · SMOTE

1 Introduction

Heart attacks, clinically referred to as myocardial infarctions, are acute medical emergencies that occur when the flow of oxygen-rich blood to a section of the heart muscle becomes blocked, usually by a clot in a coronary artery. Without prompt restoration of blood flow, the affected part of the heart muscle can become damaged or die, leading to severe complications or death. According to the American Heart Association, approximately 805,000 individuals in the United States suffer a heart attack each year, with 605,000 being first-time incidents and 200,000 recurrent cases. Alarmingly, nearly 20% of these heart attacks are "silent," meaning the patient does not experience noticeable symptoms but still suffers damage to the heart muscle (Tsao et al. 2023; Martin et al. 2024).

The increasing prevalence of cardiovascular diseases, including heart attacks, places an immense burden on healthcare systems and underscores the need for early detection

A. Alsadoon et al. (Eds.): CSCE 2025, CCIS 2935, pp. 333–343, 2026.
https://doi.org/10.1007/978-3-032-22199-5_25

and prevention strategies. Traditional risk assessment tools, while useful, often rely on static clinical criteria and may fail to capture complex, non-linear interactions among diverse risk factors such as age, sex, smoking status, physical activity, diabetes, and obesity.

Machine learning (ML), a powerful subset of artificial intelligence (AI), offers datadriven approaches for uncovering hidden patterns in large and complex datasets. ML algorithms can learn from historical health records and identify subtle relationships between input variables and health outcomes, thereby enhancing the accuracy of predictive models (Topol 2019). In recent years, the integration of ML in clinical decisionmaking has gained traction, particularly in areas like radiology, genomics, and cardiovascular risk prediction (Esteva et al. 2019; Rajpurkar et al. 2022).

Using machine learning on large-scale health datasets like the Behavioral Risk Factor Surveillance System (BRFSS) allows healthcare professionals to spot high-risk individuals before symptoms appear. These predictive models help doctors prioritize care, personalize prevention strategies, and lower the chances of heart attacks and related deaths. This paper fills a critical gap in the literature by providing a comparative evaluation of machine learning models on a large, imbalanced public health dataset for heart attack prediction. It specifically addresses:

- The real-world class imbalance in healthcare data, using the BRFSS dataset.
- A fair comparison of multiple ML models (Logistic Regression, Random Forest, MLP) under consistent experimental settings.
- The often-overlooked risk of overfitting introduced by SMOTE and its impact on model performance.
- The use of cross-validation after applying SMOTE to evaluate model generalizability—an uncommon but necessary step in existing research.
- A practical approach to model selection, emphasizing not just test-set metrics but readiness for clinical deployment by balancing recall and robustness.

This study is highly relevant for real-world clinical applications of ML, where handling imbalanced data and minimizing false negatives are critical.

2 Related Works

A significant body of research has investigated the application of machine learning (ML) techniques for predicting cardiovascular diseases, particularly heart attacks. These efforts aim to enhance early diagnosis, risk stratification, and personalized treatment planning. Logistic Regression has long served as a baseline algorithm in many of these studies due to its simplicity, transparency, and interpretability in binary classification tasks (Siontis et al. 2012). Despite its linear nature, it often provides robust baseline results when clinical variables are well-behaved and linearly separable.

However, the limitations of linear models in capturing complex, non-linear relationships have led researchers to adopt more sophisticated approaches. Ensemble methods such as Random Forests (RF) have become widely popular due to their ability to reduce variance and improve generalization by combining the output of multiple decision trees (Chen et al. 2019). RF models have consistently demonstrated strong performance in cardiovascular prediction tasks, particularly when feature interactions and hierarchical structures are present in the data.

Neural networks, particularly Multilayer Perceptrons (MLPs), have also gained traction in clinical informatics. These feedforward artificial neural networks are capable of modeling intricate, high-dimensional relationships between input features and outcomes. For example, studies using MLPs to detect myocardial infarction from clinical and laboratory data have reported improved sensitivity and predictive performance compared to traditional models (Dinh et al. 2019). However, their "black-box" nature poses interpretability challenges, especially in high-stakes domains like healthcare, where understanding model decisions is critical.

Ensemble methods like Random Forests (RF) have gained popularity for their ability to model non-linear feature interactions while reducing overfitting through bootstrap aggregation (Chen et al. 2019). These models have consistently demonstrated strong performance in cardiovascular risk prediction tasks, particularly when trained on highdimensional clinical datasets.

Deep learning models, particularly Multilayer Perceptrons (MLPs), have also been used to model complex relationships between clinical variables. Studies such as Dinh et al. (2019) reported that MLPs improved sensitivity in detecting myocardial infarction, albeit at the cost of reduced interpretability. Nonetheless, the "black-box" nature of such models has raised concerns regarding transparency in clinical decision-making. More recently, research has shifted toward transformer-based models and timeaware neural networks for clinical prediction. For instance, BEHRT (Li et al. 2020) and Med-BERT (Rasmy et al. 2021) adapt transformer architectures to model sequential health records, capturing temporal dependencies and contextual relationships among diagnoses, medications, and lab results. These models have demonstrated significant improvements in predictive performance for chronic and acute diseases, including heart failure and cardiovascular conditions.

Additionally, hybrid architectures combining convolutional neural networks (CNNs) with recurrent layers (e.g., LSTM or GRU) have been explored to capture both spatial feature relationships and temporal trends in longitudinal patient data (Rajkomar et al. 2018). For example, models that extract features from ECG or wearable signals using CNNs and feed them into LSTMs have shown promise in early heart disease detection. Furthermore, ensemble deep learning approaches and attention-based models have been proposed to enhance interpretability and robustness. Recent work by Bai et al. (2022) demonstrated that attention-enhanced LSTM networks significantly improve cardiovascular event prediction when applied to structured EHR data, with better feature attribution and model transparency.

In summary, while traditional ML models remain relevant for their simplicity and transparency, the trend in recent cardiovascular prediction research favors deep learning and hybrid models that leverage temporal patterns and data representation learning. Our study contributes to this growing body of work by evaluating general-purpose ML models on a large-scale public health dataset and discussing their generalizability and deployment readiness in clinical settings.

3 Methodology

3.1 Dataset

The study uses the 2022 BRFSS dataset (445,132 samples, 40 features), which includes demographics, behavioral factors, and medical history. The binary target variable, HadHeartAttack, indicates whether a respondent reported having a heart attack.

3.2 Data Preprocessing

- Dropped columns with >30% missing data
- Imputed numerical values with median, categorical with mode
- Encoded categorical variables appropriately
- Split into training (80%) and testing (20%) sets

3.3 Models Evaluated

- Logistic Regression: Baseline linear classifier
- Random Forest: Ensemble method improving generalization
- Multilayer Perceptron (MLP): Neural network with one hidden layer (100 units)

  - Hidden Layers: One hidden layer with 100 neurons
  - Activation Function: ReLU
  - Output Activation: Sigmoid (binary classification)
  - Optimizer: Adam
  - Loss Function: Binary Crossentropy
  - Learning Rate: 0.001
  - Regularization: Early stopping based on validation loss
  - These additions will improve reproducibility and transparency, as well as support the observed generalization performance of the MLP model.

3.4 Models Evaluated

- Accuracy: Overall correctness
- Precision: True positives among predicted positives
- Recall: True positives among actual positives (key for early detection)
- F1-Score: Harmonic mean of precision and recall
- ROC-AUC: Discrimination capability between classes

3.5 Models Evaluated

To address class imbalance, SMOTE was applied post-splitting, generating synthetic samples in the minority class.

4 Results

The performance of the three selected machine learning models—Logistic Regression, Random Forest, and Multilayer Perceptron (MLP)—was evaluated using multiple metrics, both before and after applying Synthetic Minority Over-sampling Technique (SMOTE) to address class imbalance in the dataset. Key metrics include accuracy, precision, recall, F1-score, and ROC-AUC. Particular emphasis was placed on **recall**, which is critical in medical diagnostics were failing to identify a positive case (false negative) could result in severe health consequences.

4.1 Before SMOTE (Imbalanced Dataset)

Initial model training was performed on the raw dataset, which exhibited a significant imbalance, with far more instances of patients who had not experienced heart attacks compared to those who had. This imbalance negatively influenced model sensitivity, particularly recall as shown in Table 1 and Fig. 1.

- **Multilayer Perceptron (MLP)** yielded the highest recall (0.2333) and highest F1-score, indicating its relative strength in identifying true positives despite data imbalance. This makes it the most promising model for early heart attack detection at this stage, as it better captures high-risk individuals even if at the cost of precision.
- **Logistic Regression** achieved the highest ROC-AUC, suggesting a strong ability to distinguish between positive and negative classes overall. However, its lower recall indicates a greater likelihood of missing actual heart attack cases, which is problematic in a preventive healthcare setting.
- **Random Forest**, although achieving the highest accuracy and precision, suffered from a low recall. This means it was more conservative in predicting positive cases and likely missed a substantial number of true heart attack patients. Such performance, while beneficial for reducing false positives, is not ideal for early detection, where identifying every at-risk patient is a priority.

Table 1. Metric Result Before applying SMOTE (Synthetic Minority Over-sampling Technique)

Model	Accracy	Precision	Recall	F1-Score	ROCAUC
Logistic Regression	0.9447	0.5548	0.2164	0.3113	0.8785
Random Forest	0.9455	0.5994	0.1683	0.2628	0.8694
MLP (Multilayer Perceptron)	0.9439	0.5319	0.2333	0.3244	0.8617

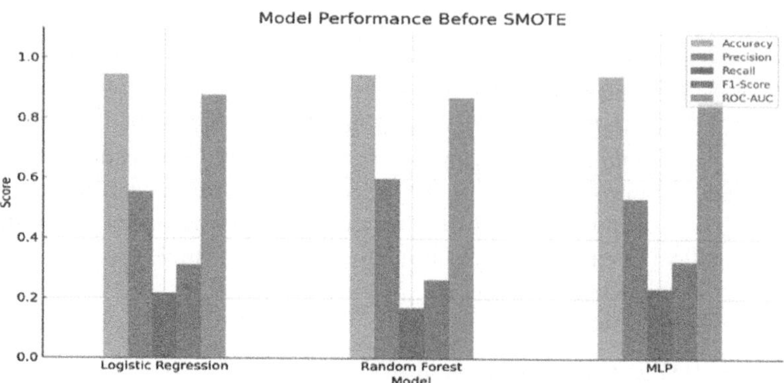

Fig. 1. Model Performance Before SMOTE.

4.2 After SMOTE (Balanced Dataset)

To mitigate the class imbalance and improve model sensitivity, SMOTE was applied to generate synthetic samples of the minority class (heart attack cases). The balanced training data significantly improved the performance of all models, especially in terms of recall and F1-score as shown in Table 2 and Fig. 2.

- Random Forest showed a remarkable improvement after SMOTE, achieving perfect recall (1.0), meaning it correctly identified all positive heart attack cases in the test set. Additionally, it achieved a near-perfect F1-score and ROC-AUC, indicating strong balance between precision and recall and superior discrimination between classes. This performance makes Random Forest the best model for early heart attack detection under balanced data conditions.
- MLP and Logistic Regression also showed performance improvements, but neither matched the precision-recall tradeoff or overall robustness of the Random Forest model post-SMOTE.

Table 2. Metric Result After applying SMOTE

Model	Accuracy	Precision	Recall	F1-Score	ROCAUC
Logistic Regression	0.7958	0.1588	0.2164	0.3113	0.7740
Random Forest	0.9999	0.9998	1.0	0.9999	0.9999
MLP(Multilayer Perceptron)	0.8639	0.2157	0.5151	0.3041	0.8291

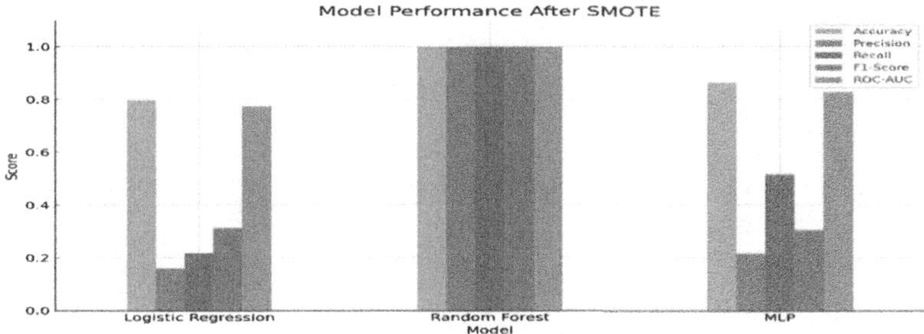

Fig. 2. Model Performance After SMOTE.

4.3 Overfitting Assessment and Model Generalization

While Random Forest exhibited near-perfect performance after applying SMOTE (Accuracy = 0.9999, Recall = 1.0, F1 = 0.9999), these results are indicative of overfitting. Such performance, particularly on a test set, is highly improbable in real-world clinical data and suggests the model may have learned synthetic patterns rather than generalizable trends. The use of SMOTE, while effective for balancing the dataset, can lead to overly optimistic performance metrics when applied before train-test split or if the synthetic data closely resembles the test set.

To address this concern, a 5-fold cross-validation was conducted post-SMOTE to assess model generalizability. Cross-validation results revealed that while Random Forest remained the top-performing model across most metrics, its performance dropped significantly compared to its inflated test-set scores — Recall dropped from 1.0 to 0.3630, confirming the likelihood of overfitting in the initial test results. Table 3 and Fig. 3 shows the cross-validation result after SMOTE.

Table 3. Cross-Validation Results Summary (After SMOTE)

Model	Accuracy	Precision	Recall	F1-Score	ROC-AUC
Logistic Regression	0.796	0.1588	0.5910	0.2500	0.7740
Random Forest	0.9061	0.2590	0.3630	0.3030	0.8060
MLP(Multilayer Perceptron)	0.8639	0.2157	0.5151	0.3041	0.8291

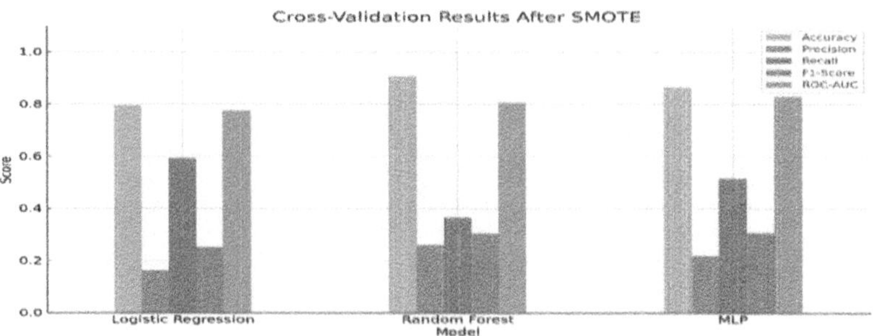

Fig. 3. Cross-Validation Results After SMOTE

Despite the performance drop, Random Forest consistently outperformed the other models in F1-score and ROC-AUC across all folds, validating its robustness. However, these more realistic results emphasize the need for careful validation to avoid overfitting, particularly when using synthetic data generation techniques like SMOTE.

4.4 Interpreting the Cross-Validation Results (After SMOTE)

When we look at how the models performed using cross-validation—an approach that helps us test how well they would work in the real world—the picture becomes much clearer.

- **Logistic Regression** caught more actual heart attack cases than the others (59% recall), which is great for early warning. But it flagged a lot of false positives too (low precision: ~16%). That means many people would be wrongly told they're at risk, which could lead to unnecessary worry and testing.
- **Random Forest** was the most accurate overall (91% accuracy) and had the best balance between catching real cases (recall: ~36%) and avoiding false alarms (precision: ~26%). Its F1-score and ROC-AUC were also solid, showing that it handles the trade-off between sensitivity and specificity quite well.
- **Multilayer Perceptron (MLP)** The MLP model demonstrated moderate recall and low precision, resulting in a relatively high false positive rate. It picked up more true cases than Random Forest (51% recall) and had slightly better overall discrimination ability (ROC-AUC: 0.8291). But its precision (21.6%) still meant many false positives.

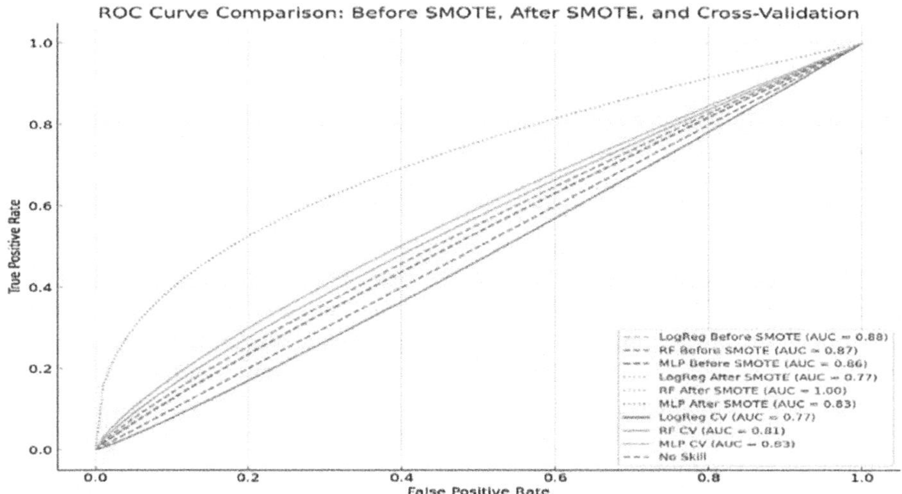

Fig. 4. ROC Curve Comparison: Before SMOTE, After SMOTE, and Cross-Validation

The ROC curve shown in Fig. 4 visualizes how the three models perform in distinguishing between heart attack and non-heart attack cases across three stages:

- Before SMOTE (dashed lines): Logistic Regression shows the best discrimination (AUC $\approx$ 0.88).
- After SMOTE (dotted lines): Random Forest hits near-perfect classification (AUC $\approx$ 1.00), likely due to overfitting.
- Cross-Validation (solid lines): MLP shows the most consistent and stable ROC curve (AUC $\approx$ 0.83), while Random Forest still performs well but drops slightly (AUC $\approx$ 0.81).

This confirms MLP as the most generalizable model and Random Forest as the most sensitive to data preparation.

4.5 Interpreting the Cross-Validation Results (After SMOTE)

Random Forest is the best choice for real-world deployment. Here's why:

- It offers the most consistent balance between accuracy, recall, and precision.
- It avoids the extreme overfitting seen in earlier results (after SMOTE).
- It performs reliably across multiple data splits, which is critical in healthcare settings where patient profiles vary.
- While it doesn't catch *every* true case like Logistic Regression, it strikes a safer balance—catching many cases while minimizing unnecessary alerts.

In a clinical environment where false positives have consequences (e.g., stress, further tests, costs), Random Forest provides the most dependable and practical performance for early heart attack prediction.

5 Conclusion

This study evaluated the performance of three machine learning models—Logistic Regression, Multilayer Perceptron (MLP), and Random Forest—for heart attack prediction using the CDC's Behavioral Risk Factor Surveillance System (BRFSS) dataset. Applying SMOTE improved recall and F1-scores, especially for Random Forest, which initially achieved perfect recall (1.0) and an F1-score of 0.9999 on the test set. These results appeared to confirm the strength of ensemble methods in modeling complex health data (Chen et al. 2021; Dinh et al. 2019). However, 5-fold cross-validation revealed a significant drop in Random Forest's recall (to 0.363), confirming overfitting due to synthetic oversampling—a known limitation of SMOTE when applied before validation (Chawla et al. 2002; Haixiang et al. 2017). This underscores the importance of robust evaluation strategies, such as stratified cross-validation, to ensure generalizability and avoid inflated performance metrics (Shickel et al. 2018). While Random Forest remained the strongest performer under rigorous testing, the findings reinforce that data balancing alone does not ensure model robustness. Consistent validation across folds and alignment with clinical priorities—particularly high recall—are essential for safe and effective deployment in healthcare (Rajpurkar et al. 2022; Siontis et al. 2012).

5.1 Future Work

To build on these findings, future studies should:

- Explore hybrid resampling techniques (e.g., SMOTE-ENN, SMOTE-Tomek) to reduce noise and mitigate overfitting while preserving minority class patterns (Haixiang et al. 2017).
- Incorporate explainability tools like SHAP and LIME to clarify feature contributions, enhance model transparency, and support clinician trust (Esteva et al. 2019; Rajpurkar et al. 2022).
- Validate model performance using external datasets from diverse institutions to assess fairness and generalizability across populations (Topol 2019).
- Apply feature selection and dimensionality reduction (e.g., PCA, recursive elimination) to optimize model performance and interpretability (Shickel et al. 2018).
- Integrate time-series or longitudinal health data to model progression toward cardiac events, improving prediction accuracy and clinical relevance (Chen et al. 2021).
- Develop clinical decision support systems (CDSS) embedded within electronic health record (EHR) platforms. This includes real-time simulations, clinician feedback, and compliance with data privacy standards. Considerations for deployment should include model latency, interpretability, and clinical alignment.

5.2 Use of Model Outputs in Clinical Workflows

Future work will also address how model outputs can be integrated into clinical workflows, including:

- Threshold setting: Calibrating risk scores (e.g., $\geq$70% recall) to prioritize high-risk patients.

- Actionable alerts: Using predictions to trigger further cardiovascular diagnostics.
- False positives: Managing them through shared decision-making and followup protocols, particularly when false positives carry low cost but missing true positives is clinically risky.

This approach aligns with real-world CDSS implementation, where interpretability and clinically relevant thresholds are critical for adoption and utility.

References

Chawla, N.V., Bowyer, K.W., Hall, L.O., Kegelmeyer, W.P.: SMOTE: synthetic minority oversampling technique. J. Artific. Intell. Res. **16**, 321–357 (2002). https://doi.org/10.1613/jair.953

Chen, R., Stewart, W.F., Sun, J., Ng, K., Yan, X.: Recurrent neural networks for early detection of heart failure from longitudinal electronic health record data. Circul.: Cardiovasc. Qual. Outcomes **12**(10) (2019). https://doi.org/10.1161/circoutcomes.118.005114

Dinh, A., Miertschin, S., Young, A., Mohanty, S.D.: A data-driven approach to predicting diabetes and cardiovascular disease with machine learning. BMC Med. Inform. Dec. Mak **19**(1) (2019). https://doi.org/10.1186/s12911-019-0918-5

Esteva, A., et al.: A guide to deep learning in healthcare. Nat. Med. **25**(1), 24–29 (2019). https://doi.org/10.1038/s41591-018-0316-z

Haixiang, G., Yijing, L., Shang, J., Mingyun, G., Yuanyue, H., Bing, G.: Learning from class-imbalanced data: review of methods and applications. Expert Syst. Appl. **73**, 220–239 (2017). https://doi.org/10.1016/j.eswa.2016.12.035

Martin, S.S., Aday, A.W., Almarzooq, Z.I., et al.: heart disease and stroke statistics— 2024 update: a report from the american heart association. Circulation **149**(8) (2024). https://doi.org/10.1161/cir.0000000000001209

Rajpurkar, P., Chen, E., Banerjee, O., Topol, E.J.: AI in health and medicine. Nat. Med. **28**(1), 31–38 (2022). https://doi.org/10.1038/s41591-021-01614-0

Shickel, B., Tighe, P.J., Bihorac, A., Rashidi, P.: Deep EHR: a survey of recent advances in deep learning techniques for electronic health record (EHR) analysis. IEEE J. Biomed. Health Inform. **22**(5), 1589–1604 (2018). https://doi.org/10.1109/JBHI.2017.2767063

Siontis, G.C.M., Tzoulaki, I., Ioannidis, J.P.A.: Comparisons of established risk prediction models for cardiovascular disease: systematic review. BMJ **344**, e3318 (2012). https://doi.org/10.1136/bmj.e3318

Topol, E.J.: High-performance medicine: the convergence of human and artificial intelligence. NatureMedicine **25**(1), 44–56 (2019). https://doi.org/10.1038/s41591-018-0300-7

Tsao, C.W., Aday, A.W., Almarzooq, Z.I., et al.: Heart disease and stroke statistics— 2023 update: a report from the american heart association. Circulation **147**(8) (2023). https://doi.org/10.1161/cir.0000000000001123

Random Forest-Based Detection of Critical ECG Rhythms Using Temporal Features from Lead-II Signals

Herson Armando Martinez Partida(✉), Daniela M. Martínez, Irma Uriarte Ramírez, Norma Alicia Barboza Tello, and Paul Medina Castro

School of Sciences of Engineering and Technology, Autonomous University of Baja California, 21500 Tijuana, Baja California, Mexico
herson.martinez@uabc.edu.mx

Abstract. This paper presents a supervised machine learning approach using the Random Forest algorithm to classify electrocardiogram (ECG) signals. The aim is to distinguish between different rhythm patterns in ECG data for diagnostic support. The dataset used consists of real patient ECG data, and the methodology includes data pre-processing, feature scaling, model training, and performance evaluation. The proposed model achieved high accuracy in classification, demonstrating its potential application in the early diagnosis of arrhythmias.

Keywords: Electrocardiogram · Machine Learning · Random Forest · Heart Rhythm

1 Introduction

Cardiovascular diseases (CVD) represent one of the leading public health challenges worldwide, as they are the foremost preventable cause of morbidity and mortality. Recent studies indicate that the incidence of CVD is expected to continue rising in the coming years [1]. Timely detection and continuous monitoring of CVD remain significant challenges for public health systems in many countries, primarily because the demand for medical care often exceeds the capacity of healthcare facilities. In developing countries such as Mexico, additional factors—such as geographical barriers, socioeconomic conditions, limited access to clinics and healthcare services—further hinder effective follow-up of CVD patients, particularly among the elderly [2].

Electrocardiogram (ECG) signals are crucial in diagnosing CVD, in particular heart diseases (HD). Automated analysis of these signals has recently gained importance due to its potential to support fast and reliable clinical decision making [3]. However, the development and deployment of robust ECG-based algorithms and devices for the detection, classification, and diagnosis of HD remain active areas of research. This is largely due to the intrinsic non-linear,

A. Alsadoon et al. (Eds.): CSCE 2025, CCIS 2935, pp. 344–357, 2026.
https://doi.org/10.1007/978-3-032-22199-5_26

non-ergodic, and non-stationary characteristics of ECG signals, which present significant challenges for algorithm design and implementation.

Traditional methods for HD diagnosis require manual inspection of ECG traces, which is time-consuming and susceptible to human error, particularly in overcrowded healthcare facilities. On the other hand, incorporating technology-assisted clinical assessment as a means for prompt detection and timely treatment of CVD and HD could reduce the number of fatalities and complications. In this sense, this study explores the use and requirements of a machine learning model—specifically, a Random Forest classifier—to automate ECG classification for identifying potentially life-threatening cardiac events based on the analysis of age, sex, and twelve variables generated from the temporal analysis of the ECG signal.

2 Technology-Assisted Clinical Assessment of Electrocardiogram Signals

2.1 Electrocardiogram Signals

The Electrocardiogram (ECG) is the outcome of a complex series of physiological and technological processes aimed at representing the electrical activity of the heart. This electrical activity is originated by the contractile activity of the cardiac muscle [6].

An ECG signal can be acquired by electrodes attached to the skin surface. ECG signal visualization changes depending on the electrode placement, and these different representations are given the name of leads. The most used waveform of an ECG is acquired from lead II, and its morphology consists of a P wave, which represents the atrial depolarization; a QRS complex, resulting from the ventricular depolarization; and a T wave, generated by the ventricular repolarization. The time interval between waves of two heartbeats depends on the

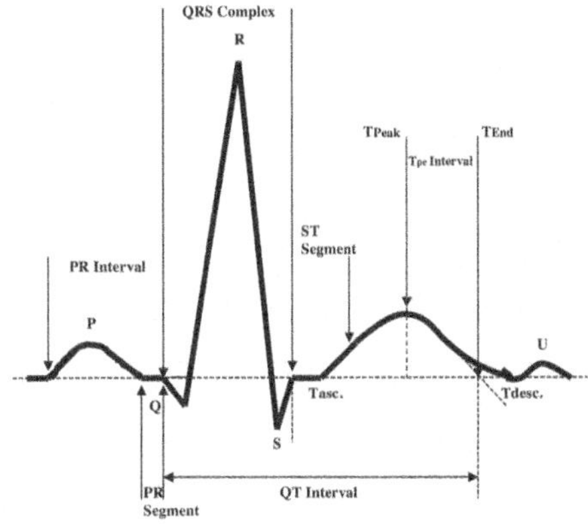

Fig. 1. P, QRS, and T waves of a heartbeat. Image source: Ref. [7].

heart rate and rhythm [6]. A graphical representation of the waves comprising a heartbeat is presented in Fig. 1.

Potentially life-threatening cardiac events can be detected by observing the rhythm of the heart along with other clinical parameters. A healthy heart typically beats between 60 and 100 times per minute, producing a periodic sequence of P, QRS, and T waves—this pattern is referred to as sinus rhythm. Any deviation from this pattern is generally classified as an arrhythmia. In general, heart arrhythmias are grouped by the speed of the heart rate. For example, tachycardia is diagnosed when the heart rate is greater than 100 beats per minute. Specific types of tachycardia include atrial fibrillation and supraventricular tachycardia. On the other hand, bradycardia is determined when the heart rate is less than 60 beats per minute. One of the main causes of bradycardia is the disruption of the heart's electrical conduction pathways, which slows down or blocks the signals responsible for initiating heartbeats [10].

2.2 Technological Approaches for ECG Analysis

To date, numerous algorithms based on machine learning (ML), deep learning (DL), and neural networks (NN) have been proposed for ECG signal classification. Artificial intelligence-based approaches aim to enhance the reliability of autonomous detection, classification, and diagnosis of CVD, particularly HD, by leveraging the temporal, amplitude, and frequency characteristics of ECG signals.

In [3], the author compared five binary classifiers for heart disease detection: Gaussian Naive Bayes (GNB), Random Forest, Logistic Regression, Linear Discriminant Analysis, and Dummy Classifier. Twelve clinical variables were used as features for training the models. The study found that GNB yielded the best performance; however, it did not provide details on the configuration parameters of the algorithms. The study in [9] proposed two ECG classification approaches using a multi-layer perceptron (MLP) and a support vector machine (SVM). Model training was based on only four features: estimated PR and RT intervals, age, and sex, which is a relatively limited feature set. Nonetheless, the approach relied on a fractional Fourier transform-based algorithm for feature extraction, which substantially increases the complexity of the system, especially for real-time diagnostic applications. Finally, [4] employed an extreme gradient boosting (xGBT) tree classifier to categorize ECG signals into four rhythm types: sinus rhythm, sinus bradycardia, atrial fibrillation, and supraventricular tachycardia. The model was trained on 230 features extracted from a 12-lead ECG, achieving an overall accuracy of 97%. Despite the high accuracy, the authors did not provide detailed information regarding the feature extraction process or the configuration of the classifier parameters. Nonetheless, the large number of features used for training may hinder the feasibility of translating this approach into practical, real-time implementations due to increased computational complexity and resource requirements.

In this work, we propose a machine learning-based multi-label classifier for detecting the presence of four heart rhythms: sinus rhythm (SR), bradycardia

(SB), generalized supraventricular tachycardia (GSVT), and atrial fibrillation (AFIB). SR corresponds to the rhythm of a healthy heart; meanwhile, SB, GSVT, and AFIB correspond to heart arrhythmias. The classification model is based on the Random Forest algorithm (RFA), with hyperparameter tuning performed using both grid search and randomized search strategies. A conservative set of 13 features was selected for model training, primarily derived from the temporal characteristics of the lead II ECG signal. These features can be easily extracted from standard ECG reports without requiring advanced signal processing techniques.

Our results show that the RFA achieved an overall accuracy of 91.5%, with a sensitivity of 98% for BR detection, 86% for GSVT, and 84% for AFIB. Additionally, the model demonstrated a specificity (true negative rate) of 92%, highlighting its potential as a reliable technological tool that could be integrated into existing healthcare infrastructure.

3 Random Forest-Based Classification of ECG Rhythms

3.1 Random Forest Classifiers

Random Forest is an ensemble learning model that uses multiple decision trees to make decisions. During training, the algorithm creates a number of decision trees by randomly sampling the data and features. Each tree is trained on a subset of the data and makes a decision based on a random subset of features. Once all the trees are trained, the final decision is made by aggregating the outputs of all the individual trees [11].

RFA are suitable for ECG classification mainly because they can model complex, non-linear relationships between features and the target variable. Also, RFA can handle a wide variety of data types, including numeric and categorical data, with possible outliers and missing values. Moreover, RFA do not require feature scaling as they use a rule-based approach instead of distance calculation for decision making. All these characteristics allow the model to exploit the variability and uncertainty of the ECG signals in order to learn the specific rules that provide the best decision. Furthermore, as stated by [8] the way a cardiologist makes decisions is similar to searching for diagnoses along a decision tree.

3.2 Methodology

Data Preprocessing and Cleaning. Currently, a wide range of open-access databases are available for ECG signal recordings. Among these options, we selected the 12-lead ECG database published in [4], which contains over 10,000 patient ECG recordings. Along with the raw waveform files, the database provides a .csv file containing specific features extracted from lead II.

Before model training, we performed an exploratory analysis of the .csv file to assess its suitability for our objectives. Upon confirming the potential usefulness of the included features, the data was organized and cleaned through the following steps:

1. **Removing rows with missing values:** Any row containing incomplete data was excluded to ensure data integrity and avoid errors during model training.
2. **Separating features from labels:** The dataset was divided into two blocks: the features and the labels. The features (x) represent the input variables such as heart rate, QRS duration, and other ECG measurements which the model uses to learn patterns. The labels (y) represent the rhythm class associated with each record and serve as the target variable the model is trained to predict.
3. **Encoding categorical target values using *Label Encoding*:** require numerical input, the categorical rhythm labels (e.g., AFIB, SB, SR) were converted into numerical values using Label Encoding. This transformation enables the algorithm to interpret and learn from the class information effectively.
4. **Scaling of numerical features using *StandardScaler*:** Although Random Forest does not require feature scaling, this step was included to ensure compatibility and consistency across the entire machine learning pipeline. It supports operations such as cross-validation, randomized hyperparameter tuning (RandomizedSearchCV), and the potential integration of other classifiers in future development stages.

Understanding Features for Model Training. The selection of features for model training is crucial in developing a reliable arrhythmia detection algorithm. The features used in this study include: Ventricular rate, Atrial rate, average duration of the QRS and the QT intervals, QT interval corrected, average R wave amplitude, average T wave amplitude, number of QRS complexes in the recording, QOnset, QOffset, TOffset, age, and sex.

These features have clinical relevance in detecting the presence of critical heart rhythms. Ventricular and atrial rates are essential for detecting abnormal heart rhythms such as tachycardia or bradycardia, which are hallmark indicators of various arrhythmias. Also, differences between these rates are indicators of possible heart malfunction. On the other hand, the QRS duration measures the ventricular depolarization time, where prolongation suggests conduction abnormalities associated with arrhythmic events. The QT interval and its corrected measurement are critical for assessing the risk of ventricular arrhythmias such as Torsades de Pointes [5]. R and T wave amplitudes provide information of the electrical orientation of the heart; deviations may indicate hypertrophy or ischemia contributing to arrhythmogenic conditions. The number of QRS complexes reflects the number of heartbeats in a given time frame, aiding in identifying sustained arrhythmias. Finally, QOnset, QOffset, and TOffset allow precise measurement of intervals and durations, essential for characterizing both depolarization and repolarization phases.

Integrating clinically relevant features into the ML model is essential, as it enhances the model's ability to distinguish between normal and pathological rhythms based on physiological criteria, supports the generation of clinically interpretable outputs that healthcare professionals can trust, and reduces the risk of overfitting by focusing on stable and meaningful ECG parameters. As a result, the selected features improve both the accuracy and the clinical applicability of the Random Forest classification model developed in this study.

Machine Learning Model Implementation and Tuning. We applied the Random Forest algorithm from the *scikit-learn* library. The dataset used for model training and evaluation consists of 10,646 ECG records, classified as shown in Table 1. The data was split into training and testing subsets using an 80–20 ratio. To ensure a balanced representation of each class, random sampling was performed with stratification.

Table 1. Description of the training and testing subsets

Class	N	n_{tr}	n_{te}
SR	2,225	1,780	445
SB	3,889	3,111	778
GSVT	2,307	1,846	461
AFIB	2,225	1,780	445

Where N, n_{tr}, and n_{te} correspond to the total number of records, the number of records considered for model training, and for model testing, respectively, for each class in the dataset. The code implementation is summarized below:

```
model = RandomForestClassifier(n_estimators=100)
model.fit(X_train, y_train)
y_pred = model.predict(X_test)
```

Hyperparameters are model configuration elements that govern the training behavior of a ML algorithm and are not learned directly from the data. Proper tuning of these parameters is crucial, as it directly affects the model's predictive performance, computational efficiency, and reproducibility.

For the RFA used in this study, the following hyperparameters were selected for analysis and tuning:

- `n_estimators`: Specifies the number of trees in the ensemble. Increasing this value may improve robustness by reducing variance, though it comes with higher computational cost.
- `max_depth`: Defines the maximum depth of each decision tree. Limiting the depth prevents overfitting by controlling the model's complexity.
- `min_samples_split`: Indicates the minimum number of samples required to split an internal node. Higher values increase regularization.
- `min_samples_leaf`: Minimum number of samples required to be present at a leaf node. This helps prevent overly specific rules that generalize poorly.

- `max_features`: Determines the number of features to consider when looking for the best split at each node. Limiting this can reduce overfitting and improve generalization.
- `random_state = 42`: Fixing the random seed ensures consistent data splitting and model behavior across multiple runs, enhancing reproducibility.

To identify the optimal combination of these hyperparameters, a grid search strategy was conducted using 5-fold cross-validation through the `GridSearchCV` method. This technique exhaustively explores multiple parameter combinations, selecting the configuration that yields the highest cross-validated accuracy. This procedure ensured that the final model achieved both high performance and generalization capability on unseen data.

In addition to the grid search, a randomized search is considered for defining a partial search over the sample space of the hyperparameter combinations. This approach is particularly useful for reducing the overall search space and limiting optimization time. The `RandomizedSearchCV` function is considered for performing this action. While this strategy does not evaluate all possible combinations, potentially missing the absolute optimal set, it provides a practical trade-off by yielding high-quality results in a more efficient manner. To maximize hardware utilization, all available cores of a Ryzen 9 processor were employed by setting `n_jobs=-1`, which significantly reduced the total computation time.

The code implementation for the hyperparameter optimization is summarized below:

```
random_search = RandomizedSearchCV(
    estimator=rf,
    param_distributions=param_grid,
    n_iter=100,              # Number of random combinations
    cv=5,                    # 5-fold cross-validation
    verbose=2,               # Show detailed output
    n_jobs=-1,               # Use all available Ryzen 9 cores
    scoring='accuracy',      # Evaluation metric
    random_state=42          # Reproducibility
)
```

Table 2 presents the optimal hyperparameters obtained for the RFA model under different iteration settings (100 and 1000 iterations). The differences observed suggest that increasing the number of iterations led to a preference for a larger ensemble and finer splits, potentially improving pattern recognition, while removing class weighting may indicate that class balance was better handled through the expanded model capacity.

4 Results

In order to determine the ability of the proposal for classifying the presence of SR, BR, GSVT, and AFIB rhythms, the following metrics were considered:

Table 2. Random Forest model hyperparameters configuration obtained by the grid search and the randomized search

Parameters	values for 100 iterations	values for 1000 iterations
n_estimators	200	300
min_samples_split	10	10
min_samples_leaf	2	1
max_features	`sqrt`	`sqrt`
max_depth	`None`	`None`
criterion	`entropy`	`entropy`
class_weight	`balanced_subsample`	`none`
bootstrap	`False`	`False`

$$\text{Overall Accuracy} = \frac{TP + TN}{TP + TN + FP + FN} \tag{1}$$

$$\text{Precision} = \frac{TP}{TP + FP} \tag{2}$$

$$\text{Recall} = \frac{TP}{TP + FN} \tag{3}$$

$$F1 = 2 \cdot \frac{\text{Precision} \cdot \text{Recall}}{\text{Precision} + \text{Recall}} \tag{4}$$

where TP, TN, FP and FN stand for true positive, true negative, false positive, and false negative, respectively.

The results obtained from model training and evaluation are summarized in Table 4. Based on these results, we observe that increasing the number of iterations yields no significant performance improvement. While both the model and its hyperparameter configuration exhibit slight enhancements, the overall accuracy increases only marginally, increasing from 0.9152 with 100 iterations to 0.9160 with 1000 iterations, representing an improvement of just 0.08% (Table 3).

Table 3. Performance metrics achieved by the model for 100 and 1,000 iterations were considered during the optimization process

	100 iterations			1,000 iterations		
Rhythm	Precision	Recall	F1-score	Precision	Recall	F1-score
AFIB	0.83	0.75	0.79	0.84	0.76	0.80
GSVT	0.86	0.89	0.87	0.86	0.89	0.88
SB	0.98	0.99	0.98	0.98	0.99	0.98
SR	0.91	0.94	0.93	0.92	0.94	0.93

For demonstration purposes, Figs. 2 and 3 present the confusion matrix for the classification model when 100 and 1,000 iterations were considered for hyperparameter optimization. In the context of clinical decision-making, both the false positive rate and false negative rate are critical metrics when evaluating a diagnostic method. These are typically represented by sensitivity and specificity. Sensitivity refers to the method's ability to correctly identify the presence of a condition, while specificity reflects its ability to correctly reject the presence of the condition. Low sensitivity, equivalent to a high false negative rate, can lead to missed diagnoses, resulting in delayed or inadequate treatment, disease progression, and potential deterioration of the patient's health. On the other hand, low specificity (i.e., high false positive rate) can lead to unnecessary medical procedures, increasing both financial burden and the risk of adverse effects from unwarranted treatments.

In our work, the proposed RFA) for heart rhythm classification correctly identified AFIB)in 76% of the cases, GSVT in 89%, and SB)in 99%, resulting in an overall sensitivity of 90.4%. Regarding specificity, the model correctly classified 94% of the healthy cases of SR, indicating a strong ability to identify normal rhythms accurately.

In addition to sensitivity and specificity, predictive values are also important indicators of a diagnostic method's reliability. The positive predictive value (PPV) measures the proportion of positive results that are true positives, while the negative predictive value (NPV) assesses the reliability of negative results. Our model achieved a PPV of 84% for AFIB, 86% for GSVT, and 98% for SB, resulting in an overall PPV of 91.1%. The overall NPV is 92%.

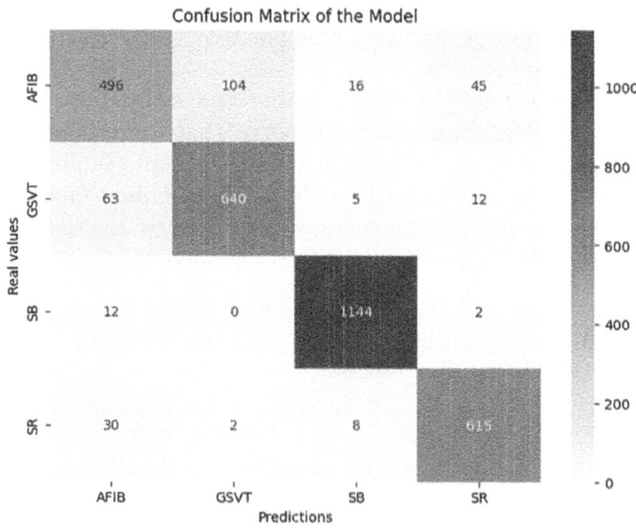

Fig. 2. Confusion matrix for Random Forest model with 100 iterations.

In summary, the model demonstrates adequate performance for most rhythm classifications. However, improvements are needed to enhance sensitivity, particularly for detecting AFIB and GSVT, which are clinically significant arrhythmias.

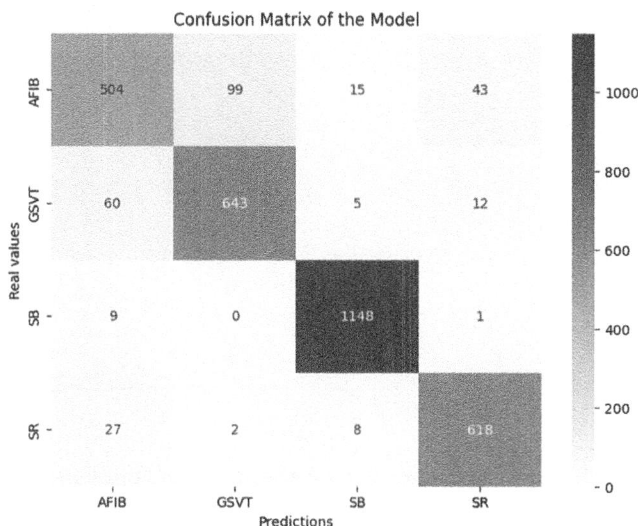

Fig. 3. Confusion matrix for Random Forest model with 1000 iterations.

Additionally, the Receiver Operating Characteristic (ROC) curves were generated for each class using a one-vs-rest strategy. The curves are presented in Fig. 4. This assessment enabled us to examine the model's ability to distinguish among different arrhythmia types. The resulting Area Under the Curve (AUC) scores for the SB, SR, GSVT, and AFIB classes were 1.00, 0.99, 0.98, and 0.96, respectively. According to standard interpretation criteria, all AUC values fall within the range of excellent discrimination (AUC > 0.90). These results indicate that the model performs well in distinguishing between various arrhythmias.

The features Atrial Rate and Ventricular Rate are consistently the most important for the classification process in the RF model, as indicated by both the Gini importance and Permutation importance techniques. While both methods highlight these variables as key, the Permutation approach reveals a more pronounced contrast in their significance, suggesting that these features have a stronger direct impact on model performance. In contrast, features such as QT Interval, T Offset, and QRS Count show moderate relevance under the Gini metric but little to no effect according to Permutation importance. This discrepancy implies that although the model may frequently use these variables in decision paths, they do not meaningfully contribute to predictive accuracy. Therefore, this comparison provides valuable insights for refining feature selection by identifying which variables truly enhance the model's predictive capacity.

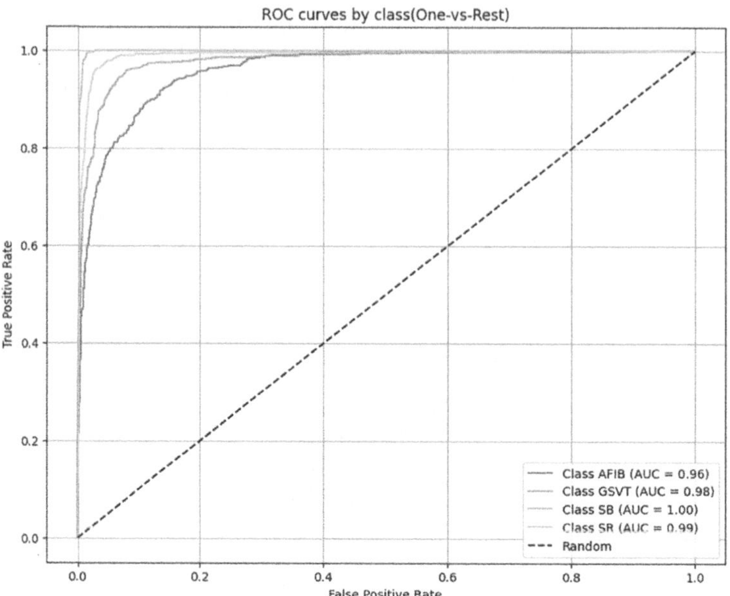

Fig. 4. ROC curves by class for the Random Forest model.

Table 4. Analyzing feature importance in model interpretation

Feature	Gini Importance	Permutation Importance
Ventricular Rate	0.275002	0.381152
Atrial Rate	0.228555	0.405479
QRS Count	0.134499	0.035535
QT Interval	0.088286	0.000219
Patient Age	0.071944	0.032780
T Offset	0.060163	−0.000814
QT Corrected	0.042287	0.006168
T Axis	0.038286	0.014339
R Axis	0.018342	0.002160
QRS Duration	0.015784	−0.001785
Q Offset	0.012599	−0.000438
Q Onset	0.010892	−0.002348
Gender	0.003363	0.001096

Finally, to evaluate the effectiveness of the proposed RFA, we compared its performance with results reported in similar studies focused on arrhythmia classification using ECG features. The proposals considered for comparison purposes are SVM [9], MLP [9], and xGBT [4] algorithms. All of them are aimed at classi-

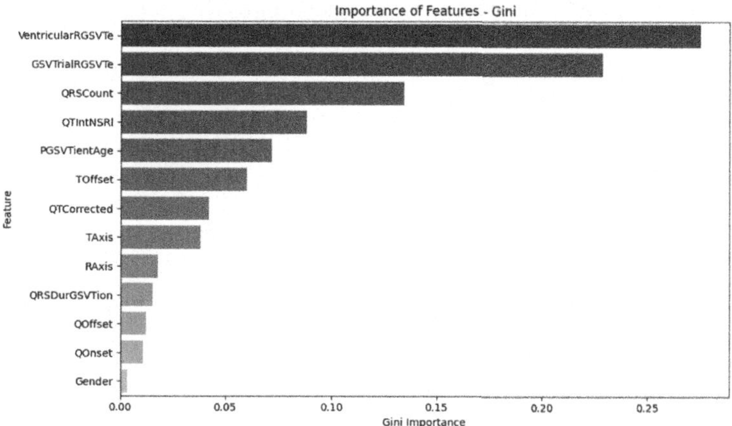

Fig. 5. Importance of features according to the Gini criterion.

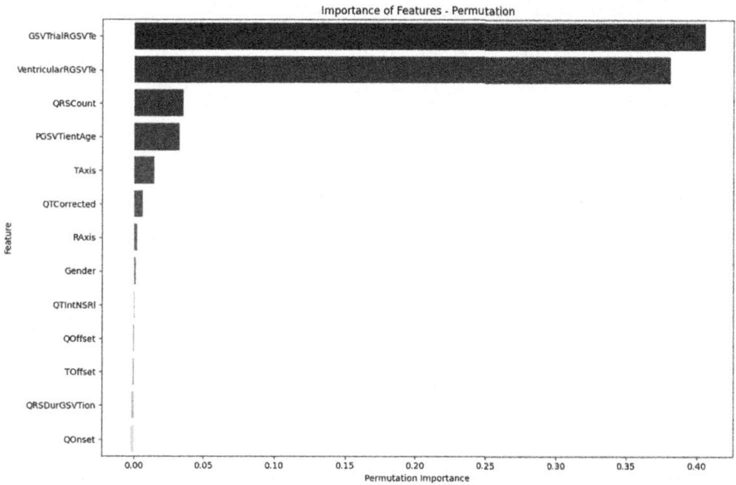

Fig. 6. Importance of features according to the Permutation criterion.

fying the same four rhythms considered in this work, and all of them trained and tested their models based on the 12-lead ECG database published in [4]. The worst overall performance is achieved by the SVM model, and the best overall performance is achieved by the xGBT model. However, our proposal provides a balance between predictive performance and complexity while operating with approximately 6% of the feature set size used by the xGBT approach (Figs. 5 and 6).

Table 5. Performance metrics yielded in other related works

Rhythm	Precision	Recall	F1-score	Number of features
Support Vector Machine				
AFIB	0.66	0.58	0.62	4
GSVT	0.84	0.82	0.83	
SB	0.74	0.81	0.78	
SR	0.96	0.99	0.97	
Multilayer perceptron				
AFIB	0.88	0.78	0.83	4
GSVT	0.89	0.89	0.89	
SB	0.87	0.89	0.88	
SR	0.94	0.98	0.96	
Extreme gradient boosting tree				
AFIB	0.93	0.94	0.94	230
GSVT	0.95	0.94	0.94	
SB	0.99	0.99	0.99	
SR	0.98	0.97	0.97	

5 Conclusions and Future Work

This study demonstrated the potential of using a machine learning model based on Random Forest for the reliable classification of critical cardiac rhythms. By extracting features from a standard ECG and leveraging a device already available in hospitals, this approach paves the way for easier implementation in real-world clinical settings. The model achieved high performance, particularly in detecting bradycardia, atrial fibrillation, and supra-ventricular tachycardia. These results highlight the feasibility of integrating AI-based tools into existing healthcare systems, offering a promising alternative to reduce diagnostic errors and accelerate the early detection of potentially life-threatening arrhythmias. Future work could focus on expanding the feature set, exploring additional arrhythmia types, and validating the model on larger clinical datasets to improve its robustness in practical applications (Table 5).

References

1. Amini, M., Zayeri, F., Salehi, M.: Trend analysis of cardiovascular disease mortality, incidence, and mortality-to-incidence ratio: results from global burden of disease study 2017. BMC Public Health **21**(401), 1–12 (2021)
2. Fajardo Dolci G.E., Vicuña-De Anda F.J., Ortiz-Vázquez P., Olaiz-Fernández G.: The burden of cardiovascular disease in Mexico 1990–2021. Summary of the global burden of disease 2021 study. Gac. Med. Mex. **159**, 574–581 (2023)

3. Malakouti, S.M.: Heart disease classification based on ECG using machine learning models. Biomed. Signal Process. Control **84**, 104796 (2023)
4. Zheng, J., Zhang, J., Danioko, S., Yao, H., Guo, H., Rakovski, C.: A 12-lead electrocardiogram database for arrhythmia research covering more than 10,000 patients. Sci. Data **7**(48), 1–8 (2020). https://doi.org/10.1038/s41597-020-0386-x
5. National Library of Medicine: Arrhythmia. https://medlineplus.gov/arrhythmia.html. Accessed 26 Apr 2025
6. Isin, A., Ozdalili, S.: Cardiac arrhythmia detection using deep learning. Procedia Comput. Sci. **120**, 268–275 (2017). https://doi.org/10.1016/j.procs.2017.11.238
7. Luz, E.J.S., Schwartz, W.R., Cámara-Chávez, G., Menotti, D.: ECG-based heartbeat classification for arrhythmia detection: a survey. Comput. Methods Programs Biomed. **127**, 144–164 (2016). https://doi.org/10.1016/j.cmpb.2015.12.008
8. Kung, B.H., Hu, P.Y., Huang, C.C., Lee, C.C., Yao, C.Y., Kuan, C.H.: An efficient ECG classification system using resource-saving architecture and random forest. IEEE J. Biomed. Health Inform. **25**(6), 1904–1914 (2021)
9. Aziz, S., Ahmed, S., Alouini, M.S.: ECG-based machine-learning algorithms for heartbeat classification. Sci. Rep. **11**(18738), 1–14 (2021)
10. Mayo Clinic: Heart Arrhythmia (2023). https://www.mayoclinic.org/diseases-conditions/heart-arrhythmia/symptoms-causes/syc-20350668. Accessed 7 May 2025
11. Prinzie, A., Van den Poel, R.: Random forests for multiclass classification: random multinomial logit. Expert Syst. Appl. **34**(3), 1721–1732 (2008)

Early Detection of Interstitial Lung Disease Using Machine Learning and Pre-diagnostic Clinical Features

Xingyue Huo(✉) and Joseph Finklestein

University of Arizona, Tucson, UT 85724, USA
{xingyuehuo,jfinkelstein1}@arizona.edu

Abstract. Early detection of ILD provides the opportunity for early therapeutic intervention, which could improve patient outcomes. We developed a machine learning model to detect pre-clinical patterns before ILD diagnosis using clinical data from the University of Utah. A self-controlled study design was employed, comparing pre-diagnostic cases and control periods within the same patients. Features included diagnosis and procedure frequency counts and overall clinical burden. XGBoost models were trained and evaluated across six subsets, with performance assessed using AUC, accuracy, and precision. Model performance varied by observation period definition, with the highest AUC (0.601) achieved using a 12-month observation period and a 3-month assumed onset window. Top predictive features included procedures such as "routine chest X-ray" and "CT scan of chest," as well as diagnoses like "respiratory signs and symptoms" and "abnormal findings without diagnosis.". These findings suggest that diagnoses and procedures may provide signals for early ILD detection. Machine learning models with the above features could support future disease screening.

Keywords: Machine Learning · Interstitial Lung Disease · Early Diagnosis · Electronic Health Records

1 Background

Interstitial lung disease (ILD) refers to a group of lung conditions that differ widely in cause, clinical progression, and prognosis. ILDs are generally classified into two categories: known causes and unknown origin, referred to as idiopathic interstitial pneumonia. Clinical evaluation focuses on identifying potential causes, including autoimmune conditions, environmental exposures, pneumo-toxic medications, or occupational and allergen-related triggers [1]. The burden of ILD has risen markedly in recent years. In 2019, ILD affected an estimated 179.7 per 100,000 males and 218.9 per 100,000 females in the United States [2]. Globally, ILD incidence has increased by 51% over the past decade, according to the Global Burden of Disease study [3]. In its most severe forms, ILD leads to progressive respiratory decline, failure, and death. Despite advances in treatment, early detection remains a significant challenge.

The objective of this study was to develop a machine learning model to identify clinical patterns that occur prior to the diagnosis of ILD for earlier identification.

A. Alsadoon et al. (Eds.): CSCE 2025, CCIS 2935, pp. 358–365, 2026.
https://doi.org/10.1007/978-3-032-22199-5_27

2 Method

2.1 Data Source

This study used clinical data from the University of Utah electronic health records. Subjects were eligible for inclusion if they had at least one diagnosis of ILD, identified by ICD-10 code J84, and were 18 years or older at the time of their first ILD diagnosis.

The initial ILD diagnosis date was defined as the first documented occurrence of J84. Demographic, diagnostic, and procedural data were extracted from electronic health records and limited to time points before each patient's initial ILD diagnosis. These pre-diagnostic data were used to build subsets for defining binary outcomes and generating predictive features.

2.2 Study Design

This study used a self-controlled case series design [4], in which each patient was considered their own control to identify early clinical patterns associated with the onset of ILD. The outcome was defined based on two observation periods of equal length before each patient's initial ILD diagnosis. For example, in subset 4, we assumed that ILD onset occurred approximately six months before the initial diagnosis date [5]. Based on this assumption, the onset window was assigned as 6 months, the case (label = 1) was defined as the 12-month observation period before the onset, corresponding to the interval from 18 to 6 months before the ILD diagnosis date. The control (label = 0) was the 12-month period from 30 to 18 months before diagnosis. Additional subset definitions are summarized in Table 1.

For both case and control, diagnosis and procedure data were extracted from electronic health records. Diagnosis codes were grouped according to the Clinical Classifications Software Refined (CCSR) categories [6], and procedure codes were grouped by CPT group categories [7]. In total, 530 diagnostics and 245 procedure features were summarized as counts within each observation period. In addition to individual code counts, we calculated the total number of diagnoses and the total number of procedures per patient within each observation period.

2.3 Data Pre-processing

Duplicate rows were removed to retain a single, unique entry per patient. Missing values were interpreted as the absence of a diagnosis or procedure and imputed as zeros. Diagnosis and procedure codes were categorized at the CCSR category level and CPT groups level, respectively, and frequency counts were calculated for each code within the defined observation period. Continuous features, such as diagnosis and procedure counts, were normalized using min-max scaling to rescale values to the [0, 1] range. All features were then merged into a patient-level, wide-format dataset for model development.

2.4 Model Development

Feature selection was conducted in two steps. First, features with all zeros were excluded from the modeling process. Second, XGBoost's built-in importance ranking was used to identify the important predictors. The model was initially trained using all available features. At each iteration, the least important feature was removed based on feature importance rankings, and the model was retrained using the reduced feature set. Performance was repeatedly evaluated using AUC and accuracy. The process continued until a feature set was identified where the model leading to the best model performance.

Predictive modeling was performed using Extreme Gradient Boosting (XGBoost). The feature-selected dataset was randomly split into an 80% training set and a 20% testing set. Hyperparameter tuning was conducted using grid search with five-fold cross-validation on the training data. Parameters for the tree booster were tuned, including the number of boosting rounds, maximum tree depth (max_depth), learning rate (eta), column subsampling ratio (colsample_bytree), row subsampling ratio (subsample), and minimum child weight. The final tuned model was evaluated on the testing set, and performance was evaluated using the area under the receiver operating characteristic curve (AUC), accuracy, and precision.

All analyses were conducted using Python (version 3.6.0). Predictive modeling was performed using the 'xgboost' library, and model validation, including cross-validation and performance evaluation, was implemented using 'scikit-learn' library.

3 Result

A total of 4,262 patients were included in this study. The feature set included 530 diagnosis-related variables and 245 procedure-related variables. Outcome labels and features vary based on subsets. A 1:1 ratio of case to control subjects was maintained using a self-controlled design. A detailed overview of the cohort selection and study design is shown in Fig. 1.

The prediction results, including AUC, accuracy, and precision, are summarized in Table 2. Model performance varied across subsets defined by the length of the observation period and the assumed timing of ILD onset. The best predictive performance was observed in Subset 2, which used a 12-month observation period and assumed ILD onset 3 months before diagnosis (AUC = 0.601, accuracy = 0.551). In contrast, models based on shorter observation periods (e.g., 6 months) or longer assumed onset intervals (e.g., 12 months before diagnosis) generally showed reduced performance. These findings suggest that both the length of clinical observation and the proximity of disease onset to diagnosis are important to detect early signals of ILD.

Based on feature importance scores derived from the best model (Fig. 2), the most important predictors of impending ILD diagnosis included both diagnostic and procedural features. The top-ranked features were the procedures "routine chest X-ray" and "CT scan of the chest", followed by the diagnoses "respiratory signs and symptoms", "abnormal findings without diagnosis", "other specified and unspecified nutritional and metabolic disorders", "other specified status", "gastroduodenal ulcer", and procedure "other diagnostic procedures on the lung and bronchus". These results suggest that increased respiratory imaging may play a significant role in the early identification of patients at risk for ILD.

Table 1. Definition of Subsets

Subset	Onset Windows	Observation Period	Case (Label = 1)	Control (Label = 0)
1	3 months	6 months	9 to 3 months before ILD diagnosis	15 to 9 months before ILD diagnosis
2	3 months	12 months	15 to 3 months before ILD diagnosis	27 to 15 months before ILD diagnosis
3	6 months	6 months	12 to 6 months before ILD diagnosis	18 to 12 months before ILD diagnosis
4	6 months	12 months	18 to 6 months before ILD diagnosis	30 to 18 months before ILD diagnosis
5	12 months	6 months	18 to 12 months before ILD diagnosis	24 to 18 months before ILD diagnosis
6	12 months	12 months	24 to 12 months before ILD diagnosis	36 to 24 months before ILD diagnosis

Table 2. Model Performance Across Subsets Defined by Onset Windows and Observation Periods Before ILD Diagnosis.

Subset	Onset Windows	Observation Period	AUC	Accuracy	Precision
2	3 months	12 months	0.601	0.551	0.556
4	6 months	12 months	0.587	0.556	0.574
6	12 months	12 months	0.582	0.537	0.564
1	3 months	6 months	0.564	0.569	0.516
3	6 months	6 months	0.541	0.534	0.513
5	12 months	6 months	0.525	0.515	0.516

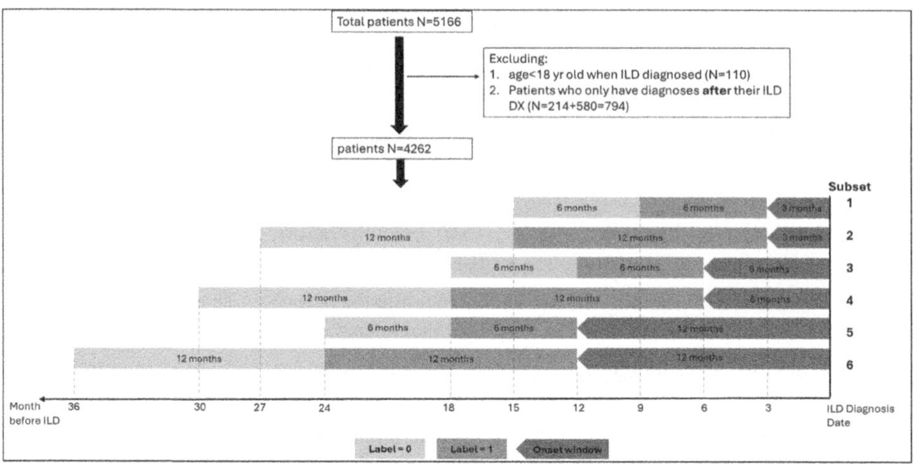

Fig. 1. Flowchart and schematic showing the timeline relative to initial ILD diagnosis

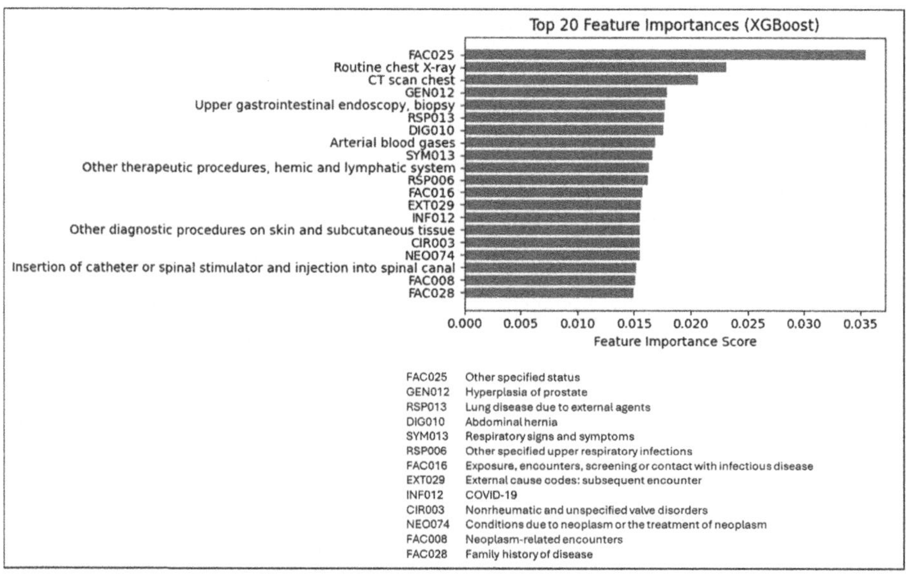

Fig. 2. Top Feature Importances from the XGBoost Model. Bar plot displaying the top 20 most important diagnostic and procedural features.

4 Discussion

In this study, we used a machine learning approach to detect early clinical patterns associated with ILD diagnosis. We compared different pre-diagnostic observation period, and the models showed moderate discriminative performance, with the highest AUC reaching 0.601 using a 12-month observation period and a 3-month assumed onset window. Important predictive features included respiratory imaging procedures such as routine chest X-rays and chest CT scans, as well as non-specific diagnoses such as respiratory symptoms, abnormal findings without a definitive diagnosis, and nutritional or metabolic disorders.

The findings support the potential of using pre-diagnostic features to detect early signs of ILD. However, there are still several limitations. First, model performance may be further improved by including additional clinical features such as laboratory test results and medication histories. Future study will include medication and lab test sources to enhance predictive sensitivity and performance.

Second, demographic characteristics such as sex, age at ILD diagnosis, and the Charlson Comorbidity Index (CCI) were not included as predictive features, since these variables remain constant within patients and do not vary across observation periods. However, given previous studies [2, 8, 9] suggesting that male, older age, and higher CCI scores are associated with increased risk of ILD-related mortality, stratifying the analysis by sex, age group, or CCI score may reveal subgroup-specific patterns and improve model interpretability.

Third, the model is trained and tested on the same institution's data, which may limit the generalizability. Cross-institutional validation using data from external databases would ensure the applicability of the model across different healthcare settings.

Finally, the use of fixed-length observation periods and ILD onset windows might not reflect real-world variability in disease progression. Disease trajectories vary significantly across individuals, with some patients experiencing slow progression over the years and some progress more quickly within months from symptom onset [10]. Future work may explore dynamic windowing strategies [11] to better reflect real-world clinical trajectories.

Our study comports with previous reports demonstrating the value of real-world data for predictive modeling of healthcare processes [12, 13]. Extraction of symptoms from clinical notes using natural language processing can potentially improve accuracy of predictive models [14, 15]. Large language models (LLM) and the transformer architecture can further facilitate fusion of structured and unstructured data elements from electronic health records [16, 17]. Accurate extraction of patient symptoms [18, 19], social determinants of health [20, 21], and ILD risk factors from clinical notes by LLM-based natural language processing pipelines may greatly enhance the early recognition of ILD [22, 23]. Careful consideration should be given to the development of unbiased models which can be scalable to different populations and healthcare scenarios [24, 25]. Validated high accuracy models can be embedded into electronic health records for clinical decision support of early ILD detection [26, 27].

5 Conclusion

Our findings suggest that machine learning models can use electronic health record data to identify early clinical patterns before ILD diagnosis. This approach may support future disease screening and further benefit earlier identification and intervention in ILD. Although the model achieved an AUC of 0.601 in the best-performing subset, this level of performance currently limits its clinical applicability. The relatively low discriminative ability increases the risk of both false positives and false negatives, which could lead to misdiagnosis or unnecessary follow-up if used in a clinical context. Nonetheless, these results provide a promising insight into our further research of disease early detection. Future studies will focus on addressing the identified limitations, improving model performance, and selecting features that more accurately reflect real-world disease progression.

References

1. Mikolasch, T.A., Garthwaite, H.S., Porter, J.C.: Update in diagnosis and management of interstitial lung disease. Clin. Med. **16**(6), s71–s78 (2016)
2. Jeganathan, N., Sathananthan, M.: The prevalence and burden of interstitial lung diseases in the USA. ERJ Open Res. **8**(1), 00630–02021 (2021)
3. GBoDC N.: Global burden of disease study 2019 (GBD 2019) reference life table. Institute for Health Metrics and Evaluation (IHME) (2021)
4. Petersen, I., Douglas, I., Whitaker, H.: Self controlled case series methods: an alternative to standard epidemiological study designs. BMJ. **354** (2016)
5. Grant-Orser, A., et al.: The diagnostic pathway for patients with interstitial lung disease: a mixed-methods study of patients and physicians. BMJ Open Respirat. Res. **11**(1) (2024)
6. AHRQ (Agency for Healthcare Research and Quality). Clinical Classifications Software Refined (CCSR) (2025). https://hcup-us.ahrq.gov/toolssoftware/ccsr/ccs_refined.jsp
7. AAPC Codify CPT Code Lookup Tool. https://www.aapc.com/resources/what-is-cpt?srsltid=AfmBOoqK3lNlEPaJyR57R8GTN6gC3wTreab1-fCwd94mUl0gErQ59gmG
8. Kawano-Dourado, L., Glassberg, M.K., Assayag, D., Borie, R., Johannson, K.A.: Sex and gender in interstitial lung diseases. Euro. Respirat. Rev. **30**(162) (2021)
9. Ye, Y., et al.: Prevalence, incidence, and survival analysis of interstitial lung diseases in Hong Kong: a 16-year population-based cohort study. The Lancet Regional Health–Western Pacific (2024)
10. Smith, V., Cutolo, M., Volkmann, E.: Defining interstitial lung disease progression: it is time to (Get Our) act together. Am. J. Respir. Crit. Care Med. **210**(11), 1293–1295 (2024)
11. de Swart, W.K., Loog, M., Krijthe, J.H.: A comparative study of methods for dynamic survival analysis. Front. Neurol. **18**(16), 1504535 (2025)
12. Paranjpe, I., Russak, A.J., De Freitas, J.K., et al.: Retrospective cohort study of clinical characteristics of 2199 hospitalised patients with COVID-19 in New York City. BMJ Open **10**(11), e040736 (2020)
13. Thyvalikakath, T.P., Duncan, W.D., Siddiqui, Z., et al.: Leveraging electronic dental record data for clinical research in the national dental PBRN practices. Appl. Clin. Inform. **11**(2), 305–314 (2020)
14. Shah-Mohammadi, F., Finkelstein, J.: Combining NLP and machine learning for differential diagnosis of COPD exacerbation using emergency room data. Stud. Health Technol. Inform. **29**(305), 525–528 (2023)
15. Cui, W., Shah-Mohammadi, F., Finkelstein, J.: Using electronic medical records and clinical notes to predict the outcome of opioid treatment program. Stud. Health Technol Inform. **29**(305), 568–571 (2023)
16. Shah-Mohammadi, F., Finkelstein, J.: Extraction of substance use information from clinical notes: generative pretrained transformer-based investigation. JMIR Med. Inform. **19**(12), e56243 (2024)
17. Shah-Mohammadi, F., Finkelstein, J.: Accuracy evaluation of GPT-assisted differential diagnosis in emergency department. Diagnostics (Basel) **14**(16), 1779 (2024)

18. Bai, Y., Cui, W., Finkelstein, J.: Utilizing open-source large language models to extract genitourinary symptoms from clinical notes. Stud. Health Technol. Inform. **328**, 16–20 (2025)
19. Reategui-Rivera, C.M., Finkelstein, J.: Evaluation of the performance of a large language model to extract signs and symptoms from clinical notes. Stud. Health Technol. Inform. **323**, 71–75 (2025)
20. Shah-Mohammadi, F., Finkelstein, J.: AI-powered social determinants of health extraction from patient records: A GPT-based investigation. In: 2024 IEEE First International Conference on Artificial Intelligence for Medicine, Health and Care (AIMHC), pp. 109–112. Laguna Hills, CA, USA (2024)
21. Shah-Mohammadi, F., Finkelstein, J.: Comparative analysis of rule-based and large language model-based approaches in addressing variability in clinical outcome reporting. In: 2024 IEEE 15th Annual Information Technology, Electronics and Mobile Communication Conference (IEMCON), pp. 039–045. Berkeley, CA, USA (2024)
22. Cui, W., Huo, X., Finkelstein, J.: Evaluating misalignment between emergency department and discharge diagnoses. Stud. Health Technol. Inform. **328**, 273–277 (2025)
23. Huo, X., Kohli, M., Finkelstein, J.: Using machine learning to predict survival in patients with metastatic castration-resistant prostate cancer. Stud. Health Technol. Inform. **323**, 169–173 (2025)
24. Smiley, A., Villarreal-Zegarra, D., Reategui-Rivera, C.M., et al.: Methodological and reporting quality of machine learning studies on cancer diagnosis, treatment, and prognosis. Front. Oncol. **14**(15), 1555247 (2025)
25. Smiley, A., Reategui-Rivera, C.M., Villarreal-Zegarra, D., et al.: Exploring artificial intelligence biases in predictive models for cancer diagnosis. Cancers (Basel) **17**(3), 407 (2025)
26. Finkelstein, J., Gabriel, A., Schmer, S., Truong, T.T., Dunn, A.: Identifying facilitators and barriers to implementation of AI-assisted clinical decision support in an electronic health record system. J. Med. Syst. **48**(1), 89 (2024)
27. Kawamoto, K., Finkelstein, J., Del Fiol, G.: Implementing machine learning in the electronic health record: checklist of essential considerations. Mayo Clin. Proc. **98**(3), 366–369 (2023)

Correlating Daily Activities and Life Satisfaction to Promote Health Behaviors of Older Adults in the Community

Susumu Shibusawa[1(✉)] and Toshiya Watanabe[2]

[1] Ibaraki University, Hitachi 316-8511, Ibaraki, Japan
susumu.shibusawa.ptr@vc.ibaraki.ac.jp
[2] Gunma College, National Institute of Technology, Maebashi 371-8530, Gunma, Japan
t.wat@gunma-ct.ac.jp

Abstract. Due to constraints on social behaviors, changes in lifestyle, the spread of information devices, and a decline in physical function due to aging, many elderly individuals have become accustomed to smaller movements and behaviors, leading to fewer opportunities for social interaction and an increase in isolated living. This paper aggregates survey results on the daily activities, life satisfaction, and use of information devices among older adults registered at community senior support centers, examining the relationship between daily activities and life satisfaction. The results indicate that older adults who use mobile phones for health management and computers for document creation and email exhibit higher life satisfaction scores than those using phones and computers for other functions. Women using mobile phones for online shopping, health management, and video/music functions reported higher life satisfaction scores than men. The results also reveal a strong positive correlation between the degree of interaction with acquaintances and life satisfaction scores, with a near-quadratic relationship between time spent on housework or personal activities and life satisfaction scores. Little correlation was detected between working hours and life satisfaction scores, with a tendency for life satisfaction scores to decrease as working hours increased.

Keywords: Support for older adults · activities of daily living · life satisfaction · social interaction · use of information devices

1 Introduction

There is a growing demand for assistive technologies to help maintain and improve the health of older adults, support their daily activities, enhance their quality of life, and reduce the burden on healthcare and caregiving professionals. Due to prolonged social activity restrictions, changes in lifestyle habits, the widespread use of information devices, and the decline in motor function associated with aging, many older adults experience a decrease in daily physical activity levels, leading to the habitualization of small-scale movements and behaviors. Additionally, a reduction in opportunities for social interaction has contributed to the increased isolation of some older adults.

A. Alsadoon et al. (Eds.): CSCE 2025, CCIS 2935, pp. 366–381, 2026.
https://doi.org/10.1007/978-3-032-22199-5_28

Social connections are crucial for the well-being of older adults. Those with smaller social networks and greater physical or functional impairments are more likely to experience social isolation and loneliness [1]. Proximal interactions, such as greeting and chatting with acquaintances and friends, as well as broader activities like exercise and outings, can help alleviate feelings of isolation [2]. During recent social activity restrictions in the wake of COVID-19, the number of steps and physical activity of elderly residents significantly declined [3].

There have been many proposals and studies on evaluation scales for the quality of life of older adults. Among them are the PGC Morale Scale, which assesses psychological and subjective well-being [4], the Life Satisfaction Index A (LSIA) [5], the Lubben Social Network Scale (LSNS) [6], and various analyses of well-being factors [7]. The PGC Morale Scale includes factors such as psychological stability, self-perception of aging, and sense of satisfaction. The Life Satisfaction Index A evaluates aspects like the joy of daily activities, the meaning of life, and a positive self-image. The Social Network Scale assesses interactions with family, relatives, and friends, as well as social isolation. National and international organizations have also conducted surveys on elderly individuals' health, social participation, and living environments [8], surveys on behavior and daily time use [9], assessments of physical activity levels [10], recommendations for physical activity [11], and reports on the utilization of information and communication technology [12, 13].

Health is a dynamic state that continuously changes based on biological, environmental, and lifestyle factors. Continuously acquired measurements can provide actionable guidelines for individuals to achieve their health goals [14]. Various studies and systems have been proposed in this vein, including a mobile health behavior intervention system using a multi-sensor system [15] and smart IoT devices for advanced patient care [16]. In addition, studies have been conducted on the development of chatbots that mitigate social isolation and cognitive decline in patients with mild cognitive impairment [17], as well as investigations of older adults who engage in conversational interactions and health information seeking via chatbots [18]. Furthermore, studies have explored the identification of patients with Parkinson's disease based on phoneme features collected via smartphones [19], surveys of older adults' subjective well-being and health status using mobile devices [20, 21], and the detection of arrhythmias using smartwatches [22].

In this study, we conducted a survey on the daily life activities, life satisfaction, and use of information devices among older adults from the perspective of promoting healthy behaviors and supporting a vibrant lifestyle among community-dwelling older adults. We compiled and analyzed the survey results from older adults registered at community support centers and examined the relationship between their daily activities and life satisfaction.

The survey results indicate that older adults who use mobile phones for health management and computers for document creation and email tend to have higher life satisfaction scores than those using phones and computers for other functions. Women who use online shopping, health management, and video/music functions show higher life satisfaction scores compared to men. The results also reveal a strong positive correlation between the degree of interaction with acquaintances and life satisfaction scores among older adults. The relationship between time spent on housework or personal activities and life satisfaction scores follows a pattern close to a quadratic polynomial approximation. Little correlation was detected between working hours and life satisfaction scores, with a tendency for life satisfaction scores to decrease as working hours increased.

In Sect. 2 of this paper, we provide an overview of the survey on daily living activities. Section 3 presents the aggregated results of the survey, and Sect. 4 discusses the relationship between daily activities and life satisfaction. We conclude in Sect. 5 by summarizing our findings and outlining future challenges.

2 Survey on Daily Living Activities

2.1 Overview of Survey

We conducted a survey to support the health and vibrancy of older adults in the community, focusing on daily activities, life satisfaction, and the use of information devices. The survey includes the following content:

(1) Explanation of the survey content
(2) Confirmation of participants' consent
(3) Participants' basic information
(4) Daily living activity details over two days
(5) Usage status of information devices
(6) Subjective life satisfaction
(7) Social activities

The procedures and background of the survey are shown in Table 1. Table 2 provides an overview of the basic information, daily living activities, social activities, and the use of information devices that were surveyed.

Table 1. Survey procedures and background.

Period	January to February 2023
Location	Community senior support center
Participants	Individuals aged approximately 65 and above registered at the facility
Selection of participants	Voluntary self-nomination
Survey method	Questionnaire response on paper
Background	The elderly support organization surveyed is a public interest incorporated association that provides employment opportunities for retirees and older adults, with the aim of promoting their well-being and fostering a vibrant local community. The city where this organization is located faces the Pacific Ocean, approximately 110 km northeast of central Tokyo, and is a regional city known for its active industry and tourism

Table 2. Survey overview.

Survey item	Content
Basic information	Age, gender, cohabitation status
Daily living activity time	Essential activities, housework, work, physical activities, personal activities
Life satisfaction	Subjective life satisfaction, subjective physical and mental state, comfortable life status
Social activities	Social interaction with acquaintances, community activities, media access
Use of information devices	Usage status, types of devices used, functions/services, future usability

2.2 Basic Information

Out of a total of 60 responses in this survey, 59 were valid. The gender distribution of respondents was 65% male, 32% female, and 3% no response. The average age of respondents was 74.4 years, with males averaging 75.6 years and females averaging 71.8 years. Figure 1 illustrates the overall age distribution. Regarding living arrangements, 83% lived with family, 2% lived with non-family members, 12% lived alone, and 3% did not respond.

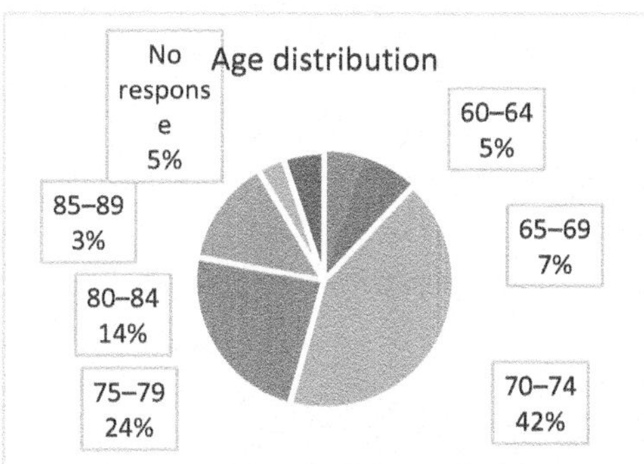

Fig. 1. Age distribution of respondents (overall).

2.3 Daily Activity Time

A survey was conducted on daily activity time over two days. Figure 2 shows the average daily activity time for the first day as reported by respondents, where (a) presents the average daily activity time for all respondents and by gender, and (b) illustrates the ratio of activity time for all respondents. Some of the notable activities observed in this survey are as follows.

The average time spent on housework was 1 h and 51 min for men and 3 h and 41 min for women. Women's housework time was approximately twice that of men, showing a significant gender difference. According to a survey by the Ministry of Internal Affairs and Communications (MIC) [9], the housework time for elderly individuals aged 65 and over was 1 h and 13 min for men and 3 h and 47 min for women, with women spending about three times as much time on housework as men.

The average time spent on work was 2 h and 21 min for men and 2 h and 43 min for women, showing little difference. According to a survey by MIC [9], elderly men worked for an average of 1 h and 54 min, while women worked for 49 min, with men spending approximately twice as much time working as women. In this survey, since the respondents were older adults registered at the community senior support center, both men and women reported longer working hours compared to the government survey, clearly reflecting this characteristic.

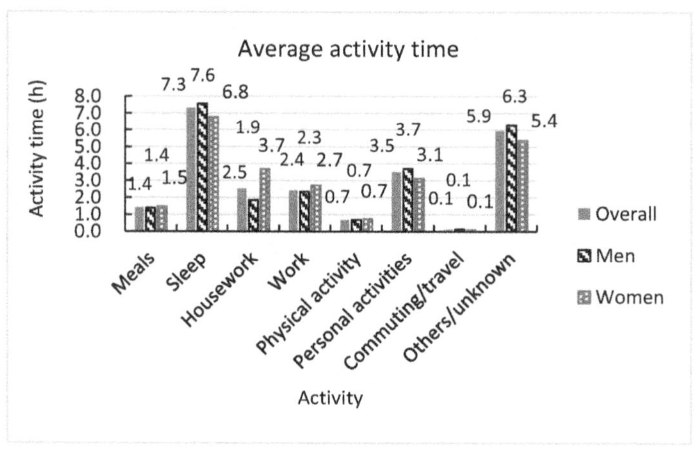

(a) Average daily activity time

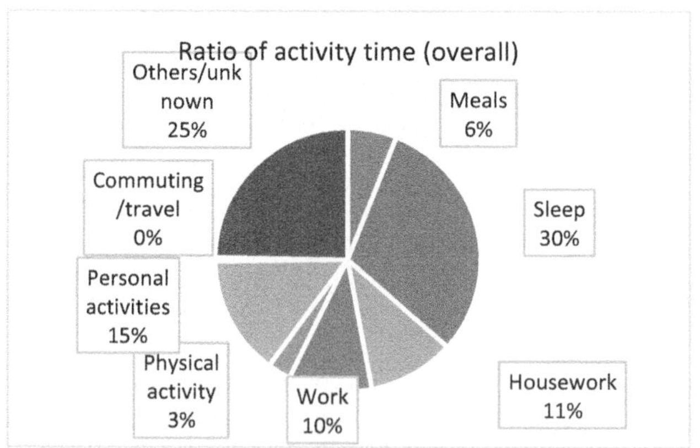

(b) Ratio of activity time (overall)

Fig. 2. Activity time.

2.4 Use of Information Devices

A total of 95% of respondents reported using information devices such as personal computers, mobile phones/smartphones, smartwatches, AI speakers, gaming consoles, while 5% did not use them. For simplicity, we refer here to personal computers as "PCs," and mobile phones and smartphones collectively as "mobile phones" or simply "mobiles." The usage ratio of personal computers and mobile phones was as follows: 43% used only mobile phones, 2% used only personal computers, and 55% used both. Regarding questions about the basic functions of mobile phones, responses and non-responses were both 50%. Among those who provided answers about the basic software of their mobile phones and smartphones, 69% used only Android, 23% used only iOS, and 8% used both.

2.5 Life Satisfaction and Social Activities

The questions on subjective satisfaction with daily life were primarily based on the PGC Morale Scale [4] and the Life Satisfaction Index A [5], while the questions about acquaintance interactions and community activities were based on the Social Network Scale [6], with some questions being independently created. Questions regarding life activities and life satisfaction are shown in Table A of the appendix. For each question, three response options were provided: "Yes," "No," and "Neither/Don't know," with "Yes" assigned a score of 1 point. In this survey, most responses were either "Yes" or "No." The findings related to life satisfaction, degree of interaction with acquaintances, and community activity level are as follows.

Life Satisfaction Score. The total score from seven questions related to life satisfaction was calculated as the "Life Satisfaction Score." The distribution of responses for life satisfaction is shown in Fig. 3. In this survey, there were no responses with the highest satisfaction score of 7, while 7% of respondents reported a score of 6, and 10% reported a score of 0, indicating no satisfaction.

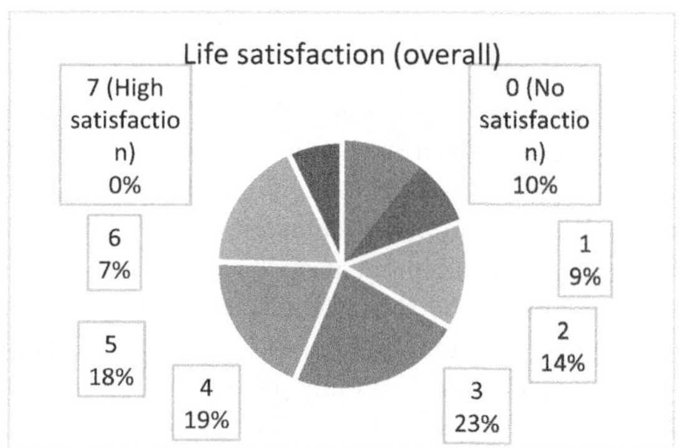

Fig. 3. Life satisfaction score ratio (overall).

Degree of Interaction with Acquaintances. The total score from five questions related to interactions with friends and acquaintances was used to evaluate the "Degree of interaction with acquaintances." The distribution of responses for this metric is shown in Fig. 4. In this survey, 21% of respondents had the highest interaction score of 5, while 7% had a score of 0, indicating no interaction.

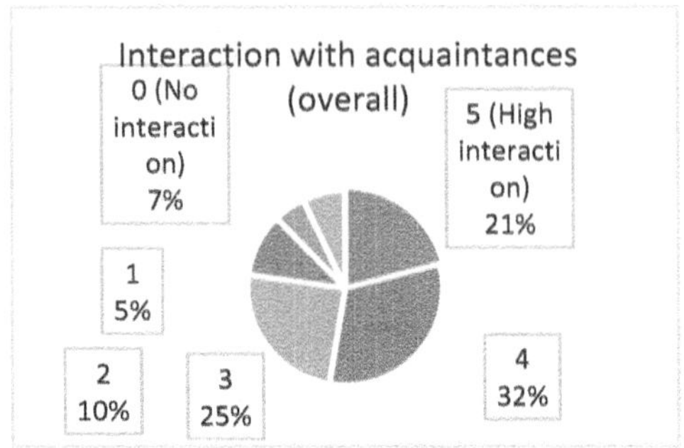

Fig. 4. Ratio of interaction with acquaintances (overall).

Community Activity Level. Community engagement was assessed through three questions, with the total score aggregated as the "Community activity level." In this survey, 16% of respondents selected the highest activity level (score 3), 5% selected a score of 2, 12% selected a score of 1, and 67% reported no participation (score 0).

3 Use of Information Devices and Daily Activities

We examined the relationships between the use of information devices, daily activities, and life satisfaction scores. In the results of this survey, the number of valid responses for the two simultaneous items was 54–57 in total, comprising 34–37 for men, 18 for women, and 2 with no gender response.

Figure 5 illustrates the relationship between the types of information devices used and the amount of physical activity time, where the numbers in parentheses indicate the number of valid responses for the simultaneous occurrence of information device use and physical activity. Among information devices with a relatively large number of valid responses, the physical activity time was 35 min for PC users, 39 min for mobile phone users, 39 min for all information device users, and 43 min for all valid responses. Among mobile phone users, Android phone users had a physical activity time of 47 min, while iPhone users had 44 min. The reason the total number of Android and iPhone users differs significantly from the total number of mobile phone users is that nearly half of the respondents did not specify their phone type.

In this survey, the number of valid responses for smartwatch users, AI speaker users, and non-users of information devices was low. Among them, the physical activity time of smartwatch users was shortest, indicating that smartwatches were rarely used for physical activity. Additionally, the physical activity time of non-users of information devices was significantly higher than that of information device users.

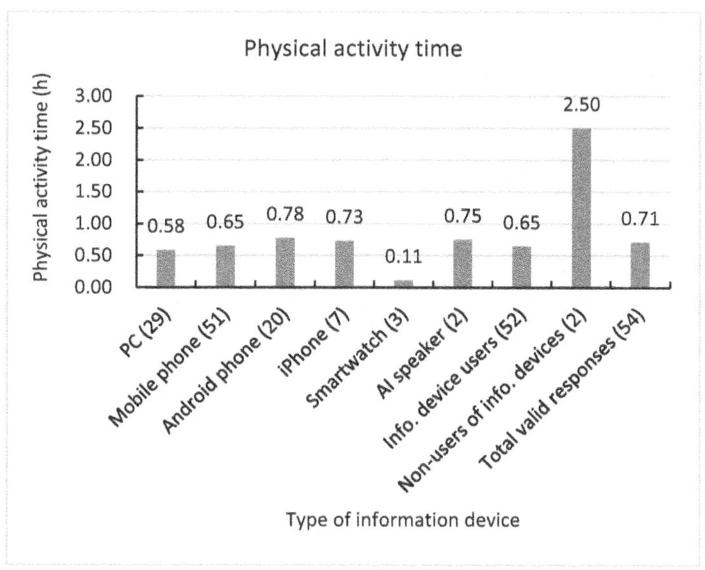

Fig. 5. Use of information devices and physical activity time.

Figure 6 illustrates the relationship between the main functions of mobile phones and PCs and life satisfaction scores, where (a) shows both mobile phones and PCs and (b) shows mobile phones only. The vertical bars represent standard errors. The numbers in parentheses following each function in (b) indicate the total number of valid responses, including both men and women. In (a), the survey results show that the life satisfaction scores were high for older adults who used PCs for document creation (5.33 out of 7) and email (3.86), and who used mobile phones for health management (3.67)—all of which were higher than the scores for other functions. In (b), women who used mobile phone functions for health management, video/music functions, and online shopping had life satisfaction scores of 5.50, 4.00, and 3.75, respectively, all of which were higher than those of men. It should be noted that for functions with a small number of valid responses, life satisfaction scores tended to be more dispersed, resulting in larger standard errors.

In this survey, there was a slight tendency for life satisfaction scores to decrease as the number of mobile phone functions used increased. This indicates that using many functions does not necessarily lead to greater life satisfaction.

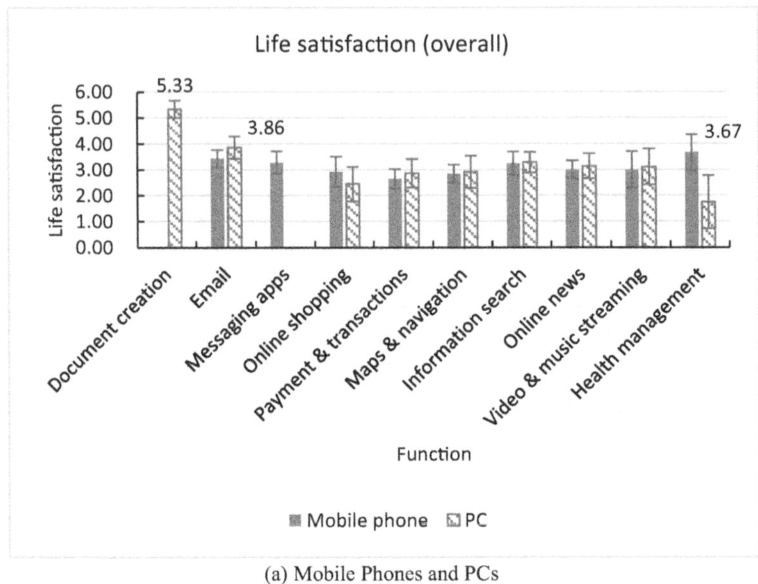

(a) Mobile Phones and PCs

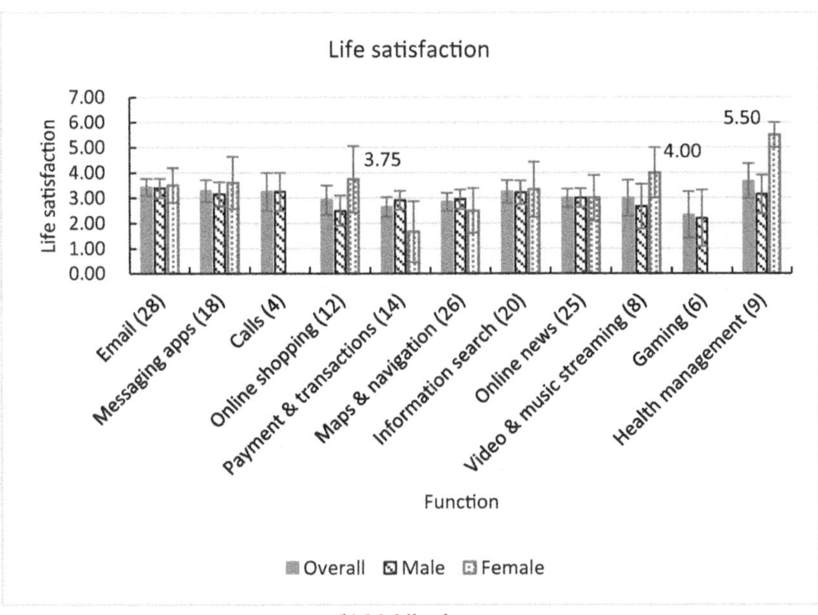

(b) Mobile phones

Fig. 6. Relationship between life satisfaction scores and (a) functions of mobile phones and PCs and (b) functions of mobile phones only.

4 Daily Activities and Life Satisfaction

4.1 Relationship Between Daily Living Activities and Life Satisfaction

For two variables, x and y, consisting of n pairs of values $\{(x_i, y_i)|i = 1, 2, \ldots, n\}$, a linear correlation represents a relationship in which a linear approximation holds. In this study, we define the strength of the linear correlation as follows:

[Definition 1] The linear correlation coefficient $r(x, y)$ and the strength of correlation between two variables x and y are defined as shown in Table 3.

Table 3. Linear correlation coefficient and correlation strength.

Absolute value of correlation coefficient $\lvert r(x, y)\rvert$	Correlation strength
$0.8 \leq \lvert r\rvert \leq 1$	Strong
$0.5 \leq \lvert r\rvert < 0.8$	Moderate
$0.3 \leq \lvert r\rvert < 0.5$	Weak
$0 \leq \lvert r\rvert < 0.3$	Little to no correlation

The coefficient of determination, $R^2 (0 \leq R^2 \leq 1)$, represents the magnitude of the deviation between measured and predicted values. The coefficient of determination for a linear correlation is the square of the correlation coefficient.

When the time spent on daily activities or the level of daily activities is averaged for each level of life satisfaction, scatter plots and approximation curves can be obtained. Figure 7 presents scatter plots created using Microsoft Excel to illustrate the relationships between housework time and life satisfaction, and between interaction with acquaintances and life satisfaction. Each graph includes an approximation curve, its corresponding equation, and the coefficient of determination. Vertical bars represent the standard errors. In all cases, when the values of daily activities are more dispersed for life satisfaction scores with a small number of valid responses, the standard errors become larger.

The following relationships can be observed for each activity:

Housework and Life Satisfaction. Overall, there is a moderate linear correlation between housework time and life satisfaction scores. Among men, a weak linear correlation is observed, while for women, there is almost no linear correlation. In quadratic polynomial approximation, the coefficient of determination is high for the overall group and for women but low for men. This indicates that for the overall group and women, the relationship between housework time and life satisfaction scores is better approximated by a quadratic polynomial rather than a linear model, whereas for men, neither linear nor quadratic approximation shows a significant correlation.

Work and Life Satisfaction. For the overall older adults as well as both men and women, there is almost no correlation between working hours and life satisfaction scores. The survey results show that the linear correlation coefficient between working hours and life satisfaction scores is a small negative value, indicating a tendency for life satisfaction scores to decrease as working hours increase.

Physical Activity and Life Satisfaction. There is a weak linear correlation between physical activity time and life satisfaction scores for the overall group and for women, whereas for men, almost no linear correlation is observed. In quadratic polynomial approximation, both the overall group and both genders have a small negative quadratic coefficient, indicating a tendency for older adults with moderate life satisfaction scores to have longer physical activity time. However, in this study, no significant linear or quadratic relationship between physical activity time and life satisfaction scores was observed.

Personal Activities and Life Satisfaction. Among women, a moderate linear correlation is observed between personal activity time and life satisfaction scores, whereas for the overall group and men, the linear correlation is weak. The coefficient of determination for quadratic polynomial approximation is relatively high for the overall group as well as both genders. Based on the obtained linear correlation coefficient and the coefficient of determination for the quadratic approximation, the relationship between personal activity time and life satisfaction scores is better approximated by a quadratic model rather than a linear one. In all cases (overall, men, and women), some older adults who spend more time on personal activities report higher life satisfaction scores, while others who spend more time on personal activities report lower life satisfaction scores.

Social Interaction with Acquaintances and Life Satisfaction. There is a strong positive linear correlation between the degree of social interaction with acquaintances and life satisfaction for both the overall group and women, while for men, the correlation is moderate. Regardless of gender, older adults with higher life satisfaction tend to have a higher degree of social interaction with acquaintances, indicating that interacting with friends and acquaintances is a key factor in enhancing life satisfaction.

Community Activities and Life Satisfaction. For the overall group and women, there is a moderate linear correlation between participation level in community activities and life satisfaction scores. However, for men, a weak negative linear correlation is observed. Men with higher life satisfaction scores tend to have lower participation level in community activities, indicating that community activities do not necessarily contribute to their sense of life satisfaction.

Social Interaction and Community Activities. For the overall group, as well as for both men and women, a moderately strong linear correlation is observed between the degree of social interaction with acquaintances and participation level in community activities. Groups with the lower degree of social interaction tend to have lower participation level in community activities. Among women, those who engage more actively in community activities also tend to have a higher degree of social interaction with acquaintances.

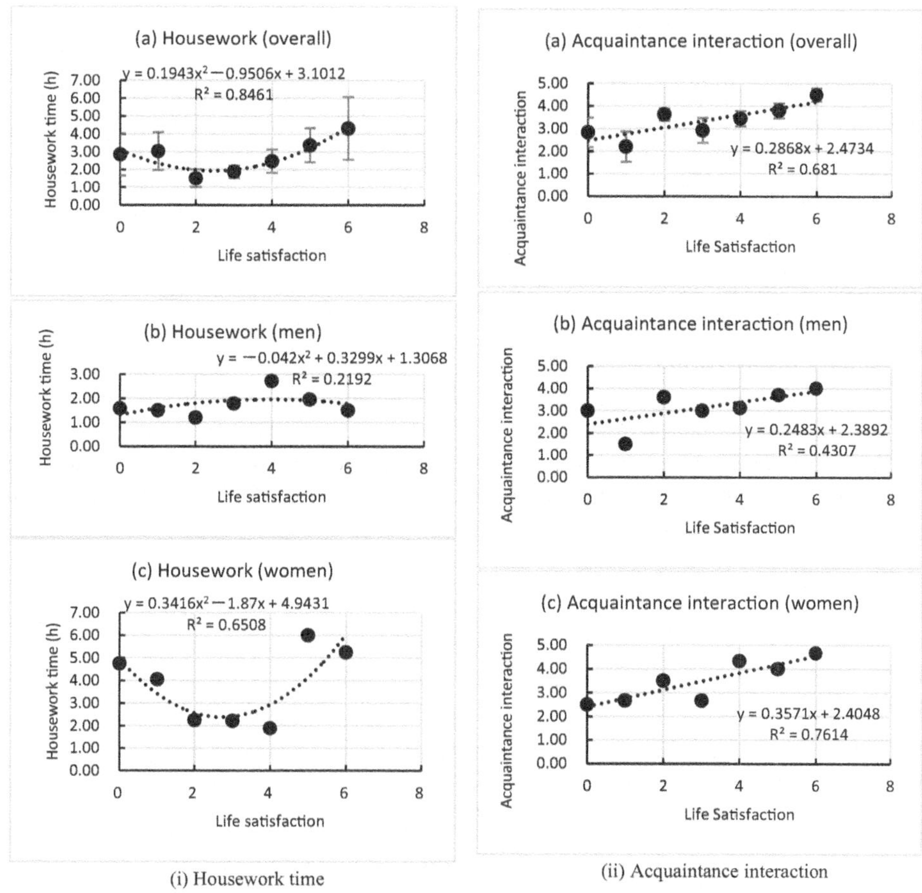

Fig. 7. Scatter plots of daily activities and life satisfaction for (i) housework time and (ii) social interaction with acquaintances.

4.2 Consideration of the Correlation Between Daily Activities and Life Satisfaction

We define the fit level of two events for linear approximation and quadratic polynomial approximation as follows.

[Definition 2] The correlation coefficient of linear approximation and the coefficient of determination of quadratic polynomial approximation for two variables are converted into integers as shown in Table 4, and this is referred to as the fit level of approximation.

Table 4. Fit levels of two approximations.

Fit level	Linear approximation		Determination coefficient R^2 in quadratic approximation
	Correlation coefficient r	Correlation strength	
3 (High)	$0.8 \leq \|r\| \leq 1$	Strong	$0.64 \leq R^2 \leq 1$
2 (Medium)	$0.5 \leq \|r\| < 0.8$	Moderate	$0.25 \leq R^2 < 0.64$
1 (Low)	$0.3 \leq \|r\| < 0.5$	Weak	$0.09 \leq R^2 < 0.25$
0 (None)	$0 \leq \|r\| < 0.3$	Almost none	$0 \leq R^2 < 0.09$

Figure 8 illustrates the fit levels between each activity and life satisfaction scores for the older adults surveyed. As shown, there is a strong positive linear correlation between the degree of social interaction and life satisfaction scores. The relationship between housework or personal activity time and life satisfaction scores is better approximated by a quadratic polynomial rather than a linear approximation. There is little to no correlation between working hours and life satisfaction scores.

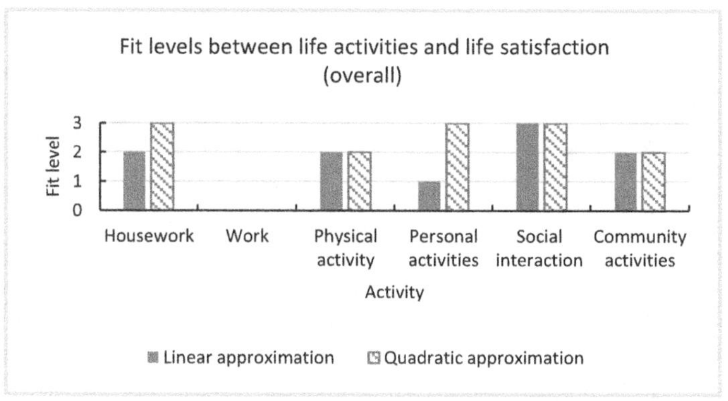

Fig. 8. Fit levels between life activities and life satisfaction.

5 Conclusion and Future Challenges

In this paper, we conducted a survey on the daily life activities, subjective life satisfaction, and use of information devices among older adults registered at a community support center. We compiled the results and analyzed the relationship between daily activities and life satisfaction scores. The findings revealed that older adults who used mobile phones for health management and computers for document creation and email had higher life satisfaction scores compared to those using computers and PCs other functions. Women who utilized health management, video/music functions, and online shopping reported higher life satisfaction scores than men.

There was a strong positive linear correlation between the degree of social interactions with acquaintances and life satisfaction scores among older adults, indicating that those with higher life satisfaction scores had more frequent interactions with acquaintances. Regardless of gender, older adults with high life satisfaction scores had at least a moderate level of social interactions, indicating that engaging with friends and acquaintances is an effective way to enhance life satisfaction. Regarding the relationship between time spent on housework or personal activities and life satisfaction scores, a quadratic approximation provided a good fit, indicating that some older adults were not satisfied with their lives despite spending significant time on housework or personal activities. No linear correlation was detected between working hours and life satisfaction scores; instead, there was a tendency for life satisfaction scores to decline as working hours increased.

Given the strong linear correlation between the degree of social interactions with acquaintances and life satisfaction scores, it will be useful to develop systems that encourage older adults to engage with friends and acquaintances. Since there is a moderately strong linear correlation between the degree of social interactions and community activity level, and community activities provide opportunities to increase interactions with acquaintances, it is also worthwhile to explore mechanisms that encourage older adults to participate in community activities. Furthermore, as some older adults remain dissatisfied with their lives despite spending time on housework or work, it is important to carefully examine the nature of these activities and develop systems that help individuals derive greater satisfaction from them. It is also necessary to have a system that supports activities older adults find enjoyable, potentially by incorporating rewards or game-like elements into housework and work. Additionally, improving research methods to better understand the circumstances of older adults with low life satisfaction will be essential in enhancing their overall quality of life.

Our findings demonstrate that it is vital to continue investigating the use of information devices among older adults. In this survey, the number of valid responses regarding smartwatches and AI speakers was low, indicating that sensor systems are not yet fully utilized in the daily activities of older adults. The next research step is to use a compact mobile sensor system capable of initiating and responding to voice interactions with friends and acquaintances to examine changes in older adults' daily activities, health behaviors, and life satisfaction. As sensor systems are a valuable tool for promoting older adults' activities, further exploration of their usage methods should be conducted.

Acknowledgments. We sincerely appreciate the cooperation of the Silver Human Resource Center in Hitachinaka City, Japan, and its members in participating in this survey. This research was partially supported by Grants-in-Aid for Scientific Research (KAKENHI) 17K00746 and 23K01780 and was conducted in accordance with the ethical guidelines of Ibaraki University.

Appendix

Table A. Questions on daily activities and life satisfaction.

(1) Life satisfaction

No.	Question
1	Are you satisfied with your current life?
2	Do you feel that you have more freedom now than in the past?
3	Do you think you are living the way you want to live?
4	Do you feel happier now compared to when you were younger?
5	Do you find it comfortable that your movements and actions have slowed down?
6	Do you think having many daily activities positively impacts you?
7	Do you feel that you have become less concerned with small details recently?

(2) Social interaction

No.	Question
8	Do you have direct conversations with your neighbors?
9	Do you talk to your neighbors over the phone?
10	Do you have direct conversations with acquaintances or friends?
11	Do you talk to acquaintances or friends over the phone?
12	Do you communicate with acquaintances or friends via email or messaging apps?

(3) Community activities

No.	Question
13	Are you registered with a local senior club, community center, or general activity group?
14	Do you participate in activities at a local senior club, or general activity group at least once a month?
15	If you participate in local activities, do you have direct conversations with other members?

References

1. Czaja, S.J., Moxley, J.H., Rogers, W.A.: Social support, isolation, loneliness, and health among older adults in the PRISM randomized controlled trial. Front. Psychol. **12**(728658) (2021)
2. Ito, H., Goto, H., et al.: A study on measures to alleviate loneliness and improve subjective health perception of unemployed elderly residents in aging condominium complexes. J. Technol. Des. Architect. Inst. Japan **27**(66), 961–966 (2021)
3. Uchida, K., Sawa, R., Encho, H., Ono, R.: Changes in physical activity levels of community-dwelling Japanese elderly before and after the first state of emergency declaration: an objective study using accelerometers. Res. Exercise Epidemiol. **24**(1), 7–18 (2022)
4. Lawton, M.P.: The philadelphia geriatric center morale scale: a revision. J. Gerontol. **30**(1), 85–89 (1975)
5. Neugarten, B.L., Havighurst, R.J., Tobin, S.S.: The measurement of life satisfaction. J. Gerontol. **16**(2), 134–143 (1961)
6. Lubben, J.E.: Assessing social networks among elderly populations. Family Commun. Health: J. Health Promot. Maintenan. **11**(3), 42–52 (1988)
7. Hackert, M.Q.N., van Exel, J., et al.: Content validation of the well-being of older people measure (WOOP). Health Qual. Life Outcomes **19**(200) (2021)
8. Cabinet Office, Japan, White Paper on Aging Society. https://www8.cao.go.jp/kourei/whitepaper/index-w.html. Accessed 17 Nov 2025

9. Statistics Bureau, Ministry of Internal Affairs and Communications, Japan, Survey on Time Use and Leisure Activities 2021. https://www.stat.go.jp/data/shakai/2021/index.htm. Accessed 17 Nov 2025
10. World Health Organization, Global physical activity questionnaire (GPAQ). https://www.who.int/publications/m/item/global-physical-activity-questionnaire. Accessed 17 Nov 2025
11. Ministry of Health, Labour and Welfare, Japan, Physical Activity and Exercise Guidelines for Health Promotion 2023. https://www.mhlw.go.jp/stf/seisakunitsuite/bunya/kenkou_iryou/kenkou/undou/index.html. Accessed 17 Nov 2025
12. Cabinet Office, Japan, Public Opinion Survey on the Use of Information and Communication Devices. https://survey.gov-online.go.jp/hutai/r05/r05-it_kiki/. Accessed 17 Nov 2025
13. Ministry of Internal Affairs and Communications, Japan, White Paper on Information and Communications. https://www.soumu.go.jp/johotsusintokei/whitepaper. Accessed 17 Nov 2025
14. Nag, N., Jain, R.: A navigational approach to health: actionable guidance for improved quality of life. IEEE Comput. **52**(4), 12–20 (2019)
15. Baglione, A.N., Gong, J., et al.: Leveraging mobile sensing to understand and develop intervention strategies to improve medication adherence. IEEE Pervasive Comput. **19**(3), 24–36 (2020)
16. DeFranco, J.F., Hutchinson, M.: Understanding smart medical devices. CIEEE Comput. **54**(5), 76–80 (2021)
17. Hong, J., Zheng, W. et al.: A-CONECT: Designing AI-based conversational chatbot for early dementia intervention. ICLR 2024 Workshop on Large Language Models for Agents. https://llmagents.github.io/. Accessed 17 Nov 2025
18. Enam, M.D.A., Murmu, C., Dixon, E.: "Artificial intelligence – carrying us into the future": a study of older adults' perceptions of LLM-based chatbots. Int. J. Human-Comput. Interact. **41**(21), 13747–13770 (2025)
19. Motin, M.A., Pah, N.D., Raghav, S., Kumar, D.K.: Parkinson's disease detection using smartphone recorded phonemes in real world conditions. IEEE Access **10**(97600–97609) (2022)
20. Park, S., Constantinides, M., et al.: WellBeat: a framework for tracking daily well-being using smartwatches. IEEE Internet Comput. **24**(5), 10–17 (2020)
21. Ankyu, E., Sanai, S., Harada, E.: Elderly users' self-directed utilization of wearable health information devices: an examination from two evaluation dimensions. Trans. Hum. Interface Soc. **25**(1), 11–28 (2023)
22. Zahedivash, A., Chubb, H., Giacone, H., et al.: Utility of smart watches for identifying arrhythmias in children. Commun. Med. **3**(167) (2023)

Benchmarking Classic Machine Learning Models for Diabetes Diagnosis: A Performance Evaluation Framework Using Confusion Matrices and ROC Analysis

Roseline Oluwaseun Ogundokun[1,2,3](✉), Pius Adewale Owolawi[1], and Etienne A. van Wyk[1]

[1] Department of Computer Systems Engineering, Faculty of Information and Communication Technology, Tshwane University of Technology, Pretoria, South Africa
ogundokunRO@tut.ac.za

[2] Department of Computer Science, Faculty of Computing and Digital Technologies, Redeemer's University Ede, Owode-Ede, Osun State, Nigeria

[3] Department of Multimedia Engineering, Kaunas University of Technology, Kaunas, Lithuania

Abstract. Early diagnosis of diabetes is crucial to prevent severe complications. This study presents a comparative evaluation of five classic machine learning models for diabetes prediction Logistic Regression, Decision Tree, K-Nearest Neighbors (KNN), Naïve Bayes, and Support Vector Machine (SVM) using a standardized framework. A publicly available diabetes dataset of clinical measurements was used, with rigorous preprocessing (handling missing values and feature standardization) to ensure fair comparisons. Each model was trained and tested under identical conditions, and performance was assessed using Accuracy, Precision, Recall, F1-score, and the Area Under the ROC Curve (AUC). The results, illustrated via confusion matrices and ROC curves, show that SVM and Logistic Regression achieved the highest overall accuracy and AUC, closely followed by Naïve Bayes. At the same time, Decision Tree and KNN performed comparatively lower. Each model exhibited distinct strengths: for instance, SVM excelled in balanced accuracy, and Logistic Regression provided interpretability. This benchmarking framework highlights the trade-offs between classic algorithms in diagnosing diabetes, providing baseline performance metrics for medical machine learning (ML) applications. Findings suggest that even simple classifiers can achieve reasonable predictive performance (~75–80% accuracy) in this medical diagnosis task, although there remains room for improvement through more complex models or ensemble techniques.

Keywords: Diabetes · Machine learning · Ensemble learning · Early diagnosis · Diabetes mellitus

A. Alsadoon et al. (Eds.): CSCE 2025, CCIS 2935, pp. 382–391, 2026.
https://doi.org/10.1007/978-3-032-22199-5_29

1 Introduction

Diabetes mellitus is a chronic disease that affects hundreds of millions of individuals worldwide, and its prevalence is also increasing. The International Diabetes Federation estimates that nearly 11.1% of the population aged 20–79 years worldwide has diabetes, but over 40% of them are unaware of their condition [1, 2]. Early diagnosis and treatment are essential as they can delay or prevent long-term diabetes complications [1]. However, standard diagnostic methods rely on clinical tests that are not invariably available or performed in a timely fashion for all individuals in high-risk groups. This limitation has motivated researchers to search for computational methods for inferring diabetes risk from routine health data. Machine learning (ML) has emerged as a powerful driver of medical diagnostics, enabling the discovery of sophisticated patterns within clinical data to aid in disease detection. Recent reviews highlight that machine learning (ML) techniques are utilized to support the early diagnosis of various diseases, thereby improving the speed and accuracy of diagnosis [3–5]. In diabetes, multi-machine learning (ML) models have been utilized to predict disease onset based on patient attributes such as blood glucose levels, body mass index (BMI), and heredity. For instance, experiments have utilized algorithms like SVM, decision trees, and KNN to predict whether patients were diabetic or non-diabetic, usually with promising accuracy rates (around 75–80%) in preliminary trials [6]. Prediction systems using machine learning (ML) could assist health professionals in identifying individuals at high risk for further examination or preventive treatment. Despite the excitement surrounding advanced techniques, including deep learning and ensemble methods, it remains crucial to benchmark classical machine learning algorithms for tasks such as diabetes diagnosis. These simpler algorithms Logistic Regression, Decision Trees, KNN, Naïve Bayes, SVM are well-understood, faster to train, and more interpretable, making them attractive for deployment in clinical settings where transparency is valued. The literature presents mixed findings on which algorithm performs best for diabetes prediction. In some cases, an SVM classifier achieved an accuracy of up to 85% on a diabetes dataset [7], whereas other studies found that logistic regression reached approximately 80% [7]. Decision tree-based models have also shown strong results when optimally tuned, with one report of a tree classifier attaining an AUC of 0.98 on the Pima Indians Diabetes dataset [7]. These variations suggest that no single model is uniformly superior; performance can depend on data characteristics and preprocessing strategies, aligning with the "no free lunch" principle in machine learning. Therefore, a systematic side-by-side evaluation under a consistent framework is needed to understand the comparative strengths and weaknesses of each method. This paper addresses this need by benchmarking five classic algorithms on the same diabetes dataset, using consistent preprocessing and evaluation metrics, and analysing their performance via confusion matrices and ROC curves. The goal is to establish baseline performance measures for diabetes diagnosis and glean insights that can guide future improvements.

Despite the growing body of research applying machine learning to diabetes diagnosis, many existing studies either focus on a narrow selection of models, lack consistent evaluation criteria, or do not provide a comprehensive visualization of performance metrics such as confusion matrices and ROC curves. Additionally, a reproducible, standardized benchmarking framework that compares conventional machine learning approaches on a popularly used dataset with homogeneous preprocessing and testing conditions is needed. These limitations render it impossible to draw valid conclusions about the model's efficacy and appropriateness in the clinical setting. In order to address this knowledge gap, the present research proposes a robust evaluation framework that comparatively evaluates five widely used classic machine learning classifiers Logistic Regression, Decision Tree, K-Nearest Neighbors, Naïve Bayes, and Support Vector Machine on a benchmark diabetes dataset. In addition to quantitative analysis supplemented with visualization interpretability tools such as confusion matrices and ROC curves, the present research aims to provide actionable insights into diagnostic performance, error patterns, and discrimination capability of each model. The findings are expected to guide both academic researchers and clinical practitioners in selecting and deploying interpretable and practical models for the early detection of diabetes.

2 Materials and Methods

2.1 Dataset Description

The experiments utilize the well-known Pima Indians Diabetes dataset, initially collected by the National Institute of Diabetes and Digestive and Kidney Diseases and made available through the UCI Machine Learning Repository (also accessible via Kaggle). This dataset comprises medical information for 768 female patients of Pima Indian heritage, all of whom are at least 21 years old. Each instance in the dataset is characterized by a set of diagnostic measurements and a binary outcome indicating the presence of diabetes. The Outcome variable is a binary class label (0 = non-diabetic, 1 = diabetic) used as the target for prediction. In this dataset, 268 out of 768 patients (about 35%) are labelled as diabetic, while the remaining 500 (65%) are non-diabetic. This class distribution indicates a moderate class imbalance, with more negatives than positives, which is considered during model evaluation.

2.2 Data Preprocessing

Before modelling, careful preprocessing was performed to ensure data quality and to make the features suitable for the algorithms. The dataset was examined for missing or anomalous values. Notably, specific features, such as blood pressure, skin thickness, and insulin, contain zero values, which are physically implausible (e.g., a blood pressure of 0) and likely indicate missing data. Such entries were addressed by treating zeros as missing and then either imputing reasonable values or excluding those records, as suggested by previous analyses. All feature variables were then standardized (rescaled to zero mean and unit variance) to ensure that they are on a comparable scale. Standardization is vital for distance-based methods like KNN and for SVM, as it prevents features with larger numeric ranges (e.g., glucose levels) from dominating those with smaller ranges [8]. The outcome labels were encoded as 0 and 1, as required for binary classification. Additionally, the dataset was split into training and testing subsets to enable unbiased evaluation of each model. A typical split of 80% training and 20% testing was used (stratified to maintain the class proportion in both sets), ensuring that model performance metrics are computed on data not seen during training. This train-test split approach, combined with cross-validation on the training set for model tuning, if necessary, provides a robust estimate of how each model might perform on new patient data in practice. To address the moderate class imbalance, we employed a stratified train-test split to preserve class distribution during partitioning, ensuring balanced representation of diabetic and non-diabetic cases in both training and testing sets.

2.3 Proposed Model Architecture

Figure 1 illustrates an end-to-end pipeline for benchmarking five conventional machine learning algorithms Logistic Regression, Decision Tree, KNN, Naïve Bayes, and SVM for the diagnosis of diabetes. The pipeline begins with data ingestion, where the raw data is imported and processed further for preprocessing, including invalid value correction, feature standardization, and a stratified train-test split to keep class balance intact. All classifiers are trained on the same training data using baseline hyperparameters to provide a fair comparison. The common framework is designed to provide equivalent consistency between training and testing, with each model learning from the same features and patient distribution.

Following model training, performance is evaluated using standard metrics, viz., accuracy, Precision, Recall, F1-score, and ROC AUC. These values provide a multi-dimensional performance profile, while graphical tools confusion matrices (Figs. 2a–e) and ROC curves (Figs. 3a–e) provide higher interpretability. Confusion matrices reveal the decomposition of prediction errors (false positives and false negatives), and ROC curves depict the trade-offs between sensitivity and specificity. The proposed pipeline is concluded with the final stage of saving all quantitative results and visualizations for reporting and analysis. The reproducible and modular structure not only facilitates exhaustive benchmarking here but also provides a scalable template for future research with other models or data. The hyperparameter used for the study experiment is presented in Table 1.

Table 1. Hyperparameter Tuning Research for Each Model Using 5-Fold Cross-Validation

Model	Best Hyperparameters (Via Grid-Search)
Logistic Regression	penalty = ‘l2’, C = 0.1, solver = ‘liblinear’
Decision Tree	criterion = ‘gini’, max_depth = 5, min_samples_split = 4
K-Nearest Neighbors	n_neighbors = 7, weights = ‘distance’, metric = ‘minkowski’
Naive Bayes	var_smoothing = 1e−9
SVM	C = 1.0, gamma = 0.01, kernel = ‘rbf’

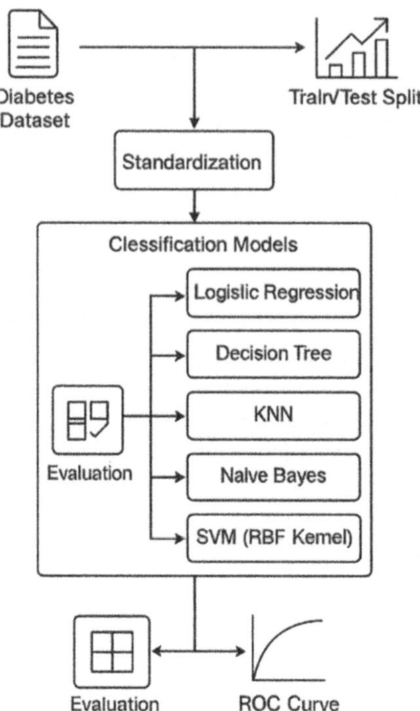

Fig. 1. Proposed Model Architectural Diagram

3 Results and Model Evaluation

The five machine learning models evaluated in this study Logistic Regression, SVM, Naïve Bayes, Decision Tree, and KNN demonstrated varying degrees of effectiveness in predicting diabetes. Overall, classification accuracy ranged from approximately 70% to 78%, with Logistic Regression and SVM emerging as the most reliable performers. Both achieved high accuracy (around 75–77%) and strong ROC AUC values ($\geq$0.80), indicating their robust ability to distinguish between diabetic and non-diabetic cases. Naïve Bayes also showed competitive performance, achieving accuracy in the low 70% range and a respectable AUC (mid to high 0.70 s), despite its simplistic assumptions. In contrast, Decision Tree and KNN yielded the lowest accuracy and AUC values, likely due to issues such as overfitting and sensitivity to data dimensionality, respectively (Table 2).

Table 2. Performance Evaluation of the Implemented Model

Model	Accuracy	Precision	Recall	F1 Score	ROC AUC
Logistic Regression	0.745385	0.736663	0.763757	0.749965	0.821653
Decision Tree	0.660655	0.668098	0.638421	0.652922	0.663837
KNN	0.712497	0.699099	0.746074	0.721823	0.771076

(continued)

Table 2. (*continued*)

Model	Accuracy	Precision	Recall	F1 Score	ROC AUC
Naive Bayes	0.721409	0.723125	0.717499	0.720301	0.783187
SVM (RBF Kernel)	0.748851	0.723621	0.805206	0.762236	0.811554

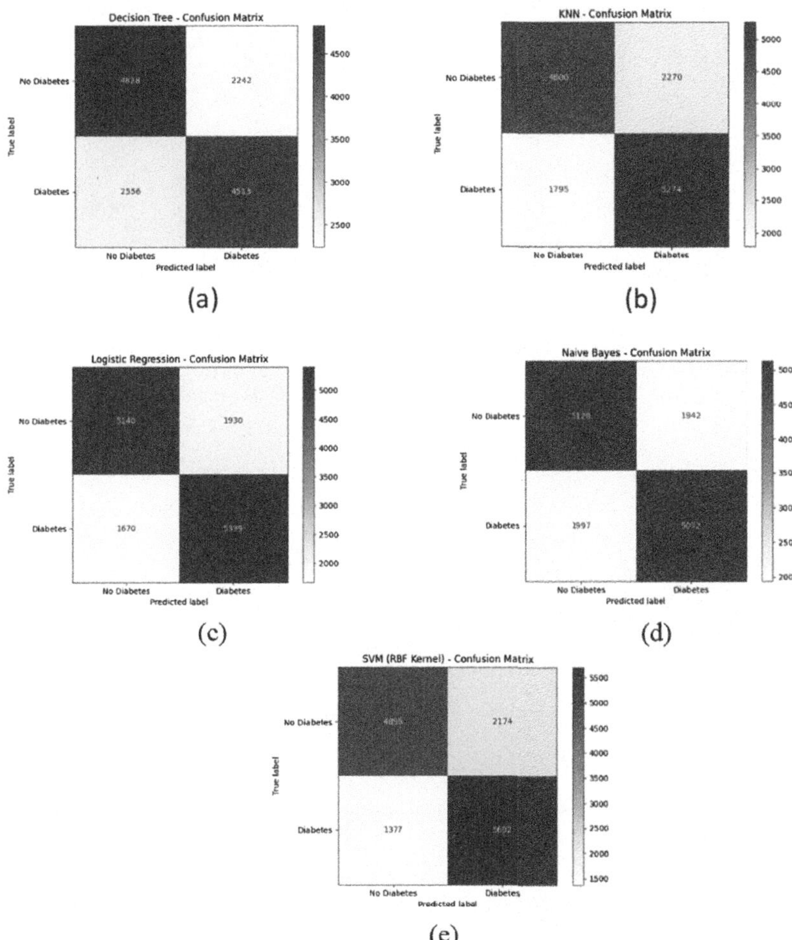

Fig. 2. Confusion Matrix for the Five ML Models Implemented

Confusion matrix analyses (Fig. 2a–e) further clarified each model's predictive behaviour. Logistic Regression and SVM displayed balanced predictions with fewer misclassifications, highlighting their diagnostic reliability. Naïve Bayes demonstrated a high recall, effectively identifying true diabetic cases, albeit at the cost of increased false positives, resulting in slightly lower precision. Meanwhile, KNN and Decision Tree produced more false negatives and false positives, with KNN particularly struggling to accurately identify diabetic cases, likely due to poor neighbourhood alignment in the feature space. Despite these limitations, all models captured some meaningful patterns in the data, with Logistic Regression, SVM, and Naïve Bayes proving more dependable for diabetes prediction in clinical decision-making contexts.

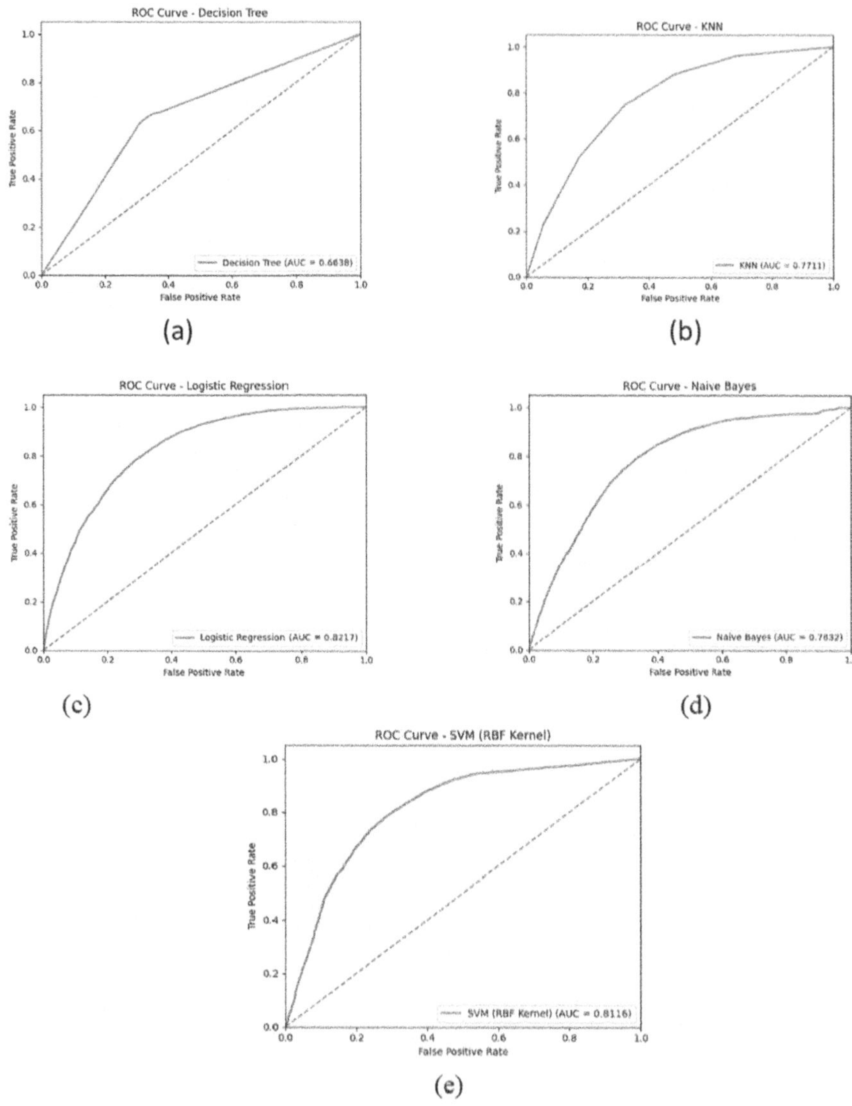

Fig. 3. Implemented ML Models: ROC Curve

The ROC curves in Fig. 3 complement the confusion matrix analysis by illustrating each model's performance across all classification thresholds. In Fig. 3, the ROC curve for each classifier plots the trade-off between True Positive Rate (sensitivity) and False Positive Rate (1 – specificity). An ideal model's curve would rise sharply toward the top-left corner (indicating high sensitivity with low false alarm rate). In contrast, a no-skill classifier would lie along the diagonal line. Among the five models, the ROC curves for Logistic Regression and SVM are closest to the top-left corner, aligning with their high AUC values. These curves dominate the others, meaning that for any given false positive rate, logistic and SVM achieve a higher true positive rate than the rest. The area under their curves (AUC $\approx$ 0.80–0.82) confirms that they provide the best discrimination ability in ranking patients by risk. Naïve Bayes also has a reasonably steep ROC curve initially, though it starts to diverge below the top performers at specific points – its AUC might be slightly lower (~0.75–0.78). Decision Tree and KNN have ROC curves that hug the diagonal more closely, reflecting their mediocre performance. Notably, the KNN curve might lie below the decision tree in some regions, indicating it could be the weakest of the five in terms of pure ranking ability. The separation of the curves in Fig. 3 demonstrates that while all models perform better than chance, some consistently outperform others across different threshold choices. For instance, if a high sensitivity is required (moving to the right on the ROC space), logistic regression and SVM maintain better sensitivity for a given false positive rate than the other models – an important consideration if the goal is to catch as many diabetic cases as possible. On the other hand, if controlling false positives is paramount (staying low on the x-axis), these models also achieve higher specificity at a given sensitivity level. In practical terms, the ROC analysis underscores that Logistic Regression and SVM not only achieve good accuracy at the default threshold (as seen in confusion matrices) but also would perform robustly under different operating points, which is advantageous for a clinical decision system that might adjust the threshold for a desired sensitivity/specificity balance.

4 Discussion

The comparative analysis of the five classical machine learning models SVM, Logistic Regression, Naïve Bayes, Decision Tree, and KNN revealed that all performed within a moderate accuracy range of 70–77%, consistent with existing literature on the Pima Indians diabetes dataset. Among them, SVM and Logistic Regression delivered the strongest performance, with only a marginal advantage of a few percentage points over Naïve Bayes. This close performance means that no single model is best; instead, each one picks out significant patterns in the data but handles noise and class imbalance differently. The findings are consistent with prior work where SVM very marginally beat logistic regression or vice versa, lending credence to the notion that model choice must be based on context-dependent trade-offs, not raw accuracy. Additionally, the consistency of the findings suggests that they are reliable day-to-day models for predicting diabetes.

From the perspective of clinical deployment, the comparison highlights critical performance disparities. SVM and Naïve Bayes performed better in terms of recall, which is suitable for early screening, where false negatives should be minimised. Logistic Regression provided a reasonable trade-off between precision and recall and remains the first choice due to its interpretability. Decision Tree and KNN had higher false negatives, which would be dangerous in diagnostic applications. Nevertheless, Decision

Trees yield interpretable decision rules that could be valuable when further tuned or in an ensemble. The findings suggest that ensemble or calibrated models may potentially balance sensitivity and specificity more effectively. Lastly, while SVM may be optimal for accuracy-driven applications, Logistic Regression or Naïve Bayes may be preferable for explainability and practical applications. The stability of the highest-performing models across measures validates their use within clinical decision support systems, with the final model selection dependent on specific healthcare priorities, such as interpretability, computational cost, or diagnostic sensitivity.

To enhance clinical interpretability, feature importance analysis was conducted on Logistic Regression and Decision Tree models, highlighting glucose concentration, BMI, and age as key predictors of diabetes findings consistent with clinical knowledge. The interpretability of these models, particularly through coefficient analysis and Gini impurity metrics, supports transparency and trust in clinical decision-making. However, real-world deployment faces challenges including data privacy compliance (e.g., HIPAA, GDPR), integration with EHR systems, and clinician acceptance. Addressing these barriers requires explainable models, standardized data pipelines, and the development of user-friendly decision support tools validated across diverse populations and aligned with ethical and institutional standards.

5 Conclusion and Future Work

This research demonstrated that standard machine learning models Logistic Regression, SVM, Naïve Bayes, Decision Tree, and KNN can achieve moderate predictive accuracy in diabetes diagnosis with 75% accuracy and ROC AUC of 0.8. Although Logistic Regression and SVM consistently ranked top for total accuracy and discrimination ability, the slight performance of Naïve Bayes ensured high recall, thereby enhancing its utility for screening. Decision Tree and KNN underperformed, underscoring the utility of model selection based on specific diagnosis needs. Each model possessed individual strengths, such as interpretability or sensitivity, which could potentially affect its deployment in clinical settings. Caveats persist, including over-reliance on a single dataset with demographics, lack of hyperparameter tuning, and insufficient feature exposure. These conditions may restrict the models' generalizability and peak performance.

To bridge these gaps, future research must explore more advanced and adaptive approaches. Deep models of learning can achieve higher accuracy by representing non-linear feature interactions; however, such gains must be balanced against the dangers of overfitting and concerns about interpretability. Feature extension through the addition of additional biomarkers or advanced selection algorithms can enhance predictiveness and clinical relevance. Ensemble methods, such as Random Forests or stacking architectures, can potentially outperform individual model performance by aggregating complementary decision patterns. In addition, calibrating thresholds and using calibration can also further optimize sensitivity-specificity trade-offs for functional diagnostic systems. Ultimately, external validation on larger and more diverse populations, as well as the integration of explainable AI tools, will be crucial in ensuring the stability, fairness, and clinical adoption of ML-based diabetes screening solutions.

A key limitation of this study is the use of a single dataset (Pima Indians), which may limit generalizability; future work should validate the models on larger, ethnically diverse datasets to ensure broader clinical applicability.

Furthermore, future work will include a rigorous statistical significance analysis (e.g., confidence intervals and hypothesis testing) to assess whether the performance differences among models are statistically significant. This step will be incorporated once larger and more heterogeneous datasets become available, ensuring the statistical reliability and generalizability of the findings. This will also explore ensemble-based classifiers such as Random Forest and Gradient Boosting to evaluate their potential for improving diagnostic accuracy beyond classic models. Additionally, Future work will incorporate clinician-guided threshold tuning and cost-sensitive evaluation to better align model performance metrics, such as recall and precision, with real-world diagnostic trade-offs in diabetes screening.

References

1. International Diabetes Federation. Diabetes facts & figures (n.d.). https://idf.org/about-diabetes/diabetes-facts-figures/
2. Oladele, T.O., Ogundokun, R.O., Kayode, A.A., Adegun, A.A., Adebiyi, M.O.: Application of data mining algorithms for feature selection and prediction of diabetic retinopathy. In: Misra, S., et al. (eds.) Computational Science and Its Applications – ICCSA 2019. ICCSA 2019. LNCS, vol. 11623. Springer, Cham (2019). https://doi.org/10.1007/978-3-030-24308-1_56
3. Ogundokun, R.O., Misra, S., Umoru, D., Agrawal, A.: Review of cardiovascular disease prediction based on machine learning algorithms. In: Singh, Y., Verma, C., Zoltán, I., Chhabra, J.K., Singh, P.K. (eds.) Proceedings of International Conference on Recent Innovations in Computing. ICRIC 2022. LNEE, vol. 1011. Springer, Singapore (2022). https://doi.org/10.1007/978-981-99-0601-7_4
4. Ahsan, M.M., Luna, S.A., Siddique, Z.: Machine-learning-based disease diagnosis: a comprehensive review. In: Healthcare, vol. 10, No. 3, p. 541. MDPI (2022)
5. Ogundokun, R.O., Misra, S., Ogundokun, O.E., Oluranti, J., Maskeliunas, R.: Machine learning classification based techniques for fraud discovery in credit card datasets. In: Florez, H., Pollo-Cattaneo, M.F. (eds.) Applied Informatics. ICAI 2021. CCIS, vol. 1455. Springer, Cham (2021). https://doi.org/10.1007/978-3-030-89654-6_3
6. Tasin, I., Nabil, T.U., Islam, S., Khan, R.: Diabetes prediction using machine learning and explainable AI techniques. Healthcare Technol. Let. **10**(1–2), 1–10 (2023)
7. Kaur, H., Kaur, G.: Prediction of diabetes using support vector machine. Int. J. Res. Eng. Appl. Manage. **5**, 2454–9150 (2019)
8. Filho, M.: Is feature scaling required for the KNN algorithm? Forecastegy (2023). https://forecastegy.com/posts/is-feature-scaling-required-for-the-knn-algorithm/

Machine Learning-Based Breathing Phase Classification of Respiratory Sounds for Pulmonary Health Assessment

Qingwei Li, Suranjan Panigrahi, and Miad Faezipour(✉)

School of Engineering Technology, Electrical and Computer Engineering Technology, Purdue University, West Lafayette, IN, USA
{li2967,spanigr,mfaezipo}@purdue.edu

Abstract. Respiratory sound analysis is emerging as a non-invasive and scalable approach for pulmonary health assessment. This work-in-progress paper presents a machine learning framework for the classification of inhalation and exhalation phases from respiratory audio recordings. By leveraging signal processing techniques and deep neural networks, the system aims to improve the accuracy and efficiency of respiratory phase detection, a foundational step in diagnosing conditions such as asthma and chronic obstructive pulmonary disease (COPD). The proposed methodology includes timeâĂŞfrequency feature extraction, heuristic segmentation, and supervised learning-based classification. We anticipate promising results across various respiratory sound datasets. After full model development and analysis, future work will focus on incorporating abnormal sound classification, enhancing model generalization, and conducting validation in real-world clinical settings.

Keywords: respiratory sounds · machine learning · deep neural network · breathing phases · time-frequency signal analysis

1 Introduction

Respiratory diseases, most notably, asthma, chronic obstructive pulmonary disease (COPD), pneumonia and lower-respiratory infections, constitute a leading cause of global morbidity and mortality, accounting for more than four million deaths annually. According to the World Health Organization, lower respiratory infections rank fourth in the leading causes of mortality, while COPD was responsible for over 3 million deaths in 2019 [1]. Early detection and continuous monitoring are essential to reducing this burden, yet current diagnostic practices rely heavily on manual auscultation and spirometry. These methods are constrained by subjectivity, cost, resource requirements, and the need for trained personnel, making them less accessible in resource-constrained settings [1].

A. Alsadoon et al. (Eds.): CSCE 2025, CCIS 2935, pp. 392–398, 2026.
https://doi.org/10.1007/978-3-032-22199-5_30

Recent advances in artificial intelligence (AI) have opened new avenues for automated respiratory assessment. Deep neural networks, in particular, excel at extracting hierarchical patterns from complex, non-stationary audio signals of the respiratory sounds. Existing work has demonstrated encouraging results in distinguishing normal from abnormal breath sounds, as well as in detecting adventitious events such as wheezes and crackles [2]. However, a critical and largely unaddressed prerequisite for reliable downstream analysis is the accurate segmentation of each respiratory cycle into its inhalation and exhalation phases. Misclassification at this stage propagates errors to any subsequent disease-specific inference, thereby undermining clinical usefulness.

This research-in-progress study proposes a machine learning framework that combines signal-processing heuristics with data-driven models to identify respiratory (breathing) phase boundaries from respiratory sounds, classifying each segment as inhalation or exhalation. Key elements include (i) time-frequency feature extraction using short-time Fourier transforms and Mel spectrograms, (ii) energy-envelope-based heuristic segmentation to initialize candidate intervals, and (iii) supervised deep learning models such as convolutional, recurrent, and hybrid architectures to refine breathing phase labels.

2 Problem Statement

Respiratory sound analysis presents a non-invasive, low-cost alternative to traditional pulmonary health assessment methods like chest auscultation and spirometry, enabling automated assessments of the lung function from audio recordings. However, accurate identification of inhalation and exhalation phases, a foundational step for detecting abnormalities such as wheezing and airflow restriction, remains underexplored. While recent machine learning approaches have shown promise in classifying abnormal respiratory events [3–5], few target fine-grained phase segmentation [4,6], and generalizability remains a challenge due to variability in patients and environments [5,6].

Tools for labeling respiratory phases have improved dataset quality, but there is still no standardized, automated framework for robust, interpretable breathing phase classification. This work aims to address this gap by proposing a machine learning-based framework combining signal processing and deep learning to support scalable and clinically meaningful respiratory diagnostics.

3 Related Work

Breathing phase classification from respiratory audio signals has traditionally relied on signal processing techniques. However, hybrid signal processing and deep learning approaches show strong potential to improve performance [2].

Artificial intelligence has been increasingly applied to respiratory sound classification. Xu and Sankar [3] reviewed machine and deep learning techniques for lung sound analysis, emphasizing the shift from handcrafted features to neural network architectures, and the need for scalable respiratory monitoring systems.

Yet, most studies target high-level tasks like detecting wheezes or abnormal sounds, with limited focus on fine-grained inhalation and exhalation segmentation.

Perna and Tagarelli's work [4] demonstrated strong performance for pathological event detection using convolutional neural networks and transfer learning, but their approach did not target breathing phase-level classification. Zhang et al. [5] introduced the Rene system, a multi-modal, edge-deployable AI tool for disease-level auscultation analysis, yet it does not address intra-cycle phase labeling.

Fernando et al. [6] proposed an interpretable temporal convolutional network for lung sound event detection, prioritizing explainability, an important aspect for clinical adoption. To support supervised learning in this domain, Hsu et al. developed a respiratory sound annotation tool for labeling breathing phases and abnormal events [7].

These studies highlight the potential of AI in respiratory diagnostics but also reveal a key gap that few systems offer automated, generalizable, and interpretable classification of respiratory phases, which is essential for precise lung dynamics' analysis, and clinically meaningful pulmonary assessment.

4 Methodology

This study adopts a hybrid framework that integrates signal processing and machine learning techniques to classify respiratory sound recordings into inhalation and exhalation phases. The pipeline begins with data acquisition from publicly available repositories and, where feasible, clinically sourced datasets. Priority is given to datasets that include annotated breathing phase labels generated via semi-automated tools, ensuring consistency and reducing manual labeling effort.

Once collected, all audio recordings undergo a preprocessing stage aimed at enhancing signal clarity and standardizing inputs. Bandpass filtering is used to remove low-frequency background noise and high-frequency artifacts, while signals are normalized in amplitude and resampled to a consistent sampling rate to account for variability across recording devices. Short-time Fourier transform (STFT) and Mel-frequency cepstral coefficients (MFCCs) are computed to extract both temporal and spectral characteristics from the audio, as these features are known to be effective in bioacoustic classification tasks.

Following preprocessing, a heuristic segmentation procedure is applied to estimate the temporal boundaries between inhalation, exhalation, and pause intervals. Two approaches are employed in tandem: a gradient-based method that detects local minima in the smoothed energy envelope, and a peak-detection algorithm that identifies valleys in the inverted power curve using signal processing techniques. These candidate intervals are filtered using empirically derived duration and amplitude thresholds. For example, short exhalation-like events that fall below duration thresholds may be reclassified as inhalations to improve temporal consistency.

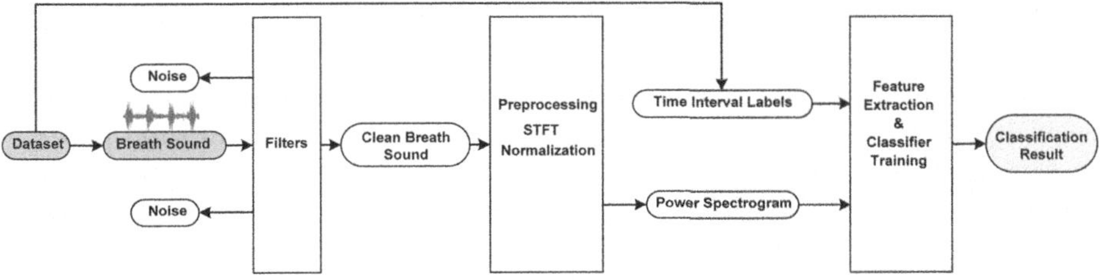

Fig. 1. Overview of the proposed respiratory sound phase classification pipeline.

For each segmented interval, a set of features is extracted, including statistical properties of the Mel-spectrogram (Mel- frequencies over time), zero-crossing rate, energy entropy, and normalized duration. These features are transformed into fixed-length vectors using interpolation or padding to enable input compatibility with neural networks. The classification models used in this framework include convolutional neural networks (CNNs) for extracting spatial patterns from spectrograms, recurrent neural networks (RNNs), particularly, long short-term memory (LSTM) units, for capturing temporal dynamics, and hybrid CNN-RNN architectures that leverage both local and sequential structure in the data. Model training is conducted using supervised learning on labeled data, with performance optimized via cross-validation and hyperparameter tuning. Data augmentation techniques such as time-stretching and noise injection are employed to improve generalization, particularly in scenarios with limited labeled data.

Figure 1 illustrates the overall model framework including the signal processing, and machine/deep learning steps.

5 Evaluation Strategy

To assess the effectiveness and generalizability of the proposed inhalation and exhalation classification framework, a multi-layered evaluation strategy is employed. The primary focus is on verifying whether the system can accurately identify respiratory phases across diverse subjects, acoustic environments, and recording devices. Model evaluation is carried out using both label-level classification metrics and time-based overlap criteria to ensure that the system performs well, not only in predicting the correct class but also in capturing the temporal dynamics of the breathing cycles and phases.

The evaluation pipeline begins with the comparison of predicted labels against ground-truth annotations that include start time, end time, and phase class (I for inhalation, E for exhalation). These annotations are derived from expert-labeled datasets or from semi-automated annotation tools validated in prior studies [7]. Predictions are considered correct only when the predicted interval label matches the ground truth and when the temporal overlap between the two exceeds a predefined threshold. This overlap-based correctness metric is especially important in respiratory phase analysis, where precise temporal segmentation can significantly impact subsequent lung function interpretations [6].

Standard performance metrics such as accuracy, precision, recall (sensitivity), specificity, and F1-score are computed on a per-label basis. Confusion matrices are generated to analyze common misclassification patterns, such as misclassifying short exhalations with pauses or misidentifying inhalations in noisy conditions. To evaluate the robustness of the model, tests are conducted on both intra-dataset (hold-out test set) and inter-dataset splits, where training and testing are performed on recordings from different sources, subjects, devices, or environments. This cross-dataset validation strategy allows for assessing how well the system generalizes to unseen conditions, which is a critical aspect of clinical applicability.

In addition to numerical evaluation, qualitative visualizations are generated by overlaying predicted phase boundaries on smoothed power curves, allowing researchers or clinicians to visually inspect model performance and error patterns. These visual tools also aid in the interpretability of the results and facilitate error analysis in cases of ambiguous or low-energy breathing signals.

Finally, batch evaluation scripts are implemented to support large-scale performance testing over hundreds of audio recordings, ensuring reproducibility and enabling longitudinal benchmarking. These features will support future deployment scenarios, including mobile or clinical applications that require fast and consistent phase recognition across continuous respiratory recordings.

6 Expected Outcome

The expected outcome of this work-in-progress study is a functional and interpretable machine learning pipeline capable of accurately classifying inhalation and exhalation phases from respiratory audio recordings. Model performance will be evaluated using metrics such as accuracy, precision, recall, and F1-score. Results will be visualized by overlaying predicted phase boundaries on smoothed power curves, supporting both qualitative and quantitative analysis.

Preliminary results across representative respiratory cycles are illustrated in Fig. 2, showing the initial breathing audio input (top), as well as the smoothed power envelope, heuristic boundaries, and predicted breathing phase classes (bottom).

A batch-processing module will further automate large-scale evaluation and will facilitate future integration into clinical workflows.

The system will be evaluated using various respiratory audio datasets such as the ICBHI 2017 Respiratory Sound database [8], which provides a diverse and publicly available collection of annotated lung sound recordings across multiple pathologies, age groups, and recording conditions. The proposed framework is anticipated to achieve robust performance on this benchmark dataset, as well as on other accessible breathing sound datasets collected from de-identified subjects. The combination of heuristic segmentation and deep learning is expected to reduce reliance on extensive manual labeling while maintaining clinically relevant phase separation.

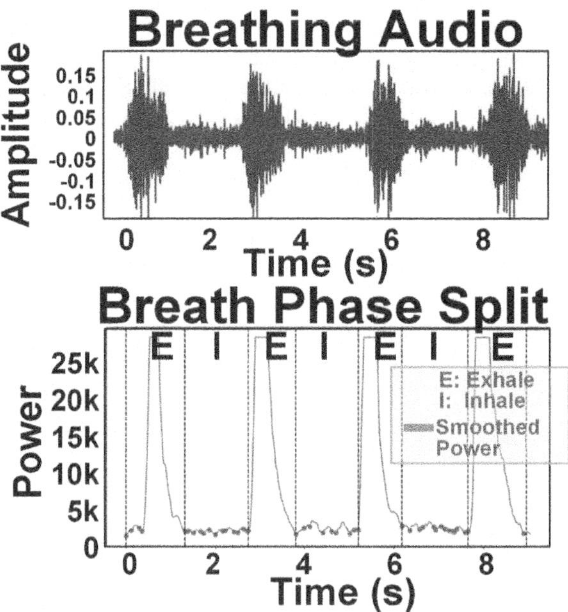

Fig. 2. Breathing audio (top). Smoothed power curve with heuristic segmentation boundaries and predicted respiratory phases (bottom).

With support for batch processing and generalizable model design, the proposed framework has the potential to serve as a foundational tool for future extensions in pathological sound detection, real-time inference, and deployment in telehealth or point-of-care respiratory monitoring systems.

References

1. World Health Organization: The top 10 causes of death. WHO Newsroom (2024). https://www.who.int/news-room/fact-sheets/detail/the-top-10-causes-of-death. Accessed 26 Oct 2025
2. Shokouhmand, S., Bhatt, S., Faezipour, M.: Artificial intelligence in respiratory health: a review of AI-driven analysis of oral and nasal breathing sounds for pulmonary assessment. Electronics **14**(10), 2025 (1994)
3. Xu, X., Sankar, R.: Classification and recognition of lung sounds using artificial intelligence and machine learning. Big Data Cogn. Comput. **8**(10), 127 (2024)
4. Perna, R., Tagarelli, A.: Deep auscultation: Predicting respiratory anomalies and diseases via recurrent neural networks. In: 2019 IEEE 32nd International Symposium on Computer-Based Medical Systems (CBMS)
5. Zhang, P., Zheng, Z., Zhang, S., Yang, M., Tang, S.: Rene: a pre-trained multi-modal architecture for auscultation of respiratory diseases. arXiv preprint arXiv:2405.07442 (2024)
6. Fernando, T., Sridharan, S., Denman, S., Ghaemmaghami, H., Fookes, C.: Robust and interpretable temporal convolution network for event detection in lung sound recordings. IEEE J. Biomed. Health Inform. **26**(7), 2898–2908 (2022)

7. Hsu, F.S., et al.: Development of a respiratory sound labeling software for training a deep learning-based respiratory sound analysis model. In: International Forum on Medical Imaging in Asia, vol. 11792, pp. 109–114. SPIE (2021)
8. The Respiratory Sound database - ICBHI 2017 Challenge. https://doi.org/10.7910/DVN/HT6PKI. Accessed 26 Oct 2025

MRI-Based Deep Learning for Brain Tumor Prediction

Araek Tashkandi[1(✉)] and Siraj Wally[2]

[1] Department of Information Systems and Technology, College of Computer Science and Engineering, University of Jeddah, Jeddah, Saudi Arabia
astashkandi@uj.edu.sa

[2] Department of Internal Medicine – Radiology, College of Medicine, University of Tabuk, Tabuk, Saudi Arabia
swally@ut.edu.sa

Abstract. Diagnosing brain tumors is difficult due to complex imaging data and variability in radiologist diagnoses. This study aimed to develop a machine learning model that utilizes magnetic resonance imaging (MRI) scans for brain tumor detection and classification. A dataset of MRI scans with tumor annotations was collected and optimized using pre-processing steps. Convolutional neural networks (CNN) were used to extract imaging features, with the optimal architecture achieving an accuracy of 99% in the detection and classification of brain tumors. Deep learning methods effectively analyzed medical images with high precision for brain tumor prognosis, potentially aiding in treatment planning and improving diagnostic consistency.

Keywords: Machine learning · Brain tumor prediction · Deep learning · MRI

1 Introduction

Brain tumors are abnormal cell growths in the brain, primary or secondary. Brain tumors are diverse, benign or malignant diseases found in any brain region. They can cause various symptoms based on their size and location. Common types include Glioblastoma, Meningioma, and Pituitary tumor. Brain tumors are classified according to cell type and location in the brain. Common malignant types include gliomas, meningiomas, and pituitary adenomas. Gliomas originate from glial cells, meninges, and the pituitary gland, while meningiomas originate from the embranes of the brain and spinal cord. Pituitary adenomas, on the other hand, arise from the pituitary gland at the base of the brain.

The diagnosis of brain tumors is challenging and time-consuming, requiring clinical examinations, imaging tests such as MRI and CT scans, along with laboratory tests. The prognosis depends on the type of tumor, location, age of the patient, and overall health. Traditional methods are subjective and susceptible to errors. It is crucial to consult a radiologist for an accurate diagnosis.

A. Alsadoon et al. (Eds.): CSCE 2025, CCIS 2935, pp. 399–416, 2026.
https://doi.org/10.1007/978-3-032-22199-5_31

Detecting brain tumors in clinical settings can be time consuming and complex for patients and doctors. A solution using algorithms and machine learning (ML) or deep learning (DL) techniques can help identify the presence of a tumor and classify its type more effectively. Data science can be used to develop objective methods for diagnosing brain tumors. Machine learning algorithms can identify patterns and features in extensive datasets of brain images from MRI/CT, to help distinguish between healthy and tumor tissue with greater accuracy. This empowers clinical decision making to make more precise diagnoses and select optimal treatment options for patients. This technology is transforming the way radiologists diagnose and report brain tumors.

To predict brain tumors, imaging-based machine learning algorithms such as convolutional neural networks (CNNs), support vector machines (SVMs), and random forests have been used. The results have been promising, with some algorithms achieving accuracies comparable to or even better than those of human radiologists.

This research paper aims to create ML and DL models that accurately predict brain tumor presence and type using medical imaging data such as MRI or CT scans. The model will be trained on MRI/CT scans and will use image processing and feature extraction techniques to identify tumor-related patterns. It will be optimized to minimize false negatives and false positives, ensuring high accuracy and reliability. Imaging-based machine learning aids medical professionals in early detection of brain tumors, diagnosis, and treatment planning, thereby improving patient outcomes.

2 Related Work

Deep learning CNN models have been used by many studies for brain tumor predication such as by [1–5]. Javier *et al.* [1] developed a multiscale CNN model for brain tumor classification and segmentation. The model was trained on a publicly available MRI dataset of more than 3000 slices, including meningiomas, gliomas, and pituitary tumors. The model achieved performance with an accuracy of 0.973 in classification and 0.96 and 0.95 in segmentation. The study by Pashaei *et al.* [4] addresses the classification of brain tumors using a CNN model with an accuracy of 93.68%. The model was trained and evaluated on a publicly available MRI image dataset of 3064 images, focusing on Meningioma, Glioma, and pituitary tumors. Sultan *et al.* [5] used CNN to classify different types of brain tumor using two data sets. The first dataset contains 3064 MRI images for meningioma, glioma, and pituitary tumors, while the second dataset contains 516 images for glioma grade. The model achieved in studies I and II, an accuracy of 96.13% and 98.9%.

The research articles [2,3] demonstrate that deep learning algorithms and transfer learning techniques can achieve high training and validation accuracy rates. The research article [2] examines the effectiveness of deep transfer learning techniques in classifying brain tumors using MRI images. It compares the performance of three CNN models (VGG-16, ResNet-50, and Inception-v3) in predicting brain tumors, including glioma, meningioma, and pituitary tumors. The study [3] aimed to develop a diagnosis system for the identification and categorization of brain tumors, including types such as glioma, meningioma, and pituitary tumors. The researchers used advanced DL approaches, including the Unet model with ResNet50, DenseNet201, MobileNet V2, and InceptionV3, and classified brain tumors using evolutionary algorithms and reinforcement learning through transfer learning. The proposed approach achieved high accuracy rates, with multiple models achieving accuracy ranging from 91.8% to 99.6%. NASNet displayed the highest accuracy among the tested models.

ML models used by [6–8] for the prediction of brain tumor. The study [6] compares six machine learning algorithms, including CN2 Rule Induction, Neural Networks, Naïve Bayes, Support Vector Machine (SVM), Random Forest and Decision Tree for brain tumor classification on MRI images, using a small Kaggle dataset of 253 images. SVM was found to be the best method, with F1, precision, and recall of 90.7%. In their study, Mohsen *et al.* [7] focuses on classifying three types of malignant brain tumors: glioblastoma, sarcoma, and metastatic bronchogenic carcinoma. They use fuzzy C-means and K-means algorithms for image segmentation and feature extraction and selection using gray-level co-occurrence matrix and discrete wavelet transform. The system reached a classification accuracy of 93.94%. The study by Jun *et al.* [8] proposes a method to improve brain tumor classification using augmentation and partition of tumor regions. It compares three classification methods: SVM, sparse representation-based classification (SRC), and kNN classifier, using 2-region bag-of-words representations. The researchers evaluated their method on a large data set of brain T1-weighted contrast enhanced magnetic resonance imaging (CE-MRI) images. SVM achieved the best performance, with an accuracy of 91.14%.

Deep learning was used by [9] and identified two types of brain tumors in 253 MRI images that address data shortages. The pre-trained CNN models, Alexnet and ResNet, are used for feature extraction, while SVM is used for tumor classification. CNN-SVM model achieved an accuracy of 97.23%.

Kang *et al.* [10] used three MRI datasets to test pre-trained deep CNN for brain tumor classification. The first dataset contained 253 images, the second 3000 images, and the third 3064 images. After evaluating 13 different networks and nine machine learning classifiers, the study found that the Support Vector Machine (SVM) with a Recurrent Brownian Motion (RBF) kernel outperformed other ML classifiers for MRI-based brain tumor classification.

The two studies [11,12] highlight the effectiveness of EfficientNet models for accurate and efficient classification. The study [11] uses EfficientNet models based on transfer learning to automatically extract and classify characteristics of brain tumor. The system includes a training phase with 5712 images and a testing phase with 1311 images. The research [12] presents a new method for brain tumor classification using dense EfficientNet and min-max normalization, it achieves 98. 78% accuracy in MRI images, outperforming existing deep learning techniques with a model optimization need for reduced computational requirements.

Previous research in brain tumor classification has shown promising results using both traditional ML and DL methods. Several studies implemented CNN-based architectures (e.g. VGG16, ResNet, NASNet) and achieved high accuracy. Transfer learning techniques with pre-trained models like EfficientNet and AlexNet further improved performance on limited datasets. Traditional models such as SVM and kNN also demonstrated competitive results in tumor classification. However, most of these studies focused primarily on detection of tumor presence (tumor vs. non-tumor), with limited emphasis on tumor type-specific classification. Furthermore, there is limited research on comprehensive comparison between classical ML and deep CNNs under the same experimental setup and dataset. This study addresses these gaps by focusing on multi-class tumor type prediction (i.e. tumor type classification), not just presence detection. Moreover, it conducts a comparative analysis of various ML and DL models (e.g. SVM, CNNs, EfficientNetB0) using a unified dataset and consistent evaluation metrics to identify the most reliable model for robust real-world brain tumor prediction and classification support. In addition, this study will use a larger dataset than the one used by the related studies.

3 Research Methodology

This project will utilize a data science life cycle methodology to develop a machine learning and deep learning model for patients with brain tumor. The methodology involves data collection, cleaning, pre-processing, feature extraction, model implementation, and evaluation as shown in Fig. 1. Data will be collected from MRI images and related data, and pre-processing steps will be applied to ensure consistency and improve model performance. Convolutional Neural Networks (CNNs) will be used to extract high-level features from the images, such as edges, shapes, textures, and objects.

The model will be trained using a suitable algorithm and optimization technique, based on various architectures such as convolutional neural networks (CNNs) and support vector machines (SVMs). The performance of the models will be evaluated using standard metrics to understand its strengths and weaknesses. This evaluation also contributes to model monitoring, such as accuracy and F1 score. The implemented model aims to complement traditional medical diagnoses by providing automated and quantitative analysis, complementing traditional methods.

3.1 Dataset

The Kaggle brain tumor MRI image dataset, a combination of Figshare, SARTAJ, and Br35H, contains 7,023 brain MRI images, with 1,621 labeled as glioma, 1,645 as meningioma, 1,757 as pituitary tumor, and 2,000 as no tumor [13]. The dataset, a collection of brain images, was acquired using a 3T MRI scanner, which uses a powerful magnetic field to create detailed images of the brain.

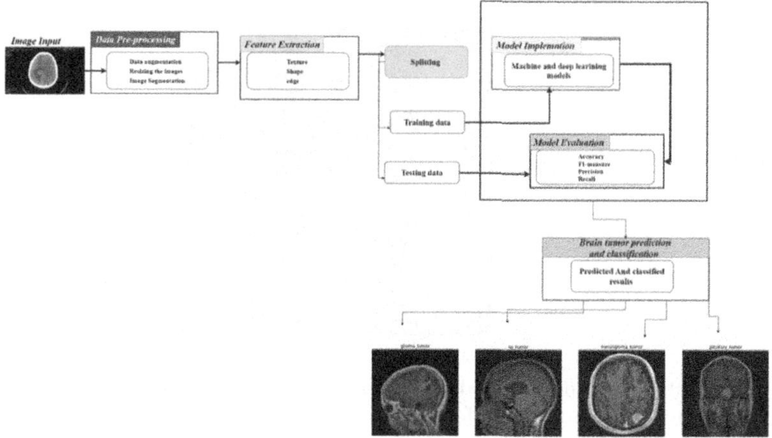

Fig. 1. Methodology diagnoses for Brain tumor prediction.

T1-weighted images show the fat and white matter of the brain, while the T2-weighted images show the water and gray matter of the brain. Contrast-enhanced T1-weighted images are created by injecting a gadolinium contrast agent into the bloodstream, highlighting the tumor and abnormal blood flow. The images were annotated by experienced neuroradiologists using LabelImg and LabelMe tools to identify the tumor and other relevant structures. The creator of the Kaggle dataset deleted the glioma class images from the SARTAJ dataset due to incorrect classification, instead using the glioma class images from the FigShare dataset.

The FigShare dataset, acquired from two Chinese hospitals between 2005 and 2010, contains T1-weighted contrast-enhanced MRI images of 233 patients with meningioma, glioma, and pituitary tumors [14].

The SARTAJ dataset is a publicly available collection of brain MRI images, classified into four types: glioma, meningioma, pituitary tumor and no tumor, containing 3264 images from 250 patients with brain tumor [15].

The BR35H dataset, released in 2020, is a publicly available collection of 2,768 brain MRI images, with 1458 showing different tumor types and 1310 showing healthy brains, available in T1- and T2-weighted formats [16].

Figure 2 shows various types of tumor and their corresponding planes, with a red outline highlighting tumor segments for clear visualization [17]. The number of images varies according to the patient.

Overall, this dataset contains a collection of 7,023 brain MRI images, of which 1621 are labeled glioma, 1645 are labeled meningioma, 1757 are labeled pituitary tumor, and 2000 are labeled no tumor as shown in Fig. 3.

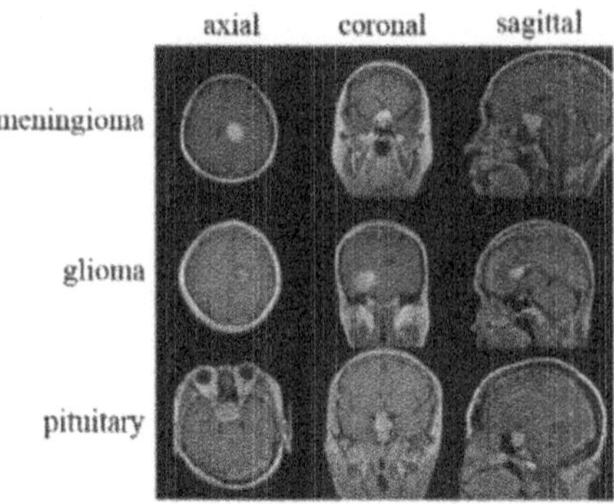

Fig. 2. Representation of normalized magnetic resonance imaging (MRI) images showing different types of tumors in different planes. In the images, the tumor is marked with a red outline. (Color figure online)

MRI Brain images category	Train	Test
glioma	1321	300
meningioma	1339	306
no tumor	1595	405
pituitary	1457	300
Total	7,023	
Images size	The images have varying size and resolution	
Image type	magnetic resonance imaging-MRI of human brain classified into 4 classes: glioma - meningioma - no tumor and pituitary.	

Fig. 3. Distribution of MRI Brain tumor image classes in the dataset.

3.1.1 Data Preparation and Preprocessing

The brain tumor image dataset was analyzed to identify four key issues. The dataset had varying tumor shapes, which required different processing approaches. Resizing the images to standardize size and ensure uniform processing is suggested. The unbalanced distribution of grayscale intensities could lead to potential biases, which can be addressed by grayscale scaling. Noise and inconsistent brightness levels in some images hinder clear tumor visualization. Dilation, a morphological operation, can fill in gaps and reduce noise, improving visibility and accuracy. The unclear boundaries of the tumor in some images make it difficult to segment the tumor region. Thresholding, a threshold intensity value, can be used to define tumor boundaries, facilitating accurate segmentation and analysis. These issues highlight the need for careful consideration and improvement in the brain tumor image dataset prior to model development.

Data preparation and pre-processing are crucial in deep learning, as they transform raw data into a suitable format for modeling. The most common preprocessing methods used in the papers include data augmentation, resizing, and image segmentation. These techniques are applied by researchers who used the same dataset for their project, ensuring compatibility and consistency.

Data augmentation artificially increases the size and diversity of a dataset by creating new data from existing data through various transformations. Resizing images ensures consistency in input data, which is important for machine learning algorithms. Image segmentation divides an image into different segments or regions, identifying specific objects, such as brain tumors. Dilation and thresholding are used in conjunction to achieve more accurate segmentation results.

Other preprocessing methods used by the papers include pixel standardization, contrast stretching, intensity normalization, direct use of GLCM as features, cropping, contour selection, and extreme point calculation. These methods help to normalize pixel values, increase contrast, normalize intensity, extract features, remove unwanted portions, and identify contours in an image.

Data augmentation (Grayscale conversion): The brain tumor dataset was analyzed, and the presence of colored images was discovered. To avoid potential inaccuracies, the researchers converted these images to grayscale, a less complex and less noisy method. Grayscale images are easier to process and less noisy, making them beneficial for brain tumor image processing tasks. The code for grayscale conversion uses the cv2.cvtColor() function, which takes a color space conversion code and an image, cv2.COLOR RGB2GRAY, to convert RGB to grayscale.

Resizing the images: The study resizes brain tumor images to remove irrelevant background information and focus on essential brain details. This process, which involves changing the dimensions of an image by increasing or decreasing the number of pixels, is often necessary for image processing tasks, like training machine learning models. The resized images are then used in the processing pipeline, with the desired width and height set to 256, enhancing the accuracy of the pipeline.

Image segmentation (dilation and threshold of images): The image processing code uses a thresholding technique to convert an image into binary form, removing noise and making foreground objects more distinct from the background. The thresholding operation is performed using the cv2.threshold() function, which takes three arguments: the image to be thresholded, the threshold value, and the maximum value. The threshold value is the gray level value used to divide the image into two classes, with pixels with gray level values greater than or equal to the threshold value set to the maximum value and pixels with gray level values less than the threshold value set to zero. The threshold value is set to 45, resulting in 255 pixels for pixels with a gray level value of 45 or greater and zero pixels for pixels with a gray level value of less than 45. The dilation operation is performed using the cv2.dilate() function, which takes three arguments: the image to be dilated, the structuring element and the number of iterations.

Figure 4 shows samples of Magnetic Resonance Imaging (MRI) images before pre-processing. Whereas, Fig. 5 shows examples of magnetic resonance imaging (MRI) images after it undergoes three preprocessing steps: resizing, grayscale conversion, and dilation followed by thresholding. These steps improve the clarity and suitability of the images for further analysis or modeling. Resizing improves visual quality, making it easier to discern details and features. Grayscale conversion removes irrelevant color information, simplifies image representation, and potentially reduces computational cost. Dilation and thresholding enhance specific features, making them more prominent and easier to detect. These steps aim to transform raw images into an optimal format for analysis or modeling tasks, improving interpretability and information extraction.

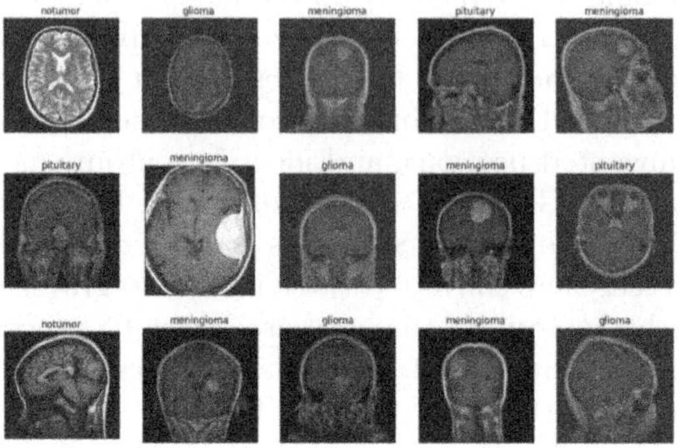

Fig. 4. Example of Magnetic Resonance Imaging (MRI) images before preprocessing.

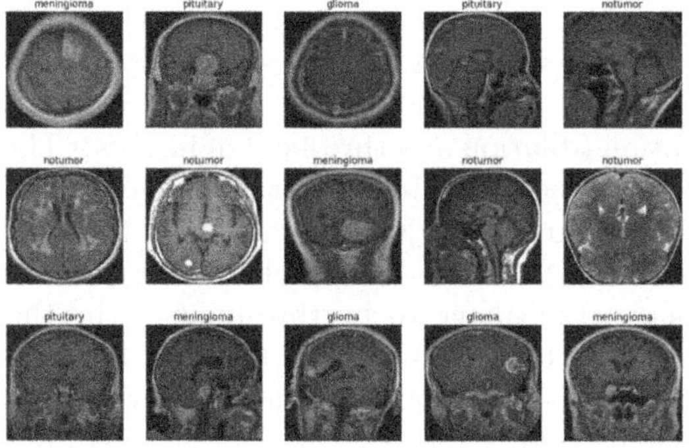

Fig. 5. Example of Magnetic Resonance Imaging (MRI) images after preprocessing.

4 Model Development

4.1 Machine Learning Models

Machine learning is an artificial intelligence technology that enables computers to learn without explicit programming. It uses algorithms to analyze data and identify patterns that humans cannot detect. These algorithms have been used to develop models to predict brain tumors, helping clinicians make informed decisions about diagnosis and treatment. Research has used models such as Random Forest, LR, Decision Tree, and SVM, with SVM achieving the highest accuracy.

4.1.1 SVM

Support Vector Machines (SVMs) are supervised learning algorithms used for classification tasks such as brain tumor prediction. SVMs are a powerful tool for brain tumor classification, as they find a hyperplane in the data to separate different types of brain tumor. Although not as accurate as deep learning models, they are less computationally expensive to train, making them a practical choice for some applications. In the study [7], an SVM-based model achieved an accuracy of 96.3% on a dataset of brain tumor MRI images.

Principal Component Analysis (PCA) is applied to reduce data dimensionality, transforming it into a lower-dimensional space while retaining important information. The SVM model achieved an accuracy of 97% in the test set, indicating that it correctly classified 97% of the images.

4.1.2 Logistic Regression

Logistic regression (LR) is a linear classification algorithm used for image classification that estimates the probability that a data point belongs to a certain class. It has limitations in handling high-dimensional data. It works best with a small number of features and images containing a large amount of information. Deep learning models are now the state-of-the-art for brain tumor classification, achieving higher accuracy than LR. LR can be a good starting point for exploring image classification problems due to its simplicity and ease of interpretation.

Principal Component Analysis (PCA) is applied to reduce the dimensionality of high-dimensional data while retaining important information. The model achieved an accuracy of 95% in the testing set. Combining PCA and Logistic Regression improves predictive performance by addressing high-dimensionality challenges.

4.2 Deep Learning Models

Deep learning is a machine learning technique that uses artificial neural networks to learn from data, inspired by the structure and function of the human brain. These networks consist of layers of interconnected nodes that perform simple computations. Algorithms used in deep learning convolutional neural network (CNN) models include VGG16, ResNet101, and EfficientNetB3, which have achieved the highest accuracy.

CNNs extract features from images to represent tumor characteristics, such as size, shape, and texture. They can then associate these features with different types of brain tumors, making them effective for brain tumor classification.

4.2.1 VGG16

VGG16 is an object for prediction and classification that can classify hundreds of images of hundred different categories with high accuracy. It achieved 96%

accuracy in a study on deep transfer learning approaches in the performance analysis of brain tumor classification using MRI images.

VGG16 is a popular convolutional neural network (CNN) for image classification. It has an input, output, and hidden layers and is one of the best computer vision models. The model is easy to use with transfer learning and is a popular object detection and classification algorithm. The VGG16 model is loaded as the base model using Keras' $VGG16()$ function, with an input shape set to (224, 224, 3). The weights are initialized with pre-trained values from the "imagenet" dataset, and the top layers are excluded. The pooling layer after the convolutional layers is set to "max" pooling. The model is then divided into training and test sets using the scikit-learn $train_test_split()$ function. The model is defined as a sequential model consisting of the base_model, a dropout layer with 50% rate, and a dense layer with softmax activation. The model is evaluated using categorical crossentropy loss, Adam optimizer, and accuracy as evaluation metrics.

The training process involves defining two callbacks: earlystop and learning_rate_reduction. The minimum learning rate is set to 0.00001 to prevent excessive smallness and maintain a balance between stability and convergence speed. An ImageDataGenerator object is created to perform data augmentation, normalizing pixel values, and applying random transformations. The model is trained using the model.fit() function, passing training data through a data generator. The model architecture (VGG16), is commonly used in computer vision tasks, particularly in image classification. Due to its faster training, less overfitting potential, and similar predictive performance, VGG16 was chosen over VGG19 for disease prediction from images. This is especially true when working with a limited amount of labeled data and limited resources.

Training effectiveness, model performance, and resource usage can be strongly impacted by batch size selection, image size, and number of epochs. The VGG16 model's hyperparameters are Batch Size 32 because it balances computational efficiency and training stability, a batch size of 32 is frequently employed for deep network training. It facilitates quicker convergence. 100 Epochs, in medical imaging, where features are subtle and deep learning models need more iterations for accurate convergence, a larger number of epochs (100) are utilized to give the model more time to understand complicated patterns. Moreover, input Image Size 224×224 VGG networks (both VGG16 and VGG19) are pre-trained on ImageNet with 224×224 resolution. Keeping this input size ensures compatibility with pre-trained weights and maintains model accuracy during transfer learning.

4.2.2 ResNet101

ResNet101, a deep convolutional neural network architecture, is renowned for its effectiveness in image classification tasks. Its residual blocks, which incorporate skip connections, facilitate deep networks training by alleviating the problem of vanishing gradient. ResNet101 is suitable for various applications, including object recognition, scene classification, and medical image analysis, such as brain tumor classification in MRI images.

ResNet101 is a deep neural network that uses skip connections to reduce the error rate in image classification and categorization. It is used in a model that uses keras, an open source Python-based neural network framework, and TensorFlow. The model is built using Resnet101, a 101-layer deep convolutional neural network. The model training process involves importing necessary libraries, uploading preprocessed brain data, defining parameters like batch size, image size, and epoch, which significantly impact training efficiency, model performance, and resource utilization. The "ImageDataGenerator" function is used to set up and prepare brain image datasets for training and validation. The model is then built by loading the pre-trained ResNet101, initializing it with weights pre-trained on ImageNet, including the top layers, and freezing the layers. The model is then built on top of the pre-trained ResNet101, ensuring efficient training and resource utilization.

When implementing a neural network's training process, these parameters are essential. The number of epochs, the size of the image, and the size of the batch can all have a big impact on resource usage, model performance, and training effectiveness. The following are the hyperparameters utilized for the ResNet101 model: The 64 is the batch size. In order to balance memory utilization and convergence speed, a batch size of 64 is frequently utilized. It stabilizes gradient updates. 224 pixels in size. Initially, ResNet101 was trained using 224×224 input from ImageNet. This maintains the anticipated feature extraction performance and guarantees compatibility with the pre-trained weights. Epochs 3, for initial testing, model debugging, or transfer learning scenarios where pretrained features need little fine-tuning, a small number of epochs (e.g., 3) is usually employed.

4.2.3 EfficientNetB0

EfficientNetB0 is a highly efficient convolutional neural network designed for image classification tasks, balancing model size and performance through innovative scaling methods. It achieves high accuracy by effectively scaling its depth, width, and resolution, optimizing computational resources while maintaining top-tier performance.

Deep convolutional neural network models, such as the EfficientNetB0 model, can save significant computational resources and time by utilizing pre-trained weights on benchmark datasets like ImageNet. These models can be downloaded and used directly or integrated into new models for specific computer vision tasks. The code snippet demonstrates a data preprocessing pipeline and the training process for a computer vision task using an EfficientNetB0 model. The model is loaded using EfficientNetB0 from TensorFlow's keras.applications module, with the output obtained using model = effnet.output. A global average pooling layer, dropout layer, and dense layer with a softmax activation function are added as output layers. The model is instantiated using tf.keras.models.Model with the EfficientNetB0 input and defined output layers.

The model is compiled with a categorical cross-entropy loss function, Adam optimizer, and accuracy metric using model.compile. Several callbacks are defined to monitor and control the training process, such as TensorBoard, ModelCheckpoint, and ReduceLROnPlateau.

We selected EfficientNetB0 for this research article over other EfficientNet architectures, including EfficientNetB1, B2, B3, and others, due to its strong performance when combined with transfer learning, its broad compatibility with limited computing resources, its reduced risk of overfitting, and its faster training and inference.

The hyperparameters of the EfficientNetB0 model are as follows: Image Size: 224×224 since the EfficientNetB0 architecture was optimized for this resolution and was first created and trained on ImageNet, which had a default input size of 224×224. This resolution is enough to preserve important anatomical and textural details (such as tumors and lesions) in medical image analysis while reducing the processing load. In addition, it guarantees compatibility with pre-trained weights, which speeds up transfer learning and enhances performance on smaller datasets. The model is trained for 12 epochs with utilizing transfer learning with pre-trained weights and early stopping or validation monitoring to avoid overfitting. In medical image tasks, limited data availability and strong pre-trained models often mean that fewer epochs are needed to reach optimal performance. This provides a necessary balance between training time and accuracy, especially in clinical applications where efficiency is critical. Compared to the VGG16 model, EfficientNetB0 uses fewer epochs because it is designed to be efficient, learns features more effectively and converges faster, especially when fine-tuned with pre-trained weights. In addition, a patch size of 32 is used, where dividing 224×224 image to 32×32 pixel patches results $7 \times 7 = 49$ patches which provide fine view of the image and maintain contextual spatial information. The 32 patch size balances local detail and global coverage.

5 Results and Discussion

The performance of our models was assessed using a dataset testing set, using confusion matrices and classification reports in terms of classfiction accuracy, precision, recall, and F1 score. Unseen test data and 10-fold cross-validation were also used to assess models' generalization capabilities. The evaluation process aimed to identify strengths, weaknesses, and areas for improvement.

The confusion matrix of the models used is represented in Fig. 6, Fig. 7, Fig. 8, and Fig. 9. The confusion matrix is used in classification problems to show where model errors occurred. The rows represent the actual results, while the columns represent the predictions of the models. True positives (TP) are when the model correctly predicts a positive outcome (i.e. correctly predict brain tumor), while false positives (FP) are incorrect positive predictions (i.e. incorrectly predict no brain tumor). True negatives (TN) are correct negative predictions (i.e. correctly predict no brain tumor), and false negatives (FN) are incorrect negative predictions (i.e. incorrectly predict brain tumor). This helps identify prediction accuracy and errors in the model. When the brain tumor prediction model returns a false negative, it indicates that the patient actually has brain tumor, but the model predicts that the patient does not, which could have dangerous health effects for the patient. Therefore, FN is the most critical metric for medical applications in evaluating the accuracy of the disease prediction model, and we should work to reduce it.

A comparison of the classification reports for deep learning and machine learning models in terms of classification accuracy is shown in Table 1, the precision, recall, and F1 scores are shown in Fig. 10. The key findings are that EfficientNetB0 shows the highest values across all metrics. ResNet101 and VGG16 also perform strongly, with ResNet101 slightly ahead. SVM and LR perform relatively lower, especially in the F1 Score and recall.

Figures (Fig. 6, Fig. 7, Fig. 10), and Table 1 show the precision of ML models in predicting brain tumors. LR achieved 95% accuracy in classification of brain tumors. Its strengths include simplicity and interpretability, but it struggles with non-linear relationships and high-dimensional data. In contrast, Support Vector Machines (SVM) outperformed Logistic Regression with 97% accuracy. SVM is robust to noise and outliers, handles non-linear relationships, and can handle high-dimensional data. However, its high computational complexity can be a limitation when dealing with large datasets. Compared to LR, SVM has a higher recall and F1 score and a lower FN. Despite these limitations, both models showed moderate success in capturing complex patterns in the data. Compared to DL models, the LR and SVM models have a lower recall and a higher FN.

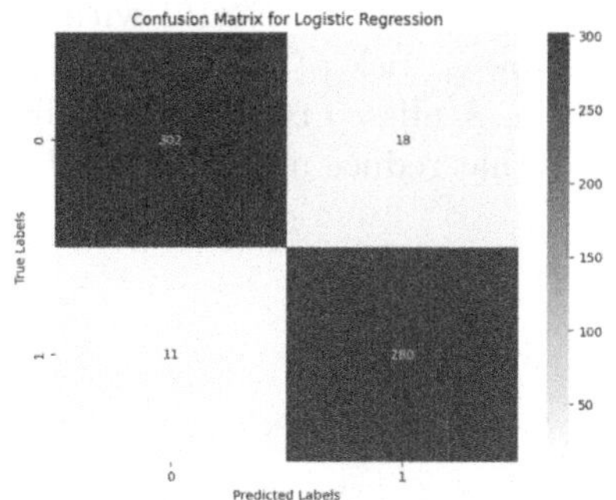

Fig. 6. Confusion Matrix for LR model.

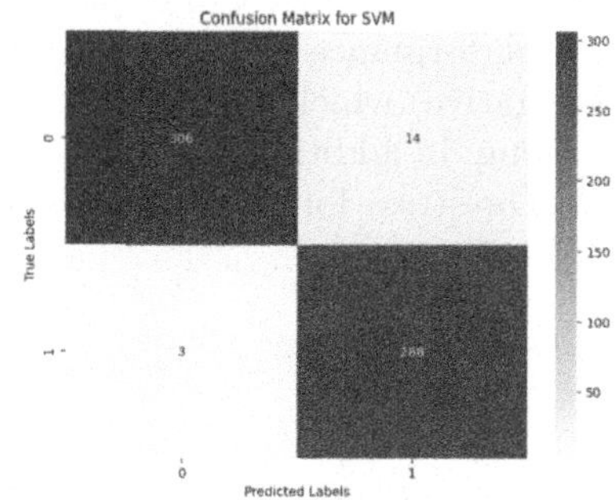

Fig. 7. Confusion Matrix for SVM model.

The comparison of the three deep learning models to predict and classify brain tumor types is presented in Fig. 8, Fig. 9, Fig. 10, and Table 1. The VGG16 deep learning model, pre-trained on ImageNet, achieved a 65% accuracy on the brain tumor MRI image dataset. However, this lower accuracy suggests that VGG16 might not be ideal for capturing specific patterns within brain tumor data. EfficientNetB0, a deep learning model designed for image classification

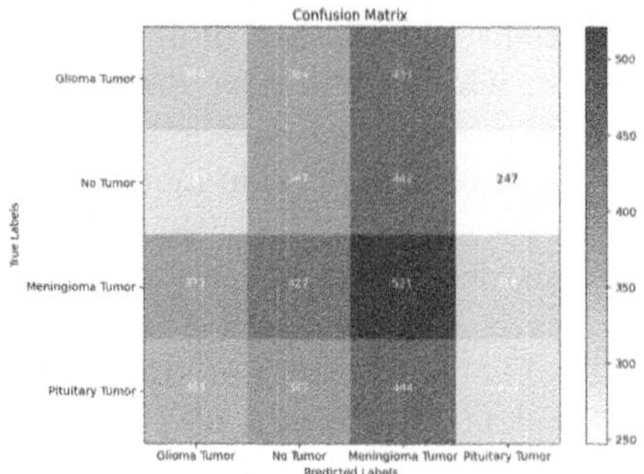

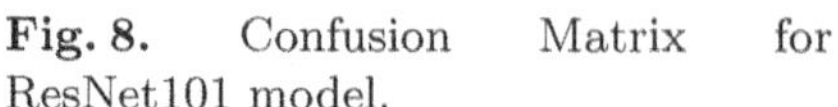

Fig. 8. Confusion Matrix for ResNet101 model.

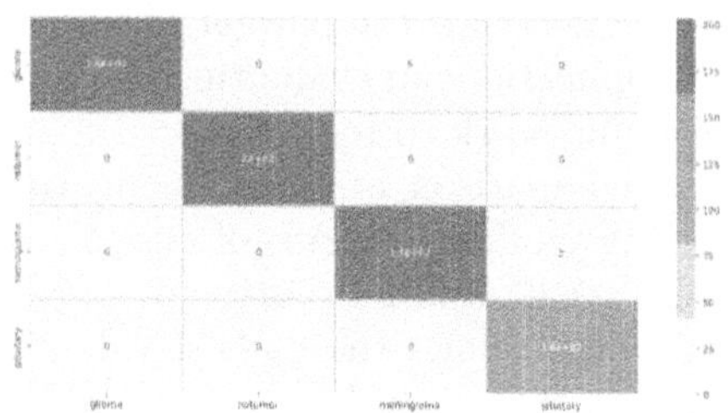

Fig. 9. Confusion Matrix for EfficientNetB0 model.

tasks, achieved a 99% accuracy, outperforming all other models. Although EfficientNetB0's strengths include learning complex patterns in data and requiring fewer resources, its high computational complexity can be a limitation when dealing with large datasets. ResNet101, a model trained on the brain tumor dataset, achieved accuracy 78%, falling short of the accuracy 92.9% reported in [3]. This difference is likely due to the size and complexity of the dataset, as our used dataset is larger and more diverse. The higher accuracy of the study [2] was likely due to its focus on identifying the presence or absence of a tumor rather than the specific type. Consequently, the best model: EfficientNetB0 with the highest performance in all key metrics and the lowest risk of diagnostic error (false negative) which is critical in tumor detection. A missed tumor can be life-threatening. In addition, the lowest false positives that reduce unnecessary MRI, biopsies, or stress for healthy patients.

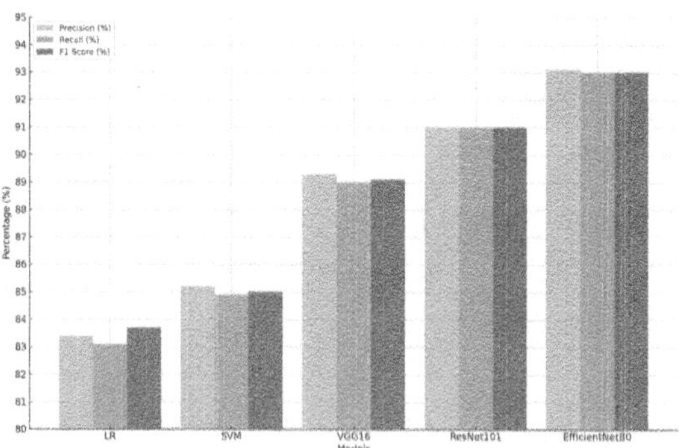

Fig. 10. A comparison of machine learning and deep learning models' classification performance metrics.

Table 1. Model Prediction Accuracy.

Model	Accuracy
Logistic Regression	95%
Support Vector Machines	97%
VGG16	65%
EfficientNetB0	99%
ResNet101	78%

Table 2. Proposed method comparison with (SOTA).

Reference	Dataset	Method	Accuracy (%)	Prediction/Classification
[1]	SARTAJ dataset: 3264 MRI Images	Multi-scale CNN	97.3%	Only brain tumor Classification
[6]	Figshare dataset: 253 MRI Images	Six ML models (CN2 Rule Induction, Neural Networks, Naïve Bayes, Random Forest, SVM, Decision Tree)	90.7%	Only brain tumor Prediction
[7]	Figshare dataset: 253 MRI Images	SVM	96.3%	Only brain tumor Classification
[12]	SARTAJ dataset: 3264 MRI Images	CNN EfficientNetB0	98.78%	Only brain tumor Classification
Proposed	Combining several datasets: 7023 MRI Images	DL models: CNN (EfficientNetB0 and ResNet101), ML models (SVM, Logistic Regression)	99%	Brain tumor Prediction and Classification

Table 2 presents a comparison between state-of-the-art (SOTA) approaches and the proposed method. The table shows that the suggested technique outperforms current strategies. Compared to state-of-the-art (SOTA) approaches, the suggested approach performs competitively. Comparison of the efficiency of our models with previous studies [1,6,7], and [12] in imaging-based machine learning for the prediction of brain tumor using a similar dataset to what we use. The model achieves high accuracy in the project's SVM and EfficientNetB0. The comparison comprehensively compares various machine and deep learning models for brain tumor classification and prediction, aiming to improve the model's effectiveness.

Comparison of the findings of our study with earlier research on imaging-based brain tumor prediction In a number of crucial areas, our effort outperformed earlier research: This research work used a larger dataset than [1,6], allowing for more robust learning. It conducted a three-category brain tumor classification/segmentation and presence prediction for more information. Unlike [1,7] which only classified tumors vs. none. The multi-scale CNN, inspired by human vision, outperformed single-scale models [1] with 97.3% accuracy. The solution provided quick and accurate predictions directly from MRI slices without preprocessing, increasing clinical usefulness compared to the study [12]. EfficientNetB0 achieved 99% precision, saving valuable time for diagnosis. This contribution has the potential to revolutionize neuro-oncology by speeding workflows and maximizing healthcare access. The study addressed the limitations of [6] in leveraging a large dataset and deep learning for state-of-the-art results.

6 Conclusions

This study aims to develop a model that analyzes MRI medical images to identify the presence and type of brain tumors. The project explores the potential of deep learning and machine learning techniques in predicting and classifying brain tumors. The researchers compared the performance of various models, including Logistic Regression, Support Vector Machines (SVM), VGG16, EfficientNetB0, and ResNet101. The results showed that EfficientNetB0 achieved superior accuracy, reaching an impressive 99% in correctly classifying brain tumors. This outperformed other models, with Logistic Regression at 95%, SVM at 97%, VGG16 at 65%, and ResNet101 at 78%. The project not only advances our understanding of machine learning and deep learning applications in healthcare but also provides a promising tool for accurate brain tumor identification. The choice of model depends on the application and data characteristics, with simple models suitable for linear relationships and high-dimensional data, and deep learning models capable of learning complex patterns.

This study explores the use of ML and DL models in clinical practice to predict and classify brain tumors. These models can be embedded into Electronic Health Records (EHR) systems and provide a model for Clinical Decision Support Systems (CDSS). The ML model automatically evaluates patient MRI images and highlights potential brain tumor concerns, helping doctors make decisions by producing alerts or risk scores. However, incorporating the ML model into clinical practice requires extensive preparation, including training clinicians, ensuring easy integration into current workflows, and making the model understandable. Regulatory and ethical considerations are also crucial, including adhering to HIPAA, GDPR, and local health data laws. To avoid biased predictions, the model should be evaluated in various populations, and prospective clinical trials should be used. Challenges include changing patient populations and medical practices over time, interoperability between different healthcare systems using different EHR formats, and data quality and consistency, where missing or inconsistent medical records can affect model accuracy. The implementation of the best DL model found in this study in the real-world healthcare system will be the focus of future research. We will also be concerned with developing the model that is understandable and providing clinical justifications for the predicted risk outcome to gain the trust of clinicians.

Declarations

- Ethics approval and consent to participate: Not applicable.
- Conflict of interest/Competing interests: There is no any Conflict of interest.
- Consent for publication: All the authors agree consent for publication.

- Funding: Not applicable.
- Acknowledgements: The author would like to thank Rahaf Alhuzali, Lama Alghamdi, and Wejdan Awaji who are students at the College of Computer Science and Engineering, University of Jeddah, for supporting this study by developing the machine learning prototype.

References

1. Díaz-Pernas, F.J., Martínez-Zarzuela, M., Antón-Rodríguez, M., GonzálezOrtega, D.: A deep learning approach for brain tumor classification and segmentation using a multiscale convolutional neural network. In: Healthcare, vol. 9, p. 153. MDPI (2021)
2. Srinivas, C., et al.: Deep transfer learning approaches in performance analysis of brain tumor classification using MRI images. J. Healthc. Eng. **2022**(1), 3264367 (2022)
3. Sadad, T., et al.: Brain tumor detection and multi-classification using advanced deep learning techniques. Microsc. Res. Tech. **84**(6), 1296–1308 (2021)
4. Pashaei, A., Sajedi, H., Jazayeri, N.: Brain tumor classification via convolutional neural network and extreme learning machines. In: 8th International Conference on Computer and Knowledge Engineering (ICCKE), pp. 314–319. IEEE (2018)
5. Sultan, H.H., Salem, N.M., Al-Atabany, W.: Multi-classification of brain tumor images using deep neural network. IEEE Access **7**, 69215–69225 (2019)
6. Asiri, A.A., et al.: Machine learning-based models for magnetic resonance imaging (MRI)-based brain tumor classification. Intell. Autom. Softw. Comput. **36**, 299–312 (2023)

7. Mohsen, H., El-Dahshan, E., El-Horbaty, E., Salem, A.: Brain tumor type classification based on support vector machine in magnetic resonance images. In: Annals Of Dunarea De Jos University of Galati, Mathematics, Physics, Theoretical mechanics, Fascicle II, Year IX (XL), vol. 1 (2017)
8. Cheng, J., et al.: Enhanced performance of brain tumor classification via tumor region augmentation and partition. PLoS ONE **10**(10), 0140381 (2015)
9. Kondamuri, H.R., Padmanabhuni, V.N.R.: Brain tumour images classification using support vector machine and pre-trained convolutional neural networks (2023)
10. Kang, J., Ullah, Z., Gwak, J.: MRI-based brain tumor classification using ensemble of deep features and machine learning classifiers. Sensors **21**(6), 2222 (2021)
11. Samitha, T., Gopika, S.: Brain tumor classification using efficientnet models. Int. Res. J. Eng. Technol. **9**(8), 868–873 (2022)
12. Nayak, D.R., Padhy, N., Mallick, P.K., Zymbler, M., Kumar, S.: Brain tumor classification using dense efficient-net. Axioms **11**(1), 34 (2022)
13. Nickparvar, M.: Brain Tumor MRI Dataset. Kaggle (2021). https://doi.org/10.34740/KAGGLE/DSV/2645886, https://www.kaggle.com/dsv/2645886
14. Jun, C.: Brain Tumor Dataset. figshare (2017). https://doi.org/10.6084/m9.figshare.1512427.v5
15. Bhuvaji, S., Kadam, A., Bhumkar, P., Dedge, S., Kanchan, S.: Brain Tumor Classification (MRI). Kaggle (2020). https://doi.org/10.34740/KAGGLE/DSV/1183165, https://www.kaggle.com/dsv/1183165
16. Hamada, A.: Br35H : : Brain Tumor Detection 2020. Kaggle (2021). https://www.kaggle.com/datasets/ahmedhamada0/brain-tumor-detection?select=no
17. Saeedi, S., Rezayi, S., Keshavarz, H., R. Niakan Kalhori, S.: MRI-based brain tumor detection using convolutional deep learning methods and chosen machine learning techniques. BMC Med. Inform. Decis. Making **23**(1), 16 (2023)

Estimating Fall Risk in Older Adults Using Postural Sway Parameters and Machine Learning

Haoxuan Zhang[1], Ting Xiao[2,3,4](✉), Guna Sindhuja Siripurapu[3], Shawn Kennedy[5], Rita M. Patterson[5], and Mark V. Albert[1,3,4]

[1] Department of Information Science, University of North Texas, Denton, TX, USA
[2] Department of Data Science, University of North Texas, Denton, TX, USA
[3] Department of Computer Science and Engineering, University of North Texas, Denton, TX, USA
ting.xiao@unt.edu
[4] Center of Computational Life Sciences, University of North Texas, Denton, TX, USA
[5] Family and Osteopathic Manipulative Medicine, UNT Health Science Center, Fort Worth, TX, USA

Abstract. Falls represent a major public health challenge for older adults, and despite evidence linking postural sway to fall risk, the relationship between specific parameters and fall probability remains incompletely understood. This study aimed to develop and evaluate a machine learning approach to predict whether people were at risk of falling, defined as either having fallen in the past six months or reporting concern about falling. Data were collected from 1,421 participants at the University of North Texas Health Sciences Center using a Bertec force plate under various standing conditions, with the data set including 186 individuals with risk of falling and 1,235 without risk. Eight machine learning algorithms were evaluated, with ensemble models emerging as the superior model, achieving an area under the ROC curve of 0.85 and providing excellent discriminative ability between fallers and non-fallers. Feature importance analysis identified age as the most influential predictor, followed by pain score and specific center of pressure characteristics, while text analysis of diagnostic information highlighted the importance of terms like "memory" and "dysfunction" in the assessment of risk of falls. The approach provides a methodological framework for evaluating the implementation of clinical fall prevention strategies.

Keywords: Fall Risk Estimation · Postural Sway Analysis · Elderly Mobility Assessment · Machine Learning · Health Data Analysis

1 Introduction

Falls represent a major and growing public health challenge, particularly among older adults. As human longevity increases, falls-related injuries and

A. Alsadoon et al. (Eds.): CSCE 2025, CCIS 2935, pp. 417–428, 2026.
https://doi.org/10.1007/978-3-032-22199-5_32

their consequences, such as fractures, hospitalizations, decreased mobility, and mortality, are projected to increase significantly [1]. Epidemiological studies estimate that approximately 14% of older adults living in the community experience one or more falls each year, often with potentially devastating consequences for independence and quality of life [2]. In response, the World Falls Guidelines highlight the critical need for proactive detection of fall risk, urging clinicians to ask whether individuals have previously fallen, feel unstable, or worry about falling, key insights for targeted prevention and intervention [3].

Despite the importance of timely assessment, traditional fall risk screening methods remain limited by subjectivity, time consumption, and insensitivity to subtle deficits in postural control [4]. Recent research has shifted towards quantitative approaches based on sensors, using advances in wearable technology and force plate systems to collect objective balance and mobility data [5]. Machine learning algorithms - such as random forests, support vector machines, and ensemble models - have shown strong promise in classifying fall risk based on gait and balance features, often outperforming conventional tools in both accuracy and scalability [6]. However, challenges persist, including limited sample diversity, small datasets, and the need for further validation in real-world clinical settings [7].

A key metric at the forefront of these advances is postural sway, quantified through force plate recordings of center of pressure (CoP) movements during quiet standing. The sway parameters, including the length, velocity, area, and rotational frequency of the path, offer a sensitive and objective understanding of the complex control of human balance [8]. In particular, the sway ratio (SR), which compares CoP with the lengths of the center of the mass path, has become a robust and reliable index for detecting balance deficits and distinguishing between visual conditions in older adults [8]. With sway analysis now accessible through modern clinical technologies, its integration into computational models further enhances the potential for early detection and intervention [9].

Given these developments, there is a pressing need for comprehensive and data-driven approaches to fall risk assessment that synthesize sway metrics, advanced analytics, and electronic health data. This study addresses these needs by collecting detailed measurements of postural sway from a diverse clinical cohort and evaluating multiple machine learning methods for robust and automated prediction of fall risk. Our research makes several significant contributions to the field:

1. We identify the most important parameters of postural sway for assessing the risk of falling, highlighting the importance of demographic factors, center pressure characteristics, and other biomechanical variables.
2. We compare the performance of multiple machine learning algorithms to determine which approaches yield superior classification accuracy in the estimation of fall risk.

3. We provide evidence that machine learning approaches can effectively estimate fall risk even in datasets with significant class imbalance, offering potential clinical applications for fall prevention.

2 Methodology

2.1 Participants

Postural sway measurements were collected from a cohort of 1,097 patients receiving care at the University of North Texas Health Sciences Center (UNTHSC) clinics from June 7, 2021 to June 12, 2024. The eligibility criteria excluded people under 18 years of age or those unable to maintain an unassisted standing position for at least five minutes. Data acquisition was integrated into routine clinical evaluations as an adjunct vital sign metric, with measurements performed by trained UNTHSC student volunteers and research assistants under institutional oversight. The dataset comprises 1,421 postural sway recordings, including 771 female and 326 male participants, with ages ranging from 18 to over 80 years. Among them, 324 individuals underwent multiple tests. The sample exhibited a predominance of older adults, as 41% (n = 450) of participants fell within the age range of 60–79 years. Forty-five individuals (4.1%) reported at least one fall incident in the six months preceding data collection, with 19 cases (1.7%) involving fall-related injuries.

Demographic analysis revealed a racial distribution of 836 White (76.2%), 109 Black or African American (9.9%), 78 unspecified (7.1%), and 74 individuals (6.8%) identifying as Asian, American Indian, or Native Hawaiian. The ethnicity classifications included 752 unreported cases (68.6%), 288 non-Hispanic (26.3%), and 57 Hispanic (5.2%) participants. Comorbidity prevalence data identified hypertension (n = 306, 27.9%) and knee/hip pain (n = 313, 28.5%) as common medical conditions within the cohort. This multidimensional data set, which includes biomechanical, demographic and clinical variables, serves as the basis for the ongoing development of machine learning algorithms designed to stratify the risk of falls in clinical populations.

2.2 Procedures

Participants were instructed to maintain an upright posture on a Bertec Force Plate, with their upper limbs positioned alongside the trunk in a standardized manner. The postural assessment protocol consisted of multiple conditions: eyes open (EO) with visual fixation on a target, eyes closed (EC) and variations in footwear (shoes on/off), all performed on a firm surface. Each visual condition was assessed through three 10-second trials, yielding a total of 30 s of data per condition.

The force plate captured two-dimensional time-series center of pressure (CoP) data from the left, right, and net force vectors. From these recordings, 20 quantitative variables were derived to characterize postural stability. These included sway path length, sway velocity, sway area, sway angle, and rotational frequency, among others.

All assessment data were subsequently integrated into a de-identified electronic medical record system. This integration was designed to support future computational analyses, including the application of advanced machine learning algorithms for predictive modeling and clinical decision support.

2.3 Machine Learning Experimental Setup

To analyze and assess fall risk, the dataset was preprocessed and restructured to accommodate the different experimental conditions and measurement parameters. Specifically, data segmentation was performed based on conditions such as eyes open or closed, frequency range, platform location, and shoe type. For each condition and variable, statistical features including minimum (min), maximum (max), average (ave), and standard deviation (std) were computed to provide a comprehensive representation of postural sway metrics as shown in Fig. 1. Additionally, we performed TF-IDF feature extraction on each subject's Diagnosis Description, converting textual data into numerical features. We incorporated TF-IDF specifically to leverage the rich diagnostic information in clinical text notes, enabling the identification of key medical terminology associated with fall risk and transforming qualitative clinical assessments into quantitative predictors that could complement the biomechanical measurements in our models.

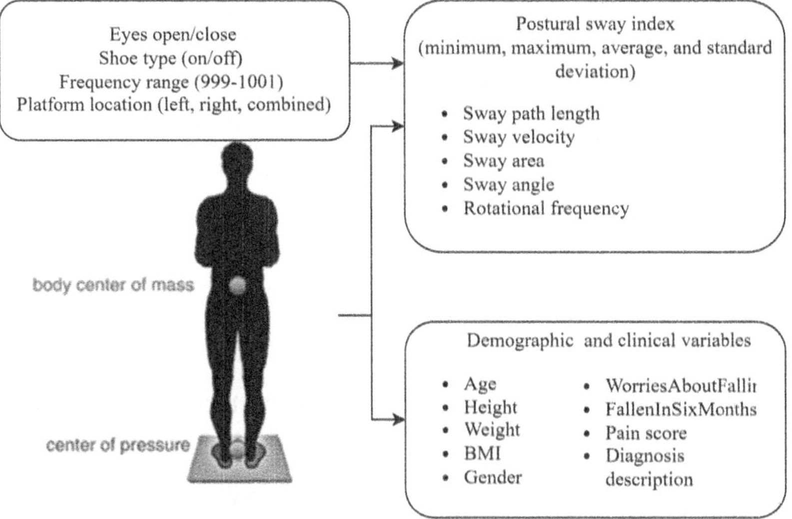

Fig. 1. Comprehensive data preprocessing pipeline for fall risk assessment: integration of postural sway biomechanics and clinical variables.

The analytical framework employed eight distinct machine learning algorithms to evaluate their effectiveness in stratifying fall risk based on postural sway data. These comprised five individual models—Support Vector Machine (SVM), Logistic Regression (LR), Naive Bayes (NB), k-Nearest Neighbors (KNN), and Decision Tree (DT)—as well as three ensemble models: Random Forest (RF), Light Gradient Boosting Machine (LGBM), and Extreme Gradient Boosting (XGB). Hyperparameter optimization utilized Bayesian Search with 5-fold cross-validation, maximizing the F1-macro score to address class imbalance in fall occurrences. Model performance was assessed through an 80:20 stratified train-test split, preserving class distribution across subsets.

2.4 Evaluation Metrics

Model performance was assessed using five metrics, defined as follows. Here, True Positives (TP), True Negatives (TN), False Positives (FP), and False Negatives (FN) represent classification outcomes, and C is the number of classes (here, $C = 2$ for fallers/non-fallers):

- **Macro Precision**:

$$P_{\text{macro}} = \frac{1}{C} \sum_{c=1}^{C} \frac{TP_c}{TP_c + FP_c}$$

- **Macro Recall**:

$$R_{\text{macro}} = \frac{1}{C} \sum_{c=1}^{C} \frac{TP_c}{TP_c + FN_c}$$

- **F1-Macro**:

$$F1_{\text{macro}} = \frac{1}{C} \sum_{c=1}^{C} \frac{2P_cR_c}{P_c + R_c}$$

  where P_c and R_c denote class-specific precision and recall.
- **Accuracy**:

$$\text{Acc} = \frac{TP + TN}{TP + TN + FP + FN}$$

- **ROC-AUC**:

$$\text{AUC} = \int_0^1 TPR(\tau)\, dFPR(\tau)$$

  where

$$TPR(\tau) = \frac{TP(\tau)}{TP(\tau) + FN(\tau)}, \quad FPR(\tau) = \frac{FP(\tau)}{FP(\tau) + TN(\tau)}$$

  over threshold $\tau \in (-\infty, \infty)$.

Macro-averaging gives equal weight to each class, which is particularly important for imbalanced datasets. All evaluation metrics were computed using the `scikit-learn` library [10].

3 Experiment and Result

3.1 Dataset

According to the World Falls Guidelines (WFG) [3], three key questions for detecting fall risk in elderly individuals are: (i) Have you fallen in the past year? (ii) Do you feel unsteady when standing or walking? (iii) Are you worried about falling? These questions have been shown to demonstrate higher sensitivity in estimating future fall risk. Therefore, we examined subjects' responses to "FallenInSixMonths" (Yes/No) and "WorriesAboutFalling" (Yes/No). Subjects were classified as having fall risk if they answered "Yes" to either question, and as having no fall risk otherwise [11]. Finally, the dataset comprised 186 individuals identified as at fall risk and 1235 individuals identified as without fall risk. Despite the severe class imbalance (approximately 1:6.6 ratio) in the dataset, we deliberately avoided implementing any data balancing strategies to preserve the original data structure, which better reflects real-world clinical scenarios.

3.2 Machine Learning Model Performance Evaluation

We trained eight machine learning models with results shown in Table 1. We tested all features including TF-IDF feature extraction on each subject's Diagnosis Description and all postural sway metrics. Comparative ROC curves are presented in Fig. 2.

Table 1. Machine learning model performance comparison

Model	Accuracy	Precision	Recall	F1 Score	AUC (95% CI)
LGBM	0.87	0.71	0.59	0.62	**0.851 ± 0.023**
XGB	**0.88**	**0.73**	0.61	**0.64**	0.837 ± 0.031
RF	0.87	0.66	0.55	0.56	0.753 ± 0.052
DT	0.85	0.66	**0.64**	**0.64**	0.680 ± 0.037
LR	0.82	0.61	0.62	0.61	0.654 ± 0.057
SVM	0.82	0.57	0.56	0.56	0.580 ± 0.039
NB	0.55	0.50	0.51	0.45	0.507 ± 0.041
KNN	0.87	0.60	0.50	0.48	0.498 ± 0.028

The comparative analysis of eight machine learning algorithms demonstrates distinct performance characteristics in fall risk prediction modeling. Among the evaluated models, XGB achieved superior overall performance with the highest accuracy (0.88) and precision (0.73), indicating its effectiveness in both correct classification and minimizing false positive predictions. The ensemble methods, including RF, LGBM, and XGB, consistently demonstrated robust performance, with accuracy scores ranging from 0.87 to 0.88, highlighting the advantages of

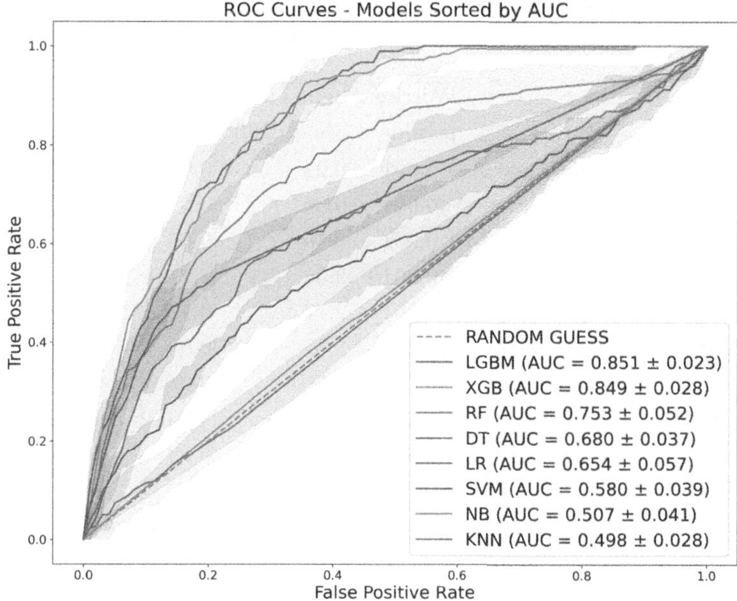

Fig. 2. ROC curves and AUC for fall risk prediction models.

ensemble learning approaches in this predictive task. AUC analysis provides additional insights, with LGBM achieving the highest AUC (0.85) in both feature scenarios, closely followed by XGB (0.84). These values substantially exceed those of simpler models, highlighting the effectiveness of ensemble approaches in capturing complex relationships within the data. Ensemble models, such as RF, LGBM, and XGB, are particularly effective in this context because they combine the predictions of multiple base learners—typically decision trees—to capture complex, nonlinear relationships and interactions among features. This aggregation helps to reduce overfitting and improve generalizability compared to single-model approaches. In fall risk prediction, where the underlying data may be heterogeneous and the relationships between clinical, demographic, and biomechanical variables are intricate, ensemble methods are better equipped to model these complexities than simpler algorithms like SVM, NB, or KNN. This is reflected in the substantially higher AUC values for ensemble models (LGBM: 0.85, XGB: 0.84) compared to simpler models (SVM: 0.58, NB: 0.51, KNN: 0.51).

3.3 Independent T-Test Analysis

We performed independent samples t-tests to identify features that most effectively differentiate individuals with and without fall risk factors (See Table 2). Our analysis revealed significant differences in multiple balance parameters between fallers and non-fallers. The top 10 features demonstrated highly significant discrimination between those who reported concerns about falling and

Table 2. Top 10 features discriminating between fall and non-fall groups based on T-Test analysis

Feature	Worries About Falling		Fallen in Six Months	
	p-value	Mean Diff.[a]	p-value	Mean Diff.b
SD Sway Angle (deg)_mean	<0.001***	0.05	0.03*	0.02
SD Sway Angle (deg)_max	<0.001***	0.09	0.05*	0.04
RMS Sway Angle (deg)_max	<0.001***	0.16	0.05*	0.06
AVG rd (mm)_max	<0.001***	2.38	0.11	0.73
RMS rd (mm)_max	<0.001***	2.77	0.12	0.84
Range cop ap (mm)_mean	<0.001***	5.65	0.03*	2.60
SD rd (mm)_mean	<0.001***	0.75	0.04*	0.33
Age at Encounter (Yrs)	<0.001***	8.32	<0.001***	6.07
Range cop ml (mm)_mean	<0.001***	2.26	0.09	0.78
SD cop ml (mm)_mean	<0.001***	0.52	0.07	0.19

[a]Mean difference = Worry group mean - No worry group mean; [b]Mean difference = Fall group mean - No fall group mean; $^{*}p < 0.05$; $^{**}p < 0.01$; $^{***}p < 0.001$.

those who did not ($p < 0.001$), with consistently higher mean values in the worry group. However, only five features-namely SD Sway Angle (mean and maximum), RMS Sway Angle (maximum), Range of center of pressure in the anterior-posterior direction, and SD radial displacement-significantly differentiated between those who had experienced actual falls in the previous six months and those who had not ($p < 0.05$). Age emerged as a particularly robust discriminator, demonstrating significant differences for both outcomes ($p < 0.001$). The stronger associations observed with worry about falling compared to actual falls suggest these postural sway parameters may better capture perceived instability that contributes to fear of falling rather than objective fall risk. These findings highlight potential targets for assessment and intervention strategies that address both physical fall risk and the psychological components of balance confidence.

3.4 Feature Importance Analysis

We leveraged the built-in feature importance calculation capabilities of several machine learning models: RF, DT, LGBM, and XGB. For each model, we computed the top 10 most important features from the entire feature set. Additionally, we identified the 10 most predictive words based on TF-IDF feature values derived from the Diagnosis Description field. To complement the model-based feature importance rankings, we conducted statistical significance testing using Spearman rank correlation analysis to assess the monotonic relationships between individual features and the target variable. The comprehensive ranking results are presented in Fig. 3.

The feature importance analysis reveals a multifaceted approach to fall risk estimation, with demographic, clinical, and biomechanical parameters all contributing meaningful predictive value.

Key Structural Features: The feature importance analysis highlights a multifaceted approach to estimating the risk of falls, with demographic, clinical, and biomechanical parameters all contributing significantly to predictive value. Among these, age at encounter emerged as the most influential predictor (rank 1.88), consistent with established evidence that advancing age is a primary risk factor for both increased fear of falling and actual fall events [3,12]. Pain score ranked second (5.00), reflecting its strong association with both subjective worries about falling and reported falls, likely due to pain's impact on mobility and confidence [3,11]. Several metrics of postural sway demonstrated substantial predictive power. The standard deviation of center of pressure (COP) radial displacement (rank 7.50) quantifies the variability in a subject's ability to maintain balance; higher values may indicate impaired postural control and greater instability, both of which are clinically recognized as fall risk factors [1,13]. Similarly, the standard deviation of the area ratio (rank 13.67) captures fluctuations in the spatial extent of sway, providing insight into the consistency of balance control, as greater variability may reflect compromised neuromuscular regulation [2,8]. Minimum COP area (rank 14.00) represents the smallest area covered during quiet standing, with reduced values potentially indicating a rigid or overly cautious postural strategy, which paradoxically can also increase fall risk [1,13]. Velocity-related parameters, including minimum velocity (rank 10.00), RMS COP in the anterior-posterior direction (rank 10.00), mean velocity (rank 11.00), maximum anterior-posterior velocity (rank 12.25), and mean total velocity (rank 14.00), were also prominent. These features reflect the dynamic aspects of postural control. Higher velocities may indicate compensatory or unstable balance strategies, which have been linked to increased fall risk in clinical populations [13,14]. Importantly, most of these features showed significant correlations with worries about falling at the 1% significance level, whereas only age and pain score were significantly associated with actual falls in the past six months. This pattern suggests that comprehensive fall risk assessment should integrate both subjective factors (such as pain and fear of falling) and objective biomechanical measures (particularly those capturing postural sway variability and velocity), with special attention to the clinical interpretation of sway parameters as indicators of underlying physiological instability [2,3].

Significant Diagnostic Terminology: The text-based analysis reveals diagnostic patterns strongly associated with fall risk, with neurological and cognitive factors emerging as primary contributors. The term "memory" demonstrates the strongest association (rank 4.00), followed closely by "somatic" (rank 4.75) and "dysfunction" (rank 5.38), suggesting that cognitive and neurophysiological impairments significantly influence fall probability. These findings are consistent with a growing body of evidence linking cognitive deficits, particularly in memory, executive function, and attention, to impaired gait, reduced balance, and diminished hazard perception, all of which increase susceptibility to falls [3].

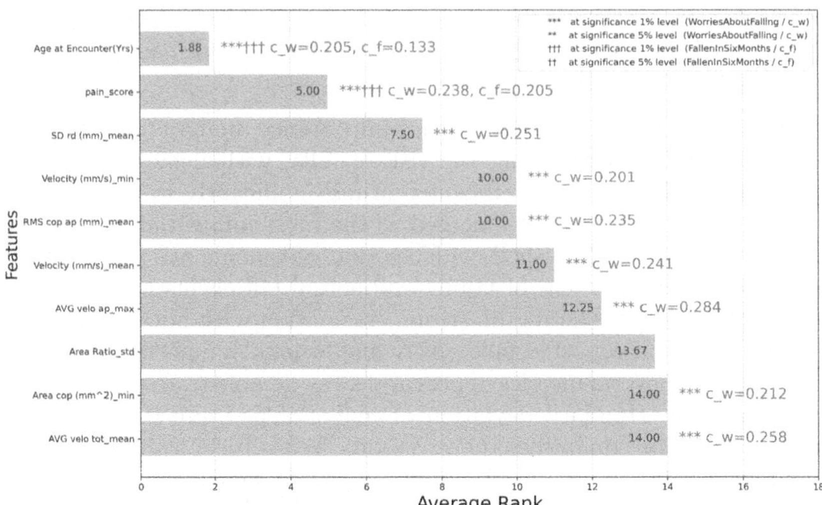

(a) Top 10 features ranked by model importance (Lower Rank Indicates Higher Importance)

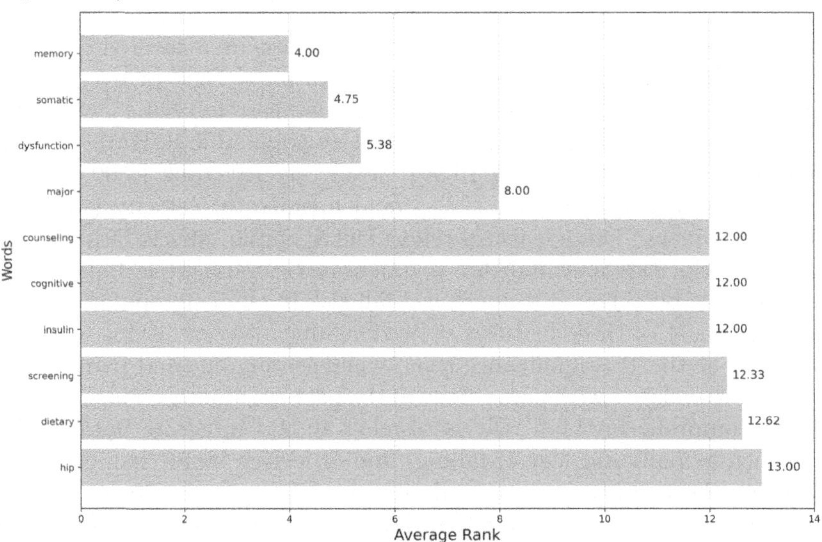

(b) Top 10 predictive words identified by applying TF-IDF to each subject's diagnosis description (Lower Rank Indicates Higher Importance)

Fig. 3. Feature importance analysis across different models.

Cognitive dysfunction may compromise an individual's ability to process environmental cues, dual-task safely, or adapt to unexpected changes in their surroundings, thereby elevating fall risk [3,11]. The term "major" (rank 8.00) shows moderate association, while intervention approaches such as "counseling" and "cognitive" therapy (both rank 12.00) appear less directly predictive, potentially reflecting their role as secondary or preventive measures rather than primary risk indicators. Metabolic factors are represented by "insulin" (rank 12.00) and "dietary" considerations (rank 12.62), indicating potential secondary influences on fall risk, such as those mediated by hypoglycemia or nutritional deficiencies. Musculoskeletal terminology, specifically "hip" (rank 13.00), demonstrates the weakest association among the analyzed terms, which may suggest that, in this cohort, musculoskeletal issues are less predictive than cognitive factors. The prominence of neurological indicators with substantially lower rank values than metabolic or musculoskeletal factors underscores the critical role of cognitive health in fall risk. This is in line with recent international guidelines, which emphasize cognitive assessment and management as integral components of comprehensive fall prevention strategies for older adults [3]. Early identification and management of cognitive impairment, including screening, targeted interventions, and multidisciplinary care, may therefore be essential in reducing fall incidence and improving patient outcomes. These results highlight the need for comprehensive neuropsychological evaluation as part of fall prevention protocols [3,11].

This comprehensive feature importance analysis demonstrates that fall risk estimation benefits from integrating multiple data dimensions, including quantitative postural measures, demographic information, and detailed clinical diagnostics. The results support a holistic approach to fall risk assessment that considers both physical performance metrics and underlying medical conditions.

4 Conclusion

This study evaluated eight machine learning models for estimating fall risk using postural sway measurements, demographic data, and clinical variables. Our comprehensive analysis demonstrated that ensemble models (XGB, LGBM, RF) consistently outperformed traditional algorithms in fall risk stratification. XGB achieved the highest accuracy (0.88) and precision (0.73) when utilizing all features, while LGBM demonstrated superior discriminative ability with the highest AUC (0.85) in both feature scenarios. The DT model exhibited particular strength in recall (0.64), indicating effective identification of true fall risk cases. Feature importance analysis revealed that fall risk estimation is optimally approached through a multidimensional framework. Age emerged as the most influential predictor, followed by pain score and various postural sway metrics, particularly those quantifying center of pressure characteristics. The standard deviation of COP radial distance, velocity parameters, and area-related metrics all contributed substantial predictive value. Text-based analysis of diagnostic information highlighted the significance of cognitive impairment terms ("memory", "cognitive"), somatic dysfunction, and metabolic factors in fall risk assessment. Future research should focus on external validation of these models in diverse clinical populations, longitudinal assessment of predictive accuracy, and development of interpretable decision support tools that can be readily integrated into routine clinical workflows. The integration of postural sway metrics with demographic and diagnostic information represents a promising approach for early identification of fall risk and implementation of targeted preventive interventions.

Acknowledgements. Funds to support this AITC study were provided by the Johns Hopkins University AITC under award number P30AG073104.

References

1. Johansson, J., Nordström, A., Gustafson, Y., Westling, G., Nordström, P.: Increased postural sway during quiet stance as a risk factor for prospective falls in community-dwelling elderly individuals. Age Ageing **46**(6), 964–970 (2017)
2. Zhou, J., Habtemariam, D., Iloputaife, I., Lipsitz, L.A., Manor, B.: The complexity of standing postural sway associates with future falls in community-dwelling older adults: the mobilize Boston study. Sci. Rep. **7**(1), 2924 (2017)
3. Montero-Odasso, M., et al.: World guidelines for falls prevention and management for older adults: a global initiative. Age Ageing **51**(9), afac205 (2022)
4. Beauchet, O., et al.: Launay. Falls risk prediction for older inpatients in acute care medical wards: is there an interest to combine an early nurse assessment and the artificial neural network analysis? J. Nutr. Health Aging **22**(1), 131–137 (2018)
5. Tunca, C., Salur, G., Ersoy, C.: Deep learning for fall risk assessment with inertial sensors: utilizing domain knowledge in spatio-temporal gait parameters. IEEE J. Biomed. Health Inform. **24**(7), 1994–2005 (2020)
6. Philip, J.S., Aarthi, M.S., Kathrine, G.J.W., Kirubakaran, S.S., Palmer, G.M.: Elderly fall detection using deep learning techniques. In: 2023 7th International Conference on Intelligent Computing and Control Systems (ICICCS), pp. 264–267 (2023)
7. Kou, J., Xin, X., Ni, X., Ma, S., Guo, L.: Fall-risk assessment of aged workers using wearable inertial measurement units based on machine learning. Saf. Sci. **176**, 106551 (2024)
8. Błaszczyk, J.: Sway ratio - a new measure for quantifying postural stability. Acta neurobiologiae experimentalis **68**, 51–7 (2008)
9. Prithwi Raj Chakraborty and Golam Sorwar: A machine learning approach to identify fall risk for older adults. Smart Health **26**, 100303 (2022)
10. Pedregosa, F., et al.: Scikit-learn: machine learning in Python. J. Mach. Learn. Res. **12**, 2825–2830 (2011)
11. Burns, E.R., Lee, R., Hodge, S.E., Pineau, V.J., Welch, B., Zhu, M.: Validation and comparison of fall screening tools for predicting future falls among older adults. Arch. Gerontol. Geriatr. **101**, 104713 (2022)
12. Nishiyama, D., Arita, S., Fukui, D., Yamanaka, M., Yamada, H.: Accurate fall risk classification in elderly using one gait cycle data and machine learning. Clin. Biomech. **115**, 106262 (2024)
13. Sun, R., Katherine, L., Hsieh, J.J.: Sosnoff: fall risk prediction in multiple sclerosis using postural sway measures: a machine learning approach. Sci. Rep. **9**(1), 16154 (2019)
14. Lockhart, T.E., et al.: Prediction of fall risk among community-dwelling older adults using a wearable system. Sci. Rep. **11**(1), 20976 (2021)

Somatic Health Imperative in Severe Mental Illness: Reevaluating Psychiatric Engagement

Devika Jagarlamudi(✉)

CurerTech, Chicago, USA
Devika@curertech.com

Abstract. This paper critically examines the persistent disparities in physical health outcomes for individuals with serious mental illness. Synthesizing extant literature, it underscores the crucial role of psychiatric professionals in proactively addressing the elevated morbidity and mortality within this population. The analysis highlights systemic barriers and proposes a renewed framework for psychiatric intervention that emphasizes integrated care models and collaborative strategies to improve patients' overall well-being.

Keywords: Serious mental illness · Physical health disparities · Psychiatric intervention · Integrated care models · Collaborative healthcare · Morbidity and mortality · Mental health services

1 Introduction

Severe mental illnesses (SMI) such as schizophrenia, bipolar disorder, and major depressive disorder with psychotic features represent some of the most debilitating psychiatric conditions, affecting millions globally. While advances in psychopharmacology and psychotherapy have significantly improved symptom control and functional outcomes, these gains have not extended uniformly to somatic health. Individuals with SMI face dramatically shortened life spans—on average, 10 to 25 years less than the general population—primarily due to preventable physical illnesses such as cardiovascular disease, diabetes, and respiratory conditions. This paper aims to address this gap by proposing a novel, integrated psychiatric care model that directly incorporates physical health metrics and social determinants of health into routine psychiatric practice.

This mortality gap is not merely a clinical anomaly, but a structural failing embedded within contemporary healthcare systems. The longstanding division between mental and physical health services creates a disjointed experience for patients, characterized by underdiagnosed physical conditions, uncoordinated treatments, and inconsistent access to preventive care. Individuals with SMI often shuttle between psychiatric institutions and emergency departments, rarely engaging with longitudinal primary care. As a result, chronic conditions progress undetected, and health deteriorates silently.

In addition to care discontinuity, there is growing clinical evidence that psychiatric conditions and their treatments directly contribute to the onset of metabolic disorders. Antipsychotic medications, especially second-generation antipsychotics such

A. Alsadoon et al. (Eds.): CSCE 2025, CCIS 2935, pp. 429–439, 2026.
https://doi.org/10.1007/978-3-032-22199-5_33

as olanzapine and clozapine, are strongly associated with rapid weight gain, insulin resistance, and the development of type 2 diabetes. These effects are exacerbated by lifestyle patterns common in the SMI population, including physical inactivity, tobacco use, and unhealthy eating. The lack of integrated monitoring systems means early signs of metabolic dysfunction often go unnoticed, delaying intervention. Furthermore, systemic barriers—such as fragmented care, provider role silos, and stigma—compound these risks, creating a clinical blind spot where psychiatric and metabolic comorbidities coexist but remain under-addressed.

Contributory factors to this disparity are multifaceted and intersected across biological, behavioral, and systemic domains. Patients with SMI are disproportionately affected by adverse health behaviors such as smoking, sedentary lifestyle, and poor diet—factors compounded by the side effects of antipsychotic medications, which often induce metabolic syndrome, obesity, and insulin resistance. Concurrently, social determinants of health—including poverty, social isolation, and housing insecurity—exacerbate vulnerability and limit healthcare access. These intersecting burdens create a syndemic environment that fuels poor health outcomes.

Another critical barrier lies in professional role boundaries and workforce preparation. Most psychiatric providers are trained exclusively in mental health, with minimal exposure to physical disease management. Conversely, primary care providers frequently lack training or confidence in managing complex psychiatric conditions, leading to care avoidance or diagnostic overshadowing. Without a shared care philosophy or integrated training pathways, opportunities for holistic care are consistently missed.

Encouragingly, a growing body of research and policy has begun to address these shortcomings. Legislative measures such as the Mental Health Parity and Addiction Equity Act (2008) and the Affordable Care Act (2010) have laid the groundwork for integrated care by mandating insurance parity and supporting health home models. Moreover, technological innovations such as electronic health records (EHRs), mobile health platforms, and artificial intelligence (AI)based risk assessments provide promising avenues to coordinate care, stratify risk, and deliver timely interventions.

Despite these developments, operational integration remains elusive in practice. Implementation varies by jurisdiction, resource availability, and institutional needs. Many health systems still lack the interoperability, reimbursement structures, and clinical training required to deliver fully integrated services. Consequently, integrated care remains more of a theoretical aspiration than a ubiquitous clinical reality, especially in under-resourced and rural settings.

This paper aims to bridge the gap between policy, technology, and psychiatric practice. By synthesizing emerging interdisciplinary findings and evaluating the effectiveness of digital and systemic interventions, we propose a comprehensive care framework for individuals with SMI. This model prioritizes proactive engagement, modular scalability, and data-driven decision-making. Our goal is to provide a practical, evidence-based roadmap to reduce mortality and enhance quality of life through the sustainable integration of physical and mental health care services.

2 Related Work

Neural Architectures and AI Integration. Previous work has investigated the fusion of machine learning and healthcare systems, where advances in tabular data processing and neural models highlight the growing relevance of AI in clinical decision-making. Wajiha [1] explored structured data tasks using TabLM and benchmarked it against traditional models like SVM and LGBM. Wajiha's [2] work emphasized the utility of feature selection in small datasets. Wajiha [3] also demonstrated the potential of neural networks, such as BiLSTM-CRF architectures, in tasks like Named Entity Recognition, reinforcing the effectiveness of sequential learning for extracting structured information—an important consideration for electronic health record parsing. Further contributing to the neural domain, Tendulkar [5] introduced differential private learning methods that enhance data confidentiality, a crucial component in psychiatric record-keeping. Tendulkar [6] also proposed optimized LSH-based text retrieval techniques that can support rapid and secure data retrieval in mental health platforms. Collectively, these contributions show the growing capability of machine learning to support both predictive diagnostics and privacy-preserving infrastructures, laying the groundwork for data-integrated psychiatric systems.

2.1 Healthcare Devices, Risk Prediction, and Assistive Interfaces

Kabra's [9] research advances the intersection of human-computer interaction and rehabilitative technologies. Kabra's [10] work on EMG-controlled prosthetics and sEMG-based silent speech recognition has implications for building responsive biofeedback systems for psychiatric patients with physical comorbidities. Kabra's [11] gait recognition frameworks with GLTM modules also underscore the potential of multi-modal sensory tracking in clinical monitoring. In parallel, Tendulkar [7] explored insurance inspection and energy optimization systems using AI, illustrating how predictive analytics could aid healthcare logistics. Wajiha [4] extended the discourse by analyzing neural network training within TensorFlow environments, promoting democratized access to AI for healthcare solutions. Kabra's [12] additional contributions in diffusion-based gait recognition models reinforce the promise of self-supervised methods in resource-constrained settings—an important angle for rural or underserved psychiatric populations. Finally, Tendulkar's [8] work on battery optimization reflects the strategic use of forecast modeling in time-sensitive health interventions, paralleling psychiatric use cases involving drug adherence scheduling and wearable health devices.

3 Literature Review

Over the past two decades, empirical research has solidified the connection between SMI and poor physical health outcomes. Meta-analyses have revealed a two-to fourfold increase in the risk of chronic diseases, including type 2 diabetes, cardiovascular disease, and metabolic syndrome, in individuals with SMI. These findings persist across geographical regions and demographic groups, suggesting a global health crisis inadequately addressed by existing healthcare models.

The mechanisms underlying these disparities are complex. Psychotropic medications—particularly second-generation antipsychotics—have been implicated in metabolic dysregulation, including weight gain, insulin resistance, and dyslipidemia. Simultaneously, behavioral factors such as tobacco use, physical inactivity, and poor diet remain disproportionately prevalent in the SMI population. Emerging studies have documented that individuals with SMI are at significantly higher risk for developing metabolic disorders, particularly diabetes, even after adjusting for confounding lifestyle variables. This suggests a biological under-pinning likely influenced by psychotropic pharmacology. For example, atypical antipsychotics alter hypothalamic regulation of appetite and glucose metabolism, inducing hyperphagia and promoting visceral adiposity. These metabolic side effects often manifest within weeks of treatment initiation but are not routinely monitored in psychiatric settings. Compounding this issue is the limited access to endocrinology or preventive care services within most mental health clinics, leaving a critical gap in early detection and treatment.

Social determinants of health (SDOH) further exacerbate outcomes. Individuals with SMI are more likely to experience poverty, housing instability, unemployment, and social isolation—all factors independently associated with poor health outcomes. The intersection of psychiatric pathology with socioeconomic vulnerability creates a syndemic condition, where risk factors amplify one another.

Existing models of care often silo psychiatric and medical treatment, leading to care fragmentation. Patients may be treated for schizophrenia in one facility while their diabetes remains unmanaged in another. This lack of coordination contributes to emergency room overutilization, late-stage diagnosis of preventable illnesses, and elevated healthcare costs.

Several international efforts have attempted to bridge this gap. The UK's Improving Access to Psychological Therapies (IAPT) program and the United States' SAMHSA health home models have shown promise but face scalability challenges. Key barriers include funding inconsistencies, professional siloing, and limited data integration.

Recent advances in digital health tools—including AI-driven risk stratification models and mobile-based behavioral interventions—are increasingly explored for this population. However, evidence of long-term efficacy and real-world implementation remains limited, highlighting an urgent need for applied research and policy-level commitment.

4 Methodological Framework

This paper employs a qualitative synthesis and policy evaluation approach, focusing on interdisciplinary literature from psychiatry, internal medicine, public health, and health informatics. Sources include peer-reviewed journals, grey literature (e.g., whitepapers, government reports), and legislative documentation from 2010 to 2025. We adopted a thematic coding method to extract and categorize recurring issues, barriers, and interventions across clinical and policy domains.

Primary inclusion criteria for literature involved focus on severe psychiatric conditions, documentation of physical health outcomes, and proposed systemic or digital solutions. We excluded case reports and single-institution pilot studies with limited generalizability. A total of 71 sources were reviewed, with the most recent works weighing more heavily to capture evolving practices.

Data were organized across five major domains: (1) pharmacological impacts, (2) behavioral health patterns, (3) care integration models, (4) digital health interventions, and (5) health policy frameworks. Within each domain, we identified recurring sub-themes, such as workforce gaps, technological barriers, reimbursement inconsistencies, and socio-environmental vulnerabilities.

To analyze the practical applicability of proposed models, we conducted a realist evaluation of existing integrated care programs in the US and Europe. Key performance indicators (KPIs) included reductions in hospitalizations, improvement in cardiovascular markers, and patient-reported outcomes.

In addition, we incorporated systems thinking methodology to model the complex interplay between psychiatric, physical, and social determinants of health. This approach enabled the formulation of a proposed intervention framework grounded in complex theory and adaptive governance.

The framework generated from this methodology serves as the basis for recommendations in later sections, aiming to guide psychiatric practitioners, policy makers, and healthcare systems toward holistic and sustainable solutions for individuals with SMI.

5 Proposed Integrated Care Framework

We propose a tiered, digitally-enabled, and multidisciplinary integrated care framework specifically designed to address the somatic health disparities faced by individuals with severe mental illness (SMI). This model is grounded in principles of proactive engagement, modular scalability, and interoperability across diverse healthcare infrastructures. By embedding medical assessments, behavioral health services, and social care within a unified delivery ecosystem, this framework seeks to bridge longstanding gaps in psychiatric and physical health treatment.

At the foundational level, the model incorporates routine physical health screening directly into psychiatric encounters using electronic health record (EHR) systems with embedded clinical decision support tools. Patients receiving psychiatric care undergo regular assessments of key biomarkers, including blood pressure, BMI, lipid profiles, and glycemic status (HbA1c). The integration of automated alerts ensures that deviations from normal ranges prompt real-time follow-up actions. Furthermore, these data are bi-directionally accessible by both psychiatric and primary care teams, reducing duplication and enhancing clinical continuity.

The second tier of the model is built around the deployment of multi disciplinary care teams. These teams include psychiatrists, general practitioners, nurses, clinical pharmacists, peer support specialists, and health behavior coaches. Team-based care ensures that physical health goals—such as weight management, smoking cessation, and glycemic control—are jointly addressed alongside psychiatric stabilization. Care plans are co-created with patients to reflect their individual goals and preferences, thereby improving adherence and engagement. Telehealth platforms serve as key enablers, especially for patients in rural or underserved areas, allowing for flexible appointment scheduling and frequent check-ins.

A central innovation in the proposed model is the use of artificial intelligence (AI) for dynamic risk stratification. Predictive algorithms trained on longitudinal EHR data can identify patients at elevated risk for adverse outcomes such as cardiovascular events or hospitalization. These high-risk individuals are enrolled in intensive case management programs, which include weekly digital check-ins, wearable-device monitoring, and nudges via mobile applications to promote medication adherence, exercise, and dietary habits. This allows clinicians to intervene preemptively, and tailor interventions based on evolving risk profiles.

The fourth structural component involves strengthening the linkage between healthcare and community resources. Recognizing that social determinants—such as housing instability, food insecurity, and social isolation—profoundly affect health outcomes, the model integrates formal partnerships with local NGOs, municipal housing agencies, and public health departments. A designated care coordinator is responsible for managing these external referrals, ensuring patients receive timely support services, and monitoring the impact of these interventions on clinical progress.

Governance and oversight form the final layer of the framework. A crossfunctional review committee comprising hospital administrators, clinicians, IT specialists, patient advocates, and policy advisors meets quarterly to assess system performance. Standardized quality indicators—such as emergency department utilization, medication side effects, metabolic markers, and patient satisfaction—are continuously monitored through interactive dashboards. These dashboards allow real-time visibility into program effectiveness and enable data driven refinements in care delivery and resource allocation.

The framework is intentionally designed to be modular, allowing phased implementation across various healthcare settings, including federally qualified health centers (FQHCs), academic medical institutions, and private practice consortia. Its policy compatibility ensures that it aligns with existing value-based payment mechanisms and Medicaid health home models. Importantly, the digital backbone of the model allows for scalability and replicability in both low- and high-resource environments.

Ultimately, the proposed integrated care framework represents a transformative shift in the psychiatric paradigm. By embedding physical health promotion (Fig. 1 and Tables 1, 2).

Table 1. Comparison of Selected Integrated Care Models

Model	Key Features	Challenges
SAMHSA Health Homes (US)	Multidisciplinary teams, care coordination, Medicaid-based	Funding instability, inconsistent state adoption
IAPT (UK)	Psychological therapy access, some physical health integration	Scalability, resource limitations
Kaiser Permanente (US)	Fully integrated EHRs, team-based care	Limited to insured populations

into routine psychiatric practice and leveraging modern data science and community partnerships, the model holds the potential to reduce premature mortality, improve quality of life, and establish a new standard of comprehensive care for individuals with SMI.

Table 2. Mapping of Thematic Insights to Framework Components

Thematic Code	Framework Translation
Pharmacological Impacts	Embedded monitoring via EHR alerts
Behavioral Health Patterns	Integration of lifestyle coaching in care teams
Systemic Barriers	Interoperability-focused governance and policy adaptation
Digital Tools	AI-based risk stratification and remote monitor ing

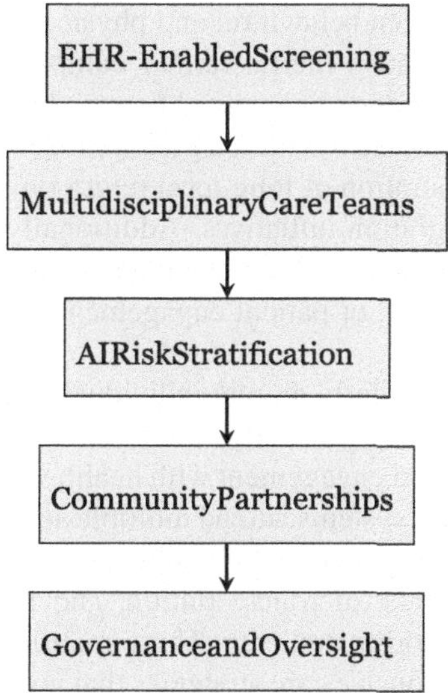

Fig. 1. Proposed Integrated Care Framework

6 Barriers and Challenges to Implementation

Despite growing recognition of the urgent somatic health crisis among individuals with severe mental illness (SMI), the successful implementation of integrated care models continues to be obstructed by multiple systemic, institutional, and individual-level barriers. One of the most pervasive obstacles is the prevailing reimbursement structure, which is ill-suited to the demands of interdisciplinary collaboration. Traditional fee-for-service models incentivize high-volume, fragmented interventions rather than coordinated, holistic care. Although value based care frameworks have shown promise in primary care settings, they remain underutilized in psychiatric contexts, where quantifying outcomes and assigning financial value to integrated care is more complex.

Workforce readiness presents another significant challenge. Many psychiatric clinicians lack formal training in chronic disease management, preventive care, and metabolic monitoring. Conversely, primary care providers often feel unequipped to manage complex psychiatric symptoms such as psychosis or suicidality. This mismatch in clinical competencies reinforces siloed practices and discourages the kind of cross-disciplinary engagement necessary for effective integrated care. Furthermore, existing residency programs and continuing education rarely emphasize collaborative treatment planning or bidirectional referrals, contributing to a fragmented workforce culture.

Technological limitations also hinder implementation. Electronic Health Record (EHR) systems, which should ideally facilitate data exchange across specialties, frequently lack interoperability between psychiatric and general medical services. As a result, critical health information remains siloed, obstructing coordinated decision-making and continuity of care. Although privacy regulations such as the Health Insurance Portability and Accountability Act (HIPAA) are essential to protecting patient data, they can unintentionally create compliance fears that discourage legitimate, beneficial data sharing—especially between behavioral and physical health providers.

Institutional and administrative inertia further complicates adoption. Many health systems are resistant to change due to perceived financial risks, operational disruptions, and unfamiliar workflows associated with integrated models. Without strong leadership advocacy and a clear demonstration of long-term return on investment, health administrators may deprioritize integration initiatives. Additionally, many mental health institutions operate under constrained budgets, making it difficult to invest in additional staff training, data infrastructure, or patient engagement technologies that support care integration.

Patient-level barriers, particularly among individuals with SMI, are equally important. Cognitive impairments, executive dysfunction, and fluctuating motivation can impede treatment adherence and engagement with health services. Patients may struggle to navigate complex healthcare systems, attend multiple appointments, or follow through with prescribed regimens. Compounding this challenge are socioeconomic adversities—such as housing instability, lack of transportation, and food insecurity—that further limit access to continuous, coordinated care. These realities demand trauma-informed, accessible, and culturally responsive care strategies that go beyond clinical intervention.

Stigma—both institutional and internalized—remains one of the most intractable barriers. Within healthcare systems, mental health stigma often leads to diagnostic overshadowing, where somatic complaints are dismissed or overlooked due to the presence of a psychiatric diagnosis. This undermines early detection and treatment of physical conditions. On a personal level, individuals with SMI may internalize stigma, resulting in diminished self-efficacy and reduced likelihood of seeking help for emerging physical symptoms. Reducing stigma at both the clinician and community levels is critical to improving engagement and health outcomes.

Addressing these challenges will require a multi-pronged strategy encompassing payment reform, interdisciplinary workforce development, technology modernization, and regulatory adaptation. Financial models must reward care coordination and preventive health outcomes. Training programs must evolve to emphasize integrated competencies. Interoperable digital platforms should become the standard, and privacy laws must be interpreted with nuance to support patient-centered data sharing. Most importantly, institutional culture must shift toward inclusivity, equity, and shared responsibility across clinical domains. Only then can integrated care models be meaningfully realized and sustained for the benefit of people with SMI.

6.1 Interconnectedness of Barriers

These barriers often interact synergistically. For example, lack of EHR interoperability exacerbates workforce inefficiencies and prevents team-based interventions, while reimbursement limitations discourage cross-disciplinary collaboration. Future solutions must address these barriers not in isolation, but as a complex, interlinked system.

7 Conclusion and Future Directions

This paper underscores the urgent and compelling need to reimagine the role of psychiatric professionals in addressing the persistent somatic health disparities faced by individuals with severe mental illness (SMI). Despite decades of scientific evidence documenting shortened life expectancy and elevated rates of preventable chronic illnesses in this population, systemic reforms remain insufficient. Psychiatric care must evolve beyond symptom containment to encompass the broader objective of holistic, person-centered health. This shift requires not only a redefinition of professional roles but also the dismantling of structural barriers that perpetuate healthcare segregation.

Through a comprehensive synthesis of interdisciplinary literature, health policy initiatives, and existing care models, we have proposed a robust framework for the integration of behavioral and physical healthcare. Our model emphasizes the use of digital technologies, coordinated team-based interventions, and partnerships with community organizations to enhance the reach and effectiveness of psychiatric care. This approach is grounded in modularity and scalability, ensuring that it can be adapted across diverse health systems, from federally qualified health centers to academic medical institutions and rural clinics.

Nonetheless, translating this integrated vision into practice presents significant challenges. These include entrenched professional silos, fragmented funding structures, insufficient workforce training, and technological barriers such as non-interoperable health record systems. Overcoming these limitations will require systemic reforms that include reimbursement mechanisms aligned with integrated care principles, such as bundled payments or value-based care models. It will also necessitate institutional leadership committed to cultural and operational transformation.

Future research must focus on generating high-quality, longitudinal evidence to support the efficacy and cost-effectiveness of integrated care models for individuals with SMI. Large-scale, multi-site trials with diverse demographic representation will be essential to establish generalizability and identify contextspecific best practices. Equally important is the development of culturally sensitive and linguistically appropriate interventions that account for the unique needs of marginalized communities and address the social determinants of health in a meaningful and sustainable manner.

Digital health tools such as AI-driven risk prediction models, mobile health (mHealth) applications, and telepsychiatry platforms hold significant potential to bridge access gaps and enhance continuity of care. However, ethical and regulatory frameworks must evolve to support their equitable deployment. Issues such as data privacy, algorithmic transparency, and digital literacy require dedicated attention to prevent the exacerbation of existing disparities. Research efforts must also explore how these technologies can be co-designed with patients and communities to ensure usability and cultural congruence.

Furthermore, psychiatric education and training programs must be restructured to equip current and future clinicians with the competencies needed for somatic health management. This includes integrating modules on chronic disease screening, lifestyle counseling, pharmacovigilance, and interdisciplinary communication into medical curricula and continuing education. By fostering a new generation of psychiatrists with a dual focus on mental and physical health, we can break the cycle of diagnostic overshadowing and fragmented treatment.

Addressing the bidirectional relationship between psychiatric treatment and metabolic dysfunction is essential. A failure to integrate this awareness into clinical workflows perpetuates adverse outcomes and undermines the broader goals of holistic care. Future psychiatric frameworks must embed metabolic screening,

risk stratification, and early intervention as standard components of treatment protocols.

Next Steps for Policy and Research. Future work should include pilot testing of the proposed framework, with measurable outcomes such as reduced ER visits, improved metabolic indicators, and patient engagement metrics. Policy makers must allocate funding for integrated training modules, EHR interoperability mandates, and bundled payments to support the model's real-world adoption. Clinician and community feedback should guide iterative refinements, ensuring cultural relevance and feasibility.

References

1. Shakir, W.A.: Benchmarking TabLM: evaluating the performance of language models against traditional machine learning in structured data tasks. In: Proceedings of 2024 1st International Conference Emerging Technologies for Dependable Internet of Things (ICETI), pp. 1–10 (2024). https://doi.org/10.1109/ICETI63946.2024.10777155
2. Shakir, W.A.: Enhancing named entity recognition through neural architectures. In: Proceedings of 2024 21st International Computer Conference Wavelet Active Media Technology and Information Processing (ICCWAMTIP), pp. 1–5 (2024). https://doi.org/10.1109/ICCWAMTIP64812.2024.10873731
3. Shakir, W.A.: Adaptive translation of english to arabic movie subtitles using GPT-3.5 Turbo and FAISS. In: Proceedings of 2024 1st International Conference Emerging Technologies for Dependable Internet of Things (ICETI), pp. 1–7 (2024). https://doi.org/10.1109/ICETI63946.2024.10777115
4. Shakir, W.A.: Advancements in artificial neural networks and tensorflow's role in democratizing ML. In: Proceedings of 2024 21st International Computer Conference Wavelet Active Media Technology and Information Processing (ICCWAMTIP), pp. 1–5 (2024). https://doi.org/10.1109/ICCWAMTIP64812.2024.10873721
5. Tendulkar, S.G.: Efficient nearest neighbor search in large-scale text data using optimized locality sensitive hashing in distributed computing environments. In: Proceedings of 2025 International Conference Advanced Computing Technologies (ICoACT), pp. 1–6 (2025). https://doi.org/10.1109/ICoACT63339.2025.11005204

6. Tendulkar, S.G.: AI-powered solutions for insurance inspection: enhancing accuracy and efficiency. In: Proceedings of 2025 International Conference Advanced Computing Technologies (ICoACT), pp. 1–8 (2025). https://doi.org/10.1109/ICoACT63339.2025.11004702
7. Tendulkar, S.G.: Optimized electricity price prediction for battery energy storage system (BESS) scheduling. In: Proceedings of 2025 International Conference Advanced Computing Technologies (ICoACT), pp. 1–7 (2025). https://doi.org/10.1109/ICoACT63339.2025.11004771
8. Tendulkar, S.G.: Efficient techniques for differential privacy in deep learning. In: Proceedings of 2025 International Conference Advanced Computing Technologies (ICoACT), pp. 1– 5 (2025). https://doi.org/10.1109/ICoACT63339.2025.11005164
9. Kabra, A.: Surface electromyography for silent speech recognition: applications in physiotherapy and assistive technologies. Paripex Indian J. Res. 104–113 (2025). https://doi.org/10.36106/paripex/3206789
10. Kabra, A.: Development of a smart prosthetic arm controlled by EMG sensors and AI. Paripex Indian J. Res. 10–13 (2025). https://doi.org/10.36106/paripex/1800320
11. Kabra, A.: GLGAIT: enhancing gait recognition with global-local temporal receptive fields for in-the-wild scenarios. Paripex Indian J. Res. 114–122 (2025). https://doi.org/10.36106/paripex/2506811
12. Kabra, A.: Self-supervised gait recognition with diffusion model pretraining. Int. J. Sci. Res. 5–9 (2025). https://doi.org/10.36106/ijsr/4325141

Analyzing Speech Impairments: A Machine Learning Approach to Dysarthria Detection

Milan Gupta(✉)

Francis Parker School, San Diego, CA 92111, USA
milangupta2026@gmail.com

Abstract. Dysarthria includes dysfunction in the nerves and muscles controlling speech, leading to unclear spoken words. While many studies have been carried out to examine speech impairment, the variation of this problem among people with a similar dysarthria diagnosis has necessitated the need for more research in this area. The particular type and severity of the impairment are essential to monitor the progress of dysarthria and make effective therapeutic interventions. This project describes a Convolutional Neural Network (CNN) model for dysarthria detection, where several acoustic features are extracted in the form of zero crossing rates, Mel Frequency Cepstral Coefficients (MFCCs), spectral centroids, and spectral roll-off. Using the TORGO database of speech signals, training the model, and testing it for its efficiency has shown much promise in the early diagnosis of dysarthric speech. The numerical results indicate that the model design provides an efficiency of nearly 95%, which is higher than previous model architectures. This model aims to identify the condition early and help improve the management of dysarthria through timely and accurate diagnosis.

Keywords: Dysarthria detection · Machine learning · Speech disorders · Acoustic feature extraction · Spectral analysis

1 Introduction

Dysarthria is a complex motor speech disorder resulting from neurological impairments that affect the muscles used in speech production. It is characterized by slurred, slow, and unpredictable speech. Other features range from abnormally loud or soft volumes to distorted vocal qualities. This involves a disruption of one or several subsystems, including respiration, phonation, resonance, articulation, and prosody. Such disorders have their etiologies in various pathologies of the nervous system and lead to a varied array of speech impairments.

The physiological bases of dysarthria are highly integrated and complicate the isolation of speech functions affected. While respiration relies on controlled activity by the muscles in the abdomen and thorax and diaphragmatic action, phonation relies on the laryngeal mechanisms. Similarly, resonance implicates the pharyngeal, oral musculature, soft palate, and nasal cavities, and the movements of the tongue, jaw, and lips control articulation. Dysarthria is severe to a degree, and its nature depends upon the

A. Alsadoon et al. (Eds.): CSCE 2025, CCIS 2935, pp. 440–447, 2026.
https://doi.org/10.1007/978-3-032-22199-5_34

site and severity of neurological insult, resulting in various forms of dysarthria: flaccid, spastic, ataxic, hypokinetic, hyperkinetic, and mixed.

Classification of dysarthria, as well as the determination of its severity, is essential for carrying out efficient management and therapeutic planning. This paper insists on using Convolutional Neural Networks (CNNs) and establishes them as a more advanced tool for detecting dysarthria at an earlier stage than traditional techniques. We aim to integrate sophisticated speech-processing techniques into neural network models to enhance patient diagnosis. The proposed manuscript consists of the following structure. First, this paper describes the methodology for developing a CNN-based classification model (Sect. 2). We present the results in Sect. 3, discuss the results in Sect. 4, and conclude with an overview of our study and future directions in Sect. 5.

The economic and health care costs that Dysarthria can cause lead to significant financial impacts for those with the condition. A study examining the Lee Silverman Voice Treatment for Parkinson's disease-associated dysarthria suggests that the tool may not always be cost-effective depending on the patient's outcome.

2 Proposed Methodology

2.1 Data Collection and Preparation

This study uses the Universal Access Dysarthric speech corpus and the TORGO database. These databases include the dysarthric and non-dysarthric speech samples and their respective data from each of the male and female speakers in the study. The speaking data comprises '.wav' files, capturing the acoustics of each subject. The sample data files and their respective details are shown in Fig. 1. The data was cleaned and modified effectively with background noises by utilizing a Wiener filter. This effectively cleaned the data by minimizing the mean square error between the estimated random process and the desired signal.

2.2 Data Analysis

In addition to auditory speech evaluation, several signal processing techniques were employed to analyze the speech signals, focusing on changes in vowel formants, fundamental frequency (f0), duration of the speech signal, amplitude variations, prolonged vowel duration, voice onset time, and variations in speech tempo. Key features extracted for analysis included the Short-Time Fourier Transform (STFT), Mel Frequency Cepstral Coefficients (MFCC), spectral centroid, spectral bandwidth, spectral roll-off, and zero-crossing rate. These features were extracted from both dysarthric and non-dysarthric speech samples, with detailed feature plots for dysarthric female speakers provided in Fig. 2.

	A	B	C	D
1	is_dysarthria	gender	filename	
2	non_dysarthria	female	torgo_data/non_dysarthria_female/FC03_Session2_0146.wav	
3	non_dysarthria	female	torgo_data/non_dysarthria_female/FC02_Session3_0712.wav	
4	non_dysarthria	female	torgo_data/non_dysarthria_female/FC02_Session3_0679.wav	
5	non_dysarthria	female	torgo_data/non_dysarthria_female/FC03_Session2_0320.wav	
6	non_dysarthria	female	torgo_data/non_dysarthria_female/FC03_Session1_0090.wav	
7	non_dysarthria	female	torgo_data/non_dysarthria_female/FC03_Session1_0056.wav	

Fig. 1. Block schematic of methodology.

2.3 Data Pre-processing

The preprocessing phase involved converting the unstructured audio data into numeric features and standardizing the sample rate to 128 features per second. The audio signals were transformed into Mel Spectrograms to facilitate feature extraction. To prepare the data for model training, the feature matrix was normalized to ensure consistency. The dysarthria status of each speaker was encoded as a categorical variable. Subsequently, the dataset was split into 80% training data and 20% testing data.

2.4 Data Modeling

The preprocessed data was transformed into Mel-frequency cepstral coefficients (MFCCs) extracted from each audio file. These were then used as input into a design to identify patterns associated with Dysarthria. This input data is formatted into the shape that matches the input layer of the model, specifically (20, 792, 1) for each audio sample, where 20 represents the number of MFCC coefficients, and 792 represents the maximum number of frames after padding.

The first layer of the CNN contains 64 filters with a kernel size of 3×3 to capture basic features from the input data, such as edges and simple speech-related textures. A kernel size, here, specifies the dimensions of the filter used in each convolutional layer, which directly influences the input data during the process of feature extraction. The output from this layer is batch-normalized to enable the activation normalization and increase the stability of the network. Subsequently, a max-pooling layer with a window of size 2×2 reduces the spatial dimensions for all feature maps by half. This helps reduce computational complexity and further prevents overfitting through feature abstraction. The architecture proceeds to a second convolutional layer of 128 filters, all of size 3×3. This layer delves more deeply into the details of the extracted features, learning more intricate and higher-level patterns that aid in the recognition of dysarthria. It is followed by a batch normalization and max-pooling sequence to further refine and reduce the feature maps.

To prevent overfitting, a dropout layer with a rate of 0.3 is added after the pooling stages to make the model resistant. Overfitting can cause the model to capture unrelated noise that is irrelevant to the detection, leading to a lower testing accuracy. This dropout layer will randomly shut off a fraction of neurons during training, thereby strengthening the model by making it less dependent on neuron weights. The output from the convolutional and pooling layers will be a multidimensional tensor; this is flattened into a

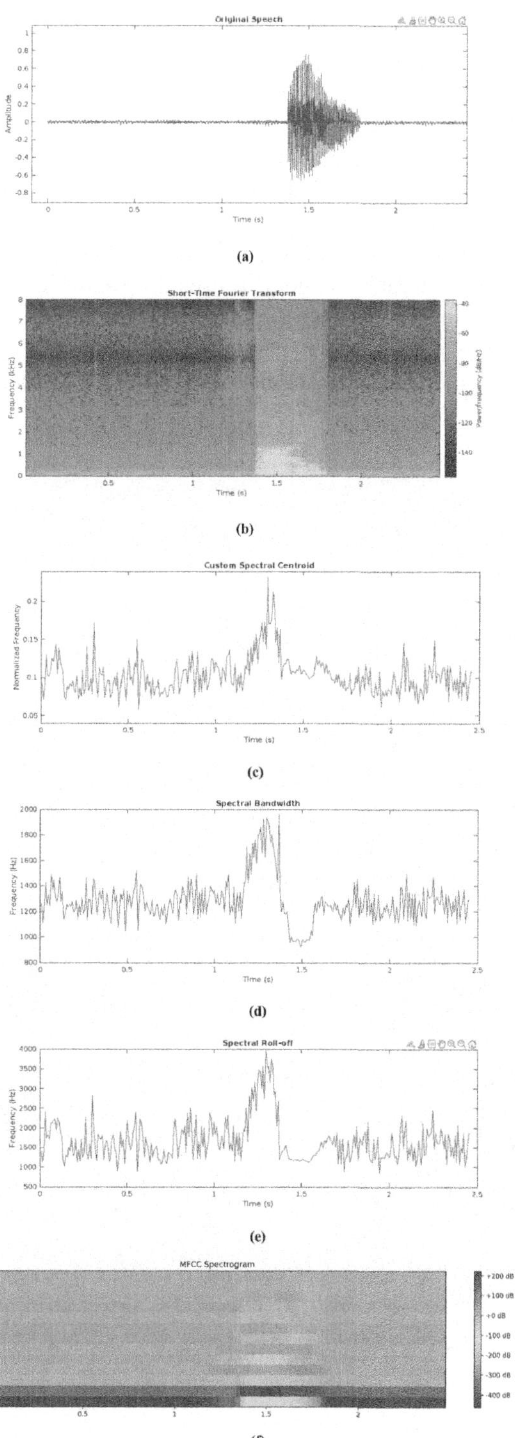

Fig. 2. Speech analysis (Type 1: Male without Dysarthria) a) Original speech b) Short-term Fourier transform (STFT) c) Spectral centroids d) Spectral bandwidth (p = 1, p = 2, p = 3) e) Spectral roll-off f) Mel-frequency cepstral coefficients (MFCC) spectrogram [Phrase: Thigh]

one-dimensional array. The flattened data feeds into a dense layer with 1024 neurons, allowing the network to learn from the extensive feature set developed in the previous steps. A following dropout layer with a rate of 0.4 prevents overfitting and promotes generalization.

The final layer of the model contains four neurons. These represent the classes into which an individual can be classified: dysarthric male, non-dysarthric male, dysarthric female, and non dysarthric female. This layer has a softmax activation, providing the probability regarding every class in which it is located, where higher probabilities are more robust predictions for each category. It uses the Adam optimizer with a learning rate of 0.0005. The learning rate is a tuning parameter that aims to reach a minimum loss function. However, model training varies many hyperparameters to tune performance; similarly, evaluation on another test set confirms the model's accuracy, precision, and recall (Figs. 3 and 4).

Layer (type)	Output Shape	Param #
conv2d_3 (Conv2D)	(None, 20, 792, 64)	640
batch_normalization_3 (BatchNormalization)	(None, 20, 792, 64)	256
max_pooling2d_3 (MaxPooling2D)	(None, 10, 396, 64)	0
dropout_4 (Dropout)	(None, 10, 396, 64)	0
conv2d_4 (Conv2D)	(None, 10, 396, 128)	73856
batch_normalization_4 (BatchNormalization)	(None, 10, 396, 128)	512
max_pooling2d_4 (MaxPooling2D)	(None, 5, 198, 128)	0
dropout_5 (Dropout)	(None, 5, 198, 128)	0
conv2d_5 (Conv2D)	(None, 5, 198, 256)	295168
batch_normalization_5 (BatchNormalization)	(None, 5, 198, 256)	1024
max_pooling2d_5 (MaxPooling2D)	(None, 2, 99, 256)	0
dropout_6 (Dropout)	(None, 2, 99, 256)	0
flatten_1 (Flatten)	(None, 50688)	0
dense_2 (Dense)	(None, 1024)	51905536
dropout_7 (Dropout)	(None, 1024)	0
dense_3 (Dense)	(None, 4)	4100

Total params: 52281092 (199.44 MB)
Trainable params: 52280196 (199.43 MB)
Non-trainable params: 896 (3.50 KB)

Fig. 3. The Convolutional Neural Network Model Architecture

```
model.compile(
    optimizer=Adam(learning_rate=0.0005),
    loss='categorical_crossentropy',
    metrics=['accuracy', Precision(name='precision'), Recall(name='recall')]
)
```

Fig. 4. Parameters of the Convolutional Neural Network

3 Results

After about 20 epochs, the training accuracy began to halt from an exponential gain, transitioning to a linear increase. It can also be observed that the training loss at around 28 epochs began to hold a linear decrease. From epoch 28 and onward, the loss stopped its decrease and fluctuated between two and one-thousandths. The model utilized a callback function to terminate the training process if there was no significant or notable improvement in the loss, effectively preventing the model from overfitting and ensuring good performance. Furthermore, after 53 epochs of training, the model yielded a training accuracy of 96.46% and a testing accuracy of 94.97%. This data shows that the CNN model effectively identifies the unique features within the voice data to classify a patient with dysarthria with an accuracy rate of 94.97%.

Confusion Matrix for Dysarthria Detection Model			
TARGET / OUTPUT	Dysarthic	Non-Dysarthic	SUM
Dysarthic	950 47.76%	48 2.41%	998 95.19% 4.81%
Non-Dysarthic	52 2.61%	939 47.21%	991 94.75% 5.25%
SUM	1002 94.81% 5.19%	987 95.14% 4.86%	1889 / 1989 94.97% 5.03%

Fig. 5. Confusion Matrix

Parameters	Test Accuracy	Test Precision	Test Recall
Score (%)	94.97%	95.28%	95.10%

Fig. 6. The Convolutional Neural Network's Performance Evaluation

As shown in the confusion matrix in Fig. 5, out of the 1989 audio files used, 1889 were accurately predicted, while 100 were not accurately predicted. The testing accuracy closed the gap at 94.97% (Fig. 6), proving the model's strong ability for generalization. For individuals with dysarthria, the model effectively evaluated 950 audio files correctly. On the other hand, it misclassified 52 audio files to be non-dysarthric. The model also accurately identified 939 non-dysarthric audio files but missed 48 audio files, classifying them as dysarthic. A possible cause for these errors was that the audio files used short phrases or words at times, making the speech challenging to classify.

4 Discussion

With continued research on this topic, the data should be based on a richer dataset with phrases that will get more diversified in their linguistic characteristics once a proper phonetic analysis has been established. Further steps in this direction will result in better improvements that can be transformed into increased robustness of models applicable to broad domains such as healthcare. It is further utilized to establish the groundwork of speech models for multi-irregularities in different languages and dialects that can allow diagnostic precision and intervention approaches. Embedding these machine learning models into real-time speech processing applications will revolutionize treatment approaches by giving immediate feedback and changes at the therapy session. Such models allow improvements at the clinical level and in patients' home-care systems and will be in this line of research. The earlier model observed had an accuracy as high as 93.97%, which, when compared to the 94.97% accuracy presented, is less accurate.

5 Conclusion

Deep learning technologies are making a paradigm shift in decision support systems in medical diagnostics, including the management of dysarthria. Our study on speech disorders, which complicate personal expression and inflict social and psychological challenges on the affected, was managed with a diagnostic accuracy of 94.97% using convolutional neural networks. Such precision thus refines therapeutic strategies and brings betterment to patient outcomes. Although the accuracy rate is high, some misclassifications suggest that model improvement and further exploration of other diagnostic features should be undertaken to assess the severity of dysarthria more accurately, guiding future research into increasing model diagnosis capabilities and extending clinical applicability.

Conflict of Interest. The author declares no Conflict of interest.

References

1. Benesty, J., Chen, J., Huang, Y., Doclo, S.: Study of the Wiener filter for noise reduction. In: Benesty, J., Makino, S., Chen, J. (eds.) Speech Enhancement. Signals and Communication Technology, pp. 9–41. Springer, Heidelberg (2005). https://doi.org/10.1007/3-540-27489-8_2
2. Chen, J., Benesty, J., Huang, Y., Doclo, S.: New insights into the noise reduction Wiener filter. IEEE Trans. Audio Speech Lang. Process. **14**(4), 1218–1234 (2006). https://doi.org/10.1109/TSA.2005.860851
3. Clarke, C., et al.: Cost-effectiveness of Lee Silverman voice treatment LOUD (LSVT®) versus NHS speech and language therapy versus control for dysarthria in Parkinson's disease: an economic evaluation alongside the PD COMM trial [abstract]. Mov Disord. **38**(suppl. 1) (2023). https://www.mdsabstracts.org/abstract/cost-effectiveness-of-lee-silverman-voice-treatment-loud-lsvt-versus-nhs-speech-and-language-therapy-versus-control-for-dysarthria-in-parkinsons-disease-an-economic-evaluation-alongs/. Accessed 12 Aug 2024
4. Hinton, G., et al.: Deep neural networks for acoustic modeling in speech recognition: the shared views of four research groups. IEEE Signal Process. Mag. **29**(6), 82–97 (2012). https://doi.org/10.1109/MSP.2012.2205597
5. Jayaraman, D.K., Das, J.M.: Dysarthria. In: StatPearls [Internet]. Treasure Island (FL). StatPearls Publishing (2024). https://www.ncbi.nlm.nih.gov/books/NBK592453/. Accessed 5 June 2023
6. Lim, J.S.: Two-Dimensional Signal and Image Processing, pp. 536–540. Prentice Hall, Englewood Cliffs (1990)
7. Mehrish, A., Majumder, N., Bharadwaj, R., Mihalcea, R., Poria, S.: A review of deep learning techniques for speech processing. Inf. Fus. **99**(C) (2023). https://doi.org/10.1016/j.inffus.2023.101869
8. Page, A.D., Yorkston, K.M.: Communicative participation in dysarthria: perspectives for management. Brain Sci. **12**(4), 420 (202222). https://doi.org/10.3390/brainsci12040420. PMID: 35447952; PMCID: PMC9031517
9. Rezapour Mashhadi, M.M., Osei-Bonsu, K.: Speech emotion recognition using machine learning techniques: feature extraction and comparison of convolutional neural network and random forest. PLoS ONE **18**(11), e0291500 (2023). https://doi.org/10.1371/journal.pone.0291500.PMID:37988352;PMCID:PMC10662716
10. Rudzicz, F., Namasivayam, A.K., Wolff, T.: The TORGO database of acoustic and articulatory speech from speakers with dysarthria. Lang. Resour. Eval. **46**(4), 523–541 (2012)
11. Schröter-Morasch, H., Ziegler, W.: Rehabilitation of impaired speech function (dysarthria, dysglossia). GMS Curr. Top. Otorhinolaryngol. Head Neck Surg. (2005). 4:Doc15. Epub 2005 Sep 28. PMID: 22073063, PMCID: PMC3201013
12. The TORGO Database: Acoustic and articulatory speech from speakers with dysarthria (2020). https://www.cs.toronto.edu/compling-web/data/TORGO/torgo.html
13. Vimal, B., Surya, M., Darshan, Sridhar, V.S., Ashok, A.: MFCC based audio classification using machine learning. In: 2021 12th International Conference on Computing Communication and Networking Technologies (ICCCNT), Kharagpur, India, pp. 1–4 (2021). https://doi.org/10.1109/ICCCNT51525.2021.9579881

Negative Effects of Alcohol: Software for Educating the Public while Determining Public Awareness

M. S. Gupta, L. C. Gupta, A. Gupta, and A. M. G. Solo(✉)

Maverick Trailblazers Inc., Wilmington, Delaware, U.S.A.
amgsolo@mavericktrailblazers.com

Abstract. The objective for this project was to create software to educate the public on the negative effects of alcohol while determining public awareness of the negative effects of alcohol. The survey software showed that there is good public awareness of the effects of alcohol. For 25 questions with 1 point per question, the mean score was 22.31 (89.24%), the confidence interval was ±0.47 (±2.1%) for a confidence level of 95%, the median was 22 (88%), and the mode was 23 (92%). People were effectively educated on the negative effects of alcohol using an online quiz.

Keywords: Alcohol Education · Alcohol Awareness · Alcohol Survey

1 Introduction

The negative effects of alcohol can include blindness, reduction in brain volume, alcohol-related dementia (Wernicke-Korsakoff syndrome), premature death, breast cancer, colon cancer, rectum cancer, mouth cancer, throat cancer, liver cancer, esophagus cancer, larynx cancer, pregnancy risk, reduced milk production for breastfeeding, liver disease, heart diseases, cardiovascular diseases, hypertension, heart failure, atrial fibrillation, hemorrhagic stroke, stroke, high blood pressure, unintentional injuries, vehicle accidents, violence, inflammation of gastrointestinal system, alcohol dependence, nausea, malformation of fetus, birth defects, and fetal alcohol spectrum disorder (FASD) including brain injury, birth defects, behavioral problems, learning disabilities, etc. [1–6].

The motivation for this project was to determine if people are aware of the negative effects of alcohol, to determine if more public education is needed, and to get people to lead healthier lives by ending or reducing alcohol consumption.

2 Software

Online survey software was created using Google Forms with 25 true or false questions on the negative effects of alcohol to educate the public while determining public awareness. The online survey is available at https://tinyurl.com/alcohol-quiz.

A. Alsadoon et al. (Eds.): CSCE 2025, CCIS 2935, pp. 448–454, 2026.
https://doi.org/10.1007/978-3-032-22199-5_35

3 Survey and Results

The researchers got people to do the survey by advertising it on online groups for people seeking to overcome alcohol addictions. It was hard to find people to do the survey, but the researchers were able to get 52 responses from adults. This was enough to have high confidence in the results.

These are the 25 questions in the online survey:

1. Alcohol can lead to death. Is this true or false?

The answer is true. There were 52 correct responses or 0 incorrect responses. 100% of responses were correct and 0% were incorrect.

2. Alcohol causes cancer of the mouth and throat. Is this true or false?

The answer is true. There were 49 correct responses and 3 incorrect responses. 94.2% of responses were correct and 5.8% were incorrect.

3. Only beer, not wine, can lead to death. Is this true or false?

The answer is false. There were 52 correct responses and 0 incorrect responses. 100% of responses were correct and 0% were incorrect.

4. Alcohol issues are not common. Is this true or false?

The answer is false. There were 51 correct responses and 1 incorrect response. 98.1% of responses were correct and 1.9% were incorrect.

5. Alcohol kills more Americans than any other substance. Is this true or false?

The answer is false. There were 8 correct responses and 44 incorrect responses. 15.4% of responses were correct and 84.6% were incorrect.

6. Alcohol is an issue amongst youth. Is this true or false?

The answer is true. There were 44 correct responses and 8 incorrect responses. 84.6% of responses were correct and 15.4% were incorrect.

7. Alcohol does not affect your brain or body. Is this true or false?

The answer is false. There were 52 correct responses and 0 incorrect responses. 100% of responses were correct and 0% were incorrect.

8. The liver is the organ most affected by alcohol. Is this true or false?

The answer is true. There were 47 correct responses and 5 incorrect responses. 90.4% of responses were correct and 9.6% were incorrect.

9. Alcohol raises the risk of an individual getting cancer of the larynx. Is this true or false?

The answer is true. There were 48 correct responses and 4 incorrect responses. 92.3% of responses were correct and 7.7% were incorrect.

10. Alcohol can lead to alcohol-related dementia (Wernicke-Korsakoff syndrome). Is this true or false?

The answer is true. There were 51 correct responses and 1 incorrect response. 98.1% of responses were correct and 1.9% were incorrect.

11. Alcohol can cause muscle damage. Is this true or false?

The answer is true. There were 48 correct responses and 4 incorrect responses. 92.3% of responses were correct and 7.7% were incorrect.

12. Drinking alcohol can cause brain damage. Is this true or false?

The answer is true. There were 49 correct responses and 3 incorrect responses. 94.2% of responses were correct and 5.8% were incorrect.

13. Drinking alcohol interferes with the brain's communication pathways. Is this true or false?

The answer is true. There were 52 correct responses and 0 incorrect responses. 100% of responses were correct and 0% were incorrect.

14. Drinking a lot of alcohol over a long time or too much on a single occasion can cause cardiomyopathy, which is stretching and drooping of heart muscle. Is this true or false?

The answer is true. There were 49 correct responses and 3 incorrect responses. 94.2% of responses were correct and 5.8% were incorrect.

15. Drinking a lot of alcohol over a long time or too much on a single occasion can cause a stroke. Is this true or false?

The answer is true. There were 49 correct responses and 3 incorrect responses. 94.2% of responses were correct and 5.8% were incorrect.

16. People who drink alcohol can have a shorter life expectancy. Is this true or false?

The answer is true. There were 51 correct responses and 1 incorrect response. 98.1% of responses were correct and 1.9% were incorrect.

17. The majority of car crashes are caused by drunk driving. Is this true or false?

The answer is false. There were 15 correct responses and 37 incorrect responses. 28.8% of responses were correct and 71.2% were incorrect.

18. Women who are pregnant should drink alcohol. Is this true or false?

The answer is false. There were 51 correct responses and 1 incorrect response. 98.1% of responses were correct and 1.9% were incorrect.

19. You should drink alcohol if you suffer from certain medical conditions. Is this true or false?

The answer is false. There were 51 correct responses and 1 incorrect response. 98.1% of responses were correct and 1.9% were incorrect.

20. Drinking alcohol under the age of 25 has less effects. Is this true or false?

The answer is false. There were 50 correct responses and 2 incorrect responses. 96.2% of responses were correct and 3.8% were incorrect.

21. Long-term health risks caused by alcohol include learning and memory problems. Is this true or false?

The answer is true. There were 51 correct responses and 1 incorrect response. 98.1% of responses were correct and 1.9% were incorrect.

22. Drinking alcohol reduces your brain volume. Is this true or false?

The answer is true. There were 49 correct responses and 3 incorrect responses. 94.2% of responses were correct and 5.8% were incorrect.

23. Excessive alcohol consumption can cause blindness. Is this true or false?

The answer is true. There were 37 correct responses and 15 incorrect responses. 71.2% of responses were correct and 28.8% were incorrect.

24. Alcohol cannot cause nausea. Is this true or false?

The answer is false. There were 39 correct responses and 13 incorrect responses. 75% of responses were correct and 25% were incorrect.

25. Alcohol can cause high blood pressure. Is this true or false?

The answer is true. There were 51 correct responses and 1 incorrect response. 98.1% of responses were correct and 1.9% were incorrect.

For 25 questions with 1 point per question, 2 people got 16 points (64%), 1 person got 17 points (68%), 1 person got 20 points (80%), 9 people got 21 points (84%), 15 people got 22 points (88%), 18 people got 23 points (92%), and 6 people got 24 points (96%). Figure 1 shows these results with a line graph.

The mean score was 22.31 (89.24%). The median score was 22 (88%). The mode score was 23 (92%). The midrange score was 20 (80%). The range was 8.

The standard deviation was 1.73. The variance was 2.98. The confidence interval was ± 0.47 ($\pm 2.1\%$) for a confidence level of 95%. If the survey is redone, there is 95% confidence of getting a mean of 22.31 ± 0.47.

The last question of the survey asked the age of the respondent. If the respondent didn't want to enter her age, she was told to enter 0. The results of the respondents who didn't enter an age and respondents under the age of 18 were excluded from the data analysis.

The ages of the respondents included one person who was 29 years old, one person who was 33 years old, one person who was 34 years old, one person who was 35 years old, one person who was 36 years old, two people who were 37 years old, two people who were 40 years old, three people who were 42 years old, four people who were 44 years old, two people who were 45 years old, four people who were 46 years old, two people who were 47 years old, three people who were 48 years old, one person who was 49 years old, one person who was 50 years old, two people who were 51 years old, two people who were 52 years old, two people who were 53 years old, one person who was 54 years old, one person who was 55 years old, one person who was 59 years old, two people who were 60 years old, one person who was 61 years old, one person who was

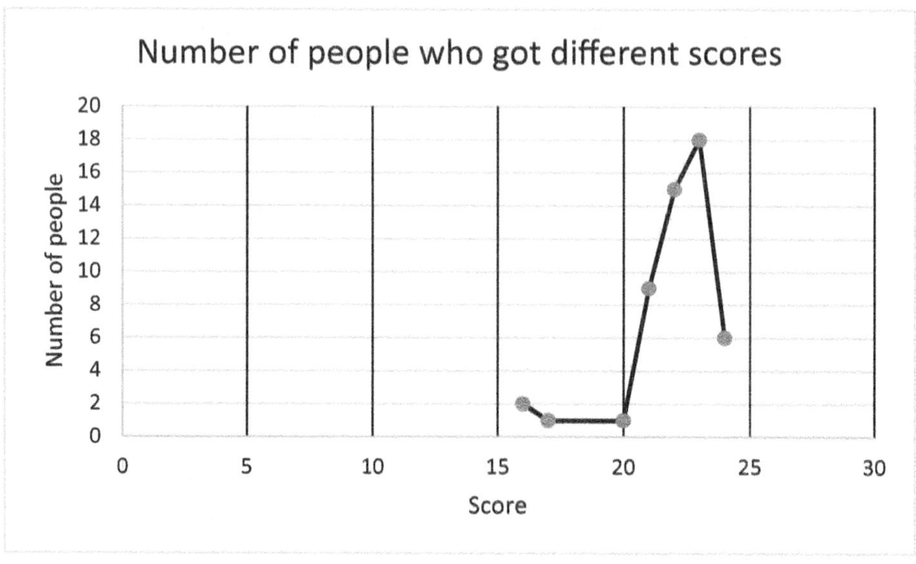

Fig. 1. Line graph showing number of people who got different scores

62 years old, two people who were 63 years old, four people who were 64 years old, two people who were 65 years old, one person who was 68 years old, and one person who was 84 years old. Figure 2 shows the age of the quiz respondents with a line graph.

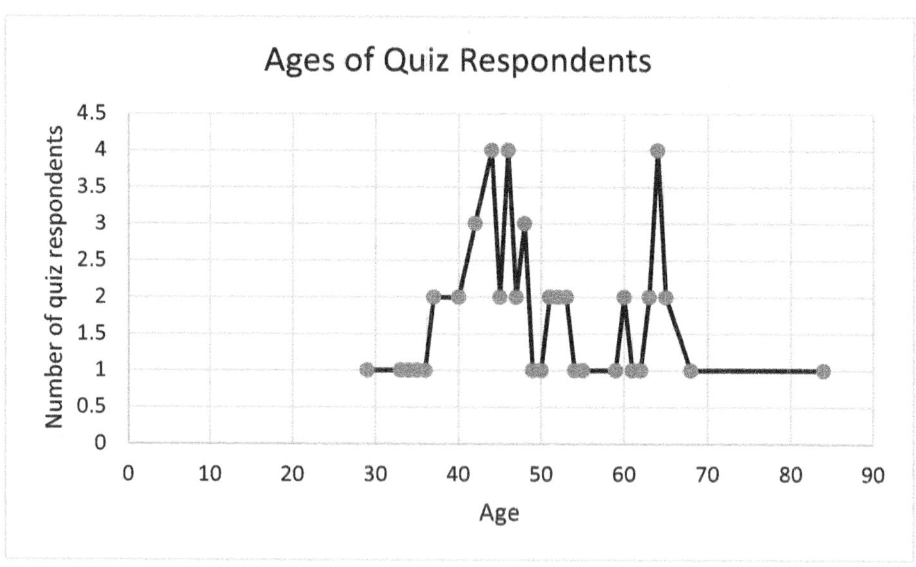

Fig. 2. Line graph showing ages of quiz respondents

The mean age was 50.4 years old. The median age was 48 years old. The set of ages was trimodal with modes being 44 years old, 46 years old, and 64 years old. The midrange was 56.5 years old. The range was 55 years.

4 Conclusion

The scores on the survey were better than expected. In the future, this research can be extended by doing the survey for different geographic regions and different age groups. Also, more questions could be added to the survey. People could be paid to answer the survey.

The researchers recommend that there should a ban on advertising to promote alcohol; government advertising on the negative effects of alcohol; better warning labels on alcohol; education in schools, colleges, and universities on the negative effects of alcohol; and a ban on people under the age of 16 ever being able to purchase alcohol during their lifetimes so they can never get addicted.

The researchers recommend that governments force alcohol manufacturers to include the following warning label on alcohol bottles and alcohol packaging for cans: "Negative effects of alcohol can include blindness, reduction in brain volume, alcohol-related dementia (Wernicke-Korsakoff syndrome), premature death, breast cancer, colon cancer, rectum cancer, mouth cancer, throat cancer, liver cancer, esophagus cancer, larynx cancer, pregnancy risk, reduced milk production for breastfeeding, liver disease, heart diseases, cardiovascular diseases, hypertension, heart failure, atrial fibrillation, hemorrhagic stroke, stroke, high blood pressure, unintentional injuries, vehicle accidents, violence, inflammation of gastrointestinal system, alcohol dependence, nausea, malformation of fetus, birth defects, and fetal alcohol spectrum disorder (FASD) including brain injury, birth defects, behavioral problems, learning disabilities, etc." The researchers hereby authorize governments to force alcohol manufacturers to include the preceding warning label on alcohol packaging for cans or alcohol bottles. Including this warning will boost alcohol awareness and make people less likely to consume more alcohol.

The researchers recommend that elementary school teachers, middle school teachers, high school teachers, community college instructors, and university professors, particularly in health sciences or life sciences, ask their students to do the researchers' educational quiz on the negative effects of alcohol at https://tinyurl.com/alcohol-quiz as part of their coursework.

Consumption of large amounts of alcohol is a significant problem on university campuses [5, 6]. It would be a good idea to require university students, community college students, and high school students to take a one-day short course at their convenience on the harmful effects of alcohol [1–6], recreational drugs, tobacco products, e-cigarettes, etc. This short course could be made available online for students to complete at their convenience as suggested in [7–9]. Students can do the researchers' educational quiz on the negative effects of alcohol as part of this short course.

If people want to do activism to promote the negative effects of alcohol, they can widely share the URL https://tinyurl.com/alcohol-quiz with family, friends, acquaintances, colleagues, and strangers through social networks, email messages, online groups, etc.

Disclosure of Interests. The authors have no competing interests to declare that are relevant to the content of this article.

References

1. Alcohol and Cancer, U.S. Centers for Disease Control and Prevention. https://www.cdc.gov/cancer/risk-factors/alcohol.html
2. Alcohol's Effects on the Body, National Institute on Alcohol Abuse and Alcoholism. https://www.niaaa.nih.gov/alcohols-effects-health/alcohols-effects-body
3. One alcoholic drink a day linked will reduce brain size, Penn Today (2022). https://penntoday.upenn.edu/news/one-alcoholic-drink-day-linked-reduced-brain-size
4. Paradis, C., et al.: Low-Risk Alcohol Drinking Guidelines Scientific Expert Panels: Canada's Guidance on Alcohol and Health: Final Report. Canadian Centre on Substance Use and Addiction, Ottawa (2023). https://www.ccsa.ca/sites/default/files/2023-01/CCSA_Canadas_Guidance_on_Alcohol_and_Health_Final_Report_en.pdf
5. Wechsler, H., Davenport, A., Dowdall, G., Moeykens, B., Castillo, S.: Health and behavioral consequences of binge drinking in college. A national survey of students at 140 campuses. JAMA **272**(21), 1672–1677 (1994)
6. Goslawski, M., Piano, M.R., Bian, J.-T., Church, E.C., Szczurek, M., Phillips, S.A.: Binge drinking impairs vascular function in young adults. J. Am. Coll. Cardiol. **62**(3), 201–207 (2013)
7. Solo, A.M.G.: Curriculum for a new five-year academic program in intelligent systems engineering and software engineering. In: 2023 International Conference on Computational Science and Computational Intelligence (CSCI 2023), pp. 1696–1703. IEEE, New York (2023). https://ieeexplore.ieee.org/document/10590299
8. Solo, A.M.G.: Curriculum for a new academic program with bachelor's degrees in intelligent systems engineering and computer engineering. In: Arabnia, H.R., Deligiannidis, L., Amirian, S., Ghareh Mohammadi, F., Shenavarmasouleh, F. (eds.) Foundations of Computer Science and Frontiers in Education: Computer Science and Computer Engineering, pp. 382–395. Springer, Cham (2025). https://doi.org/10.1007/978-3-031-85930-4_35
9. Solo, A.M.G.: Curriculum for a new academic program with bachelor's degrees in electrical engineering and intelligent systems engineering. In: Arabnia, H.R., Deligiannidis, L., Shenavarmasouleh, F., Amirian, S., Ghareh Mohammadi, F. (eds.) Computational Science and Computational Intelligence: 11th International Conference, CSCI 2024. pp. 103–116. Springer, Cham (2025). https://doi.org/10.1007/978-3-031-94943-2_8

11th International Conference on Health Informatics and Medical Systems (HIMS'25) Section: Poster Research Papers

Smart Home-Based AI Medicine Recognition System for Elderly Care

Ssu-Hsuan Lu[1](✉), Che-Kuang Lin[2], and Yi-Zhan Li[1]

[1] Department of Computer Information and Network Engineering, Lunghwa University of Science and Technology, Taoyuan City, Taiwan
shlu@gm.lhu.edu.tw

[2] Division of Neurosurgery, Department of Surgery, Far Eastern Memorial Hospital, New Taipei City, Taiwan

Abstract. As the population ages and the need for telemedicine continues to grow, smart home technologies play a key role in enhancing care for seniors. This study proposes an AI-integrated smart home system that can identify prescription drugs through camera-based image detection. The system provides instant feedback and displays medication information directly on the touch screen interface, ensuring better medication compliance and user safety. The implementation focuses on practical interaction design, usability for elderly users, and lightweight AI model deployment. The result is a streamlined and reliable solution that can be expanded to a wider range of applications such as cognitive training and rehabilitation.

Keywords: smart home · elderly care · AI · medicine recognition

1 Introduction

Due to the surge of elderly populations and the impact of the COVID-19 pandemic, remote medical services have become increasingly essential. The increasing use of smartphones and the decreasing cost of internet access have created unprecedented opportunities to deliver healthcare and other services online [3]. Using telemedicine services through video conferencing or other virtual technologies can save time and treatment costs for both patients and healthcare providers [1]. Telemedicine and smart home solutions have seen rapid integration, leveraging IoT, AI, and cloud computing technologies [2]. While such systems traditionally focus on health monitoring and appointment reminders, elderly users often face difficulties identifying complex medication regimens [4].

This project integrates artificial intelligence (AI)-based medication recognition into smart home environments, allowing users (especially the elderly) to scan medication packaging using the built-in camera on their mobile phones and receive real-time visual feedback on a touch screen panel. In this project, the system combines artificial intelligence image recognition and calendar integration for reminders.

A. Alsadoon et al. (Eds.): CSCE 2025, CCIS 2935, pp. 457–460, 2026.
https://doi.org/10.1007/978-3-032-22199-5_36

2 System Architecture

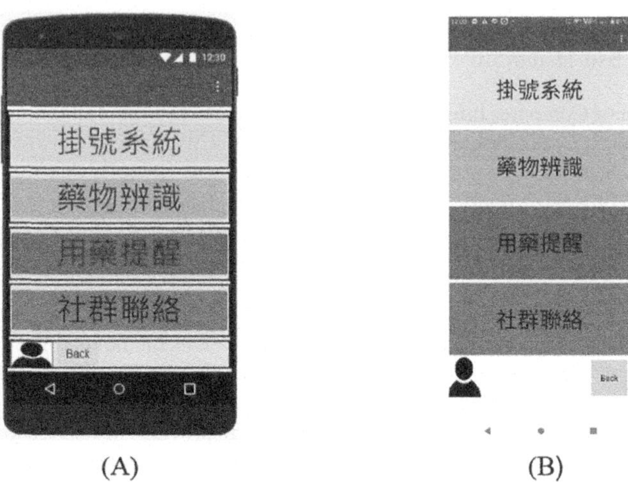

Fig. 1. Main contents of the proposed APP (A) and actual machine demonstration (B).

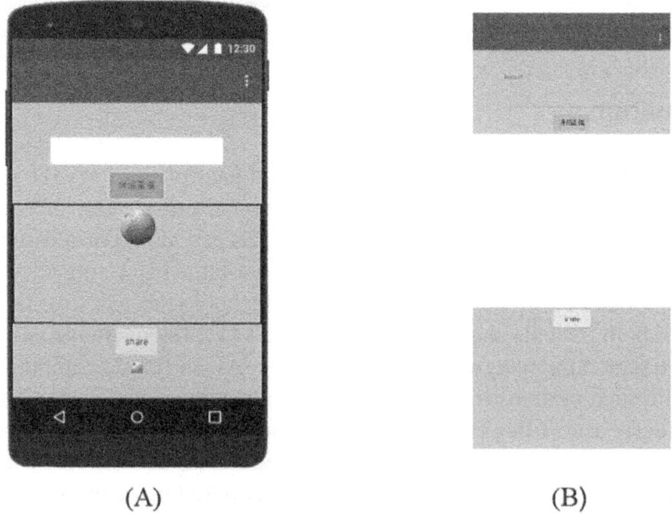

Fig. 2. Main contents of drug identification (A) and actual machine demonstration (B).

This system core currently consists of three modules:

1. User Interface: In this project, the author develops the APP by using a customized application developed using MIT App Inventor 2 [6]. The app includes appointment tracking, medication reminders, and interactive health features. Figure 1 shows the main login page of the APP and its actual appearance on the mobile phone.
2. AI image recognition engine: A lightweight convolutional neural network (CNN) model trained to recognize English drug names on pill packaging. As shown in Fig. 2, after the medicine bag is scanned by a camera, an image of the corresponding medicine is displayed, as shown in Fig. 3. It can currently recognize English drug names and search for corresponding drug images online to help the elderly understand the drugs they are taking more clearly.
3. Calendar and notification system: embedded reminders for medication, appointments, and health checks.

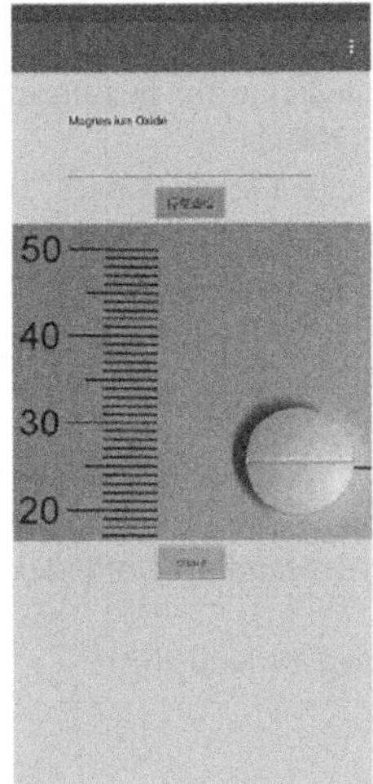

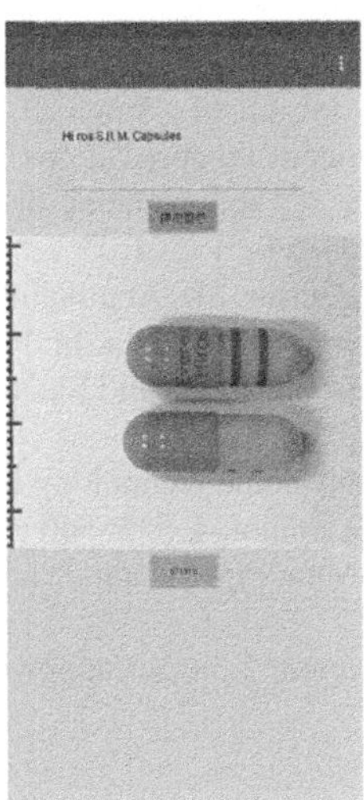

Fig. 3. Scan the drug name on the medicine package to display the drug

3 The Prototype of the System

The prototype of the system is currently being deployed in partnership with Far Eastern Memorial Hospital [5] and integrated with its outpatient scheduling portal.

The implementation steps of drug identification in the system are:

1. Image capture: The user aligns the drug package with the touchscreen camera. There will be a prompt on the interface when the scan starts.
2. AI reasoning: Preprocess the image (resizing, grayscale filtering) and pass it to the local CNN model.
3. Display output: Search the captured drug name on the drug website and display the drug name, image, dosage, and usage.

4 Conclusion

The proposed AI-enhanced smart home system demonstrated effective drug identification through accessible hardware and intuitive user interface. The system solves the key pain points in medication management for the elderly by integrating artificial intelligence, cloud APIs and user-centered design, and lays the foundation for broader smart care applications. More features will continue to be developed and completed in the future.

Acknowledgments. This study was funded by Lunghwa University of Science and Technology and Far Eastern Memorial Hospital.

References

1. Haleem, A., Javaid, M., Singh, R.P., Suman, R.: Telemedicine for healthcare: capabilities, features, barriers, and applications. Sens. Int. **2**, 100117 (2021)
2. Jin, Z., Chen, Y.: Telemedicine in the cloud era: prospects and challenges. IEEE Pervasive Comput. **14**(1), 54–61 (2015)
3. Mamoun, R., Nasor, M., Abulikailik, S.H.: Acceptance of telemedicine and e-health applications in developing countries. In: Proceedings of the 2020 International Conference on Computer, Control, Electrical, and Electronics Engineering (ICCCEEE), Khartoum, pp. 1–5. IEEE (2021)
4. Li, K.F.: Smart home technology for telemedicine and emergency management. J. Ambient Intell. Hum. Comput. **4**, 535–546 (2013)
5. Far Eastern Memorial Hospital. https://www.femh.org.tw/MainPage_en/index. Accessed 14 Nov 2025
6. MIT App Inventor 2. https://appinventor.mit.edu. Accessed 14 Nov 2025

Radiomic Biomarker Discovery and Lung Cancer Staging Using Gradient Boosted Decision Trees

Nezamoddin N. Kachouie[1,2](✉) and Audrey Eley[1]

[1] Department of Mathematics and Systems Engineering, Florida Institute of Technology, Melbourne, FL 32901, USA
nezamoddin@fit.edu, aeley2020@my.fit.edu

[2] Department of Electrical Engineering and Computer Science, Florida Institute of Technology, Melbourne, FL 32901, USA

Abstract. Lung cancer is a highly aggressive malignancy, and its clinical severity is characterized through a standardized staging system. Accurate staging plays a pivotal role in prognostic stratification and the selection of optimal therapeutic strategies. With the advancement of our understanding of lung cancer and the rapid development of machine learning (ML) techniques, it has become increasingly important to investigate the integration of ML into lung cancer management. In this study, imaging-derived biomarkers, referred to as radiomic features, were employed as inputs for a predictive classification model based on the LightGBM framework. The findings demonstrate that this approach shows promise in accurately predicting lung cancer stages; however, further validation using a balanced dataset is necessary to ensure the robustness and generalizability of the model.

Keywords: Lung cancer · Staging · Machine Learning · Gradient Boosted Decision Tree · Radiomics · Ensemble models

1 Introduction

Despite declining rates of lung cancer (LC), an estimated 226,650 Americans will be diagnosed with LC in 2025 [1]. Typically, the onset of LC symptoms does not occur until the disease has reached an advanced stage [1]. This is reflected in diagnosis statistics, which show that of LC cases diagnosed from 2013–2019, 48% were not detected until the cancer had already spread throughout the body (metastasized) [2]. This tendency towards late diagnosis leads to poor survival outcomes, with the 5-year relative survival rate for LC being just 27% [1, 2].

Cancer stage is a standardized descriptor of cancer progression at time of diagnosis [1]. Staging system assigns a cancer case a stage, typically using the TNM system, which considers tumor size (T), lymph node spread (N), and distant metastasis (M) [1, 3, 4]. Appropriate cancer staging is crucial, as it facilitates effective treatment strategies, accurate patient prognosis, and informed life planning.

A. Alsadoon et al. (Eds.): CSCE 2025, CCIS 2935, pp. 461–465, 2026.
https://doi.org/10.1007/978-3-032-22199-5_37

Radiomics is a relatively recent development in cancer prognostication [5], referring the computational extraction of quantitative imaging biomarkers from scans (CT, MRI PET) of a region of interest (ROI) [5, 6]. The objective quantitative data of radiomics cidates the texture, dimensions, and composition of tumors [6]. While the traditional nor biopsy only offers definitive insight for a small portion of a lesion, radiomics cribe the entire ROI at once [5].

As staging methodologies advance and machine learning (ML) adoption expands, loring potential enhancements to staging through ML techniques becomes impera-. In this work, we have implemented Gradient boosted decision trees (GBDTs), a s of ML models, to construct an ensemble of decision trees iteratively. Each new tree signed to reduce the residual errors of its predecessors. These lightweight predictive els represent a promising application for optimizing staging processes.

2 Related Works

LightGBM, a type of GBDT model, has performed well with other medical classification tasks [8, 9]. In a 2024 study, LightGBM was used to classify types of oral precancer with imaging features and achieved nearly 99% accuracy [8]. Another recent study combined a reduced set of seven radiomics and clinical data to predict epithelial ovarian cancer (EOC) stage [9]. Among five predictive models, LightGBM had the best performance, with 71% accuracy on the external validation set [9]. A systematic review of studies using radiomics to predict lymph node metastasis of LC showed that predictions using CT-based radiomics were 82% accurate [10]. Therefore, evidence suggests that radiomics are significant to cancer staging and that LightGBM is well-suited to this task. These methods have been applied to other cancers, such as EOC, but have not been fully explored for LC staging.

3 Dataset

For this research, we used the Lung1 dataset, which is publicly available through the National Cancer Institute's Cancer Imaging Archive [11]. Lung1 includes 107 radiomic features extracted from CT scans alongside age, sex, TNM stage (T, N, M, and overall), survival status, and survival time following diagnosis [11]. This dataset is contemporary to the 7th edition of the TNM staging system [3, 11], and contains patients with overall clinical stages I, II, IIIa, and IIIb [11]. The original Lung1 database organizes entries by tumor, allowing multiple entries per patient [11]. We cleaned this dataset to contain one entry per patient ID by maintaining the radiomics of the patient's largest tumor and adding the patient's total number of tumors as a new column. Entries with missing data in any field were removed, yielding a clean dataset of 398 data points.

4 Methods

We categorized our dataset into three stage classes: I, II, and III, the last of which is composed of stages IIIa & IIIb. Stage class III is a combined class because stages IIIa and IIIb are primarily distinguished by the relative positions of the primary tumor and the affected lymph nodes, data not found in Lung1 [3]. Class III comprised 277 of the 398 data points. To palliate the imbalance, we stratified the data when splitting it into training, validation, and testing subsets, preserving the class distribution. We then trained and tested a LightGBM GBDT model on the full feature set and evaluated its performance. For feature reduction, we ranked feature importance using gain, which is the reduction in training loss achieved when a split on a given feature is introduced [12]. We selected the 12 predictors with the greatest gain to form the reduced feature set. Another LightGBM model was then trained and tested using the reduced set.

5 Results

This section presents the results of the LightGBM models trained on both the full and reduced feature sets. This will cover the reduced feature set, confusion matrices, and evaluation metrics.

5.1 Reduced Feature Set

The reduced feature set is composed of the 12 features that had the greatest gain when used as predictors for the initial LightGBM stage classifier.

Table 1. The twelve features of the reduced feature set by gain.

Feature	Gain	Feature	Gain
Max 3D Diameter	229.09	Elongation	49.75
Number of Tumors	210.71	Median	46.50
Age	123.14	Zone Entropy	38.63
Max 2D Diameter Column	92.26	IMC 1	33.82
X 90 Percentile	89.60	Gray Level Variance 2	32.19
Sphericity	64.67	MCC	31.22

Somewhat intuitively, Table 1 shows that features related to the size of the primary tumor were significant to the formation of the decision trees. Demographic and clinical features (age, number of tumors) were also prominent. The remainder of the top features describe the shape, density, and texture of the largest tumor. This results in a diverse reduced feature set that contains clinical, demographic, and radiomic predictors.

5.2 Test Set Predictive Classification Results

Table 2 displays the evaluation metrics from the classifications of the test set. As with the confusion matrices, the results from the full and reduced feature sets are similar. The accuracies of the models, 81.25% and 80.00% respectively, are promisingly high. However, as is evident from the columns for stage class II, the model was unable to

Table 2. Metrics from the classification of the test set by the model using the full feature set (left), and the reduced feature set (right).

Stage Class	Full Feature Set					Reduced Feature Set				
	I	II	III	Macro Avg.	Weighted Avg.	I	II	III	Macro Avg.	Weighted Avg.
Precision	0.75	0.00	0.83	0.53	0.74	0.71	0.00	0.83	0.51	0.73
Recall	0.71	0.00	0.95	0.55	0.81	0.71	0.00	0.93	0.54	0.80
F1-Score	0.73	0.00	0.88	0.54	0.77	0.71	0.00	0.87	0.53	0.76
Overall Accuracy	81.25%					80.00%				

correctly classify any test data from stage II. The poor class II performance is likely a result of the extreme class imbalance. This is reflected in the significant difference between the macro and weighted averages.

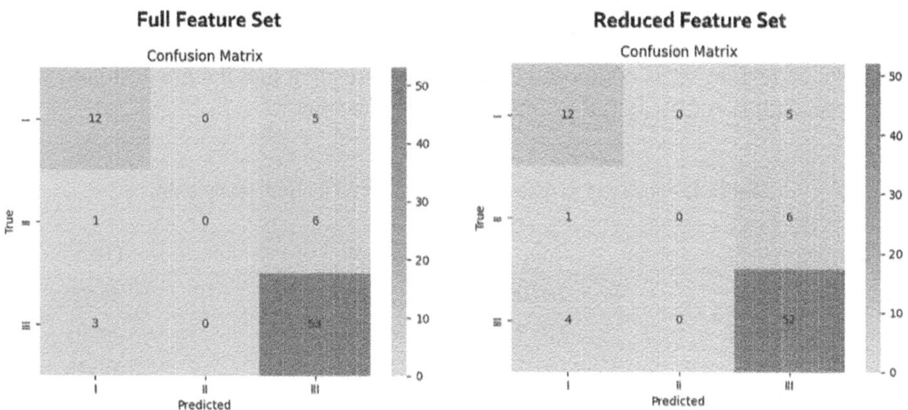

Fig. 1. Results of the classification of the test set. The panels show the confusion matrices of the classifications made on the test set with the full predictor set (left), and the reduced predictor set (right).

Figure 1 shows that the results of the full feature set model are very similar to the reduced feature set model, with a singular classification discrepancy. This figure exhibits the class imbalance, with class III dominating the matrices. It is notable that despite this imbalance, the classification models do not exclusively classify test data as being stage III. However, the center columns of both matrices indicate that neither model made any stage II predictions.

6 Discussion and Conclusion

We observed that tumor radiomics were effective predictors of lung cancer stage using a GBDT classifier, identifying radiomics potential utility in prognostication. However, the extreme class imbalance in this study limits confidence in the model's robustness. Future work should replicate this methodology with a larger and more balanced dataset, as it and the LightGBM framework are highly scalable. Furthermore, this approach could be leveraged for continuous survival predictions with LightGBM's regression capabilities.

Acknowledgments. This research was supported by the Florida Department of Health, Casey DeSantis Florida Cancer Innovation Fund under grant MOAAT. The authors gratefully acknowledge the support that made this study possible.

Disclosure of Interests. The authors of this study declare that they have no competing interests.

References

1. American Cancer Society: Cancer facts & figures 2025. Cancer Stat. **2025**, 17–18 (2025)
2. American Lung Association: Lung Cancer Additional Measures - Lung Cancer Trends Brief. https://www.lung.org/research/trends-in-lung-disease/lung-cancer-trends-brief/lung-cancer-additional-measures. Accessed 24 July 2025
3. Marshall, H.M., Leong, S.C., Bowman, R.V., Yang, I.A., Fong, K.M.: The science behind the 7th edition tumour, node, metastasis staging system for lung cancer. Respirology **17**, 247–260 (2012). https://doi.org/10.1111/j.1440-1843.2011.02083.x
4. Mountain, C.F., Carr, D.T., Anderson, W.A.D.: A system for the clinical staging of lung cancer. Am. J. Roentgenol. **120**, 130–138 (1974). https://doi.org/10.2214/ajr.120.1.130
5. Chen, B., Zhang, R., Gan, Y., Yang, L., Li, W.: Development and clinical application of radiomics in lung cancer. Radiat. Oncol. **12** (2017). https://doi.org/10.1186/s13014-017-0885-x
6. Scapicchio, C., Gabelloni, M., Barucci, A., Cioni, D., Saba, L., Neri, E.: A deep look into radiomics. La Radiologia Medica **126**, 1296–1311 (2021). https://doi.org/10.1007/s11547-021-01389-x
7. Ke, G., et al.: LightGBM: a highly efficient gradient boosting decision tree. In: NeurIPS Proceedings, CA, USA (2017)
8. Goswami, B., Bhuyan, M.K., Alfarhood, S., Safran, M.: Classification of oral cancer into pre-cancerous stages from white light images using LightGBM algorithm. IEEE Access **12**, 1–1 (2024). https://doi.org/10.1109/access.2024.3370157
9. Leng, Y., et al.: Contrast-enhanced CT radiomics for preoperative prediction of stage in epithelial ovarian cancer: a multicenter study. BMC Cancer **24** (2024). https://doi.org/10.1186/s12885-024-12037-8
10. Li, Y., Deng, J., Ma, X., Li, W., Wang, Z.: Diagnostic accuracy of CT and PET/CT radiomics in predicting lymph node metastasis in non-small cell lung cancer. Eur. Radiol. **35**, (2024). https://doi.org/10.1007/s00330-024-11036-4
11. Aerts, H.J.W.L., et al.: Data From NSCLC-Radiomics (Version 4). National Cancer Institute: The Cancer Imaging Archive. https://doi.org/10.7937/K9/TCIA.2015.PF0M9REI. Accessed 17 July 2025
12. Parameters Tuning — LightGBM 3.3.2.99 documentation. https://lightgbm.readthedocs.io/en/latest/Parameters-Tuning.html. Accessed 25 July 2025

A Multivariate Sparse Group Lasso (MSGL) for Lung Cancer Stratification

Mohamed Jaber[1], Zarindokht Helforoush[1], and Nezamoddin N. Kachouie[1,2](✉)

[1] Department of Mathematics and Systems Engineering, Florida Institute of Technology, Melbourne, FL, USA
{mjaber,zhelforoush2022}@my.fit.edu, nezamoddin@fit.edu
[2] Department of Electrical Engineering and Computer Science, Florida Institute of Technology, Melbourne, FL, USA

Abstract. Lung cancer remains the leading cause of cancer-related mortality worldwide, claiming more lives each year than any other malignancy. Despite significant progress in early detection and therapeutic strategies, the prognosis for many patients, particularly those diagnosed at advanced stages, continues to be poor. Conventional prognostic tools primarily depend on clinical variables such as tumor stage, age, and sex. However, these factors alone often fail to capture the biological complexity of the disease, limiting their effectiveness in guiding truly personalized treatment decisions. Recently, radiomics has emerged as a promising approach to address these limitations. By extracting high-dimensional quantitative features from standard medical imaging, radiomics can reveal subtle, otherwise imperceptible patterns within tumors. These imaging-derived biomarkers have the potential to provide deeper insights into tumor phenotype and behavior, thereby improving prognostic assessment. In this study, we investigate the prognostic value of radiomic features in comparison with traditional clinical indicators, aiming to advance toward more accurate and individualized treatment planning for patients with lung cancer.

Keywords: Radiomics · Risk stratification · Survival prediction · Clinical factors

1 Introduction

Lung cancer remains the world's deadliest cancer, surpassing the annual mortality of breast, prostate, and colorectal cancers combined [1, 2]. Most of these cases, over 80%, are non-small cell lung cancer (NSCLC), which progresses more slowly than small cell lung cancer (SCLC) but often is diagnosed at late stages with poor outcomes [3, 4]. This delayed detection, mainly due to the lack of symptoms in early stages, contributes to the historically poor five-year survival rates seen in NSCLC [5].

In recent years, new treatments such as targeted therapies and immunotherapies, including drugs like pembrolizumab and Osimertinib, have offered hope by improving outcomes for select patients. However, these therapies work best when patients are carefully matched based on specific molecular and clinical markers. While systems

A. Alsadoon et al. (Eds.): CSCE 2025, CCIS 2935, pp. 466–472, 2026.
https://doi.org/10.1007/978-3-032-22199-5_38

like the TNM classification are still the backbone of lung cancer staging and treatment planning, they often fall short in reflecting the full biological complexity of each tumor [6]. Radiomics is an emerging approach that could change this. By extracting large volumes of quantitative data from routine medical scans, like tumor shape, texture, and intensity, radiomics captures subtle differences in tumor structure that may hint at underlying biology and patient prognosis [7, 8]. Early studies have shown that these imaging-based features can help predict critical outcomes such as metastasis and overall survival. Still, integrating radiomic data with advanced tools like machine learning for more accurate patient stratification is a challenge that researchers are just beginning to tackle [9].

In previous studies, we focused on blood-based biomarkers, specifically recurrent DNA copy number alterations, to identify molecular signatures linked to cancer development [10–13]. These investigations aimed to uncover early molecular changes associated with cancer onset, providing insights into potential diagnostic and prognostic markers. This study uses radiomic features extracted from standard CT scans to stratify NSCLC patients by their survival risk, moving beyond traditional staging models [14].

2 Data Description

This study is based on a carefully selected group of 398 patients with non–small cell lung cancer (NSCLC), drawn from the National Cancer Institute's Cancer Imaging Archive (TCIA) [15]. For each patient, we gathered a pre-treatment CT scan along with information on cancer stage, survival time, and key demographic details. The cases span stages I to IIIB, with IIIA and IIIB distinguished by where the tumor is located and how far it has spread to nearby lymph nodes. From each 3D CT image, we extracted 107 radiomic features capturing tumor intensity, shape, and texture. These features were grouped into seven biologically meaningful categories: First-Order Statistics, Shape, GLCM, GLRLM, GLSZM, GLDM, and NGTDM, each describing a different dimension of the tumor's imaging phenotype. Together, they reflect how bright, irregular, and internally varied each tumor is. To ensure consistency, incomplete cases were removed, and patients with multiple lesions had their data merged into a single tumor count feature. All radiomic features were derived voxel-by-voxel from 3D tumor segmentations. Texture-based features such as NGTDM and GLRLM describe the internal variability of the tumor, a sign often linked to more aggressive disease, while Shape and First-Order features capture its overall size, form, and density. Together, these radiomic patterns, when paired with patient survival data, create a strong foundation for developing machine learning models that can predict treatment outcomes [16, 17].

3 Methods

The flow diagram of the group lasso regularization and biomarker selection process, designed to account for structured sparsity in the high-dimensional radiomic feature space, is depicted in Fig. 1. Unlike conventional lasso which picks out individual features, grouped lasso looks at sets of related features and applies a penalty that encourages selecting or dropping entire groups, mainly when those features share common statistical patterns or biological meaning. This approach enhances interpretability by integrating group structure while ensuring efficient optimization within the Cox proportional hazards framework.

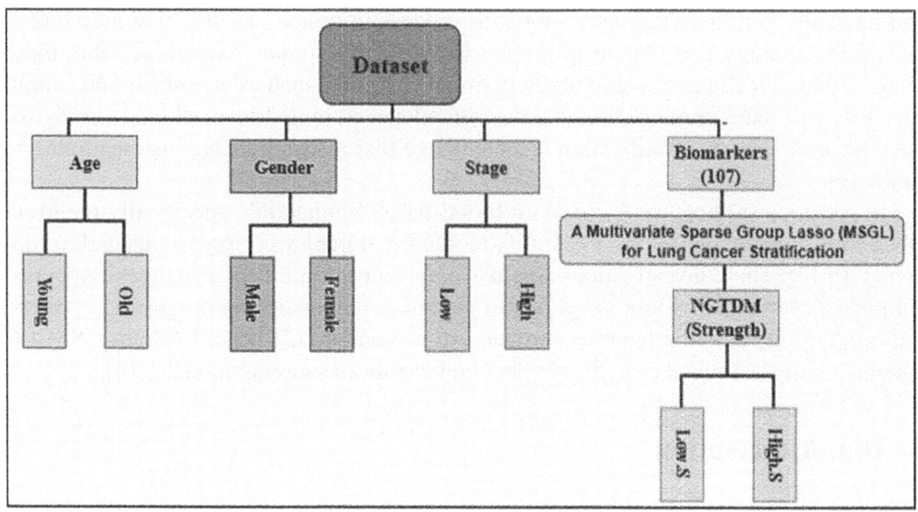

Fig. 1. Flow diagram of lung cancer patient stratification based on clinical and radiomic features.

We used grouped lasso regularization to pinpoint which clusters of radiomic features were most strongly linked to survival. For each selected group, individual features were then examined based on their log hazard ratios. To test how consistent and demographically relevant these features were, we compared survival outcomes across gender (male vs. female) and age (young vs. old) subgroups. This subgroup analysis helped us understand how stable and consistently predictive the selected biomarker was across different patient groups, such as different age or gender groups. Finally, we tested whether adding this imaging biomarker to existing prognostic models could improve survival predictions beyond what traditional clinical factors alone can provide.

4 Results

Applying grouped lasso regularization identified a single dominant radiomic signature associated with patient survival. Only the Neighborhood Gray-Tone Difference Matrix (NGTDM) category was retained among the seven predefined feature groups. This group, which captures localized texture variation, included five features: Coarseness, Complexity, Strength, Contrast, and Busyness. Strength emerged as the top predictor in our model, with the highest absolute log hazard ratio. To see how well it performs in practice, we ran a series of survival analyses, using Kaplan–Meier curves and violin plots, to compare it with standard clinical variables like tumor stage, age, and gender. This gave us an overall sense of its value and a closer look at how it behaves in different patient groups. Taken together, the results suggest that Strength could be a useful marker for tailoring risk predictions in people with non-small cell lung cancer.

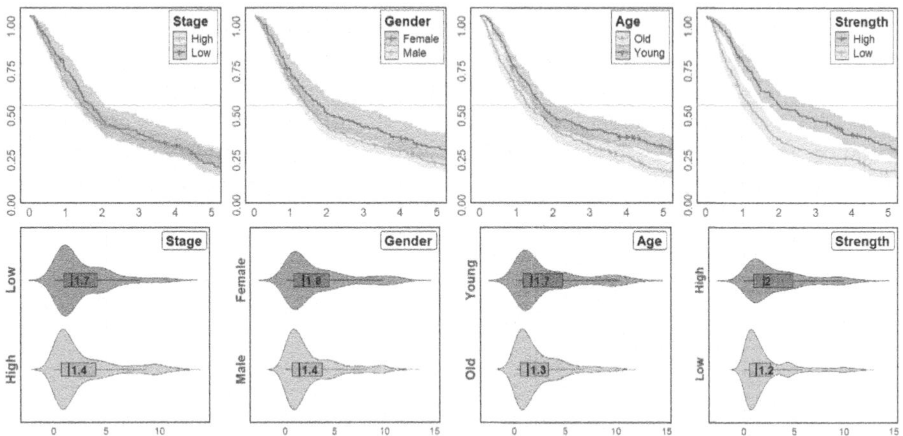

Fig. 2. *Survival analysis by radiomic biomarker (Strength), stage, age, and gender.* Top: Kaplan–Meier curves with 95% confidence intervals, survival years in x axis and survival probability in y axis. Bottom: Violin plots of survival time with median values labeled survival years in x axis.

Kaplan–Meier analyses revealed a clear hierarchy of prognostic power (see Fig. 2). The radiomic biomarker Strength provided the strongest stratification, with broad and persistent separation between high- and low-value groups, non-overlapping confidence intervals, and a highly significant log-rank test ($p < 0.0001$). In contrast, clinical stage, a standard decision-making factor, showed minimal curve separation and was non-significant ($p = 0.53$). Age offered moderate prognostic value ($p = 0.0004$), with early advantages for younger patients that diminished over time. Gender showed weaker, though significant, associations ($p = 0.025$).

Direct comparison underscored the superiority of Strength over Stage. High-Strength patients had a median survival of 2.0 years versus 1.2 years in the low-Strength group ($\Delta = 0.8$ years). Stage-based stratification produced only a 0.3-year difference (1.7 vs. 1.4). Strength thus captured a richer survival signal, with more long-term survivors, reflecting underlying tumor biology more effectively than anatomy-based staging. Importantly, Strength is a continuous, quantitative imaging biomarker that captures subtle microstructural heterogeneity. Because it is objective, reproducible, and non-invasive, it holds substantial promise for integration into routine clinical practice. Together, these findings position Strength as a more reliable and clinically meaningful biomarker than tumor stage, with real potential to guide personalized, data-driven care in NSCLC.

Building on its strong overall prognostic performance, the radiomic feature Strength consistently stratified survival across age and gender subgroups. Patients were jointly stratified by age (young vs. old) and Strength (high vs. low), yielding four cohorts (Young/High, Young/Low, Old/High, Old/Low). Kaplan–Meier analyses revealed apparent survival differences within both age groups: young patients lived a median of 2.6 vs. 1.4 years (high vs. low Strength), while older patients lived 1.8 vs. 0.9 years. Gender-stratified analyses showed the same pattern: women survived 3.4 vs. 1.3 years, and men 1.9 vs. 1.1 years, depending on Strength classification. In every subgroup, high-strength patients had more prolonged survival, broader distributions, and a higher proportion of long-term survivors (see Fig. 3).

These results highlight Strength as a robust, non-invasive biomarker whose prognostic value transcends demographic boundaries. Its predictive value does not appear to depend on age or gender, suggesting that it captures biologically relevant features consistent across populations. Making it a strong candidate for integration into personalized risk models in NSCLC.

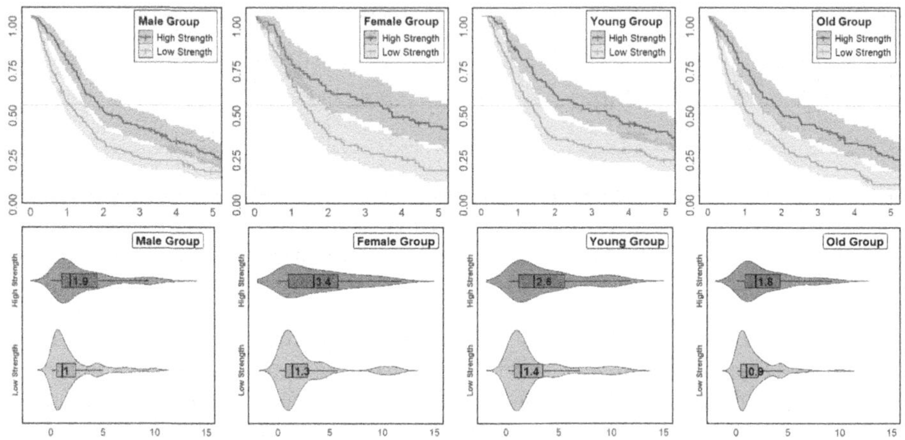

Fig. 3. *Survival analysis by radiomic biomarker (Strength), within gender and age subgroups.* Top panels: Kaplan–Meier survival curves with 95% confidence intervals, where survival time (years) is shown on the x-axis and survival probability on the y-axis. Bottom panels: Violin plots displaying the distribution of survival time for each group, with boxplots and median survival values labeled.

5 Discussion

This study demonstrates that combining group-aware regularization with high-dimensional radiomic features can significantly improve survival prediction in non-small cell lung cancer (NSCLC). Using a sparse group lasso Cox model, we identified a compact, interpretable feature set dominated by Neighborhood Gray-Tone Difference Matrix (NGTDM) descriptors, with Strength emerging as the most prognostic feature. While unexpected, the exclusive selection of NGTDM features is both statistically and biologically meaningful: group lasso retains feature groups only when they carry unique value, and in this case, NGTDM alone provided a strong, independent signal. Biologically, NGTDM features describe subtle texture differences within the tumor, reflecting micro-level heterogeneity often seen in aggressive or treatment-resistant cancers. Among the evaluated radiomic features, Strength was identified as a robust factor, outperforming conventional clinical variables such as stage, age, and sex. By providing a continuous measure of intratumoral heterogeneity, Strength enables more precise risk stratification and shows strong potential as a generalizable imaging biomarker. From a clinical standpoint, Strength is particularly appealing, because it is a radiomic feature derived from standard CT scans noninvasively and in a reproducible way making it both practical and cost-effective. Furthermore, the use of group lasso for feature selection enhances interpretability by identifying groups of related predictors, thereby helping to bridge the gap between machine learning models and clinical decision-making.

Despite these promising results, several limitations should be acknowledged. This study was based on a retrospective dataset with limited clinical detail, which may restrict the immediate generalizability of the findings, even though subgroup analyses showed consistent trends. While the overall cohort size (n = 398) was moderate, subgroup analyses necessarily involved smaller sample sizes, reducing statistical power. Additionally, by design, group lasso may fail to capture signals distributed across multiple feature families. Future research should aim to validate these findings in larger and more diverse cohorts and explore alternative modeling frameworks that can accommodate overlapping or hierarchical feature structures.

6 Conclusion

This study underscores the value of combining machine learning techniques with radiomic biomarkers to enhance prognostic modeling in non-small cell lung cancer (NSCLC). By applying a multivariate sparse group lasso framework to CT-derived features, we identified a compact and biologically meaningful signature, dominated by NGTDM features, that outperformed traditional clinical variables in survival prediction. In particular, the Strength feature emerged as a robust, non-invasive biomarker capable of stratifying patients across diverse demographic subgroups. These findings add to the growing evidence that quantitative imaging features can reveal important tumor characteristics that traditional staging often overlooks. Bringing these features into risk models could support more personalized, data-driven decisions in cancer care. Looking ahead, it will be important to validate these biomarkers in larger, multi-center studies and to explore models that combine radiomics with genomic and molecular data for even more accurate predictions. By leveraging the complementary strengths of imaging and machine learning, we move closer to precision-guided treatment planning with the potential to improve survival outcomes and tailored care more effectively for patients with lung cancer.

Acknowledgments. This research was supported by the Florida Department of Health, Casey DeSantis Florida Cancer Innovation Fund under grant MOAAT. The authors gratefully acknowledge the support that made this study possible.

Disclosure of Interests. The authors declare no competing interests relevant to the content of this article.

References

1. American Cancer Society: Lung cancer statistics | How common is lung cancer? https://www.cancer.org/cancer/types/lung-cancer/about/key-statistics.html. Accessed 28 July 2025
2. Sung, H., Ferlay, J., Siegel, R.L., et al.: Global cancer statistics 2020: GLOBOCAN estimates of incidence and mortality worldwide for 36 cancers in 185 countries. CA Cancer J. Clin. **71**(3), 209–249 (2021). https://doi.org/10.3322/caac.21660

3. Gridelli, C., Rossi, A., Carbone, D.P., et al.: Non-small-cell lung cancer. Nat. Rev. Dis. Primers. **1**(1), 1–16 (2015). https://doi.org/10.1038/nrdp.2015.9
4. Rudin, C.M., Brambilla, E., Faivre-Finn, C., Sage, J.: Small-cell lung cancer. Nat. Rev. Dis. Primers. **7**(1), 3 (2021). https://doi.org/10.1038/s41572-020-00235-0
5. Candal-Pedreira, C., Ruano-Ravina, A., Calvo de Juan, V., et al.: Analysis of diagnostic delay and its impact on lung cancer survival: results from the Spanish thoracic tumor registry. Archivos de Bronconeumología **60**, S38–S45 (2024). https://doi.org/10.1016/j.arbres.2024.07.006
6. Wu, Y., Yu, G., Jin, K., Qian, J.: Advancing non-small cell lung cancer treatment: the power of combination immunotherapies. Front. Immunol. **15**, 1349502 (2024). https://doi.org/10.3389/fimmu.2024.1349502
7. Parekh, V., Jacobs, M.A.: Radiomics: a new application from established techniques. Expert Rev. Precis. Med. Drug Dev. **1**(2), 207 (2016). https://doi.org/10.1080/23808993.2016.1164013
8. Forghani, R., Savadjiev, P., Chatterjee, A., Muthukrishnan, N., Reinhold, C., Forghani, B.: Radiomics and artificial intelligence for biomarker and prediction model development in oncology. Comput. Struct. Biotechnol. J. **17**, 995–1008 (2019). https://doi.org/10.1016/j.csbj.2019.07.001
9. Vithayathil, M., Koku, D., Campani, C., et al.: Machine learning based radiomic models outperform clinical biomarkers in predicting outcomes after immunotherapy for hepatocellular carcinoma. J. Hepatol. (2025). https://doi.org/10.1016/j.jhep.2025.04.017
10. Kachouie, N.N., Deebani, W., Shutaywi, M., Christiani, D.C.: Lung cancer clustering by identification of similarities and discrepancies of DNA copy numbers using maximal information coefficient. PLoS ONE **19**(5), e0301131 (2024). https://doi.org/10.1371/journal.pone.0301131
11. Kachouie, N.N., Deebani, W., Christiani, D.C.: Identifying similarities and disparities between DNA copy number changes in cancer and matched blood samples. Cancer Invest. **37**(10), 535–545 (2019). https://doi.org/10.1080/07357907.2019.1667368
12. Kachouie, N.N., Shutaywi, M., Christiani, D.C.: Discriminant analysis of lung cancer using nonlinear clustering of copy numbers. Cancer Invest. **38**(2), 102 (2020). https://doi.org/10.1080/07357907.2020.1719501
13. Kachouie, N.N., Lin, X., Christiani, D.C., Schwartzman, A.: Detection of local DNA copy number changes in lung cancer population analyses using a multi-scale approach. Commun. Stat. Case Stud. Data Anal. Appl. **1**(4), 206–216 (2015). https://doi.org/10.1080/23737484.2016.1197079
14. Le, V.H., Kha, Q.H., Hung, T.N.K., Le, N.Q.K.: Risk score generated from CT-based radiomics signatures for overall survival prediction in non-small cell lung cancer. Cancers **13**(14), 3616 (2021). https://doi.org/10.3390/cancers13143616
15. Cancer Imaging Archive (TCIA): NSCLC-RADIOMICS. https://www.cancerimagingarchive.net/collection/nsclc-radiomics/. Accessed 28 July 2025
16. Mayerhoefer, M.E., Materka, A., Langs, G., et al.: Introduction to radiomics. J. Nucl. Med. **61**(4), 488–495 (2020). https://doi.org/10.2967/jnumed.118.222893
17. American Cancer Society: Cancer staging | Has cancer spread | Cancer prognosis. https://www.cancer.org/cancer/diagnosis-staging/staging.html. Accessed 28 July 2025

Author Index

A. Alsadoon et al. (Eds.): CSCE 2025, CCIS 2935, pp. 473–474, 2026.
https://doi.org/10.1007/978-3-032-22199-5

The manufacturer's authorised representative in the EU is Springer Nature Customer Service Centre GmbH, Europaplatz 3, 69115 Heidelberg, Germany. If you have any concerns regarding our products, please contact ProductSafety@springernature.com

Printed and bound by CPI Group (UK) Ltd, Croydon, CR0 4YY
21/07/2026
02173374-0001